RELIGION AND POLITICS
IN AMERICA

Religion and politics are never far from the headlines, but their relationship remains complex and often confusing. This book offers an engaging, accessible, and balanced treatment of religion in American politics. It explores the historical, cultural, and legal contexts that motivate religious political engagement and assesses the pragmatic and strategic political realities that religious organizations and people face. Incorporating the best and most current scholarship, the authors examine the evolving politics of Roman Catholics; evangelical and mainline Protestants; African-American and Latino traditions; Jews, Muslims, and other religious minorities; recent immigrants and religious "nones"; and other conventional and not-so-conventional American religious movements.

New to the **Sixth Edition**

- Covers the 2016 election and assesses the role of religion from Obama to Trump.
- Expands substantially on religion's relationship to gender and sexuality, race, ethnicity, and class, and features the role of social media in religious mobilization.
- Adds discussion questions at the end of every chapter, to help students gain deeper understanding of the subject.
- Adds a new concluding chapter on the normative issues raised by religious political engagement, to stimulate lively discussions.

Allen D. Hertzke is David Ross Boyd Professor of Political Science at the University of Oklahoma. He is author or editor of several books on religion and politics, most recently *Religious Freedom in America* and *Christianity and Freedom*, vols. I and II.

Laura R. Olson is Centennial Professor in the Department of Political Science at Clemson University and Editor-in-Chief of the *Journal for the Scientific Study of Religion*.

Kevin R. den Dulk is the Paul B. Henry Chair in Political Science and Director of the Henry Institute at Calvin College. He is the coauthor of *The Disappearing God Gap? Religion in the 2008 Election* and *Pews, Prayers, and Participation: Religion and Civic Responsibility*.

Robert Booth Fowler is Professor Emeritus of Political Science at the University of Wisconsin-Madison. His published books include *Enduring Liberalism: American Political Thought since the 1960s, The Dance with Community: The Contemporary Debate in American Political Thought,* and *Unconventional Partners: Religion and American Liberal Culture.*

RELIGION AND POLITICS IN AMERICA

Faith, Culture, and Strategic Choices

SIXTH EDITION

Allen D. Hertzke
Laura R. Olson
Kevin R. den Dulk
Robert Booth Fowler

Routledge
Taylor & Francis Group

NEW YORK AND LONDON

Sixth edition published 2019
by Routledge
711 Third Avenue, New York, NY 10017

and by Routledge
2 Park Square, Milton Park, Abingdon, Oxon, OX14 4RN

Routledge is an imprint of the Taylor & Francis Group, an informa business

© 2019 Taylor & Francis

The right of Allen D. Hertzke, Laura R. Olson, and Kevin R. den Dulk to be identified as authors of this work has been asserted by them in accordance with sections 77 and 78 of the Copyright, Designs and Patents Act 1988.

Fifth edition published by Westview Press 2014

Library of Congress Cataloging-in-Publication Data
Names: Hertzke, Allen D., 1950– author. | Olson, Laura R., 1967– author. | Dulk, Kevin R. den, author. | Fowler, Robert Booth, 1940– author.
Title: Religion and politics in America : faith, culture, and strategic choices / Allen D. Hertzke, Laura R. Olson, Kevin R. den Dulk, Robert Booth Fowler.
Description: Sixth Edition. | New York, NY : Routledge, 2019. | "New to the Sixth Edition: Covers the 2016 election and assesses the role of religion from Obama to Trump. Expands substantially on religion's relationship to gender and sexuality, race, ethnicity, and class, and features the role of social media in religious mobilization. Adds discussion questions at the end of every chapter, to help students gain deeper understanding of the subject. Adds a new concluding chapter on the normative issues raised by religious political engagement, to stimulate lively discussions."—t.p. verso. | Includes bibliographical references and index.
Identifiers: LCCN 2018004050| ISBN 9781138596153 (hardback) | ISBN 9780813350578 (pbk.) | ISBN 9780429487910 (ebook)
Subjects: LCSH: Religion and politics—United States. | United States—Religion. | United States—Politics and government.
Classification: LCC BL2525 .H474 2019 | DDC 322/.10973—dc23
LC record available at https://lccn.loc.gov/2018004050

ISBN: 978-1-138-59615-3 (hbk)
ISBN: 978-0-813-35057-8 (pbk)
ISBN: 978-0-429-48791-0 (ebk)

Typeset in Minion Pro
by Florence Production Ltd, Stoodleigh, Devon, UK

Printed and bound by CPI Group (UK) Ltd, Croydon, CR0 4YY

TO BOOTH—MENTOR, COLLEAGUE, AND FRIEND

CONTENTS

ILLUSTRATIONS

FIGURES

TABLES

BOXES

PREFACE

The dynamic interactions between religion and politics are visible everywhere in the United States—and they are the focus of this book. We see continuing engagement by the conservative religious movement on abortion and traditional marriage. We observe the assertiveness of the Roman Catholic Church, which allies itself with evangelical Protestants in defending religious autonomy and traditional sexual ethics and with progressive religious groups on poverty and immigration. We spot unlikely alliances on global issues, such as human rights, humanitarian aid, and religious freedom. We cannot miss the expanding pluralism of religious advocacy. The powerful legacy of African-American churches in American politics is joined by the increasing political relevance of Latino religious expressions. We notice the prominent role of Jewish groups in American politics, especially regarding support for Israel, and the continuing efforts of the American Muslim population to gain political influence. We witness the growing secular constituency as well as the vibrant religious commitments of recent immigrants. From voting behavior to presidential actions to the persistent flood of cases in the American judicial system—everywhere one looks, religion and politics appear to be intertwined in American public life.

The aim of this book is to understand the politics of religion in the United States and to appreciate the strategic choices that politicians and religious participants make when they participate in politics. We try to make sense of how religion and politics come together in the voting booth, Congress and the state legislatures, the executive branch, the courts, the interest-group system, and the larger culture of the United States. The subject is large and complex, and it features fascinating and often contradictory currents. It is a topic of tremendous importance because we believe one can understand American politics and society today only with an appreciation of religion's role in them.

Our book also depicts the arena of struggle and strategic calculation, of the clashing ideals and necessary compromise that mark all of politics—a concept we define as conflict and agreement in public life. We shift back and forth between describing practical politics, religious traditions, and theology. At the same time, we explore the nature of citizens' faiths and the personal values that have so much effect on their political beliefs and behaviors. Only by doing both tasks may the dynamics of religion in American politics today be appreciated.

We have worked hard to make this book accessible. Although we take account of what many political scientists, historians, and sociologists have said about religion and politics, our goal has been to produce a readable and informative text, not a scholarly tome. We endeavor to strike a balance between providing enough information and cluttering the narrative with endless nuance. Historical background, we believe, is an essential part of this context, so we devote an entire chapter to historical roots, in addition to providing historical details elsewhere in the text. We also highlight cultural trends that indicate future political ramifications. To make the narrative come alive we feature real-world illustrations of political impacts, clashing religious views, and strategic alliances. Boxes profile fascinating religious activists and issues, illuminating that the contemporary scene is about real people with passionate convictions.

The complexities of religious politics preclude any single definition of religion. Moreover, we are not especially attracted to elaborate philosophical or linguistic attempts to define such a changing and fluid concept as religion. Rather, we define religion phenomenologically. That is, whatever most people and the culture generally treat as religion (or as a religion), we do, too. Despite the great religious diversity of American culture, religion is ordinarily assumed to involve the acknowledgment and worship of a transcendent god or gods, spirit, or force. Usually it is more specific than the alternate definition, which would suggest that any general system of meaning is a religion.

This sixth edition has been thoroughly updated but also revamped, with new features, such as study-guide questions at the end of each chapter. One of the challenges we have faced in preparing this edition relates to the very nature of American religion—its dynamic change and ever-expanding pluralism. Indeed, we have been astonished by how much has changed in the four years since the previous edition was prepared.

NEW TO THE SIXTH EDITION

- Covers the 2016 election and assesses the role of religion from Obama to Trump.
- Expands substantially on religion's relationship to gender and sexuality, race, ethnicity, and class.

- Reflects the political impact of growing religious pluralism.
- Features the role of social media in religious mobilization.
- Foregrounds the theories of religion, culture, and politics at the beginning of the book, for better context.
- Discusses core topics in depth and with contemporary examples, including updated feature boxes.
- Includes chapter discussion questions to help students gauge their understanding of the material.
- Adds discussion questions at the end of every chapter, to help students gain deeper understanding of the subject.
- Adds a new concluding chapter on the normative issues raised by religious political engagement, to stimulate lively discussions.
- Reorganizes the order of the chapters to help them build more logically on each other.

As with previous editions, this volume represents not just a summary of existing scholarship but also reflects our own original research and analysis. To elaborate on the bullets above, we feature the following in this new edition:

- data found nowhere else on the dramatic expansion of the use of Facebook and Twitter in religious political advocacy;
- changes in voting patterns with the Trump candidacy;
- religious clashes sparked by the rise of ethno-nationalist populism;
- new challenges and directions in church–state jurisprudence;
- growing pluralism in religious activism, both by religious tradition (Jews, Muslims, Buddhists, Hindus, Sikhs, Baha'is) and within Christianity (with immigrant communities from Latin America, Asia, Africa, and the Middle East gaining in prominence);
- the intensified engagement by Muslims and other religious minorities, as well as diverse prominence of Latino religionists;
- religious activism over sexuality and gender-identity policies;
- greater attention to the religious "nones" whose secular politics is often defined as over and against religious actors;
- the increasing global connections of religious politics in the United States; and
- consideration of moral and normative issues raised by religion in politics.

Chapter 1 of this book begins with a thematic interpretation of religion and politics in American history. We avoid presenting a merely chronological review because we are more interested in broad themes that resonate with current issues. Chapter 2 continues this thematic overview by examining broad theories that attempt to explain religious politics in America today. Looking at these big-picture interpretations should help provide the reader with a meaningful context for our presentation of the particular dimensions of religion and politics in later chapters. Chapter 3 begins an in-depth exploration of the status of religion in

America today. Here we examine the religious affiliations of the American people, their religious practices, and the theological and political outlooks of major Christian religious traditions in America—evangelical Protestantism, mainline Protestantism, and Catholicism. In Chapter 4, we turn to the politics of Judaism, Islam, and other dimensions of religious pluralism in the United States, as well as the increasingly prominent secular constituency. Not only do such traditions highlight important themes in religion and politics, they sometimes have a tangible impact on politics in the United States. In the next two chapters we extend this exploration of pluralism in religion and politics, focusing on influential ethno-religious communities of Latinos and African Americans in Chapter 5 and the dynamic intersections of gender, sexuality identity, and religion in Chapter 6.

In the next three chapters we turn to practical politics: voting and party politics in Chapter 7, lobbying and advocacy in Chapter 8, and political elites in Chapter 9. These chapters, in particular, present original research on the tangible impacts of religious political engagement. Then in Chapter 10 we extend our view by examining the intersection of religion and political culture, and especially the role that religion plays in fostering the values and norms of American democracy.

This brings us to the legal and constitutional arenas, which are the subject of Chapters 11 and 12. Here we consider clashing views about the meaning of the First Amendment's provision for religious free exercise and its prohibition of official religious establishment. We explore crucial court cases that have defined church–state law and indelibly shaped the way religion and government interact; we also examine various legal interest groups involved in the relevant legal battles both within and outside of the courtroom. As in other arenas of politics, jurisprudence is dynamic, as the courts grapple with new challenges and shifting interpretations.

In our concluding chapter, we depart from our empirical investigations to reflect on the moral and normative issues surrounding religious political activism. While we do not stake out a position in these complex intellectual debates, we do provide readers with some of the most important arguments about whether, or under what conditions, religious engagement in politics is a good thing or not.

ACKNOWLEDGMENTS

In preparing this new edition we benefited enormously from the assistance of several persons: University of Oklahoma's post-doctoral fellow Jason Pudlo, who produced voting breakdowns from diverse surveys, master's student Alexander Davis, and undergraduate students Allison Johanningmeier and Alan Murphey; Calvin College undergraduate student Abigail Schutte; and Ellen Hekman, program coordinator for the Henry Institute at Calvin, who produced the book's index. We are also especially grateful for the excellent support of our former editor at Westview Press, Ada Fung, who guided a number of the new features of this edition, as well as Jennifer Knerr and Ze'ev Sudry at Routledge.

Finally, there is one person who must be acknowledged above all, the original lead author, Robert Booth Fowler. A true pioneer in research (and teaching) on religion and politics at the University of Wisconsin, Booth Fowler wrote an early textbook and recruited his former doctoral students (the three of us) as coauthors in successive editions of this text. Though he retired from the project for this new edition, his analysis and spirit endure (as does his name on the book). Words cannot capture our profound gratitude to Booth, but we do take delight in the heartfelt gesture of dedicating this volume to him.

Allen D. Hertzke

Laura R. Olson

Kevin R. den Dulk

1

RELIGION AND POLITICAL CULTURE IN AMERICA: FROM THE HISTORICAL LEGACY TO THE PRESENT DAY

One cannot understand American politics today without knowing something about American religion. And one cannot understand either politics or religion without a sense of history, a sense of how the interplay among religion, politics, and culture has shaped the story of the United States. Since colonial days, religion has played a profound role in molding American culture, directly and indirectly, in ways that no one at the time of the founding ever could have imagined or predicted. To sort out the complex history of the relationships among religion, politics, and culture, we have organized this chapter around five themes: the Puritan temper, pluralism, the evangelical dimension, populism, and the contemporary growth of religious and spiritual individualism.

THE PURITAN TEMPER

The United States was born of religious zeal. Its colonization coincided with, and was fueled by, dramatic upheavals in Europe that had been unleashed by the Protestant Reformation. The most important of these upheavals was the Puritan revolution that shook England and inspired many to immigrate to the New World. Today, the term "puritanical" connotes a narrow-minded, self-righteous rejection of anything pleasurable. But the Puritan legacy is something quite different. The Puritans bequeathed to Americans strong civic institutions, a sense of national mission, and a reformist impulse that continues to shape American society and political culture today.

The Puritans earned their name from their desire to "purify" the Church of England and, more broadly, society itself in the late 1500s and early 1600s. Inspired by Calvinist Reformed theology, Puritans reacted vehemently against what they saw as laxity and corruption in Christian churches. Infused with a sense of moral urgency, Puritans threatened established political and religious elites, and they often suffered persecution as a result of their agitation. To many Puritans, America offered both an escape and a fresh start. Thus, many Puritans (along with other religious dissenters) found their way to American shores beginning in the early 1600s.[1]

Although the American colonies were characterized by religious diversity from the beginning, the Puritans brought with them such a powerful vision that they exercised a disproportionate influence for a century and a half before the Revolutionary War. Many people at the time, regardless of their specific denominational affiliation, embraced the central tenets of Puritanism, and several leading colonial intellectuals were Puritan ministers.[2]

To the Puritans, the new land was not just a place where they could freely exercise their religion. It was literally the New Israel, the Promised Land on which the faithful could build a holy commonwealth unencumbered by Old World corruption. The Puritans called their mission an "Errand in the Wilderness" and saw it as divinely ordained. To use the celebrated Puritan phrase, America was to be "a city upon a hill," a light to all nations. This sense of the nation's providential destiny has infused many aspects of American politics, from the "manifest destiny" of westward expansion to various initiatives by presidents. From Abraham Lincoln's determination to preserve the Union as "the last best hope of earth," to Woodrow Wilson's quest to "make the world safe for democracy," to John Kennedy's Peace Corps, to Ronald Reagan's confrontation with the Soviet Union, to George W. Bush's declared foreign-policy aim of "ending tyranny in our world," American leaders periodically have acted on a sense of special global mission and destiny.[3] On the other hand, Donald Trump's "America First" posture, with its zero-sum assessment of foreign affairs, seems to reject a wider global destiny for the nation, though many of his religious followers probably still adhere to that view. Whether, or how, a sense of divine mission should define America's global responsibilities remains a hotly debated matter.[4]

Puritan doctrine also helped to nurture self-government in the new land.[5] Puritans articulated a "covenant theology" that blatantly rejected the long-standing "divine right of kings" doctrine. As the Puritans saw it, political leaders did not derive their authority directly from God; instead, Puritans favored a model of government based on a community's covenant with God. Puritan churches were autonomous, self-governing parishes. This "congregational" tradition gave rise to a parallel political preference for community self-governance.

To be sure, the Puritan conception of democracy was hardly equivalent to today's understanding of democracy. Only the religious "elect," or church members, were allowed to participate. People could become church members only by persuading church leaders that they were predestined for salvation; this status was understood to be enjoyed by only a small percentage of the population. But even if the Puritan colonies were more theocracies than democracies, they fostered a form of self-government from the start. Christian colonists had become outraged by 1775 as England and its established church continued to assert authority over the colonies. By then, the colonists had governed themselves for more than a century, and many in the Puritan tradition believed their religious doctrine justified revolutionary action.[6]

The Puritan emphasis on all humans' tendency to sin also affected American politics, though scholars disagree on the extent. Certainly the Puritans' skeptical view of human nature contributed to the American fear of concentrated governmental power. If political leaders are as tempted by sin as other human beings, then precautions against abuse must be built into the system. Some scholars see evidence of the residual cultural influence of Puritan doctrine in James Madison's concern about diffusing and checking power in the US Constitution. Others note that during the American Revolution people largely avoided romantic and utopian thinking of the sort that led to the excesses of the contemporaneous French Revolution. A deeply ingrained understanding of sin thus tempered the early American practice of government.[7]

In addition, throughout the nation's history, many Americans have based their social practices on the Puritan understanding of the need to restrain individual sin for the good of the community. As the French observer Alexis de Tocqueville noted in the 1830s, the majority of Americans shared the Puritan conviction that "freedom" did not mean license to do anything one pleased but rather the ability to do those things that are good and right. Tocqueville found Americans remarkably faithful to this ideal in their organization of churches, schools, communities, and families. Powerful socialization forces restrained human impulses deemed destructive to the community.[8] Thus, morally intrusive laws and practices that may seem suffocating today were viewed as helpful in early America, as they could liberate the individual from "slavery to sin."[9]

Puritans emphasized the community's central role in nurturing and restraining the individual. This aspect of their outlook is receiving renewed attention today. The Puritans and their heirs could be harsh, but their focus on community meant that people were not isolated. Women were not abandoned if they became widows; orphans were cared for; people did not suffer from rootlessness. Religious mores and strong communities restrained the atomizing tendencies unleashed by political freedom. Even today, many Americans continue to align themselves at least nominally with religious groups, even if their attendance is sporadic, in part because they value precisely this sense of community in congregations.[10]

Finally, Puritanism left a legacy of moral zeal that often did not recognize that shades of gray are needed in a political system whose lifeblood is compromise. Critics note how Puritan clergy moved with equal stridency from depicting the French as anti-Christian during the French and Indian War to viewing the British in similar terms only a decade later during the American Revolution.[11] More sympathetic voices note that politics sometimes cries out for an infusion of religious conviction and fervor. Where would the nation be, they ask, without the uncompromising fervor of the abolitionists in the nineteenth century or the reformist energies of suffragists?

Whether for good or ill, we see evidence of this zeal among religionists across the political spectrum today. When today's religious leaders prophesy against the evils of society and equate their political struggles with God's cause, they are exemplifying the American Puritan tradition and keeping its cultural presence alive.

RELIGIOUS FREEDOM AND PLURALISM

Important though the Puritan legacy was and is, the reality of religious pluralism played an even more powerful role in shaping the nation's history. The roots of the dominant characteristic of American religion today—its almost bewildering multiplicity of religions, denominations, theologies, spiritualities, and organizational styles—may be traced to early colonial patterns. Moreover, the American break with the 1,500-year European tradition of maintaining a state-established church, as well as the eventual constitutional protection for religious freedom, combined to allow religious pluralism to flourish in the New World. And no one in any way planned this confluence of events.

Most colonies installed official state churches. The New England colonies formally designated the Congregational (Puritan) Church as their official faith; Maryland was at one time officially a Catholic colony; most southern colonies established the Anglican Church (the Church of England, which later became known as the Episcopal Church in the United States). This commonplace practice of establishing an official faith meant citizens had to pay a tax to support the colonial church and in some places had to be married by government-supported clergy.[12]

Despite the existence of established churches, members of other religious groups, including Jews, Quakers, Baptists, and many more, all found more room to practice their faiths in the New World than they had in Europe. If one found Massachusetts too suffocating, there was always Rhode Island, home to a host of dissenters, or New York, which had received numerous Jewish settlers by the late seventeenth century. Then there were the middle colonies—most notably Pennsylvania, where religious freedom was official policy from the start—modeling religious tolerance for the rest of the new nation. And there was always the seemingly endless wilderness, which became a haven to religious

Nonconformists and visionaries. So Catholics settled in Maryland and tolerated Protestants; Quakers settled in Pennsylvania and tolerated Lutherans; Baptists agitated for their own freedom in a number of colonies. The idea of a society in which each faith tolerated all others so it could enjoy its own freedom took root.[13]

Religious tolerance was strengthened in the late eighteenth century when the Constitution and the Bill of Rights were drafted and adopted, officially founding the United States. The framers of the Constitution faced an enormous challenge: knitting together thirteen colonies with different cultures, religions, economies, and climates. The solutions were born of necessity and compromise, as we can see in the language of the Religion Clauses of the First Amendment, which clearly are an attempt to address the complexities of religious pluralism: "Congress shall make no law respecting an establishment of religion, or prohibiting the free exercise thereof." The federal government was not allowed to favor one religion over all others, nor to limit the liberty of worship to any religion.

Then, as now, the goal of religious freedom meant different things to different people. Some of the framers, such as Benjamin Franklin, Thomas Jefferson, and James Madison, favored religious liberty in part to reduce clergy's capability of meddling in politics, which to them represented a vestige of the corrupt and oppressive European world. Those founders who took this view were Enlightenment deists who believed in a God who had set the universe on course with natural laws and then left it alone. They cherished the chance to create an enduring United States free of the intense religious squabbles involving government interference that infected the Old World.

Jefferson, a religious skeptic who wrote his own version of the New Testament in which he did not affirm Christ as God, authored the Virginia Statute of Religious Freedom (a precursor to the First Amendment). Madison shared Jefferson's belief that leaving individual conscience unfettered by the state would be the best guide in religion and morality. He therefore joined Jefferson's effort to disestablish the state-established church in Virginia. Meanwhile, fervent Baptists and other religious dissenters also strongly supported constitutional protection of religious freedom and an end to state support for Virginia's established church. Persecuted by Anglican authorities in the southern colonies and by Puritan leaders in New England, Baptists remembered times when they had been jailed for seeking marriages outside the established church or for refusing to pay the church tax. As a result, they were natural allies of separationists like Jefferson and Madison.

Even Christians who initially favored state-established churches recognized the necessity of protecting their own specific interpretations of the faith, which ultimately led most of them to support religious freedom. Given the religious pluralism already present in the prewar colonies, no one could ensure that any particular church would be the one established by the new national government.

All believers wanted freedom for themselves and concluded that the "only way to get it for themselves was to grant it to all others."[14]

The bold national experiment in religious freedom, as embodied by the First Amendment, did set the stage for an end to established churches in the states. Even though the language of the Religion Clauses was understood to prohibit only establishment by the federal government, the national model eventually swept through the states, which took it upon themselves to end their own practice of establishment. Massachusetts was the last state to do away with its official faith, disestablishing the Congregational Church in 1833.[15]

This ideal of church–state separation and religious freedom is deeply ingrained in American culture today. It is also one of the central contributions of the United States to the world. To understand the uniqueness of the American experiment, it is necessary only to observe that from the time of the Emperor Constantine in the fourth century to the founding of the American colonies in the seventeenth century, European practice and doctrine had always been to establish an official religion by law. So embedded is this practice in Europe that government support for religion continues to this day even though most European countries are largely secular. On the other hand, from the start the United States never had a state-established national religion, which has had the somewhat ironic effect of allowing religion to flourish.

By the nineteenth century in the United States, state governments continued to help organized religion in a few ways, but religious institutions were mostly on their own. Cut off from the paternalistic hand of government and largely freed from persecution, churches became voluntary associations, dependent almost entirely upon the continued support of their members for survival. And contrary to what some expected, churches thrived. Indeed, in the wake of disestablishment, remarkable religious growth and innovation occurred in the nineteenth century, spurred by those faith traditions—especially the Baptist and Methodist varieties of Christianity—that adapted best to the rapidly changing conditions of life on the frontier. Unsupported by the state and facing all the challenges of westward expansion, "voluntarist churches" sprang up as circuit-riding ministers traveled west to preach the gospel.

A new kind of entrepreneurial climate fostered the emergence of a multiplicity of worship styles and faith interpretations. If you did not like the local minister, or if you held unorthodox views, you could always join a new congregation or form your own. Such freedom was unheard of in Europe, as it is in most Islamic countries today. Churches blossomed and new faith traditions sprouted as religious entrepreneurs competed with one another for the loyalty of the faithful. In turn, religious practice adapted endlessly to changing economic and social circumstances as Americans pressed ever westward. The peculiar vitality of American religion that we observe today (in contrast to the comparatively moribund state churches of Europe) owes its origin to this unique blend of religious freedom, evangelical fervor, and frontier life.

The fruit of this nineteenth-century pioneer religious culture was a proliferation of religious experiments ranging from utopian communities to the practice of transcendentalism. Another development was the rise of millennial sects. Convinced they could divine the coming of the End Times prophesied in Scripture, charismatic leaders of the nineteenth century forged new religious traditions and contributed to the eschatological theology of modern fundamentalism. A host of movements and sects today trace their lineage to this era.

This God-intoxicated culture also produced religious movements in the nineteenth century that the Protestant-dominated society viewed as threats. The most important of these was the Church of Jesus Christ of Latter-Day Saints (LDS Church) and its faithful, the Mormons. Their story illustrates the limits of tolerance and how religious clashes in America sometimes took violent turns. The Mormon story also illustrates how the American experience can give rise to a popular new faith, one with worldwide membership that is continuing to grow rapidly in the twenty-first century.

Mormons trace their origins to the vision of Joseph Smith, Jr., of Palmyra, New York, who claimed to have found sacred tablets describing how the lost tribe of Israel migrated to the New World. A farmer's son with limited formal education, Smith published his translations of the sacred tablets in 1830, thereby writing what became known as the Book of Mormon, which Mormons take to be an additional testament of Jesus Christ. Within a few years of the book's publication, Smith's following became a serious new movement.

But the religion Smith fashioned, which was fervent, disciplined, and situated outside of the mainstream with its practice of polygamy, aroused the enmity of neighbors. Smith's followers were chased successively out of New York, Ohio, Missouri, and Illinois. Smith himself fled a near war in Missouri (where the governor issued an extermination order against Mormons). After founding the city of Nauvoo, Illinois, he was arrested by the Illinois state militia. Before Smith could stand trial, a lynch mob stormed the jail in Carthage, Illinois, and killed him. Smith's successor, Brigham Young, then led the faithful across the Rocky Mountains to safety in the Salt Lake Valley, where he founded what amounted to a theocratic nation.[16]

Mormons' safe haven was soon interrupted when the territory of Utah came under US control in 1848, following the Mexican War. To Protestant society, the Mormon practice of polygamy (which was grounded in their religious beliefs about eternal life) was repugnant, and politicians responded aggressively. President James Buchanan ordered troops to besiege Salt Lake City in 1857, and Congress followed suit by passing a series of laws outlawing polygamy in US territories. Penalties included the confiscation of church property and the loss of citizenship privileges. These actions, which the US Supreme Court upheld in its 1879 decision in *Reynolds* v. *United States*, ultimately succeeded in forcing Mormons to conform to the marital norms of mainstream American society. LDS Church leaders issued a declaration late in the nineteenth century against plural marriages and pledged loyalty to the laws of the United States. Only then could Utah be admitted to the Union, which officially happened in 1896.[17]

In addition to homegrown pluralism, of course, immigration also fueled religious diversity and continues to do so. By far the most important legacy of nineteenth-century immigration to the United States was the dramatic expansion of the Roman Catholic population. From the mid-1800s on, successive waves of immigrants from Catholic countries such as Ireland, Italy, and Poland poured into the United States. This phenomenon produced a long-enduring religious and cultural divide in American history—the Catholic–Protestant split—which shaped partisan political loyalties for over a century and a half. Indeed, one cannot understand the significance of John F. Kennedy's election to the presidency in 1960 or recent political alliances between Catholics and many evangelical Protestants without appreciating how bitter the divide between Protestants and Catholics once was.

The first large wave of Roman Catholics arrived in the 1840s and 1850s, as Irish immigrants settled in American cities and built a vigorous and public Catholic Church. A second group came from Germany beginning in the same period and continuing into the second half of the nineteenth century. A third set of Catholics came to the United States at the turn of the century, this time from southern, central, and eastern Europe. As the Catholic presence grew, some political issues took on overtones reflecting religious division. Temperance was in part a Protestant attempt to discipline Catholic drinkers; campaigns against corrupt big-city party machines also were partly a reaction against the political power of Catholic immigrants and their descendants. Even before the Civil War, there were occasional Catholic–Protestant skirmishes. Civil War draft riots in New York, in which Irish Catholics protested military conscription, reflected their resistance to the evangelical Protestant tendency to view the Civil War as a holy crusade. Political parties channeled this cultural combat, especially in the North. There, Protestant voters were disproportionately Republican, whereas most Catholics became loyal Democrats. Though some vestiges of this division linger to this day, other cleavages now shape American politics, as we discuss in later chapters.

One of the most graphic examples of the Catholic–Protestant split concerned education. Although church and state institutions were constitutionally separated in the nineteenth-century United States, Protestant domination of society produced an unofficial, cultural Protestant establishment. Public schools frequently used texts—from the Protestant King James Bible to the McGuffey Readers—that openly promoted Protestant values. Catholics developed their own parochial school system and, in places where they were strong enough, pushed for state aid for it. Protestants fought against such efforts.

After the Civil War, Catholics intensified efforts to secure public support for their church-run schools. Protestant fealty to the Republican Party produced its response: the Blaine Amendment, an attempt by the Republican administration of Ulysses S. Grant to amend the US Constitution to prohibit any state govern-mental aid to parochial schools. Introduced in the House of Representatives by James G. Blaine of Maine in 1875, the amendment became a symbol of anti-Catholic sentiment within the Protestant majority (Blaine, a Republican, became associated with the charge that the Democrats were the party of "Rum, Romanism, and Rebellion"). The proposed constitutional amendment passed the House but fell short of the two-thirds vote needed in the Senate. In the wake of that defeat, many states passed a version of the Blaine Amendment in their own constitutions, a legacy that continues to spark judicial clashes today.

But state-level restriction of parochial education did not end there. In the 1920s, for example, Catholics had to take their case all the way to the US Supreme Court when the State of Oregon decreed that all children had to attend public schools—in effect making parochial systems illegal. Catholics won, and the Oregon law was overturned.[18] With that victory, however, the battle shifted once again to state public support, which remains a major constitutional issue.

Immigration, of course, continues to expand American religious pluralism. From the nineteenth century onward, waves of Jewish immigrants, often spurred by persecution abroad, produced a vibrant Jewish community second only to Israel in total population. Since the mid-1960s, when Congress ended national quotas on immigration, new Americans have emigrated from every continent on earth.[19] This not only means that Muslims, Hindus, Buddhists, Sikhs, Baha'is, and others have assumed their place in the American civic fabric but also that Christian communities are becoming more diverse. Korean Presbyterians, Chinese Baptists, Nigerian Catholics, and Orthodox Armenians (Chaldeans), and many other representatives of global Christianity are shaping both American culture and politics in the twenty-first century.

The remarkable pluralism of American religion was not achieved without struggle. The United States has seen plenty of conflict as new religions emerged or new peoples arrived on American shores, inevitably altering the established religious equilibrium. But pluralism has flourished through it all. The evidence from US history confirms what recent global data show: protection of religious freedom and pluralism reduces religious conflict in the long run. On the other hand, repression and persecution from those in or out of government guarantees religious conflict, a lesson not to be ignored.[20]

And there are quite contemporary signs of the continuing struggle to preserve or enhance the reality of religious freedom in the United States. Examples abound today of religious individuals and groups chafing at what they see as government infringement on their religious liberty, conscience rights, or institutional autonomy.[21] Diverse new challenges—zoning bans on mosque construction, workplace discrimination on the basis of religious dress, govern-ment mandates that shutter religious adoption agencies, and lawsuits against vendors of wedding services who refuse service to same-sex couples—these and many other flashpoints are explored in later chapters.

THE EVANGELICAL DIMENSION

Intimately linked with both the Puritan heritage and the American experiment in religious freedom is the strong evangelical dimension of American religion. We mean "evangelical dimension" in two senses. First, we are referring to the branch of Protestantism that is deeply committed to the Bible as the only authoritative source of God's revelation and stresses the adult conversion ("born-again") experience and vigorous evangelizing (seeking converts).

Second, the evangelical dimension also reflects the broader fact that all major faiths, to some extent, have had to adopt strategies of evangelization to survive in the American religious marketplace. Because evangelical Protestants have been especially assertive in seeking converts, evangelical Protestantism became the paradigm of successful religious growth in America. But whether Protestant or Catholic, Mormon or Muslim, any faith must spread the word—that is, evangelize—to thrive. And given the close link between culture and politics, evangelizing can produce political fallout.

In a major study of religious growth and decline from the revolutionary era to today, Roger Finke and Rodney Stark contend that disestablishment, religious freedom, and the frontier have combined to produce an American "religious marketplace."[22] In this marketplace, religious faiths thrive or decline based on how well they serve the needs of existing members and manage to grow by evangelizing new members and "fallen away" former members.[23]

Finke and Stark's study supports what others have argued: Sometimes the intensity of the religious experience offered by a particular faith tradition wanes over time; members become comfortable and do not look outward. Clergy can contribute to this decline if they grow complacent and accommodating. When a religious message becomes watered down, it loses its power to convey any authoritative message about the meaning of life.[24] People yearning for such meaning may therefore leave fading religious traditions for other religious, spiritual, or secular settings. Evangelical faiths of all kinds seek to reach potential adherents with their distinctive messages about meaning. Religious institutions that do not convey clarity of conviction cannot expect to flourish in the long run.[25]

We observe this pattern of rising sects and the decline of once-dominant churches throughout American history. For example, Puritans of the seventeenth century, who were otherworldly and severe, saw their churches transformed into the comfortable, more liberal Congregational Church born in the eighteenth century. In general, when colonial churches became too comfortable, they lost substantial shares of their members to the new, primarily evangelical congregations that were emerging from revivals. Upstart Methodist and Baptist congregations, which had grown dramatically after the founding era, eclipsed them. The cycle continued: As Methodism became the home of an increasingly settled membership and its ministers grew less strict about enforcing traditional rules in the late nineteenth century, a fervent Holiness religious movement drew away a significant portion of its membership.

This pattern is why almost all religious groups in the United States increasingly are committed to actively reaching out to new and former members. They know that if they fail to do so, decline will follow. Thus, even the relatively insular (if large) Roman Catholic Church has an active Office of Evangelization as well as an Evangelical Catholic youth organization and formation movement. They take their lesson from growing religious traditions like the LDS Church, Islam, and evangelical Protestantism in attempting to bring their faith to others.

Throughout American history, surges of evangelical energy often have stimulated significant political upheaval. Consider several major examples of political fallout from evangelical revivalism, beginning in the eighteenth century and continuing into the modern era.

Special Case: Evangelicals, Slavery, and the Civil War

One characteristic of American evangelicalism at times has been its tendency to view politics as a struggle between good and evil. We see this evangelical temper in one of the most momentous, religiously infused movements in US history: the crusade to end slavery. No issue tormented the young nation as much as slavery, America's "original sin." Black people came to the New World in bondage, which was a contradiction with professed political ideals and Christian beliefs from the beginning. Some early leaders, such as George Washington and Thomas Jefferson, acknowledged this contradiction but did little to address it. Indeed, both men were slaveholders, though Washington freed his slaves in his will. The Quaker faith expelled slaveholding members in 1776, and antislavery societies sprouted among some churchgoing people, particularly in the North. However, the practice of slavery was so entrenched by the late eighteenth century that the Constitution itself made a "pact with the Devil" by allowing southern states to count, for purposes of allocating members in the House of Representatives, three-fifths of their enslaved population.

A revolution against slavery began in Northern thinking in the early nineteenth century as more antislavery societies sprang up after religious revivals that awakened Christian consciences against slavery. Churches increasingly became the fulcrum of antislavery agitation during the decades leading up to the Civil War. Many great revivalist preachers joined the cause. For example, during the debate over the Kansas–Nebraska Bill, which allowed the extension of slavery into new territories, Congress was presented with a petition from 3,000 New England ministers who opposed the Bill.[26]

Above all, abolitionist agitation was fueled by African-American leaders, often ex-slaves and fervent Christians, whose testimony and eloquence rebuked the hypocrisy of the nation and the church. Frederick Douglass, one of the towering figures of the nineteenth century, was not only a gifted political orator and writer but also for a time served as a lay preacher in the African Methodist Episcopal Zion Church, whose members included Sojourner Truth and Harriet Tubman. In his numerous writings and speeches, Douglass not only denounced slavery as a violation of the nation's founding creed as laid out in the Declaration of Independence but also castigated biblical justifications of slavery as a heresy against true Christianity.[27]

At the same time, heightened northern agitation against slavery served to harden Southern attitudes and enhance the regional divide. White Southern evangelicals came to view the defense of their land and institutions (including slavery) as divinely ordained.[28] The evangelical tendency to see political clashes as spiritual struggles between good and evil increasingly characterized both sides of the debate about slavery. Thus, the irreconcilable conflict was, in some sense, a clash of evangelicals.

When war came, preachers in both camps depicted their cause in religious terms. From the pulpits of both the North and South came invocations of God's wrath toward the other side in martial prayers of vivid and bloody mien. Hymns similarly carried an almost apocalyptic message, as this stanza of Julia Ward Howe's "Battle Hymn of the Republic" shows:

> I have read a fiery gospel, writ in burnished rows of steel.
> "As ye deal with my contemnors, so with you my grace shall deal";
> Let the Hero, born of woman, crush the serpent with his heel,
> Since God is marching on.

But how could both sides invoke God? And how could anyone find God's will in the carnage of the Civil War? These questions deeply vexed Abraham Lincoln, whose story is central to the religious and political history of America.[29] His thinking on the meaning of the Civil War reveals a great deal about the potential of religiously inspired politics.

The Second Inaugural Address (1865) rivals the Gettysburg Address (1863) as Lincoln's greatest speech. In it, reflecting on the bloodthirsty prayers of partisans, Lincoln observed that "both North and South read the same Bible, and pray to the same God. . . . The prayers of both could not be answered; that of neither has been answered fully. The Almighty has his own purposes." Perhaps, pondered Lincoln, God had prolonged the war as a means of eradicating slavery, something neither side had expected. Perhaps the war was also God's punishment of both North and South for the sin of slavery. Lincoln prayed for a speedy end to the war but accepted that God might will that it last until "every drop of blood drawn with the lash, shall be paid by another drawn with the sword." For Lincoln, this decision was God's. The same God expected him to articulate a forgiving vision of reconstruction and reunification once the war was over: "with malice toward none, with charity for all."[30]

Special Case: Evangelicals and the Temperance Movement

The Temperance Movement—the crusade against drinking alcohol—constitutes another example of evangelical politics, and it provides some important practical lessons for religious partisans today. The crusade, which began in the early 1800s and lasted well into the twentieth century, was a landmark effort by churches to shape American politics—and, indeed, American culture. Led by Protestant ministers and laity, it attained a remarkable public following. The Temperance Movement was largely rooted in concerns about excessive alcohol consumption that had taken root in the colonial period and continued long afterward. Alcohol use in the colonies was widespread and included the consumption of hard liquor by youth. Spurred by the difficulties of life on the frontier, consumption rose to extraordinary levels. Alcoholism was a pervasive problem, especially among men. With gender roles of the time dictating that the man must be the breadwinner, alcoholism among men posed an enormous threat to women and children and was debilitating to men's health and community life as well.

To understand the central role of churches in the Temperance Movement, especially as it led the charge to Prohibition, it is helpful to trace the history of one of the most effective pressure groups in American political history, the Anti-Saloon League. Founded in 1895 by Rev. Howard Hyde Russell, the League united devout Protestants across denominational lines in a strategic approach that led to political success. Because of its close ties to Protestant churches, which served as the grassroots basis for local organization, the League became a formidable national force, able to field 20,000 speakers nationwide for the cause. League organizers compromised when necessary, formed alliances, flooded wavering legislators with mail, and played hardball with opponents.

Though Catholics sometimes joined voluntary temperance initiatives, most were opposed to outright prohibition not only because they personally did not oppose drinking but also because they knew that behind the prohibition movement lay a good deal of anti-Catholicism.

What made the Anti-Saloon League successful was its relentless pressure and clear strategic calculation. It would start local and expand outward, overcoming the multitude of divisions within Protestantism with a simple message of democratic appeal: Fight for the right of local governments to regulate or close down saloons. Once these local "option laws" passed, the League would lobby local governments to enact restrictions on saloons or shutter them. As more and more local communities acted, remaining "wet" areas (places where the purchase and consumption was legal) became isolated, and most of a state went "dry." Then organizers fought to repeal local option laws in favor of statewide prohibition. If beer and alcohol lobbyists prevented state legislatures from acting, the League pushed for a direct vote of the people through referenda. State after state enacted prohibition in this manner. Swept by a mood of optimism, the League turned its attention to the federal government, and Congress passed the Eighteenth Amendment to the Constitution banning the production and sale of intoxicating beverages. Prohibition became the law of the land in 1920.[31]

Prohibition represented the high-water mark of the political clout of evangelical Protestantism, but its success ironically contributed to its downfall. Evangelicals increasingly became a social and political lightning rod into the 1920s. One reason for the controversy is that while Prohibition did reduce drinking, it also fueled political corruption and gangsterism and made lawbreakers out of millions of otherwise law-abiding citizens. Moreover, during the Roaring Twenties, American culture itself was changing. Religiously speaking, Catholics and Jews had grown in number and clout in just a few decades, so the religious pluralism of the nation had expanded again, eroding Protestant domination of the culture. The Great Depression was the final straw, making religio-moral concerns far less pressing than economic ones. While many Protestant churches vigorously fought the repeal of Prohibition, the nation moved on, and the Twenty-First Amendment was passed in 1933, repealing the Eighteenth.[32]

While this episode marked the passing of a particular manifestation of evangelical activism, the tradition of ardent evangelical political energy goes on. The broader impulse, motivated by a deep desire to reach the hand of God out to confront perceived evils remains strong, sometimes transforming, and often controversial when it takes a political direction. It animates many causes— sometimes surprising ones, as we will see—and emanates from people in numerous religious and spiritual groups.

THE POPULIST DIMENSION

Churches in America, as we have seen, depend on the voluntary support of the faithful to survive, let alone thrive. But thrive many do. Churches and spiritual groups were, and are, the most common means (apart from work and family) by which ordinary Americans meet voluntarily in large numbers. To a great extent, religion in America is popular religion—and the religious traditions that succeed understand this reality. Thus, popular religion often is a good way for people to discover and express their common hopes and concerns. It can be a conservative force, helping to preserve traditions people cherish. It can also be a radical force, channeling mass discontent and challenging elites with prophetic denunciations of injustice. Whatever its specific directions, popular religion often fosters populist politics that focus on mass-based democracy and hold elites accountable to the people.

This populist dimension was evident in the religious Great Awakening of the eighteenth century, which fostered grassroots evangelism and prepared colonists for the Revolution. It was present in the crusades against slavery and alcohol. It is alive today in black churches that serve as vital social and political centers for many African Americans, directing both their hopes and their challenges. There also is a kind of populism alive today among Christian conservatives who attack the hegemony of "cultural elites." To understand this manifestation of contemporary religious politics, it is helpful to survey the evolution of popular democracy and populist politics.

The framers of the Constitution did not view direct democracy or majority rule favorably at all. Key figures, such as James Madison, feared popular demagogues and knew that the masses could trample on liberty just as easily as a single tyrant could. The resulting Constitution, as well as standard suffrage restrictions (the exclusion of women and African Americans, for example) and the absence of strong political parties combined to ensure that politics in early American history remained far from fully democratic.

As historian Nathan Hatch suggests, however, a continuing democratization of Christianity advanced political democracy in the early 1800s. At the forefront of democratized religion were itinerant and often uneducated grassroots preachers (especially Baptists and Methodists) who understood the distinctive needs of people on the frontier.[33] Tent revivals, which brought souls to Christ by the thousands, originated during this period; later, Rev. Billy Graham and various other evangelists updated the setting and the technology. Clergy who arose from among the common people dominated religious life on the frontier because, as the eighteenth-century evangelist George Whitefield observed, Harvard and Yale divinity schools did not prepare their elite students "to spend half their days in the saddle going from one rural hamlet to another."[34] Circuit-riding preachers endured many hardships to spread their message to the masses and brought with them a democratic faith that all are equal before God. Many people were profoundly moved by this populist Christianity and began refusing to see themselves as inferior to others. They pushed for elimination of property restrictions on voting and other measures that advanced democratization. By the late 1820s, mass democracy (at least for white males) had come to the United States, propelled in part by evangelical Protestant forces in the young nation.

This link between popular religion and popular democracy emerged again toward the end of the nineteenth century, the era from which the term "populist" derives.[35] This was an era of great expansion in manufacturing; industrialists garnered wealth while millions of farmers and workers struggled to survive. Along with rapid economic growth and ferment came a new set of ideas—especially the gospel of wealth, conspicuous consumption, and social Darwinism. In 1859, biologist Charles Darwin had shocked religious sensibilities with the publication of *The Origin of Species*, with its central argument that life forms develop and change slowly over time by a natural process of evolution. Herbert Spencer and William Graham Sumner popularized a social counterpart to this theory, with a competitive "survival of the fittest" model of human social evolution. Some saw captains of industry as the "fittest" by virtue of their success and wealth. To critics, this new doctrine provided a suspicious justification for the plunder perpetrated by nineteenth-century robber barons.

This new age and its justifying doctrine clashed sharply with rural Christian life, where more traditional, communal norms of barter, shared work, and extended families still operated. This clash of worldviews turned into a fierce political struggle beginning in the 1880s, when hard times settled over much of agricultural America.

For our purposes, what is notable about the populist movement was its religious overtones and its combination of moral traditionalism and economic radicalism. As many populists were evangelical Protestants, the crusade took on a distinctly revivalist flavor, complete with camp meetings and stirring speeches. The crusade was "a Pentecost of politics in which a tongue of flame sat upon every man."[36] Populists sought a series of religiously connected goals aimed at a moral structuring of society, which also was reflected in the Protestant-led Temperance Movement (many populists were also "temperance men"). They concluded that the threat posed by industrialists required government to act with vigor and authority to protect the people. They proposed a variety of radical ideas, from inflationary monetary policies to outright state ownership of the railroads and the telegraph.

In 1896, the Democratic Party nominated William Jennings Bryan, a fiery speaker who shared the populist repugnance for the emerging industrial society, as its presidential candidate. Bryan could sound like a socialist one minute and a pietist preacher the next. For Bryan, as for many populists, the gospel of the New Testament was the proper basis for a good and caring society.[37] Bryan's followers lauded the pietist idea of creating a Bible-based moral social order, insisting, as Bryan did in his famous 1896 "Cross of Gold" speech, that "you shall not crucify mankind on a cross of Gold," a reference to the gold standard that Bryan hoped the United States would abandon to help farmers repay their substantial debts.[38] Bryan's campaign was inherently limited, however, because it fostered an urban–rural cleavage and undercut traditional Democratic support among Catholics and Lutherans, who were uncomfortable with his particular brand of evangelical politics. However, Bryan's populist economic message ultimately was adopted by the Progressive movement, and later brought to fruition in the New Deal.

We hear many echoes of populism today—from across the political spectrum—as religious and political leaders denounce various elites and demand that "the people" be heard.[39] But the populist impulse, fueled by resentments and prone to imagining elite conspiracies, can take a dark turn. Populist figures in the past courted nativist and anti-Semitic prejudices. Today we see the emergence of a nationalist populism that helped catapult Donald Trump into the White House, which critics see as capitalizing on antipathy toward immigrants, fear of Muslims, or, in its most extreme form, overt racism.[40] We will explore these issues more fully in subsequent chapters.

SPIRITUAL AND RELIGIOUS INDIVIDUALISM

Another theme in sharp focus today is spiritual and religious individualism, which is soaring in significance and increasingly taking place outside the doors of established religious institutions. Its most evident sign is the growth in numbers of Americans who, while describing themselves as spiritual to one degree or another, self-consciously separate themselves from traditional religious organizations. Another sign is the simultaneous and rapid increase in the number of people who are explicitly nonreligious or just indifferent to the entire realm of the religious or spiritual.

Of course, American religious history has a vibrant tradition of practicing and celebrating individual spirituality and explicitly rejecting organized religion. It also has a tradition of attacking all religions and another of behaving indifferently toward religion. These individual attitudes, though not in accord with the dominant culture, are as much a part of US history as are the Puritan temper, the evangelical impulse, or the populist dimension. Consider Thomas Paine and his late eighteenth-century Age of Reason, a relentless critique of the Bible. Consider Ralph Waldo Emerson and his historic "Divinity Address," in which he proclaimed his determination to follow his individualistic spirituality rather than any organized religion.[41] Consider Robert Ingersoll, the famous (or notorious) campaigning atheist of the second half of the nineteenth century.[42] Such dissenters were hardly alone, either. Consider Emma Goldman and other early twentieth-century radical socialists who were self-assured atheists. Consider Elizabeth Cady Stanton, iconic feminist and suffragist, who was openly skeptical of the Bible and Christianity. The presence of such "freethinking" dissenters in our history is as real as was the pressure they often faced as individualistic rebels in religious America.[43]

Recent years, however, have witnessed a rapid expansion of individualistic expressions of spirituality, religious skepticism, and indifference. During the 1950s, which reflected the "high tide of civic religion," less than 5 percent of Americans reported no religious affiliation, and most were regularly attending members of religious congregations.[44] Recent surveys report that a quarter of Americans have no religious affiliation, up 50 percent in less than a decade and a fivefold increase since the 1950s. These so-called "religious nones" include some 7 percent who say they are atheists or agnostics, but the rest responded "nothing in particular" to religious affiliation questions.[45] The religiously unaffiliated are also becoming more thoroughly secular over time, according to their responses to a battery of questions about the importance of religion and religious practices.[46] Even among people explicitly seeking a religious home, the approach today tends to be an individualistic shopping expedition for a place that fits the seeker's individual values, rooted in the assumption that the individual should not have to conform his or her values to any religious institution. The focus is on the self, not the collective.[47]

A host of interrelated explanations account for these trends. The cultural shock of the 1960s introduced a wave of rebellious, anti-institutional sentiment into American society that affected attitudes about organized religion in the name of personal freedom and distaste for authority. Successive generations of young people have been shaped by this culture of hyper-individualism and personal autonomy.[48] Since the 1960s, each generational cohort has been less conventionally religious than the one before it; thus, generational replacement propels the growth in numbers of religious nones.[49] Indeed, some 35 percent of millennials (those born between 1981 and 1996) are religiously unaffiliated.[50]

The failures of conventional organized religion, particularly scandals involving televangelists and sex abuse by clergy, also have fueled disillusionment. We also see evidence that more liberal Americans are reacting against politicized religion, particularly the close association of the Republican Party with conservative religionists, who have themselves mobilized against what they see as a secular assault on their way of life.[51]

One of the most intriguing of the explanations for the rise of secularism in the United States relates to changes in family structure and related demographic trends that we observe throughout the West, not just in the United States. Profound changes in marriage norms and habits have been shaped by economic, technological, and cultural forces. Many Americans are marrying later, not marrying at all, and having fewer children; these demographic trends all tend to weaken religious institutions.[52] In addition, more and more children today are born out of wedlock or into families that tend not to pass on religious habits. As Mary Eberstadt shows, vigorous families and vibrant religion are interdependent: they are "the double helix of society, each dependent on the strength of the other for successful reproduction." In short, profound changes in family structure undermine traditional religious affiliation.[53]

It is not clear, however, what the future may bring regarding the growth of secularism in the United States. While many of the disaffiliated have low birth rates, many of today's new American immigrants are both more religious and likely to have larger families, which may serve as a counterweight to secular trends. Still, the rise of the nones, like the broader overall expansion of spiritual individualism, is a historic phenomenon of unmistakable importance. For instance, nonreligious citizens today tend to be more liberal than the general public about a wide variety of issues. They also have become an important, if informal, voting constituency that leans heavily toward the Democrats. While not a self-conscious voting bloc, the nonreligious have become as worthy of attention for their voting behavior as evangelical Protestants, Catholics, or Jews, as we will see in Chapter 7.[54]

Another significant question posed by the growth of individualistic and anti-institutional approaches to religion concerns its potential long-term effect on religious freedom in America. The increasing number of nonreligious Americans is itself a byproduct of religious freedom, which naturally includes the freedom to opt out of traditional religious life with little or no consequence. Yet there also is a warning sign here regarding the future of religious liberty in the United States. The shift away from traditional religious commitments weakens well-established religious institutions at every level of society—local, state, and national. As some churches and synagogues empty and various Protestant denominations decline, so does their power in politics, for better or for worse. It was the perspective of James Madison and the framers of the Constitution that political power in the hands of religious leaders and groups could be dangerous—or serve as a vital check on government. Put another way, the paradox of our historical moment may be that the explosion of religious and nonreligious individualism may come to threaten the extent of religious freedom as government confronts weakened organized religion that is less able to check it. For some, this will be good news; for others, it is frightening.

CONCLUSION

Threads of American religious history, past and present, interact with each other and inevitably help frame the future. In the chapters to follow we will see how the themes explored here—the Puritan temper, pluralism, the evangelical dimension, populism, and spiritual and religious individualism—help us understand politics and religion in the United States today.

DISCUSSION QUESTIONS

1 How did the Puritans' rejection of the "divine right of kings" and their embrace of "covenant theology" influence later conceptions of authority in the political arena? Are there any similarities today?

2 During the founding years of the United States, different groups of people had different reasons for supporting freedom of religion. Identify two such groups and explain their reasoning for supporting religious freedom.

3 Reflect on the Protestant–Catholic rivalry present for much of American history. How did it play out in the political arena? What makes alliances between Catholics and Evangelicals today so shocking, historically speaking?

4 Finke and Stark coined the phrase "religious marketplace." What were they referring to?

5 How was the American Civil War infused with a religious temper?

6 Expand on the link between popular religion and popular democracy. Give an example of the populist dimension in American religious history.

FURTHER READING

Ahlstrom, Sydney, *A Religious History of the American People* (New Haven, CT: Yale University Press, 1972). The classic history of religion in the United States.

Clark, Norman H., *Deliver Us from Evil: An Interpretation of American Prohibition* (New York, NY: W. W. Norton, 1976). Still the most thoughtful modern history of the Prohibition experience.

Eberstadt, Mary, *How the West Really Lost God: A New Theory of Secularization* (Philadelphia, PA: Templeton Press, 2014). A fascinating account of the way family decline fuels religious decline.

Eck, Diana L., *A New Religious America: How a "Christian Country" Has Become the World's Most Religiously Diverse Nation* (San Francisco, CA: HarperSanFrancisco, 2002). A history with a central theme of religious diversity in the United States.

Finke, Roger, and Rodney Stark, *The Churching of America, 1776–2005: Winners and Losers in Our Religious Economy* (New Brunswick, NJ: Rutgers University Press, 2005).

Gaustad, Edwin S., and Leigh E. Schmidt, *The Religious History of America: The Heart of the American Story from Colonial Times to Today* (San Francisco, CA: HarperSanFrancisco, 2004). One of the leading historical treatments of religion in America.

Hawley, George, *Demography, Culture, and the Decline of America's Christian Denominations* (Lanham, MD: Lexington Books, 2017). Examines trends in culture, demography, and family size that explain why so many of America's largest denominations are declining in membership.

Hertzke, Allen D., *Echoes of Discontent: Jesse Jackson, Pat Robertson, and the Resurgence of Populism* (Washington, DC: CQ Press, 1993).

Jacoby, Susan, *The Great Agnostic: Robert Ingersoll and American Freethought* (New Haven, CT: Yale University Press, 2012). On religious skepticism in American history.

Marty, Martin E., *Pilgrims in Their Own Land: 500 Years of Religion in America* (Boston, MA: Little, Brown, 1984). Sweeping history by one of the nation's foremost church historians.

McLoughlin, William, *Revivals, Awakening, and Reform: An Essay on Religion and Social Change in America, 1607–1977* (Chicago, IL: University of Chicago Press, 1978). Especially useful discussion of the Great Awakening.

Morgan, Edmund, *The Puritan Dilemma: The Story of John Winthrop* (Boston, MA: Little, Brown, 1958). A readable introduction to Puritan religion and politics.

Noll, Mark, and Luke E. Harlow (eds.), *Religion and American Politics: From the Colonial Period to the Present* (Oxford: Oxford University Press, 2007). Eminent historians reflect on religion and politics in the United States.

Putnam, Robert D., and David E. Campbell, *American Grace: How Religion Divides and Unites Us* (New York, NY: Simon & Schuster, 2010). Summarizes a massive survey to make an argument about major trends in American religion.

Reichley, A. James, *Faith in Politics* (Washington, DC: Brookings Institution, 2002). A superb historical introduction to its subject.

Smith, Christian, *The Religious and Spiritual Lives of Emerging Adults* (Oxford: Oxford University Press, 2009).

Szymanski, Ann Marie, *Pathways to Prohibition: Radicals, Moderates, and Social Movement Outcomes* (Durham, NC: Duke University Press, 2003).

Wuthnow, Robert, *America and the Challenge of Religious Diversity* (Princeton, NJ: Princeton University Press, 2005).

NOTES

1. See Perry Miller, *Errand into the Wilderness* (Cambridge, MA: The Belknap Press of Harvard University Press, 1956); and Edmund Morgan, *The Puritan Dilemma: The Story of John Winthrop* (Boston, MA: Little, Brown, 1958).

2. A. James Reichley, *Faith in Politics* (Washington, DC: Brookings Institution, 2002), pp. 54–73.

3. Lincoln's quote is from his Second Annual Address to Congress, December 1, 1862; Bush made this sweeping declaration in his Second Inaugural Address, January 20, 2005.

4. Foreign-policy realists often see the missionary impulse as dangerously naive while nationalists criticize the global commitments this sense of divine mission can create.

5. John Witte Jr., "How to Govern a City on a Hill: The Early Puritan Contribution to American Constitutionalism," *Emory Law Journal*, 39 (1990): 41–64.

6. Sydney Ahlstrom, *A Religious History of the American People* (New Haven, CT: Yale University Press, 1972); and Reichley, *Faith in Politics.*

7. This point is made by Barry Allen Shain, *The Myth of American Individualism: The Protestant Origins of American Political Thought* (Princeton, NJ: Princeton University Press, 1994).

8. Alexis de Tocqueville, *Democracy in America: And Two Essays on America*, trans. Gerald E. Bevan and Isaac Kramnick (London: Penguin, 2003).

9. Shain, *The Myth of American Individualism.*

10. Robert Booth Fowler, *Unconventional Partners: Religion and Liberal Culture in the United States* (Grand Rapids, MI: Eerdmans, 1989); Robert Putnam, *Bowling Alone: The Collapse and Revival of American Community* (New York, NY: Simon & Schuster, 2000).

11. Mark Noll (ed.), *One Nation Under God? Christian Faith and Political Action in America* (San Francisco, CA: HarperSanFrancisco, 1988).

12. Ahlstrom, *A Religious History of the American People*; Leonard Levy, *The Establishment Clause: Religion and the First Amendment*, 2nd edn (Raleigh, NC: University of North Carolina Press, 1994).

13. Ahlstrom, *A Religious History of the American People*; Roger Finke and Rodney Stark, *The Churching of America, 1776–2005: Winners and Losers in Our Religious Economy* (New Brunswick, NJ: Rutgers University Press, 2005); Andrew Greeley, *The Denominational Society: A Sociological Approach to Religion in America* (Glenview, IL: Scott, Foresman, 1972); Will Herberg, *Protestant–Catholic–Jew* (Garden City, NY: Doubleday, 1955).

14. Sydney Mead, *The Lively Experiment: The Shaping of Christianity in America* (New York, NY: Harper & Row, 1963), p. 35. For an excellent general discussion of the theological and political ideas that presaged the Religion Clauses, see John Witte Jr. and Joel A. Nichols, *Religion and the American Constitutional Experiment*, 4th edn (Oxford: Oxford University Press, 2016), chapter 2.

15. Gary Glenn, "Forgotten Purposes of the First Amendment Religion Clause," *Review of Politics*, 49 (1987): 340–366; Michael Malbin, *Religion and Politics: The Intentions of the Authors of the First Amendment* (Washington, DC: American Enterprise Institute, 1978); Witte and Nichols, *Religion and the American Constitutional Experiment*, chapter 4.

16. Ahlstrom, *A Religious History of the American People*, pp. 501–509.

17. Anson Phelps Stokes, *Church and State in the United States*, vol. II (New York, NY: Harper, 1950), pp. 275–285. For a brief and engaging discussion of Mormon

experience in Utah in the mid-nineteenth century, see David Roberts, "The Brink of War," *Smithsonian Magazine*, June 2008.

18. *Pierce* v. *Society of Sisters*, 268 US 510 (1925).

19. The Immigration and Nationality Act of 1965, passed in the Civil Rights era, ended restrictions on the basis of nation of origin that had been in place since 1921. It led to the dramatic increase in immigrants from Asia, the Middle East, and Africa.

20. Brian J. Grim and Roger Finke, *The Price of Freedom Denied: Religious Persecution and Conflict in the Twenty-First Century* (Cambridge: Cambridge University Press, 2011). Georgetown University's Religious Freedom Project has built upon Grim and Finke's landmark study with commissioned research documenting the civic benefits of religious freedom and the huge costs of its repression (https://berkleycenter.georgetown.edu/rfp). A synthesis of that research is contained in a book chapter by Allen D. Hertzke, "Religious Agency and the Integration of Marginalized People," in Pierpaolo Donati and Roland Minnerath (eds.), *Towards a Participatory Society: New Roads to Social and Cultural Integration* (Vatican City: Pontifical Academy of Social Sciences, 2017).

21. For a catalogue of these emerging clashes, see Allen D. Hertzke (ed.), *Religious Freedom in America: Constitutional Roots and Contemporary Challenges* (Norman, OK: University of Oklahoma Press, 2015).

22. Finke and Stark, *The Churching of America*.

23. Laurence Iannaccone, "Why Strict Churches Are Strong," *American Journal of Sociology*, 99 (1994): 1180–1211; Donald E. Miller, *Reinventing Protestantism: Christianity in the New Millennium* (Berkeley, CA: University of California Press, 1997).

24. We use the term "church" here and in many subsequent contexts for linguistic economy. However, in this and future instances, blanket references to "church" may be read more broadly to encompass any organized faith tradition.

25. Iannaccone, "Why Strict Churches Are Strong"; Dean M. Kelley, *Why Conservative Churches Are Growing: A Study in Sociology of Religion* (San Francisco, CA: HarperSanFrancisco, 1972).

26. Luke Eugene Ebersole, *Church Lobbying in the Nation's Capital* (New York, NY: Macmillan, 1951).

27. William S. McFeely, *Frederick Douglass* (New York, NY: W. W. Norton, 1991).

28. Ahlstrom, *A Religious History of the American People*, pp. 653–654; David B. Chesebrough, *Clergy Dissent in the Old South, 1830–1865* (Carbondale, IL: Southern Illinois University Press, 1996).

29. On Lincoln and religion, see Allen C. Guelzo, *Abraham Lincoln: Redeemer President* (Grand Rapids, MI: Eerdmans, 1999); Richard J. Carwardine, *Lincoln* (New York, NY: Longman, 2003).

30. Ronald C. White, *Lincoln's Greatest Speech: The Second Inaugural* (New York, NY: Simon & Schuster, 2002).

31. Ann Marie Szymanski, *Pathways to Prohibition: Radicals, Moderates, and Social Movement Outcomes* (Durham, NC: Duke University Press, 2003).

32. Norman H. Clark, *Deliver Us from Evil: An Interpretation of American Prohibition* (New York, NY: W. W. Norton, 1976).

33. Nathan O. Hatch, *The Democratization of American Christianity* (New Haven, CT: Yale University Press, 1989).

34. As quoted in Finke and Stark, *The Churching of America*, p. 87.

35. The literature on the populist movement, including its religious dimensions, is extensive and growing. It is summarized by Allen D. Hertzke, *Echoes of Discontent: Jesse Jackson, Pat Robertson, and the Resurgence of Populism* (Washington, DC: CQ Press, 1993), chapter 2.

36. As quoted in John D. Hicks, *The Populist Revolt: A History of the Farmers' Alliance and the People's Party* (Lincoln, NE: University of Nebraska Press, 1961).

37. This point is developed more fully in Hertzke, *Echoes of Discontent*, chapter 2.

38. Paul Kleppner, *The Cross of Culture: A Social Analysis of Midwestern Politics, 1850–1900* (New York, NY: Free Press, 1970).

39. Hertzke, *Echoes of Discontent*.

40. This extreme manifestation is found in the so-called "alt-right" movement, a loose collection of provocateurs that includes overt racists, such as Richard Spencer, who espouse "white nationalism." See Graeme Wood, "His Kampf," *The Atlantic*, June 2017 and Oliver Laughland, "White Nationalist Richard Spencer at Rally Over Confederate Statue's Removal," *The Guardian*, May 14, 2017.

41. See https://emersoncentral.com/texts/nature-addresses-lectures/addresses/divinity-school-address/.

42. Susan Jacoby, *The Great Agnostic: Robert Ingersoll and American Freethought* (New Haven, CT: Yale University Press, 2012).

43. Susan Jacoby, *Freethinkers: A History of American Secularism* (New York, NY: Henry Holt & Co., 2004), chapters 2, 5, 6, and 8.

44. Robert D. Putnam and David E. Campbell, *American Grace: How Religion Divides and Unites Us* (New York, NY: Simon & Schuster, 2010).

45. The most recent figure on the percentage of religious nones, at 25 percent, is from Gregory A. Smith, "A Growing Share of Americans Say It's Not Necessary to Believe in God to be Moral," October 16, 2017, www.pewresearch.org/fact-tank/2017/10/16/a-growing-share-of-americans-say-its-not-necessary-to-believe-in-god-to-be-moral. The historical figures and trends are from the Pew Research Center, "America's Changing Religious Landscape: A Report on the Religious Landscape Study," May 12, 2015, www.pewforum.org/2015/05/12/americas-changing-religious-landscape/.

46. Michael Lipka, "Religious 'Nones' Are Not Only Growing, They're Becoming More Secular," Pew Research Center, November 11, 2015, www.pewresearch.org/fact-tank/2015/11/11/religious-nones-are-not-only-growing-theyre-becoming-more-secular.

47. Paul Heelas, *The New Age Movement: The Celebration of the Self and the Sacralization of Modernity* (Oxford: Blackwell, 1996); Robert Wuthnow, *America and the Challenges of Religious Diversity* (Princeton, NJ: Princeton University Press, 2005), chapter 4; in Christian context, a lively discussion is in Dan Kimball, *They Like Jesus but Not the Church: Insight from Emerging Generations* (Grand Rapids, MI: Zondervan, 2007).

48. Christian Smith, in this area as in so many others in the sociology of religion, has done superb work. See his *Souls in Transition: The Religious and Spiritual Lives of Emerging Adults* (Oxford: Oxford University Press, 2009).

49. Putnam and Campbell, *American Grace*.

50. Michael Lipka, "A Closer Look at America's Rapidly Growing Religious 'Nones,'" Pew Research Center, May 13, 2015, www.pewresearch.org/fact-tank/2015/05/13/a-closer-look-at-americas-rapidly-growing-religious-nones.

51. Putnam and Campbell, *American Grace*.

52. George Hawley, *Demography, Culture, and the Decline of America's Christian Denominations* (Lanham, MD: Lexington Books, 2017).

53. Mary Eberstadt, *How the West Really Lost God: A New Theory of Secularization* (Philadelphia, PA: Templeton Press, 2014).

54. Pew Research Center, "The Unaffiliated," 2009, http://religion.pewforum.org/portrait.

2

THEORIES OF RELIGION, CULTURE, AND AMERICAN POLITICS

Now that we have examined key themes in the history of religion in American politics, in this chapter we introduce several broad social-scientific theories that will help us interpret the relationships among religion, politics, and culture. These theories are efforts by scholars to comprehend the central features of the sometimes-bewildering complexity of religion's relevance to American politics by providing a cogent lens through which to understand diverse empirical facts. Some of the theoretical perspectives emphasize worldwide forces; others restrict themselves to the United States. Each has its own emphasis, makes its own case, and clearly illuminates one or more aspects of the place of religion in American political culture. Readers will find it helpful to keep these broad theories—civil religion, unconventional partners, culture wars, secularization, populism, the religious marketplace, and culture shift—in mind while reading subsequent chapters.

CIVIL RELIGION

Especially in the years after World War II, but sometimes in recent years too, some analysts have argued that something called the civil-religion thesis provides the most guidance to those seeking to understand religion, as well as the religion-politics relationship, in the United States. This perspective contends that the most politically relevant form of religion in the United States has little to do with specific organized religious traditions, religious-interest groups, or court cases about church–state separation. Instead, advocates of the civil-religion thesis assert that the religion that matters most in the United States is a shared but vague political religion that broadly celebrates America and its culture. Scholars refer to this "religion" as the civil religion. The American civil religion tends to emphasize the unique, "blessed" status of the United States among the nations of the world. It inspires in its followers a sense of divinely ordained American patriotism. The quick appearance of American flags and signs reading "God Bless America" in the days immediately following the terrorist attacks of September 11, 2001, as well as the national joy at the quick apprehension of the Boston Marathon bombers in April 2013, are among many examples analysts cite to indicate the presence of the civil religion.

Those attracted to this perspective agree that the civil religion exists alongside, not in conflict with, sectarian religions in the United States. The two do not clash because, unlike any given organized religious tradition, civil religion is nonsectarian in its assumption that God has blessed the United States, endowed it with special opportunities, and assigned it responsibilities to do good in the world. One can be a faithful adherent of one religious tradition and simultaneously celebrate the civil religion. Analysts contend that it is essential to recognize and analyze the civil religion because it enhances national stability, governmental legitimacy, and a feeling of shared destiny among citizens. After all, every nation has a "faith" of sorts, a belief in itself, a civic creed. In the United States, this civil religion is infused with a sense that God has provided Americans with unique purposes and promise, often tied to a distinctive struggle to extend liberty and equality.

Drawing from the work of the political philosopher Jean-Jacques Rousseau, the prominent sociologist Robert Bellah helped illustrate the reality of a civil religion. In his comparison of the inaugural addresses of Abraham Lincoln and John F. Kennedy, Bellah noticed that these two seminal American leaders— separated by a century—both invoked civil-religious themes in asserting that the nation had a divine purpose and calling upon God to bless the country.[1] Other scholars since have observed how much presidential inauguration ceremonies are steeped in civil-religious imagery, including the fact that incoming presidents make reference to God and the United States almost in the same breath. It also has become routine for American presidents to end major speeches with some variant of the phrase "God bless you, and God bless the United States of America."

Historian Sidney Mead documented how a "national religion" grew steadily during the early years of the Republic and established firm roots by the time of the Civil War. Mead was the first to observe that there are two distinct forms of faith in the United States: first, the faiths of specific religious groups and denominations and, second, what he terms "the American faith," or the civil religion. Both religious forms, he argued, are intertwined and mutually supportive.

In the end, the ultimate question is one of how to evaluate the validity of the civil-religion thesis. Are Bellah and Mead empirically correct in asserting that the United States has a civil religion? A good bit of evidence supports their contentions. Patriotism is palpable in some religious settings, as anyone who has seen the American flag or heard a spirited singing of "God Bless America" in a house of worship can attest. In turn, religious Americans gain affirmation of the broad significance of their faith when they hear political leaders publicly call on God, when they use currency that reads "In God We Trust," and when they repeat the Pledge of Allegiance's proclamation of one nation "under God."[2]

From Abraham Lincoln's sublime vision of the nation as the "last, best hope of earth" to Ronald Reagan's invocation of the Puritan "city on a hill" metaphor to more recent presidents' invocation of God's blessing on Americans, civil-religious images abound of an America that is connected somehow with the divine. Many religious leaders have echoed politicians' words as well; most famously, evangelist Billy Graham spent decades asking God's blessings on the nation's leaders, institutions, and purposes.

Moreover, signs of civil-religious rituals appear around major American holidays, such as Fourth of July ceremonies, Memorial Day observances, and everything surrounding that most distinctly civil-religious holiday, Thanksgiving. Each yearly ritual brings its own blend of religion and patriotism, faith and political history. The American civil religion has its own sacred places too, such as the majestic Lincoln Memorial in Washington, DC, and the hallowed battleground of Gettysburg in Pennsylvania. Some documents have symbolic sacred status as well—"scriptures," one might say, of the American creed—especially the original Declaration of Independence and the Constitution. At the National Archives in Washington, visitors wishing to view these two documents encounter a reverent atmosphere not unlike that of a grand house of worship. The area is softly lit and so quiet that conversations turn to a whisper when people enter. Visitors walk up a narrow, semicircular corridor approaching glass cases, impervious even to nuclear war, that hold these documents for the faithful to venerate. Guards prevent visitors from getting too close to the glass, and the cases are lowered underground for safekeeping every night.

Finally, there are the symbolic prophets and saviors of the American civil religion. In Washington, DC, one can read prophetic words carved in stone at the Jefferson Memorial or stare in awe at the soaring monument to George Washington. At the very center of the civil religion stands Abraham Lincoln, whom historian Clinton Rossiter labeled "the martyred Christ of Democracy's passion play."[3] The story of Lincoln's presidency, remarkable maturation, single-minded sense of purpose, and tragic assassination invokes religious images of Christ-like sacrifice and death for the nation's rebirth. Millions of citizens and foreign visitors alike make reverent pilgrimages to the Lincoln Memorial, which also commemorates the spot where another great American prophet,

Rev. Martin Luther King, challenged the nation to work toward his dream of equality and dignity for all.

It is fair to say that the civil-religion thesis holds some water despite a degree of scholarly disagreement.[4] Political scientist Christopher Chapp's study of the rhetoric of civil religion in US political life affirms this conclusion. He contends that not only is the civil religion real but also that the usual invocations of civil religion often do not amount to much. In Chapp's words, civil-religious rhetoric often is no more than "banal expressions of American national identity" that can exclude people who might not identify with either the patriotism or the implicit religiosity conveyed by the civil religion.[5] This conclusion raises the question of whether the civil-religion thesis explains any practical dimensions of religious politics—such as how religious beliefs affect voting behavior, or the agendas of religious interest groups, or church–state conflicts in America.

Finally, the ever-intensifying political polarization in America calls into question how much power civil religion has to unite people across deep cultural and partisan divides. Expanding religious diversity and the growing number of religiously unaffiliated Americans also chip away civil religion's unifying potential. Can civil religion unite when so many Americans seem "divided by God"?[6] Perhaps we are seeing the emergence of competing civil religions, with progressives invoking religious pluralism and conservatives the nation's Judeo-Christian heritage.

THE UNCONVENTIONAL-PARTNERS THESIS

Another theoretical perspective on the relationships among culture, religion, and politics in the United States is the "unconventional partners" thesis forwarded by political scientist Robert Booth Fowler.[7] Although Fowler's perspective takes some inspiration from the civil-religion thesis, it is broader, looking beyond the periodic rituals of civil religion to deeper manifestations of religion's relationship to American culture. The unconventional-partners thesis posits that religion plays a significant political role in the United States because it helps to sustain both the political culture and its governmental institutions. Religion accomplishes this task not through active engagement in politics but instead by offering Americans a clear source of meaning, morality, and community that neither the culture nor the government can provide. In doing so, it relieves pressure on—and strengthens—both the culture and the government. In turn, the government and the culture frequently accept or promote religious freedom, allowing the religious sector to thrive. But this symbiotic relationship is largely unintentional—hence the "unconventional partners" label.[8]

Like the civil-religion thesis, Fowler's unconventional-partners thesis approaches religion—in this case organized religious institutions and the beliefs they promote—as playing an essentially conservative, preservative role in

American life. By providing meaning, morality, and community for many Americans, organized religion stabilizes both society and the government. From this perspective, as long as government (at every level) allows religion a good margin of freedom, periodic clashes between religious groups do not matter much in the grand scheme of things.

An early variant of this theory was put forward by the French statesman-author Alexis de Tocqueville. Comparing conditions in the United States during the early nineteenth century to those in his native France, Tocqueville noted that the "spirits of religion and of freedom" marched in opposite directions in France but not in the young United States, where he concluded the two spirits marched together, supporting and reinforcing each other.

Tocqueville concluded that the symbiotic relationship he observed between religion and politics in the United States was due to the crucial role religion played in instilling moral self-restraint, combined with the way congregational life helped Americans overcome their isolation. When political freedom implied that a person (at least a white man) in the nineteenth century could do as he pleased, organized religion taught him he should not do things that could be destructive to his family or community. Thus, religion made liberal democracy possible by instilling core inner mores that prevented American society from plunging into chaos. In turn, religion (in general) and congregations (in particular) thrived in the United States because they were left relatively free from persecution and unencumbered by government paternalism found in Europe, which tends to debilitate organized religion.[9] Thus, an unintentional symbiosis developed between government and religion, with each sustaining the other.

Of course, the contemporary United States is a far cry from the country Tocqueville visited in the 1830s. In many ways, American culture today is far more materialistic, skeptical, and focused on the individual than was the case during the early years of the Republic. However, the intensification of American individualism has served only to strengthen the partnership between religion and culture. In its present form, organized religion paradoxically helps to sustain an individualistic society by offering people a temporary refuge from the more isolating aspects of the culture. Indeed, evidence abounds that many people who turn to organized religion do so because they are seeking something different from the circumstances in which they live and work. They crave a refuge from the enormous burden of living in a society where meaning, morality, and community mores often are confusing or entirely relative.

It is crucial, however, to understand that the unconventional-partners thesis asserts that people get involved in organized religion for temporary refuge only—not as a permanent or radical alternative to the broader society. Fowler argues that most people who are involved in religious life want religion to give them just enough communal sharing and spiritual sustenance to enable them to survive in the broader culture. Thus, religion sustains the social order by filling a gap, providing a refuge that the social order often fails to offer.[10] Without this kind of refuge, Fowler argues, society might find itself wracked by radical challenges from both the right and the left. Evidence that the 2016 presidential election unleashed such forces may suggest some fraying of this partnership.

The other side of the unconventional partnership is the fact that American culture and government both serve to assist religion. There are many ways in which they do so, despite illusions of a high wall of separation between church and state. Perhaps the most important form of assistance comes in the generous protection of religious free exercise. The First Amendment is alive and well despite inevitable and sometimes nasty disputes over its interpretation, as we will discuss in Chapters 11 and 12. The fact that both government and culture have some sympathy for religion is essential to the viability of organized religious life in the United States.

At another level, organized religion has reaped extraordinary financial advantages from both government and culture. As we discuss in Chapter 12, the United States provides all sorts of concrete financial benefits, from aid to church hospitals to freedom from property taxes for houses of worship. Although no precise figures are available for how much direct or indirect aid religious institutions receive, it is indisputably in the billions of dollars. This assistance obviously matters, but so too does the traditional American embrace of broad religious freedom. This freedom constitutes the other side of the partnership from which both religion and culture benefit.

The unconventional-partners thesis offers some perspective on conflicts between church and state. The sound and fury of such conflicts should not drown out the continuing partnership that exists between religion and American culture. This is not to say that the ordinary manifestations of the religion–politics relationship—interest groups, voting, efforts to change public policy, and court cases—are meaningless; far from it. Nonetheless, the unconventional-partners thesis reminds us that the significance of the everyday religion–politics relationship must be interpreted in light of the deep and long-standing affinity between religion and culture in the United States. That relationship will continue for as long as organized religion persists as a temporary refuge rather than an enemy of American culture, and as long as government respects religion in spite of the efforts of those who call for a complete separation of church and state.

A permanent conflict between religion and culture is unlikely given the propensity of most Americans to be religious and spiritually inclined. In an important book, *American Grace: How Religion Divides and Unites Us*, political scientists Robert Putnam and David Campbell argue that most religious people in America are broadly tolerant of other religions.[11] Even when their own religious outlook is quite strict, people tend to tolerate others' views without feeling they must embrace them to any extent. What this tolerance means, Putnam and Campbell argue, is that most Americans are authentically pluralistic even when they are deeply committed to their own religious or spiritual paths.

In short, the very existence of religious pluralism has promoted religious tolerance. As people encounter, get to know, and live with or near others of different religions, they often come to see them as ordinary people just like themselves—and tolerance naturally develops.

What remains to be seen is whether the increasing number of Americans who are either indifferent or hostile toward organized religion will damage the unconventional partnership between religion and culture in the United States. To such individuals, the partnership between religion and government may seem to be of limited value or even dangerous. A prominent book, *Why Tolerate Religion?*, captures this new skepticism, which extends to questioning the tax-exempt status of churches.[12] In turn, some influential religious people who perceive the culture and government today as irredeemably hostile to faith call for various radical changes.[13] These future potentialities remind us that there can be no partnerships when there are no longer interested partners.

CULTURE WARS

Perhaps no theory about religion and politics in the United States has received as much attention in recent decades as the "culture wars" thesis. Proponents of this theory argue that to understand religion and politics in America today one must understand the intense nature of ongoing clashes over the merits of fundamental values and lifestyles. These clashes pit two irreconcilable viewpoints against one another; each side sees the other as threatening its way of life, not just having different policy preferences. The culture-wars thesis contends that many (but by no means all) Americans fall into one of two familiar categories: conservatives and progressives. Conservatives adhere to and emphasize trad-itional values and institutional arrangements regarding religion, heterosexual marriage and family, discipline, abortion, and same-sex marriage. On the other hand, progressives stress the importance of respecting and encouraging diversity in many areas of moral significance, including religion, family, and sexuality. Culture-wars theorists note that supporters of each perspective are not just sharply critical of one another; indeed, they feel threatened by the very existence of their opponents. Each side is struggling for dominance in American culture, as (for example) recent debates about same-sex marriage clearly illustrate.

The culture-wars division cuts across many lines in American life, including traditional religious lines.[14] For example, traditional Catholics today find themselves aligned with conservative evangelicals on many social and political issues; this alliance would have been unthinkable a half century ago. Both groups decry abortion, support public expressions of faith, criticize secularism in public schools, oppose same-sex marriage, and assert a right to object to certain public policies on account of conscience rights. Theological and cultural differences remain between traditional Catholics and evangelical Protestants, to be sure, but they unite in rejecting what they see as a secular assault on time-honored traditions and values. Their cultural alliance also sometimes includes Mormons, Orthodox Jews, and conservative Muslims, creating a sort of ecumenism of orthodoxy.[15]

The other side of the culture wars is comprised of liberal Protestants, progressive Catholics, most Jews, and the religiously unaffiliated, who together constitute the progressive coalition. Thus, liberal Protestants often find that they have more in common with liberal Catholics, Jews, and secular elites than they do with Protestant conservatives.[16] In place of the socio-moral stances that resonate most with religious conservatives, adherents of the progressive coalition speak a common language, emphasizing the imperative of working for "peace and justice," and prioritize civil rights, gender equality, the right of gay and lesbian couples to marry, full acceptance of transgender people, the need to overcome economic inequalities, and the dangers of military action.

Several scholars have advanced evidence of a culture war. Political scientist James Guth and his colleagues found strong evidence that something akin to a culture war split does, in fact, divide Protestant clergy into groups (conservatives and progressives).[17] Taking a broader view, prominent sociologist Robert Wuthnow concluded that a massive restructuring of American religion occurred in the wake of World War II that had the effect of polarizing Americans within their religious traditions. Not too long ago, Wuthnow argues, being a member of one church or another meant something distinctive. Being a Methodist, Presbyterian, Catholic, Lutheran, or Baptist implied sharing a religious and ethnic heritage featuring distinctive customs and beliefs with coreligionists. Today, however, a theological and cultural divide cuts across Christian church bodies. Politically speaking, it matters more whether one is a liberal Catholic or a conservative Catholic, or a liberal Methodist or an evangelical Methodist, than whether one is a Methodist or a Catholic in the first place. Thus, a liberal Methodist might feel more comfortable with secular liberals than she would with fellow Christians, and, indeed, fellow Methodists, on the evangelical side of the theological divide.[18] We see clear evidence of these intra-denominational tensions in the ongoing debates about ordaining LGBT clergy in mainline Protestant denominations.[19]

To illustrate how this cleavage plays out, imagine two women who appear to have much in common. Both are married, both are college graduates, both are church members, and both are economically comfortable. One woman attends an independent evangelical church, views abortion as anathema, and is an avid reader of conservative religious and political websites. Deeply alienated from the public schools, which she sees as having low academic standards and promoting secular and hedonistic values, she has chosen to homeschool her children. She is an active member of a homeschool association, which provides her with Christian-based curricula and strategies for avoiding being harassed by state education authorities. She views with alarm news about Christian photographers, bakers, and florists being sued for thousands of dollars for refusing to provide their services for same-sex weddings, which to her symbolize a broader assault on American religious liberty. She is a conservative Republican who voted for Donald Trump hoping he would defend her way of life against secular threats.

The other woman says the defining experiences of her life have arisen when she has joined in struggles for racial and gender equality. She is an active member of a United Methodist congregation known for its peace and justice activism. A strong feminist who advocates legal access to abortion, she belongs to several progressive political organizations and donates to political action committees that support women candidates. She fears what she sees as right-wing evangelical influence in politics. She has gay and lesbian friends and celebrated the Supreme Court's affirmation of their right to marry. She is a liberal Democrat who was so horrified by the election of Donald Trump that she now sees herself as part of the "resistance" movement against his presidency.

The original scholarly case for the culture-wars thesis was made by sociologist James Davison Hunter. In his classic 1991 book, *Culture Wars*, Hunter charts how cultural conflict plays out in skirmishes over school curricula, same-sex marriage, battles over abortion rights, and similar issues.[20] From the moment Hunter published his book, skeptics have questioned the extent to which ordinary people really are engaged in the culture wars—or even feel comfortable with the culture-wars rhetoric. To be sure, many political elites frame issues in highly polarizing terms for political gain, but is there evidence that most Americans feel engaged in a cosmic struggle for the soul of their country?[21]

The twenty-first century, however, thus far has witnessed heightened cultural and political divisions among Americans, who are more polarized than ever according to essentially all reputable surveys. Not only are Democratic and Republican voters further apart ideologically today, but animosity between partisans has been deepening as well. Indeed, nearly half of all party identifiers (and the majority of strong partisans) say that the other party makes them feel "angry" or "afraid"; differences are not about mere policy preferences or even ideology but rather about more basic perceptions of identity (and threats to that identity).[22] This polarization seems to suggest a resurgence of the culture wars. But emerging divisions are not fueled solely by religious cleavages—as the culture-wars thesis suggests—but also by region, class, education, and geographic sorting.[23] As we will see in our discussion of populism later in the chapter, Donald Trump, en route to the White House, channeled the rising discontent of rural Americans, workers who felt threatened by immigrants and foreign competition, and cultural conservatives. It is not clear at this stage how his economic nationalist message fits with the classic culture-wars thesis.

Adding further complexity to our consideration of the culture wars is the reality that there is no longer just one culture war in American society. In a society characterized by ever-increasing religious pluralism, many newer groups struggle to preserve their traditional values—often deeply intertwined with their religion—in the diverse and often-hostile strands of American culture. Many Muslim immigrants have faced this struggle to reconcile their faith with American popular culture. For example, some interpretations of Islam demand that women's faces be covered, but most US state laws require that veiled Muslim women remove their coverings for pictures on drivers' licenses.[24] Traditionalist Muslims also insist that women not touch or have any romantic relationships with men until marriage; ordinary American customs are quite different. This tension is common across western democracies but takes on distinctive qualities in the United States, as we will see in Chapter 4.[25]

To a degree, we may downplay the ferocity of the "culture wars" metaphor by noting that many clashes are simply cultural growing pains, inevitable as American life diversifies and (to a degree) recedes toward secularism. That said, the culture-wars thesis does fit certain features of contemporary American life. In the final analysis, this theory allows only a partial accounting of the relationship between religion and politics in the United States. Just as civil religion and the unconventional-partners thesis might overemphasize harmony in the religion–politics relationship, the culture-wars thesis might be overly negative.

THE SECULARIZATION THESIS

For a time, the secularization thesis seemed dusty and dated. However, twentieth-century scholars are rediscovering its insights and potential to explain some of the realities of the relationship between religion and politics in the contemporary United States. These theorists point to increasing numbers of non-religious Americans, as well as the secularization of culturally significant institutions, as evidence that the United States is becoming a less religious society. They also argue that the recent surge of politicized religion is a reaction against its weakening social relevance and clout.

First, though, we must explore the definition and history of this broad theoretical perspective. Proponents of the secularization thesis argue that as modernization advances in all areas of human life religion's cultural centrality should be expected to decline. Secularization theorists contend that this development is an inescapable result of mere existence in today's world that already has transformed much of the Western world.[26]

Some classic advocates of the secularization thesis were giants of nineteenth-century European thought. Perhaps the most prominent of these thinkers was Karl Marx, who was certain class struggle ultimately would lead to the triumph of socialism and the relegation of religion to "the dustbin of history" as subordinated classes discovered the capitalist source of their misery. Max Weber, the great German sociologist, believed that with modernity would come forces of rationalism and bureaucratization that eventually would defeat organized religion, if not entirely eliminating religious belief. Sigmund Freud, the founder of psychoanalysis, also was quite interested in religion, especially his own Jewish tradition. Although Freud knew there was no guarantee religion would fade, he hoped "the future of an illusion" would mean an end to religion as people came to see that modernity presents the option of being free from religion.[27]

Because secularization theorists assume modernization causes religion to decline, we need to investigate what this term means. By modernization, scholars mean the embrace of scientific ways of thinking, technological advances such as the Internet, complex economic systems, contemporary mass communication and entertainment, and the growth of government bureaucracies and public education. According to secularization theorists, as rational and scientific approaches come to dominate modern societies, religious worldviews should linger only in traditional societies as more people realize they can control their environment without appealing to religion. In modernized societies, education becomes an engine of secularization when it teaches scientific explanations of earthly phenomena. The capitalist marketplace also mutes religious enthusiasm as it directs people toward a consumer culture and the competition endemic to the workaday corporate world. The decline of traditional families also appears to undercut stable, regular participation in organized religion.[28] Finally, even though some forms of religious observance remain, we may be said to live in a "secular age" because of our awareness that religious engagement is but one lifestyle choice, not a given.[29]

On the global stage, however, the secularization thesis has come under withering critique. Some critics argue that religion will never disappear because it is basic to the human condition. Though its forms do and will change and diversify, religion will endure.[30] More tangibly, religious communities around the world began to push back against marginalization during the 1970s, in what Gilles Kepel termed "The Revenge of God."[31] Today, religious adherence is surging even in the face of advancing secularization, and global demographic trends indicate that the world's population will become even more religious in the future (owing to high fertility rates among religious people).[32]

Moreover, in recent years and in many places, religion has not been content to remain in a narrow, compartmentalized realm but instead has asserted itself in the larger, public world. Indeed, religious political movements worldwide now exercise more independence from states, marshal greater resources, and command greater transnational authority than ever before, leading some scholars to conclude that "God is Back" on the global state, or that this is "God's Century."[33] Perhaps future historians will note an ironic "unsecularization"— or even sacralization—of today's secular world as a prominent characteristic of the present era.[34]

On the other hand, secularization theorists point to trends in the United States as straightforward evidence of secularization even when they acknowledge the global resurgence of religion. The most important bit of evidence here is, of course, the expanding number of Americans who eschew formal religion altogether. A generational shift away from traditional religious expressions toward an often-vague, individualized spirituality also seems to be moving many toward the kind of secular outlook that has become commonplace in much of Western Europe.[35]

Still others who study the United States argue that an "elite secularization thesis" may prove most valid and insightful. According to this view, even though religion is still relevant to most human beings, elites and elite institutions have secularized, which matters because such people and institutions have disproportionate power to shape culture. Scholars note how many legal, political, and educational elites appear bent on banishing faith-based arguments from American politics, trivializing religious devotion, or flouting religious norms.[36] Studies show that academics, reporters, media elites, and government employees are more likely to be secular than the US population at large.[37] Moreover, many major American institutions—giant corporations and banks, public schools and universities, government bureaucracies, charitable foundations, television networks, the movie and music industries, and professional sports—operate on the basis of secular concerns and logic.[38] Often these institutions ignore the religious and spiritual dimensions of life; some are positively hostile toward them. A problem with the elite-secularization thesis, however, is the unevenness of the phenomenon. For example, elected officials—members of Congress and state legislators—often better reflect the religious diversity of the population at large.[39] There also is plenty of scholarship and intellectual discourse by people of faith that belies the presumption that all intellectual elites are hostile to religion.

Another slant on secularization theory contends that the process of secularization is in reality an individual-level phenomenon that happens to Americans one at a time. According to this interpretation, the key is to understand that religion, even as it continues to exist and even thrive in some quarters, is nonetheless receding quietly into private realms of American life and culture. The true test of any version of secularization theory is not whether religion is disappearing but whether its role is diminishing in daily lives.[40] There is no doubt that numerous religious Americans compartmentalize their faith today by choosing not to manifest it in many areas of their lives.[41]

Nor should we overlook the distinctive case of millennial Americans in evaluating secularization theory. Among younger adults in the United States, as many as 35 percent say they have little interest in or commitment to organized religion, regardless of·whether they happen to believe in God.[42] This reality suggests that secularization may advance further in the United States in years to come if millennials continue to opt out of religious life as they age.

An especially provocative recent analysis of secularization in the United States may be found in Rod Dreher's 2017 book, *The Benedict Option: A Strategy for Christians in a Post-Christian Nation.* Dreher perceives that orthodox Christian faith in America—whether Catholic, Protestant, or Eastern

Orthodox—is challenged from the outside by elite secularization and hollowed out from within by the loss of young people and the decline of traditional family and community ties and arrangements. So dire is this situation, Dreher contends, that Christians must consider exiling themselves and constructing resilient, countercultural enclaves in a post-Christian America, just as ancient monks did during the Dark Ages after the fall of Rome.[43]

Despite some clear signs of secularization in the United States and its seeming triumph in western Europe, there is no consensus about whether secularization is an unstoppable train. The recent migration of immigrants and refugees into Europe and the United States is infusing new religious vitality into these societies. In the United States, there are growing communities of Muslims, Hindus, Buddhists, and other religious groups, as well as vibrant congregations of Christians from Africa, Asia, and Latin America. In short, secularization may be a feature of our times, but it is not inevitable.

POPULISM

As we noted in Chapter 1, some of the most consequential social movements in American history succeeded in part because they tapped into the energies and resources of religious communities. These populist religious movements, while they hardly tell the full story of religion and politics in America, can profoundly shake up the cultural status quo and shape political and policy outcomes. Populist movements have been key components of many chapters of the story of religion and politics.

The link between populism and religion flows in part from the nature of religious life in the United States. Religious communities that fulfill the deepest needs, frustrations, and anxieties of their members are likely to thrive. Moreover, unlike the elite membership of most interest groups, congregational membership is broad and diverse. There is no other institution or activity in which Americans of all socioeconomic strata participate in such large numbers. Especially in a highly individualistic and mobile society, congregations represent one of the few settings in which many people meet face to face—and sometimes discover common political grievances.[44] Despite some skittishness about political engagement, congregations that engage in political action can allow segments of the population that otherwise are unable to find a political voice to register their discontent. Local churches, synagogues, and mosques can become places in which to organize, develop leadership, and call upon members for sacrifice.[45]

At the national level, church-based mobilization of African Americans and the galvanization of evangelical Protestant networks have been the most vivid manifestations of this populist–religious intersection in recent decades. Each of these populist movements achieved meaningful impact on party platforms, voter alignments, public policy, and presidential politics. That the same theory can accommodate such different movements illuminates its broad utility.[46]

Black churches historically have provided most of the organizational base, leadership, money, emotion, and moral support for African-American political mobilization. Black congregations and ministers propelled the Civil Rights revolution that began in the 1950s, mobilized broader voting participation during the presidential campaigns of Rev. Jesse Jackson in the 1980s, and rallied to support President Barack Obama's election campaigns in 2008 and 2012.[47]

Similarly, from the late 1970s onward, evangelical Protestant churches and their leaders, joined more recently by some traditionalist Catholic allies, have channeled the growing discontent of their members with what they see as the decay in American society and family breakup, as well as their opposition to legal abortion, same-sex marriage, and perceived threats to religious liberty. Successive waves of populist mobilization shaped the political emergence of conservative Protestants. The first Christian right groups emerged during the Reagan era. Rev. Pat Robertson's 1988 presidential campaign led to the formation of the politically impactful Christian Coalition in the 1990s. Later, so-called "values voters" rallied in support of George W. Bush's presidential campaigns during the 2000s. Most recently, we have seen the activation of conservative religious networks to help elect Donald Trump to the presidency in 2016. Taken together, these episodes point toward sustained populist-driven energy on the socio-moral right.

Much attention today in both the United States and Europe is focused on the emergence of new forms of populism that seem to depart from previous models. This new populism channels nationalist resentments around immigration, economic competition, and globalization, as reflected in the "alt-right" movement in the United States and the successful "Brexit" vote in the UK. At first glance, this new populism seems not to involve religious concerns. Yet those who mobilize resentments against cosmopolitan global elites often do so in the name of defending traditional religion and Western (Christian-based) civilization. Steve Bannon, a conservative Catholic provocateur and former Trump adviser, has explicitly worked to unite religious traditionalists with others who chafe at what they see as a smug governing class hostile to their economic and cultural concerns. Moreover, Trump clearly gained electoral support in 2016 from Americans who felt marginalized by cultural changes that they see as threatening traditional religious and family arrangements. For example, a large majority of rural voters said they believe government favors urban areas and that Christian values are under attack. Voters like these provided the margin of victory for Trump's election.[48]

We cannot know whether this new populism will endure or evolve in unexpected ways. What we can say is that the periodic and powerful appearance of populist mobilization, often connected with religious motivation and energy, will remain a feature of the religion–politics relationship in the United States, and increasingly around the world. Populism gives us yet another theoretical means of understanding the many ways in which religion and politics interact.

THE RELIGIOUS-MARKETPLACE THESIS

Another approach to the study of religion—and the dynamics of religion and politics in the United States—is the religious-marketplace thesis. Its proponents, most importantly sociologists Roger Finke and Rodney Stark, argue that religion's relative strength in every society is largely a function of how much competition is present between and among religious traditions and the degree to which that competition is unfettered.[49] According to the religious-marketplace thesis, which draws heavily on economic theory, the future of religion in the United States looks robust, so its potential political impact should continue relatively unabated even though we see more Americans disaffiliating from organized religion.[50]

Analysts of the religious marketplace start by noting the intense competition that has always existed between and among American religious traditions. This competition, they argue, serves to draw people into the religious marketplace because it features an almost unbelievable variety of religious niches from which to choose. Congregations advertise their services just like secular businesses do, online, via billboards—sometimes even with free gifts. Some congregations market themselves as friendly places where it is not necessary to dress up on Sunday morning. Others promote themselves as offering a distinctive theological, social, or political outlook. Still others attempt to meet members' every need, offering everything from a range of worship experiences to small-group friendship groups to sports leagues to healthcare clinics. This diversity suits Americans' pluralist and individualistic tastes. Religious-marketplace theorists argue that the congregations that fare poorly are either not competing hard enough or need to change their "brand" to offer more compelling spiritual messages.[51]

In addition, although informal modes of religious "establishment" might be said to linger in the United States, the fact remains that there is no single official American religion. This lack of establishment means that most groups enjoy considerable religious freedom, especially compared to the situation in many other countries around the globe. One implication here is that because the American religious sector is strong, competitive, and relatively free, it is capable of exerting meaningful political force. Another implication is that virtually all religious groups have the incentive to defend their First Amendment religious rights. Because of this shared need to operate freely, religious competition in America is mostly friendly and civil, unlike religious strife in many other nations.[52]

Theorists argue that in a market environment that is competitive and relatively free, every individual can be a shopper, exploring different religions, denominations, churches, spiritualties, and even congregations. As more and more Americans become religious shoppers, competitive marketing challenges face each religious group. Picky shoppers "inspire" and demand competitive—and often aggressive—marketing. Failure to compete in any market, religious or otherwise, can lead quickly to decline.

Religious-marketplace theorists note that in much of western Europe, organized religion is in serious decline; consequently, its political impact has also diminished. Scholars contend that these developments are partly the result of limited competition fostered by the existence of long-standing state-established churches. The Church of England, for example, is the official state church in the UK. One of the monarch's official roles is his or her constitutional position as "Defender of the Faith," which means the king or queen is the supreme governor of the Church of England. Yet many of England's majestic churches sit virtually empty most Sundays, and research shows that Britons are no longer a particularly religious people.[53]

Religious-marketplace theory holds that when religious groups lack the fire to compete aggressively for souls, all religions pay a steep price. Competitive evangelism appears to be an essential ingredient for the success of any religious group. Tired, insular religions, which in some countries are propped up by government, face serious decline and a consequent loss of political influence.[54]

No doubt, the religious-marketplace perspective offers crucial insights about the vitality of religion in the United States as well as its causes and effects. This vitality is essential for organized religion to be a factor in American politics. But the marketplace theory also plausibly suggests why religious competition, and the pluralism it creates, may undercut the potential power of any given religious outlook or organization. Some skeptics wonder how marketplace theory can deal with the increasing number of people who do not identify with any organized religion. Marketplace analysts respond to this criticism by saying the rise of the unaffiliated represents the emergence of yet another competitor in the American religious sector. The rise of secularism may, in fact, prove to increase competitive energy, as organized religion attempts to react to and displace this new competitor.

THE CULTURE-SHIFT THESIS

Political scientist Ronald Inglehart pioneered the "culture shift" thesis, which dovetails with the secularization thesis in holding that the influence of old-time religion is dying, especially in the Western world. Inglehart explains this demise by arguing that cultures worldwide are changing in response to modernization. He argues that antiquated institutions, the tired politics of class and economics, and outdated modes of thinking are receding (despite occasional revivals) in the face of modernity.

Inglehart also says, however, that one result of modernization is not what the standard secularization thesis would predict: Spiritual concerns have not disappeared, nor will they disappear. On the contrary, spiritual concerns are as important as ever to humans, but they are now increasingly made manifest through individual journeys of the soul and spirit rather than through participation in institutionalized religion. A natural upshot of this analysis is that formal religious influence in politics will decline over time but not because interest in the spiritual world will decline. According to this view, what looks like secularization around us is instead a shift in spiritual life from the organized and public to the individual and personal. The rise of the religiously unaffiliated is not an end of influence for spiritual concerns but rather a change in what they look like and how they work.[55]

There is plenty of evidence that a culture shift is taking place in the United States. Sociologist Wade Clark Roof described the baby-boomer generation as a "generation of seekers": people who look in a wide variety of places—some of them unconventional—for spiritual fulfillment.[56] Subsequent studies have demonstrated that a similar phenomenon applies to Generations X and Y, and there is reason to believe that millennials are more likely than any previous generation to be spiritual seekers.[57] A huge portion of the United States is "spiritual, but not religious," reflecting this seeker movement. All sorts of mystical, healing, holistic, feminist, Eastern, environmental, and related spiritualties are ascendant today, just as culture-shift analysts would predict; everywhere we look, we can see the presence of this "seeker spirituality."[58] And, as sociologist Robert Wuthnow has observed, the result is a host of spiritual shoppers flooding the spiritual marketplace, looking here, there, and everywhere for spiritual fulfillment. Indeed, even among those who remain committed to one or another organized religious tradition, experimentation is commonplace. For example, church-hopping within and across Protestant denominations is routine for people in search of the right fit, often the right "spirit."[59] The Catholic Church is dismayed that more parishioners in the United States are following this Protestant lead by sampling parishes other than the one to which they are geographically assigned. The same phenomenon also applies to Jews looking for the right temple and Muslims for the right mosque that best fits their spiritual needs.

Sociologist Phillip Hammond offers a related take, arguing that American religion is undergoing a major "disestablishment" that demonstrates how widespread the culture shift has been. As Hammond describes it, American culture now honors choice, expressivism, and individualism in religion as much as it does in other social sectors. Thus, he says, traditional religions that focus on duty, uniformity, and strict collective practices are slowly losing out. Mainline Protestantism arguably is suffering the most from these pressures, though it is far from alone facing the challenges of declining numbers. In truth, all American congregations are threatened by the movement toward individualistic spirituality.[60]

A great deal of scholarship on younger Americans reports something of the same reality. Sociologist Christian Smith's study of young adults aged eighteen to twenty-four finds many who are "spiritually open" or "selectively adherent" to one or another traditional religion, which is to say they proceed as individuals, taking what they like from their faith and rejecting what they don't like. Smith also argues, though, that many young Americans also are disconnected, irreligious, and not spiritually oriented. Each of these attitudes shows a widespread indifference toward, and intentional separation from, organized religion, which again reflects the currency of individualism and skepticism toward institutions in the United States today.[61]

Meanwhile, many other young Americans—women more than men—do espouse more conventional religious beliefs and allegiances, but only about 15 percent of these emerging adults are committed religious traditionalists. Most self-declare their resistance to "blind faith" and see themselves as open and tolerant of a wide range of spiritual and religious beliefs (or the lack thereof); in short, young Americans seem especially compelled by the argument that religious matters should be up to each individual.[62] Moreover, many young people are deeply critical of organized Christianity, which they see as too rigid, judgmental, angry, hostile to diversity, and stuck in the past with outdated dogmas. The obvious consequence is a widespread reluctance to join, or even visit, a church.[63]

The discerning reader will note also how neatly the culture-shift view speaks to the contemporary discussion of the rise of the religiously unaffiliated in the United States, a topic we will discuss often in this book. Most of these unaffiliated Americans do in fact report having some degree of spiritual interest or direction. The key point to understand about these Americans is that traditional religion has fallen out of favor and individual spirituality (however defined and however deep) is what counts, the sign that the culture-shift thesis reflects reality.[64]

On the other hand, some skeptics argue that the growing drift away from organized religion is partly a statistical myth caused by survey biases that tend to over-include the less religious component of the US population.[65] Moreover, many spiritual seekers do retain ties to conventional organized religion; some of these people are prodding their traditional religious communities to adapt. For example, many evangelical Protestant churches have been revitalized by providing expressive and contemporary music and other means of worship that allow adherents to achieve a deeply felt, individualistic spirituality. Such congregations tend to radiate a decidedly unstuffy aura despite the strictness of their teachings, which often emphasize the importance of a personal relationship with Jesus Christ and support the institution of the nuclear family. For their part, many Catholic and mainline Protestant congregations have been experimenting with including some of the more contemporary aspects of evangelical worship to reach those who desire a more emotional, expressive religious experience.[66] We also detect some countertrends, in which a cadre of young Catholics, Jews, and Muslims prefer greater orthodoxy in their beliefs and fervency in their practices than members of older generations, perhaps as a reaction against the fluidity of the wider world they inhabit.

It is unclear what the long-term consequences of the seeker phenomenon will be for religion and politics in the United States. But if American religion increasingly adapts to demand for individualistic spirituality and spiritual quests,

THEORY	ARGUMENT
The Civil-Religion Thesis	Proponents of the civil-religion thesis assert that a shared but generously vague political religion that broadly celebrates America and its culture is the religion that matters most because it helps knit the nation together.
The "Unconventional-Partners" Thesis	The "unconventional-partners" thesis posits that religion plays a significant political role in the United States, helping to sustain both the political culture and its governmental institutions by offering Americans a clear source of meaning, morality, and community.
The "Culture-Wars" Thesis	This theory argues that to understand religion and politics in America one must understand the intense nature of ongoing clashes over competing fundamental values and lifestyles. These clashes draw most (if not all) Americans into mutually hostile conservative and progressive camps.
The Secularization Thesis	Proponents of the secularization thesis argue that as modernization advances in all areas of human life, religion's cultural centrality should be expected to decline. Intense political activism by religious groups represents mostly a last-gasp response to this inevitable trend.
Populism	Populist religious movements powerfully shake up the cultural status quo and alter political and policy outcomes. Local churches, synagogues, and mosques can become places in which to organize, develop leadership, and call upon members to sacrifice in national mobilization campaigns.
The Religious-Marketplace Thesis	This theory argues that religion's relative strength in every society is largely a function of how much competition is present between and among religious traditions and the degree to which that competition is unfettered. Vibrant religious engagement in America flows from the nation's "free marketplace" in religion.
The "Culture-Shift" Thesis	The "culture-shift" thesis, which dovetails with the secularization thesis in holding that the influence of old-time religion is dying, argues that cultures worldwide are changing in response to modernization. However, it differs from the standard secularization thesis in positing that spiritual concerns are as important as ever to humans but are now manifested through individual journeys of the soul and spirit rather than through participation in institutionalized religion.

TABLE 2.1 **Major Theories of Religion, Politics, and Culture**

its impact on political life likely will become less focused and organized—and thus less impactful—than it has been with organized religious groups and interests at work. On the other hand, this long-term outcome is not self-evident. If spirituality continues to grow in importance and value among Americans, it may affect their individual political outlooks and behaviors as well. We just cannot know exactly what the future will bring as American religion continues to adapt to changing historical and cultural circumstances.

CONCLUSION

It remains to be seen which of these theoretical approaches, whether alone or in combination, will be most helpful in illuminating the relationship between religion and politics in the twenty-first century United States (see Table 2.1). Though each theory offers a useful perspective, none of them can explain everything on their own. What the future will produce in terms of the theory and practice of religion and politics in the United States may surprise all of us. After all, who expected that an African-American minister named Martin Luther King Jr. would emerge in the 1950s to change how we view race and civil rights in America? Who could have known in 1960 that Catholics and evangelical Protestants one day would be forming political alliances? Who predicted the rise of the Christian right in the 1980s? Who thought that Mormons and Muslims would have begun to emerge as important political players in the United States today? And how will the growing, diverse, and assertive immigrant communities shape the face of public religion in the future? Because of their dynamism, religion and politics in the United States defy explanation with any single theory. This fact should only spur us to try even harder to understand the impact of the religion-politics relationship on the culture, politics, and, indeed, collective life of the United States.

DISCUSSION QUESTIONS

1 Define the term "civil religion" and reflect how it is made manifest in America.

2 According to the unconventional-partners thesis, how do religion and liberal democracy have a symbiotic relationship?

3 How does market theory apply the basic distinction between supply and demand to religion in America?

4 Why is disestablishment an important condition of a vibrant "religious market," according to market theorists? How does competition play a role in religious vibrancy and levels of affiliation?

5 According to secularization theory, why does increasing modernization lead to diminished religious influence? How is this influence diminished for individuals, organizations, and society as a whole?

6 How would you compare secularization theory to market theory? Are they opposed positions, or in some way complementary?

7 The theories of culture war and culture shift both assert that the role of religious traditions and institutions is less important today than in the past. But neither theory fully accepts the secularization argument. If traditions matter less today, what fills the void for each of these theories? And what are the political implications?

8 Which theory, or combination of theories, do you think is the best suited to describe religion and politics in the United States?

FURTHER READING

Chapp, Christopher B., *The Rhetoric of Religion and American Politics: The Endurance of Civil Religion in Electoral Campaigns* (Ithaca, NY: Cornell University Press, 2012). An argument that civil religion is alive and well in American politics.

Dreher, Rod, *The Benedict Option: A Strategy for Christians in a Post-Christian Nation* (New York, NY: Sentinel, 2017). A countercultural proposal for how Christians must respond to secularization in America.

Finke, Roger, and Rodney Stark, *The Churching of America, 1776–2005: Winners and Losers in Our Religious Economy* (New Brunswick, NJ: Rutgers University Press, 2005). A recent restatement of the market model from its leading proponents.

Fowler, Robert Booth, *Unconventional Partners: Religion and Liberal Culture in the United States* (Grand Rapids, MI: Eerdmans, 1989). An account of the unconventional-partners thesis.

Gorski, Philip, *American Covenant: A History of Civil Religion from the Puritans to the Present* (Princeton, NJ: Princeton University Press, 2017). An ambitious argument that civil religion has been a central idea throughout American history.

Hertzke, Allen D., *Echoes of Discontent: Jesse Jackson, Pat Robertson, and the Resurgence of Populism* (Washington, DC: CQ Press, 1993). Leading statement of the populist thesis.

Hunter, James Davison, *Culture Wars: The Struggle to Define America* (New York, NY: Basic Books, 1991). Classic articulation of the culture-wars argument.

Inglehart, Ronald, *Culture Shift in Advanced Industrial Society* (Princeton, NJ: Princeton University Press, 1990). Best statement of the culture-shift theory.

Putnam, Robert D., and David E. Campbell, *American Grace: How Religion Divides and Unites Us* (New York, NY: Simon & Schuster, 2010). On contemporary US religion.

Roof, Wade Clark, *A Generation of Seekers: The Spiritual Journeys of the Baby Boom Generation* (San Francisco, CA: HarperSanFrancisco, 1993). A pioneering work of continuing value.

Smith, Christian (ed.), *The Secular Revolution: Power, Interests, and Conflict in the Secularization of American Life* (Berkeley, CA: University of California Press, 2003). A set of provocative arguments about the reasons for American secularization.

Toft, Monica Duffy, Daniel Philpott, and Timothy Samuel Shah, *God's Century: Resurgent Religion and Global Politics* (New York, NY: Norton, 2011). A good example of the new awareness of global religion today.

NOTES

1. Robert N. Bellah, "Civil Religion in America," *Daedalus*, 96 (1967): 1–21.

2. Sidney Mead, *The Lively Experiment* (New York, NY: Harper & Row, 1975).

3. Clinton L. Rossiter, *The American Presidency*, rev. edn (Baltimore, MD: Johns Hopkins University Press, 1960), p. 102.

4. For example, see John Wilson, *Public Religion in American Culture* (Philadelphia, PA: Temple University Press, 1979).

5. Christopher B. Chapp, *Religious Rhetoric and American Politics: The Endurance of Civil Religion in Electoral Campaigns* (Ithaca, NY: Cornell University Press, 2012), pp. 134–135.

6. Ross Douthat, "Divided by God," *New York Times*, Sunday Review, April 8, 2013, pp. 1, 6.

7. Robert Booth Fowler, *Unconventional Partners: Religion and Liberal Culture in the United States* (Grand Rapids, MI: Eerdmans, 1989).

8. Fowler, *Unconventional Partners*.

9. Alexis de Tocqueville, *Democracy in America: And Two Essays on America*, trans. Gerald E. Bevan and Isaac Kramnick (London: Penguin, 2003).

10. On these points, see also Roger Finke and Rodney Stark, *The Churching of America, 1776–2005: Winners and Losers in Our Religious Economy* (New Brunswick, NJ: Rutgers University Press, 2005).

11. Robert D. Putnam and David E. Campbell, *American Grace: How Religion Divides and Unites Us* (New York, NY: Simon & Schuster, 2010).

12. Brian Leiter, *Why Tolerate Religion?* (Princeton, NJ: Princeton University Press, 2012); Mark Oppenheimer, "Now's the Time to End Tax Exemptions for Religious Institutions," *Time*, June 28, 2015.

13. Rod Dreher, *The Benedict Option: A Strategy for Christians in a Post-Christian Nation* (New York, NY: Sentinel, 2017).

14. Robert Wuthnow, *The Restructuring of American Religion: Society and Faith Since World War Two* (Princeton, NJ: Princeton University Press, 1988).

15. On the growing political affinity between evangelical Protestants and traditional Catholics, see Clyde Wilcox, "Toward a Theory of Religious Coalitions," *Politics and Religion*, 9 (2016): 234–248.

16. Wuthnow, *The Restructuring of American Religion*.

17. James L. Guth, John C. Green, Corwin E. Smidt, Lyman A. Kellstedt, and Margaret M. Poloma, *The Bully Pulpit: The Politics of Protestant Clergy* (Lawrence, KS: University Press of Kansas, 1997). See also John C. Green, James Guth, Corwin E. Smidt, and Lyman Kellstedt (eds.), *Religion and the Culture Wars: Dispatches from the Front* (Lanham, MD: Rowman & Littlefield, 1996).

18. Wuthnow, *The Restructuring of American Religion*.

19. Wendy Cadge, "Vital Conflicts: The Mainline Protestant Denominations Debate Homosexuality," in Robert Wuthnow and John H. Evans (eds.), *The Quiet Hand of God: Faith-Based Activism and the Public Role of Mainline Protestantism* (Berkeley, CA: University of California Press, 2003), pp. 265–286.

20. James Davison Hunter, *Culture Wars: The Struggle to Define America* (New York, NY: Basic Books, 1991); James Davison Hunter, *Before the Shooting Begins: Searching for Democracy in America's Culture War* (New York, NY: Free Press, 1994).

21. Morris P. Fiorina, *Culture Wars? The Myth of Polarized America* (New York, NY: Longman, 2006).

22. Pew Research Center, "Partisanship and Political Animosity in 2016," June 22, 2016, www.people-press.org/2016/06/22/partisanship-and-political-animosity-in-2016; Pew Research Center, "Political Polarization in the American Public," June 12, 2014, www.people-press.org/2014/06/12/political-polarization-in-the-american-public. See also Kevin R. den Dulk, "Looking at the Election through Polarized Lenses," *Comment Magazine*, September 21, 2016.

23. Bill Bishop, *The Big Sort: How the Clustering of Like-Minded Americans is Tearing Us Apart* (New York, NY: Mariner Books, 2009). While religious cleavages play an important part in what Bishop calls the Big Sort, he also demonstrates the importance of rural versus urban cleavages, neighborhood density, and geographic location in propelling polarization. On cleavages by education, see Pew Research Center, "A Wider Ideological Gap Between More and Less Educated Adults," April 26, 2016, www.people-press.org/2016/04/26/a-wider-ideological-gap-between-more-and-less-educated-adults.

24. Susan Martin Taylor, "A Fight for Religion or Something More?" *St. Petersburg (FL) Times*, June 15, 2003, p. 2A.

25. See J. Christopher Soper, Kevin R. den Dulk, and Stephen Monsma, *The Challenge of Pluralism: Church and State in Six Democracies*, 5th edn (Lanham, MD: Rowman & Littlefield, 2017).

26. For a general discussion of secularization theory, see Steve Bruce, *God Is Dead: Secularization in the West* (Oxford: Blackwell, 2002), chapter 1, and *Religion and Modernization* (Oxford: Oxford University Press, 1992); see also Pippa Norris and Ronald Inglehart, *Sacred and Secular: Religion and Politics Worldwide* (Cambridge: Cambridge University Press, 2004).

27. See Karl Marx's "Economic and Philosophic Manuscripts," "Critique of Hegel's Philosophy of Right," and "Critique of the Gotha Program," in *The Marx–Engels Reader*, 2nd edn, ed. Robert C. Tucker (New York, NY: W. W. Norton, 1978), pp. 53–65, 525–541; Max Weber, *The Protestant Ethic and the Spirit of Capitalism* (New York, NY: Scribner's, 1958); Sigmund Freud, *The Future of an Illusion* (Garden City, NY: Doubleday, 1964).

28. Mary Ebertsadt, *How the West Really Lost God: A New Theory of Secularization* (Philadelphia, PA: Templeton Press, 2014).

29. Charles Taylor, *A Secular Age* (Cambridge, MA: Harvard University Press, 2007).

30. Nicholas Wade, *The Faith Instinct: How Religion Evolved and Why It Endures* (New York, NY: Penguin, 2009); Norris and Inglehart, *Sacred and Secular*.

31. Gilles Kepel, *The Revenge of God* (University Park, PA: The Pennsylvania State University Press, 1994), translation of *La Revanche de Dieu* (Paris: Editions du Seuil, 1991).

32. Michael Lipka, "Why People with No Religion Are Projected to Decline as a Share of the World's Population," Pew Research Center, April 7, 2017, www.pewresearch.org/fact-tank/2017/04/07/why-people-with-no-religion-are-projected-to-decline-as-a-share-of-the-worlds-population.

33. John Micklethwait and Adrian Wooldridge, *God Is Back: How the Global Revival of Faith Is Changing the World* (New York, NY: Penguin, 2009); Monica Duffy Toft, Daniel Philpott, and Timothy Samuel Shah, *God's Century: Resurgent Religion and Global Politics* (New York, NY: W. W. Norton, 2011).

34. See, for example, Peter Berger (ed.), *The Desecularization of the World: Resurgent Religion and World Politics* (Grand Rapids, MI: Eerdmans, 1999); and Samuel P. Huntington, Jr., *The Clash of Civilizations and the Remaking of World Order* (New York, NY: Simon & Schuster, 1998).

35. Christian Smith, *Souls in Transition: The Religious and Spiritual Lives of Emerging Adults* (Oxford: Oxford University Press, 2009).

36. Richard John Neuhaus, *The Naked Public Square: Religion and Democracy in America* (Grand Rapids, MI: Eerdmans, 1984); Stephen Carter, *The Culture of Disbelief: How American Law and Politics Trivialize Religious Devotion* (New York, NY: Basic Books, 1993).

37. For a fascinating look at the religious orientations of one elite sector of American society, see Elaine Howard Ecklund and Christopher Scheitle, "Religion Among Academic Scientists: Distinctions, Disciplines, and Demographics," *Social Problems*, 54 (2007): 289–307.

38. See, for example, George Marsden, *The Soul of the American University: From Protestant Establishment to Established Nonbelief* (Oxford: Oxford University Press, 1996); and Christian Smith (ed.), *The Secular Revolution: Power, Interests, and Conflict in the Secularization of American Life* (Berkeley, CA: University of California Press, 2003).

39. A description of the nature of religion among members of Congress is found in Peter L. Benson and Dorothy L. Williams, *Religion on Capitol Hill: Myths and Realities* (Oxford: Oxford University Press, 1982).

40. David Yamane, "Secularization on Trial: In Defense of a Neosecularization Paradigm," *Journal for the Scientific Study of Religion*, 36 (January 1997): 109–122. See also Mark Chaves, "Secularization as Declining Religious Authority," *Social Forces*, 72 (1994): 749–774; Robert Wuthnow, *After the Baby Boomers: How Twenty- and Thirty-Somethings Are Shaping the Future of American Religion* (Princeton, NJ: Princeton University Press, 2007); Christian Smith, *Souls in Transition: The Religious and Spiritual Lives of Emerging Adults* (Oxford: Oxford University Press, 2009).

41. Wuthnow, *After the Baby Boomers*.

42. Among other sources in this chapter, Robert Putnam and David Campbell discuss the growth of the "nones" in the United States in their *American Grace*.

43. Rod Dreher, *The Benedict Option: A Strategy for Christians in a Post-Christian Nation* (New York, NY: Sentinel, 2017).

44. See Paul A. Djupe and Christopher P. Gilbert, *The Political Influence of Church* (Cambridge: Cambridge University Press, 2009).

45. Djupe and Gilbert, *The Political Influence of Church*; see also Paul A. Djupe and Laura R. Olson (eds.), *Religious Interests in Community Conflict* (Waco, TX: Baylor University Press, 2007); Aldon D. Morris, *The Origins of the Civil Rights Movement: Black Communities Organizing for Change* (New York, NY: Free Press, 1984).

46. Allen D. Hertzke, *Echoes of Discontent: Jesse Jackson, Pat Robertson, and the Resurgence of Populism* (Washington, DC: CQ Press, 1993).

47. Fredrick C. Harris, *Something Within: Religion in African-American Political Activism* (Oxford: Oxford University Press, 1999); R. Drew Smith and Fredrick C. Harris (eds.), *Black Churches and Local Politics: Clergy Influence, Organizational Partnerships, and Civic Empowerment* (Lanham, MD: Rowman & Littlefield, 2005).

48. *Washington Post*/Kaiser Family Foundation, "Survey of Rural America," June 2017; reported by Jose A. DelReal and Scott Clement, "Rural Divide," *Washington Post*, June 17, 2017, www.washingtonpost.com/graphics/2017/national/rural-america/?utm_term=.3374f68bdd07.

49. Finke and Stark, *The Churching of America*.

50. Finke and Stark, *The Churching of America*; Laurence Iannaccone, "Why Strict Churches Are Strong," *American Journal of Sociology*, 99 (1994), 1180–1211; Lawrence

A. Young (ed.), *Rational Choice Theory and Religion: Summary and Assessment* (London and New York, NY: Routledge, 1997); an especially funny and devastating discussion of the market reality in action is *Shopping for God* by James B. Twitchell (New York, NY: Simon & Schuster, 2007).

51. In *The Churching of America*, Finke and Stark actually make the argument that demanding faiths are the ones that grow in the religious marketplace, so their market theory is not about crass marketing of religion, as some critics allege.

52. Putnam and Campbell, *American Grace*.

53. Norris and Inglehart, *Sacred and Secular*.

54. See Finke and Stark, *The Churching of America*.

55. Ronald Inglehart, *Culture Shift in Advanced Industrial Society* (Princeton, NJ: Princeton University Press, 1990). See also Norris and Inglehart, *Sacred and Secular*; Ronald Inglehart, *Modernization and Postmodernization* (Princeton, NJ: Princeton University Press, 1997); Robert Wuthnow, *After Heaven: Spirituality in America Since the 1950s* (Berkeley, CA: University of California Press, 1998).

56. Wade Clark Roof, *A Generation of Seekers: The Spiritual Journeys of the Baby Boom Generation* (San Francisco, CA: HarperSanFrancisco, 1993); Wade Clark Roof, *Spiritual Marketplace: Baby Boomers and the Remaking of American Religion* (Princeton, NJ: Princeton University Press, 1999).

57. Richard Flory and Donald E. Miller, *Finding Faith: The Spiritual Quest of the Post-Boomer Generation* (New Brunswick, NJ: Rutgers University Press, 2008); Christian Smith, *Soul Searching: The Religious and Spiritual Lives of American Teenagers* (Oxford: Oxford University Press, 2005); Wuthnow, *After the Baby Boomers*. See also Robert N. Bellah, Richard Madsen, William M. Sullivan, Ann Swidler, and Steven M. Tipton, *Habits of the Heart: Individualism and Commitment in American Life* (Berkeley, CA: University of California Press, 1985).

58. Robert C. Fuller, *Spiritual but Not Religious: Understanding Unchurched America* (Oxford: Oxford University Press, 2001). See also Bellah et al., *Habits of the Heart*.

59. Robert Wuthnow, *America and the Challenges of Religious Diversity* (Princeton, NJ: Princeton University Press, 2005), chapter 4.

60. Phillip Hammond, *Religion and Personal Autonomy: The Third Disestablishment* (Columbia, SC: University of South Carolina Press, 1992).

61. Christian Smith, *Souls in Transition: The Religious and Spiritual Lives of Emerging Adults* (Oxford: Oxford University Press, 2009).

62. Smith, *Souls in Transition*.

63. Kenda Creasy Dean, *Almost Christian: What the Faith of Our Teenagers Is Telling the American Church* (Oxford: Oxford University Press, 2010); David Kinnaman, *Unchristian: What a New Generation Really Thinks about Christianity* (Grand Rapids, MI: Baker Books, 2007). Dan Kimball, *They Like Jesus but Not the Church: Insight from Emerging Generations* (Grand Rapids, MI: Zondervan, 2007).

64. A negative view on the result may be found in Ross Douthat, *Bad Religion* (New York, NY: Free Press, 2012); he argues the result is little more than a fog of self-expressions.

65. Rodney Stark, "The Myth of Unreligious America," *Wall Street Journal*, July 5, 2013, p. A9.

66. Donald E. Miller, *Reinventing Protestantism: Christianity in the New Millennium* (Berkeley, CA: University of California Press, 1997); Kimon Howland Sargeant, *Seeker Churches: Promoting Traditional Religion in a Nontraditional Way* (New Brunswick, NJ: Rutgers University Press, 2000); see Roof, *Spiritual Marketplace*.

3

CHRISTIANITY AND ITS
MAJOR BRANCHES

In this chapter and the next two, we analyze the status of the wide variety of religious traditions in America and chart their political impact. We open this chapter with an overview of religion in the United States, then turn to the most prominent traditions of Christianity and their enduring yet changing roles in shaping public life. In Chapter 4, we examine Judaism, Islam, and other religious expressions that, despite size constraints and pressures from the broader culture, nevertheless exercise a significant voice in American society and politics. Finally, in Chapter 5, we consider Latinos and African Americans, whose distinct spiritual traditions play a key role in American religious life and politics and illustrate the inextricable connections between race and religion in the American experience.

THE STATUS OF RELIGION IN THE UNITED STATES

At one level, organized religion has enjoyed continuous vitality in the United States. Today, some 89 percent of Americans profess a belief in God or a universal spirit, with more than 63 percent claiming to be "absolutely certain" of God's existence.[1] Moreover, 77 percent of Americans say they belong to one religious tradition or another, while 53 percent say that religion is "very important" in their everyday lives. Despite the sizable and growing segment of secular or otherwise religiously unaffiliated citizens in the United States, a large majority of Americans do continue to make religious faith part of their lives.[2]

One way to understand the significance of religion in the United States is to compare Americans with citizens of other nations, particularly those of comparable socioeconomic status. This comparison lends credence to the description of the United States as religiously "exceptional," meaning that Americans are much more likely to express religious commitments than their counterparts in other wealthy, developed nations.[3] Table 3.1 provides a striking look at various dimensions of religious commitment in the top six wealthiest countries in the world (as measured by Gross Domestic Product). On various other measures—belief that religious faith is important for children, belief in God and morality, and religious participation—the United States also consistently ranks higher than other developed nations. Only 4 percent of Swedes, 12 percent of Germans, and 14 percent of Dutch say children should be encouraged to learn religion at home, as compared with 43 percent in the United States.[4] Meanwhile, 53 percent of Americans say it is necessary to believe in God to be a moral person compared to just 20 percent in Britain and 15 percent in France.[5] Similarly, while more than a third of Americans (35 percent) report that they are active members of a church or religious organization, the same can be said of 14 percent or less of German, Dutch, and Swedish people.[6]

On the other hand, the United States is not so exceptional when compared with other nations more generally. Table 3.2 shows that levels of religiosity in the United States closely match the overall averages across fifty-seven countries where research was conducted for the highly regarded World Values Survey.[7] In this table, we also see evidence of religion's continuing strength from the Middle East to Latin America to Africa. Such data hint at the future prospects of religion across the globe. Over 60 percent of Christians live in sub-Saharan

	RELIGION IS VERY IMPORTANT IN MY LIFE	GOD IS VERY IMPORTANT IN MY LIFE	ATTEND RELIGIOUS SERVICES ONCE A WEEK OR MORE	I AM A RELIGIOUS PERSON
China	2.6%	2.1%	1.9%	12.5%
United States	40.4%	48.8%	33.3%	67.0%
India	44.2%	9.2%	24.5%	77.1%
Japan	5.4%	6.1%	2.5%	20.9%
Germany	13.1%	12.7%	9.9%	49.5%
Russia	14.3%	19.2%	4.9%	53.1%

TABLE 3.1 **Religiosity in the World's Six Wealthiest Countries**

Source: World Values Survey, Wave 6 (2010–2014). Country wealth is derived from the US Central Intelligence Agency, *World Factbook* (2016); countries represented here comprise the top decile of Gross Domestic Product.

	RELIGION IS VERY IMPORTANT IN MY LIFE	GOD IS VERY IMPORTANT IN MY LIFE	ATTEND RELIGIOUS SERVICES ONCE A WEEK OR MORE	I AM A RELIGIOUS PERSON
Average (60 countries)	50.7%	48.5%	30.6%	64.4%
United States	40.4%	48.8%	33.3%	67.0%
Mexico	58.4%	79.7%	46.2%	74.2%
Brazil	51.5%	87.5%	49.9%	79.7%
India	44.2%	9.2%	24.5%	77.1%
South Africa	55.8%	41.5%	58.1%	80.0%

TABLE 3.2 **Religiosity in Selected Countries**

Source: World Values Survey, Wave 6 (2010–2014).

Africa, Latin America, and parts of Asia, a figure projected to reach 80 percent later in this century—a clear shift from Christianity's traditional home in Europe and North America.[8] In addition, Islam, with more than a billion adherents worldwide, is the dominant faith in northern Africa, the Middle East, and other regions of Asia.[9] From this perspective, the United States is hardly unusual; it is Europe and the Pacific Rim that are the exceptions.

It is also useful to compare groups of citizens within the United States itself. Faith is especially important to women and nonwhites, for example. Nearly two-thirds (60 percent) of women in the United States say religion is "very important" in their lives, compared with just under half (47 percent) of American men.[10] And research strongly suggests that African Americans are the most religious of all groups of US citizens.[11] This high salience of religion is the basis for the significant political role of African-American churches, which we explore in Chapter 5.

Despite growing religious diversity, a majority of Americans still place themselves within the Christian tradition. Just over 70 percent associate with some form of the Christian faith, though that is down 8 points in just seven years.[12] Likewise, nearly three-quarters believe in "a heaven, where people who have led good lives are rewarded."[13] A majority of Americans have a high view of Holy Scripture as well: Six in ten believe the Bible is the word of God.[14] Roughly the same proportion (59 percent) of Americans say they experience a sense of spiritual peace at least once a week.[15] Meanwhile, 79 percent of Americans believe in miracles.[16] And for a notable portion of the population, mystical or spiritual experiences are a very real part of life.[17]

Despite some drift away from religious institutions, most Americans have considerable trust in religious institutions and clergy. The public expresses more confidence in organized religion than it does in the US Supreme Court, Congress, the healthcare system, banks, public schools, the media, organized labor, and big business.[18] Members of the clergy consistently rank among the highest sets of social leaders in terms of public regard for their ethics and honesty, and three-quarters of the US population agrees with the contention that "churches and other religious organizations protect and strengthen morality in society."[19] Here again, Americans are distinct from people in other developed Western nations. Whereas Americans express more confidence in churches than they do in public schools, for example, these confidence figures tend to be the reverse in Germany, France, Great Britain, and many other European countries.[20] Moreover, 36 percent say they attend religious services at least once a week, although some scholars argue that people are less than truthful in responding to surveys about church attendance.[21] Even if attendance figures are a bit inflated, the fact remains that religious participation is the single most common group activity in the United States.[22] Within the Christian tradition, evangelical Protestants attend services most frequently, followed by Roman Catholics, with mainline Protestants trailing behind.[23] As we will see in Chapter 7, when we discuss religion and voting behavior, this pattern has increased the political clout of evangelical voters while reducing that of mainline Protestants.

Taking a broad view, the portrait of religious and spiritual America is one of great vitality. How much difference religious and spiritual beliefs and practices make in the daily lives of Americans, let alone in their politics, is another matter. Critics suggest that religion in America is like the proverbial prairie river: a mile wide and an inch deep. They note an obvious gap between high levels of apparent faith and considerable business dishonesty, tax fraud, sexual promiscuity, marital infidelity, family breakdown, cheating in school, crime, violence, and vulgarity in popular culture. In the 1990s, pollster George Gallup, Jr., whose surveys continue to demonstrate the widespread appeal of religion in the United States in the 2010s, concluded that much of American faith is indeed shallow and marked by a gap between faith and ethics.[24] A society that celebrates the individual pursuit of happiness, pervasively shallow (and, some argue, destructive) entertainment media, and the selfish side of capitalism tends to privilege hedonism and materialism over religion.[25]

On the other hand, there is evidence that religious belief and practice do make a difference in people's lives. Research suggests that religious conviction and practice are correlated with personal happiness, physical health, and general life stability—but it is the salience and authenticity of religious conviction that matters more than nominal affiliation: the greater the faith or practice, the more intense the benefits.[26] As we discuss more fully in Chapter 10, on the social and civic level, religious people are more likely than the secular to vote, contribute to charities, and otherwise become involved in the community.[27]

One of the most important reasons why American religion—and, more specifically, American Christianity—has so much vitality is its pluralism. The simple fact is that in Europe people who become alienated from state-established churches drift away from religion, whereas in America people who leave a congregation are much more likely to join (or even form) a new one.[28] Basic economics teaches us that the greater (and more varied) the supply of religious options, the higher the demand will be for "consumption" of such options.[29] A constitutional doctrine that has protected religious freedom, a relative openness to immigration, and a powerful cultural tradition of individualism foster a bewildering diversity of religious (and specifically, Christian) practice in the United States.

Part of the pluralism within Christianity, of course, is reflected by the familiar categories of Protestant and Catholic. Diversity within Protestantism dramatically increases the pluralism of American religion overall. The United States is home to virtually all Protestant denominations (organized subgroups, such as the United Methodist Church) and sects (smaller, less mainstream subgroups), some of which are internally diverse as well. Consider the Baptists. There are black Baptists and white Baptists, fundamentalists and moderates, Northern branches and Southern ones. Indeed, several hundred different Baptist denominations exist in the United States. Moreover, within each Baptist denomination, every congregation tends to consider itself autonomous, as the broad Baptist tradition has always resisted hierarchies. We also encounter myriad independent churches, some of which are loosely affiliated with national organizations, others of which are entirely independent, or "nondenominational." Even the hierarchical Catholic Church is pluralistic on the inside. There are liberal and conservative Catholics, a host of religious orders from Jesuits to Maryknolls, and numerous religious lay groups spanning the ultraconservative to the decidedly radical. The patchwork of American pluralism also includes small pacifist churches such as the Quakers, Brethren, Mennonites, and Amish, as well as Jews, Muslims, Mormons, Jehovah's Witnesses, Native American religionists, viewers of television ministries, pre- and postmillennial fundamentalists, Pentecostals and charismatics, evangelical Presbyterians, high church Episcopalians, and members of gay congregations, just to name a few—not to mention people who join the host of new religious movements (sometimes called cults) that sprout with regularity.

While 70 percent of Americans describe themselves as Christian, measuring the religious affiliation of various self-declared Christians can be a tricky matter in practice. For instance, more than a few evangelical Protestants argue that many people who say they are Christian do not actually have a serious commitment to traditional Christian beliefs and lifestyles so ought not to be counted as Christians.[30] Social scientists use a carefully developed means of classifying people's religious affiliations based on the traditions, denominations, and movements to which they say they belong.[31] The largest religious subgroup of Americans place themselves within the Protestant tradition of Christianity; however, this proportion is in decline, and for the first time in the nation's history less than a majority of Americans today are Protestants. Just under a quarter of the US population places itself within the Catholic tradition. The remainder of the white population is comprised of small percentages of Mormons, Eastern Orthodox Christians, Jews, adherents of other faiths, and the religiously unaffiliated (see Table 3.3). One of the most important general trends we see in twenty-first-century American religion is the slight decline of Christianity and the concomitant increase in adherence to non-Christian faiths and (even more prominently) religious disaffiliation.[32] Individual American congregations also vary in every conceivable way.[33] Some congregations are tiny, with fewer than fifty members, while others have many thousands of adherents (see Box 3.1). And just getting a handle on actual church membership is harder than it might seem. Churches keep their own records, and they tend to count members (as opposed to attendees) according to their own, often differing, methods. Independent opinion surveys of people's religious affiliation (for example, evangelical Protestant, Catholic, etc.) look at another, broader picture of self-identification and do not always arrive at the same results.

	2007	2014	2007–2014 CHANGE
Christian	78.4%	70.6%	−7.8%
Protestant	51.3%	46.5%	−4.8%
Evangelical	26.3%	25.4%	−0.9%
Mainline	18.1%	14.7%	−3.4%
Historically Black	6.9%	6.5%	−
Catholic	23.9%	20.8%	−3.1%
Mormon	1.7%	1.6%	−
Orthodox Christian	0.6%	0.5%	−
Non-Christian faiths	4.7%	5.9%	+1.2%
Jewish	1.7%	1.9%	−
Muslim	0.4%	0.9%	+0.5%
Unaffiliated	16.1%	22.8%	+6.7%
Atheist	1.6%	3.1%	+1.5%
Agnostic	2.4%	4.0%	+1.6%
Nothing in particular	12.1%	15.8%	+3.7%

TABLE 3.3 Religious Affiliation of US Population, 2007–2014

Source: Pew Research Center, "America's Changing Religious Landscape," May 12, 2015.

BOX 3.1 THE MEGACHURCH PHENOMENON

Social scientists often use broad categories of religious affiliation as a measure of a person's religion. Members of the United Church of Christ, for example, are put into the mainline Protestant category; Southern Baptists are catalogued as evangelicals. What about congregations that have no association with a denomination? Their status is an important question, particularly because of the rapid growth of nondenominational churches in the United States. In fact, many of the largest churches—the so-called megachurches, with thousands of members—are nondenominational. Lakewood Church in Houston, with more than 40,000 congregants on any given Sunday, is the largest megachurch in the United States today. Joel Osteen, its senior pastor, has followed in the footsteps of his father, John Osteen, who founded the church in 1959 and went on to develop a successful television ministry. Since his father's death in 1999, Joel Osteen has presided over even more growth in the Lakewood ministry, both in person and via traditional and new media. He is a leading proponent of the prosperity gospel, an interpretation of Christian teaching that says piety will be rewarded with financial success.

Saddleback Church in southern California is another good example of a megachurch. The brainchild of Rick Warren, who is perhaps best known as the author of a runaway bestseller, *The Purpose Driven Life*, Saddleback has been a leader in the international fight against HIV/AIDS. In fact, Warren and his wife, Kay, wrote an op-ed for *USA Today* criticizing President Donald Trump's budgetary proposal to cut US funding in this area. Warren is also noted for rejecting Osteen's prosperity gospel message. Based on core religious beliefs and behaviors, most nondenominational megachurches belong in the evangelical category, often sharing the political conservatism of their denominational brethren. But their size and detachment from the traditional organization of Protestantism make them a phenomenon unlike any other in American culture.

Sources: www.lakewoodchurch.com; www.saddleback.com; Mark Chaves, "All Creatures Great and Small: Megachurches in Context," *Review of Religious Research*, 47 (June 2006): 329–346; Scott Thumma and Dave Travis, *Beyond Megachurch Myths* (Hoboken, NJ: Jossey-Bass, 2007); David Van Biema and Jeff Chu, "Does God Want You to Be Rich?" *Time*, September 10, 2006; Rick Warren and Kay Warren, "Trump Budget Would Set Back Global AIDS Fight Just When We're on Track to Win It," *USA Today*, July 25, 2017.

Nonetheless, the general outlines of affiliation (as shown in Table 3.3) provide a basic overview of American religious pluralism.

Amid all this pluralism—and underlining it—is the very real regional religious diversity in the United States.[34] Major politically significant cultural differences exist between the considerably Catholic eastern states and the largely evangelical South, and between the diverse religious and spiritual worlds of southern California and the quasi-secular environmentalist outlook of much of the Pacific Northwest. Likewise, rural America today is culturally—and religiously—worlds away from the nation's big cities.[35] Differences can be just as real at the local level as well. For example, Denver may be only 70 miles away from Colorado Springs, but the religious gulf between diverse Denver and its heavily evangelical neighbor to the south could not be more pronounced. And all these variegations matter politically.[36]

The broad political significance of religious pluralism within Christianity is manifold—and pluralism acts as a check on the political influence of any religious group. No one group dominates, nor can it, which is a pluralist reality often ignored by those who fear that any single religious group could establish a "theocracy" or otherwise use government to enforce widespread oppression of others with whom they disagree on doctrinal or moral grounds. Religious pluralism also requires a willingness on the part of religiopolitical activists to overcome theological differences in the interest of coalition building, which is vital for successful political endeavors. Deeply held convictions sometimes must be modified if effective political alliances are to result.[37]

There are four dominant Christian traditions in the United States: evangelical Protestantism, mainline Protestantism, and African-American Protestantism, and Roman Catholicism. These traditions are distinctive from one another in terms of history, theology, religious practice, and ethnic makeup. The traditions are also politically distinct, although the boundaries are often blurry. The theological orientations of many black Christians, for example, are evangelical, yet because of the American legacy of slavery and segregation, black churches developed politically in directions that diverge in significant ways from white evangelicalism. We discuss the African-American church tradition only briefly in this chapter, but Chapter 5 discusses it in detail. We treat Judaism, Islam, and several other smaller religious traditions—as well as the growing number of Americans who claim no religious affiliation—in Chapter 4.

EVANGELICAL PROTESTANTISM

As we saw in Chapter 1, much of American history has been influenced by evangelical Protestant culture. By the 1920s, evangelicalism seemed to be in retreat from society, but it reemerged decades later with considerable vigor.[38] Today, evangelical Protestantism is the largest of the four major American

Christian traditions. It also has been the most visible politically over the past several decades.

An important watershed for evangelicals came in 1976, when presidential candidate Jimmy Carter proclaimed himself a "born-again Christian." It was at that time that evangelicals burst into the broader public consciousness; a bevy of journalists made pilgrimages to the South to discover just what evangelicalism entailed. Conservative churches had grown steadily in the wake of the 1960s because they offered precisely what many people craved: strong faith, concrete answers to life's challenges, and tight bonds of community.[39] One manifestation of—and, indeed, impetus for—the growth in evangelicalism over the past several decades has been the strong presence of evangelical student organizations, such as InterVarsity Christian Fellowship, Campus Crusade, Navigators, and the Fellowship of Christian Athletes, on college campuses.[40]

The growth of evangelical Protestantism would not have been so politically significant had a social movement known as the Christian right not emerged as a political force in the late 1970s. The movement began with isolated protests by parents who were frustrated with public-school textbooks in the mid-1970s, gained momentum with the creation of the Moral Majority and other national groups by 1980, and established itself as a formidable political force by the 1990s.[41] Unlike most previous presidential candidates on both sides of the aisle, Ronald Reagan acknowledged white evangelical voters in the 1980s and embraced their concerns, once famously telling a group of evangelicals: "I know that you can't endorse me, but I want you to know that I endorse you and what you are doing." At least from a rhetorical standpoint, Presidents Bill Clinton, George W. Bush, Barack Obama, and Donald Trump have followed suit.[42] By the early twenty-first century, white evangelicals had become one of the Republican Party's most loyal constituencies, having been transformed from a mass of unorganized (and somewhat alienated) citizens into a political movement of tremendous clout.[43] According to exit polls, Trump received an extraordinary 81 percent of evangelicals' 2016 presidential votes, a larger share than they have given to any previous Republican candidate. We discuss white evangelicals and the GOP more fully in Chapters 7 and 10.

What does it mean to be an evangelical? The most telling characteristic that distinguishes many evangelical Protestants from other Christians is the essentiality of personal conversion, commonly (though not exclusively) known as a "born-again" experience or "accepting Christ" as one's personal savior. Evangelicals often ask others, "Are you saved?" or, "When did you commit your life to Christ?" Evangelicals also hold a high view of Scripture. For all evangelicals, the Bible is at a minimum the inspired word of God; for some, it is the literal word of God. Evangelicals also adhere strongly to the orthodox tenets of the Christian faith (Christ's divinity, his atoning death and resurrection, everlasting salvation or damnation in a literal heaven or hell) and are committed to Jesus's "great commission" to evangelize others by spreading the good news of salvation through personal belief in Jesus Christ.[44] Although these characteristics are hallmarks of evangelical denominations (including those with African-American and Latino roots), there are also Christians who share one or more evangelical traits scattered throughout the Protestant world. Conservative "renewal" groups with a strongly evangelical feel have sprung up within mainline Protestant denominations, for example.[45] Former president George W. Bush illustrates the point: He identifies strongly as an evangelical, having had a transformative "born-again" experience, but is a member of the United Methodist Church, a mainline denomination.

As we have previously noted, one of the most significant distinctions within American evangelicalism is racial. Normally when scholars and commentators speak of evangelicals, they are referring to white (and, to a lesser extent, Latino) evangelicals. Yet black Baptists and Pentecostals also are fervent evangelicals. Moreover, increased racial tolerance has enabled more interaction between white and black evangelicals. The Southern Baptist Convention, for example, now trumpets its growing black membership—and even elected its first-ever African-American president, Rev. Fred Luter, Jr., in 2012. The burgeoning world of Pentecostal and charismatic congregations is truly interracial, largely because the Pentecostal movement began as an interracial religious revival in early twentieth-century California.[46] White religious conservatives have been modestly successful in building alliances with black Protestants on such issues as school prayer, abortion, school choice, pornography, and traditional marriage. Some white evangelicals have called for greater attention to racial justice as well.[47]

Nevertheless, a considerable gulf remains between black and white evangelicals. African-American churches feature a unique blend of theological conservatism and political liberalism; piety combines with prophetic witness around a prevailing theme of justice and equality for all. In black churches, one hears the liberationist messages of God's mercy toward the poor, the captive, and the downtrodden. African-American Protestants also tend to express considerable confidence in government as the temporal means to change. In this sense, God is an avenging liberator who can lift up the believer and provide both a refuge from the pain of the world and a means for counteracting injustice. This combination of messages lends itself naturally to political liberalism, at least on economic and civil-rights issues.[48] We discuss these differences in greater depth in Chapter 5.

Several other significant theological and cultural divisions also exist within the evangelical world. Pluralism reigns here, just as it does across religious America. There are some evangelicals who believe Scripture is inerrant but must be interpreted by humans; this group of evangelicals is largely ambivalent, rather than outwardly hostile, toward the broader culture. On the other hand, fundamentalists, who are true biblical literalists, are deeply suspicious of those who claim to "interpret" God's word and highly critical of the "fallen" culture they see around them.[49] Meanwhile, there are premillennialists, who expect certain biblical prophecies to come true before Jesus returns for a thousand-year reign on Earth (the bestselling Left Behind book series takes this approach), as opposed to postmillennialists, who believe a Christian reign will precede Jesus's second coming. An example of a postmillennialist group is the small but influential group of Christian Reconstructionists, who hold that believers should structure society as a theocracy based on Old Testament law. Comprising another significant—and growing—category of American evangelicalism are Pentecostals and charismatics, who emphasize the availability of gifts of the Holy Spirit such as speaking in tongues, faith healing, and prophecy.[50] Despite the fact that Pentecostals and charismatics embrace orthodox scriptural interpretation and traditional moral values, fundamentalists and many mainstream evangelicals are skeptical of Pentecostals because of their strong emphasis on personal spiritualism, which they say diminishes the Bible as the sole source of divine authority.

One way to clarify the diversity within evangelical Protestantism is to think of the evangelical community as a tree with several main branches and numerous smaller ones. There are literally hundreds of evangelical denominations, the largest of which is the Southern Baptist Convention. Many, but not all, evangelical congregations belong to denominations, which serve as a coordination point for worship and religious education materials and as a touchstone for doctrine. But increasingly evangelical churches in the United States describe themselves as nondenominational, meaning they are not affiliated with any formal religious organization outside of the congregation and are therefore entirely autonomous (see Box 3.1).

The first, largest branch of evangelical Protestantism consists of mainstream evangelicals in the tradition of Rev. Billy Graham. One of Graham's most significant contributions to American religious history was his teaching that Protestants who take a high view of Scripture need not separate themselves entirely from the secular society.[51] This branch of evangelicalism is well represented by the National Association of Evangelicals (NAE), an umbrella group for numerous evangelical churches and denominations that works to transform the world spiritually; it is generally conservative politically but by no means militantly so. A second, smaller branch of the evangelical tree is fundamentalism, which historically has been separatist, biblically literalist, and rather strongly opposed to the secular world.[52] A third branch includes fast-growing Pentecostal or charismatic churches, whose members share many of the political views of fellow evangelicals but whose vibrant religious practice and emphasis on spiritual gifts set them apart.[53] Whereas a fundamentalist church service usually features traditional Bible reading and preaching, Pentecostal and charismatic congregations feature contemporary music, speaking in tongues, and an emotional, free-form worship style.[54] Finally, we see the growth of independent megachurches, often nondenominational or with only a loose connection to a particular Protestant tradition. Although these distinctions may seem trivial to outsiders, they can present a significant challenge to political unity.

Other challenges exist, too, as is inevitably the case in any large religious tradition. Although evangelicals were until quite recently a major growth sector in American religion, some argue this is no longer true. The Southern Baptist Convention, to cite one major example, is struggling to increase its numbers. Moreover, because the term "evangelical" means different things to different people, it is not clear what the actual number of evangelicals is.[55] Undoubtedly,

---

BOX 3.2 ARE MILLENNIAL EVANGELICALS DISTINCTIVE?

Many political observers have suggested that the millennial generation of evangelicals is diverging in many ways from their older counterparts, growing more liberal ideologically and expressing concern about issues that go far beyond the morality politics of the old Christian conservative movement.

In general, millennials are less religious and more liberal than people in earlier generations. Scholars have argued that millennials are rejecting organized religion because they perceive it to be too conservative, particularly on gay rights. In 2014, the Public Religion Research Institute (PRRI) found that the percentage of evangelicals aged between eighteen and thirty-four was half that of people between the ages of fifty and sixty-four. However, evangelicals disagree with the assertion that attitudes about LGBT people are driving young people away from church. In fact, the leader of the evangelical Southern Baptist Convention's Ethics and Religious Liberty Commission is quoted by Robert Jones in his book *The End of White Christian America* as saying, "If we have to choose between Jesus and Millennials, we choose Jesus."

Meanwhile, political scientist Corwin E. Smidt argues that even if there are fewer of them than in generations past, millennial evangelicals are not remarkably different from older evangelicals in terms of their religious beliefs and behaviors. To be more precise, the religious differences (church attendance and beliefs in God, prayer, and the Bible) between evangelical millennials and their older coreligionists are less striking than the differences between evangelical millennials and their age peers (see Table 3.4). Smidt also finds small cross-generational gaps among evangelicals in terms of political beliefs and behavior. For example, consider evangelicals' attitudes about homosexuality. Although there is a 14-point gap between millennial and older evangelicals, millennial evangelicals differ much more significantly

the challenge of appealing to young people is real also (see Box 3.2). A 2014 survey reports that only 10 percent of white Americans under the age of thirty—compared with 27 percent of senior citizens—are evangelical.[56] As is the case for all of organized religion, evangelicalism must contend with the reality that many millennials prefer to be self-governing and free. Any theology that places a high premium on the concept of sin often can be a difficult "sell."[57] On the other hand, the evangelical world is often more than determined to reach youth by all means possible, whether through supporting colleges and universities, such as Wheaton College in Illinois and Regent University in Virginia, staging music festivals and Bible conferences for young people, or providing counter-cultural events from contemporary hip-hop shows to skateboarding ministries.[58]

	MILLENNIALS	OLDER GENERATIONS
Evangelical Protestant	41%	26%
Mainline Protestant	70%	57%
Black Protestant	57%	40%
Catholic	79%	60%
Unaffiliated	81%	73%

TABLE 3.4 Agree that "Homosexuality Should Be Accepted by Society"

from other millennials, including mainline Protestants (29-point gap), Catholics (38-point gap), and the unaffiliated (40 points).

Likewise, large-scale surveys conducted by PRRI show that evangelical millennials stand apart from the rest of their generation with respect to a range of other issues. A majority opposes both same-sex marriage and passage of the DREAM Act, which would create a path to citizenship for undocumented immigrants who were brought into the United States as children. Evangelical millennials are also much more uniformly opposed to abortion than their peers, with eight in ten saying it should be illegal in all or most cases. Likewise, evangelical millennials are much more likely than their age peers to favor abstinence as birth control, to oppose policy that would require employers to provide birth control to employees, and to reject "moral relativism."

Sources: Robert P. Jones, *The End of White Christian America* (New York, NY: Simon & Schuster, 2016); PRRI, *Millennial Values Survey*, 2012; PRRI, *How Race and Religion Shape Millennial Attitudes on Sexuality and Reproductive Health*, 2015; Corwin E. Smidt, *American Evangelicals Today* (Lanham, MD: Rowman & Littlefield, 2013).

Evangelical attitudes about political participation have changed dramatically in recent decades as well. Evangelicals long viewed politics with distaste; political activity constituted an engagement with the sinful world God meant for them to eschew. To be sure, many evangelical churches have always stressed the civic duty of voting, but beyond occasional local issues involving gambling or alcohol, not much effort was expended on politics until the 1980s.[59] That stance left the political field open for mainline Protestantism, which rode the crest of Civil Rights and anti-Vietnam War activism in the 1960s and 1970s.[60]

But by the 1970s all of that began to change. Many evangelical leaders came to believe that the government and the broader culture had become dangerously secular, so they felt they had to fight back. Evangelical congregations were also growing rapidly by the 1970s. Their members were becoming better educated and more affluent than ever before, and their television and radio ministries were becoming more popular. They had the motivation to fight and, increasingly, the resources to do so.[61] A large majority of white evangelicals today are political conservatives, although there is a small but meaningful "evangelical left." Represented most visibly by Jim Wallis of the group Sojourners and William Barber of the group Repairers of the Breach, this movement focuses on civil rights, working to alleviate poverty, and preserving God's natural creation. Wallis was a vocal critic of George W. Bush during his second term in office and later became an active supporter of the Obama administration.[62] Barber is best known for his weekly Moral Mondays in North Carolina, which put social-justice issues, especially healthcare, into the spotlight.[63] Still, as we show in Chapter 7, most white evangelical voters have realigned into the Republican Party and now constitute a key GOP voting bloc in both national and local politics. Beneath diversity in theology and religious practice lies a broad-based consensus supporting conservative politics. How political leaders, particularly within the Republican Party, continue to court this important constituency during the Trump era will shape a key dimension of American politics in the years to come.

MAINLINE PROTESTANTISM

Mainline Protestantism is a tradition that is, and always has been, distinct and separate from evangelicalism. This branch of Protestantism carries the label "mainline" because historically its denominations represented the dominant, socially elite expression of Protestantism in the United States, a position that long translated into exceptional political access. Mainline denominations, and many of their congregations, remain among the oldest and wealthiest in the nation. In terms of lay numbers and contemporary influence, however, the "mainline" nomenclature does not fit as easily as it once did because over the past fifty years the Protestant center of gravity has shifted toward evangelicalism.

Some refer to the mainline tradition as "liberal Protestantism," with the adjective referring to theology, not politics. As theological liberals, mainline Protestants view the Bible as inspired by God but by no means as literally true in every word. They also argue that Scripture must be read in the context of history and modern science. In fact, the mainline–evangelical split crystallized in the early twentieth century, when mainline Protestants embraced modernity and scientific theories such as Darwinism, of which evangelicals were wary.[64] Mainline Protestants have hardly abandoned all the central tenets of Christian faith, but they do place more emphasis on gradual, reflective spiritual development instead of the intensely individual "born-again" conversion experience. Mainline Protestants also are skeptical of the biblical literalism of fundamentalists and of the emotionalism and faith-healing claims of Pentecostals.

As is the case within evangelicalism, considerable variation characterizes mainline Protestantism and its major denominations. Mainline Lutherans (adherents of the Evangelical Lutheran Church in America, or ELCA), for example, maintain a distinct liturgical tradition rooted in ethnic German and Scandinavian roots. Methodists stress good works in the world as a manifestation of faithfulness. Episcopalians often treasure a formal, traditional worship service that is not unlike the Catholic Mass. The United Church of Christ (UCC) is substantially more liberal in theology, official policy, and practice than the other mainline denominations (for example, the UCC has been ordaining openly gay people as clergy since 1972). Despite these differences, however, mainline Protestants share a lot in common, not only in core theology but in worship style as well. In mainline Protestant churches, one rarely hears sermons about hell or personal sin. More common are scholarly discussions of the meaning of divine incarnation or ethical insights of Jesus's teachings. Services typically are orderly and include traditional music, but, to stay current, many mainline Protestant congregations have also been implementing more contemporary worship styles. By and large, mainline Protestant churches are more accepting of skepticism about portions of the Bible than are their evangelical counterparts. Bible study, therefore, often focuses on moral precepts contained in the Bible and welcomes examinations of the context of biblical times. This is not to say that there are no traditional religionists sitting in the pews of mainline churches— there are many indeed—but most mainline church leaders do not reinforce their outlook.[65]

There is an emphasis in many mainline churches on a general call to love one's brother or sister and to be active in "this world." Moreover, Christian love is often interpreted in collective ways as well as individual ones. For over a century, many mainline clergy have argued that Christians must address the world's injustices not merely through individual charity but through collective efforts to change societal structures as well.[66] Mainline seminaries, liberal both in theological and political terms since the early twentieth century, became radicalized during the Civil Rights movement in the 1960s, which socialized clergy into theologically grounded liberal politics.[67] Many mainline seminarians still learn that unless political and economic structures change, injustice and oppression will continue irrespective of personal acts of mercy and love.[68] For mainline clergy and denominational leaders, theological liberalism often correlates with liberal political activism. Among mainline parishioners, however, the link between liberal theology and liberal politics is less well established.[69]

Mainline Protestants traditionally voted Republican, but this pattern has diminished in recent decades. In fact, since 2008, some surveys have suggested that a bare majority of mainline Protestants now identify with the Democratic Party, an indicator of a potentially significant historical shift.[70] Shifts in partisanship reflect a correlation between theological liberalism and liberal attitudes among rank-and-file mainline Protestants on a wide range of social and moral issues.[71]

The well-established Protestant denominations were the dominant force in American religion through the 1950s. Methodists, Episcopalians, Congregationalists (members of the UCC), most Presbyterians, many Lutherans, and Northern (American) Baptists, along with members of a few other smaller mainline denominations and the National Council of Churches (a parachurch organization to which they all belong), constituted the principal political and social witness from religious Americans through most of the twentieth century.[72] From Main Street to Wall Street to Washington, mainline Protestants were a presence with which to be reckoned. When progressive social movements gathered momentum in the 1960s, influential mainline leaders voiced their solidarity with activists, and many mainline Protestants became foot soldiers in the movements.[73] The 1960s exercised a strong influence on mainline Protestant leaders. They embraced—and continue to embrace—issues of poverty, racism, sexism, and oppression—and unjust social structures many of them see as perpetuating these evils. Mainline church leaders typically view much of their sociopolitical role as championing peace and justice, especially for the poor and disadvantaged.[74] As a result, many mainline clergy favor expanded government funding for welfare, healthcare, and other social programs at home and economic assistance for developing nations abroad. They also work for world peace (sometimes from a pacifist perspective) and frequently fault American foreign policy as too militaristic and too oriented toward gain for the US economy.

Two significant challenges confront mainline clergy who wish to exercise political influence. First, many lay members either do not share the ideological orientations of their national leaders and local pastors or do not wish to conform to a political vision articulated from the pulpit. As an illustration of this phenomenon, consider the recent schisms within mainline denominations and congregations around the ordination of LGBT people (see Box 3.3).[75] Indeed, the hierarchical process of political decision-making in these large denominations means lay members are not always consulted as official positions are developed.

BOX 3.3 STRIFE INSIDE THE EPISCOPAL AND PRESBYTERIAN CHURCHES

Mainline Protestantism in the United States is in decline. The Pew Research Center found that between 2007 and 2014, the percentage of Americans who affiliate with mainline Protestantism declined by 3.4 percent. During that same period, the percentage of religiously unaffiliated Americans increased by 6.7 percent—and these trends are related. In recent years, the Episcopal Church in the United States (which is the American branch of the Church of England, or Anglican Church) has been wracked by so much strife that some observers have wondered whether the denomination might break in two. Other mainline denominations, most recently the United Methodist Church, have confronted similar challenges.

The dissension in the Episcopal Church has arisen because conservative members and leaders disagree profoundly with some of the denomination's recent decisions and policies. The first great flashpoint of tension was the 2003 installation of an openly gay man, Rev. Canon V. Gene Robinson, as the Episcopal bishop of New Hampshire. After Robinson's consecration, conservative congregations began breaking ties with the US denomination and aligning themselves instead with Anglican communions in other countries where traditional doctrines hold sway, most notably the Episcopal Church of Uganda. Some of these dissident congregations have wound up in court battles pitting them against the US church over ownership of their church buildings and other property. In 2016, the worldwide Anglican Communion, of which the Episcopal Church is a member, was demoted from its status as a full participant after conservative African bishops led the charge.

Meanwhile, perhaps in an effort to avoid some of the same tensions, the deeply divided United Methodist Church's High Court voted in 2017 to deny the consecration of its first openly gay bishop, Rev. Karen Oliveto of Denver. Most of today's mainline denominations are the result of historic mergers, but their future seems more likely to involve the ongoing threat of collapse.

Sources: Pew Research Center, "America's Changing Religious Landscape," May 12, 2015; Laurie Goodstein, "A Divide, and Maybe a Divorce," *New York Times*, February 25, 2007, p. D1; Laurie Goodstein, "Methodist High Court Rejects First Openly Gay Bishop's Consecration," *New York Times*, April 28, 2017; Kimberly Winston, "Episcopal Church Suspended from Full Participation in Anglican Communion," Religion News Service, January 14, 2016.

Moreover, because mainline churches tolerate a wide diversity of theological interpretations, lay members are not accustomed to accepting concrete assertions of truth (about any matter, including politics) from their clergy. It therefore can be difficult for mainline leaders to find support within their congregations for the political causes about which they care most.[76]

A second challenge is that, numerically speaking, mainline Protestantism has sharply declined in recent decades. The Pew Research Center found that between 2007 and 2014 the number of mainline Protestant adults in the US dropped by 5 million.[77] Table 3.5 shows the clear drop-offs in both membership and number of congregations between 2000 and 2010 in the six largest mainline denominations. For a more detailed illustration, consider the Episcopal Church.

	CONGREGATIONS, 2000	CONGREGATIONS, 2010	% CHANGE	MEMBERS, 2000	MEMBERS, 2010	% CHANGE
American Baptist Churches, USA	5,555	5,243	−5.6%	1,767,462	1,560,572	−11.7%
Episcopal Church	7,314	6,794	−7.1%	2,314,756	1,951,907	−15.7%
Evangelical Lutheran Church in America	10,739	9,846	−8.3%	5,113,418	4,181,219	−18.2%
Presbyterian Church (USA)	11,106	10,487	−5.6%	3,141,566	2,451,980	−22.0%
United Church of Christ	5,863	5,225	−10.9%	1,698,918	1,284,296	−24.4%
United Methodist Church	35,721	33,323	−6.7%	10,350,629	9,860,653	−4.7%

TABLE 3.5 Change in Membership and Number of Congregations, Largest Mainline Protestant Denominations, 2000–2010

Source: Religious Congregations and Membership in the United States, 2000, and 2010 US Religion Census: Religious Congregations and Membership Study. Collected by the Association of Statisticians of American Religious Bodies and distributed by the Association of Religion Data Archives.

On a typical Sunday, less than a third of Episcopal churches have attendance of more than 100 people; one-third have forty or fewer people in attendance; and one-eighth have twenty or fewer. Moreover, the average age of Episcopalians is now in the upper fifties. This is an alarming sign suggesting a challenging future.[78]

Explanations for these losses vary. Sociologist Dean Kelley argued that mainline churches' religious, theological, and doctrinal flexibility and openness hurts them over time. The business of religion is generating meaning, and mainline churches often cannot meet the needs of people who want clear and firm religious beliefs. On the other hand, for those who do not want such standards, there often seems no point in remaining in a church at all except for social reasons, which can be fulfilled elsewhere. At another level, and an important one, mainline denominations have failed to keep pace because of the very low birth rate of many of their members.[79]

Despite their numeric decline, however, mainline churches still possess a wealth of inherited capital in the form of buildings, institutions, and endowments, as well as the loyalty of millions of lay members. Local churches continue to operate a host of food banks, meal programs, homeless shelters, clothing closets, and day-care centers, and national church organizations operate large hospitals, charitable agencies, and highly respected international development organizations. Mainline Protestant churches are also key players in city coalitions designed to alleviate poverty and injustice. Thus, extensive community involvement continues to thrive in mainline Protestantism, and mainline Protestants continue to exercise what sociologists Wuthnow and Evans term "quiet" but significant influence in American political and religious life.[80]

ROMAN CATHOLICISM

In Chapter 1, we observed that the Catholic–Protestant split played an important role in shaping American political culture during the first 150 years of the Republic. Catholics were perceived and portrayed as "other" in American society. They lived in ethnic neighborhoods and sustained separate institutions to shield themselves from the dominance of Protestant culture. The result of this reality by the 1950s was a tremendously vibrant Catholic community dominated by an ethic of cultural distinctiveness, with an impressive number of Catholic churches, schools, hospitals, and social-service agencies staffed by priests and nuns.

Although a palpable Protestant–Catholic division does linger in a few pockets of the United States, today it is mostly a memory. In the twenty-first century, suburban Catholics are hardly outsiders. Some Catholics themselves complain that the old distinctiveness of Catholic culture has been lost amid a more homogenized society. Still, Catholics remain theologically different from Protestants, preserving a sacramental approach to the "mysteries" of the faith and a unique intellectual tradition.[81] Catholics today inhabit a highly strategic position in American politics. At the mass level, they constitute a key swing demographic. At the elite level, both mainline Protestants and evangelicals frequently seek political alliances with them. Catholic bishops often make news when they speak on political issues. But Catholics, especially at the parish level, hardly speak with a unified political voice; here pluralism reigns just as it does elsewhere in religious America. This lack of unity sometimes hampers Catholic political clout, although the size of the Catholic population (almost one in every four Americans is Catholic) and the institutional strength of the Catholic Church ensure that Catholics are important players in the American system.[82]

A truly global church with a hierarchical structure headquartered in its own sovereign nation (Vatican City), the Catholic Church is literally the oldest continuously functioning institution in the world. It is inappropriate to refer to the Catholic Church as just another denomination; instead, like Protestantism (generally construed), it is a broad tradition within Christianity. The Catholic Church's internationalism adds a unique dimension to its politics.[83] One cannot focus merely on the US church; one must consider the hierarchical structure of the Catholic Church, the pope and other top church leaders, and the relationship of the US Catholic Church to this broader context. The popularity of Pope Francis, for example, buoys American Catholics, and his statements on political issues can provide political ammunition to competing groups within the church.

The Catholic organizational hierarchy is rooted in the church's long history. Local churches, or parishes, collect into larger geographic areas known as dioceses or archdioceses, each of which is headed by a bishop or archbishop appointed by the pope. Popes name select bishops, archbishops, and other top Catholic clergy from around the world to the College of Cardinals, the elite officials of the church who are responsible for electing a new pope each time the "bishop of Rome" dies or retires (as Pope Benedict XVI did in 2013).[84] At the heart of Catholic Church, structure is the doctrine of apostolic succession, the idea that the pope is literally the successor of the apostle Peter. Although hierarchy remains a defining characteristic of the Roman Catholic Church, American Catholicism leadership is nevertheless characterized by pluralism. Diverse holy orders of priests and nuns, each with a distinct focus and élan, exist alongside the traditional structure of priests, bishops, and archbishops. Thus, one finds progressive Jesuits, feminist nuns, and Maryknoll missionaries spreading calls for social justice alongside more conservative orders and groups of Catholic traditionalists (such as Opus Dei) who are fierce adherents of Catholic orthodoxy.[85]

One of the distinctive features of the Catholic Church is its appreciation of politics. Throughout much of European history, for example, the church was deeply enmeshed in statecraft. Politics was not alien to church leaders then, nor is it today. Catholic leaders and parishioners alike have been intensely involved in politics around the globe, from the Philippines to Latin America, from eastern Europe to the United States.[86] In one sense, this political comfort level is an asset: the Catholic Church and its activists do not need to overcome as much resistance to politics as one would confront historically when trying to mobilize Protestants. On the other hand, for much of US history, many non-Catholic Americans have viewed the church as a suspect institution in part because of the Vatican's involvement in world politics.

The Catholic Church's prominence in the medieval world of kings and princes, along with its historical skepticism about democracy and religious freedom, placed it at odds with the American liberal tradition. Well into the twentieth century the global church resisted many liberal democratic reforms and allied itself with authoritarian governments.[87] This history created a problem for American Catholics, whom many Protestants and others viewed as lacking a fundamental commitment to American democracy and liberal freedoms—even though most Catholics did in fact embrace the American creed of democracy and individual liberty and often were ardent patriots and anti-communists.[88] Nevertheless, criticism and questions about whether the Catholic embrace of American liberal democracy was compatible with the tenets of their faith continued unabated into the 1950s.[89]

Everything changed for American Catholics because of a profound revolution within the broader Catholic Church itself, a revolution in which the United States and its Catholic leaders played a pivotal role. In 1961, Pope John XXIII declared that the Catholic Church needed to open its windows and let in some fresh air. This declaration was just the second time in two millennia that a pope had called for a meeting of the world's bishops to modernize the Church. Vatican II, as this meeting came to be called, lasted from 1962 to 1965. It was a veritable earthquake for the church, and its effects are still being felt decades later. After Vatican II, the Catholic Church formally embraced democracy and individual liberty, and, for the first time, accepted Protestants as fellow Christians rather than viewing them as apostates. The Mass, which always had been said in Latin and thus was difficult for parishioners to follow, would thereafter be celebrated in hundreds of local languages. And bishops in each country were given greater authority to speak on behalf of the church in their respective lands. One worldwide impact of the church's change, as political scientist Samuel Huntington has argued, was to encourage a wave of democratization in formerly authoritarian Catholic nations.[90] In the United States, Vatican II legitimated the Catholic accommodation to liberal democracy and accelerated the assimilation process for American Catholics.

Even before Vatican II, leaders of the American Catholic Church had begun to assert themselves politically. After Vatican II, many others in the Catholic Church joined the bishops in political engagement. Nuns and priests marched in Civil Rights and anti-Vietnam War demonstrations. Two key Catholic organizations—Catholic Charities and the Campaign for Human Development—sponsored antipoverty projects in inner cities and rural backwaters. The Catholic Church also lent support to the farmworker movement led by

César Chávez.[91] Ultimately, Vatican II led to an increased role for the bishops' national organization, known today as the United States Conference of Catholic Bishops (USCCB). Headquartered in Washington, DC, and composed of several hundred leaders and former leaders of Catholic dioceses in the United States, the USCCB leads the Catholic Church's official social and political efforts.

The politics of the bishops are not easily categorized, which is one reason why American conservatives and liberals alike seek alliances with Catholic bishops. On social welfare, labor, civil rights, and military policy, the bishops have taken a decidedly liberal posture over the years. At least some of this agenda stems from the Catholic Church's historical concern that untrammeled industrial capitalism exploits workers and undermines the dignity of work and the vitality of community and family. However, the church's positions on abortion, divorce, and same-sex marriage have been conservative, while its support of "school choice" is libertarian in spirit.[92] Liberals celebrated when the bishops drafted "pastoral letters" on nuclear arms and the economy; conservatives applauded the bishops when they condemned abortion. Similarly, liberals welcomed the support of Catholics who lobbied against Ronald Reagan's support for the anticommunist Nicaraguan Contras in the 1980s and the US war in Iraq in the 2000s; conservatives appreciated the Catholic fight for day-care vouchers and school choice.[93] Most recently, the Catholic Church has been at the forefront of a fight over religious liberty, which is how it views its efforts to escape the federal government's healthcare rules and employer mandates. This campaign put the bishops at odds with the Obama administration, particularly over the so-called "contraceptive mandate," the provision of the Affordable Care Act requiring employers to provide birth control to employees.[94]

As important and powerful as the Catholic Church is, it also faces plenty of challenges.[95] Since Vatican II, mass attendance has fallen off, and many Catholics of European origin have left the Catholic Church over the years. Between 2007 and 2014, the Catholic share of the US population dropped from 24 percent to 21 percent, and the rate of decline is much steeper among white Catholics; the percentage of Latino Catholics is increasing, and the US Church is arguably now stronger in the West and Southwest than it is in the Northeast.[96] Overall losses are not as significant as those we observe among mainline Protestants (see Table 3.5), but they are noteworthy nonetheless. Some people have moved out of the Catholic Church to Protestant churches, some to individual spiritual journeys, and others to out-and-out secularism.

Even among committed Catholics, perhaps a third have little practical contact with the Catholic Church, though many others are deeply devoted to it. A common post-Vatican II American Catholic practice is "cafeteria-style Catholicism," where individuals choose for themselves which aspects of the Catholic faith to follow and which to reject. This is a striking example within the nation's largest religious tradition of the surge in spiritual individualism that is so characteristic of America today.

Another significant challenge for the Catholic Church is the struggle to get men to enter the priesthood and to get women to enter religious orders as nuns. For decades, there has been a severe shortage of priests in the United States, and a notable aging of those who are priests. The priest shortage has begun to lessen a bit as a more conservative Catholic Church attracts men who want to serve a church with a serious commitment to strict religious and moral tenets, but it remains to be seen whether the priest shortage will ever abate.[97] Some of the Catholic Church's challenges are rooted in a clash between its traditional teachings and practices and more relativist American norms. Thus, it defends a celibate, all-male priesthood; retains a formal, hierarchical authority structure; and opposes divorce, same-sex marriage, and "artificial" birth control. These stances have led not only to divisions within the Catholic Church but also to portrayals of Catholics in elite media and popular music that border on anti-Catholic bigotry.[98]

Other challenges, though, have been created by the Catholic Church's own leaders. Especially damaging has been the scandal that erupted in 2002, when it came to light that several American dioceses and archdioceses had failed to discipline priests who engaged repeatedly in the sexual abuse of minors. As of 2017, eighteen American dioceses, archdioceses, and religious orders have been forced to file for bankruptcy due to the high cost of financial settlements with victims of sexual abuse, and well over $1 billion has been paid out to thousands of victims.[99] To be sure, only a very small number of Catholic priests had been involved in this scandal, and sexual misconduct is hardly the exclusive domain of the Catholic Church.[100] Nonetheless, the scandal has damaged the church's credibility within its ranks and in the broader American society.[101]

Perhaps the most penetrating long-run explanation for the challenges the Catholic Church faces today is its evolution into a mainstream American religious tradition. As we saw in Chapter 1, church growth and decline in the American religious marketplace operate with a seemingly ineluctable logic. To the extent that the Catholic Church has become a mainstream institution in the United States, it has become subject to the profound encounter with the outside world, which has had great effect. This result should not surprise us. Catholics today are no longer found disproportionately among the white working class, as was the case at the turn of the twentieth century. Now white Catholics and Protestants are equals in terms of both educational attainment and income, and herein lies a paradox.[102] When American Catholics were disproportionately at the lower end of the socioeconomic scale, they represented a much more distinct and unified community—one that was much more likely to accept the authority of the Catholic Church and its teachings than is the case today. Today, many American Catholics do not feel bound by the dictates of the Catholic Church, let alone by its political efforts. Consequently, the Catholic Church does not exercise as much political clout with its rank-and-file membership as it once did, but the church's large size, clear lines of organization, and long-standing openness to politics continue to cement its role as a major player in American politics.

CONCLUSION

Christianity in America flourishes—yet it does so amid contrary secular forces, creating a profound tension. On the one hand, professed faith seems to be strong, and Christian churches remain heavily involved in society and politics. On the other hand, moral and ethical problems abound, and many powerful institutions such as the mass media, government, business, public schools, and universities, are driven primarily by secular logics that differ from religious teachings and speak for increasingly large numbers of Americans.

One of the perennial questions, therefore, is why Christianity does not exercise more political influence in the United States. The answer to this question lies in America's religious pluralism. Politicians hear a babble of competing religious voices on most issues. When religious groups do form a united front, they can be quite effective, but those instances are rare enough to prove the rule: Pluralism dilutes any group's political power.

Religious influence is also checked by the defining characteristics of the American polity. As we discuss in Chapters 11 and 12, the First Amendment's requirement of religious disestablishment has fostered a separatist tradition and ethic in the United States that features wariness—even suspicion—of interaction between religion and government. This wariness is especially pronounced among various elites in government, media, and business circles.

The framers of the Constitution constructed a political order designed to disperse, fragment, and check power. Successive majorities are required to pass national legislation, which can then be diluted or nullified by the actions of states, bureaucracies, or the courts. To achieve real clout, therefore, a movement or group must work successfully on several fronts—from the states to the national government, from Congress and the executive branch to the courts and bureaucracies, from lobbying and electoral mobilization to subtle efforts to shape public opinion through the old and new media alike. The challenge is formidable, and continuing success is rare. Although the framers saw to it that no single movement or voice can dominate the American political system, the system itself is open enough to provide access to even the smallest group.[103] Thus, the American system of government ensures many religious groups the chance to have some political influence while simultaneously blocking each one from achieving dominance.

DISCUSSION QUESTIONS

1 How is the experience of religious pluralism different in the United States compared to other Western democracies? What are the political implications of those differences?

2 What are some of the basic demographic features of American Catholicism that distinguish it from other major religious traditions in the United States?

3 Who comprises the Roman Catholic hierarchy, and what does apostolic succession have to do with their position of authority? What is the diocesan structure of the church?

4 How do Catholic theological beliefs affect political behavior? In particular, what is the political significance, if any, of the Eucharist and the Catholic emphasis on institutions? What about the notions of social justice and just war?

5 What are the major historical trends in the way Catholicism has interacted with the broader American culture? Has it adapted? Compromised? Assimilated? Resisted? Why or why not?

6 Does the comparison of Catholic and evangelical demographic trends help us understand each tradition's prospects in the political arena?

7 Evangelicals are often said to be "voluntaristic" or "individualistic" in their beliefs and practices, including worship styles. Why? Do their beliefs about the Bible, transformative ("born again") experiences, emphasis on evangelism, and the "personal walk with Christ" make political participation more or less likely, or does it matter at all?

8 What are some of the major differences among evangelicals? Is it useful to speak of fundamentalists or Pentecostals when sorting through the political motivations and behavior of evangelical Christians?

9 Why do we call certain Protestant denominations "mainline"?

10 How might the Civil Rights movement have influenced and radicalized many mainline Protestant ministers? How are those effects still seen today?

FURTHER READING

Allen, John L., Jr., *The Future Church: How Ten Trends Are Revolutionizing the Catholic Church* (New York, NY: Doubleday, 2009). Excellent book on the present and future of the Catholic Church.

Graziano, Manilo, *In Rome We Trust: The Rise of Catholics in American Political Life* (Stanford, CA: Stanford University Press, 2017). A thorough look at how Catholics and the worldwide Church intersect politically and otherwise.

Green, John C., *The Faith Factor: How Religion Influences American Elections* (Sterling, VA: Potomac Books, 2010). An updated overview of American faith traditions and their political predilections.

Jones, Robert P., *The End of White Christian America* (New York, NY: Simon & Schuster, 2016). A data-driven analysis of long-term changes in the American religious marketplace and their political consequences.

Kelley, Dean, *Why Conservative Churches Are Growing: A Study in Sociology of Religion* (San Francisco, CA: Harper, 1977). The classic work on the rise of evangelical and the decline of mainline Protestantism.

Lindsay, D. Michael, *Faith in the Halls of Power: How Evangelicals Joined the American Elite* (Oxford: Oxford University Press, 2007). Massive study of evangelical elites in the United States.

Smidt, Corwin E., *American Evangelicals Today* (Lanham, MD: Rowman & Littlefield, 2013). An evenhanded, data-driven look at evangelical Protestants in twenty-first-century America.

Weigel, George, *Evangelical Catholicism: Deep Reform in the 21st Century* (New York, NY: Basic Books, 2013). A lively argument about the Catholic Church's future.

Wuthnow, Robert, *The Quiet Hand of God: Faith-Based Activism and the Public Role of Mainline Protestantism* (Berkeley, CA: University of California Press, 2002). This text argues that mainline Protestantism's political and social influence, though "quiet," nevertheless continues to be important.

NOTES

1. Michael Lipka, "Americans' Faith in God May Be Eroding," Pew Research Center, November 4, 2015, www.pewresearch.org/fact-tank/2015/11/04/americans-faith-in-god-may-be-eroding/.

2. Pew Research Center, "US Public Becoming Less Religious," November 3, 2015, www.pewforum.org/2015/11/03/u-s-public-becoming-less-religious/; Pew Research Center, "America's Changing Religious Landscape," May 12, 2015, www.pewforum.org/2015/05/12/americas-changing-religious-landscape/.

3. Seymour Martin Lipset, *American Exceptionalism: A Double-Edged Sword* (New York, NY: W. W. Norton, 1997).

4. World Values Survey, 2010–2014, www.worldvaluessurvey.org/WVSOnline.jsp.

5. Pew Research Center, "Worldwide, Many See Belief in God as Essential to Morality," March 13, 2014, www.pewglobal.org/2014/03/13/worldwide-many-see-belief-in-god-as-essential-to-morality/.

6. World Values Survey.

7. Play with the data yourself at the World Values Survey's Online Data Analysis website: www.worldvaluessurvey.org/WVSOnline.jsp.

8. Pew Research Center, "The Changing Global Religious Landscape," April 5, 2007, www.pewforum.org/2017/04/05/the-changing-global-religious-landscape/.

9. Pew Research Center, "The Changing Global Religious Landscape." For fascinating cartographic descriptions of global religions, see Ninian Smart and Frederick Denny (eds.), *Atlas of the World's Religions*, 2nd edn (Oxford: Oxford University Press, 2007).

10. Pew Research Center, "The Gender Gap in Religion around the World," March 22, 2016, www.pewforum.org/2016/03/22/the-gender-gap-in-religion-around-the-world/.

11. Frank Newport, "Religion and Party ID Strongly Linked Among Whites, Not Blacks," *Gallup Politics*, July 1, 2013, www.gallup.com/poll/148361/Religion-Party-Strongly-Linked-Among-Whites-Not-Blacks.aspx; Pew Research Center, "US Religious Landscape Study," www.pewforum.org/religious-landscape-study/.

12. Pew Research Center, "US Religious Landscape Study"; Pew Research Center, "US Religious Landscape Study." Gallup says this figure was 75 percent in 2015 and reported it 77 percent in 2014. See Gallup, "Percentage of Christians in US Drifting Down, but Still High," www.gallup.com/poll/187955/percentage-christians-drifting-down-high.aspx.

13. Pew Research Center, "US Public Becoming Less Religious."

14. Pew Research Center, "US Public Becoming Less Religious."

15. Pew Research Center, "US Public Becoming Less Religious."

16. Pew Forum on Religion and Public Life, "Religion among the Millennials," Pew Research Center, February 2010, www.pewforum.org/2010/02/17/religion-among-the-millennials/.

17. Nancy T. Ammerman, "Spiritual but Not Religious? Beyond Binary Choices in the Study of Religion," *Journal for the Scientific Study of Religion,* 52 (2013): 258–278; Courtney Bender, *The New Metaphysicals: Spirituality and the American Religious Imagination* (Chicago, IL: University of Chicago Press, 2010); Pew Research Center, "'Nones' on the Rise," www.pewforum.org/2012/10/09/nones-on-the-rise/; Robert Wuthnow, *After Heaven: Spirituality in America since the 1950s* (Berkeley, CA: University of California Press, 1998).

18. Gallup, "Confidence in Institutions," www.gallup.com/poll/1597/confidence-institutions.aspx.

19. Gallup, "Confidence in Institutions."

20. World Values Survey.

21. Pew Research Center, "US Public Becoming Less Religious." Figures on church attendance are disputed by C. Kirk Hadaway, Penny Long Marler, and Mark Chaves, "What the Polls Don't Show: A Closer Look at US Church Attendance," *American Sociological Review,* 58 (1993): 741–752. See also Philip S. Brenner, "Investigating the Effect of Bias in Survey Measures of Church Attendance," *Sociology of Religion,* 73 (4) (2012): 361–383.

22. Robert D. Putnam and David E. Campbell, *American Grace: How Religion Divides and Unites Us* (New York, NY: Simon & Schuster, 2010).

23. Pew Research Center, "US Religious Landscape Study."

24. George Gallup, Jr., "Religion in America: Will the Vitality of the Churches Be the Surprise of the Next Century?" *The Public Perspective,* 6 (October/November 1995): 1–8.

25. This argument is made by Allen D. Hertzke, *Echoes of Discontent: Jesse Jackson, Pat Robertson, and the Resurgence of Populism* (Washington, DC: CQ Press, 1993). For a contemporary take from a prominent social critic, see Jim Wallis, *On God's Side: What Religion Forgets and Politics Hasn't Learned about Serving the Common Good* (Grand Rapids, MI: Baker, 2013).

26. Harold G. Koenig, Dana E. King, and Verna Benner Carson, *Handbook of Religion and Health,* 2nd edn (Oxford: Oxford University Press, 2012).

27. Putnam and Campbell, *American Grace*; Mark Regnerus, Christian Smith, and David Sikkink, "Who Gives to the Poor? The Role of Religious Tradition and Political Location on the Personal Generosity of Americans toward the Poor," *Journal for the Scientific Study of Religion,* 37 (1998): 481–493; Corwin E. Smidt, Kevin R. den Dulk, James M. Penning, Stephen V. Monsma, and Douglas L. Koopman, *Pews, Prayers, and Participation: Religion and Civic Responsibility in America* (Washington, DC: Georgetown University Press, 2008).

28. Pippa Norris and Ronald Inglehart, *Sacred and Secular: Religion and Politics Worldwide,* 2nd edn (Cambridge: Cambridge University Press).

29. Roger Finke and Rodney Stark, *The Churching of America, 1776–2005: Winners and Losers in Our Religious Economy* (New Brunswick, NJ: Rutgers University Press, 2005); Laurence R. Iannaccone, Roger Finke, and Rodney Stark, "Deregulating Religion: The Economics of Church and State," *Economic Inquiry,* 35 (1997): 350–364.

30. George Barna, *The Seven Faith Tribes: Who They Are, What They Believe, and Why They Matter* (Brentwood, TN: Tyndale, 2009).

31. Brian Steensland, Jerry Z. Park, Mark D. Regnerus, Lynn D. Robinson, W. Bradford Wilcox, and Robert D. Woodberry, "The Measure of American Religion: Toward Improving the State of the Art," *Social Forces*, 79 (2000): 291–318.

32. See Pew Research Center, "US Religious Landscape Study."

33. Mark Chaves, *Congregations in America* (Cambridge, MA: Harvard University Press, 2004).

34. Dante Chinni and James Gimpel, *Our Patchwork Nation: The Surprising Truth about the "Real" America* (New York, NY: Gotham Books, 2010); Pew Research Center, "US Religious Landscape Study"; Mark Silk and Andrew Walsh, *One Nation Divisible: How Regional Differences Shape American Politics* (Lanham, MD: Rowman & Littlefield, 2008).

35. Chinni and Gimpel, *Our Patchwork Nation*; Robert Wuthnow, *Red State Religion: Faith and Politics in America's Heartland* (Princeton, NJ: Princeton University Press, 2012); Robert Wuthnow, *Small-Town America: Finding Community, Shaping the Future* (Princeton, NJ: Princeton University Press, 2013).

36. Silk and Walsh, *One Nation Divisible*; Wuthnow, *Red State Religion*; Wuthnow, *Small-Town America*.

37. See Paul A. Djupe and Laura R. Olson, *Religious Interests in Community Conflict: Beyond the Culture Wars* (Waco, TX: Baylor University Press, 2007).

38. One brief and thoughtful introduction to evangelical Protestantism that also focuses on politics is Corwin E. Smidt, *American Evangelicals Today* (Lanham, MD: Rowman & Littlefield, 2013); Hankins, *American Evangelicals: A Contemporary History of a Mainstream Religious Movement* (Lanham, MD: Rowman & Littlefield, 2008).

39. Finke and Stark, *The Churching of America*; Laurence Iannaccone, "Why Strict Churches Are Strong," *American Journal of Sociology*, 99 (1994): 1180–1211; Dean M. Kelley, *Why Conservative Churches Are Growing: A Study in Sociology of Religion* (San Francisco, CA: Harper, 1977).

40. Peter M. Magolda and Kelsey Ebben Gross, *It's All about Jesus! Faith as an Oppositional Collegiate Subculture* (Sterling, VA: Stylus, 2009); John G. Turner, *Bill Bright and Campus Crusade for Christ: The Renewal of Evangelicalism in Postwar America* (Chapel Hill, NC: University of North Carolina Press, 2008).

41. For a fine discussion of the Christian right, see Clyde Wilcox and Carin Robinson, *Onward Christian Soldiers? The Religious Right in American Politics*, 4th edn (Boulder, CO: Westview Press, 2011). We discuss the political movement more fully in Chapter 10.

42. On the symbolic use of religion in politics, see Christopher B. Chapp, *Religious Rhetoric and American Politics: The Endurance of Civil Religion in Electoral Campaigns* (Ithaca, NY: Cornell University Press, 2012); Colleen J. Shogan, *The Moral Rhetoric of American Presidents* (College Station, TX: Texas A&M University Press, 2006). On the basis of Trump's early appeal to evangelicals, see Tim Alberta, "Trump and the Religious Right: A Match Made in Heaven," *Politico*, June 13, 2017.

43. David E. Campbell (ed.), *A Matter of Faith: Religion in the 2004 Presidential Election* (Washington, DC: Brookings Institution, 2007); Geoffrey Layman, *The Great Divide: Religious and Cultural Conflict in American Party Politics* (New York, NY: Columbia University Press, 2001); Corwin E. Smidt, Kevin R. den Dulk, Bryan T. Froehle, James M. Penning, Stephen V. Monsma, and Douglas L. Koopman, *The Disappearing God Gap? Religion in the 2008 Presidential Election* (Oxford: Oxford University Press, 2010); Wilcox and Robinson, *Onward Christian Soldiers*.

44. Kevin T. Bauder, Albert Mohler, Jr., John G. Stackhouse, Jr., and Roger E. Olsen, *Four Views on the Spectrum of Evangelicalism* (Grand Rapids, MI: Zondervan, 2011);

George M. Marsden, *Understanding Fundamentalism and Evangelicalism* (Grand Rapids, MI: Eerdmans, 1991).

45. Douglas E. Cowan, *The Remnant Spirit: Conservative Reform in Mainline Protestantism* (Westport, CT: Praeger, 2003).

46. Cecil M. Robeck, Jr., *The Azusa Street Mission and Revival* (Nashville, TN: Thomas Nelson, 2006); Grant Wacker, *Heaven Below: Early Pentecostalism and American Culture* (Cambridge, MA: Harvard University Press, 2001).

47. Russell Moore and Jim Wallis are evangelicals with different ideological perspectives who take similarly strong stands on racial reconciliation. See Russell Moore, "What Shootings and Racial Justice Mean for the Church," July 7, 2016, at www.russellmoore.com/2016/07/07/shootings-justice-body-of-christ/ and Jim Wallis, *American's Original Sin: Racism, White Privilege, and the Bridge to a New America* (Grand Rapids, MI: Brazos Press, 2016). For a social-scientific perspective, see Michael O. Emerson and Christian Smith, *Divided by Faith: Evangelical Religion and the Problem of Race in America* (Oxford: Oxford University Press, 2001).

48. Fredrick C. Harris, *Something Within: Religion in African-American Political Activism* (Oxford: Oxford University Press, 1999); Eric L. McDaniel, *Politics in the Pews: The Political Mobilization of Black Churches* (Ann Arbor, MI: University of Michigan Press, 2008).

49. Joel A. Carpenter, *Revive Us Again: The Reawakening of American Fundamentalism* (Oxford: Oxford University Press, 1997); Mark Dalhouse, *An Island in the Lake of Fire: Bob Jones University, Fundamentalism, and the Separatist Movement* (Athens, GA: University of Georgia Press, 1996); Marsden, *Understanding Fundamentalism and Evangelicalism.*

50. See Harvey Cox, *Fire from Heaven: The Rise of Pentecostal Spirituality and the Reshaping of Religion in the Twenty-First Century* (Reading, MA: Addison-Wesley, 1995) for a splendid account. See also Allan Anderson, *An Introduction to Pentecostalism: Global Charismatic Christianity* (Cambridge: Cambridge University Press, 2004); Donald E. Miller and Tetsunao Yamamori, *Global Pentecostalism: The New Face of Christian Engagement* (Berkeley, CA: University of California Press, 2005); Wacker, *Heaven Below.*

51. Hankins, *American Evangelicals.*

52. For a fine historical discussion of fundamentalism in the United States in the 1930s and 1940s, see Carpenter, *Revive Us Again.*

53. There is an important technical distinction between the terms "Pentecostal" and "charismatic." "Pentecostal" is used to describe denominations (and autonomous congregations) that are thoroughly grounded in spiritual gifts. "Charismatic" describes sub-movements, congregations, and even individuals *within non-Pentecostal denominations* of Protestantism (as well as the Catholic Church) that embrace gifts of the spirit. See Anderson, *An Introduction to Pentecostalism.*

54. Anderson, *An Introduction to Pentecostalism*; Cox, *Fire from Heaven.*

55. The Pew Research Center's 2014 "US Religious Landscape Study" estimates that 25 percent of Americans today are evangelical.

56. Robert P. Jones, *The End of White Christian America* (New York, NY: Simon & Schuster, 2016), p. 54.

57. See, for example, Christine Wicker, *The Fall of the Evangelical Nation: The Surprising Crisis inside the Church* (New York, NY: HarperCollins, 2008).

58. Lauren Sandler, *Righteous: Dispatches from the Evangelical Youth Movement* (New York, NY: Viking, 2006).

59. Wilcox and Robinson, *Onward Christian Soldiers*.

60. James F. Findlay, Jr., *Church People in the Struggle: The National Council of Churches and the Black Freedom Movement, 1950-1970* (Oxford: Oxford University Press, 1993).

61. See, for example, Michael Lienesch, *Redeeming America: Piety and Politics in the New Christian Right* (Chapel Hill, NC: University of North Carolina Press, 1993); Wilcox and Robinson, *Onward Christian Soldiers*.

62. David R. Swartz, *Moral Minority: The Evangelical Left in an Age of Conservatism* (Philadelphia, PA: University of Pennsylvania Press, 2012).

63. Cleve R. Wootson, Jr., "Rev. William Barber Builds a Moral Movement," *Washington Post*, June 29, 2017.

64. H. Richard Niebuhr, *Christ and Culture* (New York, NY: Harper & Row, 1951); Peter J. Thuesen, "The Logic of Mainline Churchliness," in Robert Wuthnow and John H. Evans (eds.), *The Quiet Hand of God: Faith-Based Activism and the Public Role of Mainline Protestantism* (Berkeley, CA: University of California Press, 2002), pp. 27–53.

65. Paul A. Djupe and Christopher P. Gilbert, *The Political Influence of Churches* (Cambridge: Cambridge University Press, 2009); James L. Guth, John C. Green, Corwin E. Smidt, Lyman A. Kellstedt, and Margaret M. Poloma, *The Bully Pulpit: The Politics of Protestant Clergy* (Lawrence, KS: University Press of Kansas, 1997).

66. Gary Dorrien, *Social Ethics in the Making: Interpreting an American Tradition* (Malden, MA: Wiley, 2011); Thuesen, "Logic of Mainline Churchliness."

67. Jeffrey Hadden, *The Gathering Storm in the Churches* (Garden City, NY: Doubleday, 1969); Harold E. Quinley, *The Prophetic Clergy: Social Activism among Protestant Ministers* (New York, NY: Wiley, 1974).

68. Jackson W. Carroll, Barbara G. Wheeler, Daniel O. Aleshire, and Penny Long Marler, *Being There: Culture and Formation in Two Theological Schools* (Oxford: Oxford University Press, 1997); Dorrien, *Social Ethics*.

69. John C. Green, *The Faith Factor: How Religion Influences American Elections* (Sterling, VA: Potomac Books, 2010); Jeff Manza and Clem Brooks, "The Changing Political Fortunes of Mainline Protestants," in Robert Wuthnow and John H. Evans (eds.), *The Quiet Hand of God: Faith-Based Activism and the Public Role of Mainline Protestantism* (Berkeley, CA: University of California Press, 2002), pp. 159–180; Smidt et al., *The Disappearing God Gap*.

70. Smidt et al., *The Disappearing God Gap*.

71. Green, *The Faith Factor*.

72. Findlay, *Church People in the Struggle*; Allen D. Hertzke, *Representing God in Washington* (Knoxville, TN: University of Tennessee Press, 1987).

73. Findlay, *Church People in the Struggle*; Michael B. Friedland, *Lift Up Your Voice Like a Trumpet: White Clergy and the Civil Rights and Antiwar Movements, 1954–1973* (Chapel Hill, NC: University of North Carolina Press, 1998); Mitchell K. Hall, *Because of Their Faith: CALCAV and Religious Opposition to the Vietnam War* (New York, NY: Columbia University Press, 1990).

74. Sue E. S. Crawford and Laura R. Olson (ed.), *Christian Clergy in American Politics* (Baltimore, MD: Johns Hopkins University Press, 2001); Paul A. Djupe and Christopher P. Gilbert, *The Prophetic Pulpit: Clergy, Churches, and Communities in American Politics* (Lanham, MD: Rowman & Littlefield, 2003); Guth et al., *The Bully Pulpit*.

75. Wendy Cadge, "Vital Conflicts: The Mainline Protestant Denominations Debate Homosexuality," in Robert Wuthnow and John H. Evans (eds.), *The Quiet Hand of God: Faith-Based Activism and the Public Role of Mainline Protestantism* (Berkeley, CA: University of California Press, 2002), pp. 265–286.

76. Djupe and Gilbert, *Political Influence of Churches*; Guth et al., *The Bully Pulpit*; Hadden, *The Gathering Storm in the Churches*.

77. Pew Research Center, "US Religious Landscape Study."

78. Reported in "While We Are At It," *First Things* (February 2012): 67–68. For a brief but illuminating insider look at the challenges faced by one mainline denomination, see Daniel J. Lehmann, "Facing Future with Resolve," *Lutheran*, August 2012, p. 4.

79. On the general question of mainline decline, see Finke and Stark, *The Churching of America*; Phillip Hammond, *The Protestant Presence in Twentieth-Century America: Religion and Political Culture* (Albany, NY: State University Press of New York, 1992); Iannaccone, "Why Strict Churches Are Strong"; Kelley, *Why Conservative Churches Are Growing*; Robert Wuthnow, *The Crisis in the Churches* (Oxford: Oxford University Press, 1996).

80. Nancy Ammerman, *Pillars of Faith* (Berkeley, CA: University of California Press, 2005); Djupe and Olson, *Religious Interests in Community Conflict*; Ram A. Cnaan, *The Invisible Caring Hand* (New York, NY: New York University Press, 2002); Stephen Hart, *Cultural Dilemmas of Progressive Politics: Styles of Engagement Among Grassroots Activists* (Chicago, IL: University of Chicago Press, 2001); Wuthnow and Evans, *The Quiet Hand of God*.

81. Richard John Neuhaus, *The Catholic Moment: The Paradox of the Church in the Postmodern World* (San Francisco, CA: Harper & Row, 1987).

82. Manilo Graziano, *In Rome We Trust: The Rise of Catholics in American Political Life* (Stanford, CA: Stanford University Press, 2017); Kristin E. Heyer, Mark J. Rozell, and Michael A. Genovese, *Catholics and Politics: The Dynamic Tension between Faith and Power* (Washington, DC: Georgetown University Press, 2008); Pew Research Center, "US Religious Landscape Study."

83. Graziano, *In Rome We Trust*.

84. For a general overview and thorough history through the election of Pope John Paul II, see Frederic J. Baumgartner, *Behind Locked Doors: A History of Papal Elections* (New York, NY: Palgrave Macmillan, 2003); for a particularly contemporary account, see John Thavis, *The Vatican Diaries: A Behind-the-Scenes Look at the Power, Personalities, and Politics at the Heart of the Catholic Church* (New York, NY: Viking, 2013).

85. John L. Allen, Jr., *Opus Dei: An Objective Look behind the Myths and Reality of the Most Controversial Force in the Catholic Church* (Garden City, NY: Doubleday, 2005); Mary Jo Weaver (ed.), *What's Left? Liberal American Catholics* (Bloomington, IN: Indiana University Press, 1999).

86. Graziano, *In Rome We Trust*; Paul Christopher Manuel, Lawrence C. Reardon, and Clyde Wilcox (eds.), *The Catholic Church and the Nation-State: Comparative Perspectives* (Washington, DC: Georgetown University Press, 2007).

87. For a brief survey in the European context, see Tom Buchanan and Martin Conway (eds.), *Political Catholicism in Europe, 1918–1965* (Oxford: Oxford University Press, 1996).

88. See, for example, Paul Blanshard's critique of the church in *American Freedom and Catholic Power* (Boston, MA: Beacon Press, 1949). For a balanced historical treatment, see John T. McGreevy, *Catholics and American Freedom: A History* (New York, NY: W. W. Norton, 2003). See also Anthony B. Smith, *The Look of Catholics: Portrayals in Popular Culture from the Great Depression to the Cold War* (Lawrence, KS: University Press of Kansas, 2010).

89. See John Courtney Murray, *We Hold These Truths: Catholic Reflections on the American Proposition* (New York, NY: Sheed & Ward, 1960). Murray concludes that the American experiment, properly understood, is compatible with church teachings.

90. Samuel Huntington, *The Third Wave: Democratization in the Late Twentieth Century* (Norman, OK: University of Oklahoma Press, 1991). On Vatican II, see Melissa J. Wilde, *Vatican II: A Sociological Analysis of Religious Change* (Princeton, NJ: Princeton University Press, 2007).

91. Timothy A. Byrnes, *Catholic Bishops in American Politics* (Princeton, NJ: Princeton University Press, 1991); Friedland, *Lift Up Your Voice like a Trumpet*, chapters 6–9; Marco G. Prouty and César Chávez, *The Catholic Bishops, and the Farmworkers' Struggle for Social Justice* (Tucson, AZ: University of Arizona Press, 2008).

92. Byrnes, *Catholic Bishops in American Politics*; Clarke E. Cochran and David Carroll Cochran, *Catholics, Politics, and Public Policy: Beyond Left and Right* (Maryknoll, NY: Orbis, 2003).

93. Cochran and Cochran, *Catholics, Politics, and Public Policy*; Hubert Morken and Jo Renee Formicola, *The Politics of School Choice* (Lanham, MD: Rowman & Littlefield, 1999).

94. Leslie C. Griffin, "The Catholic Bishops vs. the Contraceptive Mandate," *Religions*, 6 (2015): 1411–1432.

95. Two recent and controversial accounts of the current situation are George Weigel, *Evangelical Catholicism* (New York, NY: Basic Books, 2013), and Russell Shaw, *American Church: The Remarkable Rise, Meteoric Fall, and Uncertain Future of Catholicism in America* (San Francisco, CA: Ignatius Press, 2013).

96. Pew Research Center, "US Religious Landscape Study." See also John L. Allen, Jr., *The Future Church: How Ten Trends Are Revolutionizing the Catholic Church* (New York, NY: Random House, 2009); Jones, *The End of White Christian America*; Michael Lipka, "A Closer Look at Catholic America," Pew Research Center, September 14, 2015, www.pewresearch.org/fact-tank/2015/09/14/a-closer-look-at-catholic-america/.

97. Allen, *The Future Church*; Andrew M. Greeley, *Priests: A Calling in Crisis* (Chicago, IL: University of Chicago Press, 2004); Anne Hendershott and Christopher White, *Renewal: How a New Generation of Priests and Bishops are Revitalizing the Catholic Church* (Jackson, TN: Encounter Books, 2013).

98. Philip Jenkins, *The New Anti-Catholicism: The Last Acceptable Prejudice* (Oxford: Oxford University Press, 2003).

99. See "Bankruptcy Protection in the Abuse Crisis," www.bishop-accountability. org/bankruptcy.htm.

100. Greeley, *Priests*; "Jehovah's Witnesses Told to Pay in Abuse Case," *New York Times*, June 18, 2012, p. A14.

101. United States Conference of Catholic Bishops, *The Nature and Scope of the Problem of Sexual Abuse of Minors by Catholic Priests and Deacons in the United States*, 2004, www.usccb.org/nrb/johnjaystudy/. See also Shaw, *The Remarkable Rise*; Peter Steinfels, *A People Adrift: The Crisis of the Roman Catholic Church in America* (New York, NY: Simon & Schuster, 2004).

102. Pew Research Center, "'Nones' on the Rise", "US Religious Landscape Study."

103. David B. Truman, *The Governmental Process: Political Interests and Public Opinion* (New York, NY: Knopf, 1951).

4

JUDAISM, ISLAM, AND OTHER EXPRESSIONS OF RELIGIOUS PLURALISM

Much of the discussion of religion and politics in the United States concentrates on the political activity of Catholics and various Protestant denominations. This focus makes sense because these groups are the largest and most prominent among the complex and pluralistic mix of religions in the United States. But these familiar and well-established religious groups hardly constitute the entire story of religion—or of religion and politics—in the United States.

After all, while most Americans still describe themselves as Christians, the United States is now rightly described as "the world's most religiously diverse nation."[1] There are literally hundreds of religious groups and thousands of religious communities in the United States. There is also a growing proportion of Americans who opt out of organized religion altogether. Each American religious group (including the secular component of the population), however small, has political objectives—even if it simply wishes to be left alone. And each exercises political influence, however modest, indirect, or unintended. Smaller religious groups have important lessons to teach about what they do, how they protect themselves, and how they advance their values. Their stories become ever more relevant as the pluralism of American religion continues to grow.

We have already discussed in Chapter 1 the rise of the "nones"—the nearly quarter of the American population who surveys show do not declare any religion, much less belong to any religious group. They are an increasingly important part of the American (non)religious mosaic today.[2] So too are some "freethinking" groups that sometimes are antireligious. Examples are the legally activist Freedom from Religion Foundation (see Chapter 11) and the Secular Coalition of America, whose focus is activism in lobbying and elections. Another example is the Association of American Atheists, which claims such outspoken allies as British antireligion controversialist Richard Dawkins, ex-California Democratic congressman Peter Stark, the rock group Bad Religion, and others. American Atheists and allied groups have held yearly rallies on the National Mall in Washington, DC, to publicize their antireligious cause and their political agenda of fully separating religion from government in the United States.

It is not obvious how to study the political dimensions of smaller religious and religion-oriented groups in the United States. Too few have done so, and, as we proceed, we are acutely aware that our way represents only one possible method. It is, however, essential to approach studying smaller religious groups with respect and not treat them as strange phenomena. Religious movements deserve to be taken seriously, both on their own terms and for their political implications.

In this chapter, we divide smaller religious movements into several sections. First, we will discuss Judaism and Islam, both of which present major alternatives to Christianity in American public life, in terms of their size and public exposure. Jews have lived in the United States since before the founding of the nation, and many have carved out a highly successful niche in American society. Islam, by contrast, is a relative newcomer and faces challenges in addressing its unique political and social circumstances. Second, we will look at Mormons, a distinctive, thriving, and uniquely American Christian tradition. Third, we will explore small religious traditions that maintain a clear separation from mainstream politics and culture. Fourth, we will examine non-separatist religious traditions that engage the broader culture. Finally, we end the chapter with a discussion of secularism. For each category, we give attention to attitudes toward, and involvement in, political life. We argue that distinctive religious beliefs and behaviors combine with a host of other factors—such as geography and relative size—to explain differences in how smaller religious groups approach public life. Of course, we cannot possibly deal with all the organized smaller religious groups in the United States, not to speak of innumerable informal religious and spiritual groups and their political roles or potential. Yet, given the tremendous religious and ethnic diversity that immigration encourages, small religious groups require a careful eye for their political impact as they emerge on the American religious scene. For example, adherents of both Buddhism and Hinduism each now comprise 1 percent of the American population, though to date they have wielded relatively little political impact.[3]

JEWS AND JUDAISM

Many Jews are among the most successful members of minority groups in America in both economic and educational terms. After suffering persecution for centuries throughout the world, Jews have found the United States, with its doctrine of religious tolerance, a remarkably hospitable place.[4] This is not to say that they have not faced any serious disadvantages in the United States from outright discrimination and hostility. But the constitutional protection of religious liberty, combined with a social system that can reward strong families, hard work, and education, has enabled the majority of Jews to prosper in the United States.[5] As a group, Jews rank high on every aggregate socioeconomic measure, including income, educational attainment, and professional status. They have moved into positions of prominence in business, law, higher education, journalism, entertainment, and politics.[6]

However, we need to avoid reinforcing stereotypes of Jewish cabals ruling the world. Jewish influence can be easily exaggerated. As Jews constitute less than 2 percent of the US population, Jewish voting strength makes its largest impact only in cities and states where their numbers are concentrated, and migration patterns suggest increasing vote dilution as Jewish Americans disperse across the United States.[7] In some cases, Jews' influence on some issues— backing for Israel, for example—is enhanced due to broad support from Christians. Still, Jews often have had an impact on American politics that is more profound than their small numbers would suggest. Crucial are the factors of many Jewish citizens' openness to involvement in politics, substantial financial contributions to politicians and political candidates, and willingness to get organized for political causes and candidates.

Jews who are formally associated with a synagogue fall into one of three major groupings—Reform (35 percent), Conservative (18 percent), and Orthodox (10 percent)—or other smaller groupings within American Judaism (6 percent).[8] It might sound paradoxical to read that the majority of Jews are in fact largely secular and live a mainly or entirely secular life, but this is true: 62 percent of US Jews told the Pew Research Center that "being Jewish" is primarily a matter of ancestry and culture, while only 15 percent said it is a religious matter.[9] Seventeen percent of Jews say they do not believe in God.[10] Thus, it should come as no surprise that the most liberal large branch of Judaism, Reform Judaism, has suffered dramatic losses—up to one-third—of its adherents in the past decade as more Jews drift away entirely from any religious connection. Conservative Judaism, but not Orthodox Judaism, has also experienced major losses.[11] Partly as a result, one dimension of the politics of religion—the conflict between secular forces and religious ones in the American public square— attracts many Jewish voices strongly opposed to government interaction with religion.

Among Jews today, more and more Jews participate less and less in Jewish ceremonies, and close to a third are not at all connected with Judaism as a religion in any way. One exception is the various Orthodox Jewish communities which are growing steadily, with large families and a determined, often thoroughgoing commitment to their versions of Judaism. Many Orthodox Jews are not wealthy or highly educated, and often they are alienated from the larger culture by choice. They hardly fit the image of educated, affluent, liberal Jews so common in the United States, an image that does not reflect reality, especially among religious Jews.[12] Among other Jewish Americans, synagogue attendance rates are low and falling. Nevertheless, even most nonreligious Jews feel a connection to other Jews out of a sense of shared history and culture. Many proudly describe themselves as Jewish even if they never set foot in a synagogue.[13]

That said, a serious issue in Jewish circles today is the challenge of maintaining a distinctive Jewish culture without much of a religious dimension. Roughly half of all American Jews today marry people of other faith traditions, and children who have one Jewish parent often are raised with only a vague sense of that parent's heritage. Moreover, birth rates for non-Orthodox Jewish women are lower than the rate needed to replace the population. Myriad calls to reclaim Jewish heritage only confirm the concern.[14]

Most Jews have a well-deserved reputation for political liberalism. This was reflected in the 78 percent vote for President Barack Obama among American Jews in 2008, the 69 percent vote for him in 2012, and the 71 percent vote for Hillary Clinton in 2016.[15] Many Jewish leaders serve in political offices at all levels of government, generally as Democrats. Among members of the 115th Congress, 30 (5.6 percent) are Jewish, and only two of these individuals are Republicans.[16] Many more Jewish Americans are active in Democratic politics and the politics of liberal interest groups, from unions to environmental and other lobby groups. Indeed, political liberalism is now a well-established cultural norm among Jews. Support for gay marriage, abortion rights, gun control, civil rights, and other liberal causes often finds Jews in the vanguard.

This progressivism derives from several factors. One is that most Jews are acutely aware of the history of their persecution. The lessons of history warn of the dangers of not protecting the rights of minorities, very much including Jews, and stress church–state separation as part of that goal. Crucial as well is a secularized ethic rooted in historic religious Judaism, with its emphasis on hospitality for others, care for the poor, suffering, and oppressed, all of which are eloquently expressed in Jewish Scriptures.[17] Jews exercise political influence through a host of robust organizations. The oldest of these is the American Jewish Committee (AJC), which was formed in 1906. Such interest groups benefit from thriving local chapters, seasoned leaders, and a clear political agenda.

Even though these groups' agenda is undeniably liberal, there is pluralism within American Jewish politics as well.[18] Indeed, Orthodox Jews often oppose abortion, support government aid to religious schools, oppose gay marriage, and back various other measures to check the advance of secular culture (see Box 4.1). They also often vote Republican, a fact that may be of increasing significance as Orthodox numbers increase.[19] Another expression of Jewish conservatism has come in the form of Jewish intellectuals, including former liberals Norman Podhoretz and Irving Kristol, who initiated the neoconservative movement against perceived liberal excesses of the 1960s and 1970s.[20] That movement continues to the present day. Irving Kristol's son, William, founded and heads the conservative *Weekly Standard*. There were key links between such neoconservatives as Kristol and the administration of President George W. Bush, especially in terms of support for the Iraq and Afghanistan wars. They believed both efforts were vital for the defense of both the United States and Israel. Jewish intellectuals such as William Kristol, however, have been rather uniformly opposed to the administration of President Donald Trump.[21]

BOX 4.1 THE HASIDIM IN AMERICA

Several distinct ultraorthodox Jewish communities thrive in the United States, but the largest are the Hasidic Jews. They are concentrated primarily in several areas in New York State, New York City, Los Angeles, and New Jersey. Their numbers are growing even as many other Jewish groups shrink and as American Jews in general become more and more secular. Basic demographics are the reason for this difference. Hasidic Jews are much younger on average than other Jews, and they marry younger and have bigger families. The Hasidim are not a thoroughly unified group; they are in fact divided into several tight subgroups, each organized under a *rebbe* (master) and devoted to the laws and teachings of ancient scripture. Unlike many other ultraorthodox Jews, however, the Hasidim do not single-mindedly study the scriptures. For the Hasidim, such an approach is much too formal and scholarly; it downplays the essential importance of emotion in their worship of God.

The tradition of the Hasidim mostly has been one of political withdrawal from larger, usually Christian, societies. Hasidic Jews are like many other fundamentalist religious groups in that they seek distance from the secular elements of society, which they judge to be corrupting or otherwise dangerous to the faithful. At the same time, however, the Hasidim do sometimes participate in politics. In the United States, this has included regular voting. Because the Hasidim are social conservatives, they usually vote Republican. This may matter more in the future if the Hasidic population continues to expand. On occasion, Hasidim have run their own candidates in local or state legislative contests where issues that matter to them are at stake and where they have a chance to win (as in a few parts of New York state). Indeed, sometimes they have won.

Source: Pew Research Center, "A Portrait of American Orthodox Jews," August 26, 2015.

For some Jewish conservatives, the overwhelming Jewish orientation to liberalism reflects many Jews' drift away from Judaism as a religion and certainly from traditional Jewish religious beliefs. To them, the drift also reflects a movement away from concern for the future of the Jewish people and their ancient and present homeland of Israel. For these outnumbered critics, if there is a religion that affects dominant Jewish attitudes today, it is the religion, so to speak, of liberalism, to which Podhoretz has said, "They give the kind of steadfast devotion their forefathers gave to the religion of the Hebrew Bible."[22] Support for Israel, however, is a deeply felt cause for many American Jews across the political spectrum. Israel is more than a familiar land where close friends and relatives often live. It is also the Jewish homeland and a place that has been a refuge for Jews (off and on) for several millennia. Although there are plenty of disagreements today with certain Israeli leaders and policies and an increasing concern about the situation of the Palestinians (especially among secular, left-leaning Jews), many American Jews support Israel both politically and financially. In turn, Israeli leaders keep in close contact with Jewish leaders and organizations in the United States.[23]

MUSLIMS AND ISLAM

Islam today receives a great deal of media attention, especially after many finally became aware of American Muslims in the wake of the September 11, 2001, attacks on the World Trade Center and the Pentagon. The number of Muslims living in the United States is estimated to be 3.3 million: 1 percent of the population.[24] In 1900, there were no more than a few thousand Muslims in the United States; by the 1920s, there were at least 60,000; by 2050, the Pew Research Center anticipates Muslims to account for more than 2 percent of all of Americans.[25] Although Islam faces the same challenge other US religious groups do in retaining active faith among younger members, it is a relatively youthful faith today; 60 percent of American Muslims were under the age of forty as of 2017.[26]

The number of Muslim places of worship in the United States has grown as well. In the early 1930s, just one mosque existed in the United States, but today there are more than 2,100 mosques and Islamic religious centers, nearly doubling in numbers in the past decade.[27] A host of Muslim voluntary organizations flourish as well, including charities, civic groups, publishers, private schools, mosque-based Boy Scout troops, college clubs, and political organizations. There is also progress in higher education—for example, the establishment of Zaytuna College, in Berkeley, California, as chronicled by author Scott Korb.[28] There are many reasons to think that this pattern of growth will continue, particularly because in the aggregate Muslim Americans are young and have relatively large families.[29]

To a degree, the remarkable ethnic diversity of Muslims in the United States today limits their ability to organize effectively for political causes. Muslim immigrants have come to the United States in considerable numbers from all over the world. Forty-two percent of US Muslims today are native-born, with 20 percent identifying as African American; among the non-native born, 20 percent have roots in South Asia, 14 percent in the Middle East or North Africa, 13 percent in the remainder of the Asia-Pacific region, and the rest from sub-Saharan Africa and other locations.[30] Such ethnic diversity ensures that contemporary US Muslims represent both major traditions of Islam: Sunni and Shi'a, traditions that differ primarily over the question of who should have succeeded the Prophet Muhammad after his death. In part because of a sizable Shi'a population in southern California, Sunni Muslims have a much smaller majority in the United States than they do in the Islamic world overall (55 percent in the United States compared to roughly nine in ten world-wide).[31]

Apart from their growth in numbers, there are signs of organization that may lead to increased political influence for American Muslims. The aftermath of September 11, 2001, and subsequent terrorist activity by radicalized Muslims in organizations including Al Qaeda and ISIS have created urgent public-policy concerns in the American Muslim community. Concerns about terrorist acts by Muslim extremists are substantial among Muslims in the United States. In 2017, 66 percent of US Muslims told the Pew Research Center they were "very concerned" about extremism around the world in the name of Islam, compared to 49 percent of the general population.[32] Moreover, American Muslims are less likely than the population at large to perceive support for extremism among their fellow Muslims—and less likely than the US public to say, "targeting and killing civilians for political, social, or religious reasons is never justifiable."[33]

A variety of groups has worked to address the various social and political concerns of Muslim Americans through interfaith relations, lobbying, and partnership with government agencies. The primary umbrella organization of Islamic groups in the United States is the Islamic Society of North America. One group, the Muslim Public Affairs Council (MPAC), came to the forefront after September 11. Groups such as MPAC focus primarily on protecting the civil liberties and rights of Muslim American citizens.[34] Since September 11, MPAC and other Muslim organizations have spent much of their time confronting false perceptions that most Muslims are terrorists or even anti-American. Muslim leaders understand that such stereotypes must be dismantled if Muslims are to be fully accepted in the United States, much less gain political influence. Muslims also have rallied together in recent years to defend the construction of mosques and other Muslim gathering places in the face of skepticism and sometimes attack from the larger US population.[35] Most prominent in this regard was the uproar over the construction of the Manhattan Islamic Center—the so-called

"Ground Zero Mosque" for its proximity to the site of the September 11, 2001, attacks on the World Trade Center in lower Manhattan.[36]

Another way false stereotypes will be debunked is through the growing visibility of younger Muslims who are assimilating into American culture with relative ease. Muslims are like other Americans in the amount of time they

---

BOX 4.2 ISMAIL ROYER: A JOURNEY FROM JIHAD TO CHAMPIONING RELIGIOUS FREEDOM

Sometimes the best advocate against religious extremism is a former extremist. Ismail Royer is such a person. Born Randall Royer, the son of a Catholic mother and Baptist father, he was raised in suburban St. Louis. A self-described idealist and searcher, Royer converted to Islam in 1992 after reading *The Autobiography of Malcolm X* as a student at American University in Washington, DC. Upon his conversion, he changed his first name to Ismail. Shortly thereafter, he noticed large numbers of Bosnian refugees arriving in St. Louis's Muslim community and became transfixed by news accounts of atrocities committed against the Bosnian people by Serb forces during the Balkan wars.

Royer left college, traveled to Bosnia, joined the mujahedeen, and engaged in firefights. He later traveled to Pakistan and joined Laskar-e-Taiba, an armed Islamist group focused on ending Indian control of majority-Muslim Kashmir. After attempting to organize US Muslims to join in the Kashmir struggle, Royer was arrested and convicted on terror charges. He served thirteen years in the Supermax prison in Florence, Colorado, where many of the highest-profile federal inmates are housed. At Supermax, Royer struck up a correspondence with Richard Reid, the so-called "shoe bomber."

This correspondence led Royer to see deep flaws in jihadist ideology. By the time he got out of prison in 2017, Royer was a changed man both spiritually and ideologically. He began speaking out about how Muslims who join ISIS were being duped and subsequently was recruited to work for the Center for Islam and Religious Freedom. In that position, he presents the Muslim case against extremism and supports the chorus of religious interests working in favor of religious liberty in Washington, DC.

Source: Terrance McCoy, "Fourteen Years Ago, He Was a Convicted Jihadist. Now He's Fighting Radical Islam Steps from the White House," *Washington Post*, July 7, 2017.

spend doing ordinary activities such as playing video games and taking out the trash.[37] Moreover, just over one-third of US Muslims say most or all of their friends are also Muslim, and roughly one in ten married Muslim Americans has a non-Muslim spouse.[38] Meanwhile, though some assert that Islam and democracy are incompatible, only 30 percent of US Muslims take this view (compared to 44 percent of the general population).[39] Many also promote the idea of religious tolerance both in the United States and globally (see Box 4.2). Still others have been active in opposing what they see as inappropriate profiling and investigations of Muslims and Muslim organizations.[40]

Before 9/11, given the diversity inherent in American Islam—divisions between the native-born and non-native-born, between black Muslims and the rest of the Muslim population, between Sunni and Shi'a Muslims, and across ethnic and linguistic lines for new immigrants—collective Muslim political muscle seemed unlikely to develop. That is changing now. Like Christians, a majority of US Muslims share in common the fact that religion is "very important" in their lives, which suggests that they might be mobilized by religious elites for political action just as US Christians have been.[41] Political uniformity is emerging as well, with 66 percent of Muslims in the United States identifying as Democrats and the same share favoring "a bigger government that offers more services."[42] A large majority—78 percent—voted for Hillary Clinton in 2016, and as of 2017, 65 percent said they disapproved of the job Donald Trump was doing as president.[43] On the other hand, Muslims tend to be conservative on such social and moral issues, although the Pew Research Center reports that Muslims are growing more accepting of homosexuality at the same rate as the rest of the US population.[44]

One likely possibility going forward is that foreign-policy concerns affecting majority Muslim countries around the world will become the core of a political agenda for Muslims in the United States, mirroring many American Jews' concern for Israel. To some extent this is true already, although it has not necessarily led to a single set of policy priorities on the part of Muslim interest groups. The one exception is the existence of strong, universal support among Muslims for the Palestinian cause.[45] It may turn out that Muslims will never obtain substantial political leverage in the United States regardless of what agenda (or agendas) they pursue. Progress here will automatically be hindered if a more favorable image of Islam does not take hold, which will depend in part on whether Muslim extremists commit further high-profile acts of terrorism in the United States. Lack of leverage could also result if the Muslim community cannot bridge ethnic and racial divisions that may undercut the development of a unified political agenda. In time, however, the inevitable processes of assimilation may address all these challenges and help Islam emerge as a stronger, more unified force in religion and politics in the United States (see Box 4.3).

BOX 4.3 RELIGIOUS DIVERSITY IN CONGRESS

When asked about religion and their vote choices, Americans routinely say they are less likely to cast their ballot for candidates from religions perceived as being outside the mainstream. Hence, the election of Keith Ellison to the US House of Representatives in 2006 marked a historic moment in American political history. Ellison, a liberal Democrat representing Minnesota's Fifth Congressional District, became the first Muslim ever elected to Congress. Raised in Detroit, Ellison became a Muslim in college. Although he tends not to wear his faith on his sleeve, it inevitably became a campaign issue. Rep. Ellison also sparked criticism when, during a photo opportunity reenactment of his congressional oath-taking, he chose to place his hand on a copy of the Qur'an once owned by Thomas Jefferson. Nonetheless, he has been reelected several times and has become a respected member of the Democratic Caucus in the House. The second Muslim ever elected to Congress, Rep. Andrea Carson of Indiana, followed Ellison in 2008. Together they have been committed advocates for greater Muslim engagement in American politics, as well as for American engagement with global Islam. They prominently voiced their opposition to the Trump administration's "travel ban" barring people from select majority-Muslim countries from entering the United States.

Today, there is even more religious diversity in Congress than ever before, at least among Democrats. Although 91 percent of the 115th Congress identify as Christian, the House also includes Ellison, Carson, two Buddhists, three Hindus, and one member—Rep. Kyrsten Sinema of Arizona—who identifies as a "non-theist." In addition, Mazie Hirono of Hawaii is the first ever Buddhist US senator, elected in 2012 after serving three terms in the House of Representatives.

Source: Aleksandra Sandstrom, "Faith on the Hill," Pew Research Center, January 3, 2017; Richard Wolf, "First Muslim Lawmaker Takes Oath with Qur'an," *USA Today*, January 5, 2007, p. A4.

THE LDS CHURCH: A UNIQUELY AMERICAN CHRISTIAN FAITH

The Church of Jesus Christ of Latter-Day Saints (LDS Church), whose members are called Mormons, seems to belie the general tendency for small religious traditions to have only modest political effectiveness. Instead, Mormons constitute an important force in American politics, in large part because of their steady growth. Today, 1.6 percent of Americans are Mormon, and the church has experienced steady growth in recent decades both in the United States and abroad.[46] But this growth in numbers and political influence has not come easily. The LDS story presents a remarkable case study of a young religious group overcoming tremendous disadvantages. In their early days, Mormons had no influence. Indeed, no religious group has suffered more discrimination in the United States—often severe and deadly persecution—than did the Mormons in the nineteenth century.[47] Today, however, the Mormons' situation is entirely different. Headquartered in Salt Lake City, the LDS Church is highly organized and thriving. Its members are engaged in local, state, and national politics across the country, but especially in western states, where Mormon numbers are largest.

There is some debate about where the LDS faith fits into the rest of the Christian tradition. Most Americans know little about the Mormon religion, and some traditionalist Christian leaders argue that the LDS Church is not a truly Christian faith.[48] Such disagreements have impeded Mormon efforts to reach across religious barriers for political (and other) purposes. However, there is little doubt that the 2012 presidential candidacy of Mormon Mitt Romney softened the impact of this concern.[49]

Romney, a former Massachusetts governor who also had chaired the Salt Lake Olympic Organizing Committee, first ran (unsuccessfully) for the Republican presidential nomination in 2008. In 2012, he ran again and won the Republican nomination. He lost a tight race to President Barack Obama, securing about 48 percent of the popular vote and 206 electoral votes. Speculation abounded about whether anti-Mormon prejudice might hurt him among conservative, traditionalist Christians. However, in 2012, he received almost 80 percent of the vote of white evangelical Protestants, more than non-Mormon John McCain had received in 2008. Romney's serious contention for the presidency speaks to the LDS Church's emergence as a respected participant in the mainstream of American religion. It is important to note that at no time during any of his campaigns did the LDS Church give him an official endorsement, though unsurprisingly the vast majority of Mormons voted for him.[50] As was the case after John F. Kennedy became only the second Catholic to run for president, so too Mitt Romney's presidential campaigns seem to have led to an ebbing of prejudice against his religion.[51]

Both Christianity and Judaism inspired Joseph Smith in 1830 when he founded the LDS Church in western New York. However, his interpretations of those faiths inevitably clashed with the traditional Protestantism that dominated American culture of the time. Smith reported that the angel Moroni directed him to golden plates that he translated into the Book of Mormon. The plates explained the history of a tribal branch of Israelites who came to the Americas after about 600 BCE. This tribe was visited by Jesus Christ and eventually was destroyed because its members failed to follow God's will. Mormons believe that in his earthly life Moroni was the son of a prophet, Mormon, who repeatedly warned the tribe of its impending doom. They also hold that Mormon himself recorded most of the history recounted on the golden plates and buried them several thousand years before they were revealed to Joseph Smith.[52]

Nineteenth-century Mormon history is full of dramatic and often heroic episodes. From the founding of the LDS Church in 1830 to the murder of Joseph Smith in 1844 to the eventual settlement in Utah a few years later, Mormons clashed with the broader American culture. The result was a great deal of pain and suffering for Mormon people, who were literally chased out of the communities in which they settled and forced to cross the Rocky Mountains to escape physical danger. Anti-Mormon sentiment was especially intense because of polygamy, a long-abandoned practice in the official LDS Church. The question of statehood for Utah in some ways hinged on Mormons giving up polygamy, which Congress had banned in the Utah territories in 1862 (with the blessing of the US Supreme Court later in the 1878 case of *Reynolds* v. *United States*).

The LDS belief system affirms the three persons of the Christian Trinity—Father, Son, and Holy Spirit—but maintains that they are separate entities rather than the traditional Christian doctrine of three persons in one. Mormons also believe that all people were with God before creation and that they move on after death to live with God. The LDS Church teaches that present-day Mormons may save people who lived before Smith's revelation and thus could not have known Mormon truth. As a result, Mormons have amassed the United States' leading genealogical archive as part of their effort to identify past relatives. Mormons believe that baptizing these long-dead ancestors will help them toward eternal salvation.

Mormons are middle-class, well-educated, overwhelmingly white, and typically established in traditional family structures.[53] They are politically engaged, with high rates of voter turnout. They are quite uniformly conservative and even more reliably Republican than evangelical Protestants. In the 2016 presidential election, Mormon voters preferred Donald Trump over Hillary Clinton, but by a much smaller margin than is typically the case. Rather than the usual 80-plus percent of the Mormon vote that goes to the Republican presidential candidate, Trump secured just 61 percent—and only 46 percent in majority-Mormon Utah.[54] During the 2016 campaign, many leading Mormons reported discomfort with Trump's hardline stance on immigration, his unclear religious background, his derogatory comments about women, and his general comportment.[55] In fact, a Mormon independent candidate, Evan McMullin, ultimately won a sizable share (21 percent) of the presidential vote in Utah.[56]

Much of the reason for their political distinctiveness lies in Mormons' overriding commitments to family life, individual responsibility, and moral conservatism; many Mormons naturally link these values to the Republican Party. Another reason for their conservatism is a suspicion of government authority rooted in the nineteenth-century Mormon experience of conflict with the federal government. Mormons also tend to have tight social networks composed primarily of fellow believers, which has the effect of reinforcing their conservative political outlook. In fact, over the past century, Mormons have become more uniformly conservative, especially in Utah and neighboring states, where Mormon social networks can be rather homogeneous.[57] This is not to say that there are no Mormon Democrats; there are some, such as US Senator Tom Udall of New Mexico. However, their numbers are small, and Mormon Democrats tend to be less committed to the faith overall and live outside of the Mountain West.[58]

The LDS Church as an organization contends that it is apolitical. This is so in large part because the church does not take formal political stands unless its president, whom Mormons view as a prophet, shares a specific revelation. Like most religious groups in the United States, the LDS Church does not endorse candidates for office, nor does it contribute directly to candidate campaigns; doing so would be illegal on the part of any tax-exempt religious organization. The church learned from its nineteenth-century experience of trying to fashion a political theocracy—a nation of Zion—in Utah. That effort brought Mormons only grief, including from the federal government, in the end. Although the LDS Church lost its earlier political struggles, it learned how to fashion an effective political voice as a result.

Today, the LDS Church is political in several subtle ways, with most of its activism happening behind the scenes. Church leaders encourage members to participate in politics, and from time to time Mormons emerge as a powerfully unified political voice. For example, the LDS Church played significant roles, both financially and organizationally, in the 2008 campaign to pass Proposition 8, which amended California's constitution to recognize only heterosexual marriages as valid.[59] The approval of Proposition 8, which passed with 52 percent of the vote, illustrates the reality that the LDS Church can exercise substantial political muscle in certain circumstances.

SEPARATIST RELIGIONS

Several small religious traditions in the United States take a distinctly separatist orientation toward the broader culture. By the term "separatist," we mean that these religious communities set stricter moral boundaries for their members than do mainstream religions and that these boundaries necessarily separate members of the religious group from the larger society. Most of these groups are critical of the larger society, which they portray as immoral, evil, or wrongheaded. Some have an interest in reaching out to the larger society to gain converts, but they enjoy only limited success in such efforts because of the heavy demands placed on group members by their religious beliefs and practices.

It is helpful to subdivide small, separatist religions into two types. One includes religious traditions whose members share a common history or ethnic origin. Such characteristics provide a powerful basis for community, but they also limit growth. The other consists of groups with no such "built-in" basis for unity, so they substitute some other foundation to fashion a tightly bound community.

The Amish are a good example of a religious group whose community is based on a shared history. Most Amish originally came from the sixteenth-century Anabaptist movements that arose during the Protestant Reformation in Switzerland. The Amish broke away from one Anabaptist branch over issues that are now dusty with time. They began their formal existence as a separate religious group in 1693, although it was not until the eighteenth century that Amish people began migrating to the United States. Since 1990, the Amish population has grown dramatically. This is not surprising given their strong emphasis on having large families and their success in retaining about 85 percent of their teenagers. Today, more than 200,000 Amish reside in twenty-eight states, with their best-known communities located in southern Pennsylvania. Their buggies are visible on many country roads all over the nation.[60]

The religious beliefs of the Amish are familiar in the American Protestant context. At the same time, however, the Amish are not part of mainstream American religion or culture. Their focus on maintaining a tightly knit and separatist religious community, as well as their buggies, plain clothes, and rejection of electricity in the home, make this obvious. This separatism is especially clear to the Amish themselves as they struggle to maintain their way of life against an indifferent and occasionally hostile American culture.[61] The Amish traditionally have displayed little interest in politics or government and have sought only minimal contact with government. Their numbers are small, so their chances of having much political influence are extremely modest. Nevertheless, some Amish citizens vote, and there have been some Amish efforts to lobby state legislatures over issues of urgent importance to them. In 1972, the Amish were involved in a noted US Supreme Court case in which they won the right not to send their teenagers to high school (*Wisconsin* v. *Yoder*). Mostly, though, the Amish have turned away from politics, a stance that reflects their ethic of noninvolvement and withdrawal from the larger culture.

Political disengagement has worked well for the Amish. They have acquired a reputation as a quaint, inoffensive people who produce high-quality woodwork, baked goods, and quilts. The broader American culture seems to accept the Amish as a charming expression of a past and a people who pose no threat. Amish separatism has turned out to be a de-facto form of politics that has provided protection from the broader society.

Unlike the Amish, new religious movements, or "cults," are the prime illustration today of small, separatist religions that reach into the larger society for converts but usually encounter opprobrium. Every so often, media reports pop up about a new religious movement and the unusual activities of its members.[62] Strictly speaking, using the term "cult" can be prejudicial because its meaning is always negative. The terms "new religious movement" or "unconventional religion" are more value-neutral, but there are also many new or unconventional religions that are very unlike cults. Thus, we reluctantly continue to use the term "cult" to describe a specific type of highly dissident, alternative religion organized into tight communities in extreme tension with the broader culture.

Often such religious groups are headed by a single charismatic leader whom the group's members are willing to follow—sometimes to death, as in the case of Jim Jones and his 914 Peoples Temple followers in 1978.[63] Estimates of the number of cults in the United States range from as many as 5,000 to as few as 700 at any given moment, depending on how strict the definition. Despite a few exceptions, most such groups are peaceful, shun violence, and avoid both politics and the public eye.

In recent decades, few cults have had any political influence, but some have locked horns with the government. The fiery April 1993 demise of David Koresh and his Branch Davidian religious community outside Waco, Texas, is the most infamous example of a cult in direct conflict with the state. The Branch Davidian community was a breakaway group of another breakaway group of the Seventh-Day Adventist Church. Under Koresh, the Branch Davidians quickly became a classic illustration of a strictly separatist community with a charismatic leader. The Branch Davidians' eventual destruction had a clear political impact, especially on the Bureau of Alcohol, Tobacco, and Firearms and the Federal Bureau of Investigation, while dramatically demonstrating the Branch Davidians' own lack of political influence.[64]

More recently, the cult of Warren Jeffs and the Fundamentalist Church of Jesus Christ of Latter-Day Saints (FLDS, which is in no way connected with the mainstream LDS Church) has clashed with the government over the cult's practice of polygamy and charges of sex with underage girls. Jeffs himself is now serving a life sentence in prison in Texas after his 2011 conviction for sexual assault of a minor; nevertheless, he is said to continue to preside over the FLDS from prison.[65]

On the fringe of American religious life is the tiny but noteworthy Christian Identity movement, which is made up of small separatist organizations whose leaders preach hate through religion. Most Christian Identity groups are especially hostile toward racial and ethnic minorities, LGBT people, and those who profess faiths other than Christianity. They embrace what they term the "Israel message" that white people are chosen by God and that Jews and persons of color are subhuman. In the view of Christian Identity followers, an apocalyptic holy war will destroy all people except white Christians. As postmillennialists, Christian Identity followers see the End Times as imminent, so they arm themselves heavily and live together in remote compounds.[66]

There is little doubt that the extent of the cult phenomenon gets exaggerated when sporadic outbursts of media attention flare up. This is doubly true if we think about cults in political terms, since most of their adherents stay out of politics as much as they possibly can. They know society does not like them and that the public eye can be cruel. Although they seek converts, they also seek withdrawal from the larger society. They may not want to leave society alone, but they certainly want society to leave them alone.

OTHER SMALL RELIGIONS

Some alternative religions are not especially separatist, though their size renders their political involvement and impact modest. Eastern Orthodox Christians are one noteworthy example of a small religious faith community that participates fully in American society but lacks political impact due to its size. The Eastern Orthodox tradition is over 1,000 years old, deriving from the East–West Schism of 1054 in which the two great seats of Christianity at the time (Constantinople and Rome) split from one another over theological disputes. (Today, the Roman Catholic Church and Eastern Orthodox churches are again on good terms.) Major manifestations of Eastern Orthodoxy in the United States are Greek Orthodoxy, Russian Orthodoxy, and Serbian Orthodoxy. Eastern Orthodox make up just one-half of 1 percent of the US population, but there is some evidence of growth in their numbers.[67] In the aggregate, they are moderate Democrats who tend to take progressive positions on socio-moral issues, though this is hardly the case across the board (see Box 4.3).[68]

Another example of a small, self-sustaining sector of the American religious marketplace are self-defined Pagans or Neopagans. The largest group that falls under this rubric is the Wiccan tradition. Exact numbers are hard to come by, but there are perhaps 150,000 US Wiccans today, and related groups including the Druids may total nearly 200,000 more Americans.[69] Most of these groups worship nature and usually one or more female deities they associate with nature (for example, worship of Mother Earth). Their political impact has been very modest but is growing as they push to have their faiths recognized as legitimate parts of the American religious mosaic in this age of environmentalism.

Consider also Native American religion, a highly complex phenomenon. Native American religion includes diverse tribal practices, the most widely recognized being American Indian drumming, Christian worship, and various syncretic expressions that blend aspects of Christian worship with traditional native ritual. Most Native American religious groups today are loosely organized, though some are more institutionalized in familiar senses.

Because of its use of the drug peyote as a part of worship, the Native American Church is one of the best known of these syncretic faiths. Influenced to some extent by Christianity, this religion shares with other Native American religious expressions a belief in a supreme being; the reality and power of spirits, visions, and ghosts; life after death; and the omnipresence of a spiritual aspect, usually unseen but of great significance in the empirical world. The church has formal clergy and other facets of organization. Yet, in most instances, its formal religious institutionalization is modest in comparison with other American religions. Not surprisingly, the main political effort of this religion is defensive—such as going to court to defend peyote use, not always successfully.[70]

Although peyote use may grab headlines, a more widespread expression of Native American spirituality takes place within Christian churches both on and off reservations. Many prominent Native American leaders have been and are Christians, though others are not because they feel Christian churches represent a legacy of conquest.[71] We see this consciousness in *Custer Died for Your Sins*, a book by Vine Deloria, Jr., a Yankton Sioux and seminary graduate.[72] Although damning of the way Christian proselytizing divided people and undermined tribal ways, he embraced the vision of a more ecumenical and truly Native American Christianity. In much the way that African-American clergy have developed fresh understandings of the Christian message, Deloria and others have attempted to do the same for Native Americans.

Native American groups have become more politically involved and sophisticated in recent times, primarily because of tribal involvement in the gaming industry and the high-stakes politics surrounding it. The money and clout gaming provide are enabling some tribes to defend their sovereignty and traditions, sometimes thanks to the work of high-powered lobbyists. In Wisconsin, for example, tribal organizations are major funders of the Democratic Party, giving millions of dollars to that party every election cycle. There and elsewhere nationally, most native Americans who vote are Democrats, especially because of Democrats' support for government economic benefits, important for many still-poor Native American tribes.[73]

SECULAR AND OTHER DISAFFILIATED AMERICANS

In the twenty-first century, more and more Americans are opting out of organized religion altogether. Most surveys indicate that today more than one in every five people in the United States—and more than a third of millennials— have no religious affiliation.[74] And this shift in the American religious landscape has happened quickly. Until relatively recently, only small fractions of the US population reported having no religious affiliation. However, things began to change beginning in the 1990s. According to Gallup, 6 percent of Americans reported no religious affiliation in 1995; this figure reached 10 percent for the first time in 2002 and stood at 18 percent in 2016, though estimates vary (see Figure 4.1).[75] An additional sign of the advance of secularism in the United States is the percentage of Americans who are "absolutely certain" there is a God, which declined from 71 percent to 63 percent between 2007 and 2014.[76]

Only small shares of the religiously unaffiliated identify as atheists (those who do not believe in God) or agnostics (those who say it is impossible to know

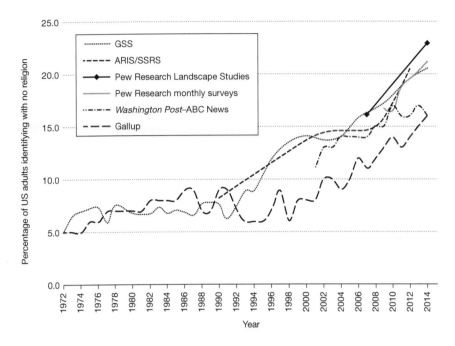

FIGURE 4.1 Population Trends of the Religiously Unaffiliated

Note: Only those who identify their religion as atheist, agnostic, none, nothing in particular, etc., are categorized here as religiously unaffiliated. Those who say "don't know" or who decline to answer when asked about their religion are not categorized as religiously unaffiliated.

Source: Pew Research Center, "US Religious Landscape Study."

whether or not there is a God); the majority of the religiously unaffiliated state simply that their religion is "nothing in particular."[77] This fact suggests that Americans are not turning to any clear-cut rejection of religious or spiritual belief; some religiously unaffiliated people report belief in God, occasional religious activity, and other signs of personal religious or spiritual engagement.[78] Instead, increasing numbers simply are turning away from traditional, organized forms of religious life.

CONCLUSION

Pluralism defines religion in the United States, but not all religious groups are politically equal. The overall political strength of most non-Christian and small Christian religious groups in the United States is modest at best. The few exceptions to this rule, such as Jews and Mormons, are comparably large groups composed of members of relatively high socioeconomic status who are well integrated into American life—and who are also willing and able to undertake political action.

Of course, size is a factor that can hardly be ignored in explaining why some religious groups play such a minor role in American politics. We know that most alternative religions are small, comprising a tiny fraction of an American population of over 300 million. Many of these faith groups are not growing, either. Only a few, such as the LDS Church, are growing rapidly enough to increase their share of the nation's population. To be sure, numbers are not everything, but they do matter: numbers furnish needed activists, supporters, and financial means, not to mention voters. A group begins at a serious disadvantage without those numbers, even if the politics it advocates is almost entirely defensive, as is the case for, say, the Amish.

The issue of isolation is important as well. Many small religious communities self-consciously choose to withdraw from the larger society because they fear its corrupting power, as is the case for Ultraorthodox Jews and the Amish. Sometimes the decision to withdraw from society also reflects a realistic analysis of the slim chances these groups have of changing the broader culture. Often, however, disengagement is rooted in a theological belief that the secular culture must be avoided.

Islam, like Judaism, may have an advantage politically because its religious principles encourage political involvement. Islam teaches that religion should pervade every aspect of life. Thus, Muslim leaders have argued that politics and government are legitimate realms in which to involve oneself. This tenet of the faith should provide hospitable theological and ideological support for Muslims as they venture further into American politics.

Geography can also influence isolation. This has been true throughout Mormon history. It is still true today, at least to some extent, because most American Mormons still reside in Utah and surrounding Mountain West states. Today, Mormons are mostly integrated into the larger culture, but this is much less true of the many Native Americans who live on reservations. For them, geography has played a major role in fostering separation. This separation can present significant but surmountable challenges for political influence. Mormons enjoy some political clout, particularly in Utah, and Native Americans have flexed some political muscle in the lobbying work they have done to preserve and strengthen their place in the gaming industry.

Socioeconomic status can also determine political effectiveness, as is the case outside the context of religion and politics. Many smaller religious traditions have a high number of adherents who lack financial resources, sometimes because of restrictions imposed by their faiths. This situation naturally limits their potential political influence. Small numbers also mean that religious minorities have fewer highly educated members to represent them politically than do larger religious communities.

Something that also matters a great deal is what we might call "respectability," or the degree to which one religious group or another is accorded sufficient legitimacy by policy-makers to advocate for itself. Many alternative religions or religious groups are unknown and thus not automatically respected. In some cases, religious minority groups acquire a reputation as less-than-respectable, especially if they are perceived as unusual or vaguely threatening, and for this they pay a considerable political price.

DISCUSSION QUESTIONS

1 Reflect on the internal divisions among American Jews. How do the three major traditions of Judaism (Reform, Conservative, and Orthodox) reflect the history and future prospects of the Jewish community in the United States?

2 What are the basic demographic and organizational characteristics associated with Islam in America? In particular, how do you think the intersection of ethnicity and Islam shapes the prospects for broad-based Islamic mobilization in the United States?

3 How did the attacks on September 11, 2001, impact the lives of American Muslims? How did the attacks affect their political presence and ideologies?

4 What do the experiences of Native American religionists tell us about how a smaller religious group might go about defending its practices or gaining political clout? What strategies are there for a smaller religious faith to exert any influence over politics?

5 The LDS Church is remarkably evangelistic and family-oriented. What are the political implications?

6 Some smaller religious groups make the decision to disengage or isolate themselves from mainstream American culture and society. Why do these groups choose to do so, and how does this choice affect their political influence?

7 Secular and other disaffiliated Americans are a growing group in the United States. What are the opportunities for and obstacles to this group forming as a political force?

FURTHER READING

Bassiri, Kambiz Ghanea, *A History of Islam in America* (Cambridge: Cambridge University Press, 2010). An excellent account.

Campbell, David E., John C. Green, and J. Quin Monson, *Seeking the Promised Land: Mormons and American Politics* (Cambridge: Cambridge University Press, 2014). The most thorough accounting of Mormons and politics ever written.

Carnes, Tony, and Fenggang Yang (eds.), *Asian American Religions* (New York, NY: New York University Press, 2004). A fine overview of the subject.

Jones, Robert P., *The End of White Christian America* (New York, NY: Simon & Schuster, 2016). A timely, provocative argument that white Christianity is declining quickly in the United States.

Marzouki, Nadia, *Islam: An American Religion* (New York, NY: Columbia University Press, 2013). A thorough, accessible look at Muslims in today's American society.

Sarna, Jonathan, *American Judaism: A History* (New Haven, CT: Yale University Press, 2004). A historian's rich treatment of Judaism's deep roots in the United States.

Treat, James, *Around the Sacred Fire: Native Religious Activism in the Red Power Era* (New York, NY: Palgrave Macmillan, 2003). A historical case study of the role of religion in Native American politics.

NOTES

1. Diana Eck, *A New Religious America: How a "Christian Country" Has Become the World's Most Diverse Nation* (New York, NY: HarperOne, 2002).

2. Robert P. Jones, *The End of White Christian America* (New York, NY: Simon & Schuster, 2016); Pew Research Center, "US Religious Landscape Study," www.pewforum.org/religious-landscape-study/.

3. Peggy Levitt, *God Needs No Passport: Immigrants and the Changing American Religious Landscape* (New York, NY: New Press, 2007); Stephen Prothero (ed.), *A Nation of Religions: The Politics of Pluralism in Multireligious America* (Chapel Hill, NC: University of North Carolina Press, 2006); on Buddhism, see Wendy Cadge, *Heartwood: The First Generation of Theravada Buddhism in America* (Chicago, IL: University of Chicago Press, 2005); Charles S. Prebish, *Luminous Passage: The Practice and Study of Buddhism in America* (Berkeley, CA: University of California Press, 1999); Richard Seager, *Buddhism in America* (New York, NY: Columbia University Press, 1999); on Hinduism, see Tony Carnes and Fenggang Yang (eds.), *Asian American Religions* (New York, NY: New York University Press, 2004); Prema Kurien, *A Place at the Multicultural Table: The Development of an American Hinduism* (Piscataway, NJ: Rutgers University Press, 2007).

4. For superb overviews of Jews and Judaism, see Pew Research Center, "A Portrait of Jewish Americans," October 1, 2013, www.pewforum.org/2013/10/01/jewish-american-beliefs-attitudes-culture-survey; "Special Report: Judaism and the Jews," *The Economist*, July 28, 2012, pp. 1–12.

5. For an excellent historical account, see Jonathan Sarna, *American Judaism: A History* (New Haven, CT: Yale University Press, 2004).

6. J. J. Goldberg, *Jewish Power: Inside the American Jewish Establishment* (Reading, MA: Addison-Wesley, 1996); Bernard M. Lazerwitz, *Jewish Choices: American Jewish Denominationalism* (Albany, NY: State University of New York Press, 1988); L. Sandy Maisel and Ira N. Forman (eds.), *Jews in American Politics* (Lanham, MD: Rowman & Littlefield, 2001); Pew Research Center, "US Religious Landscape Study."

7. In 1966, 84 percent of American Jews lived in the East; by 2014, that percentage had declined to only 41 percent, with dramatic percentage increases in the South. (Today, more than a quarter of all American Jews live in the South.) See Pew Research Center, "US Religious Landscape Study."

8. Pew Research Center, "A Portrait of Jewish Americans."

9. Pew Research Center, "A Portrait of Jewish Americans."

10. Pew Research Center, "US Religious Landscape Study."

11. Pew Research Center, "US Religious Landscape Study"; Pew Research Center, "A Portrait of American Orthodox Jews," August 26, 2015, www.pewforum.org/2015/08/26/a-portrait-of-american-orthodox-jews; Lance J. Sussman, "Prospects for American Judaism," *Jewish Review of Books*, spring 2010, pp. 27–28.

12. See Pew Research Center, "A Portrait of American Orthodox Jews."

13. Pew Research Center, "US Religious Landscape Study."

14. Samuel Freedman, *Jew vs. Jew: The Struggle for the Soul of American Jewry* (New York, NY: Simon & Schuster, 2000); United Jewish Communities, *The National Jewish Population Survey, 2000–2001* (New York, NY: United Jewish Communities); Alan Dershowitz, *The Vanishing American Jew: In Search of Jewish Identity for the Next Century* (Boston, MA: Little, Brown, 1997); Ari Goldman, *Being Jewish: The Spiritual and Cultural Practice of Judaism Today* (New York, NY: Simon & Schuster, 2000); Michael Lerner, *Jewish Renewal: A Path to Healing and Restoration* (New York, NY: Putnam, 1994).

15. Gregory A. Smith and Jessica Martinez, "How the Faithful Voted: A Preliminary 2016 Analysis," November 9, 2016, www.pewresearch.org/fact-tank/2016/11/09/how-the-faithful-voted-a-preliminary-2016-analysis/.

16. Aleksandra Sandstrom, "Faith on the Hill," Pew Research Center, January 3, 2017, www.pewforum.org/2017/01/03/faith-on-the-hill-115.

17. Norman Podhoretz, *Why Are Jews Liberals?* (New York, NY: Doubleday, 2009).

18. On this point, see Lazerwitz, *Jewish Choices*.

19. Pew Research Center, "A Portrait of American Orthodox Jews."

20. On Jewish conservatism, see Edward Shapiro, "Right Turn? Jews and the American Conservative Movement," in L. Sandy Maisel and Ira N. Forman (eds.), *Jews in American Politics* (Lanham, MD: Rowman & Littlefield, 2001), pp. 195–211.

21. See, for example, William Kristol, "Our Trump Problem," *Weekly Standard*, May 29, 2017.

22. Podhoretz, *Why Are Jews Liberals?*

23. For an interesting discussion on the possible future of Jews and American politics, see Paul A. Djupe, "The Evolution of Jewish Pluralism: The Public Opinion and Political Preferences of American Jews," in J. Matthew Wilson (ed.), *From Pews to Polling Places: Faith and Politics in the American Religious Mosaic* (Washington, DC: Georgetown University Press, 2007), chapter 8.

24. Besheer Mohamed, "A New Estimate of the US Muslim Population," January 6, 2016, www.pewresearch.org/fact-tank/2016/01/06/a-new-estimate-of-the-u-s-muslim-population/.

25. Mohamed, "A New Estimate of the US Muslim Population"; Kambiz Ghanea Bassiri, *A History of Islam in America* (Cambridge: Cambridge University Press, 2010).

26. Pew Research Center, "US Muslims Concerned about Their Place in Society, but Continue to Believe in the American Dream," July 26, 2017, www.pewforum.org/2017/07/26/findings-from-pew-research-centers-2017-survey-of-us-muslims/.

27. Ihsan Bagby, Paul M. Perl, and Bryan T. Froehle, *The Mosque in America: A National Portrait* (Washington, DC: CAIR, 2001), p. 2; Nadia Marzouki, *Islam: An American Religion* (New York, NY: Columbia University Press, 2013).

28. The college is explored in the fascinating work by Scott Korb, *Light without Fire: The Making of America's First Muslim College* (Boston, MA: Beacon, 2013).

29. Pew Research Center, "US Muslims Concerned about Their Place in Society."

30. Pew Research Center, "US Muslims Concerned about Their Place in Society."

31. Pew Research Center, "US Muslims Concerned about Their Place in Society."

32. Pew Research Center, "US Muslims Concerned about Their Place in Society."

33. Pew Research Center, "US Muslims Concerned about Their Place in Society."

34. Marzouki, *Islam*; see also the Muslim Public Affairs Council's website at www.mpac.org.

35. Marzouki, *Islam*.

36. Marzouki, *Islam*, chapter 2. Marzouki presents a brilliant account of the controversy surrounding the Manhattan Islamic Center and other mosques across the United States.

37. Marzouki, *Islam*, chapter 1.

38. Pew Research Center, "US Muslims Concerned about Their Place in Society."

39. Pew Research Center, "US Muslims Concerned about Their Place in Society."

40. Selcuk Sirin and Michelle Fine, *Muslim American Youth: Understanding Hyphenated Identities through Multiple Methods* (New York, NY: New York University Press, 2008); Scott Korb, "American Islam," *The Chronicle Review*, March 23, 2012, pp. 11–12; Brian J. Grim and Roger Finke, *The Price of Freedom Denied: Religious Persecution and Conflict in the Twenty-First Century* (Cambridge: Cambridge University Press, 2011), chapter 6; Bill George, "Eboo Patel: Uniting the Young on Religious Tolerance," *US News and World Report*, November 2009, chapter 6; Marzouki, *Islam*.

41. Pew Research Center, "US Muslims Concerned about Their Place in Society."

42. Pew Research Center, "US Muslims Concerned about Their Place in Society."

43. Pew Research Center, "US Muslims Concerned about Their Place in Society."

44. Pew Research Center, "US Muslims Concerned about Their Place in Society."

45. Yvonne Yazbeck Haddad, *Not Quite American? The Shaping of Arab and Muslim Identity in the United States* (Waco, TX: Baylor University Press, 2004); Paul A. Djupe and John C. Green, "The Politics of American Muslims," in J. Matthew Wilson (ed.), *From Pews to Polling Places: Faith and Politics in the American Religious Mosaic* (Washington, DC: Georgetown University Press, 2007), chapter 9.

46. Matthew Bowman, *The Mormon People: The Making of an American Faith* (New York, NY: Random House, 2012); see David E. Campbell, John C. Green, and J. Quin Monson, *Seeking the Promised Land: Mormons and American Politics* (Cambridge: Cambridge University Press, 2014); Pew Research Center, "A Portrait of Mormons in the US," July 24, 2009, www.pewforum.org/2009/07/24/a-portrait-of-mormons-in-the-us/; "US Religious Landscape Study."

47. Campbell et al., *Seeking the Promised Land*.

48. Campbell et al., *Seeking the Promised Land*; Richard Ostling and Joan K. Ostling, *Mormon America: The Power and the Promise* (New York, NY: HarperCollins, 2007), chapter 19.

49. Campbell et al., *Seeking the Promised Land*.

50. Campbell et al., *Seeking the Promised Land*.

51. Pew Research Center, "How Americans Feel about Religious Groups," July 16, 2014, www.pewforum.org/2014/07/16/how-americans-feel-about-religious-groups/.

52. Ostling and Ostling, *Mormon America*.

53. Campbell et al., *Seeking the Promised Land*.

54. Campbell et al., *Seeking the Promised Land*; Lauren Markoe, "White Evangelicals, Catholics, and Mormons Carried Trump," Religion News Service, November 9, 2016.

55. Michael Schwirtz, "Utah's Top Mormons in 'All-Out Revolt' against Donald Trump," *New York Times*, October 9, 2016.

56. Markoe, "White Evangelicals."

57. Campbell et al., *Seeking the Promised Land*.

58. Campbell et al., *Seeking the Promised Land*.

59. Campbell et al., *Seeking the Promised Land*.

60. Richard T. Schaeffer and William W. Zellner, *Extraordinary Groups*, 9th edn (New York, NY: Worth, 2011); Donald B. Kraybill and Carl Desportes Bowman, *On the Backroad to Heaven: Old Order Hutterites, Mennonites, Amish, and Brethren* (Baltimore, MD: Johns Hopkins University Press, 2001).

61. Tom Shachtman, *Rumspringa: To Be or Not to Be Amish* (New York, NY: North Point Press, 2006).

62. On cults and related topics in the discussion that follows, see James R. Lewis and Inga B. Tollefsen, *The Oxford Handbook of New Religious Movements* (Oxford: Oxford University Press, 2016); Catherine Wessinger, *How the Millennium Comes Violently: From Jonestown to Heaven's Gate* (New York, NY: Chatham House, 2000).

63. Rebecca Moore, *Understanding Jonestown and Peoples Temple* (Westport, CT: Praeger, 2009); Wessinger, *How the Millennium Comes Violently*.

64. See Stuart A. Wright (ed.), *Armageddon in Waco: Critical Perspectives on the Branch Davidian Conflict* (Chicago, IL: University of Chicago Press, 1995).

65. A thorough account may be found in Jesse Hyde, "A Polygamist Cult's Last Stand: The Rise and Fall of Warren Jeffs," *Rolling Stone*, February 9, 2016.

66. The Christian Identity movement is monitored closely by the Southern Poverty Law Center. See *False Patriots: The Threat of Antigovernment Extremists* (Montgomery, AL: Southern Poverty Law Center, 1996); www.splcenter.org/intel/map/hate.jsp.

67. Alexei Krindatch, "Fast Questions and Fast Answers about US Orthodox Churches," n.d., www.orthodoxreality.org/FastFactsAboutUSOrthodoxChurches.pdf; Pew Research Center, "US Religious Landscape Study."

68. Pew Research Center, "US Religious Landscape Study."

69. Pew Research Center, "The Future of World Religions: Population Growth Projections, 2010–2050," April 2, 2015, assets.pewresearch.org/wp-content/uploads/sites/11/2015/03/PF_15.04.02_ProjectionsFullReport.pdf.

70. Sam D. Gill, *Native American Religions: An Introduction*, 2nd edn (Belmont, CA: Wadsworth, 2005).

71. Joane Nagel, *American Indian Ethnic Renewal: Red Power and the Resurgence of Identity and Culture* (Oxford: Oxford University Press, 1996); James Treat, *Around the Sacred Fire: Native Religious Activism in the Red Power Era* (New York, NY: Palgrave Macmillan, 2003).

72. Vine Deloria, Jr., *Custer Died for Your Sins: An Indian Manifesto* (New York, NY: Macmillan, 1969).

73. Dale Mason, *Indian Gaming: Tribal Sovereignty and American Politics* (Norman, OK: University of Oklahoma Press, 2000); Robert Booth Fowler, *Wisconsin Votes: An Electoral History* (Madison, WI: University of Wisconsin Press, 2008).

74. Betsy Cooper, Daniel Cox, Rachel Lienesch, and Robert P. Jones, "Exodus: Why Americans Are Leaving Religion—and Why They're Unlikely to Come Back," September 22, 2016, www.prri.org/research/prri-rns-poll-nones-atheist-leaving-religion; Jones, *The End of White Christian America*.

75. Gallup, "Religion," www.gallup.com/poll/1690/religion.aspx. See also Cooper et al., "Exodus"; Jones, *The End of White Christian America*; Pew Research Center, "US Religious Landscape Study."

76. Pew Research Center, "US Religious Landscape Study."

77. Pew Research Center, "US Religious Landscape Study"; Cooper et al. "Exodus."

78. Pew Research Center, "US Religious Landscape Study."

5

LATINO AND AFRICAN-
AMERICAN RELIGION
AND POLITICS

Throughout our discussion of religious traditions in Chapters 3 and 4, we often distinguished among Americans based not just on the diversity of their religious traditions but also on their race or ethnicity. These distinctions acknowledge that racial and ethnic identity is inextricably linked with religion in the United States, and that this intersection has political significance. In this chapter, we take a step back to consider the complex interactions among race, religion, and politics in the United States.

We focus on the two largest racial and ethnic minority groups in the United States: Latinos and African Americans. In focusing on these two groups of people, we highlight their growing prominence in American politics today as well as their long histories in the American political experience. While their histories differ in crucial ways, Latinos and African Americans alike have faced similar challenges as minority groups within the broader, white-dominated culture. This reality has left a deep imprint on their religious beliefs, networks, and practices. The challenges these minority groups have faced have also had—and will continue to have—profound political implications, especially as predominant forms of white Protestantism and Catholicism in the United States decline in relative size and influence.[1]

There are many other ethno-religious groups that are relatively new, smaller, and less influential, including religiously devout immigrant communities from Asia, sub-Saharan Africa, and the Middle East. Unlike most Latinos and African Americans, who have strong connections to the Christian faith, many of these emerging communities are rooted in the non-Christian religions we discuss in Chapter 4, particularly Islam, Buddhism, and Hinduism. Indeed, the list of relative newcomers in America's ethno-religious mix is too long to discuss in a single chapter.[2] We expect that the dynamic religious experiences of Latinos and African Americans, each in their own way, provide insights about prospects for these newer groups as they confront the challenges of pluralism within American political culture.

THE CHANGING STATUS OF LATINO RELIGION

There is no better place to begin a discussion of Latino religion than with a consideration of the role of Roman Catholicism in Hispanic culture and history.[3] Hispanic Catholicism has remarkably deep roots in North America, predating the immigration of the Puritans to the United States in the early 1600s. The Spanish brought Roman Catholicism with them during their sixteenth-century conquests on the North American continent. Fueled by the efforts of Catholic missionaries who were intimately connected with Spanish colonization, Catholicism spread through the native populations of the American Southwest— a region that now includes Texas, New Mexico, Arizona, California, and the fringes of bordering states. Simply looking at a map of the region, with its hundreds of cities, streets, and public spaces named in Spanish after saints and other symbols of the Catholic faith (for example, consider the names of California's three most prominent cities—Los Angeles, San Francisco, and San Diego), we sense the unmistakable legacies of Spanish colonization and early American Catholicism.

Roman Catholicism continues to play a central role in the lives of many Latino Americans. Today, about 55 percent claim an affiliation with Catholicism, and many are intensely committed to the beliefs and practices of the institutional church.[4] Certain aspects of Catholicism resonate particularly well with Hispanics, including a strong attachment to Our Lady of Guadalupe—Mary as mother of God—reflecting the Latino emphasis on family.[5]

Worship styles and religious practices among Hispanic Catholics vary widely. Much of this diversity is tied to the fact that Latino Americans (or their ancestors) hail from many different countries of origin. Mexicans, Cubans, Puerto Ricans, Dominicans, and Latinos with other national roots often differ in their practice of the Catholic faith. The differences are especially pronounced among foreign-born Hispanics who are necessarily less well assimilated into the broader American culture.[6]

Even though expressions of Catholicism among Latino Americans are both vibrant and diverse, the relationship between the Latino community and the Catholic religious tradition sometimes has been an uneasy one. During the Spanish colonial period, for example, Latino converts often suspected Catholic missions were complicit in the brutalities of conquest. Many other Latinos over the decades have felt alienated from other immigrant groups that dominated

Catholic leadership, most notably those with roots in Ireland, Germany, Poland, and other European countries.[7]

Moreover, as second- and third-generation Latinos assimilate into American culture and join the middle class, they often shed parts of their cultural identity, including the Catholicism their parents or grandparents brought along from their countries of origin. In fact, nearly one in four Latinos in the United States today are former Catholics.[8] Many of these individuals have become evangelical Protestants or are not formally affiliated with any religious tradition.

Some Latinos who do remain in the church argue that it has ignored the unique culture and concerns of Hispanic Catholics.[9] Common complaints focus on the chronic shortages of parishes and schools in majority-Latino neighborhoods, Spanish-language masses, and Latino-oriented youth ministries, not to mention the great scarcity of Latino priests and bishops.[10] The first Mexican-American bishop, Patricio Flores, was not installed until 1970, but the number of Latino priests and bishops has grown since the 1970s.

Some bishops have been keenly attentive to both the special character and diversity of Latino spiritual expressions within American Catholicism. For example, Robert Emmett Lucey, archbishop of San Antonio from 1941 to 1969, was instrumental in raising social-justice concerns on behalf of his Hispanic parishioners, who, as immigrants, frequently faced poverty and a lack of job skills. Lucey's efforts culminated in the formation of a Committee for the Spanish Speaking in 1945. Since the 1970s, the US Conference of Catholic Bishops (USCCB) has sponsored several meetings (called Encuentros) of pastoral leaders to discuss plans for ministering to Latino Catholics. At the turn of the twentieth century, the USCCB also issued a major study addressing the need to focus on the Latino membership.[11] The US church has also sponsored major fund-raising efforts for Catholic churches in Latin American countries since at least the 1960s.[12]

The church has recently undertaken a rapid effort to enfold its Latino congregants who, by some estimates, may comprise the majority of US Catholics before 2030. Some dioceses also are addressing the shortage of Spanish-speaking priests by welcoming priests from Spain (Box 5.1). There is no doubt of the assertive outreach to Latino Catholics, but there is also no doubt that there is a long way to go.

In this situation, an intense competition has emerged between the Catholic Church and Protestant Christian groups for Latino members. Many Protestant denominations now have formal departments focusing entirely on Hispanic outreach. It is becoming standard practice to offer Spanish-speaking worship services and various forms of social and economic aid to Latino communities. While many Latino Protestants converted from Catholicism, many others are recent immigrants from Puerto Rico and Central American countries, where Pentecostalism is now flourishing.[13] Nearly a quarter of US Latinos today are Protestants, and their numbers clearly are growing (Table 5.1).

BOX 5.1 A LATINO POPE

The election of Pope Francis in 2013 was hailed widely as a change of direction for the Roman Catholic Church, in part because of the new pope's atypical origins as a non-European. Born Jorge Mario Bergoglio in Argentina, he was raised in and served the church there before his ascension to the papacy. As the first pope from either the Americas or the Southern Hemisphere, and as a man with a humble demeanor and special concern for the poor, some church observers speculated about a "Pope Francis effect": the possibility that his papacy would generate greater goodwill for the church across the globe. Catholic leaders in the United States also hoped that Pope Francis, as a Latino and native Spanish speaker himself, could help reenergize the church's ministry to the Latino world, as well as speak out on major public concerns related to poverty and immigration. The Pope did indeed make a well-received visit to the United States in 2015, and he has not been shy about taking on issues of interest to Latino Catholics, as he did in exchanges with President Donald Trump over refugee resettlement and immigration in early 2017. Nevertheless, the challenges the Catholic Church faces with its Latino members are long-standing and deep. The long-term effect of Francis's papacy among Latino Catholics remains to be seen.

Sources: Priscilla Alvarez, "Can Pope Francis Reverse the Decline of Hispanic Catholics?" *The Atlantic*, September 21, 2015; Pew Research Center, "Positive Impact of Pope Francis on Views of the Church, Especially among Democrats and Liberals" (Washington, DC: Pew Research Center, 2015).

RELIGIOUS TRADITION	PERCENTAGE OF POPULATION
Christian	77%
Evangelical Protestant	19%
Mainline Protestant	5%
Catholic	48%
Mormon	1%
Jehovah's Witness	2%
Other faiths	2%
Unaffiliated	20%

TABLE 5.1 Religious Composition of Latinos

Source: Pew Research Center, "US Religious Landscape Study," 2015.

The organization and leadership of Protestant Latino churches can differ significantly from Catholic parishes. Protestant Latino churches are much more likely than Catholic parishes to have a Latino pastor, and Protestant congregations tend to be smaller and more intimate than what one finds in large urban Catholic churches. Many of these Protestant congregations are now loosely affiliated with each other through the National Hispanic Christian Leadership Conference. Some Latino clergy, such as Wilfredo De Jesús (a.k.a. Pastor Choco) of a large Assembly of God church in Chicago, have obtained considerable attention for their active ministries. Many Protestant Latino congregations feature intense, Bible-based sermons and contemporary music, which gives them a much less formal feel than most Catholic churches.[14]

Although there is a strain of charismatic faith within Latino Catholicism that provides a vibrantly experiential and spirit-filled worship experience, the charismatic religious orientation is much more routine and central in Protestant Latino churches (many of which are expressly Pentecostal). Fully half of all Catholic Latinos use words such as "Pentecostal" or "charismatic" to describe their faith compared with just 10 percent of non-Hispanic Catholics.[15] Charismatic Latino Catholics remain loyal to the church but also are much more likely than other Catholics to report experiencing or observing divine revelations, miraculous healings, or even speaking in tongues. On the other hand, some Latino Catholics report an "ecstasy" gap in sedate Catholic churches.[16]

Thus, Pentecostal and other evangelical Protestant churches have emerged as a real alternative to the Catholic Church for Latinos. Latino Pentecostalism in America, as a young (century-old) religious movement, intentionally subordinates racial and social differences. Increasing numbers of Latino Americans are lifelong adherents of Pentecostal denominations such as the Assemblies of God and the Vineyard. Indeed, it is increasingly common for Pentecostalism in Latino American families to run generations deep.[17]

In short, the religious diversity in the Latino community is real, including differences both within and between Protestant and Catholic traditions. The size of the Latino population is expanding at precisely the same time that political elites are coming to understand that Latinos are an increasingly consequential set of Americans, particularly at the ballot box.

LATINOS IN PUBLIC LIFE

The Hispanic population includes more than 54 million Americans, 17.1 percent of the nation's population according to 2015 US Census estimates. Latinos have surpassed African Americans as the largest racial or ethnic-minority group in the United States.[18] This fact alone has enormous political implications. Elected officials and political parties have begun competing intensely for a share of the Latino electorate, even though low voter turnout in elections still diminishes some of Latinos' potential influence. Latino presence in American politics has also generated myriad policy debates, from the status of undocumented workers to affirmative action in education to English-only language requirements. The high profile of issues like these will only increase over time as the number of Latino Americans continues to grow and the challenges of pluralism intensify accordingly.

Relative population growth is likely even if economic conditions and population pressures in Mexico, Central America, and South America—or public policy in the United States—slow the rate of Latino immigration. For example, while it is true that Mexico, the largest source of Latino immigration to the United States, has a declining birth rate, other Latin American countries, such as Guatemala (at least 1 million people in the United States are of Guatemalan descent), do not. Moreover, Latinos in the United States have a relatively high fertility rate of about seventy-two births per 1,000 women of childbearing age (the overall national rate is about sixty-three). While this rate has declined significantly since 1990, it nonetheless ensures Latino growth proportionally in the United States.

The nation's Hispanic population is undergoing rapid cultural change as well. To be sure, many Latinos, particularly those who are foreign-born, maintain strong ties to their countries of origin and native cultures, whether they come from Cuba, Mexico, Puerto Rico, the Dominican Republic, or elsewhere in Latin America. Second-, third-, and fourth-generation Americans, on the other hand, have had more opportunity to assimilate into American culture. Many native-born Latinos now consider English their dominant language, although a larger proportion is bilingual. In fact, language acquisition gives us a clue as to how assimilation might affect religion because Latinos who claim to be primarily English speakers are also more likely to be members of Protestant churches.[19]

This range of dynamics accounts for the significant differences that exist between foreign- and native-born Latinos on matters of politics and culture. When the foreign versus native-born division is combined with diversity in religious tradition and country of origin, it becomes difficult to identify any monolithic Latino perspectives on public life. This fact has obvious political implications.

We can say, however, that Latinos as a group are somewhat more conservative than non-Hispanic whites on issues such as abortion, homosexuality, and other matters that touch on family life.[20] The role of family is central in the political thinking of many Latinos, with foreign-born and Spanish-dominant speakers being most likely to espouse traditionalist views. As we see with other groups, high rates of worship attendance remain a key predictor of conservatism on social and moral issues among Latinos.

On many issues, Latino opinion leans strongly toward support for government action. This is true regarding a wide range of policies focused toward the working class and the poor, groups that include many Latino people. Similarly, there is much Hispanic support for the government's financial commitment to public education. This pro-government orientation reflects the considerable economic and educational challenges many Latinos face, as well as the Catholic teachings that emphasize the legitimacy of effective government action to serve the less fortunate. The political result clearly benefits the Democratic Party (see Box 5.2). For example, Hillary Clinton won two-thirds of the Latino Catholic vote in 2016, though her percentage eroded somewhat from the 75 percent of Latino Catholics who voted for Barack Obama in 2012.[21] We explore these voting patterns more fully in Chapter 7.

The growth in number of Latino Protestant voters has political ramifications that deserve attention. Latino Protestants tend to oppose abortion and same-sex marriage even more than do Catholic Latinos. On the other hand, Latino

---

BOX 5.2 THE CATHOLIC CHURCH AND IMMIGRATION POLICY

As the electoral importance of Latinos has increased in the United States, so has attention to the millions of Latino immigrants who lack legal authorization to reside there. The Catholic Church, with its large number of Latino congregants, has taken a special interest in the US debate about immigration policy. The USCCB has consistently stated that reform of immigration laws should be a priority for the federal government, especially efforts to find a "path to citizenship" for undocumented immigrants who have demonstrated their commitment to the broader society through work and ties to family. The bishops' overall argument is rooted in their faith's concerns for social justice. Their perspective assumes that the US government ought to play an active role in alleviating poverty among undocumented immigrants, which has often placed the bishops at odds with conservatives and Republicans on the issue. The church has voiced its strong opposition to President Donald Trump's efforts to curb refugee resettlement and immigration of low-skilled laborers. On the other hand, Senator Marco Rubio (R-Florida), a Catholic Cuban American, was instrumental in pushing through a proposal for immigration reform that the Catholic Church viewed positively. The church, both in its leadership and the mobilization of its Latino laity, continues to be a major player in shaping immigration policy in the United States.

Sources: USCCB, "USCCB Committee on Migration Chair Strongly Opposes Executive Order . . . ," January 2017, www.usccb.org/news/2017/17–026.cfm; and "Catholic Church's Position on Immigration Reform," August 2013, www.usccb.org/issues-and-action/human-life-and-dignity/immigration/church teachingonimmigrationreform.cfm.

Protestants tend to share their Catholic counterparts' support for an active government role in helping the poor, sharply splitting them from many white evangelicals. Latino Protestants are more likely to vote and to be Republicans than are Catholic Hispanics, but support for the GOP has declined among both groups over time. Today, 30 percent of Latino evangelicals identify with the GOP, compared with 21 percent of Latino Catholics. Moreover, Latino Catholic and Protestant majorities have voted the Democratic candidate for president in every election from 2008 to 2016. Given evangelical Latinos' softer support for Democrats, observers will be watching closely to see whether their rising numbers cut into the Democratic advantage among Latinos in general. This possibility is far from a certainty given the Republican Party's antigovernment inclinations on economic matters, its increasingly divided views on moral issues of concern to many evangelical Hispanics, and its struggle with nationalist impulses that often accompany a stricter perspective on immigration policy.[22]

The GOP pinned some hope on Senator Marco Rubio in his bid for the presidency in 2016. But this young senator, a self-declared Latino evangelical Catholic who has personal experience in the LDS Church and Latino Protestantism, could not overcome the populist nationalism of the Trump campaign.[23] What is certain is that it will not be long before a Latino from one of the two major parties will be running for president or vice president. That person almost certainly will have a religious connection, and his or her selection will be a historic marker of the increasing influence of Latinos in the United States.

Are there other indicators of religion-inspired political behavior among Latinos? The conventional wisdom is that, aside from the religious social-service agencies that serve Latino populations, few distinctively religious groups engage in political advocacy on behalf of Latinos. It is certainly true that many prominent Latino groups—the League of United Latin American Citizens, the Mexican American Legal Defense and Educational Fund, the Latino Victory Project, and the National Council of La Raza, to name a few—are not explicitly religious in character or focus. Some research, however, suggests that the extent of faith-based Latino activism has been underestimated.[24]

The fact that there are prominent secular groups leading the way points to the myriad possibilities for political mobilization among Latinos—mobilization that religious institutions could foster. The example of César Chávez, the legendary farmworker organizer, is instructive. Spurred by a deep liberationist understanding of his own Roman Catholicism, Chávez helped unionize many thousands of Hispanic farmworkers in California from the 1950s until his death in 1993. His work with farmworkers caught the eye of many Catholic priests and other religious leaders, who subsequently provided their support to his efforts.[25]

Nevertheless, there are some challenges that may impede religion-based mobilization of Latinos. The assimilation of many second- and third-generation

Latinos has decreased the likelihood that the Latino community as a whole will emerge as a distinctive political group.[26] After all, if most Latinos become acculturated into mainstream American society, there may be nothing distinctively "Latino" about their political attitudes or behaviors after a few more generations. Latinos in the future may appear like anyone else within the religious traditions with which they affiliate.

Another challenge is that the very description of a group of Americans as "Latino" or "Hispanic" belies the many ways nonwhite Hispanics perceive their own ethnic identities. Many prefer to think of themselves as Cuban American, Mexican American, or Puerto Rican, for example, rather than Latino or Hispanic, and these categories matter both for religion and politics. Cuban Americans in south Florida often have a different political focus than, say, Mexican Americans in California or Puerto Ricans in New York city.[27] The nuances and syncretism of religious practices brought from different countries of origin reinforces variety among Latino Americans, making broad-based political mobilization more difficult than if a homogeneous group could be defined clearly.[28] Moreover, while Latino populations historically have concentrated in the South and West, recently their numbers have been growing rapidly in some counties in the Midwest and Northeast; this pattern of dispersion also poses challenges to mobilization.

As with any group, all sorts of other differences appear among Latinos when it comes to politics, such as differences in economic goals between (say) poor recent immigrants and well-established, middle-class Latino businesspeople. Variations in local or state Latino histories—for example, South Texas and Miami are hardly similar contexts—matter, too, underlining the point that one should speak of Hispanic politics and political behavior as a unitary concept with great caution.[29]

There is no doubt that Latino impact on American politics will continue to grow, especially as more Latino elected officials come to power. After the 2016 elections, there were thirty-nine Latino members of the House and Senate, a number that just a few short years ago would have been unimaginable and one that is bound to grow in the future. The majority of these individuals are Democrats. As of 2017, there were four Hispanic senators: two Republicans (Rubio of Florida and Cruz of Texas) and two Democrats (Robert Menendez of New Jersey and Catherine Cortez Masto of Nevada). In the House of Representatives there were twenty-seven Latino Democrats and eight Republicans. In most instances, these individuals represent districts that are heavily Latino, whether in rural or urban areas. There also were two Latino governors in 2017, both Republicans: Susana Martinez of New Mexico and Brian Sandoval of Nevada.

While we know that ethnic loyalty affects Latino voting behavior, what is not clear at this point is whether and how religious beliefs might influence the increasing numbers of Latino politicians.[30] In any event, Latinos are becoming more visible players in American politics. As an important part of Barack

Obama's winning coalition, they were a much-discussed voting bloc in the 2008 and 2012 presidential elections.[31] By the time of the 2016 presidential election, they were an even more central topic of discussion and attention from both the Trump and Clinton campaigns, albeit in very different ways. And while the claim that "Latinos will pick the next president" reduces a complex process at the same time that it lumps all Hispanics together politically, the fact was—and is—that Latino votes matter today in the American electoral process—and they will matter even more in the future as the population grows and disperses. What remains to be seen is whether religion will play a significant role in defining the nature and scope of Latino political mobilization, but the rich history of Catholicism and the growth of other faith traditions within the Latino community gives religion strong potential as a future political resource.

AFRICAN-AMERICAN RELIGION AND POLITICS: TOWARD A BROADER VIEW

In his fascinating and sometimes eccentric *American Religion*, scholar Harold Bloom argues convincingly that to understand African-American expressions of Christianity in the United States, one must appreciate both their evangelical side and their distinctly African-American side.[32] Just as Roman Catholicism has shaped Latino Americans, so too Protestant evangelicalism has had a huge influence on African Americans. Similarly, just as immigration and assimilation have been major factors in the history of Hispanic religious expression in the United States, so too the historical experience of slavery and racism has profoundly shaped African-American religious history.

African-American religion is overwhelmingly Protestant—and evangelical—in character. Black evangelicals, like white evangelicals, are likely to affirm the truth of the Bible and to pray daily.[33] Similarly, African-American Christian worship style is commonly quite evangelical. African-American services emphasize preaching, music, and considerable expressiveness, as is also the case in white and interracial Pentecostal worship services. There is little of the liturgy and formality that characterize most Roman Catholic and mainline Protestant worship services.

This is not to say, however, that the typical African-American worship service is indistinguishable from a white evangelical service. African-American churches demonstrate significantly more interaction between the congregation and the pastor during worship. Music plays a central role, and there is a clear connection between the call-and-response musical motif and the typical flow of an African-American service. African-American church music is important both within and outside the religious context. In worship, musical expression is a central element of emotional religious experience. In the broader culture, African-American spirituals gave rise to myriad other musical forms, from gospel to blues to jazz, rock and roll, and hip-hop.

Another similarity between white and black evangelicalism involves church organization. Both African-American and white evangelical denominations favor a loose organizational structure that tends to uphold the autonomy of the individual congregation. Such arrangements (for example, the white Southern Baptist Convention and the black National Baptist Convention, USA, Inc.) bring together many congregations under one umbrella, but, unlike hierarchical denominations such as the Episcopal Church, they usually do not supply much direction from the top.

Christianity in the black community, as in the white community, has experienced numerous and sometimes contentious conflicts that have produced permanent schisms, sometimes over doctrine and sometimes over personalities. Many African-American Baptists, who comprise more than a third of the black population, are affiliated with several different denominations, including the National Baptist Convention, USA, Inc. and the Progressive National Baptist Convention Incorporated.[34] The second largest black Protestant sub-tradition is Pentecostalism, which has been growing rapidly in the African-American community. Black Pentecostalism comprises several major denominations, most prominently the Church of God in Christ (COGIC), as well as many independent congregations.[35] Another historically prominent (and slightly less evangelical) sub-tradition is black Methodism, exemplified by the African Methodist Episcopal (AME) Church (the oldest black denomination), the African Methodist Episcopal Zion (AMEZ) Church, and the Christian Methodist Episcopal (CME) Church.

Most any evangelical congregation, regardless of its racial or ethnic composition, hires the pastor directly without involvement by a denominational apparatus. In most black churches, the pastor (who is almost always a man) is a powerful and generally dominant figure. Pastors often are the center of worship in black churches both in prayer and in dynamic sermons. They also make most important decisions about community and political activities. Their churches often rise and fall with them. Recruiting a good pastor is therefore essential for every African-American congregation.[36] Some black clergy do not have advanced theological training, although others are highly educated. For financial reasons, a significant number of African-American clergy find additional employment outside of their congregations. There are plenty of exceptions, such as Rev. Fred Luter, the barrier-breaking African American who became the leader of the 80 percent white Southern Baptist Convention in 2012 (Box 5.3).[37] But often black pastors must confront economic struggles in their personal and family lives as well as in their churches, especially when they serve small or rural congregations. This situation is often complicated by the wide range of challenging life circumstances facing many black Americans. African-American clergy who serve in urban areas must contend with issues of drug abuse, joblessness, violence, and abject poverty on a regular basis. Sometimes black pastors take personal action just to keep members of their congregations and residents of their church neighborhoods alive.[38] Samuel G. Freedman's powerful *Upon This Rock: The Miracle of a Black Church* describes some of these challenges in unmistakable terms.[39] At the same time, there are many black churches serving the ever-expanding African-American middle and upper classes.

BOX 5.3 RACE AND THE SOUTHERN BAPTIST CONVENTION

The Southern Baptist Convention (SBC) has had a complex and often painful history in the American politics of race. Today, the SBC is the largest Protestant denomination in the United States, but it originated in 1845 after a split with Northern Baptists over the question of whether slaveholders could serve as missionaries. Prominent Southern Baptists provided biblical justifications for slavery in the Antebellum South and for Jim Crow laws and other segregationist policies well into the twentieth century. However, the SBC began to respond slowly to the winds of change during the Civil Rights era. Its public outreach agency issued a statement favorable to *Brown* v. *Board of Education* (1954), the landmark desegregation case. Several decades later, in 1995, the SBC formally apologized for its complicity in the racist policies and ideologies of the past. For many leaders and ordinary parishioners alike, these were hopeful signs of change, and recent SBC leaders such as former president Fred Luter and public outreach head Russell Moore continue to push a vision of a multiracial church.

That said, the SBC's history has been difficult for it to overcome. While the denomination includes some predominantly black or multiracial congregations, it remains overwhelmingly white, and efforts to foster racial reconciliation have received an uneven reception. A recent example: At the SBC's 2017 annual meeting, Dwight McKissic, a black SBC pastor, introduced a resolution condemning white supremacy and "the racial bigotries of the so-called 'alt-right.'" A resolutions committee initially balked at this initiative, relenting only after internal chaos at the meeting and a broader public backlash (as well as a little editing). While the SBC ultimately unanimously accepted an anti-racism statement, the damage was done in the eyes of some prominent members.

Sources: SBC, "Resolution on Racial Reconciliation," 1995, www.sbc.net/resolutions/899/resolution-on-racial-reconciliation-on-the-150th-anniversary-of-the-southern-baptist-convention; Emma Green, "Southern Baptists and the Sin of Racism," *The Atlantic*, April 7, 2015; William Dwight McKissic, Sr., "I'm a Black Pastor: Here's Why I'm Staying in the Southern Baptist Convention," *Washington Post* (Acts of Faith), August 2, 2017; Lawrence Ware, "I'm Done Being a Southern Baptist," *New York Times*, July 17, 2017, p. A19.

Attracting young people is a universal challenge faced by all American religious groups that has become even more acute in recent years. Black clergy routinely worry that they have a particularly hard time attracting young black men to church. Many African-American congregations are majority female, and there is a feeling in some African-American circles that church, if not religion, is for women, except for the key position of minister.[40] One religious alternative does appeal more to men than to women: The majority of African-American Muslims are men.[41]

Because African-American women are so central to the history and culture of the black church experience, it is important to have a sense of their orientations toward life and politics. There is extensive evidence that the liberal, government-oriented political attitudes most African-American women espouse are deeply rooted in their Christian values. The emphasis here is on Christianity's concern for the oppressed, the poor, the suffering, and a Jesus who is a loving, caring, forgiving—indeed, a freeing God.[42]

It is crucial to remember that black women's (not to mention men's) Christianity is inseparable from the shared—and powerfully felt—general history of black people in the United States.[43] For several hundred years, religion has served as a crucial refuge for many African Americans. This history includes the experience of the first African Americans, slaves from Africa who brought their own indigenous religions with them, which over time melded with Christianity into African-American Christianity. In fact, the entire subject of African religious influences on the evolution of black Christianity is gaining more serious attention from scholars today.[44] During slavery times and beyond, the church was the one place where African Americans usually could be safe and free. The church remains a central institution in the black community, integral to the identities of many African-American citizens and a crucial resource for their civic activism.[45]

The distinctly African-American side of Christianity has significance that now transcends the black community. Consider, for example, that African-American spirituals, such as "Were You There?" or "Swing Low, Sweet Chariot," are now sung by Christians of all racial and ethnic backgrounds.[46] This fact is both ironic and inspiring because these spirituals emerged from the days of slavery. African slaves invented the spirituals to bring themselves hope during long days of enslaved labor. Slavery ended, but the black spiritual, with its Christian message and its theme of liberation, endures, a contribution from African-American history to the broader culture of the United States.

From the beginning, African-American Christianity has emphasized an image of God as a consoler and a liberator of the oppressed. Religion thus becomes a vehicle of hope for the weary and the downtrodden, a function that continues to be just as important for many African Americans today as it was in the days of slavery. Many religious African Americans find comfort in the assurance of heavenly peace and salvation through a belief in a benevolent God. At the same time, religion has also served as a powerful justification and mobilizing force for political activism among African Americans.[47] Relatedly, there is a long-standing effort within some theological circles to maintain a strong black liberation ideology, such as that espoused by James Cone. Cone played a crucial role in the late 1960s as elements of the civil-rights movement turned toward more radical expressions of discontent. His seminal work, *Black Theology and Black Power*, justified the Black Power movement in religious terms.[48]

HISTORY AND BLACK POLITICAL ATTITUDES

What is most striking about religion and politics in the African-American community is the close connection between the two. Politics is centrally important in black Christianity, and African-American churches often are openly involved in elections, community organizing, and other aspects of politics. There simply is no sharp division between religion and politics in most of the black religious community today; in a sense, African Americans embrace the Old Testament model in which the paths of religion and politics often crossed.

Before the Civil Rights revolution in the South, however, involvement in politics could be dangerous and sometimes deadly for African Americans. To be sure, African-American churches have long held that the Gospels emphasize social justice and equity. Even before the Civil Rights movement began, in the 1950s, plenty of African-American citizens were fighting for change, albeit behind the scenes. By and large, however, before the 1950s, most African Americans, especially in the South, justifiably saw the public arena as a dangerous place that ought to be avoided.[49] Thus, politics was relevant in the early years of black Christianity largely in a theological and symbolic sense; the image of Jesus Christ as a liberator of the downtrodden spoke poignantly to the early African-American experience.

During more than two centuries of slavery in North America, most black people adopted Christianity. Slaveholders made few allowances for black adaptations of white Christianity, but distinctly African-inspired versions of Christianity developed nonetheless. The first black Baptist congregations were organized in the South at the end of the eighteenth century, but many slaves were not allowed to attend services at these or any other churches. Often clandestine worship groups formed on plantations, coming to be known collectively as "the invisible institution."[50] At night, some slaves taught themselves to read the Bible, which provided both spiritual and intellectual refuge from the forced labor they endured during the day.

The early African-American Methodist churches were organized not by slaves but by free people living in the North who saw white churches as complicit in the perpetuation of slavery. Northern black Christians felt that by creating their own, separate churches they would have free and safe religious homes.

The beginnings of organized, separate black Protestant expression date to at least 1787, when several African Americans withdrew from St. George's Methodist Episcopal Church in Philadelphia. First, they met and prayed together informally with other African Americans. Finally, in 1794, the white Methodist bishop Francis Asbury dedicated Bethel Church of Philadelphia, the first congregation of the African Methodist Episcopal Church.[51]

African-American religion entered a new era after the Civil War. Black Christianity became more formally organized and no longer operated under any form of white tutelage. This period saw major expansion of black Baptist and Methodist denominations. In the early twentieth century, the African-American Pentecostal movement was born in California. Thus, black religion thrived, diversified, and spread out in the wake of emancipation. After Reconstruction, however, African Americans shied away from open political engagement. Most African Americans lived in the South in the late nineteenth and early twentieth centuries, and the political freedom they tasted during Reconstruction proved fleeting.

During World War I, African Americans began moving north in search of jobs and a better life outside of the segregated South. This trend accelerated during World War II and in the years afterward, when the mechanization of Southern agriculture spurred even more northward migration. Eventually, about half of all African Americans settled outside the South. Large Northern cities developed sizable black populations, which bred a comfort level that moved many African Americans to express their opinions freely and without substantial fear both in and outside of church. These changes did not, however, give rise to much political mobilization in the African-American religious community. Old suspicions remained, and evangelical theology continued to teach what previous black experiences had underlined: that politics was corrupt and dangerous. African-American churches continued to shun official political involvement and urged their members to follow suit.[52]

Everything began to change, however, in the 1950s and the 1960s, when some African-American congregations shifted dramatically toward political engagement. This shift changed history. Rev. Martin Luther King, Jr., was unequivocally the most visible pastor in the Civil Rights movement's leadership. That said, he worked in coalition with other intellectually and politically prominent African-American clergy, such as Rev. Ralph Abernathy and Rev. Fred Shuttlesworth, through the social-movement organization they founded to coordinate nonviolent protest across the South, the Southern Christian Leadership Conference.

For these pastors, the time had come to claim civil rights for all African Americans. They had few doubts about whether God supported their prophetic action, and by the late 1950s some black congregations—particularly Baptist churches—in the South were transformed into organizational centers for the Civil Rights movement. Black clergy were hardly the only force working on behalf of the Civil Rights revolution, but without the crucial support of black churches the movement never would have happened.[53] It was in church that African Americans heard the compelling message that called them into the politics of protest, and it was there that they found the moral inspiration to risk their own safety for the collective benefit of all. It was also in church that black Southerners planned strategy and developed the skills they would need to take up the fight for civil rights. And, in many ways, it was black Christian women who were the essential foot soldiers (and sometimes leaders—from Mary McLeod Bethune to Fannie Lou Hamer) in the Civil Rights movement. They were crucial then, just as today they remain the heart and soul of so much of contemporary African-American Christianity.[54]

We hear echoes of these women's activism in examples today, such as author Michele Alexander, who powerfully critiqued the link between race and mass incarceration in the bestseller *The New Jim Crow*. Alexander recently left her position as a law-school professor to join Union Theological Seminary, where she is exploring how faith and the church can build a new movement for social justice.[55]

The movement for Civil Rights in the 1950s and 1960s, however, did not win quick support from all African-American churches. Such involvement—and confrontation—with the world did not sit well with the dominant black evangelical theology, nor did it square with the painful—and sometimes fatal— experiences of African Americans who had previously dared to assert themselves politically. In fact, a strong and active resistance to the Civil Rights movement emerged from within organized black Christianity, and most black churches did not become involved in the movement. Perhaps the most visible opponent was Rev. Joseph H. Jackson, longtime head of the National Baptist Convention, USA, Inc. In his retrospective account, he portrays himself and others like him as deeply committed to traditional "Christian activism" on behalf of African Americans. But he—and many other voices of African-American religion— opposed Dr. King's form of religious politics, which relied on direct and public protest.[56]

Notably, one of the Civil Rights movement's most significant victories happened within African-American religion. The movement changed long-standing attitudes regarding political involvement, producing the political church that we find in some corners of the African-American community today. To be sure, a certain political ambivalence remains. African Americans accept and often welcome political involvement by their churches and especially by their pastors. Many, but by no means all, black pastors are at least somewhat involved in local politics. Some run local political organizations and lead marches. Some speak out frequently about politics in the local media. Some preach regularly about political issues. Some invite candidates for public office to address their congregations from the pulpit—usually Democratic politicians, most famously Presidents Bill Clinton and Barack Obama. And some black pastors even wear two hats, serving simultaneously as clergy and as elected or appointed public officials.

At the same time, like all laity, members of African-American congregations expect that political activity by their clergy will not come at the expense of visiting sick members, preaching effectively, or being available to counsel those with personal crises. There also are some African-American pastors and traditions that look at political activism with skepticism. This is particularly the case among many African-American Pentecostals.[57]

CONNECTIONS BETWEEN BLACK RELIGION AND POLITICS

"Black religion and politics remain inextricably and inescapably bound," writes historian Barbara Savage, and the principal setting for this relationship is the black church, "still the strongest and most ubiquitous of black institutions."[58] In that context, the most visible connection between black religion and American politics comes through the actions of various African-American clergy. Especially since the 1960s, many black pastors have been deeply involved in politics. Rev. Martin Luther King, Jr., became the most famous model of "black pastor as political activist" during his leadership in the Civil Rights movement in the 1950s and until his earthshaking assassination in 1968. Reverends Jesse Jackson and Al Sharpton remain as exemplars of the African-American activist pastor. Today, black clergy are engaged at all levels of politics, addressing issues, lobbying government, and serving as elected officials themselves. Some African-American clergy have even served in Congress, as does Rev. Emanuel Cleaver, a Methodist minister now representing a district in Kansas City, Missouri, in the US House of Representatives. Most often, though, it is at the local level that black clergy make the biggest impact, often a little less flamboyantly than high-profile leaders such as Sharpton and Jackson.[59]

In Jackson's presidential campaigns, especially his 1988 run that helped pave the way for Barack Obama's success in 2008, Jackson won massive support from African-American Christians. Although racial pride played a significant role in rallying support to Jackson's candidacy, a religious dimension also was significant. Specifically, many religious women were key in the Jackson campaigns, from his campaign organization to the voting booth. Jackson's support network also included such established African-American religious figures as Rev. T. J. Jemison, the former leader of the National Baptist Convention, USA, Inc. Much of Jackson's campaign rhetoric was distinctly Christian in its overtones and orientation. He emphasized empathy for the downtrodden and determination to build community despite the terrible wounds caused by poverty, drugs, and crime.[60]

The Jackson campaigns also illustrated another dimension of black religious politics that was reflected once again in the 2008 election of Barack Obama as the first African-American president: the tremendous importance of local churches. Jackson's campaigns demonstrated the potential of African-American churches as electoral precincts where rallies could be held, publicity produced, and organizations formed to ensure significant support from the black community.[61] Like Jackson's campaign, Obama's team relied heavily on the get-out-the-vote efforts undertaken by black congregations, which supported him enthusiastically and in unprecedented numbers.[62] As a former faith-based neighborhood organizer himself, Obama clearly understood the crucial political importance of mobilizing through churches.

Many black pastors and churches are convinced that political activity is a legitimate and necessary means of improving the African-American lot on earth. In many cases, there is a close congruence between what black leaders and churches propose politically and what the African-American community will support. This most certainly is the case regarding issues concerning economic opportunities for African-American citizens. After all, much of the interaction between government and African-American churches does concern economic issues and needs. In so many localities as well as at the state and national levels, a tremendous amount of informal collaboration between black churches and government takes place. This is true not just in terms of churches and church leaders working with governments to obtain economic assistance but also in terms of mobilization to support government and politicians who provide that help.[63]

The Civil Rights movement enhanced black churches' significance as a key player on the liberal side of American politics.[64] Civil Rights liberalism strengthened economic liberalism among African Americans, and both expressions of liberalism were increasingly associated with affiliation with the Democratic Party. Indeed, by the end of the 1960s, the Democratic presidential nominee could count on receiving about 85 percent of the vote from the expanding African-American electorate. Today, a typical Democratic candidate in the United States receives 90 percent or more of the African-American vote, wherever he or she may be running and for whatever office. Strong party loyalties and racial group solidarity have become core factors in black identification with the Democratic Party. African Americans also tend to have a favorable view of government and what it might do for its citizens, which in turn reinforces black support for the Democratic Party.[65]

Nevertheless, there are dimensions of African-American Christianity that do not fit well with the agendas of their liberal Democratic allies or their progressive Christian allies. African Americans who participate the most in church life tend to espouse conservative attitudes on such issues as abortion and women's equality (seen through the lens of women's roles in the church). When the National Association for the Advancement of Colored People (NAACP) endorsed legalizing same-sex marriage in 2012, many black ministers denounced that decision in no uncertain terms, as did the Conference of National Black

Churches, an umbrella organization representing most major black denominations. School choice is another issue that creates conflict between some black Americans and pro-union Democrats. There are more than a few black church-sponsored or church-supported private and charter schools across the nation. And a few high-profile African-American government officials in recent years have been conservative Republicans, including US Senator Tim Scott (R-South Carolina), former US Representative J. C. Watts (R-Oklahoma), former presidential candidate and Trump administration secretary of housing and urban development Dr. Ben Carson, and US Supreme Court Justice Clarence Thomas.

Although the picture is mixed, economic issues remain politically central in the African-American community, as does a belief that government assistance is crucial for people living in poverty. There is no reason to believe that African Americans' overwhelming support for the Democratic Party will change anytime soon; by now Democratic affiliation is deeply woven into African-American culture. Moreover, black loyalty to the Democratic Party was enhanced even further by the presidential administration of Barack Obama.

In the 2012 presidential election, President Obama received the votes of 95 percent of African-American Christians, a staggeringly one-sided result. The large US House delegation of African Americans, forty-six strong, is composed entirely of Democrats, with only one exception (Mia Love, a black Mormon representing a district in Utah). Even most self-identified black conservatives also hold that, on balance, the Democratic Party is better for the African-American community. This sense is deepened by the negative perception many black people have of white evangelicals, even though the two groups share many religious and moral values. Black suspicion of white evangelicals often centers on the perceptions that they are not trustworthy on racial issues and not sufficiently committed to the Christian gospel of helping the needy.[66]

Despite relative political homogeneity, the African-American religious community is incredibly diverse. The classic image of it as a prophetic voice for politically liberal causes often does not apply when one considers the day-to-day lives of black congregations. Most black churches have a much more mundane existence than historical images of the Civil Rights movement might project, and most are far more insular in their ordinary activities than they are activist or prophetic. Moreover, the intense support for Barack Obama in African-American congregations, especially in the context of his winning two terms in the White House, did not hint at black churches' position on the dissenting edge of American politics.[67]

Most major African-American interest groups, such as the NAACP and the Urban League, are secular organizations. Their lack of a religious orientation is an artifact of their founding in the early twentieth century. Groups such as the NAACP often were intended to be an alternative to black churches, which some activists perceived as being overly concerned with the next world and failing to

---

BOX 5.4 THE BLACK CHURCH AND THE BLACK LIVES MATTER MOVEMENT

Black Lives Matter (BLM) emerged as an anti-racist movement in 2013 and quickly gained public recognition for its protest activity against police brutality and racial inequality. BLM leaders have cited the Civil Rights movement as an inspiration, but those leaders also have expressed some ambivalence about following the strategies and tactics of that era. Their resistance extends to the appropriate role of black churches. BLM has eschewed involvement by black church leaders, including, most famously, Rev. Al Sharpton. Moreover, some of BLM's more prominent voices have described the church as too conservative and increasingly irrelevant as a motivating force for younger activists. Black churches, in their view, have lost much of their prophetic edge. And while many Christian leaders and organizations see reasons for common cause with BLM—the campus fellowship InterVarsity, for example, has thrown support to BLM—others have expressed concerns about its confrontational tactics and statements.

Sources: www.blacklivesmatter.com; Mark Oppenheimer, "A Debate Over Black Lives Matter," *New York Times*, January 23, 2016, p. A13; Rahiel Tesfamariam, "Why the Modern Civil Rights Movement Keeps Religious Leaders at Arm's Length," *Washington Post*, September 18, 2015.

---

assist African Americans in the here and now. Today, however, there is regular contact between African-American pastors and churches and branches of the NAACP and the Urban League. The eventual emergence of these connections was inevitable because the secular organizations are just as intertwined with the black middle class as are the large African-American denominations. The relationship, however, is not always smooth (see Box 5.4).

ISLAM IN THE AFRICAN-AMERICAN COMMUNITY

Today, a modest but growing number of African Americans are Muslims, many of whom are rather recent converts.[68] The story of the Muslim dimension of the African-American experience illustrates the fluidity of American religious culture and the unpredictable political consequences that arise from religious movements.

Although some Africans were followers of Islam before they were enslaved in America, only traces of that heritage survived. Modest interest in Islam existed among some nineteenth-century African Americans; certain black intellectuals saw it as an authentic African legacy that had been erased by the slave master. By the early part of the twentieth century, unorthodox, "proto-Islamic" movements emerged in some northern, urban African-American communities.[69] These were tiny, isolated groups with teachings that diverged considerably from mainstream Islam.

Most notable among these groups was Elijah Muhammad's Nation of Islam. Centered in Detroit, the Nation of Islam initially was a religion of the urban dispossessed, and it remained small and largely unrecognized until the 1960s. The Nation of Islam appealed to small numbers of African Americans in the 1950s and 1960s for two distinct reasons. First, its unique spin on mainstream Islam preached an attractive message to alienated urban blacks—particularly men and incarcerated people—that placed their plight on the shoulders of white people, a race of what Elijah Muhammad called "white devils," who were destined by Allah to be eradicated. The Nation of Islam also emphasized education, sexual discipline, hard work, cleanliness, conservative dress, economic self-sufficiency, and rejection of the white man's government assistance programs. This aspect of the faith was especially appealing to people concerned about young African Americans living a self-destructive street life.

Second, Islam's patriarchal aspect appealed to black men. In contrast to the matriarchal culture that characterizes religion in much of the broader African-American community, the Nation of Islam taught that the man was the head of the family and the woman was to be his helpmate and homemaker. Black Muslims attained a certain stature in many cities—even among some non-Muslims—for being proud, disciplined, and militantly separatist.

By 1960, the Nation of Islam still had a small membership but was making a serious effort to create a separate organizational network of schools, businesses, and radio stations, as well as a well-armed militia (the Fruit of Islam) in several US cities.[70] The political significance of the movement was magnified by Elijah Muhammad's most important disciple, Malcolm X, who burst onto the scene in the 1960s. He combined Muhammad's distinctive interpretation of Muslim theology with a call for black consciousness, assertion, and pride. Malcolm told angry African Americans that they had every right to use "any means necessary" to defend themselves against violence and discrimination by whites, challenging the very premises of both Dr. King's nonviolent approach and his goals of integration and civil rights. Malcolm X proposed separation from whites instead of integration. He declared, "We, the black man of the world, created the white man and we will also kill him"—explosive rhetoric in the fraught context of the mid-1960s.[71]

In 1964, Malcolm embarked on the Hajj, the traditional Muslim pilgrimage to Mecca. The experience transformed his understanding of Islam and led him to reject the divergent teachings of the Nation of Islam. He renounced the "white devil" theology and announced that he had taken a new name, El-Hajj Malik El-Shabazz, an indication of his embrace of mainstream Islam.[72] Cut off by the Nation of Islam, he founded his own Sunni mosque. His broadened vision of Islam was still incomplete when he was gunned down by Nation of Islam assassins in 1965.

When Elijah Muhammad himself died in 1975, his son Wallace (who took the name Warith Deen Muhammad) assumed the leadership of the Nation of Islam. Quietly but assiduously he led the movement toward a merger with mainstream Islam. Today, most African-American Muslims worship alongside other Muslims of all ethnic backgrounds in Sunni (and a few Shi'a) mosques around the United States.[73]

The movement into mainstream Islam probably facilitated the conversion of more African Americans to Islam by providing grounding in a major world religion—and one different from the "white man's" Christianity. African Americans now make up approximately 20 percent of the Muslim population in the United States. However, neither the precise size of the Muslim population nor the proportion of African Americans within it are known with great accuracy.[74]

A very small group of African Americans remains loyal to the Nation of Islam and Elijah Muhammad's separatist vision.[75] Today, the Nation of Islam is led by the fiery Louis Farrakhan, who continues to preach a mixture of militant racial separatism, black superiority, self-reliance, and traditional moral values. Critics are especially disturbed by his controversial negative statements about Jews. On abortion, LGBT rights, and government assistance for the poor, his message is pointedly conservative; he also strongly advocates for male responsibility and antidrug efforts.[76] But overall, while Farrakhan has some followers, particularly in urban areas, his political influence is small and waning.

CONCLUSION

Religion in the African-American community remains strong and often decidedly political. While that reality is likely to continue, some commentators have begun to ask whether the church might be losing the prophetic voice that sustained its politics for well over 150 years.[77] Religion is also both strong and diverse in the Latino community as well. But that diversity—and particularly the Catholic–Protestant and country-of-origin divides—also makes the connections between religion and politics for Latinos less clear. We know that Latinos will develop greater political influence in coming decades. It is less certain, however, how Latino religious expressions might shape that political presence.

DISCUSSION QUESTIONS

1 What is the legacy of immigration on both the politics and religious expressions of Latinos?

2 Why has outreach to Latino citizens become such a prevalent issue for the Catholic Church? Furthermore, why has such a competitive

atmosphere erupted between Catholic and Protestant churches as they vie for Hispanic membership?

3   Why is the Latino population becoming more of a contender in American politics? What are the implications of this trend?

4   Compare and contrast African-American Protestant churches with their non-African-American counterparts. What are some ways in which they differ, and how are they similar?

5   The black church in America has a history of political involvement, to the extent that church and politics are closely aligned. What might account for this? What are some examples of that relationship today?

6   What factors led to the growth of African-American participation in Islam during the 1960s?

FURTHER READING

Chappell, David, *A Stone of Hope: Prophetic Religion and the Death of Jim Crow* (Chapel Hill, NC: University of North Carolina Press, 2004). An account of the crucial role of churches and pastors in Civil Rights activism in the segregationist South.

Collier-Thomas, Bettye, *Jesus, Jobs, and Justice: African American Women and Religion* (New York, NY: Knopf, 2010).

Cone, James, *A Black Theology of Liberation* (Philadelphia, PA: Lippincott, 1970). The classic text on black liberation theology.

Espinosa, Gaston, *Latino Pentecostals in America: Faith and Politics in Action* (Cambridge, MA: Harvard University Press, 2014).

Espinosa, Gaston, Virgilio Elizondo, and Jesse Miranda (eds.), *Latino Religions and Civic Activism in the United States* (Oxford: Oxford University Press, 2005). A challenge to conventional wisdom that religion has had little influence on Latino civic activism.

Garrow, David J., *Bearing the Cross: Martin Luther King Jr. and the Southern Leadership Conference* (New York, NY: William Morrow, 1986). A classic account of King's political and religious activism.

Harris, Fredrick C., *Something Within: Religion in African-American Political Activism* (Oxford: Oxford University Press, 1999). An excellent examination of the role of religion in African-American political mobilization.

Hertzke, Allen D., *Echoes of Discontent: Jesse Jackson, Pat Robertson, and the Resurgence of Populism* (Washington, DC: CQ Press, 1993). Discussion of the 1988 Jesse Jackson campaign.

Jacobson, Robin Dale and Nancy D. Wadsworth (eds.), *Faith and Race in American Political Life* (Charlottesville, VA: University of Virginia Press, 2012).

Lincoln, C. Eric, and Lawrence H. Mamiya, *The Black Church in the African American Experience* (Durham, NC: Duke University Press, 1990). Superb work on African-American religion.

Martinez, Juan Francisco, *Los Protestantes: An Introduction to Latino Protestantism in the United States* (Santa Barbara, CA: Praeger, 2011).

Mulder, Mark, Aida I. Ramos, and Gerardo Marti, *Latino Protestants in America: Growing and Diverse* (Lanham, MD: Rowman & Littlefield, 2017). A helpful introduction to this growing ethno-religious group. Chapter 6 focuses especially on politics and social engagement.

Savage, Barbara, *Your Spirits Walk Beside Us: The Politics of Black Religion* (Cambridge, MA: Harvard University Press, 2008).

NOTES

1. Robert P. Jones, *The End of White Christian America* (New York, NY: Simon & Schuster, 2016).

2. Pew Research Center, "The Religious Affiliation of US Immigrants," 2013; Pew Research Center, "Asian Americans: A Mosaic of Faiths," 2012, http://assets.pew research.org/wp-content/uploads/sites/11/2012/07/Asian-Americans-religion-full-report.pdf

3. In this chapter, we use the terms "Latino" and "Hispanic" interchangeably, though the latter term is often used to denote a broader category of people with origins in Spain as well as Latin America and the Caribbean.

4. Pew Research Center, "The Shifting Religous Identity of Latinos in the United States," 2014, http://assets.pewresearch.org/wp-content/uploads/sites/11/2014/05/Latinos-Religion-07-22-full-report.pdf

5. Pew Research Center, "Shifting Religious Identity," p. 54; Hosffman Ospino and Patricia Weitzel-O'Neill, *The National Study of Catholic Parishes with Hispanic Ministry* (Boston, MA: Boston College School of Theology and Ministry, 2014).

6. Jonathan E. Calvillo and Stanley R. Bailey, "Latino Religious Affiliation and Ethnic Identity," *Journal for the Scientific Study of Religion*, 54 (1) (2015): 57–78; George E. Schultze, *Strangers in a Foreign Land: The Organizing of Catholic Latinos in the United States* (Lanham, MD: Lexington, 2006); Catherine Wilson, *The Politics of Latino Faith: Religion, Identity, and Urban Community* (New York, NY: New York University Press, 2008).

7. Schultze, *Strangers in a Foreign Land*; USCCB, Committee on Hispanic Affairs, *Hispanic Ministry at the Turn of the Millennium* (Washington, DC: USCCB, 1999).

8. Pew Research Center, "Shifting Religious Identity."

9. Janet Kornblum, "More Hispanic Catholics Losing Their Religion," *USA Today*, December 12, 2002, p. A1; Lisa Makson, "Latinos Call US Culture Hostile Climate for Faith," *National Catholic Register*, March 9–15, 2003, pp. 1, 12.

10. For numbers on parishes and schools, see Ospino and Weitzel-O'Neill, *National Survey*, p. 18. See also Jeff Guntzel, "Between Two Cultures," *National Catholic Reporter*, January 30, 2004.

11. Committee on Hispanic Affairs, *Hispanic Ministry at the Turn of the Millennium.*

12. USCCB, *Collection for the Church in Latin America: Annual Report 2015* (Washington, DC: USCCB, 2016).

13. Aida I. Ramos, Robert D. Woodberry, and Christopher G. Ellison, "The Contexts of Conversion among US Latinos," *Sociology of Religion*, 78 (2017): 119–145.

14. Mark Mulder, Aida I. Ramos, and Gerardo Marti, *Latino Protestants in America: Growing and Diverse* (Lanham, MD: Rowman & Littlefield, 2017); Mark Hugo Lopez, Jessica Martinez, and Gabriel Velasco, "When Labels Don't Fit: Hispanics and Their Views of Identity," www.pewhispanic.org/2012/04/04/when-labels-dont-fit-hispanics-and-their-views-of-identity/.

15. Pew Research Center, "Changing Faith: Latinos and the Transformation of American Religion," 2007, http://assets.pewresearch.org/wp-content/uploads/sites/11/2007/04/hispanics-religion-07-final-mar08.pdf; Pew Research Center, "Shifting Religious Identity."

16. Elizabeth Dias, "Evangelicos!," *Time*, April 15, 2013, pp. 19, 21–26, 28; Michael Warren, "Among the Evangelicos," *Weekly Standard*, April 25, 2013, pp. 31–36; Schultze, *Strangers in a Foreign Land*; "Separated Brothers," *The Economist*, July 18, 2009, p. 31; Pew Research Center, "Changing Faiths."

17. Arlene M. Sanchez Walsh, *Latino Pentecostal Identity: Evangelical Faith, Self, and Society* (New York, NY: Columbia University Press, 2003); Lopez et al., "When Labels Don't Fit."

18. See https://factfinder.census.gov/faces/tableservices/jsf/pages/productview.xhtml?pid=ACS_15_5YR_DP05&src=pt.

19. Lopez et al., "When Labels Don't Fit."

20. Pew Research Center, "Shifting Latino Religious Identity"; Pew Research Center, "Support for Same-Sex Marriage Grows," 2017, http://assets.pewresearch.org/wp-content/uploads/sites/5/2017/06/23153542/06-26-17-Same-sex-marriage-release.pdf.

21. Gregory A. Smith and Jessica Martinez, "How the Faithful Voted: A Preliminary 2016 Analysis," 2016, www.pewresearch.org/fact-tank/2016/11/09/how-the-faithful-voted-a-preliminary-2016-analysis/.

22. Lopez et al., "When Labels Don't Fit," the 2012 National Survey of Religion and Politics, conducted at the University of Akron; Jessica Hamar Martinez, Edwin Hernandez, and Milagros Peña, "Latino Religion and Its Political Consequences," in Robin Dale Jacobson and Nancy D. Wadsworth (eds.), *Faith and Race in American Political Life* (Charlottesville, VA: University of Virginia Press, 2012), pp. 149–186; Louis DeSipio, "Power in the Pews? Diversity and Latino Political Attitudes and Behavior," in J. Matthew Wilson (ed.), *From Pews to Polling Places: Faith and Politics in the American Religious Mosaic* (Washington, DC: Georgetown University Press, 2007), chapter 7; Pew Research Center, "Changing Faiths"; Pew Research Center, "How the Faithful Voted: 2012 Preliminary Analysis," 2012, www.pewforum.org/2012/11/07/how-the-faithful-voted-2012-preliminary-exit-poll-analysis/; Victoria M. DeFrancesco Soto, "Beyond Immigration," *Nation*, January 30, 2012, pp. 6, 8; Victoria M. DeFrancesco Soto, "Latino Conservatives? GOP Hopes Misplaced," *USA Today*, February 10, 2012, p. 7A; Gaston Espinosa, Virgilio Elizondo, and Jesse Miranda, Hispanic Churches in American Public Life: Summary of Findings, 2nd Ed., Institute for Latino Studies, University of Notre Dame, Norte Dame, IN, 2003; 2012 National Survey of Religion and Politics, conducted at the University of Akron.

23. See Marco Rubio, *An American Son: A Memoir* (New York, NY: Penguin, 2012).

24. Gaston Espinosa, Virgilio Elizondo, and Jesse Miranda (eds.), *Latino Religions and Civic Activism in the United States* (Oxford: Oxford University Press, 2005); Wilson, *The Politics of Latino Faith*.

25. For a discussion of Chávez's religiosity, see Frederick John Dalton, *The Moral Vision of Cesar Chavez* (Maryknoll, NY: Orbis Books, 2003); Luis D. Leon, "Cesar Chavez and Mexican American Civil Religion," in Gaston Espinosa, Virgilio Elizondo, and Jesse Miranda (eds.), *Latino Religions and Civic Activism in the United States* (Oxford: Oxford University Press, 2005), pp. 53–64; Marco G. Prouty, *Cesar Chavez, the Catholic Bishops, and the Farmworkers' Struggle for Social Justice* (Tucson, AZ: University of Arizona Press, 2008).

26. Louis DeSipio, *Counting on the Latino Vote: Latinos as a New Electorate* (Charlottesville, VA: University of Virginia, 1996).

27. Lopez et al., "When Labels Don't Fit." Rudolfo O. de la Garza, *Latino Voices: Mexican, Puerto Rican, and Cuban Perspectives on American Politics* (Boulder, CO: Westview Press, 1993).

28. For a broad discussion of Latino politics, see John A. Garcia, *Latino Politics in America: Community, Culture, and Interests* (Lanham, MD: Rowman & Littlefield, 2003), and Mulder et al., *Latino Protestantism in America*, chapter 6.

29. A useful work on the identity question is Benjamin Marquez, *Constructing Identities in Mexican-American Political Organizations: Choosing Issues, Taking Sides* (Austin, TX: University of Texas Press, 2003); Lopez et al., "When Labels Don't Fit."

30. Matt A. Barreto, *Ethnic Cues: The Role of Shared Ethnicity in Latino Political Participation* (Ann Arbor, MI: University of Michigan Press, 2013).

31. Mark Hugo Lopez and Paul Taylor, "Latino Voters in the 2012 Election," 2012, www.pewhispanic.org/2012/11/07/latino-voters-in-the-2012-election/.

32. Harold Bloom, *The American Religion* (New York, NY: Simon & Schuster, 1992), chapter 5.

33. Pew Research Center, "US Religious Landscape Study," 2014, www.pewforum.org/religious-landscape-study/ .

34. For more information about size of the specific denominations listed here, see US Member Reports for Religious Congregations and Membership Survey, available at www.thearda.com.

35. Estrelda Y. Alexander, *Black Fire: One Hundred Years of African American Pentecostalism* (Downers Grove, IL: InterVarsity Press, 2011). See also Arthur Paris, *Black Pentecostalism: Southern Religion in an Urban World* (Amherst, MA: University of Massachusetts Press, 1982).

36. The classic work is Charles Hamilton, *The Black Preacher in America* (New York, NY: Morrow, 1972); Martha Simmons and Frank A. Thomas, *Preaching with Sacred Fire: An Anthology of African American Sermons* (New York, NY: Norton, 2010).

37. Jamie Dean, "Milestone," *World*, June 16, 2012, pp. 60–62; "Luter's turn," *The Economist*, March 17, 2012, p. 36.

38. Laura R. Olson, *Filled with Spirit and Power: Protestant Clergy in Politics* (Albany, NY: State University of New York Press, 2000).

39. Samuel G. Freedman, *Upon This Rock: The Miracle of a Black Church* (New York, NY: HarperCollins, 1993).

40. Pew Research Center, "US Religious Landscape Study."

41. On this discussion and the entire subject of this chapter, see C. Eric Lincoln and Lawrence Mamiya, *The Black Church in the African American Experience* (Durham, NC: Duke University Press, 1990); for a broader discussion of men (in general) and the church, see David Murrow, *Why Men Hate Going to Church* (Nashville, TN: Thomas Nelson, 2005).

42. Lisa N. Nealy, *African American Women Voters* (Lanham, MD: University Press of America, 2009), chapter 2.

43. For a provocative discussion, see Eddie S. Glaude, Jr., *African American Religion: A Very Short Introduction* (Oxford: Oxford University Press, 2014).

44. For example, see Mary Ann Clark, *Then We'll Sing a New Song: African Influences on America's Religious Landscape* (Lanham, MD: Rowman & Littlefield, 2012).

45. See David L. Chappell, *A Stone of Hope: Prophetic Religion and the Death of Jim Crow* (Chapel Hill, NC: University of North Carolina Press, 2003); Harwood K.

McClerking and Eric L. McDaniel, "Belonging and Doing: Political Churches and Black Political Participation," *Political Psychology*, 26 (2005): 721–733; and Clyde Wilcox and Leopoldo Gomez, "Religion, Group Identification, and Politics among American Blacks," *Sociological Analysis*, 51 (1990): 271–285.

46. See J. Wendell Mapson, Jr., *The Ministry of Music in the Black Church* (Valley Forge, PA: Judson, 1984).

47. Lincoln and Mamiya, *The Black Church*.

48. James Cone, *Black Theology and Black Power* (New York, NY: Seabury, 1969).

49. See Peter J. Paris, *The Social Teaching of the Black Churches* (Philadelphia, PA: Fortress Press, 1985); Barbara Dianne Savage, *Your Spirits Walk Beside Us: The Politics of Black Religion* (Cambridge, MA: Belknap Press of Harvard University Press, 2008); James Melvin Washington, *Frustrated Fellowship: The Black Baptist Quest for Social Power* (Macon, GA: Mercer University Press, 1982).

50. Lincoln and Mamiya, *The Black Church*, chapter 2; Albert J. Raboteau, *Slave Religion: The "Invisible Institution" in the Antebellum South* (Oxford: Oxford University Press, 1978).

51. William E. Montgomery, *Under Their Own Fig Tree: The African-American Church in the South 1865–1900* (Baton Rouge, LA: LSU Press, 1993); Lincoln and Mamiya, *The Black Church*, chapter 3.

52. Savage, *Your Spirits Walk Beside Us*.

53. See Chappell, *A Stone of Hope*; David J. Garrow, *Bearing the Cross: Martin Luther King, Jr. and the Southern Christian Leadership Conference* (New York, NY: Morrow, 1986); Martin Luther King, Jr., *Why We Can't Wait* (New York, NY: Mentor, 1964); Aldon D. Morris, *The Origins of the Civil Rights Movement* (New York, NY: Free Press, 1984); and Hart M. Nelsen and Anne Kusener Nelsen, *The Black Church in the Sixties* (Lexington, KY: University of Kentucky Press, 1975).

54. Bettye Collier-Thomas, *Jesus, Jobs, and Justice: African American Women and Religion* (New York, NY: Knopf, 2010); Chappell, *A Stone of Hope*; Savage, *Your Spirits Walk Beside Us*.

55. Michelle Alexander, *The New Jim Crow: Mass Incarceration in the Age of Colorblindness* (New York, NY: The New Press, 2012).

56. Joseph H. Jackson, *A Story of Christian Activism: The History of the National Baptist Convention USA, Inc.* (Nashville, TN: Townsend, 1980).

57. Fredrick C. Harris, *Something Within: Religion in African-American Political Activism* (Oxford: Oxford University Press, 1999); R. Drew Smith and Fredrick C. Harris (eds.), *Black Churches and Local Politics: Clergy Influence, Organizational Partnerships, and Civic Empowerment* (Lanham, MD: Rowman & Littlefield, 2005); Richard L. Wood, *Faith in Action: Religion, Race, and Democratic Organizing in America* (Chicago, IL: University of Chicago Press, 2002); James H. Harris, *Black Ministers and Laity in the Urban Church* (Lanham, MD: University Press of America, 1987); Allison Calhoun-Brown, "The Politics of African American Churches: The Psychological Impact of Organizational Resources," *Journal of Politics*, 58 (1996): 935–953.

58. Savage, *Your Spirits Walk Beside Us*, p. 283.

59. Smith and Harris, *Black Churches and Local Politics*.

60. Allen D. Hertzke, *Echoes of Discontent: Jesse Jackson, Pat Robertson, and the Resurgence of Populism* (Washington, DC: CQ Press, 1993), chapters 3, 4, 6; Charles P. Henry, *Culture and African American Politics* (Bloomington, IN: Indiana University Press, 1990).

61. Hertzke, *Echoes of Discontent*.

62. Corwin E. Smidt, Kevin R. den Dulk, Bryan T. Froehle, James M. Penning, Stephen V. Monsma, Douglas L. Koopman, *The Disappearing God Gap? Religion in the 2008 Presidential Election* (Oxford: Oxford University Press, 2010).

63. Michael Leo Owens, *God and Government in the Ghetto: The Politics of Church–State Collaboration in Black America* (Chicago, IL: University of Chicago Press, 2007).

64. Harris, *Something Within*; Smith and Harris, *Black Churches and Local Politics*.

65. Hanes Walton and Robert C. Smith, *American Politics and the African American Quest for Universal Freedom*, 5th edn (New York, NY: Longman, 2007), chapter 10.

66. Angela K. Lewis, *Conservative in the Black Community: To the Right and Misunderstood* (London and New York, NY: Routledge, 2013), a fascinating discussion of its topic and see especially pp. 55–59, 114, 119, 126.

67. Lewis, *Conservative in the Black Community*, pp. 119, 126; Melissa Harris-Lacewell, "From Liberation to Mutual Fund: Political Consequences of Differing Conceptions of Christ in the African American Church," in J. Matthew Wilson (ed.), *From Pews to Polling Places: Faith and Politics in the American Religious Mosaic* (Washington, DC: Georgetown University Press, 2007), pp. 131–160; Samuel G. Freedman, "Call and Response on the State of the Black Church," *New York Times*, April 7, 2010; Savage, *Your Spirits Walk Beside Us*.

68. The "challenge of Islam" is how one of the major studies of the black church depicts the growth of the Muslim population. See Lincoln and Mamiya, *The Black Church*, pp. 388–391. Islam is one "challenge," but there are others, smaller in numbers but existent, such as Santeria and Varda; see Anthony B. Pinn, *Varieties of African American Religious Experience* (Minneapolis, MN: Minneapolis Fortress Press, 1998), chapters 1–3.

69. Pinn, *Varieties*.

70. An indication of how difficult it is to get a handle on small religious groups is the widely varying estimates of the black Muslim membership in the early 1960s. Marshall Frady, "The Children of Malcolm," *The New Yorker*, October 12, 1992, suggests its membership was as small as 10,000; Lincoln and Mamiya suggest it was as sizable as 100,000. Even the higher figure, however, is tiny compared to the black Christian population, which numbered in the millions.

71. See Frady, "The Children of Malcolm."

72. Malcolm X, with Alex Haley, *The Autobiography of Malcolm X* (New York, NY: Grove, 1964).

73. See Chapter 3 for our discussion of American Muslims and relevant bibliography.

74. Pew Research Center, "US Muslims Concerned about Their Place in Society, but Continue To Believe in the American Dream," 2017, http://assets.pewresearch.org/wp-content/uploads/sites/11/2017/07/09105631/U.S.-MUSLIMS-FULL-REPORT-with-population-update-v2.pdf.

75. Pew Research Center, "US Muslims Concerned about Their Place in Society."

76. Catherine Paden, "Political Advocacy through Religious Organization? The Evolving Role of the Nation of Islam," in Robin Dale Jacobson and Nancy D. Wadsworth (eds.), *Faith and Race in American Political Life* (Charlottesville, VA: University of Virginia Press, 2012), pp. 189–206.

77. Eddie Glaude, Jr, "The Black Church is Dead," *Huffington Post*, April 26, 2010; for a response, see "Tough Love for the Black Church," *Christianity Today*, September 16, 2015.

6

GENDER, SEXUAL
ORIENTATION, RELIGION,
AND POLITICS

In any consideration of religion and politics in the United States today, the intersectional roles of gender and sexual orientation merit attention. Americans vary in their religious, spiritual, and political attitudes based on differences in gender and sexual orientation. Gender is an especially powerful predictor of participation in religious and spiritual life, and recent issues involving lesbian, gay, bisexual, and transgender (LGBT) rights have created some of the most charged debates in American religious circles. In this chapter, we first consider aspects of gender's relationship to religion and politics in the United States, placing special emphasis on women. Then we explore several ways in which the gay-rights movement and LGBT people have left their mark on the American religiopolitical landscape.

GENDER AND RELIGION IN AMERICAN LIFE

There is no doubt that American women are, as a group, more religiously observant than men. Public-opinion polls have noted this discrepancy for many years. Consider the following findings from a massive survey conducted in 2014 by the Pew Research Center: Women are much less likely than men to be religiously unaffiliated (19 percent versus 27 percent) and more likely to have an absolutely certain belief in God or a universal spirit (69 percent versus 57 percent), to pray daily (64 percent to 46 percent), to say religion is very important in their lives (59 percent to 47 percent), and to attend worship services at least weekly (40 percent to 31 percent).[1]

If we take an even broader view and include all women who state that they are "spiritual" but not religious, age begins to matter. Traditional religious participation rates are higher among middle-aged and older women, while younger women are more likely than their older counterparts to assert that they are spiritual.[2] Some observers have been surprised at the intensity of the religiosity and spirituality of women in the baby-boom generation, which once was characterized as the least religious age cohort in American history. In fact, boomer women (who came to adulthood in the 1960s and early 1970s) did not bring about a break in the long tradition of religiosity among American women. Even in this generation of "rebels," a sizable majority of boomer women have rated religion or spirituality as very important in their lives.[3] Given the rise of religious disaffiliation among millennials, whether the youngest generation of women will continue such high levels of religiosity and spirituality is uncertain.[4]

Race also plays a role in the relationship between gender and religiosity. Specifically, African-American women tend to be more religious than white women. Black churches in the United States are much more likely to attract and retain the support of women than men, which has caused some concern in the African-American community.[5] However, as we noted in Chapter 5, African-American clergy are almost exclusively male. Traditional gender roles dominate, but this is not to say that women are not respected in African-American churches; they are, and in some historically black denominations, elder women bear the formal honorary title of "mother."

Viewed from a somewhat different perspective, it is easy to argue that African-American women have been the primary architects of black Christian history in the United States. While black (male) preachers have provided more renowned voices, there have been some consequential women leaders as well. For example, Mary McLeod Bethune, a religious organizer and liberal Democratic political activist, was among the most prominent African-American women of the first half of the twentieth century. Nannie H. Burroughs was less political than Bethune, but a no-less-central figure in the black Baptist tradition during the same era. Later, deeply religious women played critical roles in the Civil Rights movement, from the intellectual Ella Baker to the celebrated Rosa Parks to the incomparable Fannie Lou Hamer, who helped summon both the segregated South and the reluctant Democratic Party toward racial equality.[6] Politically speaking, African-American women in general tend to be sympathetic to certain aspects of feminism, including greater economic and professional opportunities for women. The experience of being a "double minority" enhances their sensitivity to the predicament of oppressed and impoverished people.

Women likewise play a central role in the operation of predominately white churches and synagogues in the United States. As we discuss below, ordination is available to women in the mainline Protestant and Jewish traditions and in a few quarters of evangelical and African-American Protestantism. In the Catholic Church, women—both laypersons and 58,000 "women religious" (nuns and sisters)—do most of the day-to-day work of parish life, serving as schoolteachers, religious catechism educators, office workers, and liturgical and music leaders.[7] For years, there was great concern that the average age of Catholic women religious (nuns) was increasing and that their numbers would eventually decline to an unsustainably low number. However, today there is some evidence of recovery as more millennial women, many inspired by Pope Francis, opt into a life of service to the church.[8] Whether the Catholic Church might one day allow women to serve as priests or deacons remains to be seen; even the progressive Francis has reaffirmed the church's stance against women priests.[9]

In addition to serving as clergy in most denominations of Judaism, some Jewish women have recently displayed renewed interest in their faith. Despite fierce debate and concern within the Jewish community about the continued vitality of Judaism—and Jewish people themselves—in the United States, many women have worked hard to preserve Jewish traditions, sometimes religious, sometimes cultural, that their parents may not have emphasized.[10] And Jewish women have been a formidable political force, particularly around progressive causes, for more than a century.[11]

Muslim women are much more recent entrants into the American religious arena, so we know less about how they might prefer to combine their religious and political viewpoints. Since Muslims face discrimination in the United States today, it stands to reason that civil rights and civil liberties might occupy a fair share of Muslim women's attention. Some Muslim-American women have decided to forgo wearing a traditional headscarf (hijab) to protect themselves from bigotry.[12] This decision reflects the findings of a 2017 survey of Muslim Americans that revealed Muslim women to be substantially more pessimistic than Muslim men about whether they are welcome in American society.[13] For example, 65 percent of Muslim men said "the American people are friendly toward Muslim Americans" compared to just 44 percent of Muslim women.[14] This perception also appears to correlate with a gender gap in party identification among American Muslims that sees women espousing more negative attitudes about the Republican Party (as is the case among American women in general).[15]

Beyond defending the Islamic community, American Muslim women have emerged as notable advocates for gender equity, religious freedom, and human rights within Islam. The national association of Muslim women lawyers, Karamah, advances those aims, as does Asma Uddin, a legal advocate and editor-in-chief of altMuslimah, an online resource on gender in Islam. Among the self-conscious feminists is journalist Asra Nomani, who has written what she describes as a "manifesto of the rights of women based on the true faith of Islam."[16] Gender dynamics in American religious life, of course, are not restricted to the roles women play. In recent times, we have seen highly publicized religious events geared specifically toward men, such as the Promise Keepers Men's Ministry, which purveys a distinctly evangelical Protestant message.[17] Today, an abundance of male-only prayer groups, reading clubs, and religious retreats operate within organized religion in the United States. These trends among men are partly a conscious effort to reverse the decline of male interest in religion; they are also a reaction to the dominance of women and recognition that in spiritual matters, as in other dimensions of life, men and women do not always have the same needs.[18] That said, men continue to comprise a vast majority of religious leaders in the United States.

WOMEN'S DIVERGING PERSPECTIVES ON RELIGION AND POLITICS

Women in the United States view the intersection between religion and politics in many different ways. This is natural since women comprise more than half of the US population. As is the case for American women in general, the political orientations of religious women defy easy characterization. Politically, religious American women are organized for social change through groups that range from the liberal Women–Church Convergence to the conservative Concerned Women for America. Theologically speaking, women span the gamut as well. Some have been active in challenging and defending traditional beliefs, practices, and structures. Others look for ways to bring their viewpoints to bear within male-dominated religious traditions, pressing for incremental change. More radical women have been involved in reviving or developing spiritual expressions that aim to transform not only religion but every aspect of social and political life. Many other women are on their own personal and informal spiritual journeys.[19] Today, the quest for meaning leads women into every corner of the pluralistic and complicated world of the spiritual and religious.

Meanwhile, American women and men increasingly have been treading divergent political paths. A gender-based difference in presidential voting behavior first appeared in 1964, when women lent the bulk of their support to Lyndon Johnson in his contest with the hawkish Barry Goldwater, reflecting women's preference for diplomatic solutions to international conflicts. Women's greater preference for Democratic presidential candidates has persisted despite small drop-offs in the 2000 and 2004 elections of George W. Bush.[20] In 2016, the gender gap in vote choice was the largest ever recorded in exit polls: women favored Hillary Clinton by 12 points while men favored Donald Trump by the same margin.[21] (For a look at how Clinton combines religion and politics, see Box 6.1.) American women are also more liberal than men on domestic-policy issues that span economics, the appropriate size and role of government, and social issues such as equality for LGBT people.[22] Is religion related to this gender gap in any consistent ways?

Conservative Intersections

Notwithstanding women's aggregate leaning toward the political left, it is hardly unusual to find religious women committed to more conservative political

BOX 6.1 HILLARY RODHAM CLINTON:
LIBERAL METHODIST

Former presidential candidate and US Secretary of State Hillary Rodham Clinton is a deeply religious person, but she has never made a point of emphasizing this aspect of her life. In part, her reticence is typical of mainline Protestants, who are by definition not evangelical about their faith. She was born into a Methodist family with roots in England, where Methodism was born. As a young woman, she attended First United Methodist Church in Park Ridge, Illinois, where she absorbed mainline theological reflections on society. As a college student, Hillary Rodham joined an interdenominational chapel society and read widely among the liberal theologians of the time. She took naturally to the intensifying social-justice activism in the United Methodist Church, which epitomized the mainline Protestant emphasis on encouraging government to promote economic and social justice for the disadvantaged.

On many Sundays when Bill Clinton was governor of Arkansas, Hillary Clinton would attend services at his Baptist church and then worship in her own Methodist congregation, where she also taught Sunday school. When Bill Clinton was president, the family frequently attended Foundry United Methodist Church, led at the time by Rev. J. Philip Wogaman, a noted progressive theologian and ethicist.

When Clinton embarked on her own political career as a US senator, and later as Secretary of State, she viewed her work as a means of quietly carrying

causes.[23] When John McCain selected former Alaska governor and evangelical Protestant Sarah Palin as his running mate in the 2008 presidential election, he rallied many evangelical Protestant women to his—or perhaps more accurately, Palin's—cause. Analysis of the 2008 campaign shows that Palin's most dedicated supporters were evangelical women, a reflection of her own evangelical Protestantism and vocally pro-life stance on abortion.[24] The presence of former House Representative Michele Bachmann (R-Minnesota), also a committed evangelical, in the 2012 race for the Republican presidential nomination has led some observers to proclaim the emergence of a new "evangelical feminism" on the political right.[25] Others insist that the thoroughgoing conservatism of women like Palin and Bachmann does not fit with feminism.[26] The clarity and power of their unique voices in American politics nevertheless marks an important breakthrough for women—and particularly religious women—in the twenty-first century.

A closely related recent manifestation of conservative religious women's political prominence has been the highly significant role they played in launching the Tea Party movement against what they see as an overly intrusive government.

out her faith as an advocate for social justice and compassion. As a presidential candidate in 2016, she vacillated between reticence and open discussion of her faith. In her acceptance speech at the Democratic National Convention, she included a teaching that most of her fellow Methodists know well: "Do all the good you can, at all the times you can, to all the people you can, as long as ever you can." Clinton also quoted Scripture frequently on the campaign trail. Historian Kristin Du Mez argues that Clinton might have reached more voters had she included more personal references to her religious life during the 2016 campaign. However, notes Du Mez, Clinton faced criticism throughout her career whenever she tiptoed toward discussing religion; conservatives shunned the progressive impulses of her mainline Protestantism while secular people saw her religious references as pandering for votes. Sometimes marrying religion and politics is much more complicated than we might assume.

Sources: Kristin Du Mez, "Can Hillary Clinton's Faith Help Her Lead a Fractured Nation?" *Religion & Politics*, July 25, 2016, http://religionandpolitics.org/2016/07/25/can-clintons-faith-help-her-lead-a-fractured-nation/; Kristin Du Mez, "Hillary Clinton's History of Faith Is Long and Rich. This Week, She Should Talk about It," *Washington Post*, July 26, 2016, www.washingtonpost.com/news/acts-of-faith/wp/2016/07/26/hillary-clintons-history-of-faith-is-long-and-rich-this-week-she-should-talk-about-it/; Paul Kengor, *God and Hillary Clinton: A Spiritual Life* (New York, NY: HarperCollins, 2007).

With Palin, Bachmann (who founded a short-lived Tea Party Caucus when she was in Congress), and Senator Joni Ernst (R-Iowa) as standard bearers, the Tea Party movement reinvigorated both a hard-right, uncompromising conservatism and an anti-establishmentarian populism. In her book on the subject, political scientist Melissa Deckman explains that the grassroots nature of the Tea Party movement was more comfortable for many conservative women than the more insider-oriented politics of organized interest groups. Women quickly gained a leadership foothold as the movement developed, often hosting local informational meetings around their kitchen tables. Women's legitimacy as leaders in the Tea Party movement was further enhanced by their decision to rely on their traditional gender roles as wives and mothers when framing controversial public-policy issues such as gun control as problems that affect families.[27] As Skocpol and Williamson described it, the Tea Party was fueled by

> women bustling about to organize things, and local meetings opening with a patriotic ritual and a prayer . . . age-old staples of grassroots

civic activism in the United States. In these respects. . . . the Tea Party . . . [has] elements that go all the way back to the US Founding Fathers—and the Founding Mothers.[28]

Although it is unclear whether the Tea Party movement has a future during and after the Trump administration, it is indisputable that the movement's rejection of politics as usual paved the way to Trump's election in 2016.

A longer-standing source of conservative religious women's political clout comes in the form of the interest group Concerned Women for America (CWA), which has been in existence since 1979. This organization has a large national membership of mostly evangelical Protestant women who take a high view of Scripture, hold conservative political beliefs, and vote Republican.[29] Beverly LaHaye founded CWA in 1979 and remained as its leader until 1998. LaHaye has written many books, including *I Am a Woman by God's Design*, in which she addresses a wide range of political issues and endorses the view that women should submit to male headship in marriage.[30] Her writings tightly interweave political conservatism and Christianity. CWA has been particularly interested and involved in "family" issues and lobbying on behalf of the pro-life cause. It operates largely through state and local chapters connected to its national headquarters.[31]

Eagle Forum is another group that is more historically significant than its currently limited size and clout might indicate. Founded in 1972 by Phyllis Schlafly, a conservative Catholic, Eagle Forum advocates for traditional stances on moral issues. Its founding and subsequent growth followed Schlafly's legendary leadership of a movement comprised largely of women that almost single-handedly defeated the proposed Equal Rights Amendment.[32] Although Schlafly died in 2016 and membership numbers continue to decline, Eagle Forum remains explicitly Christian and eager to advocate for conservative women and men around a wide range of policy matters.[33]

Interest groups such as CWA and Eagle Forum are important, but they hardly tell the entire story of religious women's involvement in conservative politics. Everywhere one looks in conservative politics today, religious women seem to be involved. For example, women often spearhead struggles at the local level over school curricula, library books, public religious ceremonies, and similar issues. Such local disputes lie at the center of religious politics in the United States. It is there that conservative women are both the generals and the foot soldiers in religiopolitical battles.[34]

That said, there are relatively few formal leadership opportunities available to women within evangelical Protestantism or the Catholic Church. Those women who do have access to the ministry or rabbinate are almost universally liberal, in part because the traditions that allow them to become religious leaders are themselves progressive.[35] Conservative religious women face greater challenges simply because their religious traditions (and related organizations, such as interest groups) tend to be more formally male-dominated. Nevertheless, there are some women leaders in evangelical Protestant circles, many of whom co-pastor churches with their husbands. And although she says she is politically neutral, religious broadcaster and author Joyce Meyer has been a trailblazer for aspiring evangelical leaders who happen to be women, even those who do not share her prosperity gospel-oriented Pentecostalism.

Indeed, conservative religious women might have better access to circles of political power if they had more opportunity to serve in formal religious leadership positions. Studies suggest some softening of opinion around the issue of women's ordination. More evangelical Protestants today favor women's ordination. On the other hand, the majority of theologically conservative Protestants—men and women alike—continue to hold to the "male headship" view of family, which teaches that the male should be the head of the household and make all major family decisions. Even this viewpoint may be in decline, however, especially among millennial evangelicals.[36]

There also is long-standing disagreement among evangelical organizations regarding the proper roles for the Christian woman. In 1987, the Council on Biblical Manhood and Womanhood developed a mediating position between patriarchy and feminism that it calls the "complementarian" view. Its advocates insist that the Bible holds that men and women are fully equal in God's eyes, but God calls them to different (and complementary) roles. Women are called to serve in the home as wives and mothers, not to enter realms traditionally reserved for men such as the ministry or head of the household. On the other hand, Christians for Biblical Equality asserts that God puts no barriers on the possibilities for humans of either gender—so roles in the church, the home, and elsewhere should be equally available to both genders. This struggle within evangelical Protestantism illustrates the lack of agreement that persists to this day about how conservative women and men seeking to follow God's word should relate to one another.[37] The most common belief among evangelical Protestant women is still acceptance of St. Paul's teachings about male headship: men are to be the heads of the household, women should submit to them, and both must submit to God. Belief does not always reflect practice for most married evangelical women in their daily lives, however. Sharing the burden rather than submitting to a husband's "rule" is the practical reality of most married women's lives—whether they are religious conservatives or not.[38] This is particularly so because many evangelical women work, use day care, and intend to continue doing so, even as others are determined to be stay-at-home wives and mothers—and, in some cases, to homeschool their children.[39] As we continue to note, the exception always disproves the rule in American religion because pluralism prevails.

Progressive and Radical Intersections

By no means should anyone assume that religious women are necessarily conservative. This is far from being the case. Nor is the connection between religious women and progressive politics a new phenomenon. For example, in 1933, Dorothy Day cofounded the Catholic worker movement, which went on to address the needs of disadvantaged people in cities across the United States.[40] Even today the movement continues in its antipoverty work, and Day is under consideration for sainthood by the Roman Catholic Church. Many people do not realize that Catholic laywomen (like Day) and nuns historically have been strong advocates of political progressivism. In fact, one analyst labeled nuns "America's first feminists."[41] The Leadership Conference of Women Religious (LCWR), which comprises 95 percent of all American nuns, engages in political action around a range of social-justice issues consistent with the long tradition of Catholic social teaching.[42] Likewise, nuns founded NETWORK, a Catholic interest group, in 1971, to "act for justice" by lobbying government on issues of poverty, racism, and violence.[43] More recently, the executive director of NETWORK, Sister Simone Campbell, has organized and led bus trips of nuns across the United States to raise awareness for various political causes. "Nuns on the Bus" began their road trips in 2012 as an action against proposed federal budget cuts to social-welfare programs.[44] They continue to cross the country— for example, in support of comprehensive immigration reform in 2013, and to raise awareness of wealth and income inequality among political candidates in 2016.[45] As Box 6.2 shows, however, NETWORK does not speak for all American nuns.

As another example, consider the long-standing witness of a group called Church Women United. This organization, which is officially interfaith, was founded in 1941 and became active politically in the 1950s and 1960s on behalf of Civil Rights causes. It moved on in the later 1960s to focus on issues of special concern to women, particularly their rights and their development as individuals. Even though fewer women today have less time available as in decades past, some do dedicate themselves meaningfully to the social-justice-oriented work of groups like Church Women United.[46]

As noted earlier in this chapter, the considerable number of African-American women who provide much time and energy fueling local African-American political causes offer yet another illustration of progressive religiopolitical intersections. For over a century, the National Association of Colored Women's Clubs has empowered black women to fight for the political and civil rights of African Americans and "work for the economic, moral, religious and social welfare of women and youth."[47] Many black women fought hard for women's suffrage as well, most famously Sojourner Truth.[48] And African-American women were integral intellectual cogs and dedicated foot soldiers in the Civil Rights movement of the twentieth century.[49] Lest one think that all black women's political activism leans in the liberal direction, consider the fact that they have spearheaded efforts to launch school choice programs and to allow federal tax dollars to fund religiously connected social services.[50]

BOX 6.2 "NUNS ON THE BUS" VS. LITTLE SISTERS
OF THE POOR

Just like other women, Catholic nuns hold different views about political issues and engagement, as we see in two groups that came to symbolize competing sides of the contentious healthcare debate. In 2010, NETWORK, the liberal "nuns' lobby," endorsed the Affordable Care Act (ACA), President Obama's signature domestic-policy initiative. Led by Sister Simone Campbell, the organization sent a letter from leaders of its member orders urging Congress to vote for the healthcare Bill, calling it "life affirming." When Republicans in Congress sought to repeal the ACA in 2017, Campbell and the NETWORK nuns mobilized again, saying the repeal effort "goes against our Catholic faith teaching."

In contrast, another order of more traditional Catholic nuns, the Little Sisters of the Poor, found themselves at the center of conflict with the Obama administration's efforts to implement the ACA's requirement that employers provide employees with contraception free of charge. The Little Sisters, whose primary mission is to serve the elderly poor, challenged the government's requirement that they accede to the provision of contraceptive services, which they said violated their religious principles. Facing millions of dollars in fines for refusing to comply, the Little Sisters, led by their Mother Provincial Loraine Marie Maguire, took their case to the US Supreme Court and became a visible symbol, especially to conservatives, of successful resistance against government mandates.

While they found themselves in different political camps, the two groups of nuns were both successful: the ACA survived, but religious organizations were excused from its contraception requirement.

Sources: "Catholic Sisters' Letter in Support of Healthcare Reform Bill," NETWORK, March 17, 2010, https://networklobby.org/20100317healthcare/; Sister Simone Campbell, *A Nun on the Bus* (New York, NY: HarperOne, 2014); Emma Green, "Even Nuns Aren't Exempt from Obamacare's Birth Control Mandate," *The Atlantic*, July 14, 2015, www.theatlantic.com/politics/archive/2015/07/obama-beats-the-nuns-on-contraception/398519/; *Zubik* v. *Burwell*, 578 US ___ (2016).

Many Jewish women are also active in liberal politics. Their work is noteworthy within the context of the Democratic Party and in a host of public actions and lobbying associations.[51] For example, the National Council of Jewish Women (NCJW), which traces its inception to 1893, is a liberal Jewish women's grassroots political organization. As its website states,

"Inspired by Jewish values, NCJW strives for social justice by improving the quality of life for women, children, and families and by safeguarding individual rights and freedoms," which translates into a political agenda that emphasizes civil liberties, civil rights and economic justice, women's issues, reproductive choice, and church–state separation.[52] NCJW also has a substantial interest in international issues, particularly those that affect Israel and its welfare. Likewise, Hadassah, a Zionist interest group specifically for women, is active in policy debates regarding Israel but also engages in progressive advocacy around domestic issues including women's health, human trafficking, and affordable childcare.[53]

It should come as no surprise, at least in the context of the broader political gender gap, that there is a radical woman-led religious witness in the United States with a political agenda that veers even further left than the progressive groups discussed above. Today, such politics emanate primarily from the Catholic, mainline Protestant, and Jewish traditions, but radicalism among religious women has a long history in the United States.

Feminist critiques of religion (which has, in the United States, usually meant critiques of Christianity) have come in three phases. The first phase was during the late nineteenth and early twentieth centuries, and its most famous expression is Elizabeth Cady Stanton's *Woman's Bible* (1895). Stanton and other critics complained that religion was too much a man's world, involving too much rejection (and even oppression) of women, and urged equality for women instead. The second phase, which occurred in the 1960s and 1970s, also stressed the need for respect and equality for women in religion and religious institutions, but it also raised serious questions about why women had been second-class citizens for so long in religious areas of life. Such questioning led to a probing of the social, sexual, and power dynamics of everything from theologies to church structures. The most recent phase, beginning in the 1980s, has continued the emphases of the two previous phases but also includes many new ideas from a wider range of religious and philosophical standpoints.[54]

The most visible radical political activity undertaken by religiously committed American women today tends to come from within Catholic circles. Between 2012 and 2015, the Vatican took the unusual step of publicly investigating and reprimanding the largest organization of American nuns, the Leadership Conference of Women Religious (LCWR). The church's original complaint against the LCWR was that it advocates "radical feminist themes incompatible with the Catholic faith . . . [and] challenge[s] the bishops, who are the church's authentic teachers of faith and morals."[55] Leftist Catholic women (and men) quickly launched a movement to support and defend the LCWR through today's leading radical American Catholic organization, Call to Action.[56] The aforementioned Nuns on the Bus movement started in part as a reaction to the Vatican's rebuke of the LCWR.[57] Ultimately, the Vatican and the LCWR patched things up—in large part because Pope Francis wished to take a much more conciliatory tone toward the nuns than his predecessor, Pope Benedict XVI, had taken.[58]

Another noteworthy radical group is Women-Church Convergence, which has been at the forefront of the attempt to develop a feminist religion with a fitting political agenda. Its theology emphasizes a vaguely Christian God, creed, and church, all of which are strongly egalitarian and communitarian. Women-Church Convergence is committed to encouraging society at large to embrace its vision and goals. Supporters share an unyielding belief in gender equality. They view God as a friend rather than a looming authoritarian presence. Women-Church Convergence also insists that political action is needed to reorient society to these ideals.[59]

A final example of leftist politics among religious women is evident in the emergence of explicitly feminist theologies. The principal goal of feminist theologians is to attack past and present male domination within religion. In advancing this goal, they raise fundamental questions about images of God as Father and the all-male hierarchies that persist in some religious traditions. Some feminist theologians seek to undermine or abolish male (and all other) hierarchies in every part of society, including the political order.[60] In this context, some feminist thinkers view the Abrahamic religions (Christianity, Judaism, and Islam) as redeemable, while others have concluded that feminism requires a complete break with all traditional religions.[61]

THE POLITICS OF WOMEN IN THE PEWS

Political debates about feminist theology and whether the Abrahamic faith traditions are redeemable dominate a good deal of today's intellectual discourse at the intersection of gender, religion, and politics. However, these matters do not appear to have engaged many rank-and-file religious women. Indeed, with the important exception of women clergy (who are markedly liberal in their political attitudes), the more deeply a woman is involved in organized religion, the more likely she is to be conservative on political and religious questions.[62] In fact, research shows that congregations with larger percentages of female members tend to be more politically conservative than congregations with a more even gender split.[63] Women who are attracted to less conventional spiritual journeys, however, are much more likely to have liberal religious and political attitudes.[64]

Consider the case of Catholic women. Not unlike the progressive nuns discussed above, lay Catholic women express a particularly strong preference for women's equality, and, as a group, they display more feminist attitudes on a wide range of issues than do Protestant women. Age is a sharp dividing line among Catholic women, with the generation of women who reached adulthood in the 1960s and early 1970s forming the clearest line of demarcation. Younger Catholic women are much more liberal on matters involving the priesthood;

they express a greater overall degree of discomfort with the Catholic Church and feel that it needs to be more respectful and inclusive of women.[65] As is the case among African-American Protestants, a majority of regular mass attendees are women. Critics raise the specter of what they call the "feminization of the Church"—a fear that fewer men will be interested in Roman Catholicism if the church comes to be seen as a female-dominated institution.[66] Perhaps as a result, the US Catholic Church has turned in a more traditional direction, and younger priests are more conservative than their predecessors have been.[67] Popes John Paul II, Benedict XVI, and Francis have all made a special point of hailing the contributions made by women to the life and work of the Catholic Church—while also reaffirming the church's commitment to an all-male priesthood.

The variety of attitudes espoused by American Catholic women in the pews is exemplified by their opinions about abortion. As we know, many of the combatants in the battle over abortion are based within organized religion.[68] The split among women on abortion along religious lines is palpable. The more deeply a woman is involved in religious life, and the more traditional her religious views, the more likely she is to oppose abortion. This does not mean that pro-life women are necessarily conservative on all other issues.[69] Nor does it mean that all active Catholic (or Protestant) women are pro-life, but it is true that the intensity of one's religious commitment is one of the best predictors of conservative abortion attitudes.[70] And religious women on both sides of the abortion debate often have more in common with each other than is often assumed. Women on both sides often share a strong belief in the intrinsic value of women—and of motherhood—as well as a sense that women ultimately must rely on themselves.[71]

As noted earlier, gender also has been a major dividing point in American voting behavior in recent years. With the exceedingly important exception of evangelical Protestants, women across religious traditions favored Hillary Clinton in the 2016 presidential election. Indeed, gender sometimes has a more significant effect on partisanship and voting behavior than does religion. Table 6.1 shows the presence of a sizable gender gap in 2016 voting behavior within every religious tradition except for evangelical Protestantism, with women much more likely than men to have voted for Clinton. Table 6.2 shows similar gender gaps among Latinos, though here evangelicals were also more likely to vote for Clinton than men.

The vast difference we observe between white evangelical women and those in other religious traditions clearly suggests that religious identity was more crucial than gender for evangelical women's vote choice in 2016. Scholars have illustrated a similar phenomenon regarding evangelical women's vote choices in the 2004 and 2008 presidential elections as well.[72] At least in the case of the 2016 election, deep-rooted distaste among evangelical women for Hillary Clinton led them to vote for Donald Trump, in spite of deep skepticism about Trump's

	EVANGELICAL PROTESTANT		MAINLINE PROTESTANT		BLACK PROTESTANT	
	M (*N=3855*)	F (*N=5030*)	M (*N=3401*)	F (*N=4167*)	M (*N=1342*)	F (*N=2927*)
Trump	80%	78%	61%	49%	13%	5%
Clinton	13%	18%	33%	46%	84%	92%
Other	6%	4%	7%	4%	3%	3%

	CATHOLIC		JEWISH		UNAFFILIATED	
	M (*N=6780*)	F (*N=7100*)	M (*N=768*)	F (*N=778*)	M (*N=5142*)	F (*N=6844*)
Trump	53%	45%	30%	25%	43%	33%
Clinton	42%	51%	64%	73%	50%	61%
Other	5%	4%	6%	2%	8%	6%

TABLE 6.1 Vote Choice by Religion and Gender, 2016

Source: Stephen Ansolabehere and Brian F. Schaffner, "CCES Common Content, 2016," v. 3, Harvard Dataverse, 2017.

Notes: Totals may not equal 100% due to rounding. Table created using suggested weighting from CCES. Evangelical defined by self-identification as Protestant, born-again, and white. Mainline defined by self-identification as Protestant, not born-again, and white. Unaffiliated defined by self-identification as "nothing in particular."

treatment of women. For decades, Clinton has symbolized the cultural move away from the traditional gender roles that many evangelicals cherish, and, to an extent, the pro-choice cause. Thus, it is arguable that in 2016 conservative evangelical women did not vote *for* Trump as much as they voted *against* Clinton.[73] It is noteworthy that Senator Elizabeth Warren (D-Massachusetts), a potential presidential contender in 2020, has been emphasizing her religious roots since Trump's election. Like Clinton, she was raised a Methodist and has tended toward reticence about her faith commitments.[74]

THE POLITICS OF WOMEN CLERGY

Another important dynamic connecting gender, religion, and US politics in the twenty-first century is the presence of women in the ministry and rabbinate. There is no broad consensus in American religious circles about whether the Bible allows or prohibits women's ordination, and the question remains a

	ALL LATINO VOTERS		LATINO CATHOLIC		LATINO PROTESTANT	
	M (N=2344)	F (N=2894)	M (N=1093)	F (N=1376)	M (N=380)	F (N=546)
Trump	30%	25%	27%	19%	57%	46%
Clinton	64%	71%	67%	78%	37%	48%
Other	6%	4%	4%	3%	6%	5%

TABLE 6.2 Vote Choice by Latino Ethnicity, Religion, and Gender, 2016

Source: Stephen Ansolabehere and Brian F. Schaffner, "CCES Common Content, 2016," v. 3, Harvard Dataverse, 2017.

Notes: Totals may not equal 100% due to rounding. Table created using suggested weighting from CCES. Evangelical defined by self-identification as Protestant and born-again.

contentious one. The passages cited most often by people who oppose women's ordination are from the epistles of St. Paul. Christian opponents of women's ordination point to scriptural passages including 1 Timothy 2:11–12, which says: "Let a woman learn in silence with all submissiveness. I permit no woman to teach or to have authority over men; she is to keep silent." However, proponents point to passages such as Galatians 3:28: "There is neither Jew nor Greek, there is neither slave nor free, there is neither male nor female; for you are all one in Christ Jesus."[75]

Today, a substantial minority of mainline and African-American Protestant pastors and Jewish rabbis are female, although clergymen still vastly outnumber clergywomen. According to the US Census, women now account for roughly one in every five American religious leaders.[76] However, only 11 percent of congregations nationwide were headed by a woman as recently as 2012.[77] This discrepancy is attributable to the fact that women tend not to serve in large, prominent churches or synagogues; in such settings, they often report to a male head minister or rabbi.[78] Research also shows that women are more likely than men to preside over small congregations.[79] The "stained glass ceiling" is not impenetrable (see Box 6.3), but it is also a reality faced by most women in the ministry and rabbinate.

Although women are not ordained in the Catholic Church, they nevertheless play essential roles. As we note above, women religious (nuns) have served the church, its schools, and its hospitals, for centuries.[80] The declining number of Catholic priests in the United States promises to increase the importance of women's informal leadership roles.[81] Neither are there many women to be found within the ranks of white evangelical Protestant pastors. In most evangelical

BOX 6.3 A MARRIED LESBIAN COUPLE WHO PASTOR
A PROMINENT BAPTIST CHURCH

It is often challenging for clergywomen to secure positions as head pastors or rabbis of large, prominent congregations. The debate about whether LGBT people should be permitted to serve as clergy remains heated today. These obstacles, however, do not mean that there are no women or LGBT people who serve in high-profile ministerial positions.

Consider the example of Revs. Sally Sarratt and Maria Swearingen, who were installed in 2017 as senior co-pastors of Calvary Baptist Church in Washington, DC. Calvary's roots in the nation's capital are long and deep; it was founded by abolitionists in 1862 and later became the founding congregation in the mainline Baptist denomination (the American Baptist Churches USA). Sarratt and Swearingen are a married couple who met while attending a prominent Baptist church in Greenville, South Carolina—a small city that sits arguably at the buckle of the "Bible belt." Their combined experience includes work in a wide range of pastoral contexts, from preaching to chaplaincy to the mission field. Moreover, Sarratt exemplifies many twenty-first-century American clergy in that the ministry is her second career.

Sources: Lauren Markoe, "Married Lesbian Couple to Lead Prominent DC Baptist Church," *Washington Post*, January 9, 2017, www.washingtonpost.com/news/acts-of-faith/wp/2017/01/09/married-lesbian-couple-to-lead-prominent-d-c-baptist-church/; Calvary Baptist Church, http://calvarydc.org/about-us/staff/.

circles, traditional gender roles and male headship preclude women from serving as clergy. Some moderate evangelical congregations—and more than a few Pentecostal churches—do allow women to serve in limited pastoral roles. Women also play many important leadership roles outside the constraints of traditional religion from formal Wiccan and neo-pagan practices to informal meetings of people who consider themselves spiritual.[82]

It took generations of struggle before any women were permitted to serve as clergy. Today's clergywomen have cause to feel feminist bonds of sisterhood with the early pioneers of the political struggle for women's equality in the United States. In 1848, Seneca Falls, New York, played host to one of the first organized public discussions of women's rights. One of the many resolutions debated at Seneca Falls during the drafting of the Declaration of Sentiments and Resolutions proposed "that the speedy success of our course depends upon the zealous and untiring efforts of both men and women, for the overthrow of the monopoly of the pulpit, and for the securing to women an equal participation with men in the various trades, professions, and commerce."[83] A generation after Seneca Falls, Frances Willard, founder of the Woman's Christian Temperance Union, saw fit to publish a book titled *Woman in the Pulpit*.[84]

Today, the simple fact of being a female religious leader remains politically significant. Some observers have argued that as more women enter the ministry the religious traditions that ordain them might move toward the political left.[85] There is some reason to think this may be a valid assessment. Research shows that clergywomen are consistently more liberal than clergymen in their political attitudes, especially on equality issues such as gender discrimination and LGBT rights.[86] Many, especially in mainline Protestant denominations, insist that the faithful must enter society and politics and work to change the world to make it more Christlike. As examples, they cite Mother Teresa, Nelson Mandela, and even Moses.[87] There are plenty of clergywomen who are not afraid to let their political voices be heard, both in their congregations and in their broader communities.

RELIGION, POLITICS, SEXUAL ORIENTATION, AND LGBT PEOPLE

No group of Americans has emerged more quickly from the shadows of discrimination and bigotry since the late twentieth century than LGBT people— or arguably caused more moral controversy in doing so. As recently as a generation ago, few LGBT people dared to be open about their sexual orientation, much less consider marrying. However, in a very short time, attitudes about LGBT people in the United States have warmed significantly, and public policy has changed in substantial ways as a result. These changes have pleased some Americans and outraged others, and religion is related to these controversies in myriad ways. What relationships exist between the politics of sexual orientation, gender identity, and religion? The answer to this question is complex and is changing quickly in an era when LGBT people are no longer subject to widespread demonization.

THE LGBT RIGHTS MOVEMENT AND AMERICAN RELIGION: CONFLICT OR COOPERATION?

Historically, Judeo-Christian teachings have emphasized restrictive attitudes about sex. In most cases, these teachings have intimated that sexual activity is appropriate only between married heterosexual partners for purposes of conceiving children. The Old and New Testaments contain several references that religious people use when teaching that same-sex relations are sinful. The strongest Old Testament prohibition appears in Leviticus 18:22, which states: "If a man lies with a male as with a woman, both of them have committed an abomination; they shall be put to death." This theme reappears several times in the New Testament, as in 1 Corinthians 6:9–10: "Fornicators, idolaters, adulterers, male prostitutes, sodomites . . . none of these will inherit the kingdom of God." In recent times, religious leaders in the United States have not been divided over whether LGBT people should live or die, but instead over how they should be received (if at all) as fellow worshipers or clergy.[88]

The rapid changes in American society's treatment of LGBT people began when the movement for gay rights followed on the heels of other movements for social change. The Civil Rights movement of the 1950s and 1960s gave other American minority groups hope that they too might one day overcome discrimination, while also providing them with a successful model of nonviolent resistance to emulate. The catalytic event that spurred the LGBT rights movement occurred in 1969 when gay people fought back in the streets after New York police raided a Greenwich Village gay bar, the Stonewall Inn. The Stonewall riots had no connection to organized religion, but in the same year an important religious Rubicon was crossed when Rev. James Stoll became the first openly gay clergyperson in US history. Stoll's coming out led his faith tradition, the Unitarian Universalist Association, to pass the first resolution by an American religious group in favor of LGBT rights in 1970.[89]

Mobilization typically begets countermobilization, especially when the cultural stakes are high. By 1977, Dade County, Florida, had passed an ordinance forbidding discrimination based on sexual orientation. Conservative activist and former Miss America Anita Bryant spearheaded a high-profile (and ultimately successful) effort to overturn the ordinance, and her leadership launched a new anti-LGBT rights movement steeped in religion and cultural conservatism. Thus, Bryant's activism contributed to the emergence of the religious right a few years later; notably, one of Rev. Jerry Falwell's first forays into politics was his effort to help Bryant in Florida.[90]

The LGBT rights movement faced several new challenges during the 1980s. At that time, most US religious voices were still united in their opposition to LGBT equality. Indeed, the culture wars that developed between moral and political conservatives and their liberal counterparts were stoked—on both sides—by rhetoric about LGBT rights. Conservatives forcefully presented their argument that homosexuality is a sin, while liberals decried what they perceived as efforts to undermine equality for all.[91]

Meanwhile, the AIDS epidemic brought increased visibility to the LGBT community because the disease initially affected gay men. AIDS served to polarize the two sides of the debate about homosexuality even further, with conservatives pointing to HIV as a concrete threat posed by gay men and liberals, arguing that the Reagan administration was complicit in the deaths of thousands of Americans due to its silence about the epidemic. Reagan was a conservative culture warrior who had very little to say about HIV/AIDS during his presidency.[92] At the end of his second term, he issued a proclamation of

"AIDS Awareness and Prevention Month" including a clear statement of his own views on the matter: "Both medicine and morality teach the same lesson about prevention of AIDS. . . . The best way to prevent AIDS is to abstain from sexual activity until adulthood and then to restrict sex to a monogamous, faithful relationship."[93] For their part, AIDS activists attracted negative attention when they disrupted a Sunday mass at St. Patrick's Cathedral in New York and an ordination ceremony at Holy Cross Cathedral in Boston, both of which were protests against the Catholic Church's own relative silence about the epidemic.[94]

The substantial challenges LGBT people faced during the first two decades of their movement for equality had the ironic effect of humanizing them before the American public. In the 1980s, relatively few Americans realized they knew anyone who was gay or lesbian because so many LGBT people remained closeted. However, media coverage of the AIDS crisis provided moving personal narratives of people mourning their lost friends and family members, many of whom were gay men. Actor Rock Hudson's public admission that he was dying of AIDS in 1985 was a turning point due to his celebrity—and because his sexual orientation had been a closely guarded secret. The AIDS Memorial Quilt project made the scope of the crisis clear for all to see as well, as grieving Americans added squares to the enormous quilt to commemorate their loved ones. And in the mid-1980s, liberal religious traditions—most notably Reform Judaism and the largely mainline Protestant National Council of Churches—began issuing statements advocating for more funding for research on HIV/AIDS and greater compassion for its victims, whether gay or straight.[95]

As the twentieth century drew to a close, public opinion about homosexuality already had taken a distinct turn in favor of LGBT people.[96] In 2002, 32 percent of Americans polled said "sexual relations between two adults of the same sex are not wrong at all" compared to just 11 percent in 1973.[97] In the same year, evangelical Protestants espoused much more negative attitudes than mainline Protestants and Catholics did about LGBT people. For example, 52 percent of evangelicals agreed with the statement "acceptance of homosexuality would be bad for the country," compared to 22 percent of mainline Protestants and 21 percent of Catholics.[98] Table 6.3 shows how attitudes changed over the course of another decade. Today, evangelical Protestants remain the most opposed to accepting LGBT people in American society, but between 2003 and 2015 even the percentage of evangelicals expressing tolerant attitudes toward LGBT people increased by 11 points. The growth in mainline Protestant acceptance is even more striking; over the same period, the percentage of mainline Protestants saying homosexuality should be accepted increased by 23 points.

With public opinion on their side, the LGBT rights movement turned a good deal of its attention to fighting for same-sex couples' right to marry. Their efforts gained initial success in some states, but they won an overwhelming victory in *Obergefell* v. *Hodges* (2015), the landmark US Supreme Court decision legalizing same-sex marriage across the land. Many organized religious

	2003	2013	2015
White Evangelical Protestant	22%	30%	33%
White Mainline Protestant	49%	68%	72%
Catholic	62%	61%	64%
Unaffiliated	–	83%	88%

TABLE 6.3 Homosexuality Should Be Accepted by Society

Source: Pew Research Center, "Support for Same-Sex Marriage at Record High, but Key Segments Remain Opposed," June 8, 2015.

traditions, including the Roman Catholic Church and nearly all evangelical and African-American Protestant denominations, formally oppose same-sex marriage. Nevertheless, public opinion moved swiftly toward support of same-sex marriage once Massachusetts became the first state to legalize it in 2003. Figure 6.1 illustrates a consistent upward trend in approval between 2005 and 2015, even among members of religious traditions opposed to same-sex marriage. We also see a yawning gap in approval between people who attend worship services regularly and who do not attend. In short, people who belong to theologically conservative churches and those who are most religiously committed are the most likely to oppose same-sex marriage, but this fact must be interpreted in the context of the steady across-the-board increase in American approval of same-sex marriage.[99]

The Obergefell decision dealt a significant blow to religious opponents of same-sex marriage. During the twelve-year interval between legalization in Massachusetts and national recognition, various religious groups exerted enormous effort to stop the spread of same-sex marriage across the country. By 2014, their efforts had contributed to the passage of constitutional amendments or laws specifically defining marriage as the union of one man and one woman in thirty-one states. An especially high-profile and contentious battle over whether to add a "defense of marriage" amendment to a state constitution happened in California in 2008. Religious actors led the way in the successful ballot initiative campaign for the amendment. The Roman Catholic Church and the LDS Church made headlines for the extensive nature of their lobbying and electioneering efforts—and for the powerful political coalition they formed by working together with evangelical Protestant groups.[100]

Since Obergefell, critics of same-sex marriage have changed their focus (out of necessity) from one of opposing the policy to finding ways of working around it. Religious individuals and groups have invoked their right to religious liberty in opting out of actions they feel would support same-sex marriage, even indirectly. In the weeks after Obergefell was handed down, a county clerk in

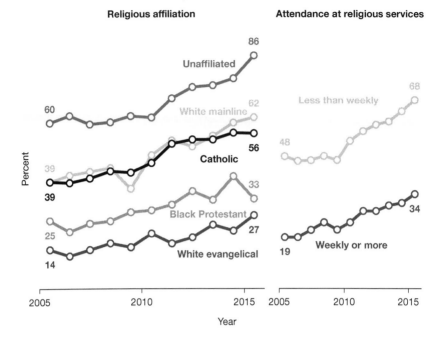

FIGURE 6.1 Approval of Legal Same-Sex Marriage

Note: Survey conducted May 12–18, 2015. Whites and blacks include only those who are not Hispanic.

Source: Pew Research Center, "Support for Same-Sex Marriage at Record High, but Key Segments Remain Opposed," June 8, 2015.

Kentucky named Kim Davis began turning away same-sex couples who came to her office to obtain marriage licenses. She defended herself using a religious-conscience argument, saying that because same-sex marriage contradicted her religious convictions, she should not be expected to sanction it by signing same-sex marriage licenses. After a lengthy legal battle, Davis went back to work and was no longer expected to sign marriage licenses.[101]

An additional battlefield in the conflict between legal same-sex marriage and religious-conscience rights is occupied by individuals who provide services at weddings, such as bakers, florists, and photographers, and oppose the Obergefell decision. In 2012, Jack Phillips, a baker in Lakewood, Colorado, refused to bake a wedding cake for a gay couple because of his religious beliefs about marriage. The men subsequently sued Phillips for discrimination. The US Supreme Court will decide their case, *Masterpiece Cakeshop* v. *Colorado Civil Rights Commission*, in 2018.[102] The Court previously had declined to hear a similar case involving two New Mexico photographers who denied their services to a lesbian couple on the same grounds Phillips invoked in his refusal to bake the cake, but it was only a matter of time before they decided these issues were ripe for adjudication.[103]

The sometimes uncomfortable relationship between organized religion and the LGBT community also involves confrontations regarding transgender people. Recently, high-profile transgender Americans including Caitlyn Jenner, Chaz Bono, and the controversial Chelsea Manning have raised awareness about transgender people and the fact that some choose to transition from one gender to the other. Concomitant debate has erupted about which public restrooms transgender people ought to use. In 2016, North Carolina passed a law requiring all individuals to use the bathroom corresponding to the gender recorded on their birth certificates. After enormous controversy and a boycott of the state by the National Collegiate Athletic Association, the law was repealed in 2017.[104]

However, debate about this issue is far from over. A recent poll revealed that 46 percent of Americans believe transgender people should be required to use the restroom of the gender into which they were born.[105] Other states such as Texas have made efforts to pass laws regulating bathroom use by transgender people.[106] Moreover, not long after taking office, Donald Trump rescinded protections put in place by the Obama administration designed to protect transgender students' right to use the bathroom of their choice in public schools.[107] He also announced in 2017 that transgender people would no longer be permitted to serve in the US Armed Forces. The frontlines of culture wars disputes about sexuality clearly have shifted in the wake of the Obergefell decision, as they almost certainly will again in the future.

LGBT AMERICANS WITHIN ORGANIZED RELIGION

Considering all the opposition LGBT people have encountered from organized religion in the United States, it is essential to consider whether and where they might find welcoming religious homes. Only recently have we had any systematic data about the religious convictions and commitments of LGBT people. The Pew Research Center found that four in ten LGBT people they surveyed were religiously unaffiliated, which is nearly twice the percentage we observe in the general population. LGBT people are also twice as likely to affiliate with a non-Christian religious tradition, and half as likely to be evangelical Protestants as members of the general population.[108]

It undoubtedly is the case that over centuries many closeted LGBT people have worshiped and prayed in every imaginable US religious context. Whether they are invited to participate in religious life while being open about their sexual orientation, however, is another matter.[109] A 2013 poll found that 29 percent of LGBT Americans have "been made to feel unwelcome at a place of worship."[110] The simple fact is that some US religious traditions formally and explicitly welcome LGBT people and others do not.

After Stonewall, mainline Protestant and Jewish denominations began wrestling with the question of how to reconcile traditional teachings about sexuality with a desire to avoid discriminating against LGBT people. One by one, each of these religious bodies worked out detailed policies regarding LGBT issues, though sometimes at great cost.[111] The numeric decline mainline Protestant denominations continue to face has been exacerbated by the exit of traditionalist members, and even some entire congregations, due to disagreement with denominational policies on LGBT issues. This fact has not diminished the mainline's desire to be a welcoming religious home for LGBT people.[112] Indeed, by 2015, most mainline Protestant denominations were allowing their clergy to officiate at same-sex weddings.[113]

Meanwhile, the Roman Catholic Church officially takes conservative positions regarding LGBT issues, but, as Table 6.3 shows, a majority of US laity are supportive of LGBT equality. Pope Francis has made history with his repeated insistence that the church should welcome gay people rather than judging them, but the degree to which his sentiments are put into action depends on the diocese, or even the parish, in question.[114] The relatively inclusive attitudes expressed both by Pope Francis and by US Catholics in the aggregate, however, bode well for the future inclusion of openly LGBT Catholic parishioners.

Most evangelical and African-American Protestant churches, though not all, have declined to adopt policies that welcome LGBT people.[115] The tide of recent elite opinion in conservative Protestant circles is exemplified by the 2017 "Nashville Statement." The Council on Biblical Manhood and Womanhood took the lead in drafting and disseminating this manifesto of renewed evangelical opposition to same-sex marriage. Among other tenets, the Nashville Statement holds:

> We affirm that it is sinful to approve of homosexual immorality or transgenderism and that such approval constitutes an essential departure from Christian faithfulness and witness. We deny that the approval of homosexual immorality or transgenderism is a matter of moral indifference about which otherwise faithful Christians should agree to disagree.[116]

Hundreds of evangelical leaders have signed the Nashville Statement, most prominently Tony Perkins of the Family Research Council, James Dobson of Focus on the Family, and Russell Moore of the Ethics and Religious Liberty Commission.

On the other hand, the Fellowship of Metropolitan Community Churches (MCC) is an evangelically oriented denomination directed specifically toward LGBT people. Founded in 1968, the global fellowship includes more than 200 congregations with thousands of members worldwide and a large headquarters in Los Angeles.[117] Its founder, Troy Perry, was a prominent leader in the fight for same-sex marriage, especially in California, illustrating how a small religious movement can sometimes make an impact by fostering group solidarity and joining alliances.[118] If the MCC ever wished to exert broader collective political clout, however, it would be hard pressed because of its modest numbers and uneven geographic presence.[119] Besides, the LGBT community in the United States is already well organized through secular organizations such as the Human Rights Campaign, the National LGBTQ Task Force, and GLAAD, all of which have divisions focusing on outreach to faith communities.

It is one thing to welcome LGBT members into a house of worship; it is quite another to ordain openly LGBT people as clergy. It should come as no surprise that relatively few religious traditions in the United States have gone this far in the direction of LGBT equality. As we note above, Unitarian Universalist Rev. James Stoll became the first openly gay clergyperson in US history in 1969. Three years later, Rev. Bill Johnson followed suit in the United Church of Christ (UCC), becoming the first openly gay American Christian pastor.[120] By the 1990s, out gay men and lesbians were welcomed as rabbis in most US Jewish traditions as well. However, mainline Protestant denominations (other than the UCC) did not quickly fall in line. It was not until 2009 that another mainline tradition, the Evangelical Lutheran Church in America, decided to allow the ordination of LGBT clergy. In 2012, the Episcopal Church and the Presbyterian Church (USA) joined the Lutherans and the UCC in allowing all LGBT people wishing to serve as clergy to be ordained. Although the United Methodist Church remains officially opposed to ordaining LGBT clergy, some do serve around the margins. However, the denomination has blocked the consecration of Rev. Karen Oliveto, who stood to become the first openly lesbian (or gay) United Methodist bishop.[121] The Methodists currently are fighting a battle much like the one that roiled Episcopalians in 2003, when Rev. V. Gene Robinson was elected as the first openly gay bishop in their church. It remains to be seen whether the United Methodist Church—one of the largest Protestant denominations in the United States—will move toward full inclusion of LGBT clergy in the years to come.

CONCLUSION

Despite many crosscurrents and plenty of diversity, women and LGBT people play important roles in American religion, and the importance of both groups is growing. There is no doubt that the relationship between religion and politics will continue to include women's voices. Indeed, women may emerge as the primary leaders of organized religion in the United States and around the world. One area to watch closely in the future is the prominence of women-led movements within American religion and reactions to the presence of such influences. Women will continue to challenge some of the theologies and practices of American religion, including questions of ordination, the proper role of religious hierarchies, and much more. Women will not just affect politics within religious circles, but they will also affect the stance and involvement of organized religion on issues of gender and family in American politics broadly construed.

It will also be important to keep an eye on continuing conflicts regarding abortion and LGBT equality in the United States. The role of conservative religious women in promoting and defending a traditionalist "pro-family agenda" may turn out to be as influential as the more progressive voices of feminist religious elites. Although a majority of female clergy are liberal, laywomen reflect a full range of political attitudes. It will also be fascinating to observe national political developments, including presidential campaigns, to see what connections they make—or attempt to make—with religious women. As the election of the first female US president inevitably draws nearer, it will be essential to analyze whether and how female candidates attempt to use religious appeals to win over women in the electorate. Will they proceed in ways that diverge from Hillary Clinton's relative religious reticence? Evangelical Protestant women were not impressed with Clinton; instead, they played a significant role in electing Donald Trump to the presidency just as they galvanized around Sarah Palin's vice-presidential candidacy in 2008. Just as there is no distinctive "women's vote" in general, the intersections between gender and politics in the voting booth will remain varied and dependent upon the individual priorities and social identities of each woman voter.

Likewise, as LGBT people gain greater acceptance in American society, we should expect to see more opportunities open for them in organized religious circles. Whether LGBT people will welcome the chance to deepen their participation in religious life, however, is another matter. Organized religion has not been kind to LGBT people. It is certainly possible that the LGBT community will continue to be overrepresented among the religiously unaffiliated even as more and more Americans across the board turn away from organized religion. The Supreme Court's decision in Obergefell, as well as the steady increase in social acceptance of LGBT people, bode well for their future equality. However, it is a near certainty that a minority of religious conservatives will continue to fight for their right to dissent on issues involving LGBT people. If even a plurality of the LGBT community continues to be religiously unaffiliated, their political clout should be expected to come primarily through secular networks and organizations rather than religious ones.

In short, it remains to be seen exactly how gender, sexual orientation, and gender identity will continue to intersect with religion in ways that are politically significant, but we can rest assured that studying these topics will be an important enterprise for decades to come.

DISCUSSION QUESTIONS

1 Women and men differ in their levels of religiosity and often play different roles in American religious life. What types of roles do women play, and how does this differ in various traditions?

2 Compare progressive and conservative approaches to the role of women in religious and public life. How do these approaches connect to broader religious traditions?

3 Some trends in feminist thought suggest that most traditional religion is irredeemably sexist. What are some alternatives for religious involvement for those who might subscribe to such thinking?

4 What are the resources for cooperation between the LGBT rights movement and religion in the United States? Where are the key points of conflict?

5 How has the state, and particularly the judiciary, shaped the tensions between religion and LGBT concerns?

FURTHER READING

Alvare, Helen M. (ed.), *Breaking Through: Catholic Women Speak for Themselves* (Huntington, IN: Our Sunday Visitor, 2012). Law professor Helen Alvare assembled this collection of personal accounts by traditionalist Catholic women who resist being typecast.

Chaves, Mark, *Ordaining Women: Culture and Conflict in Religious Organizations* (Cambridge, MA: Harvard University Press, 1997). An excellent study of conflict over women's ordination in religious groups.

Collier-Thomas, Bettye, *Jesus, Jobs, and Justice: African American Women and Religion* (New York, NY: Knopf, 2009). Masterful history of the many little-known roles women have played in black churches throughout US history.

Fetner, Tina, *How the Religious Right Shaped Lesbian and Gay Activism* (Minneapolis, MN: University of Minnesota Press, 2008). An in-depth look at one of the most significant battlefields in the culture wars.

Griffith, R. Marie, *God's Daughters: Evangelical Women and the Power of Submission* (Berkeley, CA: University of California Press, 1997). An examination of women and feminism within evangelical (particularly Pentecostal) Protestantism.

Nomani, Asra Q., *Standing Alone: An American Woman's Struggle for the Soul of Islam* (New York, NY: HarperOne, 2005). A journalist's lively account of her embrace of Islamic feminism.

Olson, Laura R., Sue E. S. Crawford, and Melissa M. Deckman, *Women with a Mission: Religion, Gender, and the Politics of Women Clergy*, Tuscaloosa, AL: University of Alabama Press, 2005. An analysis of the political orientations of women clergy.

Rayside, David, and Clyde Wilcox (eds.), *Faith, Politics, and Sexual Diversity in Canada and the United States* (Vancouver: University of British Columbia Press, 2012). An excellent collection of studies spanning the US and Canadian contexts.

NOTES

1. Pew Research Center, "US Religious Landscape Study," 2015, www.pewforum.org/religious-landscape-study/.

2. See, for example, Christian Smith, *Souls in Transition: The Religious and Spiritual Lives of Emerging Adults* (Oxford: Oxford University Press, 2009); Christian Smith and Melinda Lundquist Denton, *Soul Searching: The Religious and Spiritual Lives of American Teenagers* (Oxford: Oxford University Press, 2005); Robert Wuthnow, *After the Baby Boomers: How Twenty- and Thirty-Somethings Are Shaping the Future of American Religion* (Princeton, NJ: Princeton University Press, 2007).

3. Wade Clark Roof, *A Generation of Seekers: The Spiritual Journeys of the Baby Boom Generation* (San Francisco, CA: HarperSanFrancisco, 1993); Wade Clark Roof, *Spiritual Marketplace: Baby Boomers and the Remaking of American Religion* (Princeton, NJ: Princeton University Press, 1999).

4. Smith, *Souls in Transition*; Smith and Denton, *Soul Searching*; Wuthnow, *After the Baby Boomers*.

5. An excellent discussion of the historical gender divide in black churches is found in C. Eric Lincoln and Lawrence H. Mamiya, *The Black Church in the African American Experience* (Durham, NC: Duke University Press, 1990), chapter 10. See also Bettye Collier-Thomas, *Jesus, Jobs, and Justice: African American Women and Religion* (New York, NY: Knopf, 2009); Barbara Dianne Savage, *Your Spirits Walk Beside Us: The Politics of Black Religion* (Cambridge, MA: Harvard University Press, 2008).

6. Collier-Thomas, *Jesus, Jobs, and Justice*; Savage, *Your Spirits Walk Beside Us*.

7. John L. Allen, Jr., *The Future Church: How Ten Trends Are Revolutionizing the Catholic Church* (New York, NY: Random House, 2009), pp. 178–216.

8. M. B. Caschetta, "The Comeback of the American Nun," *New York Times*, September 24, 2015, http://nytlive.nytimes.com/womenintheworld/2015/09/24/nuns-why-theyre-suddenly-hot-again.

9. Joshua J. McElwee, "Pope Francis Confirms Finality of Ban on Ordaining Women Priests," *National Catholic Reporter*, November 1, 2016, www.ncronline.org/news/vatican/pope-francis-confirms-finality-ban-ordaining-women.

10. Lynn Davidman, *Tradition in a Rootless World: Women Turn to Orthodox Judaism* (Berkeley, CA: University of California Press, 1991).

11. Melissa R. Klapper, *Ballots, Babies, and Banners of Peace: American Jewish Women's Activism, 1890–1940* (New York, NY: New York University Press, 2013); Deborah L. Schultz, *Going South: Jewish Women in the Civil Rights Movement* (New York, NY: New York University Press, 2001).

12. Harry Bruinius, "To Protect Themselves, More American Muslim Women Give Up Hijab," *Christian Science Monitor*, December 20, 2016, www.csmonitor.com/USA/Politics/2016/1220/To-protect-themselves-more-American-Muslim-women-give-up-hijab.

13. Claire Gecewicz, "In Many Ways, Muslim Men and Women See Life in America Differently," Pew Research Center, August 7, 2017, www.pewresearch.org/fact-tank/2017/08/07/in-many-ways-muslim-men-and-women-see-life-in-america-differently.

14. Gecewicz, "In Many Ways."

15. Gecewicz, "In Many Ways."

16. Asma Uddin is director of strategy for the Center for Islam and Religious Freedom and editor of altMuslimah, or altM, www.altmuslimah.com/. Karamah: Muslim Women Lawyers for Human Rights, http://karamah.org/. See also, Asra Q. Nomani, *Standing*

Alone: An American Woman's Struggle for the Soul of Islam (New York, NY: HarperOne, 2005), p. ix.

17. John P. Bartkowski, *The Promise Keepers: Servants, Soldiers, and Godly Men* (New Brunswick, NJ: Rutgers University Press, 2004).

18. Rodney Stark, "Physiology and Faith: Addressing the 'Universal' Gender Difference in Religious Commitment," *Journal for the Scientific Study of Religion*, 41 (2002): 495–507. See also W. Bradford Wilcox, *Soft Patriarchs, New Men: How Christianity Shapes Fathers and Husbands* (Chicago, IL: University of Chicago Press, 2004).

19. Courtney Bender, *The New Metaphysicals: Spirituality and the American Religious Imagination* (Chicago, IL: University of Chicago Press, 2010).

20. Karen M. Kaufmann, "The Gender Gap," in Laura R. Olson and John C. Green (eds.), *Beyond Red State, Blue State: Electoral Gaps in the Twenty-First Century American Electorate* (Upper Saddle River, NJ: Prentice Hall, 2008), pp. 92–108.

21. Danielle Paquette, "The Unexpected Voters behind the Widest Gender Gap in Recorded Election History," *Washington Post*, November 9, 2016, www.washington post.com/news/wonk/wp/2016/11/09/men-handed-trump-the-election/.

22. Lonna Rae Atkeson and Ronald B. Rappoport, "The More Things Change, the More They Stay the Same: Examining Gender Differences in Political Attitude Expression, 1952–2000," *Public Opinion Quarterly*, 67 (2003): 495–521; Gregory M. Herek, "Gender Gaps in Public Opinion about Lesbians and Gay Men," *Public Opinion Quarterly*, 66 (2002): 40–66; Karen M. Kaufmann and John R. Petrocik, "The Changing Politics of American Men: Understanding the Sources of the Gender Gap," *American Journal of Political Science*, 43 (1999): 864–887.

23. Melissa Deckman, *Tea Party Women: Mama Grizzlies, Grassroots Leaders, and the Changing Face of the American Right* (New York, NY: New York University Press, 2016); Michelle Nickerson, *Mothers of Conservatism: Women and the Postwar Right* (Princeton, NJ: Princeton University Press, 2012); Catherine E. Rymph, *Republican Women: Feminism and Conservatives from Suffrage through the Rise of the New Right* (Chapel Hill, NC: University of North Carolina Press, 2008).

24. Kim Severson, "They Raise Children, Pray and Rally around a Running Mate," *New York Times*, September 5, 2008, www.nytimes.com/2008/09/05/us/politics/05women.html.

25. See D. Michael Lindsay, "Michele Bachmann Leads a New Form of Evangelical Feminism," *Washington Post*, June 20, 2011, www.washingtonpost.com/business/on-leadership/michele-bachmann-leads-a-new-form-of-evangelical-feminism/2011/06/20/AGztUGdH_story.html; Virginia McCarver, "The Rhetoric of Choice and 21st Century Feminism: Online Conversations about Work, Family, and Sarah Palin," *Women's Studies in Communications*, 34 (2011): 20–41; Lisa Miller, "Evangelical Women Rise as New 'Feminists,'" *Washington Post*, July 28, 2011, www.washingtonpost.com/national/religion/evangelical-women-rise-as-new-feminists/2011/07/27/gIQA EbuGfI_story.html?utm_term=.515feb016e68.

26. Marie Griffith, "The New Evangelical Feminism of Bachmann and Palin," *Huffington Post*, July 6, 2011, www.huffingtonpost.com/marie-griffith/evangelical-feminism_b_891579.html; McCarver, "The Rhetoric of Choice."

27. Deckman, *Tea Party Women*.

28. Theda Skocpol and Vanessa Williamson, *The Tea Party and the Remaking of Republican Conservatism* (Oxford: Oxford University Press, 2012), p. 44. See also Ronald P. Formisano, *The Tea Party: A Brief History* (Baltimore, MD: Johns Hopkins University Press, 2012); Clarence Y. H. Lo, "Astroturf versus Grass Roots: Scenes from Early Tea

Party Mobilization," in Lawrence Rosenthal and Christine Trost (eds.), *Steep: The Precipitous Rise of the Tea Party* (Berkeley, CA: University of California Press, 2012), pp. 98–129.

29. Concerned Women for America, https://concerned women.org.

30. Beverly LaHaye, *I Am a Woman by God's Design* (Old Tappan, NJ: Revell, 1980). For a general analysis of evangelical views on male headship and submissiveness, see Brenda E. Brasher, *Godly Women: Fundamentalism and Female Power* (New Brunswick, NJ: Rutgers University Press, 1998); R. Marie Griffith, *God's Daughters: Evangelical Women and the Power of Submission* (Berkeley, CA: University of California Press, 1997).

31. Concerned Women for America, https://concernedwomen.org/about/.

32. On Schlafly's STOP ERA movement, see Jane J. Mansbridge, *Why We Lost the ERA* (Chicago, IL: University of Chicago Press, 1986).

33. Eagle Forum, www.eagleforum.org/.

34. Stephen Bates, *Battleground: One Mother's Crusade, the Religious Right, and the Struggle for Control of Our Classrooms* (New York, NY: Poseidon Press, 1993); Melissa M. Deckman, *School Board Battles: The Christian Right in Local Politics* (Washington, DC: Georgetown University Press, 2004).

35. Laura R. Olson, Sue E. S. Crawford, and Melissa M. Deckman, *Women with a Mission: Religion, Gender, and the Politics of Women Clergy* (Tuscaloosa, AL: University of Alabama Press, 2005).

36. For a wider discussion of these issues, see Sally Gallagher, *Evangelical Identity and Gendered Family Life* (Piscataway, NJ: Rutgers University Press, 2003); Griffith, *God's Daughters*; Julie Ingersoll, *Evangelical Christian Women: War Stories in the Gender Battles* (New York, NY: New York University Press, 2003); James M. Penning and Corwin E. Smidt, *Evangelicalism: The Next Generation* (Grand Rapids, MI: Baker Books, 2002), p. 81.

37. Gallagher, *Evangelical Identity*; Ingersoll, *Evangelical Christian Women*, especially chapter 1; Christel Manning, *God Gave Us the Right: Conservative Catholic, Evangelical Protestant, and Orthodox Jewish Women Grapple with Feminism* (New Brunswick, NJ: Rutgers University Press, 1999).

38. Gallagher, *Evangelical Identity*; Manning, *God Gave Us the Right*.

39. Gallagher, *Evangelical Identity*; Molly Worthen, "Housewives of God," *New York Times Magazine*, November 14, 2010, pp. 52–57.

40. See Dorothy Day, *The Long Loneliness: The Autobiography of the Legendary Catholic Social Activist* (New York, NY: Harper & Row, 1952).

41. John Fialka, *Sisters: Catholic Nuns and the Making of America* (New York, NY: St. Martin's Press, 2003). See also Carol K. Coburn, *Spirited Lives: How Nuns Shaped Catholic Culture and American Life, 1836–1920* (Chapel Hill, NC: University of North Carolina Press, 1999).

42. Laurie Goodstein, "Nuns, Rebuked by Rome, Plan Road Trip to Spotlight Social Issues," *New York Times*, June 5, 2012; Mary Fainsod Katzenstein, *Faithful and Fearless: Moving Feminist Protest Inside the Church and Military* (Princeton, NJ: Princeton University Press, 1998); Leadership Conference of Women Religious, https://lcwr.org/social-justice.

43. NETWORK: A National Catholic Social Justice Lobby, https//networklobby.org.

44. Goodstein, "Nuns, Rebuked by Rome."

45. NETWORK, "Nuns on the Bus," 2016, https://networklobby.org/bus2016/events/.

46. Church Women United, www.churchwomen.org; R. Marie Griffith, "The Generous Side of Christian Faith: The Successes and Challenges of Mainline Women's Groups," in Robert Wuthnow and John H. Evans (eds.), *The Quiet Hand of God: Faith-Based Activism and the Public Role of Mainline Protestantism* (Berkeley, CA: University of California Press, 2002), pp. 80–107.

47. National Association of Colored Women's Clubs, "Who We Are," www.vmbcsc.org/who-we-are.

48. Collier Thomas, *Jesus, Jobs, and Justice*, chapter 5.

49. Collier-Thomas, *Jesus, Jobs, and Justice*; Aldon D. Morris, *The Origins of the Civil Rights Movement: Black Communities Organizing for Change* (New York, NY: Free Press, 1984); Savage, *Your Spirits Walk Beside Us*, chapter 4.

50. Collier-Thomas, *Jesus, Jobs, and Justice*; Cheryl Townsend Gilkes, *If It Wasn't for the Women . . . Black Women's Experience and Womanist Culture in Church and Community* (Maryknoll, NY: Orbis, 2001); Savage, *Your Spirits Walk Beside Us*.

51. Joyce Antler, "Activists and Organizers: Jewish Women and American Politics," in L. Sandy Maisel and Ira N. Forman (eds.), *Jews in American Politics* (Lanham, MD: Rowman & Littlefield, 2001), pp. 231–250.

52. National Council of Jewish Women, www.ncjw.org/about/.

53. Hadassah, www.hadassah.org/advocate/domestic-advocacy.html.

54. See Heather W. Reichgott, "What Is Feminist Theology?" Voices of Sophia, https://voicesofsophia.wordpress.com/what-is-feminist-theology/.

55. Laurie Goodstein, "Vatican Reprimands a Group of US Nuns and Plans Change," *New York Times*, April 18, 2012, www.nytimes.com/2012/04/19/us/vatican-reprimands-us-nuns-group.html.

56. Call to Action Nun Justice Project, http://nunjustice.org.

57. Goodstein, "Nuns, Rebuked by Rome"; see also see also Laurie Goodstein, "National Nuns' Group Dodges Showdown with Vatican, Seeking 'Dialogue,'" *New York Times*, August 11, 2012, www.nytimes.com/2012/08/11/us/national-nuns-group-seeks-dialogue-with-vatican.html.

58. Laurie Goodstein, "Vatican Ends Battle with US Catholic Nuns' Group," *New York Times*, April 16, 2015, www.nytimes.com/2015/04/17/us/catholic-church-ends-takeover-of-leadership-conference-of-women-religious.html.

59. Women-Church Convergence, www.women-churchconvergence.org; see also Rosemary Radford Ruether, *Women-Church: Theology and Practice of Feminist Liturgical Communities* (San Francisco, CA: Harper & Row, 1985).

60. The classic work here is Mary Daly, *Beyond God the Father: Toward a Philosophy of Women's Liberation* (Boston, MA: Beacon, 1973).

61. For example, see Elaine Pagels, *Adam, Eve, and the Serpent* (New York, NY: Random House, 1988). Also, reading Rosemary Radford Ruether, *Feminist Theologies: Legacy and Prospect* (Minneapolis, MN: Augsburg Fortress, 2007) provides a good way to get an idea of the diversity of feminist theology and of where one might want to go to pursue it.

62. Olson et al., *Women with a Mission*.

63. Andre P. Audette, Maryann Kwakwa, and Christopher L. Weaver, "Reconciling the God and Gender Gaps: The Influence of Women in Church Politics," *Politics, Groups, and Identities*, January 24, 2017, www.tandfonline.com/doi/full/10.1080/21565503.2016.1273121/.

64. Roof, *A Generation of Seekers*, pp. 222–223.

65. Elaine Howard Ecklund, "Catholic Women Negotiate Feminism: A Research Note," *Sociology of Religion*, 64 (2003): 515–524; Katzenstein, *Faithful and Fearless*; Jane Redmont, *Generous Lives: American Catholic Women Today* (New York, NY: William Morrow, 1992); Roof, *A Generation of Seekers*, pp. 231–232; Mary Jo Weaver, *New Catholic Women: A Contemporary Challenge to Traditional Religious Authority* (New York, NY: Harper & Row, 1995).

66. Cf. Allen, *The Future Church*; Leon J. Podles, *The Church Impotent: The Feminization of Christianity* (Dallas, TX: Spence, 1999); Kevin Sack, "Nuns, a 'Dying Breed,' Fade from Leadership Roles at Catholic Hospitals," *New York Times*, August 20, 2011, www.nytimes.com/2011/08/21/us/21nuns.html; Ruth A. Wallace, *They Call Her Pastor* (Albany, NY: SUNY Press, 1992).

67. On the increasing conservatism of American priests, see Ted G. Jelen, "Roman Catholic Priests," in Corwin E. Smidt (ed.), *Pulpit and Politics: American Politics at the Advent of the Millennium* (Waco, TX: Baylor University Press), pp. 235–246; Paul J. Levesque, "The Correlation between Political and Ecclesial Ideologies of Catholic Priests: A Research Note," *Sociology of Religion*, 66 (2005): 419–429; Gregory Allen Smith, *Politics in the Parish: The Political Influence of Catholic Priests* (Washington, DC: Georgetown University Press, 2008).

68. Kristin Luker, *Abortion and the Politics of Motherhood* (Berkeley, CA: University of California Press, 1984).

69. Helen Alvare (ed.), *Breaking Through: Catholic Women Speak for Themselves* (Huntington, IN: Our Sunday Visitor, 2012).

70. Elizabeth Adell Cook, Ted. G. Jelen, and Clyde Wilcox, *Between Two Absolutes: Public Opinion and the Politics of Abortion* (Boulder, CO: Westview Press, 1992), chapter 7.

71. Faye D. Ginsburg, *Contested Lives: The Abortion Debate in an American Community* (Berkeley, CA: University of California Press, 1989).

72. Karen M. Kaufmann, "The Partisan Paradox: Religious Commitment and the Gender Gap in Party Identification," *Public Opinion Quarterly*, 68 (4): 491–511; Melissa Deckman, "A Gender Gap among Evangelicals? An Examination of Vote Choice by Gender and Religion in the 2008 Presidential Elections," *Journal of Women, Politics, and Policy*, 35 (3): 199–221.

73. Sarah Pulliam Bailey, "The Deep Disgust for Hillary Clinton That Drives So Many Evangelicals to Support Trump," *Washington Post*, October 9, 2016, www.washingtonpost.com/news/acts-of-faith/wp/2016/10/09/the-deep-disgust-for-hillary-clinton-that-drives-so-many-evangelicals-to-support-trump/.

74. Victoria McGrane, "Religion Is Constant Part of Elizabeth Warren's Life," *Boston Globe*, September 6, 2017, www.bostonglobe.com/news/nation/2017/09/02/religion-constant-part-warren-life/ndGztmfK5veAGMI6A4OKEI/story.html.

75. Mark Chaves, *Ordaining Women: Culture and Conflict in Religious Organizations* (Cambridge, MA: Harvard University Press, 1999).

76. The figure was 17.6 percent in 2016. See United States Department of Labor, Bureau of Labor Statistics, "Employed Persons by Detailed Occupation, Sex, Race, and Hispanic or Latino Ethnicity" (2016), www.bls.gov/cps/cpsaat11.htm.

77. David Masci, "The Divide over Ordaining Women," Pew Research Center, September 9, 2014, www.pewresearch.org/fact-tank/2014/09/09/the-divide-over-ordaining-women/.

78. National Congregations Study, www.soc.duke.edu/natcong/ (2017); Aleksandra Sandstrom, "Women Relatively Rare in Top Positions of Religious Leadership," Pew

Research Center, March 2, 2016, www.pewresearch.org/fact-tank/2016/03/02/women-relatively-rare-in-top-positions-of-religious-leadership/.

79. National Congregations Study.

80. Allen, *The Future Church*.

81. Charles E. Zech, Mary L. Gautier, Mark M. Gray, Jonathon L. Wiggins, and Thomas P. Gaunt, *Catholic Parishes of the 21st Century* (Oxford: Oxford University Press, 2017).

82. Bender, *The New Metaphysicals*; Helen A. Berger, *A Community of Witches: Contemporary Neo-Paganism and Witchcraft in the United States* (Columbia, SC: University of South Carolina Press, 2013); Sarah Pike, *New Age and Neopagan Religions in America* (New York, NY: Columbia University Press, 2004), chapter 6.

83. The *Declaration of Sentiments and Resolutions* was a bold assertion of women's equality modeled on the Declaration of Independence: https://sourcebooks.fordham.edu/mod/senecafalls.asp.

84. Frances E. Willard, *Woman in the Pulpit* (Chicago, IL: Woman's Christian Temperance Publication Association, 1889).

85. James Davison Hunter and Kimon Howland Sargeant, "Religion and the Transformation of Public Culture," *Social Research*, 60 (1993): 545–570. See also Olson et al., *Women with a Mission*.

86. Olson et al., *Women with a Mission*.

87. See Susan K. Williams Smith, *Crazy Faith: Ordinary People, Extraordinary Lives* (Valley Forge, PA: Judson Press, 2009).

88. James W. Button, Barbara A. Rienzo, and Kenneth D. Wald, *Private Lives, Public Conflicts: Battles over Gay Rights in American Communities* (Washington, DC: CQ Press, 1997); Keith Hartman, *Congregations in Conflict: The Battle over Homosexuality* (New Brunswick, NJ: Rutgers University Press, 1996); Dawne Moon, *God, Sex, and Politics: Homosexuality and Everyday Theologies* (Chicago, IL: University of Chicago Press, 2004); Andrew L. Whitehead, "Religious Organizations and Homosexuality: The Acceptance of Gays and Lesbians in American Congregations," *Review of Religious Research*, 55 (2): 297–317.

89. Mark Oppenheimer, "Haunted Man of the Cloth and Pioneer of Gay Rights," *New York Times*, September 18, 2010, www.nytimes.com/2010/09/18/us/18beliefs.html.

90. Tina Fetner, *How the Religious Right Shaped Lesbian and Gay Activism* (Minneapolis, MN: University of Minnesota Press, 2008).

91. Fetner, *How the Religious Right*.

92. Fetner, *How the Religious Right*; Randy Shilts, *And the Band Played On: Politics, People, and the AIDS Epidemic* (New York, NY: St. Martin's, 1987).

93. Ronald Reagan, *Proclamation 5709: AIDS Awareness and Prevention Month*, September 29, 1987, www.presidency.ucsb.edu/ws/index.php?pid=33469; Shilts, *And the Band Played On*.

94. Albert R. Jonsen and Jeff Stryker (eds.), *National Research Council Panel on Monitoring the Social Impact of the AIDS Epidemic* (Washington, DC: National Academies Press, 1993); Fetner, *How the Religious Right*.

95. Fetner, *How the Religious Right*.

96. Jeni Loftus, "America's Liberalization in Attitudes toward Homosexuality, 1973 to 1998," *American Sociological Review*, 66 (5) (2001): 762–782.

97. Pew Research Center, "Religious Beliefs Underpin Opposition to Homosexuality," November 18, 2003, http://assets.pewresearch.org/wp-content/uploads/sites/11/2003/11/religion-homosexuality.pdf.

98. Pew Research Center, "Religious Beliefs."

99. Whitehead, "Religious Organizations and Homosexuality."

100. Matthai Kuruvila, "Catholics, Mormons Allied to Pass Prop. 8," November 10, 2008, www.sfgate.com/news/article/Catholics-Mormons-allied-to-pass-Prop-8–3185965. php; Jesse McKinley and Kirk Johnson, "Mormons Tipped Scale in Ban on Gay Marriage," *New York Times*, November 14, 2008, www.nytimes.com/2008/11/15/us/politics/15marriage.html.

101. Alan Blinder and Tamar Lewin, "Clerk in Kentucky Chooses Jail over Deal on Same-Sex Marriage," *New York Times*, September 3, 2015, www.nytimes.com/2015/09/04/us/kim-davis-same-sex-marriage.html.

102. Adam Liptak, "Cake Is His 'Art,' So Can He Deny One to a Gay Couple?" September 16, 2017, www.nytimes.com/2017/09/16/us/supreme-court-baker-same-sex-marriage.html.

103. Robert Barnes, "Supreme Court Declines Case of Photographer Who Denied Service to Gay Couple," *Washington Post*, April 7, 2014, www.washingtonpost.com/politics/supreme-court-wont-review-new-mexico-gay-commitment-ceremony-photo-case/2014/04/07/f9246cb2-bc3a-11e3–9a05-c739f29ccb08_story.html.

104. Mark Berman and Amber Phillips, "North Carolina Governor Signs Bill Repealing and Replacing Transgender Bathroom Law amid Criticism," *Washington Post*, March 30, 2017, www.washingtonpost.com/news/post-nation/wp/2017/03/30/north-carolina-lawmakers-say-theyve-agreed-on-a-deal-to-repeal-the-bathroom-bill/.

105. Pew Research Center, "Where the Public Stands on Religious Liberty vs. Nondiscrimination," September 28, 2016, www.pewforum.org/2016/09/28/where-the-public-stands-on-religious-liberty-vs-nondiscrimination/.

106. Sandhya Somashekhar, "Transgender 'Bathroom Bill' Fails Again in Texas as Special Session Ends," *Washington Post*, August 16, 2017, www.washingtonpost.com/news/post-nation/wp/2017/08/16/transgender-bathroom-bill-fails-again-in-texas-as-special-session-ends/.

107. Jeremy W. Peters, Jo Becker, and Julie Hirschfeld Davis, "Trump Rescinds Rules on Bathrooms for Transgender Students," *New York Times*, February 22, 2017, www.nytimes.com/2017/02/22/us/politics/devos-sessions-transgender-students-rights.html.

108. Caryle Murphy, "Lesbian, Gay, and Bisexual Americans Differ from General Public in Their Religious Affiliations," May 26, 2015, www.pewresearch.org/fact-tank/2015/05/26/lesbian-gay-and-bisexual-americans-differ-from-general-public-in-their-religious-affiliations/.

109. Laura R. Olson, Wendy Cadge, and James T. Harrison, "Religion and Public Opinion about Same-Sex Marriage," *Social Science Quarterly*, 87 (2) (2006): 340–360; Whitehead, "Religious Organizations and Homosexuality"; Melissa M. Wilcox, "When Sheila's a Lesbian: Religious Individualism among Lesbian, Gay, Bisexual, and Transgender Christians," *Sociology of Religion*, 63 (4) (2002): 497–513.

110. Pew Research Center, "A Survey of LGBT Americans," June 13, 2013, www.pewsocialtrends.org/2013/06/13/a-survey-of-lgbt-americans/.

111. Wendy Cadge, "Vital Conflicts: The Mainline Protestant Denominations Debate Homosexuality," in Robert Wuthnow and John H. Evans (eds.), *The Quiet Hand of God: Faith-Based Activism and the Public Role of Mainline Protestantism* (Berkeley, CA: University of California Press), pp. 265–286.

112. Wendy Cadge, Laura R. Olson, and Christopher Wildeman, "How Denominational Resources Influence Debate about Homosexuality in Mainline Protestant

Congregations," *Sociology of Religion*, 69 (2) (2008): 187–207; Laura R. Olson and Wendy Cadge, "Talking about Homosexuality: The Views of Mainline Protestant Clergy," *Journal for the Social Scientific Study of Religion*, 41 (1): 153–167.

113. David Masci and Michael Lipka, "Where Christian Churches, Other Religions Stand on Gay Marriage," December 21, 2015, www.pewresearch.org/fact-tank/2015/12/21/where-christian-churches-stand-on-gay-marriage/.

114. Joshua J. McElwee, "Francis Explains 'Who Am I to Judge?'" *National Catholic Reporter*, January 10, 2016, www.ncronline.org/news/vatican/francis-explains-who-am-i-judge.

115. Darren E. Sherkat, Kylan Mattias De Vries, and Stacia Creek, "Race, Religion, and Opposition to Same-Sex Marriage," *Social Science Quarterly*, 91 (1) (2010): 80–98.

116. Council on Biblical Manhood and Womanhood, "The Nashville Statement," 2017, https://cbmw.org/nashville-statement.

117. "Metropolitan Community Churches: Fact Sheet," 2013, http://mcchurch.org/overview/press/.

118. John Dart, "The Pastor Behind the Gay Marriage Ruling: Troy Perry," *The Christian Century*, June 17, 2008, www.christiancentury.org/article/2008-06/pastor-behind-gay-marriage-ruling.

119. Melinda D. Kane, "LGBT Religious Activism: Predicting State Variations in the Number of Metropolitan Community Churches, 1974–2000," *Sociological Forum*, 28 (1): 135–138.

120. Cadge, "Vital Conflicts."

121. Laurie Goodstein, "Methodist High Court Rejects First Openly Gay Bishop's Consecration," *New York Times*, April 28, 2017, www.nytimes.com/2017/04/28/us/methodist-high-court-rejects-first-gay-bishops-consecration.html.

7

VOTING AND RELIGION IN
AMERICAN POLITICS

Throughout American history, religious currents have flowed powerfully, defining partisan attachments and influencing how citizens vote. In this chapter, we chart the voting patterns of key American religious traditions and offer evidence for religion-based cleavages in the American electorate. We also explore the opposite direction of influence, that is, how parties and election campaigns attempt to shape the preferences of religious voters and mobilize their support.

A HISTORICAL REVIEW

Religion has played an important role in national elections since the founding of the United States. In the first contested presidential campaign (in 1800), Thomas Jefferson's Democratic-Republican Party challenged the Federalists, who were led by incumbent president John Adams. Adherents of the era's established religions, especially Episcopalians and Congregationalists, aligned closely with the status-quo Federalists, whereas Jefferson gained support from the religious innovators of the day, such as Baptists, Methodists, and Presbyterians. The class profiles of these churches explain part of this alignment: Members of higher-status churches often supported the Federalists; populist upstarts backed Jefferson.[1]

The debate about state establishment of religion was also related to social class. Even though the Constitution prohibited a national religion, several states retained legally established churches. Federalists generally backed this sort of religious establishment, but the Jeffersonians did not. Religious minorities thus aligned with Jefferson despite the fact that he was not a particularly religious person. During the 1800 campaign, in fact, the Federalists mounted attacks accusing Jefferson of rejecting the Christian faith. But Jefferson's personal beliefs were less important to his supporters than the fact that he was committed to protecting religious minorities and ending government preferences for one faith over others at all governmental levels. Thus, Baptists, with their commitment to the separation of church and state, flocked to Jefferson.[2]

The Nineteenth Century

Emigration of Catholics from Europe, which increased significantly in the 1830s and continued until 1920, resulted in a softening of earlier cleavages between Protestant denominations, which were replaced with something far more durable: a Catholic–Protestant cultural political divide. This division profoundly shaped political and voting patterns for more than a century. While Catholics quickly became heavily Democratic, northern Protestants gravitated toward their opponents: first the Whigs, then the Republicans. This alignment also shaped partisan positions on important issues. State aid to Catholic parochial schools, a perennial issue in American politics, found its strongest resistance among Republicans, who took many of their cues from Protestant activists. Moreover, the Republican Party's platforms of the late nineteenth and early twentieth centuries contained "strict separationist" planks designed to block Catholics from growing in social influence.[3]

The Catholic–Protestant split was not the only way in which religion played itself out in nineteenth-century elections and politics. Careful historical studies suggest that those Protestants least prone to evangelical pietism often joined Catholics in voting Democratic in the nineteenth and early twentieth centuries. Thus, one way to understand the division of the electorate was that it pitted pietists against others, who sometimes were termed "ritualists."[4] The pietist–ritualist political division, which also was tied to ethnic differences, drew deep and enduring lines on the American political map. The pietists included evangelical Methodists, Baptists, Congregationalists, Presbyterians, and less ritualistic Lutherans. These groups were overwhelmingly Republican in nearly every region, from California to Rhode Island. The ritualists included Roman Catholics as well as many German (but not Scandinavian) Lutherans; both of those groups voted Democratic.

What distinguished pietists from ritualists was their incompatible visions of the "good life" and the role government ought to play in it. As heirs to the Puritan evangelical spirit, pietists stressed religion's connection with morality. They saw themselves as moral reformers, and they favored active government involvement through laws and policies designed to accomplish their moral ends. Whether the perceived evil was alcoholism, gambling, dueling, or the breaking of the Sabbath, pietists were comfortable bringing their desire to reform society into the public realm, just as modern-day religious moralists favor government regulation of abortion, gambling, pornography, and violence in entertainment media and video games.[5] Ritualists, on the other hand, emphasized church liturgies and sacraments, as opposed to moral crusades, in their conception of religion. Compared with pietists, they were less likely to support government regulation of morals. This religious and cultural divide between pietists and ritualists was powerful enough to transcend class and immigrant status. In the North, Catholics were usually Democrats and Methodists were Republicans regardless of their socioeconomic status.[6] Today, as we will see, perceived threats from advancing secularism increasingly unite the heirs of these former adversaries.

In the South, of course, the politics of race and regional pride often co-opted or supplanted religion as a political force. During post-Civil War Reconstruction (1865–1877), Southern whites saw the Republican Party literally as a conquering army of occupation, so they voted Democratic. African Americans voted overwhelmingly for Republicans, but when Southern whites seized control of politics in the South, where most African Americans resided, they disenfranchised African Americans and made the South solidly Democratic. Thus, despite the fact that the white Southern population was heavily Baptist and Methodist, these pietists voted Democratic—unlike their Northern counterparts.[7]

The Twentieth Century

The economic upheavals of the Great Depression in the 1930s produced a partisan realignment of voters and created a relatively stable majority for a new Democratic coalition. Roosevelt's New Deal coalition rested on three interrelated factors: region, class, and religion.[8] A fourth dimension, race, was not a central factor during Roosevelt's time—the black electorate was small because of the systematic disenfranchisement of Southern black voters under Jim Crow policies. Only later did African Americans, securely enfranchised by the Voting Rights Act of 1965, come to represent a major voting bloc. Starting in the 1930s, black voters increasingly supported the Democratic Party and its candidates.[9]

President Roosevelt received his highest vote margins in the solidly Democratic white South. The Civil War legacy and the Democratic Party's total domination of Southern politics played key roles here. But so did Roosevelt's activist policies regarding the economy; his initiatives to overcome the Great Depression were popular among many white Southerners, the majority of whom were poor evangelical Protestants who had been hit especially hard by the Depression. The kind of moral cleavages we see in today's American politics were largely absent from national partisan politics in the 1930s and thus presented few cross-pressures for Southern Democrats.[10] In the rest of the United States as well, class cleavages were vital to President Roosevelt's electoral fortunes (as well as successor presidents Truman and Kennedy). He was popular among many urban poor and working-class voters, labor-union members, and others of modest means. His support among some Northern pietists (both traditional evangelicals and Pentecostals) flowed from the fact that many of them were far less affluent than their mainline Protestant counterparts.

This same kind of appeal brought Northern black voters into the New Deal coalition despite their previously long-standing loyalty to the party of Lincoln.

Despite the political significance of social class in the early twentieth century, various religious groups also formed quite cohesive elements of the New Deal coalition. Catholics at every socioeconomic level were far more likely to identify themselves as Democrats and vote that way than were similarly situated Protestants. Indeed, Catholics constituted one of the central New Deal constituencies.[11] Jewish voters were also solidly aligned with the Democrats under Roosevelt. In earlier years, many Jews had been Republicans because they viewed the GOP as the more liberal party. The Depression and Roosevelt led Jews to gravitate heavily to the Democratic Party, where most have stayed ever since.[12]

Who, then, opposed Roosevelt? Northern white Protestants (especially those from mainline denominations), wealthier individuals, and traditional Yankee Republicans formed the core of his opposition. Many modest-income Protestants in the North remained loyal to the GOP, especially in more traditional rural areas. The problem for the Republicans, of course, was that this base was too narrow to overturn the Democratic Party's hegemony. Republican war hero Dwight Eisenhower interrupted the Democrats' dominance at the presidential level in the 1950s, but Roosevelt's coalition enabled the Democrats to remain the majority party nationally through the late 1960s.[13]

The point here is that religion combined with socioeconomic status and region to shape voting patterns and political outcomes in the Roosevelt years and for several decades after his death. However, beginning in the 1960s, divisive new cultural issues began to fracture the New Deal coalition, producing political alignments that have elevated religion's political significance. Scholars attribute these phenomena to the nature of postindustrial society.[14] Value differences and disputes over moral issues began to join traditional class-based and ethnic differences to structure voting patterns. In addition, since the mid-1960s, the immigration of Hispanics, Asians, Muslims, and others has added new ethnoreligious communities to the tapestry of American life. Religious currents intersect these value-based concerns and ethnoreligious identities in complex ways. This process has a powerful and sustained effect on American citizens' political attitudes and behaviors.

The Contemporary Era

To comprehend the role of religion in recent elections, we must note both voting patterns and turnout. Over the long term, we must also consider demographic changes. With respect to turnout, just over 60 percent of eligible citizens in the United States vote in a given presidential election.[15] Diverse religious groups have different rates of voting participation, however, which shapes their electoral clout. High voting rates among Jews and Mormons increase their relative share of the electorate, whereas lower turnout among Hispanics (whether Catholic or Protestant) reduces their share. We also know that people active in social groups, such as religious congregations, vote at higher rates than unattached people. Thus, it is not surprising that while the nonreligious portion of the adult population has grown to nearly 23 percent, their share of the electorate in 2016 was much smaller (though still significant) at 15 percent.

Specific circumstances or candidates from election to election can also affect turnout and thus the makeup of the electorate. For example, Barack Obama's unprecedented candidacy in 2008 and his reelection in 2012 dramatically expanded the black electorate.[16] However, with Hillary Clinton at the top of the ticket in 2016, African-American voting participation fell while white turnout increased, in part owing to Donald Trump's mobilization of working-class white voters.[17] This switch in turnout was decisive in a number of the swing states that Trump won in 2016.[18]

Beyond such short-term electoral factors, long-term demographic trends will be fateful for religious alignments and electoral fortunes. And what we know is that the electorate will become more religiously and ethnically diverse. While the makeup of the electorate lags behind demographic changes (recent immigrants and the undocumented do not vote, but their children will), certain trends reflect fertility and immigration patterns. The Census Bureau reported that minority births outnumbered whites in 2013 and continued to grow in the following years, which means that the population will become increasingly diverse in terms of race and ethnicity. Indeed, before the middle of this century, whites will no longer be the majority in America.[19] Thus, over time, we expect to see a rise in non-Christian voters, such as Buddhists, Muslims, Hindus, and Sikhs. But the Christian population will also become more diverse, with growing numbers of Latinos, Asians, Filipinos, Africans, Chaldeans, etc. The other trend is the anticipated rise of the nonreligious electorate, as older, more religious cohorts die out and are replaced by less religious generations. Both of these broad trends favor the Democrats, as we will see in looking at the partisan affiliation and voting patterns of different groups.

To help us dive into the data on recent elections, we start with two snapshots: Table 7.1, which features a few broad categories of the religious electorate from 2008 to 2016; and Table 7.2, which provides a more detailed breakdown for 2012. As we observe in Box 7.1, readers should not dwell on precise figures (which are subject to sampling error) but strive to grasp the broader patterns and trends.[20] Keeping in mind the relative sizes of different religious groups will help underscore the significance of voting patterns, both for the outcomes of elections and for the makeup of party coalitions.

The basic structure of faith-based voting is durable, even if the shares of groups change over time. Certain religious groups, for example, strongly affiliate with one political party or another. Others are not as uniformly partisan but nevertheless cast their votes in regular patterns (with some variation from

BROAD RELIGIOUS TRADITION	2008	2012	2016	NET CHANGE 2012–2016
Protestant/other Christian	54%	53%	52%	−1%
Catholic	27%	25%	23%	−2%
Jewish	2%	2%	3%	+1%
Other faiths	6%	7%	8%	+1%
Religiously unaffiliated	12%	12%	15%	+3%
White, born-again/evangelical Christian	26%	26%	26%	–

TABLE 7.1 **Religious Makeup of the Electorate**

Source: Pew Research Center, "How the Faithful Voted: A Preliminary 2016 Analysis."

RELIGIOUS TRADITION	% OF VOTING AGE POPULATION	% OF VOTING ELECTORATE
Evangelical Protestants*	23.6%	24.9%
Mainline Protestants*	15.1%	17.5%
Hispanic Protestants	4.1%	2.9%
African-American Protestants	10.0%	10.5%
Hispanic Catholics	6.5%	5.2%
Non-Hispanic Catholics	17.3%	18.3%
Jews	1.1%	1.6%
Mormons	1.3%	2.0%
Other faiths	2.1%	1.4%
Unaffiliated	16.7%	14.3%

TABLE 7.2 **Percentage of Voting Age Population and Electorate by Religious Tradition, 2012**

Source: 2012 National Survey of Religion and Politics, conducted at the University of Akron.

Note: Evangelical Protestant and Mainline Protestant categories include whites and small numbers of minorities other than African Americans or Hispanics for all tables and figures unless otherwise indicated.

BOX 7.1 THE CHALLENGE OF ASSESSING
THE RELIGIOUS VOTE

Given the growing complexity of the religious electorate, it is no surprise that assessing the religious vote is a challenge. No survey is perfect (all have limitations), and a growing problem is that some potential respondents are refusing to participate. Among the largest and most useful surveys are exit polls conducted by news organizations on the day of the election. Their large sample size allows us to capture smaller voting groups more accurately, plus they survey actual voters leaving polling places. However, such polls cannot ask many questions, and news organizations are notorious for not always asking the same religion questions from election to election. Exit polls also suffer from bias since the younger population is more likely to complete them than the older population, and some states are also omitted each year from these polls.

The largest scholarly survey is the Cooperative Congressional Elective Study (CCES), which matches samples to US Census data. But the CCES overrepresents the unaffiliated electorate, probably because it focuses heavily on swing states. Another sophisticated but smaller survey is the American National Election Study, but because it excludes counties of less than 50,000 in population, it underrepresents conservative Christian voters.

A final problem with most general surveys is that they underrepresent Hispanics to varying degrees, which is especially problematic for measuring the Hispanic Protestant vote. For all of these reasons, we use multiple sources in this chapter. The important thing is to grasp general patterns and not dwell on precise statistical summaries. One final note: We realize that speaking of "whites" in religious breakdowns is reductionist and subsumes older ethnic identities (Irish, German, Italian, Polish, Scandinavian, etc.), and we know that a growing number of American families represent a blend of racial and ethnic backgrounds. But race remains a powerful factor in voting, and drawing this simpler distinction gives us the best purchase on religious voting with the least complication.

election to election). As Table 7.3 shows, white evangelicals are strongly Republican in their party identification, but large majorities of African-American Protestants, Jews, and Hispanic Catholics identify as Democrats. Other groups fall somewhere between. Smaller religious groups, such as Mormons, are even more Republican than white evangelicals, whereas Muslims, Buddhists, and Hindus are quite strongly Democratic. Although party identification is not a

RELIGIOUS TRADITION	REPUBLICAN/ LEAN REPUBLICAN	NO LEAN	DEMOCRAT/ LEAN DEMOCRAT
Evangelical Protestant	56%	16%	28%
Hispanic Evangelical	31%	28%	41%
Mainline Protestant	44%	16%	40%
Historically Black Protestant	10%	10%	80%
Catholic	37%	19%	44%
Hispanic Catholic	21%	28%	51%
Mormon	70%	11%	19%
Orthodox Christian	34%	22%	44%
Jehovah's Witness	7%	75%	18%
Jewish	26%	9%	64%
Muslim	17%	21%	62%
Buddhist	16%	16%	69%
Hindu	13%	26%	61%
Unaffiliated	23%	22%	54%

TABLE 7.3 **Party Affiliation by Religious Tradition**

Source: **Pew Research Center "US Religious Landscape Study."**

perfect predictor of vote choice in a given election, it is one of the strongest indicators.[21]

The outcome of a given election, however, can hinge on the context of the time and the salience of particular issues. With the economic meltdown of 2008, for example, cultural issues took a back seat to economic concerns, and Barack Obama was able to gain greater vote shares of white Catholics and evangelicals than normal for a Democrat. In 2016, on the other hand, support by those groups surged for Republican Donald Trump, who spoke to economic and cultural anxiety that simultaneously appealed to working-class whites and moral traditionalists.[22]

As this brief overview suggests, religious influence on voting is more complex than it ever was in the past. It manifests itself in three different ways:

1 Religious affiliation, or the religious tradition to which people belong, has a direct effect on vote choice. Because of the political significance of different theological traditions, it matters politically whether people are evangelicals, mainline Protestants, Catholics, Mormons, Jews, or Muslims.

2 Ethnoreligious identity, in which racial or ethnic ties blend with religion
   to create distinct political groups, also matters. Out of their collective
   experience, for example, African-American Protestants and Latino
   Catholics have developed cultural and political identities that are
   distinct from their white counterparts. We also see a similar
   phenomenon (across US history) for new immigrant groups.
3 Religious salience, in which the intensity of religious practice creates
   subgroups within religious traditions, significantly affects religious
   voting. Religious salience typically is measured by frequency of worship
   attendance, and Republican voting routinely goes up with church
   attendance rates.[23] But we also see interesting variations. In 2016, for
   example, Donald Trump did better among self-identified mainline
   Protestants who seldom or never attend church than he did among
   frequent attenders.

We can begin to see how these factors operate by looking at Table 7.4 (from
the exit polls) and Table 7.5 (from the CCES). As Republican nominees, both
Romney in 2012 and Trump in 2016 gained the overwhelming majority of the
white evangelical vote, as well as strong majorities of white Catholics and other
Christians. The Democratic nominees, Obama in 2012 and Clinton in 2016,
gained the votes of non-Christians, the unaffiliated, and ethno-religious
minorities. But we also see intriguing variations. Republicans do better among
Latino evangelicals than Latino Catholics. Trump did much worse than Romney
among Mormons, a traditionally heavily Republican constituency.

To better understand how various religious factors operate in today's
American electoral politics, we now analyze in more detail the voting behavior
of each of the major American religious groups, noting evolution over time as
well as short-term shifts from one election to another. The reader may find
it useful to refer back to Table 7.4 and Table 7.5, which provide different
breakdowns of the 2016 religious vote and changes from previous elections.

ROMAN CATHOLICS: A DEMOGRAPHIC
TRANSFORMATION

Roman Catholics vividly illustrate how religious, demographic, and sociological
changes interact and affect American elections. The transformation of the
Catholic electorate is an important part of the story of recent American politics.
It illustrates the dynamic nature of religious life and the different ways in which
religion operates to shape voting behavior. To understand this transformation,
we begin in 1960, the election in which the old Catholic–Protestant cleavage
began to give way to different—and more complex—voting patterns.

From the middle of the nineteenth century through the 1960s, Democrats
could count on the votes of a large majority of Catholics. Indeed, Catholics,
comprising about a quarter of the electorate, provided more than a third of the

RELIGIOUS GROUP	2008		2012		2016		DEMOCRAT CHANGE 2012–2016
	OBAMA	MCCAIN	OBAMA	ROMNEY	CLINTON	TRUMP	
Protestant/other Christian	45%	54%	42%	57%	39%	58%	–3%
Catholic	54%	45%	50%	48%	45%	52%	–5%
White Catholic	47%	52%	40%	59%	37%	60%	–3%
Hispanic Catholic	72%	26%	75%	21%	67%	26%	–8%
Jewish	78%	21%	69%	30%	71%	24%	+2%
Other faiths	73%	22%	74%	23%	62%	29%	–12%
Religiously unaffiliated	75%	23%	70%	26%	68%	26%	–2%
White, born-again/evangelical Christian	24%	74%	21%	78%	16%	81%	–5%
Mormon	n/a	n/a	21%	78%	25%	61%	+4%

TABLE 7.4 Presidential Vote by Religious Affiliation and Race

Source: Pew Research Center, "How the Faithful Voted: A Preliminary 2016 Analysis."

	2012			2016			DIFFERENCE FROM 2012	
RELIGION	ROMNEY	OBAMA	OTHER	TRUMP	CLINTON	OTHER	REPUBLICAN	DEMOCRAT
White Evangelical	75%	23%	2%	78%	16%	5%	+3%	−7%
White Mainline Protestant	51%	47%	2%	55%	40%	5%	+4%	−7%
Black Protestant	4%	95%	0	8%	89%	3%	+4%	−6%
Hispanic Protestant	50%	47%	3%	51%	44%	6%	+1%	−3%
Other Protestant	61%	37%	2%	57%	34%	6%	−4%	−3%
Non-Hispanic Catholic	54%	45%	1%	54%	42%	5%	0	−3%
Hispanic Catholic	25%	73%	1%	23%	73%	4%	−2%	0
Orthodox	54%	44%	2%	60%	36%	3%	+6%	−8%
Mormon	82%	16%	2%	52%	23%	25%	−30%	+7%
Buddhist	10%	86%	4%	20%	67%	14%	+10%	−19%
Hindu	12%	88%	1%	18%	82%	0	+6%	−6%
Jewish	32%	66%	1%	28%	68%	4%	−4%	+2%
Muslim	16%	82%	2%	14%	81%	5%	−2%	−1%
None/Unaffiliated	25%	72%	3%	30%	63%	7%	+5%	−9%

TABLE 7.5 Comparison of Three-Party Vote by Religion, 2012–2016

Source: CCES Common Content, 2016; CCES Common Content, 2012.

Notes: Totals may not equal 100% due to rounding. White evangelical = Protestant + born-again + white. White mainline = Protestant + not born-again + white. None = "nothing in particular" or atheist or agnostic.

total Democratic presidential vote during the New Deal and subsequent elections. The cultural divide between Catholics and Protestants continued to be a strong predictor of both partisanship and voting behavior through the early 1960s, especially when Catholic voters were directly mobilized. This especially happened when Catholic John F. Kennedy earned the Democratic presidential nomination in 1960. His candidacy electrified the Catholic world, and he received an overwhelming 80 percent of the votes of self-identified Roman Catholics, who provided an astounding 47 percent of his entire vote.[24] Kennedy's candidacy also provoked intense Protestant opposition. Both mainline and evangelical leaders expressed grave reservations about having a Catholic in the White House. Would his loyalties be divided? Would he be under pressure to take directions from the Vatican? As a Catholic, how could he serve the entire American population? Anti-Catholic tracts appeared by the thousands, reminiscent of nineteenth-century broadsides against "Romanism" and "papists."[25]

In spite of Kennedy's adroit political handling of these critics, his Catholicism nearly cost him the election. Gains among Catholic voters were more than offset by losses among the larger group of Protestant Democrats, particularly in border states, but also in places as different as Pennsylvania, New Mexico, California, and Wisconsin.[26] Some Protestant leaders campaigned against Kennedy, and he probably lost about 1.5 million votes because of his religion.[27] His razor-thin victory margin of 100,000 votes could easily have vanished had he not personally blunted at least some of the anti-Catholic prejudice that was circulating around his candidacy by his deft reassurance that he would never allow the pope to determine US government policy.[28] In the end, however, Kennedy's presidency and assassination, coupled with changes in the Catholic Church after Vatican II, put to rest the deep political cleavage between Catholics and Protestants that had existed for more than a century.

Kennedy's election represented the high-water mark of Catholic loyalty to the Democratic Party. It also marked a high point for Catholic Church internal solidarity in general—a time of plentiful priests and nuns, well-appointed parochial schools, high Mass attendance, large families, and general success in passing the faith on to the next generation. The brief Kennedy years also represented the end of an era of Catholic solidarity reinforced by ethnic pride (among Irish Catholics, Polish Catholics, Italian Catholics, etc.), embeddedness in parish life, and complementarity between Catholic social teaching and the platform and policies of the Democratic Party (such as support for labor unions and a social safety net).[29] Today, there is no longer a cohesive Catholic electorate. Instead, Catholic voting differs by frequency of Mass attendance, ethnicity, race, gender, and generation. Moreover, religious switching and immigration are changing the composition of the Catholic population in politically salient ways.

Catholic loyalty to the Democratic Party has trailed off dramatically since 1960, especially among whites who attend Mass weekly. In part, this is due to factors that reduced Catholic–Protestant tension. Over successive generations, white Catholics have assimilated into the broader society, as time separated them from the social significance of the immigrant experience. Assimilation also was facilitated by Vatican II (1962–1965), which replaced the use of Latin in Mass with local languages, eliminating one of the principal features that set Catholics apart from Protestants. Most white Catholics, now well-educated and relatively affluent, have moved out of ethnic enclaves to the suburbs, where they often send their children to public schools with all sorts of other religious backgrounds.[30]

Unlike the majority of evangelicals, though, Catholics have not yet become reliably or overwhelmingly Republican. As we saw in Table 7.3, Catholics as a group are almost evenly split in identification between the two major parties, with a sizable share of independents. One reason is the distinctive Catholic ideological blend of conservatism on abortion and marriage and progressivism on other matters, such as immigration, expansive social-safety nets, and environmental protection.[31] These stances are not idiosyncratic, either; Catholic social teaching emphasizes the imperative of affirming and supporting life in all its forms, so the Catholic inclination is to protect, defend, and improve human life from the moment of conception until the moment of natural death.[32] Thus, depending on the candidates and the salience of particular issues in a given election campaign, many Catholics remain swing voters. Since the 1980s, in fact, the overall Catholic vote has switched back and forth, acting like a bellwether predicting the outcome of the general election. Ronald Reagan won the Catholic vote in 1980 and 1984, whereas Bill Clinton carried it in 1992 and 1996. Al Gore had the edge among Catholics in 2000 in an election in which he won the popular vote, but George W. Bush carried Catholics in 2004.[33] Recent elections repeat that pattern. As we saw in Table 7.4, Barack Obama won the overall Catholic vote in his two elections, strongly in 2008 and by a closer margin in 2012.

The outcome in 2016 is less clear. According to exit polls, the Catholic vote swung back to Trump in 2016 (52 percent to 45 percent for Clinton), which would be a departure from the norm because Trump actually lost the popular vote (see Table 7.4). The CCES survey, on the other hand, reported a much closer Trump margin (see Table 7.6), while the American National Election Study gave Clinton the plurality over Trump, 48 percent to 45 percent.[34] One reason for this discrepancy, as we will discuss later, is that exit polls probably overestimated Trump's support among Hispanics, who represent a growing share of the Catholic vote.[35]

As this discussion suggests, beneath the surface of the overall Catholic vote lies a complex story, or stories. The Catholic share of the electorate is shrinking, especially among whites. The Catholic electorate is also increasingly diverse, with growing shares of Hispanics and other minorities. In turn, Hispanic voting support for Democrats has masked the rather steep decline in white support for the party of Roosevelt. And finally, voting patterns in the Catholic electorate have splintered in a number of different ways. Let us explore these related stories.

	TRUMP	CLINTON	OTHER
All Catholics	49%	47%	4%
Non-Hispanic	53%	42%	4%
Hispanic	23%	73%	4%

TABLE 7.6 Catholic Vote by Ethnicity

Source: CCES Common Content, 2016.

A key part of the American Catholic story is that the Catholic Church in the United States has lost the vitality and solidarity it enjoyed in the heyday of the early 1960s. Mass attendance is down, fewer children attend parochial schools, fewer adults choose religious vocations (resulting in a priest shortage), and there is considerable lay dissent from church teachings on birth control, clerical celibacy, and divorce.

The Catholic Church has also lagged behind many other religious groups in passing on the faith from one generation to the next. According to the Pew Research Center, some 13 percent of the total American population are former Catholics, while the Church only gained 2 percent of new converts, the most lopsided ratio of losses to gains of any other religious tradition. Between 2007 and 2014, the Catholic share of the population declined from 24 percent to 21 percent, and among the millennial generation the affiliation is only 16 percent.[36]

Theoretically, this could produce a more cohesive, if much smaller, Catholic electorate. And, indeed, there are some recent signs of renewed vitality among those who remain in the fold: young people more intensely connected to devotional practices, more men joining the priesthood, and movements toward religious unity among the church leadership. Since the election of Pope Francis in 2013, some commentators have also wondered about the potential "Francis effect," the idea that the popular pope might draw more former Catholics back into the fold. But the fact remains that for the past few election cycles the Catholic electorate has continued to decline (see Table 7.1) without evidence of greater cohesiveness.[37]

Another influence on Catholic voting is the emergence of a challenging new political environment. While Catholics no longer confront an overbearing Protestant majority, Catholic leaders now perceive threats from hostile secular forces armed with government power. Clashes between the Catholic Church and liberal authorities over abortion, same-sex marriage, and religious conscience rights have created powerful cross-pressures for Catholic Democrats and pushed a cohort of devout white Catholics toward the Republican Party.

No issue so epitomizes these cross-pressures as abortion. Most Democratic politicians today embrace an abortion-rights position that the American bishops decry because it is contrary to Catholic Church teaching. In fact, a few bishops have made news by saying they will withhold communion from Catholic politicians who stray from church teaching on abortion.[38] Yet many lay Catholics hold pro-choice views, which is a source of frustration for church leaders.

Here a real divide has emerged between less-observant Catholics, who tend to have more liberal social views, and weekly Mass attenders, who register stronger pro-life sentiment. One study found that whereas 47 percent of Catholics thought abortion should be legal in most cases, only 30 percent of weekly attenders held that view.[39] Moreover, a distinct Catholic pro-life subculture has arisen that expresses tension with the broader culture and consciously votes that way, normally for Republicans who endorse their position.

In response, prominent lay Democrats have striven to counteract the view that their party is hostile to Catholic values, in part by arguing that their healthcare and social-welfare policies would reduce the need for abortions.[40] But this effort has been undercut as clashes erupted over federal contraceptive mandates, abortion funding, and same-sex marriage, which represented threats to conscience rights of Catholic institutions. American Catholic bishops and clergy, primed by a sense of growing government threats to religious autonomy, were unusually vigorous in calling upon the faithful to defend religious liberty and the conscience rights of their religious institutions. Even Catholics who disagree with the church's stands on birth control, abortion, or marriage could identify with the right of Catholic institutions, such as Notre Dame University, to adhere to church teaching. This new environment helps to explain decline in white Catholic support for Democrats in the past three presidential election cycles (see Table 7.4).

Another key feature of the Catholic story is demographic. The decrease in the white (European ethnic) Catholic population at large has been partly compensated by a massive infusion of new Catholic immigrants, especially from Latin America, but also from Asia, Africa, and elsewhere. According to the Pew Research Center, by 2014, the US Catholic population was 59 percent white and 34 percent Latino, with the rest being Asian, African American, or mixed ethnicities. With the exception of Asian Americans, these minority Catholics are far more Democratic in their voting loyalties than their white counterparts. As we see in Table 7.6, Clinton won at least 73 percent of the Hispanic vote (with other surveys putting that at above 80 percent), while she lost the non-Hispanic or white vote to Trump.[41] The growing minority share of the Catholic electorate, therefore, has masked the significant erosion of older ethnic loyalties (Irish, Italian, Polish, etc.) away from the Democratic Party.

Another cleavage is generational. As we see in Table 7.7, the youngest generational cohort of Catholics, the millennials (aged between eighteen and thirty-five), backed Clinton over Trump, and was the only age cohort to do so among whites. On the other hand, a previous survey in the 2012 presidential election found that the youngest (and most observant) white Catholics (age between eighteen and twenty-four) tilted toward the GOP as the pro-life party.[42]

	SILENT	BOOMER	GEN. X	MILLENNIAL
All Catholics				
Trump	65%	55%	47%	35%
Clinton	33%	42%	48%	59%
Other	2%	3%	5%	6%
White Catholics				
Trump	68%	60%	57%	44%
Clinton	30%	37%	38%	49%
Other	2%	3%	6%	6%

TABLE 7.7 Catholic Vote by Generation

Source: CCES Common Content, 2016.

Trump's weakness among young voters may be operating here, or there may be a split between older millennials and younger ones.

A final divide is along gender lines. As in the population at large, Catholic women are more likely than Catholic men to vote Democratic, a reflection of female resonance with liberal safety-net policies. Among all Catholics, Trump won the male vote (53 percent to 42 percent for Clinton), while Clinton won the female vote (51 percent to 45 percent for Trump). Even among frequent Mass attenders, Catholic men and women diverge on the salience of issues that shape their votes.[43] Here, as elsewhere, complexity reigns in the Catholic electorate.

At over a fifth of the electorate, Catholics will continue to be courted by politicians and parties. One way to understand this importance is to assess the Catholic portions of party coalitions. Given that the overall Catholic vote hovers near the total vote division between the two parties, we can say that Catholics comprise roughly equal shares of each party's vote coalition (around 23 percent). But for Democrats that electoral group is comprised mostly of ethnic minorities, along with segments of less frequent Mass attenders, youth, and women. For Republicans, that electoral group is predominately white, with heavy representation of frequent Mass attenders, older voters, and men. What this demonstrates is that general appeals to Catholics inevitably will give way to the targeting of specific subgroups. Perhaps this confirms the adage making its way around political circles: There is no Catholic vote, but the Catholic vote matters.

WHITE EVANGELICAL PROTESTANTS: PIETIST SUPPORT FOR THE GOP

As we discussed in Chapter 5, the evangelical community in the United States includes a large number of minorities, and differences between white and minority evangelicals matter profoundly to politics. We consider here white evangelicals specifically. They are not only the largest group of religion-based voters (about a quarter of the US electorate), but they also stand out as an integral voting bloc within the Republican Party.

Two momentous developments have influenced the partisanship and voting behavior of white evangelical Protestants. The first has been the growth of evangelical churches over the past several decades and the decline of mainline denominations. In 1960, more than 40 percent of all white adults claimed membership in mainline denominations, compared with only 27 percent in evangelical churches. Today there are many more evangelicals than there are mainline Protestants. Moreover, because regular church attendance and other measures of commitment tend to be lower in mainline churches than in evangelical ones, this estimate exaggerates the number of people who are involved in mainline church life.[44] Thus, whereas mainline Protestants remain an important segment of the electorate, evangelical Protestants have moved toward the strategic center of the Protestant world.

The second development has been the realignment of evangelical Protestants to the Republican Party that began in roughly 1980—a development made all the more significant by their numerical growth over the past several decades. These two developments have altered the dynamics of internal GOP politics dramatically. The old Republican Party was an alliance of business interests and mainline Protestants, but the new GOP also relies heavily on its "values constituency," which is composed primarily of evangelicals.[45] At the same time, the Democratic Party's strategy has also changed, particularly by solidifying Jewish and secular support for Democrats.[46]

For much of the twentieth century, many Baptists, Pentecostals, and other evangelicals were Democrats, in spite of general Protestant loyalty to the Republican Party. Many evangelicals, especially conservative Baptists and Methodists, lived in the South, where loyalty to the Democratic Party was almost universal, reflecting the Civil War legacy of opposition to the party of Lincoln.[47] Second, a class dimension reinforced Democratic tendencies among evangelicals. During the New Deal era, for example, lower-status Protestants (most of whom were evangelical) were more likely to vote for Franklin Roosevelt than were upper-class Protestants, who tended to belong to mainline denominations. Thus, Pentecostals, independent Baptists, and other evangelicals were quite a bit more likely to be Democrats than were Presbyterians, Episcopalians, United Methodists, and Congregationalists.

Things began to change in the 1960s. The 1960s and 1970s introduced a new kind of cultural politics associated with the counterculture, the sexual revolution, newly legalized abortion, women's rights, and gay rights. As liberalism—and, by extension, the Democratic Party—became associated in some minds with rapid social change and rejection of tradition, including traditional religion, Republicans made sizable gains among conservative Protestants.[48]

Jimmy Carter, a born-again Baptist from Georgia, temporarily stalled the transition of evangelical voters into the Republican Party with his 1976 presidential victory. Analysts concluded that Carter did better at the polls among evangelicals than he did among mainline Protestants.[49] But many evangelicals later felt betrayed by Carter's policy priorities as president, and simmering cultural forces combined to bring about the emergence of a new religious conservative movement—the "Christian right"—on the eve of the 1980 presidential election. Ronald Reagan courted the evangelical constituency, who were ripe for mobilization by conservative forces, and they proved a major factor in his 1980 victory over Carter. While many evangelicals were not part of the burgeoning Christian right movement, and some movement activists were not evangelicals, white evangelicals provided most of the energy behind this conservative surge into Republican politics.

From the 1980s onward, evangelicals' loyalty to the Republican Party grew. White evangelicals have become increasingly Republican since then, routinely providing some three-quarters of their votes to Republican presidential candidates. Republican get-out-the-vote drives specifically target the evangelical community, as was most famously the case with George W. Bush's 2004 presidential campaign.[50] But religious salience generally matters for evangelicals: Republican voting is magnified by religious observance. For example, weekly attenders provided some 80 percent of their votes for Romney in 2012 as opposed to 67 percent of the less observant.[51] As a rule, however, evangelicals across the board are more reliably Republican than either Catholics or mainline Protestants, as we see especially clearly in the 2016 election, when three-quarters of evangelicals who seldom or never attend services voted for Donald Trump.

Although many contemporary evangelicals vote Republican on economic issues, a strong element of cultural conservatism clearly is behind the evangelical–Republican marriage. Evangelicals are more conservative than other Americans on a host of issues, from abortion and marriage to healthcare reform and national defense.[52] Evangelical clergy, too, are most likely to be politically active (and Republican partisans) when they are cultural conservatives.[53] Unlike the electorate as a whole, evangelicals rank the nexus of abortion and "family values" as more important than economic issues. Moreover, the salience of socio-moral issues is even higher for frequent church attendees and middle-aged citizens, who often are involved in raising children—and who are most likely to vote.[54] The relevance of these issues may wax and wane with the times but is likely to endure. Indeed, the issue of same-sex marriage, which cuts to the core of conservative evangelical concerns about traditional family values, has reinforced the place of evangelicals within the Republican Party due to its persistent opposition to the legalization of same-sex marriage.[55]

The Democratic Party has attempted to make some inroads among evangelical voters. In 2008, Barack Obama made broad overtures to evangelicals especially through the work of Joshua DuBois, a young black Pentecostal minister, who served as Obama's chief religious campaign liaison.[56] DuBois later was appointed head of the White House Office for Faith-Based and Neighborhood Partnerships.[57] In the immediate aftermath of Obama's victory, exit polls showed that he gained 26 percent of the white evangelical vote, up five points from the 21 percent John Kerry won in 2004, with most of that increase coming from young evangelicals.[58]

But that Democratic success was short-lived. According to the CCES (see Table 7.5), Obama's share of the evangelical vote fell in 2012 (down to 23 percent), a slide that continued in 2016, when Hillary Clinton garnered only 16 percent compared to Trump's 78 percent. The 2016 exit polls reported a slightly higher—but symbolically important—number: 81 percent of white evangelicals voted for Trump, a larger percentage than any election since exit polls began measuring evangelicals.[59]

White evangelical voters were not always so strongly supportive of a Trump presidency. Most were uneasy with Trump in the primaries, when they gave their strongest support to candidates with clearer conservative bona fides. Why, then, did they eventually converge on the Republican standard-bearer? Part of the reason is undoubtedly that they had nowhere else to go. Many could not imagine Clinton as a viable alternative on policy issues such as marriage and abortion, even if it meant voting for a twice-divorced casino owner with an irreverent tone and a reputation for philandering. But the nearly monolithic white evangelical vote in 2016 also reveals the power of the partisan identity that the Republican Party had cultivated over four decades. Evangelicals even shifted their attitudes about the relevance of personal morality to elective office: In 2011, only 30 percent of evangelicals said that elected officials who commit an immoral act in their personal life can still act ethically in their political work; by October 2016, a few months after Trump's nomination, that number had climbed dramatically to 72 percent.[60] As we shall see in Chapter 10, not even the deep misgivings of conservative clergy and other evangelical leaders were enough to soften party loyalties among ordinary evangelical voters.

MORMONS: CONSERVATIVE BUT DISTINCT

Mormons—adherents of the Church of Jesus Christ of Latter-Day Saints (LDS)—share the cultural conservatism of evangelicals. With their high levels of religious practice, conservative moral values, large families, and relative affluence, Mormons form a cohesive political community, strongly identify with the Republican Party, and routinely give nearly three-quarters of their votes to Republican candidates. Although Mormons still are a relatively small group, the LDS Church is growing, and Mormons' geographic concentration in a few states in the mountain West magnifies their impact there.[61] Sociologists liken the Mormon population to an ethnic group characterized by clear cultural boundaries, distinct religious practices, high marriage rates within the fold, and success in passing the faith to the next generation.

In a way, the Mormon voting constituency came of age in the 2012 election, when the Republican Party nominated Mitt Romney, the first Mormon to head a major presidential ticket, as its standard-bearer. Some commentators thought that Romney would lose some of the normal Republican evangelical vote, given the unconventional theology of the LDS Church (evangelical bookstores still contain tracts warning against the "Mormon cult"). But the Obama administration's social liberalism, coupled with Romney's defense of traditional marriage and religious rights, appear to have overcome any such qualms.[62]

Romney's candidacy, however, did represent a laboratory test of Mormon ethnic solidarity. According to one survey, Romney gained fully 90 percent of the Mormon vote, up from 72 percent for McCain in 2008, a margin almost matching African-American support for Obama.[63] In yet another irony of American politics, a group vilified by Republicans and evangelicals alike in the nineteenth century provided near monolithic backing for the Republican nominee.

The 2016 election was a different story entirely. Donald Trump's bombastic style and stigmatization of ethnic minorities and immigrants offended many Mormons, who remember when they were the victims of religious repression. Romney publicly criticized Trump during the Republican primaries, and Evan McMullin, a Mormon, mounted an independent candidacy for president in 2016 (see Box 7.2). The voting results were striking. According to the CCES survey (Table 7.5), Trump lost an astounding 30 points among Mormons, barely gaining a majority. And the falloff was not just to McMullin, since he did not get on the ballot in most states. Rather, as we see in Table 7.8, Mormons

2012 VOTE	2016 VOTE	CHANGE FROM 2012
Romney 82%	Trump 52%	−30%
Obama 16%	Clinton 23%	+7%
Other 2%	Other 13%	+11%
–	McMullin 12%	+12%

TABLE 7.8 **Comparison of Mormon Presidential Vote, 2012–2016**

Source: CCES Common Content, 2012, 2016.

BOX 7.2 EVAN MCMULLIN: MORMON INDEPENDENT

Evan McMullin was serving as chief policy director for the Republican Conference in the House of Representatives in 2015 when Donald Trump announced his candidacy for president. A former CIA operative and investment banker, McMullin fit the profile of a traditional Republican conservative, but he detected "telltale signs of authoritarianism" in Trump's attacks on the press and stigmatization of religious and ethnic minorities. He raised these concerns with posts on Facebook, then tried to recruit another Republican to run as an independent against Trump in the general election. When these efforts failed, he launched his own candidacy, running as an Independent on a ticket with Mindy Finn, a Jewish media strategist from Texas who had worked for President George W. Bush.

McMullin lacked the resources and visibility to compete nationally and failed to get on the ballot in most states. But his religious roots and message resonated with enough Mormon voters in Utah that he gained 21 percent of the state's presidential vote, significantly lowering Trump's margin. After the election McMullin and Finn teamed up to create Stand Up Republic, a non-profit organization devoted to defending "democratic ideals, norms, and institutions" and promoting civic engagement. The organization produced a series of videos critical of what they saw as President Trump's violations of those principles.

Source: David Haglund, "Evan McMullin is Trying to Save Democracy," *The New Yorker*, February 2, 2017.

---

not only increased their votes for Hillary Clinton, the Democrat, but cast significant votes for other candidates in addition to McMullin. The concentration of Mormons in heavily Republican states prevented this revolt from affecting the Electoral College outcome, but the Mormon constituency bears watching into the future.

MAINLINE PROTESTANTS: THE NEW SWING VOTERS?

As already noted, the size of the mainline Protestant component of the American electorate has declined over the past several decades. Nevertheless, mainline voters remain a significant electoral force despite their declining numbers because they tend to be well educated and often have a strong commitment to civic participation, which makes them likely voters.[64] Along the way, this constituency has also become less conservative and Republican. Many mainline

Protestants seem to be reevaluating their ties to the Republican Party because of the heavy emphasis it has placed on moral issues since the Reagan era. As we see in Table 7.3, mainline Protestants now provide only a slight edge to the GOP on their party identification (44 percent to 40 percent for the Democratic Party). Moreover, whereas two-thirds reliably voted for the GOP a generation ago, that margin now hovers at 50 percent or so.

It is fair to say that mainline Protestants now make up an important swing constituency, even if they are not collectively mobilized as such.[65] For example, mainline voters gave George W. Bush a 51 percent margin in 2004, shifted to Obama in 2008 (54 percent), then switched back to give Romney a 51 percent edge in 2012.[66] The Trump margin of 55 percent in 2016, as we analyze below, represented almost entirely a surge in the votes of mainline Protestants only loosely connected to actual congregations.

A movement toward the Democratic Party is particularly strong among mainline clergy, a substantial majority of whom are solidly Democratic and liberal across a range of issues. It now appears that more laity, especially those who attend church frequently, are following this lead.[67] This partisan shift among mainline Protestants is a striking political development. In a reversal of a pattern over a century old, for the first time in American history, in 2008 the majority of mainline Protestants voted for the Democratic presidential candidate (Obama) while the majority of white Catholics backed the Republican. As recently as the 1960s, no observer would have thought such a voting outcome would be possible.

Equally telling is the liberal shift of mainline political attitudes. Mainline Protestants are more liberal than evangelicals and, in some cases, Roman Catholics, especially on social issues such as abortion and same-sex marriage.[68] And because many hold liberal positions on many other economic and foreign-policy issues, they may be ripe for mobilization by Democratic candidates.[69]

It is important, however, not to overstate the mainline migration toward the Democratic Party. Romney still gained 51 percent of the white mainline vote in 2012, and Donald Trump increased that margin to 55 percent in 2016 (see Table 7.5). But Trump earned the same percentage (51 percent) as Romney among frequent mainline church attenders, while he gained an enormous 87 percent of those who identify with a mainline Protestant denomination but "seldom" attend church.[70] This conforms to broader patterns that emerged in 2016, where Trump's populist economic nationalism appealed especially to alienated or socially disconnected voters. Mainline voters enmeshed in their congregations, on the other hand, are more likely to be exposed to liberal messages from their clergy and activist members, even if they remain moderate Republicans. Because it is too soon to detect a clear long-term trend, both parties can potentially benefit from appeals to different segments of this emerging swing constituency.

JEWS, LIBERALISM, AND DEMOCRATIC LOYALTY

In one sense, American Jews have always been in the vanguard of a secular vision of American politics. The vast majority of Jews in the United States are liberals who celebrate the Enlightenment ideal of the nonsectarian state. Thus, most behave like secular voters, are very socially liberal, and show loyalty to the Democratic Party. Their commitment to liberalism extends to economic and civil-rights issues.

Jewish voters remain one of the true paradoxes of American politics. It is only a slight exaggeration to say that, although they look like Episcopalian Republicans in socioeconomic status, they vote more like Hispanic Democrats. Here we see the impact of a kind of value-based voting that is independent of social class. And, in this case, the values are liberal ones because, as political scientist Lee Sigelman puts it, liberalism constitutes a kind of "lay religion" among American Jews.[71] Jews are among the most liberal of all American voting groups and are far more likely than other citizens to describe themselves as progressives or liberals.[72] This commitment to liberal ideals helps explain the loyalty of many Jews to the Democratic Party.[73] Jewish Democratic loyalty solidified during the New Deal era (during which Roosevelt received an estimated 85 percent of the Jewish vote), continued through the 1960s (when John F. Kennedy, Lyndon Johnson, and Hubert Humphrey each also received more than 80 percent), and remains strong to this day, if weakening somewhat.[74]

In the post-9/11 era, one might have expected to see Republican gains in the Jewish electorate. Concern over Israel's security has been heightened since the 9/11 attacks, and Republicans have often assumed the more hawkish stance toward Israel's adversaries. President George W. Bush, for example, took an aggressive posture toward regimes (Iraq and Iran) and movements (Hamas and Hezbollah) which were viewed as serious threats to the Jewish state, while President Obama was seen as being more critical of Israel and more accommodating of Iran. Moreover, many adherents of Orthodox strains of Judaism share the moral conservatism of evangelicals and traditional Catholics, which has led them to vote Republican in the past few elections.[75]

But we have yet to see broad Republican gains among Jewish voters. Orthodox Jews comprise only about a tenth of the Jewish population, so their conservatism alone will not register as a major shift. In addition, despite vigorous attempts by Republican leaders to court the broader Jewish community, and despite a sustained effort by vocal Jewish neoconservatives to dismantle traditional Jewish liberalism, Jewish voters have not abandoned the Democratic Party.[76] They remain solidly on one side of the cultural divide.

The 2016 election results show not only continuity in Jewish support for the Democratic nominee (with Clinton gaining 71 percent according to exit polls) but also distinct weakness in Trump's candidacy—he lost 6 points from Romney's share in 2012 (see Table 7.4). Given Jewish commitment to civil liberties, Trump's divisive ethnonationalist appeal likely alarmed some conservative and Republican Jews, thus reducing his Jewish vote.

A long-term concern for Jews is that their share of the US population, always modest, has declined in the past generation, though it has stabilized recently.[77] High voting rates compensate somewhat for this decline and may account for the reported increase in the Jewish share of the electorate in 2016 (though it is likely that exit polls merely oversampled in areas with concentrated Jewish populations). With little new infusion of immigrants, Jewish population growth simply has not kept pace with most other religious groups. With the exception of Orthodox communities, Jews tend to have small families. Intermarriage is also a challenge, especially for the non-Orthodox, as it tends to dilute Jewish identity with each generation. Although it was once as high as 4 percent, the Jewish share of the population is now around 2 percent.[78]

These combined trends portend a demographic transformation in the Jewish electorate over time. As alluded to above, in contrast to other Jews, Orthodox Jews have large families and are successful in passing their faith to the next generation. In fact, while Orthodox Jews constitute only a tenth of Jewish adults, more than a quarter of Jewish children are being raised in Orthodox homes.[79] This indicates that the Jewish population will become more Orthodox and conservative over time. Whether this trend increases Republican voting patterns will depend on candidates, parties, and the salience of issues.

AFRICAN-AMERICAN PROTESTANTS: LOYAL DEMOCRATS WITH A TRADITIONALIST TWIST

As we noted in Chapter 5, African Americans are overwhelmingly Christian and mostly evangelical. Well over half of all African Americans, for example, consider themselves born-again Christians and biblical literalists.[80] Moreover, religious salience is quite high in the African-American community: 85 percent (more than in any other demographic or ethnic group) say that religion is important in their lives, and a sizable majority say they attend worship services at least once a week.[81]

Even though a great many African Americans are evangelicals, they are also decidedly Democratic in their voting behavior. Part of the African-American outlook is explained by the uniquely American tradition of black Christianity, which often blends evangelical pietism with prophetic and liberationist messages. Many African-American Christians, and especially their clergy, see themselves as carriers of God's prophetic message of justice to a troubled land. What this means is that black voters often combine religious and moral traditionalism with decided support for government welfare policies and civil rights. Thus, black voters surpass white voters in their support for school choice and school prayer and are less liberal than Jews, secularists, and mainline white Protestants on same-sex marriage and abortion. Yet they are far more liberal than other groups in their support for government jobs programs, healthcare, civil rights, and affirmative action.[82] However, this blend of issue positions often receives little attention in voting studies of African Americans because what really seems to matter most is their almost monolithic presidential voting support (routinely around 90 percent) for the Democratic Party.

Black church life also affects political behavior in ways that aggregate voting studies cannot capture. First, because the church has traditionally been the central social institution in the African-American community, it is a focal point for political organizing, voter registration drives, and overt campaigning. Unlike most white clergy, many African-American pastors invite political candidates to speak to their congregations from the pulpit. Some also endorse specific candidates at election time. The church is often a precinct for black politics. Democrats now routinely campaign in black churches. It is no wonder that in the African-American community, church membership connects people to politics and increases voter turnout. Black church members are far more likely to vote than nonmembers. And, contrary to the pattern for whites, frequent church attendance is correlated with increased identification with the Democratic Party.[83]

Another important development has been the expansion of the African-American voting population. Strong black support for Democratic candidates tells us nothing about the relative size of that proportion of the electorate and its impact on national politics. The Voting Rights Act of 1965 officially ended the systematic disenfranchisement of African-American voters in the South, but its promise was not realized immediately. After relatively slow progress, black voter registration mushroomed in the 1980s, especially in the South, owing in part to Rev. Jesse Jackson's presidential bids in 1984 and 1988. The black electorate soared again as African Americans, inspired by the candidacy of Barack Obama, flooded the polls in 2008 and 2012. The Obama elections increased African-American turnout by 3 million votes, raising it to a rate that surpassed white turnout for the first time in history (66 percent compared to 64 percent in 2012).[84] Although many organizations played a part in voter registration and mobilization, African-American churches have been crucial to the galvanizing of the black portion of the US electorate.

The growing number of African-American voters has a profound effect on the political strategies of numerous political figures. It has also enhanced the clout of black leaders in the Democratic Party.[85] Obama not only expanded the black electorate, he earned the highest percentage of the black vote in the history of presidential elections, 95 percent by some estimates. Whereas African-American Protestants comprised 13 percent of John Kerry's electoral base in 2004, they were 20 percent of Obama's base in 2012.[86]

Hillary Clinton, however, could not equal that enthusiasm among African Americans in 2016; their voting participation fell 7 points to 59 percent, and her margin of victory among African-American Protestants also dropped to

88 percent.[87] There are clearly gender differences beneath the surface of near-monolithic voting support for Democrats: Donald Trump won 13 percent of the votes of black Protestant men versus only 5 percent of the women.

Finally, because of their relatively conservative views on many socio-moral issues, including abortion and gay rights, African-American Protestants are often courted as potential allies by white religious conservatives. These efforts are based on the premise that even though African Americans vote for Democrats, moral conservatism may lead some African Americans to join in issue-based coalitions with white evangelicals. This emerged most dramatically in various state and local ballot initiatives on LGBT rights. Many African-American pastors campaigned actively against same-sex marriage, and black voters responded in kind. For example, in 2008, some 70 percent of African Americans in California (who turned out in record numbers for Barack Obama) voted in favor of the Proposition 8 ballot initiative against same-sex marriage, while the majority of whites voted in favor.[88] Thus, Obama's candidacy ironically undercut a progressive cause he ultimately championed. Similarly, in 2015, African Americans provided the decisive votes against a highly touted Houston ordinance that would prohibit discrimination on the basis of gender identity and sexual orientation.[89] While the Supreme Court has nationalized same-sex marriage rights, the majority of black Protestants (like white evangelicals) continue to support traditional marriage, which may have some bearing on emerging battles over the conscience rights of religious institutions in the new era of marriage equality.[90]

LATINOS: A DIVERSE AND GROWING CONSTITUENCY

One of the fastest growing groups in America is the diverse Latino ethnic constituency. As a heavily immigrant population, its share of the electorate will rise significantly in the coming years (especially as the children of immigrants come of voting age), making the Latino vote increasingly important to the electoral fortunes of candidates and parties. Latinos also illustrate the themes of this chapter, how religious voting patterns are shaped by the interweaving strands of religious beliefs, church involvement, and ethnic solidarity.

Like African Americans, Latinos in the United States combine high levels of religiosity with a deep consciousness of ethnic identity. Nearly eight in ten claim a religious affiliation, and 60 percent say religion is very important to them.[91] Religious affiliation and commitment among Latinos account for a certain degree of social conservatism, but ethnic solidarity is just as important in shaping Hispanic views on other issues and voting. On many issues related to immigration, government health insurance, and services for poor people, Latinos lean to the left of the ideological spectrum and routinely give at least two-thirds of their votes to Democratic candidates.

To explore the dynamics of the Latino vote, we must first understand the religious composition of the population. As we saw in Chapter 5, while heavily Christian, it is diverse and dynamic. A clear trend over the past few years has been the significant decline in the Catholic population and the increase in both the evangelical and unaffiliated constituencies.[92] Indeed, it appears that successive immigrant generations become less Catholic over time. While some two-thirds of Latino Catholics are foreign-born immigrants, most Latino evangelicals were born in the United States.[93]

The Latino electorate roughly tracks the broader Latino population in its religious composition, but the enormous gap in size between the two is an important part of the story. Latinos now comprise nearly 18 percent of the total US population, compared to 13 percent for African Americans. Yet the Latino and black shares of the electorate in 2016 were comparable, 11 percent and 12 percent respectively (according to exit polls).[94] This gap between the Latino population versus the Latino electorate is due both to the substantial number of non-citizen Latinos and to their lower voter turnout compared to other groups. Indeed, for the past two decades, the number of eligible Latino voters who did not vote slightly exceeded those who did.[95] If a party or campaign mobilized Latinos at higher rates, the impact would be enormous.

Catholics still represent the largest share of Latino voters, but a growing percentage of Latino Americans (nearly 20 percent) have found church homes within Pentecostalism and other branches of evangelical Protestantism.[96] The distinction between Protestant and Catholic Latinos explains some significant differences in political attitudes and partisan voting.[97] Evangelical Latinos are more likely to describe themselves as conservative and to prioritize socio-moral issues (see Box 7.3). They strongly oppose gay marriage and legalized abortion, and are less likely than Latino Catholics to identify as Democrats (41 percent versus 51 percent).[98] On the other hand, the growing number of Latinos who express no religious affiliation (especially prevalent among the young) tilt even more to the Democratic Party than either religious group.

Before we analyze the Latino vote in detail, it is important to acknowledge that different polls produce widely different voting breakdowns (see Table 7.5 and Table 7.9). In 2016, for example, exit polls suggested that Donald Trump did much better than expected among Latino voters (gaining 29 percent, up 2 points from Romney's total in 2012), despite his harsh rhetoric about Mexicans and his pledge to deport undocumented immigrants. But a systematic investigation by the research group Latino Decisions suggested that the exit polls were skewed in several ways. The exit polls did not sample in precincts with high Latino populations, nor did they employ many Spanish-language pollsters, even though a third of Latino voters are primarily Spanish speakers. Because dominant English speakers were more likely than bilingual or Spanish speakers to vote for Trump, this helps explains the overestimate of his Latino vote.[99] A survey on the eve of the election by Latino Decisions, however, found only 18 percent of Latinos

BOX 7.3 REVEREND SAMUEL RODRIGUEZ:
LATINO EVANGELICAL LEADER

As the President of the National Hispanic Christian Leadership Conference, Rev. Dr. Samuel Rodriguez functions as the leader for over 100 million Hispanic Evangelical Christians across the globe. As the leading voice for that Latino population in the United States, he is afforded a great deal of political clout, and, thus, he has an increasingly prominent position of influence. Rodriguez moves in diverse circles: He was honored as the first ever Latino keynote speaker at the Martin Luther King, Jr. 40th Anniversary Commemorative Service, in addition to being distinguished as an influential leader by *Charisma Magazine, Time Magazine, CNN, Fox,* and the *Wall Street Journal,* among others. Additionally, Rodriguez's book, *Be Light,* earned him a place on the *LA Times* Bestsellers List.

Rodriguez has been active on the political scene for a number of years, having served under President Obama's White House Task Force on Fatherhood and Healthy Families, acting as an informal White House adviser, and delivering a prayer at the inauguration of President Trump in 2017. As an evangelical, he strongly supported the conservative positions in the 2016 Republican platform on abortion, marriage, and religious liberty. But as a Latino leader, he criticized other aspects of President Trump's executive agenda, particularly immigration. Rodriguez's clout as a leader continues to gain traction, making him an increasingly significant player in the religious political landscape.

Sources: "Rev. Samuel Rodriguez," https://nhclc.org/about-us/rev-samuel-rodriguez/; Mark Woods, "President Trump, Please Think Again: Evangelical leaders Plead for Rethink on Refugee Ban," *Christian Today,* January 30, 2017, https://www.christiantoday.com/article/president.trump.please.think.again.evangelical.leaders.plead.for.rethink.on.refugee.ban/104256.htm?email=1.

intending to vote for Trump. On the other hand, we cannot know whether all those who said they intended to vote actually turned out.[100]

Despite these caveats, all surveys show big differences by Christian tradition. In other words, the most important religious distinction within the Latino community is a familiar one: Catholic versus Protestant. In the Latino Decisions poll, for example, the vote for Hillary Clinton was 22 points higher among Latino Catholics (at 82 percent) than among born-again Protestants (at 60 percent) (see Table 7.9). In the CCES survey, the gap was 29 points, though at lower overall levels (73 percent among Catholics to 44 percent among Protestants) (see Table 7.5).

	2012		2016		DEMOCRAT CHANGE 2012–2016
	OBAMA	ROMNEY	CLINTON	TRUMP	
All Latinos	75%	23%	79%	18%	+4%
Catholic	81%	17%	82%	15%	+1%
Born Again	54%	44%	60%	37%	+4%

TABLE 7.9 Latino Vote by Christian Tradition

Source: Latino Decisions, "2016 Election Eve Poll"; ImpreMedia/Latino Decisions, "2012 Latino Election Eve Poll."

The growth and conservative tilt of the Hispanic Protestant population initially buoyed Republican strategists, who hoped to make inroads into this growing evangelical constituency. Indeed, in 2004, President George W. Bush won over 60 percent of the Hispanic Protestant vote.[101] As governor of Texas, Bush worked closely with Hispanics and understood the overwhelming significance of immigration to this population. Later, as president, he pressed for comprehensive immigration reform that would have provided some means for unauthorized workers to move toward legal status or citizenship.

But the Republican hope of gaining support in the growing evangelical segment of the Latino electorate was undercut by a changing issue landscape. Bush's push for immigration reform ignited vehement opposition among conservatives. That turned into a populist revolt among working-class whites when President Obama took executive initiatives to shield certain groups from deportation.[102]

Latino voters thus provide a clear illustration of how one issue, in this case illegal immigration, can influence electoral fortunes. Though most Latinos in the United States are citizens, a shared culture makes sympathy for the undocumented a pressing concern.[103] Of the 11 million unauthorized immigrants in the United States, about two thirds are from Mexico and other Latin American countries. The majority have lived in the country for a decade or more, leaving millions of them vulnerable to possible deportation or family separation. Thus, President Obama's 2012 executive order, Deferred Action for Childhood Arrivals (DACA), which provides a legal means for young adults brought to the United States as children to work and go to college, is widely popular among Latino voters.

Whatever the merits of various policy arguments, many Latinos perceived hostility in conservative or populist calls for deportation, and the Republican Party has paid a price, especially among the Latino evangelicals, an otherwise natural GOP constituency. One survey of religion and politics found a dramatic reversal in the votes of evangelical Latinos, from 57 percent support in 2008 for Republican John McCain, who supported immigration reform, to only 35 percent support in 2012 for Mitt Romney, who called for self-deportation of the unauthorized.[104] Donald Trump, who pledged to crack down on illegal immigration, appears to have lost by a similar margin among born-again Latinos (see Table 7.9). To be sure, short-term Republican gains among working-class whites in 2016 compensated for the loss. But as the Latino electorate expands, continued erosion of Latino support for Republicans, especially among otherwise conservative evangelicals, remains a problem acknowledged by GOP strategists.[105]

In sum, ethnoreligious identity operates for the Latino community as a whole, but differences among subgroups are also salient. Cuban Americans are more Republican than Mexican Americans; evangelical Latinos are more Republican than Catholics. Religious observance, too, plays a role by magnifying moral traditionalism; the most conservative Latinos are weekly attending evangelicals. Finally, as we learned in Chapter 6, gender differences are also salient, with Latino women modestly favoring Democratic candidates even more than men. Among Latino evangelicals, however, the gap is even larger, with men in this community much more likely than women to give the edge to Republicans.[106] Because the Latino electorate will continue to grow in the years to come, these distinctions will play an increasingly significant role in American politics.

MUSLIMS AND OTHER RELIGIOUS MINORITIES: GROWING DEMOCRATIC CONSTITUENCIES

As the increasing religious pluralism of American society washes through the electorate, observers of voting behavior are paying attention. To be sure, Muslims, Buddhists, Hindus, Sikhs, and other religious minorities in America represent small shares of the national vote, but they are growing, and together they will become important voting constituencies in the future. All are intensifying their broader civic engagement, so it behooves us to investigate their voting patterns.

The first thing we notice is the strong Democratic Party affiliation of Muslims, Hindus, and Buddhists, a reflection of broader patterns noted throughout this chapter (see Table 7.3). Not surprisingly, the overwhelming share of their votes go to Democratic candidates. In 2016, Donald Trump only earned 20 percent or less from each of these religious traditions, as we saw in Table 7.5. The one exception is the distinct Christian minority in America, the Eastern Orthodox, whose voting patterns are solidly Republican, if not as high as evangelicals.

No group has received as much attention as American Muslims, whose civic participation has been forged in the crucible of the post-9/11 world. Muslims comprise slightly less than 1 percent of the American voting public, but their concentration in certain states, rapid growth, and heightened political consciousness make them more important than their numbers might suggest.

As a political community, American Muslims are ideologically complex. They tend to oppose same-sex marriage, abortion, and pornography, and they support public vouchers for families to send their children to private religious schools.[107]

We might easily hypothesize that this cultural conservatism, combined with solid socioeconomic status, high marriage rates, and entrepreneurial skills, would make Muslims look like typical Republican voters. Indeed, before 9/11, many Muslims were drawn to the GOP, and Republican operatives actively courted them. In 2000, a coalition of American Muslim leaders made a strategic decision to flex their political muscle by collectively endorsing George W. Bush, and he won a plurality of the Muslim vote—but not quite a majority because of a large number of votes cast for Independent candidate Ralph Nader, who is of Lebanese descent. When African and African-American Muslims are separated out, the margin for Bush among other Muslims increased to nearly 60 percent.[108]

This support earned Muslim leaders invitations to White House functions and some access to executive-branch agencies. White House sensitivity to the Muslim population continued in the immediate aftermath of the attacks of September 11, 2001. President Bush proclaimed Islam a religion of peace, called upon Americans not to discriminate against Muslim citizens, and spoke about protecting "women of cover." He also hosted end-of-Ramadan Eid celebrations at the White House.

Muslim attitudes, however, never fully conformed to the economically libertarian agenda of today's Republican Party. Perhaps reflecting both their immigrant status and the social-justice tradition of Islam, American Muslims overwhelmingly favor universal healthcare, government assistance to the poor, stricter environmental protection, funding for after-school programs, and increased foreign aid to impoverished nations.[109] These views incline Muslims toward the agenda of the Democratic Party, and, combined with growing complaints about Republican foreign policies, they moved with alacrity into the Democratic camp.

Indeed, American politics seldom has seen such a rapid electoral turnaround as the shift in the Muslim electorate between 2000 and 2004. Questions about the USA PATRIOT Act of 2001, domestic surveillance of Muslim groups and citizens following 9/11, the detention of several thousand Muslim people in prison camps, and the war in Iraq combined to make the Bush administration highly unpopular among American Muslims by 2004. Not only did they overwhelmingly give their votes to John Kerry (82 percent), but increasing numbers had come to identify themselves as Democrats.[110] This trend strengthened with the candidacy of Barack Obama, who enjoyed substantial support from the American Muslim community. Not surprisingly, Donald Trump's candidacy, his rhetoric about "Islamic terrorism," and his proposal to shut down immigration from some Muslim nations, solidified this Muslim loyalty to Democrats. As we saw in Table 7.5, both Obama in 2012 and Clinton in 2016 earned over 80 percent of the Muslim vote. Given that the US Muslim population is young and growing, its electoral impact will expand. For the foreseeable future, the mobilization of the growing Muslim vote will provide a boost to Democratic candidates.

THE SECULAR VOTE: A GROWING DEMOCRATIC STRONGHOLD

In 1960, Americans were decidedly a society of churchgoers. The Democrats depended on churchgoing Catholics and some evangelicals (especially in the South) to offset Republican strength among most Protestant faithful. Only a small percentage of the population claimed no religious preference, and those who were not religious had relatively low voting rates. Thus, secular citizens had a negligible influence on American elections.

By the 2000s, however, religious observance had declined among a much larger segment of the American public, and secular citizens were voting differently from the religiously observant. Figure 7.1 shows a significant partisan gap by frequency of worship attendance, especially pronounced between those who attend church at least weekly and those who never do. It appears that the less embedded people are in religious communities, the more they vote for Democratic candidates. This pattern is especially pronounced among whites, where ethnic or racial solidarity does not confound the influence of worship attendance on moral traditionalism.

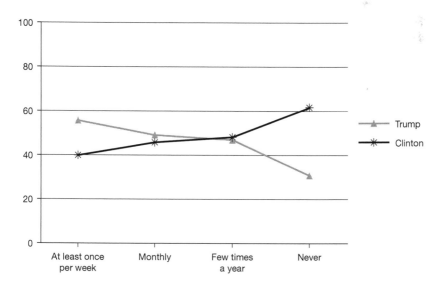

FIGURE 7.1 **Vote by Church Attendance, 2016**

Source: **Pew Research Center, "A Preliminary Analysis: How the Faithful Voted."**

This finding indicates the need to explore secular or unaffiliated voting behavior. The unaffiliated, or "nones," include a small percentage of self-identified atheists or agnostics. But that group also includes "seekers," who consider themselves "spiritual but not religious," along with others simply indifferent to religion. Although seemingly disparate, these voters share secular political values and increasingly vote in cohesive and predictable ways. Until recently, this socially liberal but economically moderate group lacked clear political direction. Some would vote for Republican candidates who emphasized libertarian themes of limited government. But, as polarization on social and moral issues has come to define the two parties, secular voters have moved increasingly away from a Republican Party that is closely associated with religious traditionalism. As secular voters have grown in number and shown greater cohesiveness over time, they have become a crucial part of the Democratic coalition. Owing to this fact, President Obama specifically mentioned "nonbelievers" during his first inaugural address.[111] In 2016, the unaffiliated comprised more than a fifth of Hillary Clinton's total voter base.

This partisan split along religious lines traces its roots to the 1970s. Prior to that time, as political scientists Louis Bolce and Gerald De Maio observe, "There was something of a tacit commitment among elites in both parties to traditional Judeo-Christian values regarding authority, sexual mores, and the nuclear family."[112] In the 1970s, secular activists began to take a more prominent place in some state- and local-level Democratic Party organizations. Ever since, Democratic activists have been far more likely than their Republican counterparts to describe themselves as secular or marginally attached to religion.[113]

Over time, this division has trickled down to average voters. President Obama received strong majorities of religiously unaffiliated voters, as did Hillary Clinton, though by a somewhat smaller margin (see Table 7.5). In fact, the voting gap between secular and religious Americans is larger than differences in education, gender, income, age, and numerous other factors.[114]

This new voter cohort presents challenges to both parties. Some Democrats fear that secularism within the party may alienate important religious voters.[115] In turn, Republican appeals to secular voters and socially liberal young people could alienate their religious backers. The growing importance of the secular voting bloc within the Democratic Party, coupled with the continuing loyalty of religious conservatives to the Republican Party, portends continued religious–nonreligious polarization along partisan lines.

But here, too, we see wrinkles from election to election. In 2012, the partisan gap by church attendance was particularly pronounced and emerged within the different religious traditions as well as overall. But in 2016 Donald Trump's distinct appeal to disconnected voters produced mixed patterns. With mainline Protestants, as we noted, Trump did much better among those who "seldom" attend church than among those embedded within congregations, and he lost major ground with frequently attending Mormons. With other groups, no clear patterns emerged. While truly secular voters remain a strong constituency for Democratic candidates, and frequent-attenders a Republican constituency, Trump's hedonistic personality and loose connection to organized religion (see Chapter 9), seems to have flattened those patterns somewhat.

CONCLUSION

The growing divide between religiously observant and more secular Americans has led some commentators to wonder whether a European-style party alignment is emerging in the United States, pitting a Christian conservative party (the Republicans) against a more secular, liberal party (the Democrats). As we have seen, this analysis is only partly accurate because many progressive mainline Protestants, Catholics, religious minorities, and immigrant groups inhabit the same political coalition as secular voters. What this chapter illustrates, instead, is how dynamic and complex religious voting is in the United States. It is dynamic because we see important changes over time—sometimes dramatic ones. It is complex because religion can play a role on several different levels, often simultaneously. One simply cannot understand elections in the United States, however, without comprehending the impact of religion upon them. There is no doubt that religion remains a defining characteristic of American political life.

DISCUSSION QUESTIONS

1 Describe the ways in which religious culture helped shape the political atmosphere during the early nineteenth century and how it impacted the development of the early US government.

2 How has the legacy of John F. Kennedy—his campaign, his time in office, his assassination—helped to resolve the fierce tensions between Catholics and Protestants that raged in the United States for much of its history?

3 In general, what role might religion play, if any, in where citizens get their party identification, whether citizens will vote, and how citizens will vote?

4 The chapter describes the voting behavior of many different religious groups and traditions. Compare and contrast their voting patterns. Why do we see big partisan gaps in some traditions (e.g., white evangelicals, Mormons, black Protestants) and small gaps in others (e.g., Catholics, mainline Protestants)?

5 What is the impact of the growing secular vote in American elections?

6 How do Latinos as an ethnoreligious group illustrate the themes of this chapter?

7   What accounts for the different vote outcomes of Mormons and white evangelicals in 2016?

8   What might the theories we covered in Chapter 2 suggest about how religious people vote?

FURTHER READING

Claasen, Ryan, *Godless Democrats and Pious Republicans? Party Activists, Party Capture, and the "God Gap"* (Cambridge: Cambridge University Press, 2015). An intriguing argument that demographic change accounts for religion-based cleavages in party activism and voting.

Green, John C., *The Faith Factor: How Religion Influences American Elections* (Westport, CT: Praeger, 2007). A thorough, empirical look at the various ways in which religion affects American electoral politics.

Layman, Geoffrey, *The Great Divide: Religious and Cultural Conflict in American Party Politics* (New York, NY: Columbia University Press, 2001). A provocative examination of the changing role of religion and culture in American voting patterns.

Menendez, Albert, *Religion at the Polls* (Philadelphia, PA: Westminster, 1977). The classic study of religious voting in American politics.

Reichley, A. James, *Faith in Politics* (Washington, DC: Brookings Institution, 2002). In a rich book, a good discussion of the voting behaviors of various religious groups placed in historical perspective.

Wilson, J. Matthew (ed.), *From Pews to Polling Places: Faith and Politics in the American Religious Mosaic* (Washington, DC: Georgetown University Press, 2007). Contains in-depth case studies of the political attitudes and voting behavior of different religious traditions.

NOTES

1. A. James Reichley, *Faith in Politics* (Washington, DC: Brookings Institution, 2002).

2. Edwin S. Gaustad, *Sworn on the Altar of God: A Religious Biography of Thomas Jefferson* (Grand Rapids, MI: Eerdmans, 1996); Reichley, *Faith in Politics.*

3. On the subject of Catholics and the Republican Party during this period, see Reichley, *Faith in Politics.*

4. See Paul Kleppner, *Continuity and Change in Electoral Politics, 1893–1928* (Westport, CT: Greenwood Press, 1987); and Paul Kleppner, *The Cross of Culture: A Social Analysis of Midwestern Politics, 1850–1900* (New York, NY: Free Press, 1970).

5. Robert Booth Fowler, *Religion and Politics in America* (Metuchen, NJ: Scarecrow Press, 1985), chapter 3. See also, Andrew R. Murphy, *Prodigal Nation: Moral Decline and Divine Punishment from New England to 9/11* (Oxford: Oxford University Press, 2009).

6. Robert Booth Fowler, *Wisconsin Votes: An Electoral History* (Madison, WI: University of Wisconsin Press, 2008).

7. For an excellent history of religion and politics in the African-American experience, see Barbara Dianne Savage, *Your Spirits Walk Beside Us: The Politics of Black Religion* (Cambridge, MA: Belknap Press of Harvard University Press, 2008).

8. A good summary of the New Deal coalition appears in Everett Carll Ladd, Jr., with Charles D. Hadley, *Transformations of the American Party System: Political Coalitions from the New Deal to the 1970s*, 2nd edn (New York, NY: W. W. Norton, 1975). On critical electoral realignment, see Walter Dean Burnham, *Critical Elections and the Mainsprings of American Politics* (New York, NY: W. W. Norton, 1970).

9. Fredrick C. Harris, *Something Within: Religion in African-American Political Activism* (Oxford: Oxford University Press, 1999); Savage, *Your Spirits Walk Beside Us.*

10. Lyman A. Kellstedt, John C. Green, James L. Guth, and Corwin E. Schmidt, "Has Godot Finally Arrived? Religion and Realignment," in John C. Green, James L. Guth, Corwin E. Smidt, and Lyman A. Kellstedt (eds.), *Religion and the Culture Wars: Dispatches from the Front* (Lanham, MD: Rowman & Littlefield, 1996), pp. 291–299; V. O. Key, Jr., *Southern Politics in State and Nation* (New York, NY: Knopf, 1949); Ladd and Hadley, *Transformations of the American Party System.*

11. Ladd and Hadley, *Transformations of the American Party System.*

12. Ladd and Hadley, *Transformations of the American Party System*, chapter 1.

13. Earl Black and Merle Black, *The Rise of Southern Republicans* (Cambridge, MA: Harvard University Press, 2002).

14. Ronald Inglehart, *Culture Shift in Advanced Industrial Society* (Princeton, NJ: Princeton University Press, 1990); Ronald Inglehart, *The Silent Revolution: Changing Values and Political Styles among Western Publics* (Princeton, NJ: Princeton University Press, 1977).

15. If we measure using voting *age* population, which includes some people who cannot vote (e.g., felons in some states), the number falls about five percentage points. See the data at the United States Election Project at www.electproject.org/2016g.

16. Mark H. Lopez and Paul Taylor, "Dissecting the 2008 Electorate: Most Diverse in US History," Pew Research Center, April 30, 2009, http://pewhispanic.org/reports/report.php?ReportID=108; United States Census Bureau, *Diversifying the Electorate—Voting Rates by Race and Hispanic Origin in 2012 and Other Recent Elections*, May 2012, www.census.gov/content/dam/Census/library/publications/2013/demo/p20-568.pdf.

17. Tom File, "Voting in America: A Look at the 2016 Presidential Election, United States," United States Census Bureau, May 10, 2017, www.census.gov/newsroom/blogs/random-samplings/2017/05/voting_in_america.html.

18. Willian H. Frey, "Census Shows Pervasive Decline in 2016 Minority Voter Turnout," Brookings, May 18, 2017, www.brookings.edu/blog/the-avenue/2017/05/18/census-shows-pervasive-decline-in-2016-minority-voter-turnout/.

19. D'Vera Cohn, "It's Official: Minority Babies Are the Majority among the Nation's Infants, but Only Just," Pew Research Center, June 23, 2016, www.pewresearch.org/fact-tank/2016/06/23/its-official-minority-babies-are-the-majority-among-the-nations-infants-but-only-just/.

20. All surveys have their limits so we rely on a variety of them to assess religious voting patterns. Exit polls seemed to have been particularly skewed in 2016 because they undersampled among solidly Republican and heavily religious states. Because it focused on swing states, the CCES survey overrepresented the unaffiliated electorate even more, roughly twice the percentage that is believed to have voted, and it underrepresented both the Christian and the evangelical segments. Regarding the American National Election Study, because it excluded rural counties under 50,000 in population, which were heavily Christian and voted strongly for Trump, it overestimated Clinton's vote (5 percent over Trump while her actual margin was 2 percent). Properly sampling the Hispanic population requires Spanish-speaking surveyors in certain precincts, as noted by the

research group Latino Decisions, which did its own poll of Latinos that we feature, http://latinodecisions.com/2016-election-eve-poll/. In previous editions of this book, we were able to use the National Survey of Religion and Politics, conducted by the University of Akron, which was the most attentive to religious nuances. That survey was not repeated in 2016, but we still occasionally refer back to its findings in previous election cycles.

21. The classic statement of the relationship between party identification and vote choice is Angus Campbell, Philip E. Converse, Warren E. Miller, and Donald J. Stokes, *The American Voter* (Chicago, IL: University of Chicago Press, 1960), especially chapter 6.

22. Pew Research Center, "Independents Take Center Stage in Obama Era: Trends in Political Values and Core Attitudes: 1987–2009," May 21, 2009, http://people-press.org/report/517/.

23. John C. Green, *The Faith Factor: How Religion Influences American Elections* (Westport, CT: Praeger, 2007).

24. Robert Axelrod, "Presidential Election Coalitions in 1984," *American Political Science Review*, 80 (1986): 281–284.

25. Albert Menendez, *Religion at the Polls* (Philadelphia, PA: Westminster, 1977).

26. Shaun Casey, *The Making of a Catholic President* (Oxford: Oxford University Press, 2009).

27. Phillip E. Converse, *Religion and Politics: The 1960 Elections* (Ann Arbor, MI: University of Michigan Survey Research Center, 1961).

28. Casey, *The Making of a Catholic President*.

29. Clarke E. Cochran and David Carroll Cochran, *Catholics, Politics, and Public Policy: Beyond Left and Right* (Maryknoll, NY: Orbis, 2003); Matthew J. Streb and Brian Frederick, "The Myth of a Distinct Catholic Vote," in Kristin E. Heyer, Mark J. Rozell, and Michael A. Genovese (eds.), *Catholics and Politics: The Dynamic Tension Between Faith and Power* (Washington, DC: Georgetown University Press, 2008), pp. 93–112.

30. Andrew M. Greeley, *The Catholic Revolution: New Wine, Old Wineskins, and the Second Vatican Council* (Berkeley, CA: University of California Press, 2005).

31. Cochran and Cochran, *Catholics, Politics, and Public Policy*.

32. Joseph L. Bernardin, *The Seamless Garment: Writings on the Consistent Ethic of Life*, ed. Thomas A. Nairn (Maryknoll, NY: Orbis, 2008).

33. Pew Research Center, "How the Faithful Voted: 2012 Preliminary Analysis," November 7, 2012, www.pewforum.org/Politics-and-Elections/How-the-Faithful-Voted-2012-Preliminary-Exit-Poll-Analysis.aspx#attend; Pew Research Center, "How the Faithful Voted: A Preliminary 2016 Analysis," November 9, 2016, www.pewresearch.org/fact-tank/2016/11/09/how-the-faithful-voted-a-preliminary-2016-analysis/

34. Michael J. O'Loughlin, "New Data Suggest Clinton, Not Trump, Won Catholic Vote," *America Magazine*, April 6, 2017, www.americamagazine.org/politics-society/2017/04/06/new-data-suggest-clinton-not-trump-won-catholic-vote.

35. Latino Decisions, "Lies, Damn Lies, and Exit Polls," November 10, 2016, www.latinodecisions.com/blog/2016/11/10/lies-damn-lies-and-exit-polls/.

36. Pew Research Center, "America's Changing Religious Landscape," May 12, 2015, www.pewforum.org/religious-landscape-study/.

37. Pew Research Center, "US Catholics Open to Non-Traditional Families," September 2, 2015, www.pewforum.org/2015/09/02/u-s-catholics-open-to-non-traditional-families/.

38. Margaret Ross Sammon, "The Politics of the US Catholic Bishops: The Centrality of Abortion," in Kristin E. Heyer, Mark J. Rozell, and Michael A. Genovese (eds.), *Catholics and Politics: The Dynamic Tension between Faith and Power* (Washington, DC: Georgetown University Press, 2008), pp. 11–26; Peter Slevin, "St. Louis Prelate Aims to Bring Flock in Line," *Washington Post*, May 29, 2007, p. A2.

39. Pew Research Center, "Obama, Catholics, and the Notre Dame Commencement," April 30, 2009, http://pewforum.org/docs/?DocID=413.

40. Amy Sullivan, *The Party Faithful: How and Why the Democrats Are Closing the God Gap* (New York, NY: Scribner, 2008); Douglas W. Kmiec, *Can a Catholic Support Him: Asking the Big Questions about Barack Obama* (Woodstock, NY: Overlook Press, 2008).

41. Latino Decisions, "2016 Election Eve Poll," www.latinovote2016.com/app/#catholic-national-all.

42. The 2012 National Survey of Religion and Politics, conducted at the University of Akron, found that over 58 percent of Catholics in the eighteen to twenty-four cohort voted for Romney, producing his strongest showing among all age groups.

43. Stephen Ansolabehere and Brian F. Schaffner, "CCES Common Content, 2016," v. 3, Harvard Dataverse, 2017, available at https://doi.org/10.7910/DVN/GDF6Z0.

44. Pew Research Center, "Attendance at Religious Services," "US Religious Landscape Study," 2014, www.pewforum.org/religious-landscape-study/attendance-at-religious-services.

45. Geoffrey Layman, *The Great Divide: Religious and Cultural Conflict in American Party Politics* (New York, NY: Columbia University Press, 2001); Clyde Wilcox, "Of Movement and Metaphors: The Coevolution of the Christian Right and the GOP," in Steven Brint and Jean Reith Schroedel (eds.), *Evangelicals and Democracy in America*, vol. II (New York, NY: Russell Sage, 2009), pp. 331–356.

46. Layman, *The Great Divide*; Louis Bolce and Gerald De Maio, "Our Secularist Democratic Party," *The Public Interest*, 154 (fall 2002): 3–20.

47. Key, *Southern Politics*.

48. Black and Black, *The Rise of Southern Republicans*.

49. Paul Lopatto, *Religion and the Presidential Election* (New York, NY: Praeger, 1985). Lopatto concluded that Carter split the theologically conservative (or evangelical) vote with Ford but lost among Protestants more generally. See also Menendez, *Religion at the Polls*. Menendez gave the evangelical edge to Ford but also concluded that Carter did better with evangelicals than he did with mainline Protestants (who backed Ford by a wide margin).

50. J. Quin Monson and J. Baxter Oliphant, "Microtargeting and the Instrumental Mobilization of Religious Conservatives," in David E. Campbell (ed.), *A Matter of Faith: Religion in the 2004 Presidential Election* (Washington, DC: Brookings, 2007), pp. 95–119.

51. The 2012 National Survey of Religion and Politics, conducted at the University of Akron.

52. Corwin E. Smidt, *American Evangelicals Today* (Lanham, MD: Rowman & Littlefield, 2013), chapter 7.

53. James L. Guth, Linda Beail, Greg Crow, Beverly Gaddy, et al., "The Political Activity of Evangelical Clergy in the Election of 2000: A Case Study of Five Denominations," *Journal for the Scientific Study of Religion*, 42 (2003): 501–514; James L. Guth, John C. Green, Corwin E. Smidt, Lyman A. Kellstedt, and Margaret M. Poloma, *The Bully Pulpit: The Politics of Protestant Clergy* (Lawrence, KS: University Press of Kansas, 1997).

54. For a fuller discussion of the issues important to evangelicals and other religious groups, see Smidt, *American Evangelicals Today*; Green, *The Faith Factor*; Andrew Kohut, John C. Green, Scott Keeter, and Robert C. Toth, *The Diminishing Divide: Religion's Changing Role in American Politics* (Washington, DC: Brookings Institution, 2000), chapter 4; Clyde Wilcox and Carin Robinson, *Onward Christian Soldiers? The Religious Right in American Politics*, 4th edn (Boulder, CO: Westview Press, 2011).

55. Republican Platform 2016, available at https://gop.com/platform/.

56. Corwin E. Smidt, Kevin R. den Dulk, Bryan T. Froehle, James M. Penning, Stephen V. Monsma, and Douglas L. Koopman, *The Disappearing God Gap? Religion in the 2008 Presidential Election* (Oxford: Oxford University Press, 2010).

57. Alex Altman, "Joshua DuBois: Obama's Pastor-in-Chief," *Time*, February 6, 2009.

58. Pew Research Center, "How the Faithful Voted," 2012.

59. Gregory A. Smith and Jessica Martinez, "How the Faithful Voted: A Preliminary 2016 Analysis," 2016, Pew Research Center, www.pewresearch.org/fact-tank/2016/11/09/how-the-faithful-voted-a-preliminary-2016-analysis/. The 2016 CCES, which we display in Table 7.5, shows a similar result: 15 and 79 percent for Clinton and Trump, respectively.

60. Robert P. Jones and Daniel Cox, "Clinton Maintains Double-Digit Lead (51 Percent vs. 36 Percent) over Trump," Public Religion Research Institute, 2016, www.prri.org/research/prri-brookings-oct-19-poll-politics-election-clinton-double-digit-lead-trump/.

61. David E. Campbell and J. Quin Monson, "Dry Kindling: A Political Profile of American Mormons," in J. Matthew Wilson (ed.), *From Pews to Polling Places: Faith and Politics in the American Religious Mosaic* (Washington, DC: Georgetown University Press, 2007), pp. 105–130.

62. Pew Research Center, "Election 2012 Post Mortem: White Evangelicals and Support for Romney," December 7, 2012, www.pewforum.org/2012/12/07/election-2012-post-mortem-white-evangelicals-and-support-for-romney/.

63. The 2012 National Survey of Religion and Politics, conducted at the University of Akron, provided that 90 percent figure. The CCES survey put Romney's Mormon vote at 82 percent, while exit polls probably undercounted his margin at 78 percent.

64. Laura R. Olson and Adam L. Warber, "Mainline Protestants and the American Presidency," in Gaston Espinosa (ed.), *Religion, Race, and the American Presidency* (Lanham, MD: Rowman & Littlefield, 2008), pp. 27–54.

65. Olson and Warber, "Mainline Protestants."

66. The 2012 National Survey of Religion and Politics, conducted by the University of Akron.

67. James L. Adams, *The Growing Church Lobby in Washington* (Grand Rapids, MI: Eerdmans, 1970); Guth et al., *The Bully Pulpit*; Ted G. Jelen, *The Political World of the Clergy* (Westport, CT: Praeger, 1993); Norman B. Koller and Joseph D. Retzer, "The Sounds of Silence Revisited," *Sociological Analysis*, 41 (1980): 155–161.

68. See also Pew Research Center, "Changing Attitudes on Gay Marriage," June 26, 2017, www.pewforum.org/fact-sheet/changing-attitudes-on-gay-marriage/.

69. Olson and Warber, "Mainline Protestants."

70. CCES Common Content, 2016, vote by church attendance for white mainline Protestants. Trump earned 87 percent of those who identify as mainline Protestant but seldom attend church.

71. Lee Sigelman, "Jews and the 1988 Election: More of the Same?" in James L. Guth and John C. Green (eds.), *The Bible and the Ballot Box: Religion and Politics in the 1988 Election* (Boulder, CO: Westview Press, 1991); see also Anna Greenberg and Kenneth D. Wald, "Still Liberal after All These Years: The Contemporary Political Behavior of American Jewry," in L. Sandy Maisel and Ira N. Forman (eds.), *Jews in American Politics* (Lanham, MD: Rowman & Littlefield, 2001), pp. 161–193.

72. Norman Podhoretz, *Why Are Jews Liberals?* (New York, NY: Doubleday, 2009); Leon Weiseltier, "Because They Believe," *New York Times Book Review*, September 13, 2009, pp. 1, 8–9; Richard Baehr, "Chosen People, Choosing Left," *Wall Street Journal*, September 25, 2009, p. A13; "Modern Liberalism Is Deeply Rooted in Jewish Values," Letters to the Editor, *Wall Street Journal*, September 14, 2009, p. A14, and September 17, 2009, p. A22.

73. For an argument that most Jews are secular liberal voters, see Peter Beinart, "Why Jews Vote Like Atheists," *Newsweek*, January 20, 2012, p. 5.

74. Sigelman, "Jews and the 1988 Election."

75. Greenberg and Wald, "Still Liberal"; Ron Kampeas, "Poll Shows Hillary Clinton Trouncing Donald Trump among Jewish Voters," *Jewish Telegraph Agency*, September 13, 2016, www.jta.org/2016/09/13/news-opinion/politics/poll-shows-hillary-clinton-trouncing-donald-trump-among-jewish-voters.

76. Edward Shapiro, "Right Turn? Jews and the American Conservative Movement," in L. Sandy Maisel and Ira N. Forman (eds.), *Jews in American Politics* (Lanham, MD: Rowman & Littlefield, 2001), pp. 195–211.

77. Elliott Abrams, *Faith or Fear: How Jews Can Survive in a Christian America* (New York, NY: Free Press, 1997).

78. Pew Research Center, "US Religious Landscape Study," 2015, www.pew forum.org/religious-landscape-study/importance-of-religion-in-ones-life/.

79. Shlomo Vile, "American Jewish Population Rapidly Becoming More Orthodox," *Israel National News*, December 12, 2016, www.israelnationalnews.com/News/News. aspx/221990.

80. Pew Research Center, "Evenly Divided and Increasingly Polarized: 2004 Political Landscape," 2003, http://www.people-press.org/2003/11/05/the-2004-political-landscape/.

81. Pew Research Center, "US Religious Landscape Study," www.pewforum.org/religious-landscape-study/importance-of-religion-in-ones-life/.

82. Harris, *Something Within*; Pew Research Center, "US Religious Landscape Study."

83. Harris, *Something Within*, chapters 6–7; see also Steven Peterson, "Church Participation and Political Participation: The Spillover Effect," *American Politics Quarterly*, 20 (1992): 123–139.

84. Lopez and Taylor, "Dissecting the 2008 Electorate: Most Diverse in US History"; US Census Bureau, *Diversifying the Electorate*.

85. This development is elaborated in Allen D. Hertzke, *Echoes of Discontent: Jesse Jackson, Pat Robertson, and the Resurgence of Populism* (Washington, DC: CQ Press, 1993).

86. The 2012 National Survey of Religion and Politics, conducted at the University of Akron.

87. CCES Common Content, 2016, https://dataverse.harvard.edu/dataset.xhtml? persistentId=doi:10.7910/DVN/GDF6Z0.

88. Karl Vick and Ashley Surdin, "Most of California's Black Voters Backed Gay Marriage Ban," *Washington Post*, November 7, 2008.

89. Emily Deruy, "How Houston's Black Voters Stopped the Equal-Rights Ordinance, *The Atlantic*, November 5, 2015, www.theatlantic.com/politics/archive/2015/11/how-houstons-black-voters-stopped-the-equal-rights-ordinance/433335/.

90. Pew Research Center, "Changing Attitudes on Gay Marriage."

91. Pew Research Center, "Religious Composition of Latinos," www.pewforum.org/religious-landscape-study/racial-and-ethnic-composition/latino.

92. Pew Research Center, "Shifting Religious Identity of Latinos in the United States," 2014, http://www.pewforum.org/2014/05/07/the-shifting-religious-identity-of-latinos-in-the-united-states/.

93. Pew Religious Landscape Study, "Evangelical Protestants Who Identify as Latino," Pew Research Center, 2014, www.pewforum.org/religious-landscape-study/racial-andethnic-composition/latino/religious-tradition/evangelical-protestant/.

94. "Exit Polls," *CNN*, November 23, 2016, www.cnn.com/election/results/exit-polls.

95. Jens Manuel Krogstad and Mark Hugo Lopez, "Black Voter Turnout Fell in 2016, Even as a Record Number of Americans Cast Ballots," May 12, 2017, www.pewresearch.org/fact-tank/2017/05/12/black-voter-turnout-fell-in-2016-even-as-a-record-number-of-americans-cast-ballots/.

96. Pew Research Center, "US Religious Landscape Study," 2015, www.pewforum.org/religious-landscape-study/.

97. Nathan J. Kelly and Jana Morgan Kelly, "Religion and Latino Partisanship in the United States," *Political Research Quarterly*, 58 (2005): 87–95; Nathan J. Kelly and Jana Morgan, "Religious Traditionalism and Latino Politics in the United States," *American Politics Research*, 36 (2008): 236–263.

98. Elizabeth Dias, "¡Evangélicos! Sunday Worship at Calvary," *Time*, April 15, 2013. The article cites statistics from the Pew Research Center and Gallup.

99. Latino Decisions, "Lies, Damn Lies, and Exit Polls."

100. Latino Decisions, "2016 Election Eve Poll." As a survey of over 5,000 Latinos with special attention to language needs and precinct concentrations, this poll is probably the most accurate reflection of the sentiment in the Latino population, even if it may inflate actual votes.

101. University of Akron, Fourth National Survey of Religion and Politics, 2004.

102. Richard Wolffe, Holly Bailey, and Evan Thomas, "Bush's Spanish Lessons," *Newsweek*, May 29, 2006, p. 24.

103. Pew Research Center, "Changing Faiths: Latinos and the Transformation of American Religion," 2006, http://assets.pewresearch.org/wp-content/uploads/sites/11/2007/04/hispanics-religion-07-final-mar08.pdf; Gaston Espinosa, Virgilio Elizondo, and Jesse Miranda (eds.), *Latino Religions and Civic Activism in the United States* (Oxford: Oxford University Press, 2005).

104. The 2012 National Survey of Religion and Politics, conducted at the University of Akron.

105. Growth and Opportunity Project, Republican National Committee, March 18, 2013.

106. Ansolabehere and Schaffner, "CCES Common Content, 2016." The largest gender gap was among Latino evangelicals, an 11-point difference, according to this survey.

107. Project MAPS, *American Muslim Poll 2004*, www.wr.mea.com/archives/Dec._2004/0412058.html.

108. Ahmed Younis, national director of the Muslim Public Affairs Council described how the American Muslim Political Coordinating Council, consisting of several of the

major American groups, endorsed Bush because the candidate came out against secret evidence. Younis, who felt that this position was not enough to warrant an endorsement, described the 2000 initiative as a "fiasco." Ahmed Younis, personal interview with Allen Hertzke, Washington, DC, June 14, 2006.

109. Project MAPS, *American Muslim Poll 2004.*

110. Project MAPS, *American Muslim Poll 2004.*

111. Pew Research Center, "Clinton and Giuliani Seen as Not Highly Religious," September 6, 2007, http://pewforum.org/surveys/campaign08/.

112. Louis Bolce and Gerald De Maio, "Secularists, Antifundamentalists, and the New Religious Divide in the American Electorate," September 6, in J. Matthew Wilson (ed.), *From Pews to Polling Places: Faith and Politics in the American Religious Mosaic* (Washington, DC: Georgetown University Press, 2007), pp. 251–276, at p. 256.

113. Layman, *The Great Divide.*

114. Laura R. Olson and John C. Green, "The Religion Gap," *PS: Political Science & Politics*, 39 (2006): 455–459.

115. Tony Carnes, "Swing Evangelicals," *Christianity Today*, January 9, 2004.

8

THE POLITICS OF ORGANIZED
RELIGIOUS GROUPS

Even though Americans love individualism and celebrate the heroic individual in literature and history, political power in the United States flows mostly from collective action. Organizing is an essential key to success in American politics. In this chapter, we examine the organized religious groups that work to affect politics and policy.[1] We trace their roots, explore their growth, and chart their stands on front-burner political issues.

The most systematic data on religious advocacy groups is contained in the online report of the Pew Research Center, "Lobbying for the Faithful," which identified over 200 organizations engaged in national religious lobbying or religion-related advocacy.[2] In this chapter, we draw extensively on that report, along with other sources that bring the narrative up to date. Though particular circumstances will change with time, the general patterns we document here provide a durable portrait of the size, scope, and diversity of religious advocacy.

Once dominated by a few mainline denominations, religious advocacy now represents a dizzying pluralism of religious traditions, values, constituencies, and institutions. Figure 8.1 provides a picture of this diversity by religious affiliation. Roman Catholic, Protestant, and Jewish groups remain the most numerous (57 percent of the total). But they have been joined by a growing number (16 percent) that represent faiths with smaller numbers of American adherents, such as Baha'i, Buddhism, Hinduism, Islam, Sikhism, and small Christian sects. The remaining quarter of the groups—more than the number of groups devoted to any single faith—represent interreligious constituencies that advocate for particular concerns.

Although religious interest groups vary widely in organizational style, ideology, and focus, collectively they engage in the full range of political

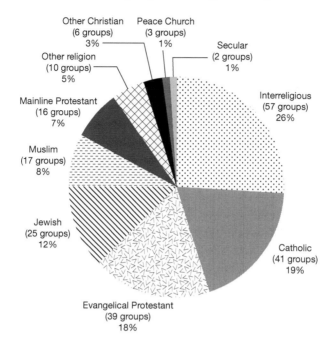

FIGURE **8.1** Advocacy Groups by Religious Affiliation

Source: Adapted from Pew Research Center, "Lobbying for the Faithful" (updated May 2012).

activities—lobbying legislatures and executive-branch officials, mobilizing their constituents, attempting to influence public opinion and sometimes elections, and litigating in the courts. Together, religious advocacy groups spend at least $350 million and employ more than 1,000 professionals in the nation's capital each year.[3]

Religious advocacy obviously includes efforts to influence public policy by actual religious denominations, institutions, and communities, such as Catholic Charities USA, the American Jewish Committee, the Muslim American Society, or the Seventh-Day Adventist Church. But it also encompasses efforts by organizations which do not represent a particular faith but which have predominantly religious constituencies, such as the National Right to Life Committee, or advocate from a religious perspective, such as the National Coalition to Abolish the Death Penalty. It also includes groups that do not see their organization as a religious lobby but have religion-related policy goals. For example, the American Israel Public Affairs Committee (AIPAC), with its mission of defending "the Jewish state of Israel," along with its predominantly Jewish constituency, qualifies as a religion-related advocacy group under the broad definition employed here. Finally, religion-related advocacy includes groups that explicitly reject religion and intentionally seek to reduce its influence. Because most of these secular groups have focused on church–state issues in courts, we discuss them in Chapter 11.

Religious group leaders generally eschew the term "lobbying," with its unsavory connotations of shady dealings and corruption, and instead often speak of themselves as "advocates." Many religious group leaders also have a practical reason for avoiding the term "lobbying." Most operate as tax-exempt nonprofit organizations that, under Section 501(c)(3) of the Internal Revenue Code, cannot devote a "substantial" part of their time and resources to actual "lobbying" as defined by the Internal Revenue Service (IRS) (attempts to influence specific pieces of legislation or ballot initiatives). This is generally not a problem for large organizations that undertake a wide range of activities, and the law is sufficiently vague that most groups can avoid officially registering as "lobbies" (which would result in forfeited tax-exempt status).

Such tax-exempt groups can, and do, advance moral principles to guide policy-making, mobilize their constituents or conduct "public-education campaigns" on issues, and provide information to policy-makers from their various ministries by testifying at hearings or meeting directly with officials, among other strategies. But they cannot legally endorse candidates or engage in electoral campaigns.

Nevertheless, some groups are organized as more overtly political entities under Section 501(c)(4) of the tax code, which allows them to hire registered lobbyists and permits greater flexibility in direct lobby strategies. In some cases, groups embrace the "lobby" moniker. For example, Bread for the World calls itself a "Christian hunger lobby"; NETWORK, "a Catholic social justice lobby"; and the Friends Committee on National Legislation, "a Quaker lobby in the public interest." Donations to such groups are not tax-exempt.[4]

Political-action committees (PACs), which make campaign contributions and endorse candidates in the religious community, are rare. For most religious groups, partisan electioneering is simply too divisive and risky, although some "Christian right" groups have striven to influence elections, and black churches can be formidable venues for electoral mobilization. The Pew study found that only 7 percent of advocacy groups supported candidates in elections.

The dominant characteristic of religious advocacy is its tremendous diversity, which tends to check the power of any single group. Despite claims to the contrary by one group or another, no religion or coalition has been politically dominant in our modern times, and continued pluralism makes such dominance unlikely in the future. To be sure, some religious groups are bigger or clearly play the political game better than others, but even the best operate in a challenging environment and can appreciate that their political fortunes naturally rise and fall with the times.

THE EVOLUTION OF NATIONAL RELIGIOUS LOBBYING

Religious advocacy, as we saw in Chapter 1, is as old as the Republic. At first, this advocacy was episodic and restricted to the state and local level, largely because the federal government's role in the lives of American citizens was limited. Issues of importance to religious people, such as child welfare, prison reform, and education, were state and local matters, and the common pattern was that coalitions of religious groups would come together temporarily when issues arose.

As the nation grew, however, religious groups periodically were drawn into national lobbying campaigns, from battles over Sunday mail delivery and dueling to the momentous issues of slavery and Native American removal.[5]

With the expanding role of the federal government in the late nineteenth century, a permanent religious advocacy infrastructure began to emerge in the nation's capital. The Roman Catholic Church, for example, established the Bureau of Catholic Indian Missions in 1881, partly to capitalize on the federal policy of contracting with church organizations to run schools, orphanages, and social programs on reservations. Among Protestants, as the formidable movement against alcohol gained strength, several temperance groups established Washington offices, including the Women's Christian Temperance Union in 1895 and the Anti-Saloon League in 1899, which set up an office across the street from the US Capitol. These organizations spearheaded the religiously based coalition behind passage of the Eighteenth Amendment in 1919, banning the sale of alcoholic beverages throughout the nation.[6] Although these groups no longer exist, they set the precedent that religious constituencies needed organized representation in the nation's capital.

Early advocacy groups included the Seventh-Day Adventists, who established a Washington office in 1901 to advance religious-freedom concerns; the Methodist Federation for Social Action (1907), an expression of social gospel progressivism; the Hebrew Immigrant Aid Society, established in 1913 to assist Jewish refugees fleeing European persecution; and the National Catholic Welfare Conference (precursor to the United States Conference of Catholic Bishops [USCCB]), which set up shop in 1919.

This era also spawned precursors to prominent contemporary groups. The Federal Council of Churches of Christ, formed in 1908 to represent historically mainline Protestant denominations and allied bodies, formalized itself as the National Council of Churches in 1950. Another Progressive Era group, the Methodist Episcopal Church's Board of Temperance, Prohibition and Public Morals, formed in 1916 to advance prohibition and social-reform causes. In 1923, the Board of Temperance opened an imposing building (now known as the United Methodist Building) on Maryland Avenue next to the Supreme Court. When various Methodist bodies joined in 1968 to form the United

Methodist Church, the Board of Temperance was reconstituted into the General Board of Church and Society, the most funded of the liberal Protestant advocacy groups in Washington, DC. Today, the United Methodist Building houses a number of mainline Protestant groups, advocacy coalitions, and allies. Thus, the "house that Prohibition built" now serves as a hub for liberal religious lobbying in the nation's capital.

The crisis leading up to and including World War II led to a spurt in national religious advocacy. As Nazi persecution of Jews intensified, B'nai B'rith International established its capital presence in 1937, followed by the American Jewish Committee in 1944. In 1943, the Quakers opened the first full-time "registered lobby"—the Friends Committee on National Legislation—primarily to protect conscientious-objector status. It was joined by advocacy offices representing mainline Protestant denominations, including Lutherans, Presbyterians, and Congregationalists. The National Association of Evangelicals, formed as a competitor to liberal Protestantism, began its operations during the war. Widespread Protestant fears of Catholic institutional power also led to the formation of such groups as the Baptist Joint Committee and Americans United for Separation of Church and State, which advanced "strict separationist" policies in church–state law.[7]

By 1950, at least twenty-five national religious groups had offices in Washington representing Protestant, Jewish, and Catholic constituencies.[8] After the World War II spurt, religious advocacy grew at a modest pace over the next two decades so that by 1970 some thirty-seven advocacy groups operated.

THE EXPLOSION OF RELIGIOUS ADVOCACY

Beginning in the 1970s, spectacular growth occurred in national religious advocacy, and it accelerated through each successive decade. As we see in Figure 8.2, the number of organizations engaged in religious lobbying or religion-related advocacy in the nation's capital increased roughly fivefold in the past four decades, from fewer than forty in 1970 to more than 200 today. While secular lobbying activity in Washington also expanded greatly during this time period, especially in the sheer number of registered lobbyists and amount of money spent, the growth in the number of religious groups has even outpaced the growth in the number of other lobbying organizations. Religious interests appear to have disproportionately established Washington offices as the means of public policy advocacy.[9]

Why all of this growth in the organized political representation of religious interest groups? One reason is the flowering of American religious pluralism. As the American religious landscape has become increasingly diverse, many small religious groups established Washington offices, both to advance their policy concerns and as a way to signify their place at the American civic table. Pluralism within religious communities also drives advocacy growth. Catholic

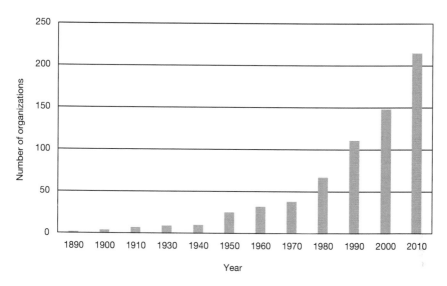

FIGURE 8.2 Growth of DC-Based Religious Advocacy Organizations

Source: Adapted from Pew Research Center, "Lobbying for the Faithful" (updated May 2012).

nuns operate their own groups apart from the Catholic bishops. Reform and Orthodox Jewish traditions sponsor separate advocacy offices. Competing Muslim groups vie with one another to define Islamic mandates for public policy.

Another explanation is the growing regulatory reach of the federal government. As the federal government's size and scope of responsibility have expanded, many groups have arisen to monitor its impact on their religious organizations and protect basic religious freedom. Thus, a striking trend in religious advocacy is the extensive national representation of associations of religious hospitals, schools, colleges, charitable organizations, and development agencies. Protecting the prerogatives and autonomy of these civil-society institutions has become an urgent priority of national representatives.

The third reason is that many religious people have come to the conclusion that they must get organized and enter politics to promote or defend their religious values. This impulse can be seen as a part of a larger global trend in assertive public religion evident from the 1970s on.[10] Often, the emergence of groups advancing one set of religious values sparks formation of rival organizations. For example, the 1973 *Roe* v. *Wade* Supreme Court decision sparked competing membership groups on both sides of the abortion debate that endure to this day. More recently, the judicial nationalization of same-sex marriage has galvanized religious advocacy groups that defend traditional conjugal marriage, as well as a faith-based countermobilization by the Human Rights Campaign, a gay-rights group.

Finally, the huge influence of the United States on the global stage serves as a catalyst for groups seeking to shape its foreign policy. As a nation of immigrants and a haven for refugees and exiles from abroad, America provides fertile ground for groups seeking support for their persecuted fellow believers abroad. Falun Gong adherents, Chinese Christians, Chaldean believers, Tibetan Buddhists, Egyptian Copts, Kashmiri Muslims, Palestinians, Russian Jews, and Iranian Baha'is—all have champions in Washington. In addition, sundry international relief and development organizations, refugee agencies, human-rights groups, and international justice ministries operate Washington lobbies because their work can be magnified, or undermined, by American aid, trade, diplomatic, or military policies.

For these reasons, the diversity, scope, and number of religious groups lobbying in Washington has never been greater.

Spending on Religious Advocacy

Political advocacy requires financial resources; thus, the scale and importance of religious lobbying is reflected in the fact that well over 200 organizations have established, funded, and staffed offices in the greater Washington area. To be sure, political advocacy for some groups represents only a part of their overall mission, but a substantial part of the growth in advocacy has been by groups with explicit political aims.

By any definition, spending is considerable. But, as Figure 8.3 demonstrates, religious groups range greatly in size, from tiny groups with budgets under $100,000 to giants with annual expenditures in the millions. This range can reflect the potential clout of different religious constituencies and interests. But, after a certain threshold, additional spending does not automatically translate into proportional clout. Budgets in the $2–3 million range, for example, seem modest compared with those of $10 million and above, but such organizations can support well-appointed offices, pay upward of twenty or so professional staff plus interns, and maintain extensive communications networks to mobilize constituents. Moreover, size alone does not always determine impact. A small group with a focused agenda and sympathetic cause can achieve notable success.

Table 8.1 shows the top thirty groups in expenditures, which together comprise more than three-quarters of all advocacy expenditures. Much like the Dow Jones Industrial average, this list provides a good snapshot of the big players and suggests a number of patterns. First, many of these large organizations are not tied to specific denominations but are member-based or interest-driven. Second, Jewish and pro-Israel groups are well-funded operations. (The American Israel Public Affairs Committee [AIPAC] is in a class by itself, spending more annually than the next seven combined.) Third, the pro-life cause emerges as one of the better-funded advocacy concerns.

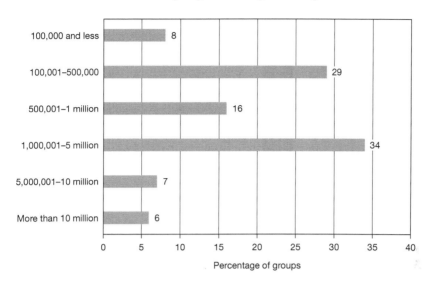

FIGURE 8.3 Groups' Annual Advocacy Expenditures

Source: Adapted from Pew Research Center's "Lobbying for the Faithful" (updated May 2012).

Fourth, conservative organizations advancing "traditional" values—the Family Research Council, Concerned Women for America (CWA), Traditional Values Coalition, and Focus on the Family—represent a sizable advocacy sector. Fifth, the progressive "social-justice" lobby, which focuses on such issues of hunger and poverty, also has considerable spending levels, especially backed by such groups as Bread for the World and Sojourners. Finally, we notice again the enormous diversity in political advocacy, from the Catholic Church and the Southern Baptist Convention to the International Campaign for Tibet and the Muslim American Society.

The Dynamic Churn in Political Advocacy

In addition to the growth in the number and overall spending of religious advocacy groups, there is also considerable churn in religious advocacy. New groups form while others fade away; some groups grow while others cut back. In some cases, this reflects a conscious decision by religious bodies, such as the Church of the Brethren and the Lutheran Church–Missouri Synod, that the cost of political advocacy no longer can be justified.

Part of the churn in advocacy is also related to the rise and fall of the importance of political issues. Temperance groups, once a mainstay in the capital, have vanished from the scene. On the other hand, groups focused on religious freedom, both at home and abroad, have proliferated.

EXPENDITURES	
American Israel Public Affairs Committee	$87.9 million
Family Research Council	$14.3 million
American Jewish Committee	$13.4 million
American Center for Law and Justice	$13.4 million*
Concerned Women for America	$12.6 million
Bread for the World	$11.4 million
National Right to Life Committee	$11.4 million
Home School Legal Defense Association	$11.3 million
CitizenLink (A Focus on the Family Affiliate)	$10.8 million
United States Conference of Catholic Bishops	$10.0 million **approximate
Traditional Values Coalition	$9.5 million
National Organization for Marriage	$8.6 million
People for the American Way	$7.8 million
World Vision	$7.0 million
American Life League	$6.7 million
Americans United for Separation of Church and State	$6.3 million
Sojourners	$5.5 million
Save Darfur Coalition	$5.4 million
United Methodist Church General Board of Church & Society	$5.4 million
Unitarian Universalist Service Committee	$4.6 million
International Campaign for Tibet	$4.2 million
United Church of Christ Justice and Witness Ministries	$4.0 million
Muslim American Society	$4.0 million
Human Life International	$3.8 million
Religious Coalition for Reproductive Choice	$3.4 million
Americans United for Life	$3.3 million
Southern Baptist Convention Ethics & Religious Liberty Commission	$3.3 million
Jewish Institute for National Security Affairs	$3.1 million
Friends Committee on National Legislation	$3.0 million
Catholics for Choice	$3.0 million
Religious Action Center of Reform Judaism	$2.9 million

TABLE 8.1 **Top Religious Groups in Advocacy Expenditures 2008–2009**

Source: Unless otherwise designated, all figures are from the Pew Research Center's "Lobbying for the Faithful" (updated May 2012).

Notes: *The American Center for Law and Justice figure is from its 2009 IRS 990 form.

**While advocacy expenditures for the USCCB are considerable, it was not able to provide detailed documentation that would conform to Pew decision rules. Therefore, Pew removed the USCCB from its summary calculations. (See www.pewforum.org/uploadedFiles/Topics/Issues/Government/all-expenditures.pdf.) The USCCB does designate $26 million as "Policy Activities Expenses." That figure, however, includes $9 million for the Catholic Campaign for Human Development, which is local grants, and $7 million for media activities, only part of which supports advocacy. Subtracting these from the total provides the $10 million estimate.

Advocacy spending by organizations also exhibits dramatic change over time, reflecting the changing fortunes of groups. The Christian Coalition, one of the most formidable conservative religious groups in the 1990s, had an annual budget of $12 million in 1993, thousands of grassroots activists, and the ability to turn elections.[11] It is now a shell of its previous self, with a budget barely a tenth of that of its peak and a modest Washington presence. On the other hand, Sojourners, a progressive evangelical group, has grown into a nearly $5-million operation.

The salience of issues—the sense of opportunity or threat experienced by religious constituencies—also affects the ability of groups to raise funds. For example, the National Organization for Marriage caught the wave of activism among Catholic and evangelical constituencies devoted to the defense of traditional matrimony against gay-marriage initiatives. Its budget grew from less than half a million dollars in 2007 to more than $8.5 million in 2009.[12] Then, after losing sweeping battles at the Supreme Court on the issue of same-sex marriage, its revenues dropped significantly.

A WIDE-RANGING ISSUE AGENDA

Religious advocates address a vast array of issues. Although groups cannot actively campaign for every issue of concern in a given year, the numerous issues listed on their websites suggest an enormous policy agenda. Indeed, at

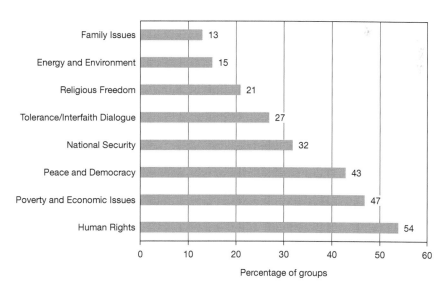

FIGURE 8.4 Percentage of Groups that Advocate on International Issues

Source: Adapted from Pew Research Center's "Lobbying for the Faithful" (updated May 2012).

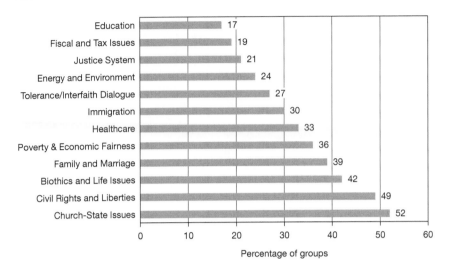

FIGURE 8.5 Percentage of Groups that Advocate on Domestic Issues

Source: Adapted from Pew Research Center, "Lobbying for the Faithful" (updated May 2012).

least 300 different issues are collectively addressed by religious groups, touching on just about every imaginable public-policy concern. Whereas in the past century religious advocacy focused mainly on domestic affairs, today, roughly as many groups focus on international issues as domestic ones, and nearly two-thirds (63 percent) work on both.

Figure 8.4 and Figure 8.5 provide breakdowns of the major categories of issues tackled by religious groups, one showing international agendas and the other domestic concerns. Several patterns emerge from an analysis of these breakdowns. First, more groups address international human rights or poverty than tackle such hot-button domestic concerns as abortion or gay marriage.

Second, the issue agenda reflects wide diversity of theological and ideological stances. Collectively, the "religious lobby" is neither predominantly liberal nor conservative as those terms are commonly used, but ranges and mixes across the political spectrum. Religious groups can be found on opposite sides of many issues, sometimes even within the same religious tradition. But alliances of strange bedfellows also emerge, as some concerns transcend conventional ideological categories.

Third, the issue agenda extends beyond what might seem as obvious religious concerns. Because many religious organizations apply their moral principles expansively, any issue that touches on questions of justice, rights, poverty, opportunity, family integrity, human dignity, or peace potentially falls under their purview.

These patterns vividly portray how deeply engaged religious advocates are, or hope to be, in public policy.

A MODEL OF RELIGIOUS GROUP EFFECTIVENESS

What makes for religious group effectiveness?[13] We suggest that five factors contribute to success: (1) amenable traditions and theological beliefs; (2) internal strength and unity; (3) strategic location; (4) constraints and opposition from other groups; and (5) a favorable "spirit of the times"—that is, whether the political culture is open to a group's political advocacy.

Traditions and Theological Beliefs

Historical traditions and theological beliefs influence whether a religious group will enter politics at all, and, if so, how it will approach that task. Some religious traditions are so otherworldly that they eschew politics altogether; others get involved only when they feel a direct threat. The Jehovah's Witnesses are a group that generally stays out of politics, with the exception of occasional forays into the courts to protect their religious freedom. Others, such as Lutherans, have a deep tradition of teaching civic responsibility for the individual but resisting corporate political witness by the church, a tendency that frustrates some Lutheran activists.[14]

Other religious traditions lend themselves to political action more readily. The American Catholic Church has long been at ease with politics and has a deep scholastic tradition of reflection on statecraft. Jewish groups, drawing upon a theology rooted heavily in justice, tend to approach public action with enthusiasm. Muslims, though they are newcomers to the advocacy scene, also arise from a religious tradition steeped in government and law. And, more than any other American religious group, African-American Protestantism has long been deeply involved in political activism. The Civil Rights movement was organizationally based in black churches, and many African-American clergy say they could not imagine their pastoral role without a political component.[15]

Internal Strength and Unity

No religious group will be able to make much of a political impact without supportive lay members. It is strategically important to have a large and unified membership. At the same time, the existence of internal dissent, disputes among leaders, and resistance from members all detract from political clout. This is a major challenge within American Catholicism because some lay members, including important political officials, dissent from the official positions of the Catholic hierarchy.[16] Catholic Democrats in Congress mostly take pro-choice positions on abortion, for example.

Equally important is the intensity of group members' commitment. Are laity willing to write only an occasional letter to Congress? Or are they ready to sacrifice hours of their time in building the organization, participating in telephone trees, and attending endless meetings? Are they willing to speak, vote, demonstrate, or even go to jail for their convictions?

Even the most committed participants need effective leaders. Strong leaders must exhibit energy, drive, and conviction. They must also have the ability to think strategically, form alliances, and articulate their messages in an appealing manner—often to elites who do not share their religious values. As in any organization, however, there is a risk that leaders may become inattentive to the members themselves.[17] Because this situation can diminish members' sense of having a stake in the organization, the best leaders try to balance the inevitable need for management at the top with attentiveness to the goals and energies of members at the grassroots level. Some religious groups, as we shall see, have been highly successful at achieving this balance, but others struggle.

Finally, resources, especially financial resources, are an absolute necessity for any political organization. Are members affluent, and are they willing to make financial contributions? Do they have time for politics? Are they well connected already, as contributors to political parties, as personal friends of members of Congress, or as leaders in their communities? Do they have expertise that the organization might need, perhaps in legal advocacy, policy analysis, or marketing? Many Jewish groups, for example, combine all of these components of internal strength and unity and are therefore politically effective, as are Quakers. Other groups enjoy a different kind of resource base. The International Campaign for Tibet, which represents the exiled community of Tibetan Buddhists, benefits from a large and intense international following of the Dalai Lama and the support of Hollywood celebrities.

Strategic Location

Another factor that is crucial to political success is a religious interest group's "strategic location." Does the group enjoy natural access to elites in government? Or does it have to beat down the door just to get noticed? Meaningful access does not just involve securing one meeting with a few members of Congress or their staffs. It means getting serious hearings with congressional leaders and committee chairs, top White House officials, high-ranking bureaucrats and administrators (who formulate much policy), and the courts. Meaningful access also involves working with the assorted network of think tanks, law firms, foundations, and influence-peddlers in Washington who know how the political game is played. It is useful to have connections with state and local officials, some of whom retain enormous influence over the federal government as well. The best access of all is to the elite national press. In a town where the words of the *Washington Post*—or the broadcasts of Fox News—often matter a good deal, the ability to gain favorable media exposure is crucial.

Constraints and Opposition

The power, intensity, and access of a group's opponents matter. Some groups, of course, ignite more opposition than others. This has perennially been the case for Christian conservatives, who face such groups as the Interfaith Alliance or People for the American Way, which intentionally present themselves as opponents of the Christian right. Muslim groups, too, face serious opposition from vehement critics and the serious constraint of skeptical public opinion. In mainline Protestant and Catholic circles, we often see tougher struggles against opposition within their own ranks. Such opposition is sometimes based in policy disputes. In other instances, members simply see political involvement of any kind as a divisive diversion from their view of the church's mission—to provide meaning, spiritual comfort, forgiveness, or conciliation. Moreover, suspicion of religious activism is endemic in American culture. The tradition of church–state separation in the United States encourages skepticism about church involvement in politics. How effectively a group overcomes these hurdles often determines how far it can go politically.

Zeitgeist: Spirit of the Times and Political Context

The fortunes of a religious group are governed in part by how well its agenda conforms to the spirit of the times and the dominant political context. A spirit of liberal political activism in the 1960s aided mainline Protestant churches, just as a more conservative tone in the 1980s helped conservative evangelicals.[18] Rising concern for religious persecution in the 1990s buoyed the political fortunes of religious minorities, from Baha'is to Tibetan Buddhists, whereas the environment since September 11, 2001, has presented a major challenge to Muslims. More recently, progressive religious aspirations soared with the presidency of Barack Obama while evangelical populists gained currency with the election of Donald Trump.

STRATEGIES FOR EFFECTIVE ADVOCACY

In one sense, the politics of "pressure groups" has not changed fundamentally since the nineteenth century. Effective advocacy is—and always has been—a combination of outside pressure and inside influence coalescing in favorable circumstances.

Outside Pressure

To be effective, interest groups must rely on a loyal network of members or influential institutions at the grassroots level that can bring pressure to bear on members of Congress and state legislators. The threat of electoral defeat remains a powerful motivator of modern politicians.[19] All elected officials know that groups with many members or well-heeled contributors can have an effect on their fortunes on Election Day. The kinds of outside pressure brought by interest groups vary tremendously by group and context. Mass mobilization, a technique commonly used by conservative Protestant organizations, represents one approach. Television and radio ministry connections, huge lists of contributors, and affiliated activist churches can generate a groundswell of communication to elected officials, which can attract attention and occasionally affect policy.[20]

Mass mobilization is necessary but rarely sufficient for success. Members of Congress often discount the "artificially inseminated" constituent communication that results from mass mobilization. More modest but well placed and informed constituent communication can be as effective. Members of the liberal nuns' lobby, NETWORK, for example, have some influence because their members are well read, knowledgeable about politics, and looped into informational networks around the globe through their religious orders.[21]

As a supplement to mass mobilization, sophisticated groups also activate smaller lists of key contacts that may be reached via phone, email, texts, or Twitter for a quick response. This is effective because sometimes a few influential community leaders and party contributors who personally know their member of Congress can have greater clout than relatively unsophisticated supporters or newcomers to politics. But not all groups are equally adept or positioned to do this. Jewish groups are renowned for deploying key contacts because local rabbis or Jewish civic leaders tend to be prominent members of their communities. The same is true of Catholic bishops, pastors of megachurches, and leading African-American clergy.

Money, of course, speaks loudly in contemporary politics. Most religious groups, however, do not form PACs, organizations that donate money to candidates. Nor are clergy normally in the position to make substantial individual contributions to candidates, political parties, or PACs, with a few exceptions. Jewish organizations, especially pro-Israel groups, do support PACs; they constitute important sources of money for both individual congressional candidates and political parties. Some Jewish citizens are also major contributors and fund-raisers—particularly for the Democratic Party—and this provides access. Like other religious bodies, African-American churches are tax-exempt institutions and thus cannot form PACs or make direct financial contributions, but they do sometimes allow their property to be used for political fund-raisers. They also frequently invite candidates to speak during services. Because overt political involvement is more accepted in the African-American religious community than in the rest of organized religion in the United States, favored candidates are sometimes able to raise money through direct appeals made in churches.

By and large, however, religious actors are not big players in the political money game. Some argue that this protects them from the corrupting influences of fund-raising and allows them to present a clearer moral message to leaders. And sometimes this may be true; religious leaders, at their best, present politicians with visions of the public good undiluted by narrow self-interest. But money does speak, and religious leaders often resign themselves to the fact that they will not have that tool at their disposal.

When a religious interest group demonstrates the ability to shape public opinion, it brings indirect pressure on politicians. Strategies and success rates for this activity vary, however. Events staged for media coverage have become common. Demonstrations, dramatic testimony, publicized fact-finding reports, and statements by bishops are all aimed at the mass media and the broader public.

Here it is crucial that the religious group enjoy the sympathies of the elite press. Conservative evangelicals, pro-life activists, and defenders of traditional marriage complain bitterly that they are not given a fair hearing in the mass media and that they are either ignored or stereotyped. As surveys of elite journalists show, there is some truth to this analysis.[22]

Inside Influence

No matter how much outside pressure an interest group can mount, it means little if group leaders are not skilled at gaining and keeping elite access. To have any measure of political success, a group needs the chance to tell sympathetic policy-makers about its agenda. Here, too, not all religious groups are equal. Some enjoy excellent access; others have to fight for every bit.

The quality of interest-group leadership matters greatly.[23] Some groups employ lobbyists with years of experience and strong reputations; others suffer from lack of experience or little perceived gravitas. Experienced interest-group leaders have a strong strategic sense, developing a clear, limited set of attainable objectives on the basis of the current political climate. Jewish groups enjoy the reputation for this kind of leadership. On the other hand, one of the recurrent problems faced by mainline Protestant lobbies is a lack of sharp focus and a tendency to take on too many issues at the same time, although some mainline leaders are striving to address this problem.[24]

Propitious circumstances work to a group's advantage. Sojourners founder Jim Wallis, as a self-proclaimed "progressive" evangelical, captured the attention of then senator Barack Obama, who spoke on the "proper connection" between faith and politics at a Sojourners gathering in 2006. With Obama's election to the presidency, Wallis gained the kind of access most religious leaders only dream of—and put Sojourners into a leadership role among progressive religious groups.[25] The election of Donald Trump in 2016, on the other hand, propelled groups like the conservative Family Research Council (FRC) into the limelight. Suddenly it was Tony Perkins, president of the FRC, who enjoyed enviable access.

The size of the religious community does not always determine the sophistication of the lobbying operation. The Society of Friends, or Quakers, has a tiny membership in the United States. Its members, however, are affluent, well educated, and highly motivated to make a political difference, so the Quakers support one of the better-staffed and more sophisticated religious lobby operations in Washington.

In spite of the growing presence and diversity of religious lobbies, most remain modest affairs compared with such giants as the National Education Association, the American Association for Retired Persons, or the National Association of Manufacturers (the one exception is the huge American Israel Public Affairs Committee). A large religious lobby may have twenty-five staff (a few have upward of seventy or so), but many operate with only a handful of people. A major secular lobby, on the other hand, could have 300 or more professional staff. This is part of the reason that—despite periodic exceptional cases of high impact—religious organizations exercise mostly modest political influence in the grand scheme of Washington, or statehouse, politics.

Blending Strategies for Impact

The best lobbies, of course, combine outside pressure and inside access. The cultivation and mobilization of key contacts, for example, can achieve a perfect marriage of Washington operation and grassroots pressure. To appreciate the effectiveness of this strategy, imagine a member of Congress expressing skepticism at a hearing about a group's favored legislation. The lobbyist in the room dashes off a text to her office, and immediately communication flows to influential contributors, community leaders, or even personal friends of the member. Stories circulate in Washington about how some groups are able to deliver high-level personal protests to members of Congress even before a day's hearing is over. Even if this occurs rarely, members of Congress pay attention if they know a group has this kind of reach.

An increasingly common strategy that blends grassroots pressure and more traditional insider lobbying is the Washington "lobby day" or "voter summit." Here a group brings members from around the country to the capital for a multiday conference that features prominent speakers, provides training on issues and strategies, organizes visits to congressional offices, and then sends participants back home with instructions to mobilize others.

Among the largest of these gatherings are AIPAC's annual meeting and the Values Voter Summit, sponsored by Focus on the Family, the Family Research Council, and other social conservative groups. Progressive Protestants, on the other hand, host an annual Ecumenical Advocacy Day, whereas a host of Catholic groups join at the Catholic Social Ministries Gathering.

The Sikh Coalition employs an imaginative approach, called the Sikh Advocate Academy, which brings a small cadre of activists from around the country to receive "a week-long, all expenses paid, experiential learning course in Washington, DC." Upon completion, participants receive "certification" as members of the volunteer Sikh Coalition Advocacy Corps.[26]

THE CYBER REVOLUTION

A treatment of outside pressure and inside influence would be incomplete without a discussion of the cyber revolution, which has transformed mobilization and woven it deeply into the policy-making process. Previous studies of religious advocacy found that most religious groups lacked the means of operating large direct-mail operations to generate constituent pressure on policy-makers.[27] Today, maintaining a large email list and a Facebook or Twitter presence is relatively cheap, and, with the click of a mouse, constituents can register their views with their congressional representatives.

Previously, constituent communication was mostly one-way—flowing from national offices to grassroots members—but today communications are more interactive. Facebook posts, online surveys, bulletin-board postings, Twitter, blogs, and podcasts can connect lobbyists, laypersons, and policy-makers in an increasingly interactive web. National religious leaders now receive feedback readily from members who interact with one another and potentially with policy-makers.

Social media can speed responses to developments in Washington. When email turnaround is deemed too slow, a Twitter pop-up can generate an immediate and targeted constituency response to a wavering member of a congressional committee. Social media can also magnify the grassroots reach of advocacy groups. When revelations of "enhanced interrogation techniques" surfaced during the second Bush administration, the Friends Committee on National Legislation initiated a national cyber campaign against torture. The campaign went viral and generated as many as 160,000 messages to Congress, more than twice the number of people the Friends Committee has on its email list (60,000).[28]

As we see in Table 8.2 and Table 8.3, social media has grown tremendously in the five years between 2012 and 2017—in some cases by exponential margins. Thus, many citizens potentially can be mobilized by religious groups on an array of issues. This seems especially the case for large globally engaged organizations, such as World Vision, the International Justice Mission (IJM), and Catholic Relief Services. We also notice that use of social media varies widely, indicating that not all groups have the capacity to maximize this resource. While the size and scope of an organization is reflected in Facebook and Twitter followings, this is not the dominant pattern. AIPAC may have the largest budget of all the groups, but it is dwarfed on social media by at least half a dozen other organizations. Finally, the exceptionally dramatic increase in the Facebook following of the American Center for Law and Justice (ACLJ) from 50,000 to 4 million cries out for explanation. In part, this reflects the group's growing budget and global reach. But it also owes to the prominence of its director, Jay Sekulow, an influential figure in conservative evangelical circles and recent legal adviser to President Trump. In addition to heading ACLJ and a network

ADVOCACY ORGANIZATION	TWITTER FOLLOWERS IN 2012	TWITTER FOLLOWERS IN 2017
World Vision	31,051	1,191,023
International Justice Mission	27,330	177,820
United States Conference of Catholic Bishops	18,907	121,849
American Center for Law and Justice	13,510	119,795
Sojourners	25,037	102,584
International Christian Concern	9,600	75,393
American Israel Public Affairs Committee	12,615	74,796
Catholic Relief Services	13,875	67,274
Anti-Defamation League	4,766	57,523
Salvation Army	10,532	55,764
Republican Jewish Coalition	6,361	53,667
Council on American-Islamic Relations	4,763	41,175
Family Research Council	4,866	28,724
Adventist Development and Relief Agency International	5,024	26,778
Jewish Federations of North America	4,247	25,026
J Street	6,069	21,354
Evangelical Lutheran Church in America	5,646	20,823
Bread for the World	5,975	17,575
World Relief	3,786	16,908
Save Darfur Coalition	13,337	15,961
Human Life International	4,217	15,023
United Methodist Church, General Board of Church and Society	3,841	14,306
American Jewish World Service	4,228	13,162
International Campaign for Tibet	4,260	12,534
Religious Action Center of Reform Judaism	3,728	12,344
Lutheran World Relief	3,690	11,931
Sisters of Mercy of the Americas	3,276	10,413
Prison Fellowship, Justice Fellowship	3,682	7,290

TABLE 8.2 Religious Advocacy Organizations by Twitter Followers

Source for 2012: Katherine Rose, "Facebook and Religious Advocacy: The Great Equalizer," Honors Research Paper, University of Oklahoma, May 8, 2012. Source for 2017: Data collected by Alan Murphey, Undergraduate student, University of Oklahoma.

ADVOCACY ORGANIZATION	FACEBOOK FOLLOWERS IN 2012	FACEBOOK FOLLOWERS IN 2017
American Center for Law and Justice	56,291	4,082,237
World Vision	888,854	1,204,510
International Christian Concern	162,425	861,929
Catholic Relief Services	41,958	380,711
International Justice Mission	57,273	312,331
Adventist Development and Relief Agency	66,798	252,252
United States Conference of Catholic Bishops	38,793	200,741
American Israel Public Affairs Committee	30,219	157,477
Americans for Peace Now	43,987	153,479
Council on American-Islamic Relations	21,488	135,921
Sojourners	25,213	113,929
International Campaign for Tibet	26,197	90,918
Sisters of Mercy of the Americas	7,868	63,680
Bread for the World	13,033	51,676
Hadassah, Women's Zionist Organization	7,650	49,921
American Friends Service Committee	7,534	48,859
J Street	15,632	40,831
American Jewish World Service	7,191	39,039
World Relief	11,789	36,196
Save Darfur Coalition	35,521	35,831
Mennonite Central Committee	11,390	28,964
Lutheran World Relief	6,488	28,433
Church World Service	5,894	23,330
Human Life International	7,760	18,841
Religious Action Center of Reform Judaism	6,517	15,785
Unitarian Universalist Service Committee	6,371	15,583

TABLE 8.3 Religious Advocacy Organizations with Global Concerns by Facebook Followers

Source for 2012: Katherine Rose, "Facebook and Religious Advocacy: The Great Equalizer," Honors Research Paper, University of Oklahoma, May 8, 2012. Source for 2017: Data collected by Alan Murphey, Undergraduate student, University of Oklahoma.

of affiliated enterprises, Sekulow hosts syndicated daily radio broadcasts and a weekly television program, which attract a large following to his social conservative advocacy.

A national lobby's effectiveness, of course, is ultimately governed by the total quality of its operation, resources, staff, research facilities, technological capacity, and institutional support, as well as the depth, sophistication, and commitment of constituents. Social media can enhance effectiveness but cannot compensate for organizational limits or constraints in the political environment.

COALITION BUILDING IN THE LEGISLATIVE PROCESS

At the heart of the legislative process—whether in Congress or in statehouses—is consensus-building. The American constitutional system frustrates swift action. The numerous checks and veto points that are built into the system delay proposals and allow many groups the chance to block proposed legislation. Political insiders know this, so they work to build the strongest possible coalition of supporters, including occasional "strange bedfellows" alliances.[29]

Religious leaders realize that it is essential to build coalitions with other lobbies to magnify their voices. Coalitions are effective because a kind of specialization operates: Different groups rotate the lead in different lobbying campaigns because of their special expertise or focus. Thus, Quakers might lead the coalition on nuclear proliferation, but Bread for the World would do so on hunger. Different groups have access to different policy-makers, so when groups join hands, the collective clout is greater.

Sometimes temporary alliances form around a single issue. The conservative evangelical group CWA teamed up with Muslim groups and the Catholic Church to spearhead a United Nations resolution banning cloning. Legislation to enable the Food and Drug Administration to regulate tobacco was backed by the Southern Baptist Convention and the United Methodist Church, two bodies that tend to disagree on hot-button cultural issues. On the prevention of prison rape, Prison Fellowship, a conservative evangelical group, teamed up with liberal groups to gain passage of legislation trying to curb the problem. On fighting poverty, the conservative Family Research Council teamed up with the liberal Evangelicals for Social Action to propose policies that would enhance the take-home pay of working-class and poor Americans.[30]

On other issues, normal allies have become serious ongoing adversaries. On Israel, for example, liberal Protestant groups part company with their Jewish counterparts in staking out a critical posture toward Israeli policies that they see as unjust to Palestinians. Most evangelical Protestants, on the other hand, are strongly supportive of Israel, both because of a theology that sees the formation of Israel as providential and because Israel represents a bulwark against what they see as the militant Islamist forces arrayed against the United States.[31]

The religious community can be formidable when groups across the ideological and theological spectrum band together. From the late 1990s through to the first decade of the twenty-first century, this occurred with coalitions backing international religious freedom, debt relief for poor countries, funding to fight AIDS in Africa, and multiple measures against human trafficking.[32]

To show how all these factors influence the actions and effectiveness of different American religious groups, we now turn to some examples.

Progressive Protestant Groups

As we noted in Chapter 2, mainline Protestants enjoyed a strategic location in American society through much of the twentieth century. Moreover, beginning with the Social Gospel movement of the early twentieth century, mainline church leaders came to share a liberal theology that encouraged, and even expected, their involvement in "this world," which would include the political realm.[33] Thus they were, and continue to be, both receptive to political action and in a position to have some influence.

The most vivid illustration of this combination came with the Civil Rights movement. Inspired by Dr. Martin Luther King, Jr., mainline denominational leaders became pivotal advocates and strategists for the landmark Civil Rights Act of 1964. They mobilized laity and brought delegations of clergy to Washington to lobby members of Congress, which was especially effective in gaining the swing votes of Midwestern Republicans who belonged to their denominations.[34] The 1960s, however, represented the high-water mark for the mainline denominations in Washington. Weakened by declining church memberships and diminishing financial support from the pews, and sometimes criticized as being out of touch with lay members, mainline church lobbies are no longer as prominent as they were in the past.[35] This is especially the case for their umbrella organization, the National Council of Churches. On the other hand, mainline lobbyists today are buoyed by the proliferation of allied groups, so it is helpful to treat mainline Protestants more generally and examine the alliances they form with Catholics, Jews, progressive evangelicals, and secular liberals.

The political agenda of progressive Protestants is wide-ranging. The National Council of Churches and affiliated religious bodies, for example, took a turn to the left on foreign policy in the late 1960s and early 1970s, repeatedly objecting to US military activities abroad. Most recently, they have objected to the wars in Afghanistan and Iraq. On domestic affairs, progressive Protestants have embraced a broad agenda that includes issues relating to poverty, healthcare, women's equality, the environment, affirmative action, and, in some cases, abortion rights and gay rights.[36]

The progressive Protestant lobbying community in Washington does include the government-relations offices of the mainline denominations, particularly the Episcopal Church, the Evangelical Lutheran Church in America, the Presbyterian Church (USA), the United Church of Christ, the American Baptist Churches USA, and the United Methodist Church. Their work is bolstered by the robust organizational presence of the peace churches—the Quakers and the Mennonites (see Box 8.1), Unitarian Universalists, and African-American denominations.

One of the more intriguing developments is the way in which progressive evangelical groups, such as Evangelicals for Social Action and Sojourners, have provided fresh energy for causes dear to religious liberals. The broadening of the agenda of the usually conservative National Association of Evangelicals to include poverty and environmental concerns has created new alliance opportunities as well.[37]

One of the challenges facing progressive Protestant groups is convincing lay members of the value and urgency of their agenda. Sometimes this challenge reflects an ideological gap between clergy and laity, and sometimes it demonstrates a lack of effort by leaders to persuade and mobilize members. But, with the technological revolution, most progressive Protestants have expanded grassroots networks.[38] Some evidence suggests that the "clergy–laity gap" may not be as salient in low-income urban congregations, where economic hardship presents incentives for political action through churches, as well as heightened resonance of the social-justice message.[39]

BOX 8.1 MENNONITE CENTRAL COMMITTEE: A PACIFIST LOBBY

The story of the Mennonite Central Committee illustrates how the actions of the federal government have spurred the growth of church lobbies. One of the perennial issues for pacifist denominations such as the Mennonites is how to protect their members from compulsory military service. Thus, the Mennonites were shocked in 1967 when they learned that proposed selective service legislation during the Vietnam War would not allow the kind of broad conscientious-objector provisions that had protected them from military service during World War II. Church leaders traveled to Washington, testified at congressional hearings, and ultimately saw changes made in the law. The Mennonite Central Committee established a permanent Washington office in 1968. Although it is small by Washington standards, the Mennonite office remains a visible player in the religious community.

Source: Keith Graber Miller, *American Mennonites Engage Washington: Wise as Serpents, Innocent as Doves?* (Knoxville, TN: University of Tennessee Press, 1996).

Roman Catholic Groups

Representing nearly a quarter of the population and a host of national and international institutions, Catholic leaders are formidable players in national politics. From the New Deal onward, Catholic interest groups enjoyed an advantageous strategic location in American politics, along with corresponding access to political decision-makers. On the one hand, most Catholic leaders are generally comfortable with—and in some cases stand to the left of—the Democrats' approach to such issues as welfare spending, labor laws, the death penalty, and immigration reform. On the other hand, they join with the Republicans in opposing abortion, preserving traditional marriage, defending conscience rights, promoting parental-choice options in education, and criticizing some elements of popular culture. Thus, religious political activists across the spectrum—from conservative evangelicals to ecumenical liberals—often view Catholics as potential allies.[40] Among the strengths of the Catholic lobby are a theological comfort with politics and a scholastic tradition of serious reflection on issues. Given the formal authority of clergy in the Catholic Church, these attitudes provide an important resource for mobilization.[41]

The USCCB represents the official political positions of the Catholic Church. The clear Catholic organizational structure, along with a strong hierarchical tradition, allows its leaders to speak with authority for the Catholic Church. This fact represents a distinct political advantage. Thus, even if lay opinion is divided on an issue, the official Catholic Church position can be articulated clearly.

The Catholic lobby, however, is far from monolithic. It includes a host of associations, religious orders, and membership organizations. In most cases, these groups do not oppose the bishops directly, but there are large differences in emphasis and even ideology. On the left, we find groups such as Pax Christi, known for its opposition to wars, the Maryknoll order, known for its support of liberation theology, and NETWORK, the lobby of liberal nuns.[42] These groups are decidedly more liberal than the USCCB, especially on foreign-policy issues. We also see such groups as the Jesuit Conference, the Franciscan Action Network, and Catholic Charities, which focus tightly on social justice for the poor.

A different picture emerges, however, from large associations of Catholic hospitals, parochial schools, and universities, which have tangible financial concerns to protect as well as broader public-policy goals on health and education policy. On church–state issues, we see the Catholic League for Religious and Civil Rights, headed by William Donohue, which vigorously combats anti-Catholic bigotry in news and entertainment media. There are also organizations sustained in part by sizable Catholic memberships, including National Right to Life, the nation's oldest antiabortion group, and the National Organization for Marriage, which opposed state recognition of same-sex marriage and now defends the rights of religious institutions to operate in accordance with their traditional teachings.

Since the nineteenth century, the American Catholic Church has battled to obtain state support for its school system, in recent times especially by promoting legislation allowing choice in education through state support in the form of vouchers for parents sending their children to nonpublic schools. The Catholic Church has faced vigorous and effective opposition from public teacher unions, civil-liberties groups, Protestant organizations such as the Baptist Joint Committee, and the formidable Americans United for Separation of Church and State.

Ever since the US Supreme Court struck down restrictive state abortion statutes in *Roe* v. *Wade* in 1973, the Catholic Church has also been at the center of pro-life lobbying, both in Washington and in state legislatures.[43] Despite the church's enormous investment of political capital in the issue, its successes have been modest: a few restrictions on late-term abortions, fragile conscience protections for healthcare providers with moral convictions against abortion, and some restraint on federal funding on abortions. And all of these gains came under pressure during the Obama administration.

One of the weaknesses of Catholic political groups is the diversity of opinion in the pews and among Catholic politicians.[44] Although polls on abortion sometimes are ambiguous, there is no question that a sizable number of Catholics support some degree of reproductive freedom, and women who identify themselves as Catholic appear as likely to have abortions as are non-Catholic women. Although support for the church's position is strongest among those who most faithfully attend Mass, the lack of lay unity impairs the Catholic Church's political impact.

Until recently, Catholic groups enjoyed great success regarding the public funding of various domestic social-service agencies associated with the church. Part of the reason for this is the Catholic tendency to separate religion from the actual method of providing the service. Unlike evangelical "gospel missions" and other pervasively religious groups, Catholic agencies, such as Catholic Charities, do not expect clients to engage in religious behavior as a condition of receiving food assistance, job training, housing, or other benefits. Consequently, federal and state grants worth millions of dollars have flowed through Catholic social-service agencies.[45]

Catholic leaders, however, now see new threats to these partnerships, even towards their ability to operate at all in civil society. Legal enforcement of marriage equality and mandates for contraception and abortion confront Catholic hospitals, colleges, adoption programs, and charities with the choice of either defying the law or violating church teachings. Long-standing Catholic adoption agencies in Massachusetts, Washington, DC, and Illinois, for example, were forced to shut down because governments provided no conscience exemptions for the requirement that the agencies place children with same-sex couples rather than refer such couples to other adoption programs. A Catholic refugee-resettlement program also lost its contract with the federal government because it would not provide abortion services. During the Obama administration, Catholic institutions confronted a mandate that they provide free contraceptive services in their health plans, in violation of church teaching. In a celebrated case, an order of nuns that serve the indigent elderly, the Little Sisters of the Poor, faced millions of dollars in fines for refusing to comply with the mandate. Only after lengthy litigation did the nuns gain relief from a Supreme Court ruling.[46]

In response to this new zeitgeist, Catholic leaders increasingly invoke the defense of "life, marriage, and religious liberty" as their prime political task. The Catholic bishops formed an ad-hoc Committee on Religious Freedom in 2011 and then made it permanent in 2017, sponsored sermons and rallies across the country in defense of religious conscience rights, and issued statements to be read at Mass on threats to religious freedom and Catholic teaching on sacramental marriage. The overall campaign, which produced a steady flow of blog postings, church bulletin inserts, editorials in Catholic publications, and the like, showcased the mobilizing capacity of the hierarchy. But to Catholic progressives, this campaign seemed to move the bishops sharply to the right on the political spectrum, as indicated by provisions in the 2016 Republican Party platform endorsing the church's positions. Again, we see how thorny are the strategic challenges confronting Catholic interest groups in the United States.

Jewish Groups

The Jewish proportion of the population in the United States is small—less than 2 percent—but it is also highly educated, relatively affluent, and politically active. These characteristics by themselves translate into significant political resources.[47]

Jewish theological diversity is reflected in national organizations of the three major branches of Judaism—Reform, Conservative, and Orthodox—which are active in civic and political affairs. In Washington, both the Reform and Orthodox branches of Judaism maintain national lobbying offices. Of these, the most active is the Religious Action Center of Reform Judaism, which represents the largest branch of American Judaism and is decidedly liberal. Orthodox Jews, represented by the Union of Orthodox Jewish Congregations of America, part company with their more liberal counterparts on abortion, marriage, and school vouchers.

Of course, no discussion of Jewish advocacy would be complete without attention to AIPAC, one of the most formidable lobbies in Washington. AIPAC's sole aim is to coordinate American support for the Jewish state of Israel, and it has become a model for a whole range of other interest groups that wish to influence US foreign policy. With a staff of at least 250 in Washington and an equal number in branches around the country, AIPAC is respected and sometimes even feared in Washington political circles. It has combined excellent research resources in its Washington office, a grassroots network of activist members, and a host of affiliated PACs that contribute money to pro-Israel candidates for federal office. And there is, in fact, tangible evidence of AIPAC's effectiveness in Congress. Largely because of AIPAC's efforts, the billions of dollars in foreign aid that the United States sends to Israel no longer comes in the form of loans; it is now given as outright grants.[48]

AIPAC has not gone unchallenged. Critiques of the "Israel lobby" charge AIPAC with distorting US foreign policy and undermining American interests in the Middle East.[49] And, in 2008, a group of progressive Jews formed a new lobby group, J Street, to counter what they see as AIPAC's uncritical support for Israeli occupation of Palestinian territory, which they view as undemocratic and threatening to Israel's long-term security. Describing itself as "the political home for pro-Israel, pro-peace Americans," J Street promotes diplomacy that would provide Palestinians with a sovereign state in return for Israel's security.[50]

These challenges have not yet seriously dented the clout of AIPAC, in part because American public opinion remains strongly supportive of Israel, but also because organized Christian Zionist groups, such as Christians United for Israel, generally back AIPAC's position.[51] On most issues, Jewish political groups are liberal. They have championed abortion rights, opposed school prayer and school voucher programs, sought strict separation of church and state, and backed gay rights and full gender equality. They have consistently opposed the Christian right in the political realm.[52] The growing political clout of Orthodox Jews has increased the pluralism of the American Jewish political witness.

On such issues as opposition to abortion and gay rights and support for public recognition of faith, Orthodox Jews often have the same perspective as evangelicals and conservative Catholics. The Rabbinical Council of America—the national organization of Orthodox rabbis—has also become more politically active on such issues as public support for religious schools.

Why do Jewish groups enjoy such excellent elite access in Washington and elsewhere? First, Jewish faith and tradition promote political participation. In Jewish Scripture, for example, the ancient Hebrews lived under God's mercy and judgment on the basis of how faithfully they organized their communal affairs. Jewish communities in America also foster a robust public life in which people feel at home with the debates and compromises of politics. Indeed, if one compares Jewish Americans with other Americans of similar economic standing, it is striking how much more interested in the world of politics many Jews tend to be. This ease with politics is, of course, a major benefit. Jewish leaders do not have to spend time and energy convincing their members that politics is a legitimate activity because their members are already politically involved.[53]

Second, Jewish political organizations build on many internal resources. At the local level, American Jews operate vibrant community organizations and chapters of national groups. Thus, when national leaders seek to mount political pressure, they can call upon a wide range of people and organizations. Even in regions with small Jewish populations, prominent Jewish citizens sometimes know their congressional representatives personally. Relative affluence is also a real plus—and one that leaders have no timidity about tapping. Jews are major contributors to a range of interest groups and to political parties, candidates, and pro-Israel PACs.[54]

Jewish political resources are maximized by a host of strong leaders. Indeed, some of them have been legends in Washington: confidants of presidents, friends of members of Congress, quintessential insiders.[55] One reason for this sustained access is the longevity of senior Jewish leadership, a product of stability in the Washington community. For example, Rabbi David Saperstein headed the Religious Action Center of Reform Judaism in Washington, DC, for more than three decades, then was selected by President Obama to serve as ambassador for international religious freedom. Longevity fosters not only wisdom in the ways of politics but a long view of lobbying strategy.

Third, Jews enjoy excellent strategic access to political elites. In part, their strategic location is a function of the presence of Jews in a variety of elite circles. It is, of course, hard to speak of this fact without promoting unfair stereotypes or feeding conspiracy theories that suggest a vast Jewish ruling cabal. The truth is that many American Jews strongly embrace education and civic engagement. This results in a mathematical overrepresentation of Jews at elite levels of government, media, and the academy.

Jewish leaders employ resources to cultivate political elites throughout the system. They also work assiduously with top bureaucrats and cabinet members. They cultivate the media, and they build alliances with the vast network of Washington lobbies and law firms. Finally, they benefit from the broadly positive sentiment non-Jewish Americans have of Jews.[56]

Evangelical Protestant Groups

No other organized religious advocacy has received as much attention as the efforts of evangelicals in the past three decades. Evangelical Protestantism thrives in the free marketplace of American religion, producing many entrepreneurial leaders, a vital resource for interest-group formation and maintenance. Moreover, as political scientist Robert Putnam observes, American evangelicals have built "the largest, best organized grassroots" social movement network of the past quarter century.[57] Thus, such well-funded groups as Family Research Council, CWA, Focus on the Family, and the ACLJ draw upon the resources of a host of conservative Protestant denominations and the extensive network of nondenominational megachurches, local activist groups, alternative schools, Christian colleges, parachurch organizations, broadcast ministries, and publishing houses. Lobbying activity is melded into a political movement—the Christian right—which combines multifarious activities of institutional development, electoral mobilization, litigation, media campaigns, and demonstrations.[58]

Despite periodic announcements of its death, the Christian right movement has endured, with successive waves of mobilization since its birth in the 1970s and 1980s. (We discuss the roots of the Christian right more fully in Chapter 10.)

When the movement's first major organization, the Moral Majority, went defunct, Pat Robertson founded a new group, the Christian Coalition, to pick up the mantle. When the Christian Coalition foundered, the Family Research Council moved into the breach. As long as cultural discontent with American society remains, there very likely will be Christian-right interest groups at all levels of society. Indeed, a heightened sense of threat—as felt by some evangelical leaders over the nationalization of same-sex marriage—often leads to increased fund-raising and group formation.

Like black church organizations, but unlike most other religious interest groups, Christian-right groups focus heavily on electoral mobilization, and some have even formed PACs to help finance campaigns, a rarity among religious lobbies. From the Moral Majority to the Christian Coalition to the Family Research Council, evangelical groups have engaged in massive voter mobilization initiatives so successfully that a definable Christian conservative voting bloc has become an important part of the Republican Party.[59] The paradox, as Wilcox and Robinson note, is that the Christian right has been "the most successful social movement in influencing elections and party politics over the past century," but it has been largely unsuccessful in winning major policy change around its core agenda.[60] The structure of American national government, with its numerous veto points and opponents' countermobilization, ensures that most Christian conservative victories will be modest and incremental.

It is also important to note that, even among evangelicals, pluralism reigns. Not all expressions of organized evangelical advocacy fit the stereotypical mold of the Christian right. Indeed, the National Association of Evangelicals recently has moved away from an exclusive focus on the core Christian-right issues of abortion and family structure to embrace concern for the poor, "Creation Care" environmental concerns, and international human rights. And some evangelicals, such as the aforementioned Jim Wallis, are in overt opposition to the Christian right.[61] There also is diversity among conservative evangelicals. There are legal advocacy groups, such as the Christian Legal Society, which take a self-consciously moderate posture, whereas others, such as the ACLJ, present a harder edge. The Southern Baptist Convention's Ethics and Religious Liberty Commission (ERLC) mixes conservative stances on abortion and gay marriage with more liberal positions on immigration reform and race relations. The head of ERLC, Russell Moore, earned the ire of fellow evangelicals for his criticism of Donald Trump during the 2016 election. There are single-issue groups, such as the Home School Legal Defense Fund, led by Michael Farris, which see themselves in a fierce battle to maintain autonomy against an overweening state. Other groups, such as Prison Fellowship, created by the late Charles Colson, promote prison reforms also embraced by liberals.

One of the unmistakable legacies of organized evangelical mobilization of all kinds has been a kind of citizen education. Conservative and progressive evangelical groups have invested enormous resources in "leadership schools" and various voter-awareness programs that explain such matters as where to register to vote and how to attend a caucus. Some initiatives generate understandable controversy, such as the practice of some Christian-right groups of distributing voter guides in churches that attempt to circumvent IRS guidelines against endorsements by showing side-by-side comparisons of presidential candidates' stands on issues that leave little doubt for whom congregation members should vote. In other cases, citizen-awareness programs constitute basic civic education, leading at least one scholar to argue that the Christian right promotes "democratic virtues."[62] Whatever one thinks of the Christian right, one thing is clear: We will continue to hear about evangelical groups across the ideological spectrum.

Muslim Groups

Relative newcomers to organized politics, American Muslims illustrate several crucial themes regarding religious lobbying: the growing pluralism of religious advocacy, its globalization, and the ways new groups adapt over time to the norms of the system.

In the current political environment, Muslims face unique challenges. Critics charge that some American-Muslim interest groups are fronts for militant Islamist movements abroad, and exposés have documented the influence of foreign (especially Saudi) money in promoting a fundamentalist strain of Islam in some American mosques that is hostile to Jews, Christians, and liberal democracy. Muslim groups also operate under intense scrutiny by the US government. Yet American Muslim organizations are also crucial government allies in rooting out and combating potential terrorists, so they enjoy a considerable degree of political access to law-enforcement agencies and other government officials.[63]

In the wake of the September 11 attacks in 2001, Muslim Americans have responded in a characteristically American fashion: increasing their civic engagement and getting organized to lobby for their interests. Groups have intensified fund-raising, registered voters, and expanded operations in Washington.

American-Muslim groups voice understandable concern about US foreign policy toward Muslim nations, but they also object to domestic surveillance, profiling, and detentions. On these issues, they have gained Jewish allies committed to civil liberties, illustrating how sometimes Middle Eastern adversaries can work together. Muslim groups also lobby on social-justice issues, such as healthcare, poverty, and the environment.

One indication of growing sophistication is that groups are carving specialized niches. The Muslim American Society emphasizes grassroots mobilization; the Muslim Public Affairs Council lobbies government agencies; the Council on American Islamic Relations focuses on civil liberties; the Center for Islam and

Religious Freedom supports scholarship; and the Institute for Social Policy and Understanding serves as a policy think tank. A key umbrella organization is the Islamic Society of North America, whose annual convention attracts some 30,000 participants.

But pluralism reigns in the American Muslim community, as elsewhere, and a vigorous debate is occurring about the proper direction of Muslim advocacy. Indeed, a growing number of groups and individuals have emerged to challenge some Muslim organizations they see as compromised by Islamist ideology. Among these self-conscious reformist groups are the World Organization for Resource Development and Education (a Sufi-based group), the American Islamic Forum for Democracy (headed by Zudhi Jasser), the Center for Islamic Pluralism, and the American Islamic Congress, headed by Zainab Al-Suwaij (see Box 8.2).

BOX 8.2 ZAINAB AL-SUWAIJ: AN AMERICAN MUSLIM LEADER WITH A GLOBAL FOCUS

The granddaughter of the leading cleric in Basra, Iraq, Zainab Al-Suwaij was one of the few women to join the armed Shi'ite uprising against Saddam Hussein in the wake of the First Gulf War in 1991, at one point part of a group that stormed a prison to free dissidents. When Hussein crushed the rebellion, she was injured, went into hiding, fled to Jordan, and eventually made her way to the United States.

Al-Suwaij was teaching at Yale University in 2001, but the shock of seeing the attacks of September 11 occur in the name of her religion led her to create the American Islamic Congress. Headquartered in Washington, DC, and with offices in Boston, Cairo, and Basra, the organization promotes "responsible" moderate Muslim leadership, interfaith understanding, women's equality, and civil rights. Al-Suwaij runs women's empowerment programs in Iraq, sponsors an essay contest on civil rights for Muslim youth in the Middle East, and leads workshops on nonviolent reform for young Arab activists. Her organization widely distributes an Arabic-language comic book on the Montgomery bus boycott led by Rev. Martin Luther King, Jr. A critic of some American Muslim groups she sees as being too sympathetic to Islamist militants, she also organizes a Capitol Hill lecture series on Muslim issues. She vividly illustrates the globalization of American religious advocacy.

Source: American Islamic Congress, "Our Team," https://aicongress.org/who-we-are/our-team/; personal interview with Allen D. Hertzke, December 2008.

THE GLOBALIZATION OF RELIGIOUS ADVOCACY

From the beginning of the Republic, national religious interest groups periodically have focused on international relations. Mainline Protestant groups, for example, were pivotal in pressing for the United Nations' 1948 Universal Declaration of Human Rights, and most religious groups since then have been drawn into contentious foreign-policy issues—from the Vietnam War, to clashes over communism in Central America, to the Iraq war and terrorism.[64] However, globalization—the process by which people around the world increasingly are interlinked through commerce, travel, and communication—has heightened international awareness and increased international engagement by religious interest groups. Still, that does not guarantee their global advocacy. Consider that many North American Protestant denominations have been slow to respond to the urgent problem of persecution across the globe, even in Syria and other areas with threatened Christian populations.[65] Nevertheless, the capacities of religious groups in the United States are extensive, and the conditions worldwide have led many groups to answer what they see as a global call to justice.

Because the United States is a land of immigrants and a haven for exiles and refugees, specific American religious groups often lobby on behalf of their coreligionists in other regions of the world. Jews lobby for Israel; Uyghurs for counterparts in China; Ahmadis for their persecuted brethren in Pakistan.

But advocacy is more than just defense of fellow religionists. Falun Gong members have become adept at breaking computer firewalls that Chinese authorities erect against dissent. Because other dissidents around the world piggyback on this technology, advocacy groups have lobbied for the US government to fund this Falun Gong initiative.[66]

We also see globalization in advocacy specific to the mission of particular groups. The LDS Church maintains a Washington staff but does little congressional advocacy. Instead, it maintains relationships with embassies of foreign governments to facilitate access for its thousands of Mormon missionaries. Similarly, the ultra-Orthodox Hasidic Jewish movement, Chabad-Lubavitch, which also has a missionary impulse, opened a Washington office to help its members navigate complex laws of foreign countries.

In some cases, American religious groups actually lobby before agencies of the United Nations and other international organizations. Advocates for global religious freedom and human rights, in particular, realize that the US government can only do so much; they must make their case before international tribunals. To advance this agenda, a number of groups have established offices or affiliates abroad. For example, the American Center for Law and Justice, formed to fight for religious rights and traditional values at home, now has affiliated groups in Strasbourg and Moscow. Advocates International, an evangelical network of attorneys, supports six regional organizations and 100 national lawyer organizations to litigate for religious rights and equitable justice around the world. The international program of Becket has litigated religious-freedom cases in Europe and Asia, and its lawyers frequently testify before the United Nations Human Rights Council and the Organization for Security and Co-operation in Europe.[67]

In other cases, religious groups have concluded that they need to lobby on the international level to defend their values at home. Cultural issues, in fact, have migrated globally as the United Nations (UN) and other international entities debate women's rights, population control, secularism, or any number of other issues with socio-moral implications. Thus, conservative religious groups that often criticize the UN nevertheless have found themselves drawn into its orbit, sometimes lobbying against the positions of the US government. Leaders of CWA, for example, have joined delegates from developing nations at the UN who espouse conservative views on marriage or abortion. In one instance, representatives of CWA worked with such delegates to pass a resolution recommending a ban on all cloning.[68]

Nowhere has this global engagement manifested itself so vigorously as in campaigns for religious freedom and human rights abroad. Over the past two decades, a diverse movement of unlikely religious allies has sought to advance human rights through the machinery of American foreign policy. Thanks to the successful lobbying of Congress, this movement effectively built a new human-rights structure in American government.[69] Initially activated by concern about religious persecution abroad, religious groups across the theological spectrum fought for passage of the International Religious Freedom Act of 1998. This legislation established a permanent office in the US Department of State charged with reporting on the status of religious freedom in every country on Earth, and it required that actions be taken by the US government against countries that egregiously persecute religious believers. Many advocates, critical of what they see as the lack of commitment to the law by the State Department and the White House, continue to lobby for more vigorous enforcement. This effort is led by the International Religious Freedom Roundtable, a coalition of religious groups and nonprofit representatives that meets monthly in Washington to plan strategies and coordinate efforts. Many disparate groups join in lobbying for more aggressive American-government promotion of international religious freedom, from the Church of Scientology to Shia Rights Watch, from Seventh-Day Adventists to the USCCB, and many others.

One of the more dramatic examples of faith-based international involvement concerns human trafficking. Each year, as many as 1 million women and children are sent across international boundaries into prostitution and other forms of forced labor; many are bought and sold until they die of disease and abuse.[70] An unusual alliance of Jewish, evangelical Protestant, and secular feminist groups mounted a lobby campaign to address this modern-day slavery, and Congress responded by passing the Trafficking Victims Protection Act of 2000 and subsequent strengthening legislation.[71] The law targets crime syndicates that run the traffic, penalizes countries that fail to criminalize and appropriately punish trafficking, and provides protection for victims. The law also established an anti-trafficking office at the State Department, which has become an important center of human-rights advocacy in the federal government.[72]

A pivotal organization behind anti-trafficking initiatives is the IJM, an evangelical group with a distinct focus on combating egregious forms of injustice. With operations in at least a dozen countries in Asia, Africa, and Latin America, it works to improve justice systems by defending victims of trafficking, or unpaid labor. The organization is the creation of Gary Haugen, a Harvard graduate who worked in the Justice Department's civil-rights division during the Clinton administration. His life was transformed when he served as the chief investigator for the Rwanda war-crimes tribunal, which led him to searing interviews with victims and perpetrators and to the mass graves of the genocide. This experience challenged his faith and led him to the conviction that Bible believers slighted the powerful critique of injustice and the command to fight it. The "good news about injustice," as he wrote in a book by that title, is that God is against it.[73] So Haugen established the IJM and built it into a well-funded and highly respected operation with a nearly $60 million global budget. The IJM has received multimillion-dollar contributions from the Gates Foundation and Google to fight trafficking and slavery.[74]

One driving force behind this global agenda is the tectonic shift of the globe's Christian population to the developing world. Whereas in 1910, 80 percent of Christians lived in Europe and North America, today over 60 percent of all Christians are found in Asia, Africa, and Latin America. This shift will accelerate to an estimated 80 percent by 2050, nesting Christian congregations amid vulnerable people afflicted by poverty, violence, exploitation, and per-secution.[75] Global communication, travel, and international mission and development networks channel awareness of these conditions to American churches and advocacy groups, which lobby for ameliorative US policies.

To illustrate how many American denominations are now smaller arms of larger global ministries, consider the Seventh-Day Adventist Church. Although the Adventist faith was born in the United States, today only 1 million of its 16 million members are American. The Adventist Relief and Development Agency, headquartered in Washington, now operates with indigenous leadership in more than 100 countries. Thus, when its leaders testify on global food security, they draw upon research from their field offices around the world. This global perspective lends tremendous legitimacy to Adventist efforts to affect public policy in the United States.

The growing international role of nongovernmental organizations (NGOs) that promote economic development, peace, or human rights also has a substantial religious component. Large relief and development agencies, such as World Vision, Catholic Relief Services, Lutheran World Relief, and Church World Service, have moved from solely delivering services to engaging in political advocacy. With teams on the ground in some of the most forbidding places on earth, workers in these organizations gain unique insight into US military, trade, and aid policies, which they share in testimony before Congress or in meetings with executive agencies. Because of the size of the US government's footprint on the global stage, NGO leaders have become aware of how small changes in US policy can magnify their efforts. The US government contracts with NGOs to deliver famine relief, provide refugee services, and undertake development projects, which creates another powerful motivation for political advocacy.[76]

NGOs also can raise awareness of issues previously invisible to the international community. World Vision, for example, noticed that illegal diamond traffic in central Africa was fueling violent militias and exploiting child soldiers. In cooperation with other organizations and business, World Vision succeeded in its effort to establish an international protocol on the sad costs of "conflict diamonds." The 2006 movie *Blood Diamond* documented this issue.

Poverty, disease prevention, and economic development increasingly receive the attention of the religious advocacy community. In 2000, Pope John Paul II joined American religious groups, secular organizations, and such celebrities as Bono in the "Jubilee 2000" campaign for global debt relief. The problem this coalition had identified was that interest payments on debt accumulated by deposed governments represented a crushing burden on poor countries, which were unable to fund health, education, and economic-development programs. Taking its inspiration from the "Year of Jubilee" in Hebrew Scripture in which debts were forgiven, the movement sought debt write-offs by lender nations, the International Monetary Fund, and the World Bank.[77] The nexus of global religion, American religious groups, and US foreign policy is also illustrated by the distinct role evangelicals played in the development of the President's Emergency Plan for AIDS Relief (PEPFAR), which was launched in 2003. Evangelical development organizations, such as World Vision, saw the devastating impact of HIV/AIDS at first hand, especially in Africa, and had begun developing their own relief programs in the 1990s. In addition, many lay members learned about the AIDS crisis in Africa as a result of the growing number of mission trips sponsored by American congregations. Employing the access they enjoyed with President George W. Bush, evangelical leaders joined with Catholics and Jewish groups to lobby the president on AIDS, and he ultimately made it a signature issue. From the launch of the PEPFAR initiative in 2004, AIDS funding more than tripled.[78]

DO RELIGIOUS GROUPS PLAY A DISTINCTIVE ROLE IN AMERICAN DEMOCRACY?

Religious group leaders may disagree with each other substantially about public policy, but one conviction they share is that they contribute to the political system. Evidence suggests that collectively they do act as a modest counterweight to what scholars describe as the "elite bias" of the system. The fact is that most of the thousands of activists engaged in secular lobbying represent the self-interests of the well-heeled who have the financial resources to form national organizations or hire high-priced lobbyists. In light of this reality, religious advocates are distinctive in broadening the representativeness of the lobby world.[79]

Religious advocates also provide a moral perspective on public policy. Most of the time they are not lobbying in their own self-interest; rather, they focus on what they see as the humanitarian impulse of their tradition. A review of the mission statements of the 216 groups in the Pew Research Center's study reveals how deeply most see public policy advocacy as a natural expression of the moral mandates of faith.[80] Virtually all religious traditions have something to say about justice and the most vulnerable members of society, and the most skilled religious activists apply these moral and theological principles in conducting policy analysis of, and lobbying around, complex issues. Indeed, religious advocates often see themselves as representing "the least, the lost, and the left out."[81]

Self-interest also plays a role in religious lobbying. Some religious groups, for example, have aggressively sought a budgetary earmark for their local institutions, a practice derided as "pork barrel spending."[82] Others receive government grants for faith-based social services or international development ministries and lobby to defend their liberties and autonomy in doing so. But religious leaders make the argument that this kind of government support merely facilitates their charitable work. By representing the interests of their social institutions at home and abroad, such as charities, international relief organizations, treatment programs, homeless shelters, refugee resettlement operations, schools, colleges, and hospitals, religious lobbyists work to protect services that assist a large number of people in need. Religious advocacy, in this sense, represents a swath of civil society that transcends organized religion: the volunteer, nonprofit, nongovernmental sector. One of the things religious lobbyists do is protect the autonomy of this entire sector from governmental intrusion, enabling it to continue contributing meaningfully to society.

CONCLUSION

As this chapter shows, religious advocacy is an important part of the American political scene today. But how effective are religious lobbies? Most religious advocacy results in modest gains. For example, in spite of enormous effort over several decades, religious pro-life groups have gained only moderate, and tenuous, restrictions on abortion but not much else.

When religious lobbies do have a meaningful impact on public policy, it is usually the result of creative problem-solving and coalition-building. Religious advocacy was a driving force in the successful campaign to secure major debt relief for poor countries, in increasing funding to address world hunger, to combat AIDS in Africa, and to work to end human trafficking. When religious groups come together, their impact can be dramatic, but those occasions are rare, so we must be cautious about claiming too much for the religious advocacy community.

DISCUSSION QUESTIONS

1 Reflect on the concept of religious advocacy. In your own words, formulate a definition of it. Consider what types of groups might participate in it, what its potential benefits and downfalls might be, how it has developed over time, and the driving forces behind it.
2 In the past few decades, religious advocacy has exploded in numbers and significance. What factors might have contributed to this burst of activity?
3 What are some factors that contribute to success in religious advocacy? How do particular religious groups try to leverage these factors for their own success?
4 Why do groups (religious and otherwise) foster coalitions? What are the obstacles to religious groups in forming those coalitions?
5 What patterns emerge in the budgets of the different religious advocacy groups?
6 Have social-media tools, like Facebook and Twitter, transformed religious advocacy? Why or why not?
7 Religious advocacy has "globalized." What does that mean, and what are the implications?

FURTHER READING

Cleary, Edward L., and Allen D. Hertzke (eds.), *Representing God at the Statehouse: Religion and Politics in the American States* (Lanham, MD: Rowman & Littlefield, 2006). A collection of essays about religious lobbying at the state level.

Djupe, Paul A., and Laura R. Olson (eds.), *Religious Interests in Community Conflict* (Waco, TX: Baylor University Press, 2007). A valuable resource on local religious advocacy.

Hertzke, Allen D., *Freeing God's Children: The Unlikely Alliance for Global Human Rights* (Lanham, MD: Rowman & Littlefield, 2004). A detailed look at coalition-building among religious groups around issues of international religious freedom and human rights.

---- *Representing God in Washington: The Role of Religious Lobbies in the American Polity* (Knoxville, TN: University of Tennessee Press, 1988). The classic guide to religious interest groups today.

Hofrenning, Daniel J. B., *In Washington but Not of It: The Prophetic Politics of Religious Lobbyists* (Philadelphia, PA: Temple University Press, 1995). The most recent book-length treatment of religious lobbies, which is comprehensive and stimulating in its perspective.

Wood, Richard L., *Faith in Action: Religion, Race, and Democratic Organizing in America* (Chicago, IL: University of Chicago Press, 2002). The classic study of the role of religion in community organizing.

NOTES

1. For a summary of the political-science literature on religious interest groups, see Allen D. Hertzke, "Religious Interest Groups in American Politics," in Corwin E. Smidt, Lyman A. Kellstedt, and James L. Guth (eds.), *Oxford Handbook of Religion and American Politics* (Oxford: Oxford University Press, 2009), pp. 299–329.

2. Allen Hertzke directed "Lobbying for the Faithful," a project for the Pew Research Center. Published in November 2011 and updated in May 2012, the study identifies some 216 organizations engaged in national religious lobbying or religion-related advocacy. That report and this chapter have some overlap in passages. See www.pew-forum.org/lobbying-religious-advocacy-groups-in-washington-dc.aspx.

3. Because these figures are for 2011, when the Pew report was issued, spending and staffing are likely larger today.

4. The Pew report found that the vast majority of groups register as tax-exempt organizations, with only 17 percent of them officially registered as lobbyists: www.pew-forum.org/Government/Lobbying-for-the-faithful-tax-status.aspx.

5. Daniel J. B. Hofrenning, *In Washington but Not of It: The Prophetic Politics of Religious Lobbyists* (Philadelphia, PA: Temple University Press, 1995).

6. Ann-Marie Szymanski, *Pathways to Prohibition* (Durham, NC: Duke University Press, 2003).

7. Sarah Barringer Gordon, *The Spirit of the Law: Religious Voices and the Constitution in Modern America* (Cambridge, MA: Harvard University Press, 2010), chapter 3, "The Almighty and the Dollar."

8. For an account of the formative years, see Luke Eugene Ebersole, *Church Lobbying in the Nation's Capital* (New York, NY: Macmillan, 1951). Ebersole analyzed twenty-two groups, but the Pew study identified three others. It is likely that there were additional groups that have since vanished from the scene.

9. Jeffrey M. Berry and Clyde Wilcox, *The Interest Group Society*, 5th edn (New York, NY: Pearson-Longman, 2009), chapter 2. Berry and Wilcox document a doubling of national associations between 1970 and 2005, less than the growth of the number of religious advocacy organizations. On the other hand, the number of lawyers in the DC Bar Association—an indirect indicator of lobby growth—increased from just above 10,000 to more than 80,000 in the same period (not all Washington attorneys are lobbyists, but many are hired for advocacy), and the same period saw the growth of public-relations firms that also support lobby campaigns. So what appears to have happened is that religious interests have disproportionately established Washington offices while other interests rely more on hired lobbyists or public-relations firms.

10. José Casanova, *Public Religions in the Modern World* (Chicago, IL: University of Chicago Press, 1994; Ronald Ingelhart, *Culture Shift in Advanced Industrial Society* (Princeton, NJ: Princeton University Press, 1990).

11. The 1993 figures for religious interest-group spending come from W. Landis Jones and Paul J. Weber, *US Religious Interest Groups: Institutional Profile* (Westport, CT: Greenwood, 1994).

12. Lou Chibbaro, "Anti-Gay Group to Fight Marriage Efforts in DC," *Washington Blade*, August 21, 2009, www.washblade.com.

13. This model is a revised version of one developed by Robert Booth Fowler, *Religion and Politics in America* (Metuchen, NJ: Scarecrow Press, 1985).

14. Lawrence Kersten, *The Lutheran Ethic: The Impact of Religion on Laymen and Clergy* (Detroit, MI: Wayne State University Press, 1970).

15. R. Drew Smith and Fredrick C. Harris (eds.), *Black Churches and Local Politics: Clergy Influence, Organizational Partnerships, and Civic Empowerment* (Lanham, MD: Rowman & Littlefield, 2005).

16. Gregory Allen Smith, *Politics in the Parish: The Political Influence of Catholic Priests* (Washington, DC: Georgetown University Press, 2008).

17. Theda Skocpol, *Diminished Democracy: From Membership to Management in American Civic Life* (Norman, OK: University of Oklahoma Press, 2003).

18. Allen D. Hertzke, *Representing God in Washington: The Role of Religious Lobbies in the American Polity* (Knoxville, TN: University of Tennessee Press, 1988); Harold E. Quinley, *The Prophetic Clergy: Social Activism among Protestant Ministers* (New York, NY: Wiley, 1974); Clyde Wilcox and Carin Robinson, *Onward Christian Soldiers? The Religious Right in American Politics*, 4th edn (Boulder, CO: Westview Press, 2011).

19. David R. Mayhew, *Congress: The Electoral Connection* (New Haven, CT: Yale University Press, 1974).

20. On interest-group strategy, one good source is Kenneth M. Goldstein, *Interest Groups, Lobbying, and Participation in America* (Cambridge: Cambridge University Press, 1999).

21. Hertzke, *Representing God in Washington*; Hofrenning, *In Washington but Not of It*.

22. S. Robert Lichter, Stanley Rothman, and Linda S. Lichter, *The Media Elite* (Bethesda, MD: Adler, 1986). In this controversial work, the authors argue that elite journalists are in fact highly secular in their behavior and attitudes. But see also John Schmalzbauer, *People of Faith: Religious Conviction in American Journalism and Higher Education* (Ithaca, NY: Cornell University Press, 2003).

23. This is especially true for public-interest groups, a category into which many religious lobbies fit. See Anthony J. Nownes and Grant Neeley, "Public Interest Group Entrepreneurship and Theories of Group Mobilization," *Political Research Quarterly*, 49 (1996): 119–146.

24. See Laura R. Olson, "Mainline Protestant Washington Offices and the Political Lives of Clergy," in Robert Wuthnow and John H. Evans (eds.), *The Quiet Hand of God: Faith-Based Activism and the Public Role of Mainline Protestantism* (Berkeley, CA: University of California Press, 2002), pp. 54–79. Interviews by Allen Hertzke for the Pew Research Center in 2009 suggest that some mainline leaders are developing more strategic focus in their work.

25. Jane Lampman, "Rev. Jim Wallis Searches for Old-Time Justice," *The Christian Science Monitor*, March 12, 2008; Jim Wallis, *God's Politics: Why the Right Gets It Wrong and the Left Doesn't Get It* (San Francisco, CA: HarperOne, 2005).

26. On the Sikh Advocate Academy, see www.sikhadvocates.org/.

27. Previous studies of religious lobbying before the cyber revolution found that few groups had extensive grassroots networks. See Hertzke, *Representing God in Washington*; and Hofrenning, *In Washington but Not of It*.

28. Interview with the Executive Secretary of the Friends Committee on National Legislation by Allen Hertzke, 2009.

29. Kevin W. Hula, *Lobbying Together: Interest Group Coalitions in Legislative Politics* (Washington, DC: Georgetown University Press, 1999).

30. Poverty Forum, http://thepovertyforum.org/.

31. Deborah Caldwell, "Why Christians Must Keep Israel Strong: An Interview with Richard Land," available at www.beliefnet.com; Todd Hertz, "The Evangelical View of Israel?" *Christianity Today*, June 11, 2003; Tatsha Robertson, "Evangelicals Flock to Israel's Banner," *Boston Globe*, October 21, 2002, p. A3.

32. Allen D. Hertzke, *Freeing God's Children: The Unlikely Alliance for Global Human Rights* (Lanham, MD: Rowman & Littlefield, 2004).

33. James L. Guth, John C. Green, Corwin E. Smidt, Lyman A. Kellstedt, and Margaret M. Poloma, *The Bully Pulpit: The Politics of Protestant Clergy* (Lawrence, KS: University Press of Kansas, 1997); Quinley, *The Prophetic Clergy*.

34. James F. Findlay, Jr., *Church People in the Struggle: The National Council of Churches and the Black Freedom Movement, 1950–1970* (Oxford: Oxford University Press, 1993).

35. Allen D. Hertzke, "An Assessment of the Mainline Churches since 1945," in James E. Wood, Jr., and Derek Davis (eds), *The Role of Religion in the Making of Public Policy* (Waco, TX: Dawson Institute of Church-State Studies, Baylor University, 1991), pp. 43–79; Olson, "Mainline Protestant Washington Offices and the Political Lives of Clergy."

36. Lynette Clemetson, "Clergy Group to Counter Conservatives," *New York Times*, November 17, 2003, p. A17.

37. Brantley W. Gasaway, *Progressive Evangelicals and the Pursuit of Social Justice* (Chapel Hill, NC: University of North Carolina Press, 2014).

38. Olson, "Mainline Protestant Washington Offices."

39. Sue E. S. Crawford and Laura R. Olson, "Clergy as Political Actors in Urban Contexts," in Sue E. S. Crawford and Laura R. Olson (eds.), *Christian Clergy in American Politics* (Baltimore, MD: Johns Hopkins University Press, 2001), pp. 104–119; Laura R. Olson, *Filled with Spirit and Power: Protestant Clergy in Politics* (Albany, NY: State University of New York Press, 2000).

40. Timothy A. Byrnes, *Catholic Bishops in American Politics* (Princeton, NJ: Princeton University Press, 1991).

41. Ted G. Jelen, "Catholic Priests and the Political Order: The Political Behavior of Catholic Pastors," *Journal for the Scientific Study of Religion*, 42 (2003): 591–604, at p. 597; Smith, *Politics in the Parish*.

42. Liberation theology, which originated in Latin America, teaches that churches must work to liberate those who are oppressed by economic and political inequality. See Paul E. Sigmund, *Liberation Theology at the Crossroads* (Oxford: Oxford University Press, 1990).

43. See Timothy A. Byrnes and Mary Segers, *The Catholic Church and Abortion Politics: A View from the States* (Boulder, CO: Westview Press, 1991).

44. William D'Antonio (ed.), *Laity, American and Catholic: Transforming the Church* (Kansas City, MO: Sheed & Ward, 1996).

45. Stephen V. Monsma, *When Sacred and Secular Mix* (Lanham, MD: Rowman & Littlefield, 1996).

46. These new threats to conscience rights and institutional autonomy are catalogued by Allen D. Hertzke, "Introduction: A Madisonian Framework for Applying Constitutional Principles on Religion," in Allen D. Hertzke (ed.), *Religious Freedom in America:*

Constitutional Roots and Contemporary Challenges (Norman, OK: University of Oklahoma Press, 2015), pp. 3–32. The Little Sisters of the Poor gained judicial relief when the Supreme Court instructed the Department of Human Resources to find means of accommodating the group's conscience concerns (*Zubik v. Burwell*, 578 US __, 2016), and the new Trump administration promulgated an executive order codifying this requirement: "Presidential Executive Order Promoting Free Speech and Religious Liberty," May 4, 2017.

47. L. Sandy Maisel and Ira N. Forman (eds.), *Jews in American Politics* (Lanham, MD: Rowman & Littlefield, 2001).

48. American Israel Public Affairs Council, www.aipac.org.

49. John J. Mearsheimer and Stephen M. Walt, *The Israel Lobby and US Foreign Policy* (New York, NY: Farrar, Straus, & Giroux, 2008).

50. Pew Research Center, Religion & Public Life Project, "Lobbying for the Faithful," Online Directory, Profiles, http://projects.pewforum.org/religious-advocacy/j-street/.

51. Christians United For Israel, www.cufi.org/site/PageServer.

52. Eun Lee Koh, "Robertson's Speech Backing Israel Gets Ovation at Temple," *Boston Globe*, April 14, 2003, p. B1.

53. Maisel and Forman, *Jews in American Politics*.

54. Maisel and Forman, *Jews in American Politics*.

55. Maisel and Forman, *Jews in American Politics*.

56. Nearly three-quarters of Americans say they have either a very favorable or mostly favorable opinion of Jews, and only 9 percent have unfavorable feelings. See Pew Research Center, "2003 Religion and Public Life Survey," June 24, 2003, available through the Roper Center, www.ropercenter.uconn.edu.

57. Robert Putnam, *Bowling Alone: The Collapse and Revival of American Community* (New York, NY: Simon & Schuster, 2000), p. 162.

58. Wilcox and Robinson, *Onward Christian Soldiers?*

59. Lyman A. Kellstedt, John C. Green, Corwin E. Smidt, and James L. Guth, "Faith Transformed: Religion and American Politics from FDR to G. W. Bush," in Mark A. Noll and Luke E. Harlow (eds.), *Religion and American Politics: From the Colonial Period to the Present*, 2nd edn (Oxford: Oxford University Press, 2007), pp. 269–295.

60. Wilcox and Robinson, *Onward Christian Soldiers?*

61. Frances FitzGerald, *The Evangelicals: The Struggle to Shape America* (New York: Simon & Schuster, 2017).

62. Jon A. Shields, *The Democratic Virtues of the Christian Right* (Princeton, NJ: Princeton University Press, 2009).

63. Information for this section is from Allen D. Hertzke, "American Muslim Exceptionalism," in Stig Jarle Hansen (ed.), *Borders of Islam* (London: C. Hurst, 2009), pp. 271–287.

64. John Nurser, *For All Peoples and All Nations: Christian Churches and Human Rights* (Washington, DC: Georgetown University Press, 2005).

65. Kevin R. den Dulk and Robert Joustra, *The Church and Religious Persecution* (Grand Rapids, MI: Calvin Press, 2015). See also Daniel Philpott, Thomas F. Farr, and Timothy Samuel Shah, "In Response to Persecution" (South Bend, IN: University of Notre Dame, 2017), http://ucs.nd.edu/assets/233538/ucs_report_2017_web.pdf.

66. Vince Beiser, "Digital Weapons Help Dissidents Punch Holes in China's Great Firewall," *Wired Magazine*, November 1, 2010.

67. Allen D. Hertzke, "The Globalization of Religious Advocacy: Implications for US Foreign Policy." Presented at the British International Studies Association and

International Studies Association Joint Conference, Edinburgh, Scotland, June 20–22, 2012.

68. From an interview by Allen Hertzke with Wendy Wright, president of CWA, May 2009. See also www.cufi.org/.

69. Hertzke, *Freeing God's Children.*

70. William Branigin, "A Different Kind of Trade War," *Washington Post*, March 20, 1999; "Trafficking in Persons Report 2013," US Department of State, www.state.gov/j/tip/rls/tiprpt/2013/index.htm.

71. Elisabeth Bumiller, "Evangelicals Sway White House on Human Rights Issues Abroad," *New York Times*, October 26, 2003; Victims of Trafficking and Violence Protection Act of 2000, Public Law 106-386, October 28, 2000.

72. Hertzke, *Freeing God's Children.*

73. Gary A. Haugen, *Good News about Injustice* (Downers Grove, IL: InterVarsity Press, 1999).

74. Because most of this spending is for programs around the world, the IJM budget was not included in the Pew report, but, as we see here, advocacy is about more than Washington lobbying. See IJM, 2016 Annual Report financial statement, www.ijm.org/financials/2016-annual-report.

75. David Masci, "Christianity Posed to Continue Its Shift from Europe to Africa," April 7, 2015, www.pewresearch.org/fact-tank/2015/04/07/christianity-is-poised-to-continue-its-southward-march/.

76. Stephen V. Monsma, "Faith-Based NGOs and the Government Embrace," in Elliott Abrams (ed.), *The Influence of Faith: Religious Groups and US Foreign Policy* (Lanham, MD: Rowman & Littlefield, 2001), pp. 203–224.

77. Joshua William Busby, "Bono Made Jesse Helms Cry: Jubilee 2000, Debt Relief, and Moral Action in International Politics," *International Studies Quarterly*, 51 (2007): 247–275.

78. Scott Baldauf and Jina Moore, "Bush Sees Results of His AIDS Plan in Africa," *The Christian Science Monitor*, February 20, 2008, p. 7.

79. For a summary of scholarship on interest groups and religious advocacy, see Hertzke, "Religious Interest Groups in American Politics."

80. The profiles of each of the 216 groups in the Pew Research Center's Searchable Directory contain excerpts from their mission statements.

81. Hertzke, *Freeing God's Children.*

82. Diana B. Henriques and Andrew W. Lehern, "Religious Groups Reap Federal Aid for Pet Projects," *New York Times*, May 13, 2007; and interview of Henriques by Allen Hertzke.

9

RELIGION AND POLITICAL
AND CULTURAL ELITES

Religious activism, as we have seen, may be directed toward shaping culture, influencing elections, or lobbying government. To a large degree, the success or failure of religious activism hinges on the accessibility and responsiveness of elites—leaders in government, media, the charitable sector, academia, and entertainment. As we turn now to explore the ways in which American elites approach and confront the politics of religion, we must keep one crucial question in mind: How much do elites listen and respond to religious groups and activists? We pose this question knowing that elites are not empty vessels. Their own religious backgrounds, worldviews, and biases affect how open they are to religious groups and faith-based arguments.

One might think we would know a good deal about elites' religious views, but in reality we know substantially less about their religious outlooks than we do about those of the general public. In part, this reflects the challenge of getting access to elites. For example, busy members of Congress, executive branch officials, party leaders, and judges often do not answer questionnaires or provide more than the most cursory interview. What's more, public officials are aware that religion can be a sensitive subject, so they are often selective in how they describe their own faith convictions. Thus, we have very little data on elites to compare with standard national surveys of the public (such as those that polling organizations like Gallup and the Pew Research Center regularly conduct). Nevertheless, we do have enough information to provide a basic understanding of religion's relevance in the lives and work of political and social elites.

As we chart what we know about the religious perspectives of elites and the broader environments in which they work, we will observe some degree of religious diversity. But we also note that the religious perspectives of elites as a group are not necessarily representative of those of the general public. Some religious perspectives are overrepresented, and others are underrepresented—and this fact has political implications.

RELIGION AND THE PRESIDENCY

The outcomes of presidential elections matter as much to religious activists as they do to any other group of politically engaged Americans. After all, the president appoints top officials in the executive branch, federal judges, US Supreme Court justices, and diplomats. The president also charts the nation's defense and foreign policies and has influence on the domestic-policy agenda as well. The occupant of the Oval Office can be a powerful ally or foe for activists who wish to further one or another political agenda based on religious principles. For their part, presidents recognize the importance of religious constituencies and religious interest groups, and for many years they have designated White House officials to serve as liaisons to them.[1]

But every president also must contend with a wide range of compelling demands. Pragmatic and partisan priorities easily can override the moral pleas of religious petitioners, many of whom have conflicting views. Moreover, in every administration a host of White House aides jockey for influence, calling on religious leaders when it is expedient but ignoring them when it is not. The late Charles Colson, a disgraced Nixon administration official who went on to found the well-respected ministry organization Prison Fellowship, recalled how he and other aides to President Nixon consciously coopted religious leaders to add legitimacy to his presidency, awing them with tours of the White House to mute potential criticism. Religious leaders, Colson noted, often are well-meaning but gullible people who understand little of the cutthroat nature of White House politics.[2] Religious critics of different stripes have voiced pointed concerns about every recent presidential administration, most recently that of Donald Trump. Even though it is difficult at best to sort out religious motivations from political calculations, it is worth our time to consider presidents' religious orientations.[3]

Any president's response to religious groups is affected by the uniquely religious dimension of the presidency. As head of state, the president serves an important civil-religious function.[4] Part of every president's responsibilities includes offering prayers to grieving families of soldiers killed in action and invoking God's blessings on holidays such as Thanksgiving and Memorial Day. Because of the nation's religious pluralism, presidents typically avoid clearly sectarian references on these occasions and employ only broad, vague kinds of religious imagery. In fact, President Barack Obama gained substantial notice for breaking with this precedent in his first inaugural address, when he noted, "We are a nation of Christians and Muslims, Jews and Hindus—and nonbelievers."

Americans' expectation that the president will serve as an informal "pastor of the nation" can have the ironic effect of diminishing the political clout of the religious tradition to which the president personally belongs. The classic illustration of this phenomenon involved John F. Kennedy. His election to the presidency in 1960 brought enormous legitimacy to the US Catholic population, but his policy priorities did not reflect the agenda of the Catholic Church (for instance, he did not promote government support for parochial schools), in part because Kennedy bent over backwards to avoid any hint of favoritism. Some Catholic critics at the time argued that this hesitation made the Kennedy administration even less hospitable to the Catholic Church than previous administrations had been.[5]

All recent US presidents have professed to be Christians. Harry Truman was a Baptist, Dwight Eisenhower joined a Presbyterian church, and Lyndon Johnson was a member of the Disciples of Christ (a small mainline Protestant denomination). But in the past four decades or so, religion's symbolic and substantive place in the White House has become increasingly visible and important. This visibility is a direct manifestation of the growing politicization of religion.[6] By comparing presidents from Jimmy Carter to Donald Trump, we can see both the scope and the limits of religious influence at 1600 Pennsylvania Avenue from 1977 to the present day.

Jimmy Carter

Jimmy Carter's presidency (1977–1981) is a good place to begin our quick sweep through presidential history. As a born-again Southern Baptist, a Sunday-school teacher, and a devout man, Carter has always linked his faith and his politics.[7] Morality drove Carter's understanding of the presidency as a trusteeship: He believed he should act in the public interest first and foremost.[8] Carter also sometimes connected his faith to his policy priorities. For example, he based his approach to environmental politics on a framework of biblical stewardship of God's creation. The religion–politics connection was most obvious of all in Carter's foreign policy, where he sought to advance what he viewed as Christian mandates of human rights and peace. As president, Carter brokered the historic 1979 peace agreement between Egypt and Israel that stands to this day. He has continued his faith-inspired work for peace, human rights, and economic development in the decades since he left office and was rewarded for his efforts with the 2002 Nobel Peace Prize.

Carter's greatest triumph as president—the Camp David Accords, which sealed the peace between Egypt and Israel—reflected specific elements of his personal faith. His belief in redemption, his stubborn determination to foster reconciliation, and his embrace of both sides of the conflict (Egypt and Israel) as religious kin of the "blood of Abraham" helped smooth the delicate negotiations. Carter's international role since his presidency has taken him to Bosnia, North Korea, Haiti, Africa, and the Middle East, among many other conflict-riddled regions, as he has sought to advance peace and reconciliation among people and nations. Some critics say Carter has behaved naively in these endeavors, but his efforts have marked his continued commitment to the same understanding of Christian service that he tried to embody as president.[9] Ironically, some critics of Carter's presidency argued that his religious scruples prevented him from taking tough action in the face of international threats, such as his response to the protracted Iranian hostage crisis. Perhaps Carter was "too Christian" for realpolitik.[10]

Ronald Reagan

Carter's commitment to living out his version of his faith cost him support from members of his own religious tradition—white evangelical Protestants—during the course of his presidency. Not only did many evangelicals reject Carter, but many began to reject the Democratic Party as well.[11] Evangelicals had become upset because President Carter did not work to restore prayer in public schools, prevent government interference with conservative Christian schools, fight to end abortion, or witness strongly enough for evangelical Christianity from the White House. Carter's opponent in the 1980 election, Ronald Reagan, understood this discontent. Speaking before a convention of mostly evangelical religious broadcasters in 1980, Reagan acknowledged that as religious leaders they could not endorse him without risking their organizations' tax-exempt status. He assured Christian evangelicals, however, that he supported their policy goals, making his position clear in one succinct declaration: "I endorse you."

Many evangelicals supported Reagan's 1980 and 1984 candidacies, although some skeptics noted that he was not much of a churchgoer and had been divorced. They also pointed out that his wife, Nancy Reagan, put stock in astrology. Still, Reagan was popular among evangelicals because he sincerely affirmed conservative Christianity, speculated about the End Times in Christian Scripture, and defended such traditional values as the nuclear family and patriotism with rhetorical skill.[12] Moreover, his White House staff paid close attention to evangelicals, as well as to Jews and Catholics, while shunning most liberal religious groups.

Reagan's vigorous denunciation of the Soviet Union, which he called the "Evil Empire," led him to form ties with Pope John Paul II. Because this connection had a historic global impact, it was arguably the most substantial and important manifestation of religion's power to shape politics to arise during the Reagan administration. Prior to his election as pope, John Paul II served as archbishop of Kraków, Poland, and he was a leader in the Polish opposition to communist rule. As pope, he set about using his authority and freedom to travel as a means of subtly encouraging opposition to communist regimes in Eastern Europe.[13] The Reagan administration was aware of these efforts and bolstered them with initiatives of its own aimed at ending Soviet rule. The alliance between Reagan, John Paul II, and British prime minister Margaret Thatcher that resulted in the collapse of communism was a dramatic example of the effectiveness of religious and political authorities working together.[14]

Nevertheless, questions persisted about what, if anything, evangelicals and other religious conservatives gained during the Reagan years (1981–1989). To be sure, many applauded Reagan's stand against communism and his appointment of moderate-to-conservative jurists to the US Supreme Court and the lower federal courts. But most conservative evangelical policy priorities went nowhere during the Reagan years.[15] For example, legal abortion continued with few restrictions, and prayer stayed out of public schools.

Bill Clinton

Bill Clinton, who was president from 1993 to 2001, was immersed in evangelical Protestantism from an early age and remained at ease with its messages and cadences as an adult. Although he was not always an active church member, Clinton was raised in Bible Belt Arkansas, where he attended Baptist churches and Pentecostal summer camps as a youngster. As governor of Arkansas, he joined a prominent Baptist church in Little Rock. He is fluent in the evangelical language of sin and redemption, and he is equally comfortable in both black and white evangelical congregations (often joining in gospel singing from memory). However, Clinton's liberalism on social issues hurt any support he might have received from conservative evangelicals or other religious traditionalists. By the 1990s, a powerful "religion gap" had come to characterize partisan politics, with many white evangelicals and many conservative Catholics favoring the Republican Party and its candidates by substantial margins.

Until sexual scandal tarnished it, Clinton's presidency was a boon to the liberal religious community. From the National Council of Churches to the United Methodist Church, religious activists who had lacked White House access during the Reagan years were welcomed back. Clinton also proved intensely popular among African Americans and was always welcomed with enthusiasm when he visited black churches.[16]

George W. Bush

George W. Bush, who served as president from 2001 to 2009, was raised a mainline Protestant in west Texas. He attended a Presbyterian church with his family until he left Texas for an elite preparatory school (and later college and graduate school) in the Northeast. Upon returning to Texas, years later, he became a respected and dutiful member of the congregation which his wife, Laura Bush, attended. However, his personal relationship to religion changed dramatically when he began participating in a Bible study during a time of personal struggle with alcohol and family life. In 1986, Bush gave up drinking and embraced evangelical Christianity.

This conversion became part of his public life, too—first during Bush's stint as a liaison to evangelicals during his father's 1988 presidential bid, then as governor of Texas, and finally as president. During a 2000 presidential debate, for example, he famously declared that Jesus was his favorite philosopher, and he repeatedly said that Jesus "changed my heart." Such statements resonate deeply with many evangelicals.

Some of President Bush's policy initiatives underlined his religious credentials. Invoking the language of "compassionate conservatism" that was popular in evangelical circles, he established the White House Office for Faith-Based and Community Initiatives to foster partnerships between the federal government and religious organizations that participate in welfare-delivery programs.[17] His administration's efforts to combat AIDS in Africa and global human trafficking were also strongly backed by a wide range of religious groups.

Critics saw a more troubling side to Bush's evangelicalism in his response to the terrorist attacks of September 11, 2001. Animated by a sense of religious destiny, the president developed an expansive, preemptive foreign-policy strategy (the "Bush Doctrine"), justifying military action in Afghanistan, Iraq, and elsewhere. He famously declared that the United States was facing an "axis of evil" comprised of Iraq, Iran, and North Korea, and he spoke of leading a "crusade" against global terrorism, confirming for critics that he saw himself on a (dangerous) religious mission.[18] During Bush's second term, skeptics charged that his administration's much-touted commitment to evangelicals was mostly for political gain.[19] Indeed, it is a thorny task to separate genuinely religious motives from strategic and partisan considerations.

Barack Obama

President Barack Obama was not raised in a religious environment; his mother was a religious skeptic, and his father was not a part of his life. Obama embraced Christianity as an adult while working with a faith-based community-organizing group in Chicago. There he attended Trinity United Church of Christ, a large African-American congregation headed by Rev. Jeremiah Wright. Wright became a highly controversial figure during the 2008 presidential campaign, when inflammatory clips from some of his sermons appeared online. Obama cut ties with Wright and went on to surround himself with a variety of less controversial clergy.[20] The most visible religion-relevant action Obama took during his first term was his outreach to the Muslim world, including a speech given in Cairo in which he emphasized "the truth that America and Islam are not exclusive, and need not be in competition."

Although President Obama rarely attended church during his presidency, except for ceremonial functions, he reported starting each morning with prayer and regularly participated in a variety of Washington politicians' prayer breakfasts. He asserted that the true test of a Christian or any religious person is to be found in action, and he was fond of quoting the Christian Gospel of Luke's declaration that "For unto whom much is given, much shall be required," or the Golden Rule, "treating others as you want to be treated."[21]

President Obama also recast the faith-based initiative Bush had created to facilitate government aid for faith-based charities. Obama renamed it the White

House Office of Faith-Based and Neighborhood Partnerships. From 2009 to 2013, its director was Joshua DuBois, a black Pentecostal minister who focused on forging connections between religious leaders and Obama administration officials, while also providing daily devotionals to the president.[22] His successor, Melissa Rogers, a Baptist lawyer from Wake Forest University, had been closely associated with both President Obama and the Pew Research Center, an influential force in the study of religion in the United States.

Obama's faith-based initiative, however, was criticized on both sides of the ideological spectrum. Secular and liberal organizations did not appreciate its religious connection, which they insisted violated the Establishment Clause. Supporters meanwhile complained that the Obama administration's efforts in this area were not very effective and that the office seemed more like a device to build support for the president than a serious effort to help faith-based groups.[23]

More clashes erupted over the Obama administration's rules requiring religiously affiliated institutions (except for congregations themselves) to provide contraception to employees. The furor was predictable as the government was imposing rules on religious institutions. Secular and some liberal religious groups insisted women's freedom to gain access to contraception should be the primary policy goal, but the majority of religious leaders expressed serious concern about the implications of the policy for religious freedom.[24]

President Obama's conservative religious critics also were outraged when he put the weight of his office into promoting same-sex marriage equality and federal protection for transgender rights. Along with the rules about employer-provided contraceptives, many conservative religious leaders perceived the Obama administration's actions as threatening their religious liberty and their right to live according to religious principles. Various Republican leaders and 2016 presidential candidates, particularly Donald Trump, seized on this sense of threat and incorporated into the GOP platform provisions pledging to reverse Obama policies and protect conscience rights and religious liberty. In this sense, Obama's presidency set the stage for the surprising election of Donald Trump, a man with no clear religious background or identity, to the White House.

Donald Trump

No figure in recent American politics has sparked such a vigorous and divisive response in the religious community as President Donald Trump. During the Republican primary season, more than a few prominent conservative Catholics and evangelicals joined religious liberals in criticizing what they saw as Trump's bullying style, impulsiveness, thin skin, and "narcissistic" character traits as unsuited for the presidency.[25] On the other hand, Trump actively courted Christian conservatives, especially evangelicals, and gained the endorsements of some key leaders. Once Trump secured the Republican nomination, some of his previous critics in the evangelical community offered grudging support, while others continued to withhold their endorsement. Trump received the overwhelming majority of the evangelical vote in the election, but this enduring rift at the elite level bears watching.[26]

By all reports, Trump is only loosely connected to organized religion. There is little evidence that he has had any serious ties to churches as an adult.[27] He was confirmed in a mainline Protestant congregation, First Presbyterian Church, in Jamaica, New York, but the greatest religious influence on him seems to have been Norman Vincent Peale, famously known at "God's Salesman" for his "power of positive thinking" doctrine. Trump's family attended Rev. Peale's Marble Collegiate Church in Manhattan, where Peale officiated Trump's first marriage (to Ivana Trump). Trump credits Peale's "believe in yourself" message of self-confidence as sustaining him through financial crises.[28]

Critics allege that Trump appears unaffected by faith considerations in his personal life. He is, after all, a twice-divorced man who has bragged about affairs with married women; has built a financial empire that included casinos, bankruptcies, reality TV, and lawsuits by suppliers he failed to pay; has claimed he had little reason to ask for forgiveness; and was videotaped boasting about freely groping women. On the other hand, Trump's religious defenders argue that God often uses flawed people for good purposes and point to Trump's forceful commitment to defend social conservatives against hostile government and secular forces.[29]

Among Trump's conservative Christian critics are Catholics Robert George and George Weigel, both of whom had backed Mitt Romney in the prior presidential election. Even more notably, evangelical critics included Russell Moore, head of the Ethics and Religious Liberty Commission of the Southern Baptist Convention (SBC); Michael Farris, president of the Home School Legal Defense Association; Michael Gerson, *Washington Post* columnist and former speechwriter for George W. Bush; Deborah Fikes, prominent leader of the World Evangelical Alliance; and Jennifer Hatmaker, popular Christian author and speaker. In addition, *Christianity Today* and *World*, two of the leading US evangelical magazines, issued editorials critical of Donald Trump. A group of evangelical leaders, including prominent progressives and minority representatives but also some conservative voices, circulated a "Declaration by American Evangelicals Concerning Donald Trump" signed by over 20,000 supporters.[30]

Despite these rifts, Trump skillfully courted evangelical voters and backed socially conservative planks in the GOP platform that provided elites with a justification for backing him. In fact, Trump earned the energetic support of prominent figures in Christian-right circles. Jerry Falwell, Jr., president of Liberty University, endorsed Trump in January 2016, on the eve of the Republican primaries, which sparked a protest by students at the university, suggesting a generational gap with likely implications for the future.[31] As the campaign progressed through the nomination, Trump also received backing by such evangelical leaders as Franklin Graham, Robert Jeffress, Ralph Reed, David Barton, James Dobson, Tony Perkins, Eric Metaxas, Pat Robertson, Jay Sekulow, and Paula White.[32] As we learned in Chapter 7, when faced with the choice between Donald Trump and Hillary Clinton and their respective parties' positions, eight out of ten white evangelicals voted for Donald Trump.

Moreover, despite the turmoil early in his presidency, Trump was able to deliver key victories to religious conservatives. He placed Neil Gorsuch, a conservative defender of religious freedom, on the Supreme Court, nominated a host of conservatives to the lower federal courts, and signed executive orders striving to reverse Obamacare's "contraceptive mandate," "pro-abortion" policies, and initiatives for transgender rights.

While Christian-right figures applauded these initiatives, other religious constituencies experienced more fraught responses to Trump's actions. Catholic bishops generally welcomed relief from the contraceptive mandate, but they criticized Trump's tone and actions around immigration policy. Religious progressives mobilized against the Trump administration across the board. But perhaps no group experienced as much angst as the Trump era began as did American Muslims. As we observed in Chapter 4, Muslims in the United States express great satisfaction with their lives and overwhelming pride in being Americans. However, more than two-thirds say that President Trump makes them feel worried. Muslim leaders have spoken out against policies they see as discriminatory toward the Muslim community, such as Trump's travel ban against people from certain Muslim-majority nations.[33]

Beyond these specific dynamics, the electoral forces Trump ignited may portend new divisions in the religious community. The emergence of the so-called "alt-right," which encompasses overt forms of white nationalism, has attracted some religious conservatives and repelled others. For years, critics of the Christian right claimed that the movement in part reflected white Southern resistance to integration and African-American empowerment. Some figures in the alt-right movement overtly embraced that connection, but this fusion of white nationalism and religion also sparked countermoves in the religious community. Most notably, the SBC, at its annual convention in June 2017, passed a resolution explicitly condemning all forms of racism and ethnic hatred, including "alt-right white nationalism," as a "scheme of the devil" antithetical to the gospel.[34] This resolution reflected, in part, the growing influence of black (and other nonwhite) people within the SBC.[35]

RELIGION AND CONGRESS

The US Congress today reflects the religious pluralism of America more than many other elite institutions. Even so, the membership of Congress does not mirror the population perfectly. Christians generally, and mainline Protestants and Catholics in particular, are overrepresented, while religious "nones" are vastly underrepresented. Jews are overrepresented relative to their small proportion of the US population, whereas evangelicals are underrepresented. Several factors are at work here, including different religious groups' socio-economic status, their openness to politics, and their geographic concentration.

Patterns in the religious affiliation of members of Congress have varied over time. In the 1950s, for example, congressional membership was weighted heavily toward mainline Protestant denominations, while Catholics, evangelical Protestants, and other religious groups were dramatically underrepresented. The first big change in this pattern occurred in 1958, when huge Democratic gains in midterm elections brought an unprecedented number of Catholics to Congress. Indeed, it was this influx of Catholics, coupled with Kennedy's presidential candidacy two years later, that motivated scholars and journalists alike to begin studying religion among members of Congress. Thus, we now have detailed data over time on the changing religious composition of Congress (see Table 9.1).[36]

But one must interpret these data with caution. After all, it is one thing to list a religious affiliation, which can often be politically advantageous to claim, and quite another for that affiliation to matter greatly in anyone's life. We know that the best guide to almost all Congress members' voting behavior is their party affiliation, not their religious affiliation, though their religious commitments may have led them to their party commitment or involvement. We also need to remember that while almost all members of Congress do claim some religious affiliation, vague labels such as "Protestant" tell us little. A small number of members of Congress (2 percent) refuse to list a religious affiliation. Sometimes, a religious affiliation tells us more about an individual's cultural background than it does about any specific religious commitments. Senator Bernie Sanders (I-Vermont), for example, was raised Jewish but during his presidential run in 2016 remarked that he does not belong to a synagogue and is "not particularly religious."[37]

Moreover, a large congressional representation hardly translates into automatic clout for a religion or a denomination on Capitol Hill. Members of Congress, even those who share the same religious affiliation, can and do disagree with one another on political issues. They also vary enormously in terms of how much religion matters in their personal and political lives. In some instances, the religious backgrounds of a member's constituents matter more than their own personal convictions regarding congressional voting behavior.[38]

The Religious Affiliations of Members of Congress

With these caveats in mind, let us look at what the patterns tell us about religious affiliation among members of Congress. One key pattern is that congressional membership has become more diverse over time, as we see in Table 9.1. Mainline Protestant denominations, particularly Methodists, Presbyterians, Episcopalians, and Congregationalists, were overrepresented in 1961 but have seen their

	TOTAL IN CONGRESS	% OF CONGRESS	% OF US ADULTS	% CHANGE IN CONGRESS SINCE 1961	% REPUBLICANS IN CONGRESS	% DEMOCRATS IN CONGRESS
Christian (total)	485	90.7%	71%	−4.2%	99.3%	80.2%
Protestant (total)	299	55.9%	48%	−25.3%	67.2%	42.1%
Baptist	72	13.5%	15%	+15.4%	15.7%	10.7%
Methodist	44	8.2%	5%	−54.9%	9.2%	7.0%
Presbyterian	35	6.5%	2%	−52.6%	9.2%	3.3%
Episcopalian	35	6.5%	1%	−47.6%	6.8%	6.2%
Lutheran	26	4.9%	4%	+25.6%	5.1%	4.5%
Congregationalist	5	0.9%	1%	−82.4%	0.7%	0.8%
Pentecostal	2	0.4%	5%	+∞	0.7%	–
Adventist	2	0.4%	1%	+∞	–	0.8%
Christian Scientist	2	0.4%	<1%	−50%	0.7%	–
Friends/Quakers	–	–	<1%	−100%	0.0	–
Other/Unspecified Protestant	76	14.2%	5%	+65%	15.4%	7.9%
Catholic	168	31.4%	21%	+67%	27.0%	36.8%
Mormon	13	2.4%	2%	+84.6%	4.1%	0.4%
Orthodox Christian	5	0.9%	<1%	+∞	1.0%	0.8%
Jewish	30	5.6%	2%	+143%	0.7%	11.6%
Hindu	3	0.6%	1%	+∞	–	1.2%
Buddhist	3	0.6%	1%	+∞	–	1.2%
Muslim	2	0.4%	1%	+∞	–	0.8%
Unitarian Universalist	1	0.2%	<1%	–	–	0.4%
Unaffiliated	1	0.2%	23%	+∞	–	0.4%
Don't Know/Refused	10	1.9%	1%	+98.9%	–	4.1%

TABLE 9.1 Religious Affiliation of Members of Congress, 2017

Source for 1961: Pew Research Center, "Faith on the Hill: The Religious Composition of the 113th Congress," November 16, 2012.

Source for 2017: Aleksandra Sandstrom, "Faith on the Hill: The Religious Composition of the 115th Congress," Pew Research Center, January 3, 2017.

numbers decline by more than 40 percent. Today, a wider range of Christian traditions are represented on the Hill, including Pentecostals, Seventh-Day Adventists, and Eastern Orthodox Christians (none of which had any members in Congress in 1961). There are now also more Jews, Mormons, Baptists, and Catholics (who are especially theologically and politically diverse). In addition, there are now a handful of Hindu, Buddhist, and Muslim members of Congress.

We also observe religious differences between the two chambers of Congress (not shown in Table 9.1 but available online through the Pew Research Center's website).[39] The Senate, as the more elite body, still overrepresents mainline Protestant denominations. In particular, there are thirteen Presbyterian senators (13 percent of the Senate versus 2 percent of the US population). Compared to the House, there are also disproportionately more Mormon senators (six) and Jewish senators (eight), which to an extent reflects the regional concentration of those religious communities.

A telling, and relatively recent, pattern is the difference in religious affiliations we see between the two political parties. Congressional Democrats are far more religiously diverse than their Republican counterparts. Every Hindu, Muslim, Buddhist, and unaffiliated member of the 115th Congress is a Democrat, as are all of those who refused to list a religion. Overall, as of 2017 the Democratic congressional membership is 42 percent Protestant, 37 percent Catholic, 12 percent Jewish, and 20 percent non-Christian or unaffiliated. Meanwhile, over 99 percent of Republican members of Congress identify as Christian, with two Jews rounding out the GOP membership. (There are no unaffiliated Republicans.) This pattern reflects both the Republican Party's political constituency as well as the overrepresentation of Republicans from rural and suburban communities, which feature less religious diversity than the urban areas Democrats tend to represent.

Drilling down further, we discover more noteworthy patterns. Although the Catholic share of the US population recently has been in slight decline, Catholic representation in Congress has grown by a full ten percentage points since 1961 to 31 percent. Politically, however, Catholic members of Congress hardly constitute a monolith in terms of party affiliation, ideology, issue priorities, or anything else beyond formal religious identification. Their political disagreements, including on some issues of importance to the Catholic Church, usually are between more liberal Catholic Democrats and more conservative Catholic Republicans. In 1961, most Catholic members of Congress were Democrats, but today that party enjoys only a slight edge (eighty-nine Democrats versus seventy-nine Republicans). The composition of the Democratic delegation continues to change today, with a growing number of Catholic Latino Democrats being elected to Congress.[40] In the Senate, this group includes Catherine Cortez Masto (D-Nevada), the first Latina ever elected to the Senate, and former presidential candidate Marco Rubio (R-Florida).[41] In the House, we find Latino individuals including Adriano Espaillat (D-New York), the first

Dominican American to serve in Congress; Darren Soto (D-Florida), who is of Puerto Rican descent; and Linda Sanchez (D-California), vice-chair of the House Democratic Caucus.

As we note above, mainline Protestant denominations continue to be overrepresented relative to their share of the US population even though their congressional numbers generally have declined since 1960, paralleling declines in mainline church membership.[42] This fact reflects the political power of socioeconomic status. Mainline Protestants are comparatively well educated and economically advantaged, which matters a lot when it comes to running for Congress.

In 1961, only 2 percent of members of Congress were Jewish, which was less than their share of the total population at the time. In 2017, by contrast, nearly 6 percent the congressional membership was Jewish (and 8 percent in the Senate), which is considerably more than their 2 percent of the US population today. Among the reasons for this change over the past half century are the increased acceptance of American Jews at large, relatively high political interest within the Jewish community, and above-average Jewish economic status and educational attainment. Of the thirty Jews in the 115th Congress, all but two are Democrats, reflecting the Democratic leanings of most politically active Jews.[43] The highest-ranking Jewish member of Congress is Senate minority leader Chuck Schumer (D-New York), who has emerged as the leader of the congressional Democratic opposition to the Trump administration. Other prominent liberal Jewish senators include Dianne Feinstein (D-California) and Al Franken (D-Minnesota).

We do not have detailed data on evangelical members of Congress because they belong to so many different denominations. For example, some Presbyterian members of Congress belong to the evangelical Presbyterian Church in America (PCA) rather than its mainline counterpart, the Presbyterian Church (USA). The number of evangelical members of Congress has increased since 1960, but they remain underrepresented relative to their share of the population compared to the overrepresentation of mainline Protestants and growth in Catholic representation. This underrepresentation has consequences, too: White evangelical voices sometimes are heard more in the country in general than they are in Congress. The Baptist contingent in Congress, which includes many traditional evangelicals, illustrates this fact. Baptist representation has increased since 1961, but Baptists remain slightly underrepresented in comparison with their numbers in the US population.[44] The Baptist congressional delegation is also diverse. It encompasses a healthy share of black and white Baptists, whose politics often diverge, as well as some adherents of the American Baptist Churches USA, a liberal mainline denomination. One of the most prominent Baptists in Congress is Senator Ted Cruz (R-Texas), who is a part of the growing Latino evangelical tradition. Cruz, who kicked off his presidential run in 2016 at Liberty University (founded by Rev. Jerry Falwell), was popular among evangelicals before being bested by Trump's unconventional campaign.

The LDS Church had 1.3 percent of the Congress in 1961, but this share nearly doubled by 2017. Today's Mormon congressional delegation (2.4 percent) is slightly larger than the Mormon share of the US population, which has been growing steadily but which is still under 2 percent.[45] Mormons are mostly middle-class, with access to the educational and financial resources that matter in politics, but their substantial presence in Utah and neighboring western states is the key to their expanded representation in Washington; Mormons are often able to win elections in states with large Mormon populations. Reflecting the heavily conservative and Republican profile of the Mormon community overall, all but one of the thirteen Mormons in Congress are Republicans. New Mexico Senator Tom Udall is the lone Democrat.

Another significant change in congressional religious affiliations since 1961 is the increasing number of members who come from non-Judeo-Christian religious backgrounds. Just as the United States has experienced significant growth in the population of Muslims, Hindus, and Buddhists since 1961, so too each of these religious traditions can now claim one or more members of Congress. Until 2007, no member of any of these faiths had ever served in Congress.[46] Currently, two members are Buddhists, three are Hindus, and two are Muslims. Muslims may have the greatest potential to increase their representation in Congress because their numbers are growing quickly in the population at large. However, as a heavily immigrant community, to win seats they will need to advance in economic and educational terms and become better organized.

The presence of these new faith voices in Congress illustrates well the complexities of religious identification. Tulsi Gabbard, a Democratic representative from Hawaii, identifies as Hindu but sees herself more as a spiritual person than as a strict follower of Hinduism. Meanwhile, Senator Mazie Hirono, another Democrat from Hawaii, is the first Buddhist to serve in the Senate, but she stresses that she is nonpracticing. Also noteworthy here are several members of Congress who explicitly avoid declaring any religious affiliation, such as Senator Tammy Baldwin (D-Wisconsin), or who explicitly affirm their secularism, such as Rep. Kyrsten Sinema (D-Arizona), who blogged for the Secular Coalition for America before her election to Congress.[47]

The Effect of Religion on Members' Legislative Behavior

The crucial empirical question here, however, is not about members' declared religious affiliations (or lack thereof), but rather about how their religious backgrounds might affect their legislative voting behavior: Do Catholic, mainline Protestant, Jewish, Baptist, or other religious affiliates in Congress comprise distinct voting blocs based on their religious loyalties? There is little evidence that they do, except for unified Jewish support for Israel.[48] While there is evidence that many evangelical members of Congress tend to agree about taking conservative approaches to socio-moral issues, there is also diversity among evangelical Protestant legislators. Most significantly, white evangelical members of Congress often have little in common with their African-American evangelical colleagues.[49]

Might religious affiliation instead have a subtler impact on congressional politics? After all, religious affiliation is often less important than how one experiences faith.[50] If we could get inside the minds of members of Congress, we might see how their religious worldviews (as opposed to their formal religious affiliations) shape their votes on Capitol Hill. This was exactly the approach of an ambitious study by Peter Benson and Dorothy Williams titled *Religion on Capitol Hill*.[51] Through in-depth interviews with a large sample of members of Congress in the 1980s, the authors explored religious themes that reached beyond affiliation to understand how the personal experience of faith might affect political decision-making. Benson and Williams discovered that members of Congress fell into six religious "types": legalistic, self-concerned, integrated, people-concerned, nontraditional, and nominal. These categories did not correlate with either religious affiliation or political party, but they proved predictive of voting behaviors. In fact, members' religious attitudes predicted their voting records even better than did their party affiliations.

What Benson and Williams help us appreciate is the complexity of religious experience and its relationship with elite-level politics. A "legalistic" Catholic member of Congress may have more in common with a legalistic Protestant colleague than with a fellow Catholic whose faith experience falls into a different category.[52] As Benson and Williams and subsequent scholars, especially political scientist Elizabeth Oldmixon, have shown, members of Congress are not empty vessels. Rather, they bring to their jobs many years of socialization and religious experiences that mold their worldviews. Those views, in turn, contribute both consciously and unconsciously to their politics.[53]

Another way to study the impact of religion in Congress is to examine specific members for whom we know their religion matters a great deal. One illustration here concerns members of minority-faith traditions. Mormons in Congress, for example, tend to mirror the LDS Church's strong commitment to conservatism on cultural and family issues. Prominent examples are Senators Mike Lee and Orrin Hatch, both of whom are Republicans from Utah. Yet religious conservatism among Mormons can also take an independent turn.[54] As we noted in Chapter 7, Mormon independent presidential candidate Evan McMullin gained significant votes from Mormon voters who were disturbed by Donald Trump's character traits. In Congress, the first vocal challenge to Trump from a Republican was offered by Mormon Senator Jeff Flake (R-Arizona), who wrote a book, *Conscience of a Conservative*, criticizing what he describes as Trump's "erratic" and "undignified" behavior, as well as his "dehumanization" of Muslims and Mexicans. To Flake, stigmatization of any ethnic or religious group recalls the nineteenth-century persecution of Mormons.[55]

Other Republicans self-consciously connect their faith to their politics. Rep. Chris Smith (R-New Jersey) is a devout Catholic who traces his political convictions to his religious upbringing. As the former director of New Jersey Right to Life, Smith entered Congress in 1981 as a fierce opponent of abortion, which led some observers to lump him in with conservative adherents of the Christian right. But throughout his career Smith also has been supportive of labor unions, government aid for impoverished children, international relief programs, and global human rights. For Smith, this blend of issue positions reflects his Catholicism. Describing himself as a "Matthew 25 Christian," Smith sees both his pro-life and international humanitarian work as flowing from the same scriptural injunction: "Whatsoever you do to the least of my brethren, you do to me." Smith has held hundreds of hearings on human-rights abuses and has sponsored legislation on such diverse issues as promotion of religious freedom, support for victims of torture, and sanctions against human trafficking.[56]

Another example is Nebraska senator Ben Sasse, a rising figure in the Republican Party with deep religious roots and training. Sasse was baptized as a child into the Lutheran Church-Missouri Synod, a conservative evangelical branch of Lutheranism. As an adult, he moved into the Reformed tradition by joining the traditionalist Presbyterian Church in America. Before his election to the Senate, Sasse served as the president of a Lutheran college and as a board member of a Reformed Protestant seminary. He wrote his undergraduate thesis at Harvard on Martin Luther and his master's thesis at Yale on John Calvin, and he calls himself a "Lutero-Calvinist" to capture his affiliation with these two giants of the Protestant Reformation. Sasse also wrote his doctoral dissertation at Yale on the religious roots of Reagan-era political alignments. A strong defender of religious freedom both domestically and globally, Sasse sees the American constitutional order as flowing from natural law and God-given rights. He gained prominence in 2016 when he wrote an open letter to his constituents explaining why he could not support Donald Trump for president, and he has continued to chart his own political course during the Trump era.[57]

Among Democrats there also are plenty of examples. Two such examples are Senator Tom Carper of Delaware and Rep. Keith Ellison of Minnesota. Senator Carper, a Presbyterian whose congregation is affiliated with the more liberal branch of the Presbyterian family (the Presbyterian Church USA), exemplifies the presence of quietly religious figures to be found on Capitol Hill. A devout Christian, Vietnam veteran, former Delaware state treasurer and governor, member of the US House of Representatives, and US senator since 2001, Carper has long been involved in prayer and Bible study groups that are self-consciously bipartisan. Like his membership in Third Way, an organization seeking to overcome partisan divisions whenever possible for the common good, Senator Carper's self-declared vision is to find the means to walk a moderate path amid the extreme polarization of Washington. He sees this goal as an expression of his Christian faith, reflecting concern for all people—and thus all perspectives.[58]

A second example of how faith affects politics on the Democratic side of the aisle comes in the form of Minnesota's Keith Ellison, a Democratic member of the House of Representatives since 2007. An African American, Ellison's district comprises the city of Minneapolis and a few of its suburbs. Raised as a Catholic in Detroit, Ellison converted to Islam in college and is one of two Muslims in the House (the other is Rep. André Carson, a Democrat from Indiana). Ellison is a dynamic voice for liberal causes who has served as co-chair of the Progressive caucus in the House and who was selected co-chair of the Democratic National Committee in 2017. A lawyer and former community activist, Rep. Ellison is known as a vigorous guardian of the rights and liberties of his fellow Muslims. He was particularly affected by his Hajj pilgrimage to Mecca in 2008, which he termed "transformative."[59]

Given what we know about the heritage of black churches in the United States, we might expect many African-American members of Congress to bring religious influences to bear on their legislative work. Indeed, in the past, some black members of Congress were also ministers; however, this path to Congress is now much rarer in the African-American community. Most black members come to Congress by rising through political party ranks, just like non-black members do. That said, some African-American representatives are deeply religious, and for them the fight for social justice and equal rights are goals shared by both the Democratic Party and their Christian faith. The same is true of quite a few Latino Catholic Democratic members of the House of Representatives.

One of the most prominent liberals in Congress during the twenty-first century has been House Minority leader Nancy Pelosi (D-California), a politician of impressive accomplishment who was the first woman Speaker of the House from 2009 to 2011. Pelosi's self-description as a "conservative Catholic" means for her that her Catholic upbringing—religiously observant and respectful of tradition—forged key aspects of her character. At a time when the old norm of the large Catholic family was becoming rarer, Pelosi raised five children as a full-time mother before embarking on her political career. Nevertheless, Pelosi has attracted the enmity of Catholic leaders up to and including former Pope Benedict XVI for her unyielding pro-choice position on abortion and her support of same-sex marriage.[60]

Sorting out religious motives from other factors, of course, is impossible, but probing these alliances suggests that the impact of religion in Congress is far from trivial. Another testament to the importance of religion, whatever its guise, is the thriving religious culture on Capitol Hill. For example, both the House and Senate have employed official chaplains throughout the history of Congress. The House chaplain, Fr. Pat Conroy, is a Jesuit Catholic priest who was nominated by former House Speaker John Boehner, a Catholic, in consultation with minority leader Pelosi. The Senate chaplain, Rev. Barry Black, is the first

African American and Seventh-Day Adventist to serve in that position. Like their predecessors, Conroy and Black keep busy presiding over weekly prayer breakfasts and Bible study groups, offering counseling sessions, and opening daily Senate and House sessions with prayer. Black, a retired Navy admiral and chief of Navy chaplains, points out that there is lots of "spirituality among the lawmakers," and declares from his personal experience that "there are saints on Capitol Hill." At times, he concedes, his work involves "singing the Lord's song in a strange land," but he appreciates that his calling allows him to minister to members on both sides of the aisle.[61]

Members of Congress also attend various DC-area churches and religious fellowships, and Capitol Hill Bible studies (in addition to those run by the congressional chaplains) have proliferated. Sometimes these groups cross party lines, allowing members of Congress to ease the frustrations and stresses of political life by praying together, sharing their stories, and offering each other solace and support. The National Prayer Breakfast, an annual affair, is perhaps the most well-known "religious" event on the Hill. It is attended by members of Congress from both parties, administration leaders, and prominent religious and secular leaders. Traditionally, it has been organized by the Fellowship Foundation (the "C Street Group"), a Washington, DC, ministry that seeks to encourage religious fellowship among Christian politicians from both parties. Several of its congressional members found themselves embroiled in sexual scandal in 2009, however, embarrassing the organization and reminding everyone that professing religious faith and escaping what one's religion defines as sin are hardly mutually exclusive.[62]

Separately, the Congressional Prayer Caucus, with some ninety members from the House and Senate, focuses specifically on religious freedom. Its membership is heavily Republican with a decidedly evangelical tilt. It is headed by Rep. Mark Walker (R-North Carolina) and Senator James Lankford (R-Oklahoma), both of whom served as Baptist ministers before election to Congress. Backed by an outside foundation, the caucus has grown extensively since its founding in 2005, even establishing connections with several similar state-level legislative religious caucuses.[63]

To be sure, these religious activities also involve plenty of opportunities for political networking with politicians who are constantly involved in strategic calculation and hardball politics. Religious practice on Capitol Hill and elsewhere is, like so much else in life, complex.

RELIGION AND OTHER POLITICAL ELITES

Think Tanks and Policy Institutes

Outside the White House and the halls of Congress are many other political elites who have a keen interest in the interaction of religion and politics. For example, consider the proliferating think tanks and policy institutes that

BOX 9.1 PATRONS OF RELIGION IN PUBLIC LIFE

A great deal of the research and reflection scholars do about religion and politics today would not be possible without funding from a small number of large philanthropic organizations. Since the early 1980s, foundations such as Lilly, Templeton, and Pew have provided tens of millions of dollars for the exploration of religion's role in public life. Many of the patrons who created these foundations were themselves deeply committed religious believers. The late J. Howard Pew, for example, head of the Sun Oil Company from 1912 to 1947 and a lifelong Presbyterian, established the Pew Charitable Trusts in 1948 with his siblings to support evangelical parachurch organizations and other religion-based enterprises, including the evangelical magazine *Christianity Today* and Gordon-Conwell Theological Seminary. Today, the Pew Charitable Trusts, in partnership with the John Templeton Foundation, actively supports academic research and superb data-gathering about religion. On its own, Templeton also funds scholarship on the challenges and benefits of global religious freedom. Scholars of religion and politics owe Pew, Templeton, and other charitable foundations that fund their research a great and continuing debt.

Sources: Michael S. Hamilton and Johanna G. Yngvason, "Patrons of the Evangelical Mind," *Christianity Today*, July 8, 2002, p. 42, Pew-Templeton Global Religious Futures Project, www.globalreligiousfutures.org/; Pew Research Center: Religion and Public Life, www.pewforum.org/.

contribute to the debates between partisans in Washington and elsewhere, as well as organizations that fund efforts to understand religion in public life (see Box 9.1). Here, too, we see evidence of a meaningful religious presence that has made a difference. Important examples include the Ethics and Public Policy Center, the Center for Public Justice, the Center for American Progress, Faith in Public Life, and the Institute on Religion and Democracy in Washington, DC, as well as the Institute on Religion and Public Life in New York. These organizations conduct policy seminars and produce a flood of publications designed to produce new ideas about how to solve problems facing society. Aware that religion must make its case to skeptics, these groups offer intellectual grounding for an active role for religious influences in policy debates. They also provide various means of support for their political allies.

Executive Branch Officials

The federal bureaucracy is one governmental sector in which religious influence might seem to be suppressed. Decisions about how laws should be implemented are almost never made in overtly religious contexts, and, as such, the federal bureaucracy has at times been accused of being "antireligious."[64] However, public administration does not lend itself to applying faith to politics and therefore does not often attract employees who are particularly interested in this goal.

On the other hand, presidential appointees do sometimes bring distinct religious influences to their work. A current example is Nikki Haley, former Republican governor of South Carolina and ambassador to the United Nations (UN), appointed by Donald Trump in 2017. Born Nimrata Nikki Randhawa to Sikh immigrants from India, she experienced being a cultural outsider in the small South Carolina town where she was raised. When she married her husband, Michael Haley, in 1996, they had two ceremonies: one Methodist and the other Sikh. She was later baptized in the United Methodist church and has raised her children as Methodists, but she periodically attends her parents' Sikh gurdwara and other Sikh ceremonies, including a 2014 visit to the Sikh Golden Temple in India. Haley's personal experience with religious diversity seems a unique asset in her position at the UN.[65]

In addition, there are a few federal executive positions that require religious sensitivity, such as the ambassador for international religious freedom in the State Department and companion members of the US Commission on International Religious Freedom. Those who serve in such positions may come from different parties, but they often share similar commitments (see Box 9.2).

The Federal Courts

The federal courts play a highly significant role in the American policy-making process, far more so than in other nations. Judicial review is a powerful tool, and many judges do not hesitate to use it when they see fit. At the level of the US Supreme Court, we have little evidence about whether—or to what extent—religious convictions might influence judicial decisions, partly due to a lack of access to the very private, even reclusive, justices. It is nonetheless remarkable that no fewer than five of the nine current Supreme Court justices are Catholics, but they are hardly a monolith; instead, they mirror the wide range of political views we generally see among Catholic laity. Three justices are Jewish, and the most recent addition, Neil Gorsuch, was raised Catholic but now belongs to an Episcopalian congregation. Although no systematic research has been conducted on the effect of religion on Supreme Court jurisprudence, at least one study of lower courts suggests a modest impact of faith on judicial decision-making, especially among the most religiously committed evangelicals.[66]

Political Parties

Political parties have become more ideologically polarized—and therefore arguably more powerful—in recent years. Access to parties and their leaders can be a major resource for religious groups. One indication of this access is the

BOX 9.2 UNLIKELY ALLIES AT THE
STATE DEPARTMENT

It would be difficult to find two political figures farther apart on the ideological spectrum than Rabbi David Saperstein and former Kansas Governor Sam Brownback. For three decades, Saperstein led the political-action program of Reform Judaism, the most liberal of the Jewish denominations. A venerable figure in Washington, DC, he lobbied for abortion rights and same-sex marriage and maintained progressive stances on taxes, welfare, and civil liberties. Brownback, on the other hand, was first elected to the House of Representatives in 1994 as an insurgent Republican conservative, moving on to the Senate in 1996. After seventeen years as a leading pro-life advocate in Congress, Brownback was elected governor of Kansas, where he established himself as a staunch fiscal conservative.

Despite their obvious differences, Saperstein and Brownback have been close allies in the areas of international religious freedom and human rights. Saperstein was a key lobbyist in favor of the International Religious Freedom Act, the Trafficking Victims and Protection Act, and the Sudan Peace Act, all of which were sponsored by then Senator Brownback. Saperstein also served as chair of the US Commission on International Religious Freedom and was appointed by President Obama in 2014 to head the State Department's Office of International Religious Freedom as its ambassador-at-large. Saperstein was succeeded by Brownback, who was appointed to the position by Donald Trump in 2017. He was eventually confirmed by the Senate in January 2018. Saperstein earned praise across the political and religious spectrum for his aggressive advocacy for persecuted religious groups, including Christian minorities. Brownback's appointment, in turn, was lauded by religious-freedom advocates, including the outgoing ambassador, his ally Rabbi Saperstein.

Sources: J. C. Derrick, "The Advocate: Why Religious Liberty Ambassador and Obama Appointee David Saperstein is Earning Praise from both Republicans and Democrats," *World Magazine*, October 1, 2016; J. C. Derrick, "An Experienced Hand: Trump Taps Gov. Sam Brownback for Religious Freedom Post," *World Magazine*, July 27, 2017; Allen D. Hertzke, *Freeing God's Children: The Unlikely Allies for Global Human Rights* (Lanham, MD: Rowman & Littlefield, 2004).

language contained in party platforms hammered out every four years at the parties' nominating conventions. While often dismissed as symbolic, party platforms do matter; they help set the agenda of legislators and executive officials. In 2016, religious conservatives were given a great deal of access to the GOP platform writing committee, which produced an unusually detailed set of policy proposals on abortion, marriage, and religious liberty. The 2016 Republican platform also contained an unprecedented number of religious references, as we see in Figure 9.1. In turn, religious liberals and secular activists helped shape the Democratic platform, demonstrating how deeply religious and cultural cleavages now separate the two major parties (see Table 9.2).

State and Local Government

Finally, state and local politics may also be influenced by the religious makeup of elected and appointed officeholders. From school board members to governors, state and local political elites make a profound difference on the ordinary lives of citizens—perhaps more so than any official of the federal government. Unfortunately, we have little systematic information about the religious affiliations and attitudes of governors, state legislators, or other local officials, much less on whether their religious backgrounds matter in the

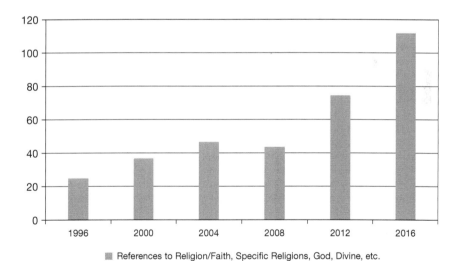

■ References to Religion/Faith, Specific Religions, God, Divine, etc.

FIGURE 9.1 GOP Platform Language on Religion, the Supernatural, and Specific Faiths, 1996–2016

Source: Authors' analysis of Republican Platforms, 1996–2016. Data from Kevin den Dulk, "The GOP, Evangelical Elites, and the Challenge of Pluralism," in Paul Djupe and Brian Calfano (eds.), *The Evangelical Crackup: Will the Evangelical-Republican Coalition Last?* (Philadelphia, PA: Temple University Press).

ISSUE	2016 DEMOCRATIC PLATFORM	2016 REPUBLICAN PLATFORM
Abortion	"We will appoint judges who . . . protect a woman's right to a safe and legal abortion. . . . [We are] committed to protecting and advancing reproductive health . . . [and favor] repealing the Hyde Amendment . . . [and] no cost contraception."	"We assert the sanctity of human life and affirm that the unborn child has a fundamental right to life. . . . [We] will not fund or subsidize healthcare that includes abortion coverage. . . . [We favor] codification of the Hyde Amendment."
Marriage	"Democrats believe that LGBT rights are human rights. . . . LGBT people . . . have the right to marry the person they love. . . . [We] will promote LGBT human rights and ensure America's foreign policy is inclusive of LGBT people around the world."	"Traditional marriage . . . is the foundation for a free society. . . . We support the right of the people to conduct businesses in accordance with their religious beliefs. . . . Every child deserves a married mom and dad."
Religious Freedom	"We support a progressive vision of religious freedom that respects pluralism and rejects the misuse of religion to discriminate. . . . [and believe] our lives are made vastly stronger and richer by faith in many forms."	"the first freedom [matters]. . . . We pledge to defend the religious beliefs and rights of conscience of all Americans. . . . [and] we strongly support the freedom of Americans to act in accordance with their religious beliefs. . . . [Religious organizations] should not be subject to taxation."
Interfaith Issues	"We reject Donald Trump's vilification of all Muslims. . . . The vast majority of Muslims believe in a future of peace and tolerance. . . . We are horrified by ISIS's genocide . . . of Christians and Yazidis and crimes against humanity against Muslims . . . [and] we will look for ways to help [those] who are fleeing persecution."	"We must apply special scrutiny to those foreign nationals seeking to enter the US from terror-sponsoring countries. . . . We must stand up for our friends, challenge our foes, and defeat ISIS. . . . Radical Islamic terrorism poses an existential threat to personal freedom and peace around the world."

TABLE 9.2 Comparison of Select Planks in the Democratic and Republican Party Platforms, 2016

policy-making process. This lack of information is unfortunate, as religious attitudes do matter in some instances. At the state and local levels, lobbyists, legislators, and other government officials struggle over issues such as abortion restrictions, school policies, and anti-discrimination initiatives on sexual orientation and gender identity.[67]

RELIGION AND CULTURAL ELITES

The News Media

Elites beyond public officials also shape American public life. The news media plays a highly significant role in shaping American social and political discourses. One matter of considerable debate is whether the media displays bias toward one or another religious perspective. For example, many conservative evangelicals and Catholics insist that the media is hostile to their perspectives, a frequent refrain among 2016 Republican presidential candidates. Another complaint, sometimes leveled by journalists themselves, is that the media either pays too little attention to religion or covers it inaccurately.[68] Yet some journalists are either religious themselves or serious about studying religion, and some media outlets provide considerable coverage of both religion and the interactions between religion and politics. The *New York Times*, the *Wall Street Journal*, the *Washington Post*, the *Atlantic Monthly*, among others, all have dedicated reporters on the religion beat, and the Religion News Service is a premier newswire source for religion stories. Nonetheless, there still is good reason to conclude that religion remains underreported by the US media.[69]

In addition to religion-beat journalists, others write about politics for religious publications such as *Christianity Today*, the *Christian Century*, *World*, *Sojourners*, and the *National Catholic Reporter*. Many Protestant denominations also sponsor publications staffed by journalists (for example, the mainline Protestant *Living Lutheran* and the SBC's *SBC Life*), and virtually every US Catholic diocese publishes a newspaper on a regular basis. All these publications at least occasionally include stories that are politically relevant.

The Popular Media

Another set of elites who have substantial influence on the American public, and thus on its religious and political discourses, are those who create popular media: movies, television, music, books, websites, apps, and magazines. Some analysts argue that the world of popular culture is secular or even hostile toward religion, but other scholars remind us that such criticisms are not the whole story.[70]

Let us first consider the movies. The film industry has released a smattering of major motion pictures in the past few decades that focus explicitly on religious themes, including *The Apostle* (1997), *The Green Mile* (1999), *The Passion of the*

Christ (2004), *Doubt* (2008), *Of Gods and Men* (2010), *For Greater Glory* (2012), *The Way* (2012), *Noah* (2014), and *Silence* (2016). Other films explore the experiences of Muslims and other religious minorities, such as *The Kite Runner* (2007), *Arranged* (2007), *Mooz-Lum* (2011), and *Life of Pi* (2012). A larger number of Hollywood productions emphasize broader spiritual themes such as redemption or the triumph of basic goodness, and some religious critics (liberal and conservative alike) sometimes assess secular movies as decent, quality entertainment.[71] Still, only a small fraction of today's movies are religious or arguably even spiritual. Critics such as Michael Medved complain that some Hollywood elites use the movies to undermine traditional religious values.[72]

On television, the typical show is entirely secular in focus. For example, some shows contradict the teachings of evangelical Protestantism or are critical of traditional perspectives on marriage, child-rearing, and the like. Some of these shows' writers and producers have indicated their commitment to advancing secular, progressive messages, and their efforts have had public impact.[73] On the other hand, changes in television-series production, spurred by premium networks like HBO and Showtime and the increasing popularity of streaming services such as Netflix and Amazon Prime, have generated a much greater range of content than has previously been possible. This means there are now more shows in which religion does play a prominent role, and not always a negative one. From *The Americans* to *House of Cards* to *The Vikings* to *The Leftovers*, there is no shortage of highly acclaimed contemporary television that portrays characters who find themselves searching for religious meaning, even if those quests might take irreverent or unconventional forms.[74]

Religious Media

Christian and non-Christian religious media help fill the void some perceive in more mainstream outlets. The marketplace has supported a remarkable demand for popular media sympathetic to Christianity. Christian bookstores, both in brick-and-mortar form and online, help meet that demand through a panoply of popular non-fiction and fiction series, not to mention a range of other "Christian lifestyle" products.[75] There have been fewer explicitly Christian movie productions due to the great cost of making commercial films, but some occasionally break through. Radio and television, however, remain the most important media for religious communication today. There are all sorts of Christian radio shows in both local and national markets, and some groups— for example, the Catholic Church—have made establishing diocesan radio stations a priority. One can listen to a wide range of religious radio programming online and download literally thousands of religious podcasts. National TV networks that are religious in nature also are now a fact of life. The Catholic EWTN (Eternal Word Television Network) and the evangelical CBN (Christian Broadcasting Network), for example, are offered by most cable, satellite, and streaming service providers.

Meanwhile, all manner of religious groups are represented on Facebook, Twitter, Instagram, and other social media, and more and more religious apps are being developed every day. For example, Pope Francis has a Twitter account (@pontifex), and Muslims can download an app that reminds them when it is time to pray during the day. There are also a plethora of blogs, support groups, wikis, and other online communities designed for a wide variety of religious groups, some of which are nonpolitical. It is also possible to "attend" worship services online, and some multi-site megachurch services consist at least in part of listening to a sermon that is streamed in from another location.

Academia

While one might not think of the world of academic elites as a stronghold of religious strength, there is plenty of religious commitment and spiritual concern among some academic leaders, especially in many religiously oriented colleges and universities. Some of these religious academic elites have engaged in politics. A few religiously inclined academics who work in secular colleges and universities have taken their faith into the political arena from time to time. Perhaps none of these scholars is as prominent as Princeton University political scientist Robert George, an expert in constitutional law and political thought, whose assertive conservative Christianity and politics have made him controversial both in academia and outside of it. George often joins his friend and former Princeton colleague Cornel West, a Christian socialist with deep roots in African-American Protestantism, in vigorous public debates about religion and politics.[76]

Music

Finally, religious themes show up in a great deal of contemporary music. The explicitly Christian music industry features two large and flourishing sectors: gospel and contemporary music. Gospel is a distinctively American form of music with a long and distinguished history. It has affected nearly every American form of music, from blues to jazz to rock and roll and hip-hop. Gospel's audience is primarily African American, but its musical and cultural influence reaches across racial and ethnic lines.[77] An even larger, if significantly different, audience exists for contemporary Christian music. In its innumerable forms and fashions, this music mimics every variety of secular music, though its lyrics, of course, are different. Some groups are explicitly Christian in their lyrics; others, such as Jars of Clay, are less so. There also is a thriving sector of hip-hop that conveys underlying Christian messages. It is not unusual to hear leading rappers like Chance the Rapper, Lecrae, Sho Baraka, and others, speak with a faith-inspired prophetic voice on racial injustice or other issues of political relevance.[78] The Christian music business is flourishing, and iTunes, Spotify, and other online streaming services feature an extensive Christian and gospel section.

The entertainment industry is also an increasingly important outlet for Muslims seeking to counter stereotypes and affirm their place in the American civic fabric. There is a flourishing group of US Muslim rappers including old-school stars such as Ice Cube, Busta Rhymes, and Q-Tip as well as newer artists such as Lupe Fiasco and Omar Offendum. Likewise, Muslim comedians such as Hasan Minhaj, who prominently roasted President Trump at the White House Correspondents' Association in the spring of 2017, are gaining prominence in the United States.[79]

CLERGY AND OTHER RELIGIOUS ELITES

Any discussion of elites, religion, and politics in the United States today needs to appreciate the presence of religious elites themselves in the mix. They obviously play a significant role in elite-level connections between religion and politics, and they constitute the best counterexample to the argument that all American elites are hostile to organized religion.

Which sorts of religious leaders have the most clout in the United States in the twenty-first century? Small, alternative religious and spiritual groups do not supply highly visible religious leadership, just as we would assume. Equally predictably, mainline Protestantism is no longer home to the religious elites with the most political or cultural clout. But we do find some religious leaders, especially from within Catholicism and evangelical Protestantism, who operate on the national stage.

Take, for example, the national visibility of leading Catholic bishops such as the Archbishop of New York, Cardinal Timothy Dolan. His 2009 appointment in New York, subsequent election as president of the US Conference of Bishops in 2010, and his elevation to College of Cardinals in 2012 are indications of his rapidly increasing influence in US Catholic circles. Today he is arguably the most important Catholic cleric in the United States. Many Catholics admire Dolan for his engaging public persona, down-to-earth charm and warmth, and unusually effective ability to communicate. His willingness to argue the church's views on controversial issues have enhanced his prominence and garnered some criticism. Cardinal Dolan is unabashed in his defense of religious freedom and his opposition to abortion and same-sex marriage. He has not hesitated to criticize top elected officials, such as House Democratic leader Nancy Pelosi, for supporting abortion rights, though he refuses to deny communion to Catholic politicians who diverge from the church.[80] He gave the invocation at the inauguration of Donald Trump, invoking Solomon's prayer for wisdom as his theme.

A different example is Jim Wallis, whose ministry is well known due to the journal Sojourners and his work as an author and speaker. Wallis is an evangelical Protestant of undoubted commitment who is known for his progressive politics. Wallis is ardent in his approach to foreign affairs, which has included determined opposition to all US military action abroad. He is equally committed to a ministry of service and support for the poor and disadvantaged, insisting that this view, like his perspective on war, is a witness to Christ's teachings. A close ally of former President Obama, Wallis now often leads opposition to President Trump.

As we noted previously, prominent evangelical leaders emerged as pivotal Trump supporters in 2016, cementing their role as major players in contemporary politics. One of the most visible, and controversial, of these leaders is Dr. Robert Jeffress—prolific author, radio and television personality, Fox News contributor, and senior pastor of First Baptist Church in Dallas, a leading American megachurch. Jeffress campaigned for Trump, preached at his inauguration (comparing the new president to the biblical leader Nehemiah), served on Trump's evangelical advisory board, and endorsed his policy initiatives. When tensions rose over North Korea's nuclear weapons during the summer of 2017, Jeffress famously said that "God has given Trump authority to take out Kim Jong-un" (the North Korean dictator), which delighted Trump partisans but horrified those who feared escalating rhetoric on both sides could lead to a catastrophic war.[81]

Alongside religious leaders with national influence are other religious elites with clout at the local level. Their names will not be known nationally, but local religious leaders exercise as much or more influence day to day, year to year, as any famous figures.[82] Indeed, no group of religious elites has more potential reach and collective influence than the US's local clergy.

Thanks to a creative new study, we have unique data on their partisan affiliations.[83] By accessing directories of congregations, Eitan Hersh and Gabrielle Malina obtained the names of some 180,000 Christian and Jewish pastors across forty religious denominations. Using public voter registration records, they identified the party registration of the majority (130,000) of those pastors. With this massive dataset, Hersh and Malina illuminate striking patterns of clergy partisanship in different American religious traditions. For example, more than 80 percent of rabbis in Reformed Judaism are Democrats, while less than 10 percent of Missouri-Synod Lutheran pastors share that party affiliation. The pattern of partisanship tracks what we would expect, with Jewish, African American, and mainline denominations having the largest proportions of registered Democrats among their clergy, while evangelical denominations have the largest percentage of registered Republican clergy. On the other hand, Roman Catholic, Eastern Orthodox, and Seventh-Day Adventist congregations had the largest shares of registered Independents among their clergy. A *New York Times* headline captured these patterns in a pithy way: "Your Rabbi? Probably a Democrat. Your Baptist Pastor? Probably a Republican. Your Priest? Who Knows."[84] For readers interested in exploring further, the Hersh and Malina study and the *New York Times* report provide vivid graphs depicting partisan patterns among clergy.[85]

While these patterns roughly conform to the partisanship of the lay members of the clergy's religious traditions, Hersh and Malina's study found that clergy in a specific tradition are somewhat more unified in their party affiliations than members of the congregations they serve. Clergy in liberal traditions are consistently more Democratic than their congregants, while pastors in conservative traditions are routinely more Republican than their congregants. For example, while 55 percent of Episcopalians in the pews identify as Democrats, 76 percent of Episcopal priests do. In the Evangelical Lutheran Church of America (ELCA), 46 percent of members are Democrats compared to 73 percent of ELCA clergy.

Given the substantial number of registered Independents among Catholic clergy, they constitute a swing group in the electorate. However, the study also found evidence of regional variation among Catholic clergy: "Catholics in states like Kansas, South Dakota, and Oklahoma are more Republican, while those in Massachusetts, Rhode Island, and Maryland are more Democratic."[86]

These findings suggest that the polarization we see in American politics today is affecting clergy.[87] Further evidence for this emerging pattern is found in the partisanship of seminary faculty. Hersh and Malina note that seminary faculty are even more uniform in their partisanship than pastors. For example, while Southern Baptist parishioners are 60 percent Republican in identification and their pastors 77 percent, Baptist seminary faculty are 83 percent Republican. Democratic-leaning religious traditions are even more one-sided. United Methodist congregants and clergy are 45 percent and 51 percent Democratic, respectively, but their seminary faculty are 95 percent Democratic.[88]

These findings still leave open the questions of whether and how the partisanship of religious elites matters for mass-level politics. Clergy can influence the views of their congregants, but they also represent the communities they serve. The extreme partisan sorting in seminaries suggests we might see the effects of ideological and partisan socialization among new clergy as the century wears on, which would almost certainly do nothing to mitigate the political polarization currently gripping the US population.

CONCLUSION

The religious views of political and cultural elites do matter. For some, faith clearly shapes worldviews and orientations to politics. But having a religious faith, much less sharing the same faith, does not necessarily engender predictable political views—far from it. As we know, people who belong to the same religious tradition do not always interpret their faith in the same way, whereas people from divergent faith backgrounds sometimes share identical positions on political issues. At the same time, religion is not a major part of the calculus of many political and cultural elites. Many other factors—party, constituency, the marketplace, and personal experience, to name just a few—often have greater influence on elites' political priorities and strategies. Nor should we ignore evidence of indifference and hostility to religion that many Americans perceive among political, media, and cultural elites. Although the picture is complicated, it is essential to explore the ways various elites experience the religious and the spiritual in their lives and those of others—as well as the political implications that follow.

DISCUSSION QUESTIONS

1 Why do you think some religious groups have representation in Congress out of proportion to their population?
2 The House of Representatives is often perceived as "more religious" than the Senate. What distinguishes the two houses that might explain these differences in religiosity?
3 Why is civil religious behavior so conspicuous in the presidency? In what other ways does religion play a distinctive role in the presidency?
4 Is religion more or less important in other areas of elite behavior (e.g., courts, culture)? Why or why not? Is the "culture war" really nothing more than a conflict among elites?
5 How does the religious affiliations—or lack thereof—of the elite press and creators of media impact the religious and political landscape of the product they create?

FURTHER READING

Benson, Peter L., and Dorothy L. Williams, *Religion on Capitol Hill: Myths and Realities* (Oxford: Oxford University Press, 1982). The pioneering study of how members of Congress experience their faith and connect it with politics.

Holmes, David L., *The Faiths of the Postwar Presidents: From Truman to Obama* (Athens, GA: University of Georgia Press, 2012).

Lindsay, D. Michael, *Faith in the Halls of Power: How Evangelicals Joined the American Elite* (Oxford: Oxford University Press, 2007). Massive study of evangelical elites in the United States.

Marshall, Paul, Lela Gilbert, and Roberta Green Ahmanson, *Blind Spot: When Journalists Don't Get Religion* (Oxford: Oxford University Press, 2009). Case studies that illustrate how journalists miss or misinterpret major stories when they don't understand their religious dimensions.

Oldmixon, Elizabeth Anne, *Uncompromising Positions: God, Sex, and the US House of Representatives* (Washington, DC: Georgetown University Press, 2005). An outstanding analysis of the legislative ramifications of religious and cultural conflict.

Sandstrom, Aleksandra, "Faith on the Hill: The Religious Composition of the 115th Congress," Pew Research Center, January 3, 2017, www.pewforum.org/2017/01/03/faith-on-the-hill-115/.

Schmalzbauer, John, *People of Faith: Religious Conviction in American Journalism and Higher Education* (Ithaca, NY: Cornell University Press, 2003). An excellent introduction to its subject.

Smidt, Corwin E., *Pastors and Public Life: The Changing Face of American Protestant Clergy* (Oxford: Oxford University Press, 2016). A careful study of the changing perspectives and roles of Protestant clergy over recent decades.

Smith, Gary Scott, *Religion in the Oval Office: The Religious Lives of American Presidents* (Oxford: Oxford University Press, 2015). A broad historical examination that uses select presidents' own words, religious participation, relationships, and policies to assess the role of faith in their administrations.

NOTES

1. Allen D. Hertzke, "Faith and Access: Religious Constituencies and the Washington Elites," in Ted G. Jelen (ed.), *Religion and Political Behavior in the United States* (New York, NY: Praeger, 1989). On the broad topic of religion and the American presidency, see David Holmes, *The Faiths of the Postwar Presidents: From Truman to Obama* (Athens, GA: University of Georgia Press, 2012); Gaston Espinosa (ed.), *Religion and the American Presidency: George Washington to George W. Bush* (New York, NY: Columbia University Press, 2009); Mark J. Rozell and Gleaves Whitney (eds.), *Religion and the American Presidency* (New York, NY: Palgrave Macmillan, 2007).

2. Charles Colson, *Kingdoms in Conflict* (Grand Rapids, MI: Zondervan, 1987), especially pp. 306–310.

3. Gary Scott Smith, *Religion in the Oval Office: The Religious Lives of American Presidents* (Oxford: Oxford University Press, 2015).

4. Vanessa B. Beasley, *You, the People: American National Identity in Presidential Rhetoric* (College Station, TX: Texas A&M Press, 2004); Richard V. Pierard and Robert D. Linder, *Civil Religion and the Presidency* (Grand Rapids, MI: Zondervan, 1988).

5. Thomas J. Carty, "Religion and the Presidency of John F. Kennedy," in Gaston Espinosa (ed.), *Religion and the American Presidency: George Washington to George W. Bush* (New York, NY: Columbia University Press, 2009), pp. 283–309.

6. Randall Balmer, *God in the White House: How Faith Has Shaped the Presidency from John F. Kennedy to George W. Bush* (New York, NY: Harper, 2008).

7. D. Jason Berggren and Nicol C. Rae, "Jimmy Carter and George W. Bush: Faith, Foreign Policy, and an Evangelical Presidential Style," *Presidential Studies Quarterly*, 36 (2006): 606–632; Most of Carter's many books have strong religious themes: see, for example, Jimmy Carter, *Living Faith* (New York, NY: Random House, 1996) and *A Call to Action: Women, Religion, Violence, and Power* (New York, NY: Simon & Schuster, 2014). Carter severed tied with the SBC in 2000 over its views of women, but he continued to attend his local Baptist church in Plains, Georgia.

8. See Charles O. Jones, *The Trusteeship Presidency: Jimmy Carter and the United States Congress* (Baton Rouge, LA: Louisiana State University Press, 1988).

9. Carter, *Living Faith*; Kenneth E. Morris, "Religion and the Presidency of Jimmy Carter," in Gaston Espinosa (ed.), *Religion and the American Presidency: George Washington to George W. Bush* (New York, NY: Columbia University Press, 2009), pp. 321–344; Jeff Walz, "Jimmy Carter and the Politics of Faith," in Mark J. Rozell and Gleaves Whitney (eds.), *Religion and the American Presidency*, 3rd edn (New York, NY:

Palgrave, 2018), pp. 171–188. See, for example, Frank J. Gaffney, "Tyranny's Enabler," *Washington Times*, April 15, 2008, p. A16; Holmes, *The Faiths of the Postwar Presidents*, pp. 143–172.

10. Jeane Kirkpatrick, "Dictatorships and Double Standards," *Commentary Magazine*, November 1979.

11. Clyde Wilcox and Carin Robinson, *Onward Christian Soldiers? The Religious Right in American Politics*, 4th edn (Boulder, CO: Westview Press, 2011).

12. Paul Kengor, *God and Ronald Reagan: A Spiritual Life* (New York, NY: HarperCollins, 2004); Wilcox and Robinson, *Onward Christian Soldiers?*; Holmes, *The Faiths of the Postwar Presidents*, pp. 193–196.

13. Jo Renee Formicola, *John Paul II: Prophetic Politician* (Washington, DC: Georgetown University Press, 2002).

14. Paul Kengor, *A Pope and President: John Paul II, Ronald Reagan, and the Extraordinary Untold Story of the 20th Century* (Wilmington, DE: ISI, 2017) and *The Crusader: Ronald Reagan and the Fall of Communism* (New York, NY: HarperPerennial, 2007); James Mann, *The Rebellion of Ronald Reagan: A History of the End of the Cold War* (New York, NY: Viking, 2009).

15. Robert Booth Fowler, "The Failure of the Religious Right," in Michael Cromartie (ed.), *No Longer Exiles: The Religious New Right in American Politics* (Washington, DC: Ethics and Public Policy Center, 1993), pp. 57–74.

16. Holmes, *The Faiths of the Postwar Presidents*, pp. 215–236; Geoffrey Layman, *The Great Divide: Religion and Cultural Conflict in American Party Politics* (New York, NY: Columbia University Press, 2001); Laura R. Olson and John C. Green, "The Religion Gap," *PS: Political Science & Politics*, 39 (2006): 455–459.

17. David Aikman, *Man of Faith: The Spiritual Journey of George W. Bush* (Nashville, TN: Thomas Nelson, 2004); Paul Kengor, *God and George W. Bush: A Spiritual Life* (New York, NY: HarperCollins, 2004); Stephen Mansfield, *The Faith of George W. Bush* (New York, NY: Tarcher, 2003); Holmes, *The Faiths of the Postwar Presidents*, pp. 240–269; Berggren and Rae, "Jimmy Carter and George W. Bush"; Amy E. Black, Douglas L. Koopman, and David K. Ryden, *Of Little Faith: The Politics of George W. Bush's Faith-Based Initiatives* (Washington, DC: Georgetown University Press, 2004).

18. On the Bush Doctrine and the religious overtones inherent in Bush's foreign policy, see Ivo H. Daalder and James M. Lindsay, *America Unbound: The Bush Revolution in Foreign Policy* (Washington, DC: Brookings Institution, 2003); Kevin R. den Dulk, "Evangelical 'Internationalists' and US Foreign Policy during the Bush Administration," in Mark J. Rozell and Gleaves Whitney (eds.), *Religion and the Bush Presidency* (New York, NY: Palgrave Macmillan, 2007), pp. 213–234; Michael J. Mazarr, "George W. Bush, Idealist," *International Affairs*, 79 (2003): 503–522; Ilan Peleg, *The Legacy of George W. Bush's Foreign Policy: Moving beyond Neoconservatism* (Boulder, CO: Westview Press, 2009); Bob Woodward, *Bush at War* (New York, NY: Simon & Schuster, 2002). As a small sampling of the criticism aroused by the evangelicalism of Bush's foreign policy, see Jane Lampman, "New Scrutiny of Role of Religion in Bush's Policies," *The Christian Science Monitor*, March 17, 2003; Ewen MacAskill, "George Bush: 'God Told Me to End the Tyranny in Iraq,'" *The Guardian*, October 7, 2005.

19. David Kuo, *Tempting Faith: An Inside Story of Political Seduction* (New York, NY: Simon & Schuster, 2006).

20. For personal accounts of Obama's religious journey, see Barack Obama, *The Audacity of Hope: Thoughts on Reclaiming the American Dream* (New York, NY: Three Rivers Press, 2006), chapter 6; *Dreams from My Father: A Story of Race and Inheritance*

(New York, NY: Three Rivers Press, 2004); and "My Spiritual Journey," *Time*, October 16, 2006; Jodi Kantor, "A Candidate, His Minister and the Search for Faith," *New York Times*, April 30, 2007; on Jeremiah Wright and the dustup during the 2008 presidential campaign, see Steven Gray, "The Unretirement of Reverend Wright," *Time*, June 4, 2008; Jodi Kantor, "Obama Denounces Statements of His Pastor as 'Inflammatory,'" *New York Times*, March 15, 2008. See also Amy Sullivan, "The Obamas Find a Church Home—Away from Home," *Time*, June 29, 2009; see also Holmes, *The Faiths of the Postwar Presidents*, pp. 270–320.

21. David Jackson, "Obama Urges Respect among Politicians," *USA Today*, February 3, 2012, p. 4A.

22. Many are collected in Joshua DuBois, *The President's Devotional: Daily Readings that Inspired President Obama* (New York, NY: Harper, 2013).

23. Laurie Goodstein, "White House Director of Faith Based Office Is Leaving His Post," *New York Times*, February 8, 2013, p. A17; Rachel Weiner, "Melissa Rogers Promises Continuity in Faith-Based Office," *Washington Post*, March 22, 2013, www.washingtonpost.com/news/post-politics/wp/2013/03/22/melissa-rogers-promises-continuity-in-faith-based-office/?utm_term=.e12c0e28dd79; Edward Lee Ottis, "Invisible Hands," *World*, April 24, 2010, pp. 47–49; Peter Wallsten, "Faith Policies Part of Political Calculus," *Wall Street Journal*, February 5, 2010, p. A3; Lisa Miller, "Heaven Help Him," *Newsweek*, February 8, 2010, p. 15; Carrie Johnson, "That Troublesome Bush Holdover," *Washington Post*, September 21–27, 2009, p. 15; Mollie Ziegler Hemingway, "Faith-Based Double Standards, *Wall Street Journal*, September 11, 2009, p. W13.

24. See Chapters 11 and 12 for a fuller discussion of this controversy.

25. Michael J. O'Loughlin, "With GOP Ticket Set, Catholic 'Never-Trump' Camp Remains Defiant," *America*, July 26, 2016, www.americamagazine.org/content/all-things/gop-ticket-set-catholic-never-trump-camp-remains-defiant; Andy Crouch, "Speak Truth to Trump," *Christianity Today*, October 10, 2016, www.christianitytoday.com/ct/2016/october-web-only/speak-truth-to-trump.html.

26. Laurie Goodstein, "Donald Trump Reveals Evangelical Rifts That Could Shape Politics for Years," *New York Times*, October 17, 2016, www.nytimes.com/2016/10/17/us/donald-trump-evangelicals-republican-vote.html?mcubz=3. See also Kevin R. den Dulk, "The GOP, Evangelical Elites, and the Challenge of Pluralism," in Paul Djupe and Brian Calfano (eds.), *The Evangelical Crackup? The Future of the Evangelical-Republican Coalition* (Philadelphia, PA: Temple University Press, 2018).

27. M. J. Lee, "God and the Don," *CNN*, June 4, 2017, www.cnn.com/interactive/2017/politics/state/donald-trump-religion/.

28. Gwenda Blair, "How Norman Vincent Peale Taught Donald Trump to Worship Himself," *Politico*, October 6, 2015, www.politico.com/magazine/story/2015/10/donald-trump-2016-norman-vincent-peale-213220.

29. Lance Wallnau, *God's Chaos Candidate* (Keller, TX: Killer Sheep Media, 2016); Kyle Mantyla, "David Barton: Christians Who Refuse to Vote for Donald Trump Will Have to Answer to God," *Right Wing Watch*, August 10, 2016, www.rightwingwatch.org/post/david-barton-christians-who-refuse-to-vote-for-donald-trump-will-have-to-answer-to-god/.

30. Michael Gerson, "Evangelical Christians Are Selling Out Faith for Politics," *Washington Post*, June 23, 2016, www.washingtonpost.com/opinions/evangelical-christians-are-selling-out-faith-for-politics/2016/06/23/f03368de-3964–11e6–8f7c-d4c723a2becb_story.html?utm_term=.4b6aa1475c60; Marvin Olasky and The Editors, "Unfit for Power," *World Magazine*, October 29, 2016; O'Loughlin, "With GOP Ticket

Set"; George Weigel, "'A Tiny Bit of a Man': Evelyn Waugh's Anticipation of Donald Trump," *National Review Online*, www.nationalreview.com/article/432744/donald-trump-evelyn-waughs-rex-mottram-prefigured-him-remarkably; Crouch, "Speak Truth to Trump"; Michael Ferris, "Trump's Meeting with Evangelical Christian Leaders Marks the End of the Christian Right," *The Christian Post*, June 21, 2016, www.christian post.com/news/trump-meeting-evangelical-leaders-end-of-the-christian-right-165473/; Deborah Fikes, "Why I Resigned My Evangelical Leadership Roles to Support Hillary Clinton," *Christianity Today*, September 27, 2017, www.christianitytoday.com/edstetzer/2016/september/why-i-support-hillary-clinton.html; "A Declaration by American Evangelicals Concerning Donald Trump," 2017, www.change.org/p/donald-trump-a-declaration-by-american-evangelicals-concerning-donald-trump.

31. Jerry Falwell, Jr., "Jerry Falwell Jr.: Trump Is the Churchillian Leader We Need," *Washington Post*, August 19, 2016, www.washingtonpost.com/opinions/jerry-falwell-jr-trump-is-the-churchillian-leader-we-need/2016/08/19/b1ff79e0–64b1–11e6-be4e-23fc4d4d12b4_story.html?utm_term=.057ec8a2c43b.

32. Michael Gerson, "Evangelical Christians Are Selling Out Faith for Politics," *Washington Post*, June 23, 2016, www.washingtonpost.com/opinions/evangelical-christians-are-selling-out-faith-for-politics/2016/06/23/f03368de-3964–11e6-8f7c-d4c723a2becb_story.html?utm_term=.58770d54fa08; Jack Jenkins, "Evangelical Advisory Board," *Think Progress*, thinkprogress.org/meet-donald-trumps-new-evangelical-advisory-board-6a5bfc5460d7/; Elizabeth Dias, "Inside Donald Trump's Private Meeting with Evangelicals," *Time*, June 20, 2016, http://time.com/4375975/donald-trump-evangelical-conservative-leaders-meeting/.

33. Pew Research Center, "US Muslims Concerned about Their Place in Society, but Continue to Believe in the American Dream," July 26, 2017, www.pewforum.org/2017/07/26/findings-from-pew-research-centers-2017-survey-of-us-muslims/.

34. Southern Baptist Convention, Phoenix, Arizona, "On the Anti-Gospel of Alt-Right White Supremacy," June 14, 2017, www.sbc.net/resolutions/2283/on-the-antigospel-of-altright-white-supremacy.

35. Sarah Pulliam Bailey, "Southern Baptists Voted Overwhelmingly to Condemn 'Alt-Right' White Supremacy," *Washington Post*, June 14, 2017.

36. In January 1961, *Congressional Quarterly* began listing the religious affiliation of members of Congress. Data are now summarized by Aleksandra Sandstrom, "Faith on the Hill: The Religious Composition of the 115th Congress," Pew Research Center, January 3, 2017, www.pewforum.org/2017/01/03/faith-on-the-hill-115/.

37. Daniel Burke, "The Book of Bernie: Inside Sanders' Unorthodox Faith," *CNN*, April 15, 2016, www.cnn.com/2016/04/14/politics/bernie-sanders-religion/.

38. James L. Guth, "Religion in the American Congress: The Case of the US House of Representatives, 1953–2013," in Kevin R. den Dulk and Elizabeth A. Oldmixon (eds.), *Mediating Religion and Government: Political Institutions and the Policy Process* (New York, NY: Palgrave, 2014), pp. 109–134; John C. Green and James L. Guth, "Religion, Representatives, and Roll Calls," *Legislative Studies Quarterly*, 16 (November 1991): 571–584; James L. Guth and Lyman A. Kellstedt, "Religion and Congress," in Corwin E. Smidt (ed.), *In God We Trust: Religion and American Political Life* (Grand Rapids, MI: Baker Academic, 2001), pp. 213–233; Elizabeth Anne Oldmixon, *Uncompromising Positions: God, Sex, and the US House of Representatives* (Washington, DC: Georgetown University Press, 2005); Elizabeth A. Oldmixon and Brian Calfano, "The Religious Dynamics of Moral Decision-Making in the US House of Representatives, 1993–2002," *Journal for the Scientific Study of Religion*, 46 (2007): 55–70; Lauren Edwards Smith,

Laura R. Olson, and Jeffrey A. Fine, "Substantive Religious Representation in the US Senate: Voting Alignment with the Family Research Council," *Political Research Quarterly*, 63 (2010): 68–82.

39. Sandstrom, "Faith on the Hill."

40. Elizabeth A. Oldmixon and William Hudson, "Catholic Republicans and Conflicting Impulses in the 109th Congress," *Politics & Religion*, 1 (2008): 113–136.

41. Suzanne Gamboa, "Latinos See Historic 'Firsts' as New Congress Gets Started," *NBC News*, January 3, 2017, www.nbcnews.com/news/latino/latinos-see-historic-firsts-new-congress-gets-started-n702411.

42. Sandstrom, "Faith on the Hill."

43. Sandstrom, "Faith on the Hill."

44. Sandstrom, "Faith on the Hill."

45. Sandstrom, "Faith on the Hill."

46. Sandstrom, "Faith on the Hill."

47. Mark Oppenheimer, "Politicians Who Reject Labels Based on Religion," *New York Times*, November 9, 2012, www.nytimes.com/2012/11/10/us/politics/politicians-who-speak-of-religion-in-unaccustomed-ways.html.

48. Oldmixon, *Uncompromising Positions*; David Yamane and Elizabeth A. Oldmixon, "Affiliation, Salience, Advocacy: Three Religious Factors in Public Policy-Making," *Legislative Studies Quarterly*, 31 (2006): 433–460; Elizabeth A. Oldmixon, Beth Rosenson, and Kenneth D. Wald, "Conflict over Israel: The Role of Religion, Race, Party and Ideology in the US House of Representatives, 1997–2002," *Terrorism and Political Violence*, 17 (2005): 407–426; Beth Rosenson, Elizabeth A. Oldmixon, and Kenneth Wald, "US Senators' Support for Israel Examined through Sponsorship/Co-Sponsorship Decisions, 1993–2002: The Influence of Elite and Constituent Factors," *Foreign Policy Analysis*, 5 (2009): 73–91.

49. Guth and Kellstedt, "Religion and Congress," p. 229. See also Peter L. Benson and Dorothy L. Williams, *Religion on Capitol Hill: Myths and Realities* (Oxford: Oxford University Press, 1982); Oldmixon, *Uncompromising Positions*.

50. David C. Leege, Kenneth D. Wald, Brian S. Krueger, and Paul D. Mueller, *The Politics of Cultural Differences: Social Change and Voter Mobilization Strategies in the Post-New Deal Period* (Princeton, NJ: Princeton University Press, 2002).

51. Benson and Williams, *Religion on Capitol Hill*.

52. See also Oldmixon, *Uncompromising Positions*. Benson and Williams' work presages the literature on the declining relevance of denomination; see Robert Wuthnow, *The Restructuring of American Religion: Society and Faith since World War Two* (Princeton, NJ: Princeton University Press, 1988).

53. Benson and Williams, *Religion on Capitol Hill*; Oldmixon, *Uncompromising Positions*; Elizabeth A. Oldmixon, "Religious Representation and Animal Welfare in the US Senate," *Journal for the Scientific Study of Religion*, 56 (2017): 162–178.

54. David E. Campbell, John C. Green, and J. Quin Monson, *Seeking the Promised Land: Mormons and American Politics* (Cambridge: Cambridge University Press, 2014).

55. Jeff Flake, *Conscience of a Conservative* (New York, NY: Random House, 2017).

56. Flake, *Conscience of a Conservative*.

57. J. C. Derrick, "Ben Sasse: A Reformed Reformer," *World Magazine*, October 15, 2016, https://world.wng.org/2016/09/ben_sasse_a_reformed_reformer; Benjamin Eric Sasse, "The Anti-Madalyn Majority: Secular Left, Religious Right, and the Rise of Reagan's America," doctoral dissertation, Yale University, May 2004; Ben Sasse, "An Open Letter to Trump Supporters," February 28, 2016, www.facebook.com/sassefornebraska/posts/561073597391141.

58. Edward Lee Pitts, "The Senate's Shepherd," *World*, June 5, 2010, pp. 54–56.

59. Tim Murphy, "Keith Ellison Is Everything Republicans Thought Obama Was. Maybe He's Just What Democrats Need," *Mother Jones*, March/April 2017, www.mother jones.com/politics/2017/02/keith-ellison-democratic-national-committee-chair/; Mitch Anderson, "Ellison: Hajj was Transformative," *Star Tribune*, December 18, 2008, www.startribune.com/ellison-hajj-was-transformative/36417549/.

60. Rachel Donadio, "Visiting Pope, Pelosi Hears a Call to Protect Life," *New York Times*, February 19, 2009, p. A17.

61. Pitts, "The Senate's Shepherd."

62. Emily Belz, "Unmoved," *World*, December 19, 2009, pp. 53–54.

63. Edward Lee Pitts, "Debate Changer," *World*, June 19, 2010, pp. 60–62.

64. John Aloysius Farrell, "US 'Antireligious Bias' Alleged: Bush Report Decries Faith-Group Hurdles," *Boston Globe*, August 17, 2001, p. A2.

65. Shaila Dewan and Robbie Brown, "All Her Life, Nikki Haley was the Different One," *New York Times*, June 13, 2010, www.nytimes.com/2010/06/14/us/politics/ 14haley.html; Manoj Kumar, "In India's Punjab, Haley Relatives Cheer Appointment as UN Envoy," *Reuters*, November 24, 2016, www.reuters.com/article/us-usa-trump-haley-india-idUSKBN13J10O; Biography, "Nikki Haley," www.biography.com/people/nikki-haley-20939217.

66. Donald R. Songer and Susan J. Tabrizi, "The Religious Right in Court: The Decision Making of Christian Evangelicals in State Supreme Courts," *Journal of Politics*, 61 (1999): 507–526.

67. But see Melissa M. Deckman, *School Board Battles: The Christian Right in Local Politics* (Washington, DC: Georgetown University Press, 2004); and David Yamane, "Faith and Access: Personal Religiosity and Religious Group Advocacy in a State Legislature," *Journal for the Scientific Study of Religion*, 38 (1999): 543–550.

68. Daniel Okrent, the public editor for the *New York Times*, offers a rich exploration of the bubble in "Is the *New York Times* a Liberal Newspaper?" *New York Times*, July 25, 2014. See also Jack Shafer and Tucker Doherty, "The Media Bubble is Worse than You Think," *Politico*, May/June 2017. The blog "Get Religion"—www. getreligion.org— and its companion podcast "Crossroads" regularly chronicle the media bubble's effect on religion reporting. See also Paul Marshall, Lela Gilbert, and Roberta Green Ahmanson (eds.), *Blind Spot* (Oxford: Oxford University Press, 2009). For an alternative perspective, see John Schmalzbauer, *People of Faith: Religious Conviction in American Journalism and Higher Education* (Ithaca, NY: Cornell University Press, 2003).

69. The Pew Research Center used to sponsor a page called "Religion in the News," but no longer does so.

70. But see William D. Romanowski, *Reforming Hollywood: How American Protestants Fought for Freedom at the Movies* (Oxford: Oxford University Press, 2012) and *Eyes Wide Open: Looking for God in Popular Culture* (Grand Rapids, MI: Brazos Press, 2001); Robert Joustra and Allison Wilkinson, *How to Survive the Apocalypse: Zombies, Cylons, Faith, and Politics at the End of the World* (Grand Rapids, MI: Eerdmans, 2016); Kathryn Lofton, *Oprah: The Gospel of an Icon* (Berkeley, CA: University of California Press, 2011).

71. See Eric Michael Mazur (ed.), *Encyclopedia of Religion and Film* (Santa Barbara, CA: ABC-Clio, 2011); Robert K. Johnston, *Reel Spirituality: Theology and Film in Dialogue* (Grand Rapids, MI: Baker Academic, 2000).

72. Michael Medved, *Hollywood v. America* (New York, NY: HarperPerennial, 1993).

73. Marco Della Cova, "Hollywood: The Best Men of Gay Marriage," *USA Today*, June 27, 2013, pp. D1–D2.

74. Alyssa Rosenberg, "How TV Made Christianity Radical Again," *Washington Post*, February 19, 2015; Elijal Siegler, "God in the Box: Religion in Contemporary Television Cop Shows," in Eric Michael Mazur (ed.), *God in the Details: American Religion in Popular Culture* (London and New York, NY: Routledge, 2001), pp. 201–215; and Lisle Dalton, Eric Michael Mazur, and Monica Siems, "Homer the Heretic and Charlie Church: Parody, Piety, and Pluralism in *The Simpsons*," in Eric Michael Mazur (ed.), *God in the Details: American Religion in Popular Culture* (London and New York, NY: Routledge, 2001), pp. 231–247.

75. See Heather Hendershot, *Shaking the World for Jesus: Media and Conservative Evangelical Subculture* (Chicago, IL: University of Chicago Press, 2004). For a fascinating analysis of evangelical diet plans, see R. Marie Griffith, *Born Again Bodies: Flesh and Spirit in American Christianity* (Berkeley, CA: University of California Press, 2004).

76. Robert P. George, *Conscience and Its Enemies: Confronting the Dogmas of Liberal Secularism* (Wilmington, DE: ISI Books, 2013). See "A Statement by Robert P. George and Cornel West," March 14, 2017, https://jmp.princeton.edu/statement.

77. For a history of gospel music, see James R. Goff, Jr., *Close Harmony: A History of Southern Gospel* (Chapel Hill, NC: University of North Carolina Press, 2002).

78. Sho Baraka, "Why I Can't Vote for Either Trump or Clinton," *Christianity Today*, September 23, 2016; Imade Nibokun, "Christian Hip-Hop Still Isn't Quite Sure What to Make of Chance the Rapper," *LA Weekly*, March 7, 2017; Michelle Boorstein, "This Rapper Is Trying to Get His Fellow Evangelicals to Talk about Race. Not Everyone Is on Board," *Washington Post*, July 1, 2016.

79. Kate Beaudoin, "7 Muslim Rappers Who Are Shattering Stereotypes about Islam," Mic.com, June 18, 2015, https://mic.com/articles/120901/7-muslim-rappers-who-embrace-their-faith-through-hip-hop#.t7XUxjneJ; Kate Shellnutt, "Meet Hasan Minhaj: The Muslim Comedian Who Roasted Trump in Front of Reporters," *Washington Post*, April 30, 2017, www.washingtonpost.com/news/acts-of-faith/wp/2017/04/30/meet-hasan-minhaj-the-muslim-comedian-who-roasted-trump-in-front-of-reporters/?utm_term=.657df532f3ff.

80. John Allen, Jr., *A People of Hope: Timothy Dolan in Conversation with John L. Allen, Jr.* (New York, NY: Image, 2012), "What a Card!" *New York Post*, February 19, 2012, pp. 1, 4–9, "Cardinal Rules: Tim Will Be a Major Player in US Politics," *New York Post*, February 19, 2012, p. 9, "Timothy M. Dolan," *Newsweek* (February 27–March 5, 2012), p. 7; Robert Kolker, "The Archbishop of Charm," *New York Magazine*, September 28, 2009, pp. 36–41.

81. Ed Kilgore, "Trump's Spiritual Adviser Authorizes Him to Smite North Korea," *New York Magazine*, August 9, 2017, http://nymag.com/daily/intelligencer/2017/08/trumps-spiritual-adviser-authorizes-him-to-smite-n-korea.html; Daniel Burke, "Inflammatory Pastor Preached to Trump before Inauguration," *CNN*, January 22, 2017, www.cnn.com/2017/01/19/politics/trump-jeffress-pastor/index.html.

82. For a superb discussion of politics and Protestant clergy in general, see Corwin E. Smidt, *Pastors and Public Life: The Changing Face of American Protestant Clergy* (Oxford: Oxford University Press, 2016); and Lyman A. Kellstedt, James L. Guth, Corwin E. Smidt, and John C. Green, "The Bully Pulpit, Revisited," *Books and Culture*, September/October 2010, pp. 32–33. See also Gregory A. Smith, *Politics in the Parish: The Political Influence of Catholic Priests* (Washington, DC: Georgetown University Press, 2008).

83. Eitan D. Hersh and Gabrielle Malina, "Partisan Pastor: The Politics of 130,000 American Religious Leaders," 2017, www.eitanhersh.com/uploads/7/9/7/5/7975685/

hersh_malina_draft_061117.pdf. See also Emma Green, "Clergy Are More Partisan than Their Parishioners," *The Atlantic*, June 12, 2017.

84. Kevin Quealy, "Your Rabbi? Probably a Democrat. Your Baptist Pastor? Probably a Republican. Your Priest? Who Knows," *New York Times*, June 12, 2017, www.nytimes.com/interactive/2017/06/12/upshot/the-politics-of-americas-religious-leaders.html.

85. Hersh and Malina, "Partisan Pastor"; Quealy, "Your Rabbi? Probably a Democrat."

86. Hersh and Malina, "Partisan Pastor."

87. For an analysis of moral worldviews of clergy in varying congregational contexts, ranging from congregations with serious disagreements to those without, see Paul A. Djupe and Amanda Friesen, "Moralizing to the Choir: The Moral Foundations of American Clergy," *Social Science Quarterly*, forthcoming.

88. Djupe and Friesen, "Moralizing to the Choir."

10

RELIGION, CIVIL SOCIETY, AND POLITICAL CULTURE

The question of what makes a "good" citizen has rarely been more urgent in the United States than it is in the current political climate. American confidence in political institutions—indeed, in most social institutions—has been declining for three decades, and many people feel indifference and alienation that tend to diminish their political participation and civic-mindedness. Commentators from across the political spectrum worry about citizens' declining sense of trust in one another and increasing cynicism about government. They watch helplessly as polarization—the deep political divide—continues to roil the American political process. They also lament fading levels of civic knowledge and enthusiasm for public service. While no group is immune from these concerns, young people have been hit especially hard by what some see as a crisis of citizenship.

In previous chapters, we have painted a portrait of a religious and spiritual America that often is deeply involved in public life. Such involvement means that organized religion has a stake in the challenges to good citizenship that we see all around us. While in many ways religion can exacerbate division and distrust, it also has remarkable capacities both to focus the public's attention on shared goals and to motivate collective action. The combined American legacies of religious freedom and popular sovereignty allow robust participation for people of all religious persuasions in the political process. As we have already seen in earlier chapters, religious attitudes and allegiances in the United States shape voting patterns, views about policy issues and the role of government, partisan attachments, interest-group strategies, and elite-level political choices.

The political activism and attitudes of religious people and groups have generated immense interest among political and intellectual observers, especially in recent decades. Some critics have envisioned the political involvement of religious groups with fear or even antagonism; others have been welcoming of religious contributions to public life and political discourse. But whatever the motivations that bring people to study the intersections of faith and politics, most have been impressed by religion's vigorous civic engagement, its diverse array of political expressions, and its remarkable ability to adapt to changing political realities.

In this chapter, we turn to the role of political culture and civil society in fostering high levels of religious participation in politics in the United States, as well as the effect of religion on political culture itself. By political culture, we mean the widely shared values and attitudes people have about politics and government.[1] Some of these values and attitudes have to do with the appropriate role of government, including how well public policy reflects such core ideals as freedom, equality, and justice. But political culture also encompasses citizens' dispositions toward public life, such as their levels of political interest and knowledge; their embrace of certain civic "virtues"; their attitudes about political authority, partisanship, and groups they oppose; and their perceptions of whether government cares about and responds to their concerns. It is essential in any democracy for the political culture to support widespread political participation by ordinary citizens.

In the United States, religion and political culture intersect in countless ways. Here we focus on how religion shapes the American political culture—and how that culture in turn shapes religion. We also consider the effects of the increasing number of Americans who are indifferent or hostile toward organized religion.

THE TENSION BETWEEN RELIGION AND POLITICAL CULTURE

As we discussed in Chapter 1, some aspects of religion have a deep historical resonance within political culture. The Puritans left a legacy of self-government, a sense of national mission ("the city on a hill"), and an emphasis on religion's ability to shape citizens' moral character for the public good. From the colonial period to the present, there has also been a remarkably steady growth of religious pluralism, fueled by waves of immigration and homegrown religious experimentation. That diversity has meant competition, and competition has created incentives for intense religious outreach for new members. This evangelical zeal has often carried over into public life, sometimes in the form of a moral campaign (for example, the Temperance Movement).

The need for religious groups to compete for adherents is coupled with an enduring strain of populism that emphasizes grassroots participation in the work of churches and other religious groups. Historically, direct participation by American laity in the leadership and administration of congregations was unusual in comparison to the norms in Europe, where ordinary church members were more accustomed to an experience of religion mediated through clergy and other elites. As we discussed in Chapter 2, American-style populism reflected a certain cultural confidence that individuals working collectively can have enormous impact. This confidence frequently appears in great political movements for social change. It is also a favorite resource for insurgent political leaders, who pit the "people" against elites they see as out of touch. The 2016 presidential election, which saw anti-elitist undercurrents in both the Bernie Sanders and Donald Trump campaigns, suggests the persistence of populist confidence in American political culture. Just as we saw in 2016, religion has always played a role in these populist movements and campaigns.

Moreover, as American culture today grows ever more pluralistic in its religious and spiritual orientations, with many adults pursuing spiritual quests outside of traditional religious organizations and many others choosing to drop away from religion altogether, there are ramifications for the political culture. The rise of the religiously non-affiliated has emerged at the same time as voters have grown more inclined to self-declare as "independents" and distance themselves from organized political parties and most other governmental structures. As we discuss later in this chapter, the fact that disaffiliation from both organized religion and political parties has occurred nearly simultaneously is not a coincidence; in many ways, the former reinforces the latter.

While religion exerts many varied influences on political culture, the influence does not move in only one direction. Political culture itself can and does shape religion. For many religious believers, this is reason enough to approach political culture with considerable ambivalence. On the one hand, people of faith may perceive the broader culture as an important battleground in a conflict over core values or national identity. Religious believers may also insist that they have an obligation to engage in that conflict—and that they expect the political system to respond to their efforts. On the other hand, the faithful may worry about meeting stiff resistance from a political culture that is already deeply influenced by values they reject—and they have good reason for that concern.[2] People of faith may even be faced with the need to compromise their own values in the political arena. Political engagement, then, seems a quixotic affair at best and downright dangerous at worst.

The Christian Conservative Movement: A Case Study

The contemporary Christian conservative movement illustrates this tension. Political activism by adherents of the movement, sometimes called the Christian right, began primarily among white evangelical Protestants in the late 1970s and early 1980s.[3] The movement's origin is a complicated story. Clearly, part of the story is about religious conservatives' growing concern at the time, especially in the wake of the sexual revolution of the 1960s, that the United States was straying from traditional values regarding family, reproduction, and child-rearing. Race was likely another factor. As we discussed in Chapter 5, race intersects with evangelicalism in complex ways, creating ideological and partisan distinctions between white evangelicals and their black coreligionists.[4] Some scholars have argued that the rise of the Christian right—a largely (though not exclusively) white phenomenon—is partly a legacy of the politics of this racial division.[5] A third argument about the movement's origins suggests that increasing religious diversity and disaffiliation led many of the conservative faithful to embrace politics as a means of trying to institutionalize and maintain established cultural values.[6] Each of these explanations of the Christian right differ in specific focus, but they share a basic theme: Christian conservatives in the late 1960s and 1970s were struggling with the challenges posed by new forms of pluralism in American society.

The movement's leaders insist they are not disguised theocrats wishing to establish Christianity as the official religion of the United States. Instead, they aim to foster an atmosphere in which committed Christians can practice their religion and see its morality honored in and by the broader culture. They contend that ultimately Christian renewal is the only way to reverse what they perceive as a fraying of the cultural fabric in the United States. But absent that mass return to traditional faith, movement leaders and activists have often attempted to use government to foster cultural change.

When the Moral Majority emerged in 1979 as the first major Christian-right organization, its founder, the late Rev. Jerry Falwell, and other leaders saw an opportunity to address discontent among conservative people of faith with the political direction of the country, as epitomized in US Supreme Court decisions declaring state-sponsored prayer in schools and restrictions on abortion to be unconstitutional. Although the Moral Majority was never as influential as its media coverage suggested (it eventually collapsed in 1988), the broader Christian-right movement took stock of the experience and reemerged by the early 1990s with much greater sophistication and organizational acumen.[7] Tapping into stores of religious populism and evangelical intensity, leaders channeled the energy of the movement's activists into effective grassroots organizations. The Christian Coalition and other movement organizations became a powerful force in the Republican Party at the state and local level during the 1990s. They were widely hailed as a key bloc in the Republicans' historic victories in the 1994 midterm elections, when the GOP took majority control of both the US Senate and the House of Representatives for the first time in four decades.[8]

By the late 1990s, however, Christian conservative leaders were expressing second thoughts about political activism as a means of cultural renewal. Twenty years after the founding of the Moral Majority, some of Jerry Falwell's key advisers suggested that Christian conservatives had lost their religious moorings and had become "blinded" by political power.[9] Their concerns reflected events on the ground. Christian conservatives undoubtedly did achieve some electoral and policy victories in the 2000s, most notably the election and reelection of President George W. Bush and the passage of significant foreign-policy legislation on religious freedom and human rights.[10] That said, the movement lost some steam around the turn of the century. The Christian Coalition, the Family Research Council, and other Christian conservative groups have experienced leadership changes, budget shortfalls, and staff reductions, all of which until recently pointed to a waning interest among many rank-and-file members and shifting political fortunes.

Nevertheless, the pendulum of political influence would appear to have shifted back toward the Christian right with the 2016 presidential election. Several prominent Christian-right leaders threw their support behind Donald Trump, and conservative evangelical voters reprised their role as stalwarts in the Republican electoral coalition. The GOP crafted a party platform at its national convention that emphasized issues including abortion, same-sex marriage, religious liberty, and other matters that appealed to the Christian conservative base—and placed greater emphasis on these issues than had any other Republican platform since the 1980s.[11] Immediately after his inauguration, Trump signaled his own "religion agenda," including, most notably, his intention to nominate conservative justices to the cultural battleground of the Supreme Court.[12]

But the Trump candidacy also laid bare the same kinds of rifts among Christian conservatives as were present in the late 1990s. Russell Moore, a key public leader in the Southern Baptist Convention, raised pointed concerns about Trump's character and a drift within the Republican Party toward what he called an "ethno-nationalist populism."[13] Many other conservative theologians, pastors, public intellectuals, and political operatives expressed similar worries. Some religious leaders, including conservative blogger Rod Dreher, in his bestselling book, *The Benedict Option*, reignited the debate about stepping away from politics versus retrenching to engage a "post-Christian" culture.[14] Moreover, it is not clear that Christian conservative organizations played a significant role in voter mobilization in 2016, especially compared to past get-out-the-vote efforts. While it remains an open question whether the 2016 election and its aftermath are the last gasp of the Christian right, it clearly exposed significant tensions within the movement.[15]

These experiences underline both the appeal and the perils of religious interactions with political culture. The Christian right sought to engage the broader public in a conflict over values but risked losing its own grounding, a challenge for any religious group that enters the public square.[16] Moreover, the story of the Christian right points to the risk of alienating the very culture that a religious group or movement hopes to transform. For many ordinary citizens who were not part of the movement, Christian-right groups represent key combatants in a "culture war" over values in the United States.[17] Indeed, conservative leaders reinforced the idea of a culture war in their own language, often using the metaphors of battle or war to describe their efforts and to define an enemy. We addressed the scholarly theory of the culture war in Chapter 2, but it is essential to note here that some observers perceived the Christian right as fanning the flames of cultural conflict and polarization. This perception led to a large-scale reaction against the movement's tactics and goals. In the wake of the 2016 election, for example, the Pew Research Center found that Americans had more favorable attitudes (compared to 2014) toward every major religion-based group, including atheists and Muslims, with one exception: white evangelicals, the backbone of the Christian right (see Box 10.1).[18]

This concern about backlash highlights a peculiar aspect of religion's potential to shape political culture that helps explain the cultural ambivalence of some religious groups. By the early nineteenth century, Alexis de Tocqueville, the

---

BOX 10.1 HAVE MILLENNIALS LEFT RELIGION BECAUSE OF POLITICS?

Compared to older generations, so-called millennials—young people who reached adulthood during the first two decades of the twenty-first century—are much more likely to answer "none" when asked about their religious affiliation on surveys. What's more, fewer young people today claim an affiliation than adults of the same age did in previous decades; since the 2000s, about a quarter of young people say they have no affiliation, compared with a little more than a tenth of similarly aged adults during the 1970s and 1980s. The reasons for this generational change are clearly very complex, but one factor that appears to explain some of the change is the controversial role of religion in politics. Political scientists Robert Putnam and David Campbell, for example, have suggested that it is not a coincidence that the rise of the Christian conservative movement was followed by a decline in affiliation rates among young people, whose increasingly liberal attitudes about issues such as marriage and the environment fit uneasily with the messages they hear from some of the most vocal religious leaders. At the same time, social scientists have found that among millennials who remain affiliated, religious intensity is no different than it is for other age groups, and within certain traditions—evangelicalism, for example—political attitudes among the young and old are quite similar.

Sources: David E. Campbell and Robert D. Putnam, "God and Caesar in America: Why Mixing Religion and Politics is Bad for Both," *Foreign Affairs*, 91 (2012): 34–43; Corwin E. Smidt, *American Evangelicals Today* (Lanham, MD: Rowman & Littlefield, 2013); Pew Research Center, "Religion among the Millennials," http://assets.pewresearch.org/wp-content/uploads/sites/11/2010/02/millennials-report.pdf; Michael Hout and Claude S. Fischer, "Explaining Why More Americans Have No Religious Preference: Political Backlash and Generational Succession, 1987–2012," *Sociological Sciences* 1 (2012): 423–447.

French social theorist and author of the classic *Democracy in America*, had already identified a counterintuitive characteristic of religion's public role in the United States. After comparing the politics of clergy in the United States and Europe, he observed that religion maintained greater influence over political values and attitudes in America precisely when it was perceived as most detached from political culture. By remaining aloof from the nitty-gritty of politics, religion was not identified with the self-interest and corrupting influences of political life. This tendency toward reticence gave religious leaders greater credibility when they did decide to speak in broad moral terms about political issues of the day. Detachment also allowed religion to present itself as an appealing refuge from the vagaries of public life, with its unrelenting emphasis on the pursuit of individual self-interest.[19]

Of course, for some religious traditions, this entire discussion is irrelevant because they are not ambivalent about cultural engagement; they are indifferent or even hostile to it. The Amish, Jehovah's Witnesses, and numerous other religious sects seek to remain separate from political culture, engaging it only when necessary to protect their own cultural space. But many religious groups feel compelled to go beyond defense of their own territory. Religionists with very different goals and tactics often share the same desire to use politics and government to embed their values in the political culture. In this broad sense, a liberal Catholic calling for more government spending to ameliorate poverty, or a pacifist mainline Protestant marching against the government's use of drone strikes, reflect an orientation toward political culture much like that of Christian conservatives. They, too, are convinced that their values deserve a place in public life and that through their activism they may be able to speak prophetic truth to power.

To be sure, the experience of the Christian right suggests that political engagement risks significant costs. Groups must learn to live with the challenges American political culture can pose to their goals and identity. Steps religious groups take toward political engagement may even lead them to withdraw entirely when it appears that political culture is impervious to their efforts. Yet the appeal of the public moral campaign can be difficult to resist for those who dedicate themselves to promoting a specific interpretation of goodness and truth.

POLITICAL CULTURE AS A CONTEXT FOR RELIGIOUS PARTICIPATION

To this point, we have examined the potential tension between religion and political culture. But we might also look at the interaction of religion and political culture from a different perspective. Although political scientists often examine religious efforts to shape the values of public life, they also are interested in how American culture provides opportunities for individuals and groups to engage in politics in ways that are in line with their religious or spiritual perspectives.

Despite an abstract cultural commitment to the separation of church and state, most Americans also accept the idea that individuals have a right to bring their religious beliefs into the public square. It is one thing to insist that government ought not to support religion through financial support or other resources; it is quite another to argue that private citizens should suppress their religious commitments when they vote, contribute money to political organizations, or advocate for their values or policy views before political leaders. American political culture is much more accepting of political activism by religious individuals and groups than it is of government support for religion.[20] Indeed, the enduring openness to religious participation in public life is often cited as one feature of American "exceptionalism" that distinguishes the United States from its closest political cousins in Western Europe.[21] On this score, religion and political culture are mutually supporting. Religious groups in the colonial era and the early Republic realized that it was in their interest to distinguish the separation of church and state from the separation of religion and politics. Many groups believed that keeping government out of religious affairs was a way of protecting their religious liberty—a belief we chronicle much more fully in Chapters 11 and 12. Yet that same freedom, which complements the Madisonian emphasis on fostering competing interests in a system of checks and balances, gave religious groups an opportunity to take part in the democratic process itself, thereby adding their voices to the pluralism of American politics. As we have seen, many religions have welcomed this opportunity to participate.

American political culture has not always been open to all manifestations of religious engagement in the world of politics. The history of the United States is replete with examples of religious minorities losing political access when they are perceived as being too far outside the mainstream. As we discussed in Chapter 4, Mormons and other smaller religious groups have confronted serious challenges to their religious beliefs and practices; in many cases, they have suffered harsh treatment when seeking redress through political means. Even some larger religious traditions have faced discrimination and violence at the hands of the dominant American political culture. For example, Catholics, Jews, and Muslims alike have faced painful stereotyping and ostracism at different points in US history, and African-American churches were burned and bombed during the Civil Rights era.

In contemporary politics, we can see American preferences about religion in public life quite clearly in mass attitudes about political elites. Opinion surveys consistently reveal that voters are much more likely to cast their ballots for a member of any religious tradition than they are to vote for an atheist. But these surveys also suggest that voters employ an implicit hierarchy of preferences when assessing the religious identity of a candidate for office. Hence, they are more willing to vote for a Muslim than for an atheist but less likely to vote for a Muslim than for a Mormon, a Mormon than for an evangelical, and so on. Perhaps the best recent example of this phenomenon came in both the 2008 and 2012 Republican presidential primary campaigns, when Mitt Romney had to address persistent questions about his Mormon faith.

In comparative terms, religious liberty has been more widely practiced in the United States than in most other places around the globe, despite occasional threats to religion and religious liberty by intolerant majorities or insensitive governments, past and present. And that liberty speaks to a broader point: American political culture nurtures a set of norms and values that encourage the democratic participation of religious groups and individuals.

RELIGION, CIVIL SOCIETY, AND CITIZENSHIP

We usually assume that a vibrant citizenship will include both a set of values (such as a cautious trust in political institutions and a belief that one's participation matters) and competencies (such as a basic level of knowledge of how the political system works). Throughout much of American history, these assumptions have shaped public discussion of the contours of a distinctively democratic political culture. In recent decades, however, many observers have become alarmed at what they perceive as an erosion of the democratic political culture in America. A flood of scholarship has chronicled declining levels of civic engagement ranging from voting to grassroots participation in voluntary organizations.[22] For some scholars, the key explanation of decreasing civic engagement is a widespread lack of political knowledge.[23] Others have suggested that American disengagement is the result of diminishing "social capital," norms of trust and reciprocity in social interactions that foster collective action.[24] Still other analysts point to underdeveloped civic skills (such as leadership and strategic communication) and other basic citizen capacities.[25]

Whatever their explanations, scholars agree that the diminishing scope and quality of civic engagement they perceive cries out for a response. Numerous associations and individuals have proposed a host of solutions, ranging from beefed-up civic education to radical reform of political institutions.[26] These efforts to address perceived civic decline raise a complex and controversial question: Does religion's engagement in politics improve the quality of public life? Or has it been one of the sources of decline?

Tocqueville again helps us answer these key questions. In *Democracy in America*, he expressed his astonishment at the democratic norms developing in the young republic, to which he traveled in the 1830s. He was especially captivated by a pervasive sense of equality among citizens, which he appreciated in comparison to political culture on the European continent at the time, with its rigid social hierarchies rooted in inherited status. But Tocqueville also worried about the risks of American-style egalitarianism; left to its own devices, he thought it naturally would lead to individualism and a drift toward a kind of "democratic despotism" as citizens focused on their own self-interests rather than the public good. For Tocqueville, it was a marvel that the United States had not yet succumbed to those tendencies.

What intervened, he observed, was the participation of ordinary Americans in what we might today call civil society: those myriad associations and institutions that point citizens away from their self-isolation and toward the interests of others. Family, professions, neighborhoods, voluntary associations, and—perhaps most important—religion helped to dampen the powerful appeal of individualism in democratic societies.

Tocqueville's observations continue to influence thinking about political culture today. Some contemporary commentators have argued, for example, that civil society acts as a set of "mediating structures" between the individual and the state.[27] Not only does civil society act as a powerful source of core political values, but it also places a buffer between the state and the individual citizen who otherwise would be left without much power against the encroachments of government, even to the extreme point of totalitarianism. In other countries, it is often the emergence of a civil society that poses the greatest threat to authoritarian regimes. And religion is distinctive in its ability to maintain autonomy under such regimes, providing a relatively strong position from which to challenge authoritarianism.[28]

Other scholars and practitioners tout civil society as a "seedbed" for civic virtues and competence.[29] Most of the nation's founders, for example, suggested that constitutional design would not sustain the American republic by itself. John Adams declared that "pure virtue" is the "only foundation of a free Constitution."[30] Thomas Jefferson touted the importance of individual character and virtue, finding it most fully developed in the yeoman farmer.[31] Even James Madison, who placed great stock in the institutional design of government, nevertheless argued that it could not work without "sufficient virtue" among citizens.[32] But even though one might agree that any government is only as good as its citizens, government cannot necessarily make its citizens good. For many social theorists, instead it is our interactions in our day-to-day networks within civil society that provide opportunities to learn respect for the rights of others, tolerance, interpersonal trust, and a work ethic, among other virtues.[33]

It should not be surprising, then, that religion would be a key component of the discussion about civil society.[34] In the United States, it is no exaggeration to say that religious institutions make up the largest single component of civil society. More than half of all volunteering in the United States happens within religious settings; nearly 60 percent of Americans are members of a house of worship; well over a third are associated with religious groups besides houses of worship.[35] With such a presence in civil society, religion is bound to have an impact on the thinking and engagement of citizens.

Civic Capacities: Skills, Interest, and Knowledge

One way religious institutions play an important role in fostering a healthy American civic life is by helping citizens develop their own civic capacities: their own internal resources for participation. In a huge study of civic voluntarism, a team of scholars headed by political scientist Sidney Verba found that churches provide a crucial venue in which people often develop what they term "civic skills."[36] The argument is that people are more likely to participate in politics— and to be more effective participants—when they have experience doing a variety of things that occur frequently in church settings, such as organizing meetings, writing letters, and speaking in public. The basic assumption is that leadership, communication, and other skills are transferable; what is learned in one context may be put to use in another. Thus, people who are deeply involved in religious life usually possess relatively high levels of civic skills. Indeed, because they are central social institutions that host numerous public discussions, self-help groups, and other community activities, congregations foster civic skills even among nonmembers.[37] Churches and other religious associations are important for skill-building simply because they provide opportunities that participants would not otherwise have.

To be sure, because religious experiences are not all alike, possibilities for skill development are not equally distributed. Some religious traditions expose their members to a greater range and number of opportunities (in particular, the mainline Protestant and Jewish traditions), while others offer fewer possibilities (for example, Roman Catholicism).[38] Regardless of tradition, larger congregations generally have many small groups and other resources available to their members, which heightens the likelihood of skill development compared with smaller congregations that are resource-poor.[39] Even within a specific congregation, members often cluster in socially homogeneous groups, crowding out others from opportunities for skill development.[40] Nevertheless, whatever a person's experience, more committed religionists generally are more likely to be presented with skill-building activities and to take advantage of them.

Another aspect of a citizen's civic capacity focuses more on interest in and knowledge about politics. Most democratic theorists insist that an informed and attentive public is a key ingredient of representative government, and empirical scholars have long known that higher levels of political knowledge and interest are strongly associated with more and better civic engagement.[41] Like civic skill development, however, opportunities and motivations for obtaining knowledge or generating interest can vary dramatically. Some factors, including level of education or socioeconomic status, clearly are more important than others.

In their study of civil society and religion, political scientist Corwin E. Smidt and his colleagues found that although religion does not have a direct effect on levels of political knowledge, it is strongly associated with higher levels of interest in public life—a factor that is itself correlated with political knowledge.[42] Why would religion generate that interest? For one thing, religious institutions are prolific in supplying information to their members. Whether it is an urgent communiqué about human-rights abuses from a missionary abroad, a flyer about a pro-life rally, or a homily about poverty at Mass, active members of congregations often receive targeted messages. Too much information can confuse and suppress interest as much as it can generate it, but well-crafted communications, especially from trusted cue-givers such as clergy, can carry substantial weight among devout religionists.[43]

Social Capital and the Civic Virtues

In a different vein, a variety of scholars argue that places of worship facilitate interactions among people that contribute to what political scientist Robert Putnam and others have termed "social capital," the norms and networks that foster participation and collective decision-making.[44] Houses of worship, of course, are a prime area of interest for social-capital scholars. On the one hand, these scholars note that churches, synagogues, and other religious institutions often display social cohesion and support vibrant social networks that facilitate political mobilization.[45] On the other hand, as we have discussed in previous chapters, trends toward religious disaffiliation raise the question of whether congregations will continue to play an important role in public life in the future.

The social networks that form in congregations are a source of civic dispositions—what theorists have traditionally called virtues—that foster higher-quality interactions among citizens.[46] And recent research does indeed suggest that religion plays a role in fostering some of those dispositions. For example, those who attend religious services regularly and engage in private religious practice (prayer or meditation) are more likely than others to place stock in obeying the law, believe that government is generally trustworthy and responsive (what political scientists call "external political efficacy"), and cherish a strong work ethic.[47] Each of these virtues lends stability to the political and economic systems and fosters greater democratic participation.

Another important disposition is interpersonal trust. The reason for its importance is simple: Citizens are more likely to cooperate with other people when they trust that all the decision-makers will live up to their word and that the decision-making process is not rigged in anyone's favor. But the factors that generate interpersonal trust are not always straightforward. Putnam and his coauthor David Campbell have found that religious adults (for example, those who regularly attend worship services) are generally more trusting (and are perceived as being more trustworthy) than secular people.[48] A key mechanism appears to be the informal connections and powerful friendships believers build within their religious network. These networks help religionists develop a more general disposition of trust with people outside their networks. At the same time, certain kinds of religious beliefs (for example, fundamentalist views of human nature or the end times) can diminish levels of trust, though it is not precisely clear why those views have that effect.[49]Additionally, the trust a citizen might build with fellow members of a congregation (that is, social or inter-personal trust) does not necessarily translate into high levels of political trust: trust in the responsiveness, competence, and reliability of government.[50]

Tolerance is an even more complex matter. Although most studies suggest that tolerance is inversely correlated with religiosity (the more devout, the less tolerant, and vice versa), the findings depend on how tolerance is defined, measured, and analyzed.[51] Just as in studies of trust, one of the key questions in the literature on tolerance is the difference between political and social tolerance. Whereas religionists (or anyone else) may disapprove intensely of the values and lifestyles a particular group represents (social intolerance), they may still defend the right of members of that group to express themselves in public life (political tolerance).[52] Many studies confuse these two forms of tolerance, as well as other dispositions such as prejudice or acceptance. Sometimes, as a result, the most devout religious believers have been perceived as unusually politically intolerant rather than as socially intolerant or prejudiced.

Moreover, a high level of tolerance is often related to the diversity of a person's networks or exposure to messages about inclusion from religious leaders. Some very observant religionists with diverse social networks may be more tolerant than equally observant believers whose networks are more closed.[53] And of course social scientists work hard to disentangle the effects of religion from other demographic forces—education, race, income, and so on—that might be correlated with religion. It can often look as though religion has an effect on tolerance, for better or worse, when the effect is actually related to other factors that are associated with religion.

The stakes in understanding these civic dispositions are higher today than at any time in recent history, as the United States faces the twin challenges of growing polarization and declining engagement at the same time and in perhaps unprecedented ways. Trust, tolerance, and other key democratic norms are indeed at risk. While religion can fuel distrust and intolerance, it also has tremendous capacity to build these dispositions in healthy ways. On balance, religious participation in the United States has encouraged civic attitudes vital to a flourishing democracy. In fact, religious social networks may be the most important source of that encouragement.

Civic Engagement

Religious commitment also translates frequently into various forms of civic activism. This activism often goes hand in hand with evangelism: the effort to win converts or bring new members to one's religion. Recruitment is vital for congregations in the competitive environment of American religion, where some religions grow and others decline on a regular basis. For example, the Assemblies of God, a conservative Pentecostal denomination, has grown rapidly in recent times, partly because of its intensive outreach to Latinos, whose numbers have exploded to 22 percent of total denominational membership.[54]

The thriving LDS Church also illustrates well the importance of active evangelism. The church sends out thousands of young missionaries each year, worldwide, and the LDS Church's remarkable growth rates and aggressive missionary activity have led some to predict that it could be one of the major world religions by the middle of the twenty-first century.[55]

Religious commitment to civic activism also often leads people to join the full range of civic associations, including secular ones. Those who belong to congregations are quite likely to belong to nonreligious groups as well—twice as likely, in fact, as those who are not affiliated with a congregation.[56] Religious Americans epitomize the view that the United States is composed of a people who are joiners.

Congregations apply their tremendous human resource to a great deal of work in American society. A large share of the charitable giving in the United States is done in and by congregations; indeed, frequent worship attendees regularly give money to social causes and volunteer to do charitable work at a dramatically higher rate than do those who rarely or never attend religious services.[57] People of modest means are particularly likely to donate almost exclusively through religious outlets. This generosity enables congregations to operate an impressive array of social organizations, hospitals, schools, universities, charitable agencies, and international relief organizations.[58] Eighty-seven percent of American congregations participate in some form of social service or community development activity designed to assist people outside the walls of their church, synagogue, or mosque.[59] Smaller religious traditions often have an outsized presence. The Seventh-Day Adventists, with about 1.2 million members in North America, support fourteen colleges and universities, more than sixty healthcare institutions, and dozens of K-12 schools and welfare agencies.[60]

Private education, of course, is a major activity of many religious groups. Approximately 10 percent of all elementary and secondary students attend private schools, and over two-thirds of those schools have a religious identity. The Catholic Church operates the largest religious educational system in the United States, with nearly 7,000 elementary and secondary schools attended by 2.1 million students; evangelical and other religious schools enroll another 2 million children in more than 16,000 schools.[61] Although many religionists are concerned about the decline in religious-school enrollments over the past few decades, faith-based schooling remains an integral part of many religious traditions' outreach.[62] Moreover, the latest research suggests that those schools often do as well, and in some cases do better, as secular counterparts when preparing students for active citizenship, though results vary depending on school type and forms of civic engagement.[63] The growing practice of homeschooling, which today includes 1.8 million children (for perspective, that is 3.4 percent of school-aged children), also has relied heavily on networks created by and through religious institutions. About two-thirds of homeschooling

BOX 10.2 SHOULD GOVERNMENT SUPPORT FAITH-BASED SOCIAL SERVICES?

In 2001, President George W. Bush established the White House Office of Faith-Based and Community Initiatives as part of his administration's broader efforts to expand public support for religious organizations that help deliver social services. Eight years later, President Barack Obama placed his own imprint on the initiative. He changed the name to the White House Office of Faith-Based and Neighborhood Partnerships—a nod to his background as a faith-based community organizer in Chicago—and added an interfaith advisory council. While President Trump has yet to say what he will do with the office, he has signaled support for faith-based organizations.

The efforts of the Bush and Obama administrations reflect a long history of government partnering with organized religion to shape and implement public policy. Indeed, billions of public dollars annually flow through religiously based nonprofit organizations, usually in the form of government contracts, grants, or patron vouchers. These partnerships are not surprising: National, state, and local governments address an array of policy areas, including health, education, criminal justice, and employment. Church–state partnerships work well from the standpoint of government because nonprofit organizations are closer to the communities they serve, less bureaucratic, more flexible, and arguably more effective at achieving public-policy goals. In turn, religious institutions receive support for their extensive networks of charities, hospitals, relief agencies, and other means of delivering social services.

Government support for faith-based nonprofits, however, has come under greater scrutiny in recent decades. Many opponents say that this support violates constitutional principles by allowing government dollars to go to organizations that might require religious behavior on the part of clients or discriminate based on religion when hiring staff. Other critics worry that the promise of public money might persuade religious groups to water down their faith-based vision and activity. Even proponents of church–state partnerships have been critical. Welfare reforms in 1996 included so-called charitable choice provisions, which allowed a wider range of religious social services to compete for public money than had been the case in the past. These advocates say the federal government has not opened up the competition to its fullest extent.

Sources: www.whitehouse.gov/administration/eop/ofbnp; Stephen V. Monsma, *Pluralism and Freedom: Faith-Based Organizations in a Democratic Society* (Lanham, MD: Rowman & Littlefield, 2012); Amy E. Black, Douglas L. Koopman, and David K. Ryden, *Of Little Faith: The Politics of George W. Bush's Faith-Based Initiatives* (Washington, DC: Georgetown University Press, 2004).

parents cite providing "religious instruction" as a key reason for their educational choice, and a sizable proportion obtain curricular materials through faith-based sources.[64] In addition, many religious traditions support their own network of colleges and universities. Catholic institutions of higher learning are numerous (about 250) and quite prominent, including many prestigious schools such as the University of Notre Dame and Georgetown University. The Council for Christian Colleges and Universities represents a host of other faith-based institutions that are more evangelical in orientation.[65]

Social involvement by churches has clear political ramifications. Church-run charities, adoption agencies, educational institutions, and international relief programs operate in a milieu that is heavily influenced by government. Interaction between these institutions and government is inevitable. Many religious hospitals and social-service organizations, for example, receive government money to perform their services (Box 10.2). Politicians in both major parties clearly understand that debates about any major healthcare policy changes—most recently around "repealing and replacing" the Patient Protection and Affordable Care Act, also known as "Obamacare"—have enormous implications for religious hospitals.[66]

CONCLUSION

It should come as little surprise to learn that religion is so intimately tied to American political culture. But the breadth and depth of religion's role is remarkable. Part of its influence lies simply in its immense size: Religion is the most prominent mainstay of civil society in the United States. Yet religion's role in political culture is also marked by the unique goals and intensity of the individual members of religious associations. And the clear message of this chapter is that religious believers tend to be more engaged and possess greater capacity for engagement than their secular counterparts.

Given religion's powerful influence in political culture, changing patterns in religious belief or affiliation inevitably will impact public life. The question is, How? Will the recent drift away from traditional religious loyalties impoverish civil society and, as a result, diminish civic skills, social capital, and civic engagement? These are difficult matters to predict, especially in a social sector as dynamic and complex as religion. Perhaps we will see historical faiths repackaged in high-tech or less structured forms, or we will see new modes of spirituality organized in ways we cannot yet foresee. To the extent that the social networks fostered by religious life could be lost in these new dynamics, however, we might expect that political culture will change in potentially negative ways as a result. But, of course, political culture can adapt as well. Perhaps changes in the American experience of religion will be met with innovations in civic engagement itself. New technology is now essential in community organizing, political campaigns, and unconventional forms of protest (for example, in Black

Lives Matter), especially among younger people.[67] It remains to be seen whether newer, virtual modes of participation can be sustained without robust institutions, religious or otherwise.

DIS5CUSSION QUESTIONS

1 In your own words, what is political culture?

2 What prompted the emergence of the Christian conservative movement? What have been some of its driving motivators and goals? How does it serve as an example of the potential benefits and risks inherent in religious political activism?

3 Consider the difference between "separation of church and state" and "separation of religion and politics." What is the difference, and what makes that difference significant for the American political and religious landscapes?

4 Given that religious groups make up the largest portion of civil society, how do they contribute to society? What benefits do they offer to citizens who are involved with them?

5 Define "social capital." In what ways do religious institutions help generate it, and why do some scholars see it as vital to the political system of the United States?

FURTHER READING

Berger, Peter, and Richard John Neuhaus, *To Empower People: From State to Civil Society* (Washington, DC: American Enterprise Institute, 1995). A discussion of religion (and civil society in general) as "mediating structures."

Cnaan, Ram A., Stephanie Boddie, Charlene McGrew, and Jennifer Kang, *The Other Philadelphia Story: How Local Congregations Support Quality of Life in Urban America* (Philadelphia, PA: University of Pennsylvania Press, 2006). An excellent case study of religion's role in urban life.

Djupe, Paul A. (ed.), *Religion and Political Tolerance in America: Advances in the State of the Art* (Philadelphia, PA: Temple University Press, 2015). A fine collection of essays that explores the complex effects of religion on political and social tolerance.

Monsma, Stephen V., *Pluralism and Freedom: Faith-Based Organizations in a Democratic Society* (Lanham, MD: Rowman & Littlefield, 2012). An argument for church-state partnership in serving human needs.

Putnam, Robert D., and David E. Campbell, *American Grace: How Religion Divides and Unites Us* (New York, NY: Simon & Schuster, 2010). A data-rich examination of the dynamic role of religion in American political culture.

Smidt, Corwin, Kevin R. den Dulk, James M. Penning, Stephen V. Monsma, and Douglas L. Koopman, *Pews, Prayers, and Participation: Religion and Civic Responsibility in America* (Washington, DC: Georgetown University Press, 2008). An expansive analysis of religion, civil society, and civic life.

Smith, Mark A., *Secular Faith: How Culture Has Trumped Religion in American Politics* (Chicago, IL: University of Chicago Press, 2015). A provocative examination of the influence of secular culture on the American experience of religion and politics.

Verba, Sidney, Kay Scholzman, and Henry E. Brady, *Voice and Equality: Civic Voluntarism in American Politics* (Cambridge, MA: Harvard University Press, 1995). The seminal study of civic skills, including religion's role in developing them.

Wuthnow, Robert, *Boundless Faith: The Global Outreach of American Churches* (Berkeley, CA: University of California Press, 2010). A fresh look at how American churches support political and economic development both at home and abroad.

NOTES

1. This description of political culture draws from standard discussions in political science. The seminal work is Gabriel Almond and Sidney Verba, *The Civic Culture: Political Attitudes and Democracy in Five Nations* (Princeton, NJ: Princeton University Press, 1963). For deeper dives on the interaction of religion and political culture, see Laura R. Olson, "The Essentiality of 'Culture' in the Study of Religion and Politics," *Journal for the Scientific Study of Religion,* 50 (2011): 639–653; Corwin E. Smidt, Kevin R. den Dulk, James M. Penning, Stephen V. Monsma, and Douglas L. Koopman, *Pews, Prayers, and Participation: Religion and Civic Responsibility in America* (Washington, DC: Georgetown University Press, 2008); and Robert D. Putnam and David E. Campbell, *American Grace: How Religion Divides and Unites Us* (New York, NY: Simon & Schuster, 2010).

2. For a provocative argument along these lines, see Mark A. Smith, *Secular Faith: How Culture Has Trumped Religion in American Politics* (Chicago, IL: University of Chicago Press, 2015).

3. Exactly who belongs to the Christian right is a matter of dispute, but it is important to bear in mind that the term "Christian right" does not describe the entire evangelical population of the United States. Moreover, some nonevangelicals, including some conservative Catholics, have an affinity for the movement (though that affinity is often an uneasy one). There have been many efforts to measure "membership" in the Christian right; no one has struggled harder with these issues than Clyde Wilcox. See Clyde Wilcox and Carin Robinson, *Onward Christian Soldiers? The Religious Right in American Politics,* 4th edn (Boulder, CO: Westview Press, 2011).

4. Michael Emerson and Christian Smith, *Divided by Faith: Evangelical Religion and the Problem of Race in America* (Oxford: Oxford University Press, 2000).

5. Randall Balmer, "The Real Origins of the Religious Right," *Politico Magazine,* May 27, 2014.

6. Robert Wuthnow, *America and the Challenges of Religious Diversity* (Princeton, NJ: Princeton University Press, 2005).

7. For scholarly assessment of the Christian right at its earliest stages, see Steve Bruce, *The Rise and Fall of the New Christian Right* (Oxford: Clarendon, 1988); and Robert Booth Fowler, "The Failure of the Religious Right," in Michael Cromartie (ed.), *No Longer Exiles: The Religious New Right in American Politics* (Washington, DC: Ethics and Public Policy Center, 1993), pp. 57–74. For a different and longer historical perspective, see Daniel K. Williams, *God's Own Party: The Making of the Christian Right* (Oxford: Oxford University Press, 2012).

8. Edward L. Cleary and Allen D. Hertzke (eds.), *Representing God at the Statehouse: Religion and Politics in the American States* (Lanham, MD: Rowman & Littlefield, 2006); Kimberly H. Conger and John C. Green, "Spreading Out and Digging In," *Campaigns and Elections*, 5 (2002): 58–65; Mark J. Rozell and Clyde Wilcox (eds.), *God at the Grassroots: The Christian Right in the 1994 Elections* (Lanham, MD: Rowman & Littlefield, 1995).

9. See, for example, Cal Thomas and Ed Dobson, *Blinded by Might: Can the Religious Right Save America?* (Grand Rapids, MI: Zondervan, 1999).

10. Allen D. Hertzke, *Freeing God's Children: The Unlikely Alliance for Global Human Rights* (Lanham, MD: Rowman & Littlefield, 2004). For a wide-ranging discussion of the Christian right's foreign-policy involvement, see Mark R. Amstutz, *Evangelicals and American Foreign Policy* (Oxford: Oxford University Press, 2013).

11. Kevin R. den Dulk, "The GOP, Evangelical Elites, and the Challenge of Pluralism," in Paul Djupe and Brian Calfano (eds.), *The Evangelical Crackup? The Future of the Evangelical-Republic Coalition* (Philadelphia, PA: Temple University Press, 2018).

12. Ian Lovett, Jacob Gershman, and Louise Radnofsky, "Agenda on Religion Shifts," *Wall Street Journal*, February 3, 2017, p. A1.

13. Russell Moore, "President Trump: What Now for the Church?" November 9, 2016, www.russellmoore.com/2016/11/09/president-trump-now-church/.

14. Rod Dreher, *The Benedict Option: A Strategy for Christians in a Post-Christian Nation* (New York, NY: Sentinel, 2017).

15. Robert P. Jones, "Trump Can't Reverse the Decline of White Christian America," *The Atlantic*, July 4, 2017.

16. Smith, *Secular Faith*.

17. James Davidson Hunter, *Culture Wars: The Struggle to Define America* (New York, NY: Basic Books, 1991). Political scientists have examined religion's role in the culture wars in various ways, often using the Christian right as a case study. See, for example, Paul A. Djupe and Laura R. Olson (eds.), *Religious Interests in Community Conflict: Beyond the Culture Wars* (Waco, TX: Baylor University Press, 2007); John C. Green, James L. Guth, Corwin E. Smidt, and Lyman A. Kellstedt, *Religion and the Culture Wars: Dispatches from the Front* (Lanham, MD: Rowman & Littlefield, 1996); and Geoffrey C. Layman and John C. Green, "Wars and Rumours of Wars: The Contexts of Cultural Conflict in American Political Behaviour," *British Journal of Political Science*, 36 (2006): 61–89.

18. Pew Research Center, "Americans Express Increasingly Warm Feelings toward Religious Groups," 2017, http://assets.pewresearch.org/wp-content/uploads/sites/11/2017/02/15093007/Feeling-thermometer-report-FOR-WEB.pdf.

19. Alexis de Tocqueville, *Democracy in America: And Two Essays on America*, trans. Gerald E. Bevan and Isaac Kramnick (London: Penguin, 2003), p. 340. For contemporary discussions, see Giorgi Areshidze, *Democratic Religion from Locke to Obama: Faith and the Civic Life of Democracy* (Lawrence, KS: University Press of Kansas, 2016); and Robert Booth Fowler, *Unconventional Partners: Religion and Liberal Culture in the United States* (Grand Rapids, MI: Eerdmans, 1989).

20. Corwin E. Smidt, Kevin R. den Dulk, Bryan T. Froehle, James M. Penning, Stephen V. Monsma, and Douglas L. Koopman, *The Disappearing God Gap? Religion in the 2008 Presidential Election* (Oxford: Oxford University Press, 2010), p. 29.

21. Seymour Martin Lipset, *American Exceptionalism: A Double-Edged Sword* (New York, NY: W. W. Norton, 1997).

22. Thomas E. Patterson, *The Vanishing Voter: Public Involvement in an Age of Uncertainty* (New York, NY: Knopf, 2002); Robert Putnam, *Bowling Alone: The Collapse*

and Revival of American Community (New York, NY: Simon & Schuster, 2001); Stephen Macedo, *Democracy at Risk: How Political Choices Undermine Citizen Participation and What We Can Do about It* (Washington, DC: Brookings Institution, 2005); Theda Skocpol, *Diminished Democracy: From Membership to Management in American Civic Life* (Norman, OK: University of Oklahoma Press, 2004).

23. Michael X. Delli Carpini, "In Search of the Informed Citizen," *The Communication Review*, 4 (2000): 129–164; Michael X. Delli Carpini and Scott Keeter, *What Americans Know about Politics and Why It Matters* (New Haven, CT: Yale University Press, 1996).

24. Putnam, *Bowling Alone*; see also Kevin R. den Dulk, "Liberal Democracy Has 'Trust Issues,'" *Comment Magazine*, spring 2017.

25. Sidney Verba, Kay Scholzman, and Henry E. Brady, *Voice and Equality: Civic Voluntarism in American Politics* (Cambridge, MA: Harvard University Press, 1995).

26. See, for example, James S. Fishkin, *When the People Speak: Direct Democracy and Public Consultation* (Oxford: Oxford University Press, 2009); Macedo, *Democracy at Risk*; National Commission on Civic Renewal, *A Nation of Spectators: How Civic Disengagement Weakens America* (College Park, MD: University of Maryland, 1998); Alison Rios, Millett McCartney, and Elizabeth A. Bennion (eds.), *Teaching Civic Engagement: From Student to Active Citizen* (Washington, DC: American Political Science Association, 2013).

27. Peter Berger and Richard John Neuhaus, *To Empower People: From State to Civil Society* (Washington, DC: American Enterprise Institute, 1995); Richard John Neuhaus, *The Naked Public Square* (Grand Rapids, MI: Eerdmans, 1984); William A. Galston, "Civil Society and the 'Art of Association,'" *Journal of Democracy*, 11 (2000), 64–70.

28. Kenneth D. Wald, Adam L. Silverman, and Kevin S. Fridy, "Making Sense of Religion in Political Life," *Annual Review of Political Science*, 8 (2005): 121–143. A good illustration is Poland, which cast off a military government in the late 1980s largely due to the efforts of the Solidarity labor-union movement and the support of the Catholic Church.

29. Mary Ann Glendon and David Blankenhorn (eds.), *Seedbeds of Virtue: Sources of Competence, Character, and Citizenship in American Society* (Lanham, MD: Rowman & Littlefield, 2005).

30. John Adams, "Letter to Zabdiel Adams, June 21, 1776," in *Letters of Delegates to Congress, 1774–1789*, vol. IV, ed. Paul H. Smith (Washington, DC: Library of Congress, 2000), p. 279.

31. Thomas Jefferson, "Notes on the State of Virginia," in *The Portable Jefferson*, ed. Merrill D. Peterson (New York, NY: Penguin, 1975), p. 217.

32. James Madison, "Virginia Ratifying Convention, June 20, 1788," in *The Papers of James of Madison*, vol. XI, ed. William T. Hutchinson (Chicago, IL: University of Chicago Press, 1977), p. 163.

33. Don E. Eberly, *America's Promise: Civil Society and the Renewal of American Culture* (Lanham, MD: Rowman & Littlefield, 1998); Don E. Eberly and Ryan Streeter, *The Soul of Civil Society: Voluntary Associations and the Public Value of Moral Habits* (Lanham, MD: Rowman & Littlefield, 2002); and Glendon and Blankenhorn, *Seedbeds of Virtue*.

34. Corwin E. Smidt (ed.), *Religion as Social Capital: Producing the Common Good* (Waco, TX: Baylor University Press, 2003); Corwin E. Smidt et al., *Pews, Prayers, and Participation*; Robert Wuthnow, *Saving America? Faith-Based Services and the Future of Civil Society* (Princeton, NJ: Princeton University Press, 2004).

35. Putnam and Campbell, *American Grace*, pp. 444–446; Smidt et al., *Pews, Prayers, and Participation*, p. 78.

36. Verba et al., *Voice and Equality*.

37. Ram Cnaan, *The Other Philadelphia Story: How Local Congregations Support Quality of Life in Urban America* (Philadelphia, PA: University of Pennsylvania Press, 2006).

38. Smidt et al., *Pews, Prayers, and Participation*, pp. 148–155. See also Robert Wuthnow and John H. Evans (eds.), *The Quiet Hand of God: Faith-Based Activism and Mainline Protestantism* (Berkeley, CA: University of California Press, 2002).

39. Wuthnow and Evans, *The Quiet Hand of God*, pp. 171–172. See also Mark Chaves, *Congregations in America* (Cambridge, MA: Harvard University Press, 2004).

40. Paul A. Djupe and Christopher P. Gilbert, *The Political Influence of Churches* (Cambridge: Cambridge University Press, 2009), chapter 4.

41. Delli Carpini and Keeter, *What Americans Know about Politics*.

42. Smidt et al., *Pews, Prayers, and Participation*, pp. 166–168.

43. Sue E. S. Crawford and Laura R. Olson (eds.), *Christian Clergy in American Politics* (Baltimore, MD: Johns Hopkins University Press, 2001); Djupe and Gilbert, *The Political Influence of Churches*, chapter 3; James L. Guth, John C. Green, Corwin E. Smidt, Lyman A. Kellstedt, and Margaret M. Poloma, *The Bully Pulpit: The Politics of Protestant Clergy* (Lawrence, KS: University Press of Kansas, 1997); and Corwin E. Smidt (ed.), *Pulpit and Politics: Clergy in American Politics at the Advent of the Millennium* (Waco, TX: Baylor University Press, 2004).

44. Robert D. Putnam, *Making Democracy Work: Civic Traditions in Modern Italy* (Princeton, NJ: Princeton University Press, 1993).

45. Djupe and Gilbert, *The Political Influence of Churches*; Kenneth D. Wald, Dennis E. Owen, and Samuel S. Hill, Jr., "Churches as Political Communities," *American Political Science Review*, 82 (1988): 531–548; Kenneth D. Wald, Dennis E. Owen, and Samuel S. Hill, Jr., "Political Cohesion in Churches," *Journal of Politics*, 52 (1990): 197–215.

46. Jacob R. Neiheisel, Paul A. Djupe, and Anand E. Sokhey, "Veni, Vidi, Disseri: Churches and the Promise of Democratic Deliberation," *American Politics Research*, 20 (2006): 1–30.

47. See, generally, Smidt et al., *Pews, Prayers, and Participation*, chapter 7.

48. Putnam and Campbell, *American Grace*, pp. 471–472.

49. Putnam and Campbell, *American Grace*, pp. 468–470.

50. Den Dulk, "Liberal Democracy Has 'Trust Issues.'"

51. The typical approach is to have a survey respondent identify a particularly disliked group and then to determine how much the respondent would allow a member of that group to engage in public activities (e.g., teach at a school, give a speech). For applications to religion, see Marie A. Eisenstein, *Religion and the Politics of Tolerance: How Christianity Builds Democracy* (Waco, TX: Baylor University Press, 2008); Smidt et al., *Pews, Prayers, and Participation*, pp. 192–201; Putnam and Campbell, *American Grace*, pp. 485–489; and Paul Djupe (ed.), *Religion and Political Tolerance in America: Advances in the State of the Art* (Philadelphia, PA: Temple University Press, 2015).

52. For a discussion of the problems involved in tolerance studies, see James L. Gibson, "Enigmas of Intolerance: Fifty Years after Stouffer's Communism, Conformity, and Civil Liberties," *Perspectives on Politics*, 4 (2006): 21–34.

53. Political scientist Diana Mutz makes this point about the effects of "cross-cutting networks" of all types. See *Hearing the Other Side* (Cambridge: Cambridge University Press, 2006).

54. Data available at https://ag.org/About/Statistics (2016). See also Donald E. Miller and Tetsunao Yamamori, *Global Pentecostalism: The New Face of Christian Social Engagement* (Berkeley, CA: University of California Press, 2007); Arlene Sanchez Walsh, *Latino Pentecostal Identity: Evangelical Faith, Self, and Society* (New York, NY: Columbia University Press, 2004).

55. Rodney Stark, "Modernization and Mormon Growth: The Secularization Thesis Revisited," in Marie Cornwall, Tim B. Heaton, and Lawrence A. Young (eds.), *Contemporary Mormonism: Social Science Perspectives* (Urbana, IL: University of Illinois Press, 2001), pp. 13–23.

56. Smidt et al., *Pews, Prayers, and Participation*, pp. 77–78.

57. Arthur C. Brooks, *Who Really Cares: The Surprising Truth about Compassionate Conservatism* (New York, NY: Basic Books, 2006); Smidt et al., *Pews, Prayers, and Participation*, chapter 4; Putnam and Campbell, *American Grace*, pp. 447–449.

58. Nancy Tatom Ammerman, *Pillars of Faith: American Congregations and Their Partners* (Berkeley, CA: University of California Press, 2005); Ram A. Cnaan, *The Invisible Caring Hand: American Congregations and the Provision of Welfare* (New York, NY: New York University Press, 2001).

59. National Congregations Study, *Religious Congregations in 21st Century America*, 2015, www.soc.duke.edu/natcong/Docs/NCSII_report_final.pdf, p. 22.

60. Office of Archives and Statistics, Seventh-Day Adventist Church, *Adventist Online Yearbook 2016*, www.adventistyearbook.org.

61. Stephen Broughman and Nancy Swaim, *Characteristics of Private Schools in the United States: Results from the 2013–14 Private School Universe Survey* (Washington, DC: National Center for Education Statistics, 2016).

62. Chester E. Finn and Andy Smarick, "Our Endangered Catholic Schools," *Washington Post*, April 21, 2009.

63. See, for example, Jonathan Hill and Kevin R. den Dulk, "Religion, Volunteering, and Educational Setting: The Effect of Youth Schooling Type on Civic Engagement," *Journal for the Scientific Study of Religion*, 52 (2013): 179–197; and Ray Pennings, Jr., David Sikkink, and Ashley Berner, "Cardus Education Survey: 2014 Report" (Hamilton, ON: Cardus, 2014).

64. Jeremy Redford, Danielle Battle, and Stacey Bielick, *Homeschooling in the United States: 2012* (Washington, DC: National Center for Education Statistics, 2017).

65. See www.cccu.org.

66. The late Steve Monsma was the foremost scholar of these public-private partnerships. See Stephen V. Monsma, *Pluralism and Freedom: Faith-Based Organizations in a Democratic Society* (Lanham, MD: Rowman & Littlefield, 2012); Stephen V. Monsma and Stanley Carlson-Thies, *Free to Serve: Protecting the Religious Freedom of Faith-Based Organizations* (Grand Rapids, MI: Eerdmans, 2015); Stephen V. Monsma, *Putting Faith in Partnerships: Welfare-to-Work in Four Cities* (Ann Arbor, MI: University of Michigan Press, 2004); and Stephen V. Monsma, *When Sacred and Secular Mix: Religious Nonprofit Organizations and Public Money* (Lanham, MD: Rowman & Littlefield, 1996).

67. Richard Dalton, *The Good Citizen: How a Younger Generation Is Reshaping American Politics* (Washington, DC: CQ Press, 2009); Craig A. Rimmerman, *The New Citizenship: Unconventional Politics, Activism, and Service* (Boulder, CO: Westview Press, 2010).

11

THE POLITICS OF RELIGION
IN THE LEGAL SYSTEM

Soon after his inauguration in 2017, President Donald Trump issued an executive order that barred entry into the United States for Syrian refugees and anyone from a set of other Muslim-majority countries. Although many of the president's supporters cheered the decision as a strong move in favor of security and a bulwark against what they perceived as a cultural threat from the Middle East, others protested that the order was an affront to the American values of equality and hospitality to people suffering harm for their faith or ethnicity. As the debate intensified in various media, on college campuses, and even at airports and in the streets, it was hard to miss the conflict's close resemblance to past controversies about the status of religious and ethnic groups in the United States that did not fit the majority mold.

Almost immediately, both supporters and opponents of the ban turned to a familiar and distinctly American tactic to help settle the conflict: They went to court. Within days of Trump's announcement of the order, several federal judges were already weighing the legality of the order under ordinary statutes and the US Constitution itself. Several judges thought the order violated constitutional norms about religious freedom and therefore ruled that portions of the order could not be enforced, setting up a series of efforts to redesign the Trump administration's actions to meet judicial demands. The conflict culminated in a showdown before the US Supreme Court, the highest court in the land.[1]

In this chapter and the next, we enter this complex realm of law and the courts. The controversy surrounding Trump's immigration ban is just one recent illustration of the powerful influence state and federal courts have on public policy related to religion in the United States. Citizen groups from all sides are passionately involved in countless legal struggles, including religion's role in such hot-button issues as defining marriage, shaping K-12 and university education, providing welfare services to those in need, or regulating personal behaviors ranging from drug use to sexuality. As a result, American courtrooms are a setting not merely for considering technical matters of law and process but also for the airing of cultural disagreements about religion's general role in society and its interactions with politics. The stakes are high, and the legal conflicts often are intense.

No one should make the mistake of thinking the American legal system exists independently of politics. Typical political pushing and shoving are just as much a part of settling legal disputes as they are of the rest of the policy-making process. Lawyers and judges plot strategy; bargain with each other; seek public support, money, and other resources; and pursue their policy goals through favorable legal decisions. None of this is shocking nor necessarily lamentable; it is simply reality. That said, we should not assume that conventional politics completely defines the American legal system. The legal system has its own internal norms, such as the principle of *stare decisis* (which means preserving and standing by previous court decisions) and the high value placed on due process. Moreover, many judges are eminently fair and strive not to allow personal prejudices to color their rulings.

In this chapter, we examine the efforts of religiopolitical forces to affect legal outcomes. We consider some of the reasons for these efforts and the specific resources that help make groups effective in the legal arena. In the process, we introduce the most significant organizations involved in legal struggles surrounding religion and politics. After reflecting on the implications of these struggles, we consider broader normative debates about how organized religion ought to relate to government. These theories are important not only because they often have shaped the legal arguments of the courts and various advocacy groups, but also because they reflect many of the assumptions that ordinary citizens have about church–state relations. In Chapter 12, we examine specific disputes about religion and politics that have arisen under the US Constitution—and how courts and legislatures have attempted to resolve those disputes.

JUDICIAL POLITICS

Since the mid-twentieth century, it has become routine for religious groups to work through the courts to try to achieve—or protect—objectives they cannot accomplish in any other way. Some of these objectives have become a familiar part of the legal landscape. When religious groups challenge government about the teaching of evolution in public schools or state-mandated insurance coverage for contraception, we hear echoes of similar disputes about education and reproduction, among myriad other issues, that have occupied religious groups in previous decades.

A large variety of legal organizations help to shepherd religion-related disputes through the courts, often by recruiting aggrieved parties and providing lawyers and funding for a case. Another common approach that religious (and other) groups use in judicial politics today is the filing of *amicus curiae* (friend of the court) briefs: opinions filed with a court that allow third parties to register their views on pending cases. Even if the court does not pay attention to the views of a particular group filing as *amicus curiae*, group leaders can trumpet their efforts to their membership. And there is a host of other tactics, too: Lobbying about the selection of judges to the federal courts (see Box 11.1), seeking favorable implementation of court rulings, and influencing elite and mass opinion about the meaning of law.

Why do religious groups turn to the courts? The strategy partly reflects changes in the national political system, which has become larger and more centralized over time. While the roots of this growth lay in the Civil War, it accelerated in the 1930s and 1940s during the administration of President Franklin D. Roosevelt, who fought the Great Depression and World War II from the national level. FDR's efforts had the result of expanding the size and the influence of the federal government, a trend that has continued to the present day. The increasing focus on the national government presented an opportunity for some key advocacy groups to nationalize their agendas.

BOX 11.1 SELECTING SUPREME COURT JUSTICES

Presidents have the exclusive power to nominate federal judges, including new justices on the US Supreme Court. They consider a range of factors when making these choices—education and experience, policy compatibility, and so on—but most presidents also have used nominations to strengthen their political support among allied groups. Does religion play a role in the selection of federal judges? There is some evidence it does. President Dwight Eisenhower's nomination of William Brennan, a Catholic Democrat, was partly seen as an effort to generate electoral support within the growing population of Catholics in the United States. More recently, numerous religious conservative groups hailed Donald Trump's appointment of Neil Gorsuch as a win for religious liberty and for traditionalist views on abortion and same-sex marriage. Gorsuch's positive reception among conservative faith-based groups is evidence that the key question has moved from shared religious identity to whether the nominee is likely to advance particular ideological convictions—in recent years Gorsuch has attended an Episcopal church, hardly a conservative house of worship.

Groups such as the National Association for the Advancement of Colored People (NAACP), founded in 1909, and the American Civil Liberties Union (ACLU), founded in 1920, fostered a "rights revolution" by actively supporting litigation that tested the boundaries of civil-liberties protections.[2]

These efforts happened at a time when certain perspectives about judicial authority were changing at the federal level, most notably within the Supreme Court. The First Amendment holds that "*Congress* shall make no law respecting an establishment of religion, or prohibiting the free exercise thereof" (our emphasis). Before the 1940s, almost all legal disputes involving church and state were considered state matters and were resolved in state courts. The Religion Clauses of the First Amendment were viewed as essentially jurisdictional; the assumption was that Congress had no authority over religious matters but that states did.[3] Because the US Supreme Court had interpreted the First Amendment to apply only to actions of the national government for 150 years, states had never been forced to comply with the Religion Clauses of the First Amendment, so church–state disputes were almost never addressed in federal courts. In the 1940s, however, the Court shifted this long-standing interpretation of the First Amendment's meaning and began ruling on a wide range of religious debates from the state and local levels. The Court insisted that national standards were necessary and acceptable—and should supersede state and local norms.

The Supreme Court accomplished the goal of extending national standards to the state and local levels by interpreting parts of the Fourteenth Amendment, which was passed in the wake of the Civil War, to mean that the First Amendment applies to state and local governments just as much as it applies to the federal government. The relevant part of the Fourteenth Amendment holds that: "No State shall . . . deprive any person of life, liberty, or property, without due process of law." According to the Court, this clause means that no state should be allowed to abridge religious freedom protected by the First Amendment, despite the wording of the amendment that "Congress shall make no law," not "Congress and the state legislatures." Since the 1940s, this interpretation has been the Court's standard—and thus the nation's—of determining the proper venue for resolving disputes about the First Amendment's Religion Clauses. In interpreting the Constitution this way, the Court extended the "doctrine of incorporation," its general argument that the states are bound by the Fourteenth Amendment to guarantee their citizens the civil liberties set forth in the Bill of Rights.

Imagine the dramatic implications of moving from constitutional restrictions on one institution of government (Congress) to more than 90,000 (the combined total of all state and local governments in the United States, which include towns, cities, counties, independent school districts, and many other regional authorities). This change sent the message that religious groups, and many others, could turn to the federal courts for resolution of their problems with any and all governmental institutions and policies.

Other factors were also at work during the twentieth century that facilitated the move of religious groups toward the courts. The simple reality of expanding religious pluralism increased the role of the judiciary. The influence of minority religions can be exaggerated, but there is no doubt that every year sees the emergence and strengthening of new religious movements in the United States. The growth of this pluralism began in earnest with the arrival of Catholic immigrants and the birth of new Protestant offshoots and sects in the nineteenth and early twentieth centuries. As religious pluralism broadened even more in the late twentieth century, an increasing number of religious groups, especially from the Middle East and Asia, found themselves in conflict with the government, the society around them, or both.

Some of these groups, especially small ones, have petitioned the federal courts to seek redress for discrimination they encounter. Leaders of such religious groups often believe that Congress and the executive branch would be less responsive to a small religious minority than would the federal courts. They have hoped, with mixed success, that the courts would protect them from domination by more powerful groups and perspectives. Indeed, often there is little else small religious groups can do when they meet with discrimination. Legislatures, after all, operate as majoritarian institutions. Federal and state courts, some of which insulate judges from elections, can therefore seem a more amenable place for minority interests. While that belief might underestimate legislatures, the success of the Jehovah's Witnesses (see Box 11.2) and other religious minorities in court has encouraged many to view the federal courts as both a possible and proper realm for addressing the unique problems faced by minority interests.[4] In effect, small religious groups encourage the federal courts to take an active role in shaping the politics of religion in the United States. Since the 1940s, what was once a trickle of cases has become a flood as the conflict between religion and politics increasingly plays out in US courts. The Supreme Court alone has decided more than 180 cases dealing with religion since 1940.[5]

The nature of the courts' rulings, especially those of the Supreme Court, has magnified legal conflicts rooted in church–state disputes and other religious matters. As we note in Chapter 12, the Supreme Court's pronouncements in these areas too often have been unclear—some say contradictory—and thus have resolved little. This uncertainty not only ensures further dispute and more litigation in the federal courts, but it also has created an opening for increasing state-level legislation about religion. Some scholars and jurists, including most prominently Justice Clarence Thomas, have even suggested that the courts ought to disincorporate the First Amendment's religion clauses to allow states more flexibility in defining the limits of religious freedom.[6] Whatever the merits of that argument, the trend toward state-level policy-making regarding religion inevitably has shifted some of the attention of key groups away from the federal level. Even religious groups that have been successful in the national arena

BOX 11.2 JEHOVAH'S WITNESSES: PIONEERS OF
FIRST AMENDMENT ACTIVISM

The US Supreme Court first decided to apply the Free Exercise Clause of the First Amendment ("Congress shall make no law ... prohibiting the free exercise [of religion]") to the states in *Cantwell v. Connecticut* (1940). In that case, the Court held that the state of Connecticut violated free-exercise rights by preventing Jehovah's Witnesses from assertively spreading their religious message. According to the Court, "The Fourteenth Amendment has rendered the legislatures of the states as incompetent as Congress to enact laws which violate the provisions of the First Amendment." During the 1940s, Jehovah's Witnesses continued to seek relief in the federal courts from assorted local and state regulations, including the requirement to salute the American flag. Such regulations severely limited the Witnesses' freedom to practice their religion, which demands active proselytizing and prohibits pledges of loyalty to anything except God. In many instances, the Witnesses succeeded in securing their free-exercise rights and came to exemplify success in the strategy of constitutional advocacy in courts.

Source: *Cantwell v. Connecticut*, 310 US 296 (1940); *West Virginia v. Barnette* 319 US 624 (1943); Shawn Francis Peters, *Judging Jehovah's Witnesses: Religious Persecution and the Dawn of the Rights Revolution* (Lawrence, KS: University Press of Kansas, 2000).

realize that they must be participants in every major playing field, including the courts at all levels, if they are going make their mark on American politics.[7]

KEY PLAYERS

The legal system today bursts with activity as religious groups and organizations attempt to influence court rulings. Although none of these groups represents a majority of the American public, many have had a significant impact on judicial politics at the federal, state, and local levels. Many of the key players have long represented what may be termed the "separationist coalition," which supports complete separation between church and state. Recently, however, such groups have been challenged by groups that prefer more accommodation of religion in the public square, most prominently groups affiliated with evangelical Protestantism.

Separationist organizations come in three varieties. Some trace their roots to a separationist Protestant tradition that goes back to the Puritan leader Roger Williams in colonial Rhode Island. Its members are often quite religious.

Their goal is to nurture their faith partly by protecting it from the external control of government. As Williams himself envisioned it in 1644, separationists believe there should be a "wall of Separation between the Garden of the Church and the Wilderness of the World."[8] Williams' legacy lives on today in such notable separationist organizations as the Baptist Joint Committee (BJC), which draws support from a variety of Baptist denominations to advocate for church–state separation, and Americans United for Separation of Church and State, which was founded in 1947 out of Protestant opposition to state support for (largely) Catholic parochial schools.[9]

Also integral to the separationist coalition are a number of Jewish organizations and their legal arms.[10] The most prominent is the American Jewish Committee, but other important groups include the American Jewish Congress and the Anti-Defamation League. Most Jewish groups have been involved in legal battles to promote separation of church and state as a way of protecting Jews (and other religious minorities) from any official establishment of Christianity. When a crèche (manger scene) appears on public property, or staff lead Christian prayers in public schools, or other potential violations of the separation of church and state arise, it is common to find the American Jewish Committee and its allies going to court to combat these practices.

A third, and perhaps more uneasy, partner in the separationist coalition today represents the truly nonreligious portion of the movement. The American Civil Liberties Union (ACLU) is the best-known member of the separationist wing. It is committed to full separation of church and state, but that often means supporting free-exercise rights for small religious minorities that have been affected negatively by the state. Other organizations exist to advance secular values and institutions only, which is a fair description of the objective of the American Atheists, the Freedom from Religion Foundation, the Secular Coalition for America, and the Center for Inquiry (see Box 11.3).

Until the late 1970s, separationist groups were largely unopposed by other advocacy groups in the courts.[11] But the activity of separationist advocates, and public perceptions of their success, have provoked a counterreaction. Regardless of separationist motivations, many have worried that strict church–state separation would result in a diminished role for religion in public life. Today, religious groups that are determined to fight back in court are well established. Most of these groups are associated with evangelical Protestantism, but many also include allies sympathetic to their efforts regardless of religious background.[12]

Some Christian conservative legal organizations have existed for decades. The Christian Legal Society was founded as an attorney fellowship in 1962, for example. Most, however, were born in the 1980s and 1990s, when conservative groups discovered that whatever one's influence on legislatures, executives, or the people in general, the courts matter, too. This realization heightened religious groups' concern about the judicial selection process and strengthened their

---

BOX 11.3 ADVOCATES FOR SECULAR AMERICANS

Organizations that aim to represent secular Americans have grown in number, reflecting the broader trend toward religious disaffiliation in the United States. The Freedom from Religion Foundation is a good illustration. Mother–daughter team Ann Gaylor and Annie Laurie Gaylor founded the organization in 1976 in Madison, Wisconsin, out of their conviction that religion was the chief impediment to women's equality. Today, the foundation has over 20,000 members, a network of state chapters, and several on-staff attorneys. It operates nationally as a leading advocate of nontheism. That advocacy has often taken the form of vigorous legal activism, including opposition to the National Day of Prayer and religious symbols in schools, public buildings, or other public displays. The Freedom from Religion Foundation combines this work with intensive efforts at public education, including writing and speaking engagements of their copresident, evangelical-preacher-turned-atheist Dan Barker, and prominent advertising in social media, national newspapers, and billboards. Likewise, the Secular Coalition for America works to further an agenda of strict church–state separation in the United States. Founded in 2002, it is the result of mergers among five smaller forerunner organizations that have come together to strengthen their collective voice. Thus far, its efforts have been directed more at Congress and the executive branch than they have been at the federal courts, but watch for them to move toward the judicial strategy more aggressively in years to come.

Sources: www.ffrf.org; www.secular.org/.

---

resolve to have their say about court decisions. In some instances, mass-membership groups such as the Moral Majority or Concerned Women for America created legal departments within their organizations. In other cases, Christian conservative groups were developed to focus on specific issues, such as the Home School Legal Defense Association. But leaders soon recognized a need to establish stand-alone groups to focus broadly on religious freedom and other cultural matters in court.

Two of the most prominent religious legal organizations with Christian conservative roots are the American Center for Law and Justice (ACLJ) and the Alliance Defending Freedom (ADF, formerly Alliance Defense Fund). The ACLJ—clearly named to strike a contrast to the ACLU—quickly became a major evangelical player in legal politics after Rev. Pat Robertson and his associates founded the organization in 1990. The ACLJ has weighed in on countless legal disputes in various capacities, and it has been remarkably active at the Supreme

Court level. Jay Sekulow, its media-savvy chief litigator, has argued more than a dozen religious-freedom and free-speech cases before the Court.[13] Another group of prominent evangelicals created the ADF in 1994 to empower such allies as the ACLJ through financial and other forms of support.[14] In its early years, the group funded many notable cases, including *Rosenberger* v. *University of Virginia* (1995), in which several Christian college students won their challenge to a state university policy of denying certain funds to religious groups. Today, the ADF has branched out to take cases directly into litigation rather than merely funding other organizations to do so.

But not all non-separationist legal groups represent Christian conservatives and their interests. The Office of the General Counsel of the United States Conference of Catholic Bishops (USCCB) provides the bishops and various ecclesial departments with legal advice and represents the US Catholic Church in litigation, both directly as a party and indirectly by filing *amicus curiae* briefs.[15] Given the Catholic Church's many interests, from immigration to reproductive issues to clergy abuse allegations (not to mention more mundane issues of property-tax exemptions, pension plans, and so on), the Church's lawyers keep very busy. Many Protestant denominations also undertake their own legal efforts, particularly as *amicus curiae*. The pro-life Lutheran Church–Missouri Synod, for example, frequently files *amicus* briefs with the Supreme Court in abortion cases. And the Becket Fund for Religious Liberty and other groups with no explicit faith identity also get significant religious support and commit themselves to defending the claims of religious believers.[16]

It is also important to note that, while the ACLU, the ACLJ, the Becket Fund, and similar groups deliberately seek to advance their perspectives through the judicial system, other groups have been far more reactive and defensive than intentional in their legal activity. They are often thrust into legal conflicts by circumstances largely out of their control. Mormons and Jehovah's Witnesses are among the most prominent examples. Both faith traditions repeatedly ended up in court in the late nineteenth and early twentieth centuries as their non-mainstream beliefs and practices ran afoul of the majority's preferences.

FACTORS FOR SUCCESS

What contributes to the success or failure of advocacy organizations when they turn to the courts regarding church–state matters? Of course, sympathetic judges and propitious times always help, but what other dynamics contribute to legal success? One crucial factor is money; litigation and other forms of legal advocacy are expensive. This fact is often an awkward matter, especially for mass-membership groups that rely on their constituents for direct donations of time and money. There can be substantial competition among various legal-action organizations for limited donors and dollars. Moreover, fund-raising efforts require both time and money, leaving less of both for actual legal advocacy.

Still, the politics of legal action offers distinct financial advantages compared to other strategies. Taking politics to the courts requires neither a large membership nor elite access in Washington or with the national media. And while legal advocacy does require money, groups do not need the vast financial resources consumed in conventional lobbying or election campaigns.

Equally important are experience and expertise, both of which take time to develop. We have already noted that in building effective lobbying organizations, people who know their way around Congress or the statehouses are indispensable. The same applies to religious associations in the legal arena. After all, they are essentially interest groups that happen to be involved in legal advocacy, lobbying the courts on behalf of their self-defined interests. The lawyers who spearhead these efforts must know both the legal and religious terrain. Indeed, it helps to have lawyers with the passion that comes with being personally committed to a group's cause, especially because groups must often rely on the volunteer labor of those attorneys. New groups, including those from the evangelical perspective, slowly have come to nurture what social scientists call "cause lawyers" by creating formal networks of like-minded lawyers and sponsoring litigation workshops.[17]

A third factor for success is support for legal activism within broad advocacy networks. External support in the form of coalition-building is valuable because it can facilitate a division of labor, often by allowing religious legal organizations to pursue a wider variety of goals. Some groups may focus on education, others on abortion, and still others on marriage, but they offer mutual support at the same time. Government support has also been of great assistance at times. This tends to be true for many conservative Christian legal organizations when a Republican is in the White House, as they find themselves in the favorable position of working with more conservative Justice Department lawyers on the same cases, toward the same ends. But the sword can cut in the opposite direction: Those same attorneys have often felt stymied by lawyers serving Democratic administrations. A notable example is the 2013 legal challenge to California's Proposition 8, a state ban on same-sex marriage that California's Democratic Governor Jerry Brown refused to defend in court. Without government support, the ADF stepped in as cocounsel to defend the ban, eventually losing its argument before the US Supreme Court in *Hollingsworth* v. *Perry* (2013).[18]

Legal activism related to religion appears to be growing during the twenty-first century. This makes sense in light of the increasing religious pluralism of American society. Today, less than half of US citizens claim to be Protestant.[19] Moreover, the fault lines within Protestantism over moral and political issues have now become as deep as those that divide Protestants and members of other religious traditions. The same could be said of Catholics. And, as we discussed in Chapter 4, we must add to these Christian traditions a wide array of other religious groups, including growing populations of Muslims and Buddhists (see Box 11.4), as well as the increasing numbers of religious "nones." In short,

BOX 11.4 MUSLIMS AND RELIGIOUS LIBERTY

American Muslims today face many of the same challenges Mormons and Jehovah's Witnesses dealt with earlier in American history. Islamic centers across the United States have faced repeated barriers to erecting buildings, and individual Muslims have confronted restrictions on their behavior ranging from wearing beards or headscarves in the workplace to securing Halal meals or times for prayer in prisons. Groups such as Council on American–Islamic Relations and the Muslim Public Affairs Council have become quite active in asserting rights in both the courts and in the realm of public opinion. We should expect to see even more advocacy for Muslim religious freedom and civil rights in the future.

Source: Asma T. Uddin, "American Muslims, American Islam, and the American Constitutional Heritage," in Allen D. Hertzke (ed.), *Religious Freedom in America: Constitutional Roots and Contemporary Challenge* (Norman, OK: University of Oklahoma Press, 2015), pp. 224–248.

American society faces an ever-expanding religious pluralism accompanied by moral pluralism. Because moral conflicts often land in court, religious groups with a moral stake in judicial decisions find themselves advocating in court.

In American religion, as elsewhere, the truth today is as James Madison suggested it should be in "Federalist 51": Interest checks interest, and ambition checks ambition. Such a situation almost compels those who seek social change into the courts, for it is often the case that judges alone make authoritative decisions breaking the organized pluralist stalemate that so often holds sway. The courts can render clear decisions; they can break impasses; and they can side with even the smallest religious interest if they feel the law or the Constitution directs such a decision.

The strategy of resolving conflicts between religion and politics in the legal system presents mixed blessings. There is much dispute about whether controversies arising from the interaction of religion and politics ought to be resolved in a democratic arena or a federal courtroom. Should religious freedom be subject to definition by the majority? Should the limits of government establishment of religion be outlined by the majority? Indeed, some participants in today's church–state debates wonder whether democracy is an important value in the first place. Those who point out that democracy is not enshrined in the Bible or any other sacred text refuse to worry about whether the courts contribute to or hinder democracy.

For such individuals, the real issue is the need to protect rights, whether they are the rights of the Amish, strict separationists, Mormons, or some other constituency. By this view, if the courts serve as a setting where such questions may be addressed—without inflaming the biases that often accompany religious diversity, free exercise, and official establishment—then they contribute immeasurably to a healthy society. And, one may argue, sometimes the result is a flowering of democracy because freedom and democracy go hand in hand.

CHURCH AND STATE: HOW SHOULD THEY RELATE?

Amid the legal struggle for advantage in debates about religion and politics today lie a variety of approaches to the relationship between church and state. There is much at stake—not simply how government relates to religious institutions, but also fundamental beliefs about the normative role of religious values in politics and society. How should the courts and those who appeal to them for recourse establish relationships between church and state, and between religion and politics?

The Supreme Court has often framed the answer in terms of neutrality—broadly speaking, the idea that government ought not to play favorites when it comes to religion. The Supreme Court formulated its most prominent version of the neutrality doctrine in the classic case *Lemon* v. *Kurtzman* (1971). In this case, the Court held that if a law has a secular purpose and a secular effect (i.e. the "primary effect" of government's actions must "neither advance nor inhibit religion"), and does not result in excessive entanglement between religion and government, then it is constitutional. By this view, incidental government support for religion is acceptable, but only as a byproduct of a law that is secular both in intent and primary effect. Similarly, it is acceptable to impair religious freedom, but only as a byproduct of a law with a secular purpose and a secular effect.

Nearly all groups involved in church–state debates invoke the value of neutrality; very few would suggest that government should be allowed to prefer a specific religious faith or set of faiths over all others, at least in an intentional way. However, groups that accept the general idea of neutrality often take opposite positions—and vehemently so—about how neutrality ought to be put into practice. There is also widespread frustration with the Court's way of handling neutrality, though for different reasons. Chapter 12 will examine some of the specific church–state matters that the federal courts have adjudicated. Here, however, we introduce two classic perspectives on neutrality in church–state relations and discuss the extent to which the federal courts have embraced each in recent decades.

The Separationist Approach

For a church–state separationist, the First Amendment's Religion Clauses— "Congress shall make no law respecting an establishment of religion, or prohibiting the free exercise thereof"—mean that government cannot be involved with religion in any way.[20] Separationists look with pride to those chapters in colonial history that were part of the journey toward the constitutional enshrinement of church–state separation. They honor Roger Williams, founder of Rhode Island, for his determination to separate church and state, and William Penn, founder of Pennsylvania, for his commitment to Quaker tolerance of other religious faiths. They respect the histories of such colonies as New York and Pennsylvania that pioneered the tradition of separatism. Such colonies were sure that true free exercise was possible only when the state and the law were kept far away from organized religion.

Although church–state relations during the colonial and revolutionary eras were complicated, there is no doubt that the separationist point of view united many people. Church–state separation formed an umbrella under which those who feared state religions and those who were skeptical of religion in any form could gather.[21] Separating church from state also accommodated those whose ardent commitment to minority and dissenting religions made them worry about how they—and thus their own beliefs—would fare if the government were to become involved in religious matters. From these diffuse roots, ranging from the skeptical Thomas Jefferson to the earnest New England Baptists, the separationist tradition grew. Sophisticated separationists, however, were—and are—well aware that even after the adoption of the Constitution and the Bill of Rights, many would seek a closer connection between church and state. After all, organized religion (especially Christianity) had been deeply connected with, and often supported by, the state over centuries of Western history.

Thus, there has been much for separationists to litigate. Separationists have been concerned about prayers and other religious references offered at the opening of sessions of state legislatures and Congress, the president's inauguration, and even the opening session of the US Supreme Court itself. They worry about the employment of government-sponsored chaplains in the military and government aid for religious hospitals, religious social-service agencies, and religious colleges. They note with displeasure the references to God on US currency and in the Pledge of Allegiance. They dislike seeing crèches on public land in December and hearing government officials invoke the name of God on Thanksgiving. In short, separationists argue that American culture is ambivalent at best, and hypocritical at worst, in its theoretical commitment to the principle of separatism considering that it is far from truly separationist in practice.

Meanwhile, public attitudes about church–state separation are equally mixed. Studies consistently demonstrate that Americans reflexively endorse the phrase "separation of church and state" and oppose the mixing of religion and politics in the abstract. But there is often considerable support for specific actions that hardly fit with such a view. Consider opinion about the role of religion in public schools: 60 percent of Americans support allowing audible prayer in classrooms at public schools;[22] three-quarters agree that public schools should be allowed to invite citizens to offer prayers at graduation ceremonies; and four in five agree that religious accounts of the origin of the human species should be taught alongside evolution in public schools.[23] Separationists hold that preventing the official sanctioning of religion by government (on the one hand) and religious free exercise (on the other) are inseparable. They believe that the more government remains separate from religion, the more citizens will be able to enjoy religious freedom because they will not be forced to support beliefs they personally reject. Separationists also claim to have good company in some key framers of the Constitution, including James Madison, the chief author of the Bill of Rights. In short, separationists believe that an activist government presents a substantial threat when it becomes involved with religious institutions.

Hence the Supreme Court's efforts to address church–state relations through the Lemon test (which looks for laws to have a secular intent and effect regardless of potential outcomes for religious groups) and other legal approaches often frustrate separationists. Separationists appreciate that these approaches do eliminate flagrant, overt aid to organized religion and forbid any formal establishment of religion. However, they also want the court to take religion into account to ensure that no matter what a law's main purpose or principal effect might be, religion cannot obtain any government benefits. For separationists, what the Supreme Court calls "neutrality" can be (and has been) used by courts as a means of turning a blind eye toward the clever ways government aids and supports religious purposes under seemingly secular objectives and language. For example, state laws that allow nonprofit groups freedom from taxation draw strict separationists' ire. Under the Supreme Court's predominant approach, such laws would be constitutional because they have a secular purpose and mainly secular effects (because they apply to nonprofit groups of all types). In practice, though, such rules grant an enormous privilege to religious nonprofit organizations. Since they are nonprofits, they may receive substantial state benefits—especially because they are not required to pay taxes. Separationists argue that to be fully neutral, government ought not to support religion in any shape or form, even if that support is secondary to a secular purpose.

Accommodationist Perspectives

In contrast to strict separationists, other groups advocate for an accommodating stance toward religion on the part of government. This position on the church–state relationship comes in many forms. Some members of the Supreme Court, for example, have offered a modified version of the Court's Lemon doctrine that one justice termed "benevolent neutrality."[24] Supporters of this approach approve of neutrality as the proper stance for the courts because they are confident it will prevent organized religion from playing a role in government decisions. At the same time, however, benevolent neutrality tries to have it both ways. Its advocates argue that the religious effects of secular government actions and laws should be at least occasionally accepted.

Supporters of the benevolent-neutrality position maintain that applying the Lemon (secular purpose/secular effect) test avoids government sponsorship of religion, but they also insist that this test must not be followed so rigidly that religious freedom is sacrificed. In short, government must neither sponsor religion nor destroy it. Although government generally should stay neutral, it must do so in a benevolent mood, and no fixed formula can make that happen. As Chief Justice Warren Burger once put it, the Lemon test should not be understood as "an easy, bright-line approach" to church and state issues but rather as a pragmatic "signpost."[25] Thus, according to the benevolent-neutrality view, judgment is needed on a case-by-case basis.

A stronger statement of church–state accommodation is known as the "equal treatment" approach. Its supporters maintain that the courts should sanction government assistance to religious groups as long as this is done for all of them equally (equal treatment) and if it would encourage free exercise of religion. Those in favor of equal treatment assert that free exercise often benefits from state action on behalf of religion. Thus, separationists may not necessarily be correct when they argue that free exercise expands when separation between church and state grows.[26] Historically, this was, in effect, part of the case made by groups (primarily Catholics) who felt that state aid for religious schools was a good idea. From time to time, this approach succeeded. For example, in the years after the Civil War, President Ulysses S. Grant undertook an effort to promote peace between whites and Native Americans by encouraging the assimilation of Native Americans through education. To provide such education, he granted churches the opportunity to establish schools on reservations. For the last three decades of the nineteenth century, Congress directly funded several religious groups that chose to take part in this effort, including the Catholic Church. In 1899, however, the program came to an end, in part because Protestant groups objected to the funding of Catholic schools.

This education program was very much the exception rather than the rule. A part of the traditional argument in favor of state aid for Catholic schools was practical: Catholics wanted and needed the money to keep their schools going. Another part of the case for state aid that some Catholics have made is that access to religious school education is vital to meaningful free exercise of religion. The only way to achieve this goal, proponents argue, is through government assistance. In recent years, some Protestant supporters of Christian education have come to embrace this traditionally Catholic view (see Box 11.5).

Outside the context of education, equal treatment garners more support. There is widespread agreement that nonprofit religious organizations should not be required to pay taxes. There is no doubt that such policies help organized religion in a material sense and may therefore encourage its existence. Recent efforts to expand public funding for faith-based social services have also been based explicitly on the equal-treatment view. Proponents of broader funding argue that government support of religious agencies is constitutionally

---

**BOX 11.5 SHOULD GOVERNMENT PROVIDE
VOUCHERS TO PAY FOR PRIVATE SCHOOLS?**

American history is filled with fierce battles over government aid to parochial (church-operated) and other religious schools. A recent flare-up in that conflict is the argument for school "choice." The basic idea of school choice is that when the state compels parents to obtain an education for their children, it should provide options outside conventional public schools. One way to provide such an alternative is an educational voucher, a grant of money that parents could use toward paying tuition at a school of their choice, including private religious schools. Two cities—Milwaukee and Cleveland—have well-established voucher programs, and some states and other cities are implementing similar programs. Proponents of school choice, such as Trump administration Education Secretary Betsy DeVos, say that if every parent has access to a voucher, school choice amounts to equal treatment under the law. Some proponents further argue that vouchers foster religious freedom by enabling parents who otherwise could not afford to do so to take their children out of what they may perceive as objectionable public schools. Separatists flatly disagree. In Chapter 12, we explore how the Supreme Court has addressed the constitutionality of such programs.

Source: Erica L. Green, "Saying Money Isn't the Answer, DeVos Calls for More School Choice," *New York Times*, March 30, 2017, p. A18.

---

permissible if money is made available to all groups, religious and nonreligious alike.

Just as separationists invoke Madison and Jefferson as historical allies, accommodationists assert that history is on their side. For proponents of equal treatment, sweeping historical claims that the framers were separationists are simply untrue. As they read it, the historical record reveals a complex pattern in which there was once widespread state-level establishment and accommodation of religion that did not involve either the sacrifice of free exercise or the establishment of a single faith. They point out that when the First Amendment was adopted, most states continued to maintain official religions. Massachusetts, the last to give up its established church, did not do so until 1833, and even after that time states supported Christianity in myriad ways, both in schools and in other institutions.[27] Moreover, whereas Congress operated in the early years as though the First Amendment prohibited all government connection with religion, at other times it gave a contrary signal. The very year Congress approved the First Amendment, for example, it also reenacted the Northwest Ordinance, the document governing much of the western US territory (now the Midwest). Section III of the Northwest Ordinance observed that "religion, morality, and knowledge being necessary to good government and the happiness of mankind, schools and the means of learning shall forever be encouraged."[28]

Advocates of state aid to religion also take issue with portrayals of crucial constitutional framers such as Thomas Jefferson and James Madison as radical separationists. They argue that neither Jefferson nor Madison believed that there needed to be dogmatic lines separating church and state and that, normatively speaking, such lines should not be drawn in a complex, diverse polity.

CONCLUSION

More than 150 years ago, Alexis de Tocqueville discussed the American inclination to try to resolve policy disputes in the courts. He saw the legal system as a way for people in the United States to avoid messy, contentious political fights. Instead, Tocqueville saw Americans using "neutral" judges and courtrooms to work out resolutions. Today, many more factors, including the presence in the United States of more than a million lawyers, incline people to turn to the legal system to address policy conflicts.

In any event, Tocqueville probably would be astounded at how often policy conflicts are today addressed and sometimes resolved in the courts. This is certainly true regarding church and state. The legal system is perhaps the favorite avenue for religious politics, and its most basic assumptions—especially neutrality—are contested with all the resources and political skills that can be mustered by interested parties. Thus, it is essential for any religious group entering the political realm in the United States to know how judicial politics works.

Courts are inescapably political institutions, and remain so when dealing with matters of church and state. They can help achieve compromises that respect the past while acknowledging the more diverse present. The results may often be messy and short on neat logic, but few things in politics are neat and logical, and, given human nature, perhaps that is just as well.

DISCUSSION QUESTIONS

1 In the 1940s, the Supreme Court began ruling that the First Amendment was applicable to both state and federal governments. What were some impacts of that change on the religious-political landscape?

2 What is the "separationist coalition"? Who are some of its most notable participants? What factors have motivated them? Why and how have its critics responded?

3 In "Federalist 51," James Madison wrote on the importance of "ambition counteracting ambition." How is that concept reflected in the current relationship between religious groups and the courts?

4 Separationists and accomodationists both claim to espouse "neutrality." Why, then, do they come to such opposed positions?

FURTHER READING

Bennett, Daniel, *Defending Faith: The Politics of the Christian Conservative Movement* (Lawrence, KS: University Press of Kansas, 2017). A thorough chronicle of the history and recent efforts by Christian conservative groups to engage the courts.

Fisher, Louis, *Religious Liberty in America: Political Safeguards* (Lawrence: University Press of Kansas, 2002). A provocative study that suggests courts do no better than the legislative process in protecting religious liberty.

Green, Steven K., *The Bible, the School, and the Constitution: The Clash That Shaped Modern Church-State Doctrine* (Oxford: Oxford University Press, 2012). A sweeping historical analysis of how eighteenth- and nineteenth-century concerns about schoolchildren led to modern views of church and state.

Kramnick, Isaac, and R. Laurence Moore, *The Godless Constitution: A Moral Defense of the Secular State*, 2nd edn (New York, NY: W. W. Norton, 2005). A probing separationist interpretation of the founding period.

Meyerson, Michael I., *Endowed by Our Creator: The Birth of Religious Freedom in America* (New Haven, CT: Yale University Press, 2012). An intensively researched study of the varied perspectives that coalesced to support religious freedom in the early United States.

Monsma, Stephen V. and Stanley Carson-Thies, *Free to Serve: Protecting the Religious Freedom of Faith-Based Organizations* (Grand Rapids, MI: Brazos, 2015).

Pfeffer, Leo, *Religion, State, and the Burger Court* (Buffalo, NY: Prometheus, 1984). The classic defense of separationism.

Soper, J. Christopher, Kevin R. den Dulk, and Stephen V. Monsma, *The Challenge of Pluralism: Church and State in Five Democracies*, 3rd edn (Lanham, MD: Rowman & Littlefield, 2017). A superb cross-national analysis of church–state relations in the United States and abroad.

NOTES

1. *Donald J. Trump* v. *International Refugee Assistance Project*, 582 US ___ (2017); Michael D. Shear and Adam Liptak, "Supreme Court Takes Up Travel Bann Case, and Allows Parts to Go Ahead," *New York Times*, June 26, 2017.

2. Charles R. Epp, *The Rights Revolution: Lawyers, Activists, and Supreme Courts in Comparative Perspective* (Chicago, IL: University of Chicago Press, 1998).

3. Steven D. Smith, *Foreordained Failure: The Quest for a Constitutional Principle of Religious Freedom* (Princeton, NJ: Princeton University Press, 1999). While courts generally accepted state restrictions on religious activity, scholars disagree about whether this jurisdictional perspective is an appropriate interpretation of the framers' purposes.

See Ellis M. West, *The Religion Clauses of the First Amendment: Guarantees of States' Rights?* (Lanham, MD: Lexington Books, 2011).

4. Allen D. Hertzke, "The US Congress: Protecting and Accommodating Religion," in Derek H. Davis (ed.), *The Oxford Handbook of Church and State in the United States* (Oxford: Oxford University Press, 2010), pp. 370–386; Louis Fisher, *Religious Liberty in America: Political Safeguards* (Lawrence, KS: University Press of Kansas, 2002).

5. John Witte, Jr. and John A. Nichols provide an exhaustive listing of religion liberty cases in their *Religion and the American Constitutional Experiment*, 3rd edn (Oxford: Oxford University Press, 2016), appendix 3. We have added some cases that have been decided since the publication of Witte and Nichols' book. We discuss a sample these cases more fully in Chapter 9.

6. See, for example, Justice Thomas's concurrences in *Cutter* v. *Wilkinson* 544 US 709 (2005) and *Elk Grove Unified School District* v. *Newdow* 542 US 1 (2004).

7. Kevin R. den Dulk and J. Mitchell Pickerill, "Bridging the Lawmaking Process: Organized Interests, Court-Congress Interaction, and Church-State Relations," *Polity*, 35 (2003): 419–440; Kevin T. McGuire, "Public Opinion, Religion, and Constraints on Judicial Behavior," in Kevin T. McGuire (ed.), *New Directions in Judicial Politics* (London and New York, NY: Routledge, 2012), pp. 238–256.

8. Roger Williams, "Mr. Cotton's Letter Lately Printed, Examined and Answered," in Daniel L. Driesbach and Mark David Hall (eds.), *The Sacred Rights of Conscience* (University Park, IL: Liberty Fund, 2009), p. 147.

9. This does not include the largest Baptism denomination, the Southern Baptist Convention, which withdrew its support from BJC in 1991 because of disagreements over the nature of church–state separation and concerns over BJC's purported liberal drift.

10. On this topic, see Gregg Ivers, *To Build a Wall: American Jews and the Separation of Church and State* (Charlottesville, VA: University of Virginia Press, 1995).

11. Frank Sorauf, *The Wall of Separation: Constitutional Politics of Church and State* (Princeton, NJ: Princeton University Press, 1976).

12. Daniel Bennett, *Defending Faith: The Politics of the Christian Conservative Movement* (Lawrence, KS: University Press of Kansas, 2017); Kevin R. den Dulk, "In Legal Culture, but Not of It: The Role of Cause Lawyers in Evangelical Legal Mobilization," in Austin Sarat and Stuart Scheingold (eds.), *Cause Lawyering and Social Movements* (Palo Alto, CA: Stanford University Press, 2006), pp. 197–219; and Kevin R. den Dulk, "Purpose-Driven Lawyers: Evangelical Cause Lawyering and the Culture War," in Austin Sarat and Stuart Scheingold (eds.), *The Cultural Lives of Cause Lawyers* (Cambridge: Cambridge University Press, 2008), pp. 56–78; Steven P. Brown, *Trumping Religion: The New Christian Right, the Free Speech Clause, and the Courts* (Tuscaloosa, AL: University of Alabama Press, 2002).

13. See, for example, *McConnell* v. *FEC*, 540 US 93 (2003); *Locke* v. *Davey*, 540 US 712 (2004); and *Pleasant Grove City* v. *Summum*, 125 S. Ct.1125 (2009).

14. ADF's founders included James Dobson of Focus on the Family, D. James Kennedy of Coral Ridge Ministries, and Bill Bright of Campus Crusade for Christ, among others.

15. See www.usccb.org/about/general-counsel/index.cfm.

16. See www.becketfund.org.

17. Den Dulk, "In Legal Culture, but Not of It."

18. *Hollingsworth* v. *Perry*, 570 US _____ (2013).

19. Pew Research Center, "US Religious Landscape Study," 2014, http://religions.pewforum.org/.

20. Perhaps the leading writer in support of separationism has been Leo Pfeffer, former chief attorney for the American Jewish Congress. See Leo Pfeffer, *Religion, State, and the Burger Court* (Buffalo, NY: Prometheus, 1984).

21. The list of excellent and often provocative studies on the history of religious freedom in the United States is quite long. A few examples include Leonard Levy, *The Establishment Clause: Religion and the First Amendment*, 2nd edn (Raleigh, NC: University of North Carolina Press, 1994); David Sehat, *The Myth of American Religious Freedom* (Oxford: Oxford University Press, 2011); Michael I. Meyerson, *Endowed by Our Creator: The Birth of Religious Freedom in America* (New Haven, CT: Yale University Press, 2012); Steven K. Green, *The Bible, the School, and the Constitution: The Clash that Shaped Modern Church-State Doctrine* (Oxford: Oxford University Press, 2012); Jon Meacham, *American Gospel: God, the Founding Fathers, and the Making of a Nation* (New York, NY: Random House, 2006); William L. Miller, *The First Liberty and the American Republic* (New York, NY: Knopf, 1986); and Steven Waldman, *Founding Faith: Providence, Politics, and the Birth of Religious Freedom in America* (New York, NY: Random House, 2008).

22. Rebecca Riffkin, "In US, Support for Daily Prayer in Schools Dips Slightly," Gallup, September 26, 2014. See also Philip Schwadel, "Changes in Americans' Views of Prayer and Reading the Bible in Public Schools: Time Periods, Birth Cohorts, and Religious Traditions," *Sociological Forum*, 28 (June 2013): 261–282, at p. 267.

23. Riffkin, "Support for Daily Prayer"; Scott Keeter and Juliana Horowitz, "On Darwin's 200th Birthday, Americans Still Divided about Evolution," 2009, www.pewresearch.org/2009/02/05/on-darwins-200th-birthday-americans-still-divided-about-evolution/.

24. Chief Justice Warren Burger explicitly argued for this position for the first time in *Walz* v. *Tax Commission*, 397 US 664 (1970). For approaches somewhat sympathetic to "benevolent neutrality," see Robert T. Miller and Ronald B. Flowers (eds.), *Toward Benevolent Neutrality: Church, State, and the Supreme Court* (Waco, TX: Baylor University Press, 1987); and A. James Reichley, *Faith in Politics* (Washington, DC: Brookings Institution, 2002), chapter 3.

25. See Burger's dissent in *Wallace* v. *Jaffree* 472 US 38 (1985).

26. For an exploration of the equal treatment approach, see Stephen V. Monsma and Stanley W. Carlson-Thies, *Free to Serve: Protecting the Religious Freedom of Faith-Based Organizations* (Grand Rapids, MI: Brazos, 2015). For a cross-national perspective, see J. Christopher Soper, Kevin R. den Dulk, and Stephen V. Monsma, *The Challenge of Pluralism: Church and State in Six Democracies*, 3rd edn (Lanham, MD: Rowman & Littlefield, 2017).

27. Steven K. Green, *The Bible, the School, and the Constitution: The Clash that Shaped Modern Church–State Doctrine* (Oxford: Oxford University Press, 2012).

28. 1 Statute 50, 52, Article III.

12

CHURCH AND STATE IN
THE COURTS

Religious liberty has been called America's "first freedom," and rightly so. Religious pluralism in the United States would be impossible without wide latitude for religious beliefs and practices. The framers of the Constitution put religious freedom front and center in the first sixteen words of the Bill of Rights' First Amendment: "Congress shall make no law respecting an establishment of religion, or prohibiting the free exercise thereof."

But securing religious freedom in practice has often been a struggle—even to the present day—because permitting religious practices often requires trading off other societal goals and values. Should public schools accommodate controversial religious perspectives on science, including non-evolutionary views about the origin of human beings or the universe? To what extent should religion define how we understand marriage, reproduction, or human sexuality? Should government provide funding to faith-based nonprofits (for example, hospitals or schools) that work toward meeting basic human needs? In light of these weighty concerns, it is no wonder that safeguarding the first freedom is also an invitation to heated conflict.

The first Congress of the United States adopted the First Amendment and its religion clauses. Congress began its work on this task in the spring of 1789 after demands were made for the inclusion of a list of guaranteed civil liberties in the Constitution during the debates about ratification. Chief among the proponents of the Bill of Rights were the Antifederalists, who feared that the expansion of the federal government under the new Constitution would curtail personal liberty, including religious freedom. Records of the congressional debate indicate that bargaining and compromise were vital to the eventual agreement on the content and wording of the First Amendment. James Madison introduced the proposed amendment in its first form in June 1789.

It subsequently went through several revisions before a conference committee agreed on a Bill that passed Congress in September 1789 and was later sent to the states, all of which duly ratified it.

Madison knew he had to fashion an amendment that would satisfy critics who feared the Constitution was hostile to religion (and suspected the same of him). He wanted to include what he called "rights of conscience" in the First Amendment, but some critics thought the provision of such rights might result in government neutrality between religion and atheism, so it was dropped. Madison also failed in his attempt to eliminate the official establishment of religion at the state level. As we discussed in Chapter 11, the final version of the First Amendment limited only the federal government ("Congress shall make no law . . .").

From the beginning, the issues of church–state policy that have arisen from disagreements about the meaning of the First Amendment have included (1) how to balance free exercise of religion with otherwise constitutional laws that interfere with it; and (2) how to decide when government activities that somehow involve or even benefit religion amount to an unconstitutional establishment of religion. In most of this chapter, we explore these two concerns separately, following the Supreme Court's own practice of fashioning precedents and complex tests that address "free exercise" of religion and "establishment" of religion as separate and independent concepts. We conclude the chapter, however, by discussing a "free speech" alternative to the religion clauses, as well as the many ways in which free exercise and establishment interact and at times conflict.

THE ROOTS OF RELIGIOUS FREE EXERCISE

An astonishing range of free-exercise disputes have arisen under the First Amendment since its passage in 1789. The recent past is illustrative: The US Supreme Court has been asked to address questions as varied as whether owners of private businesses can refuse to pay benefits or provide services they perceive to be an affront to religious values, the extent to which faith-based schools can receive state funding or use religion as a basis for hiring and firing teachers, and the authority of student groups at public universities to exclude members who do not share the group's religious identity.[1] Meanwhile, lower federal and state courts settle hundreds more cases and controversies involving religion every year.

The framers of the Constitution could never have imagined either the diversity or the volume of today's free-exercise concerns, but they nevertheless understood that there would always be much at stake in the relationship between religion and the government. Many of the framers thought government posed a constant threat to the free exercise of religion, especially for religious minorities and dissenters. They based this view on their sometimes negative experiences with the British government and even with their own colonial governments. Thus, the framers were eager to protect the free exercise of religion from political interference, especially as they crafted a constitution that augmented the power of the national government. For them, protecting free exercise meant curtailing or eliminating government establishment of, and interference with, religion.

Thomas Jefferson, who wrote the Declaration of Independence, and James Madison, the principal author of both the Constitution and the First Amendment, were among the strongest proponents of religious free exercise. Both had been active in opposing the establishment of religion in colonial Virginia and in bringing about the disestablishment of the Anglican (now Episcopal) Church there. Neither Jefferson nor Madison advocated complete separation of church and state during their subsequent presidencies, but both tried to move in that direction. Political reality, however, forced them to accept some compromises to accommodate organized religion at the federal level. And as presidents they did nothing to interfere with the states, where there was sometimes very little separation between church and state. Still, both men made important contributions to the development of American free-exercise rights.[2]

Historically and in comparative perspective, Americans have enjoyed broad rights of religious free exercise.[3] The majority of early Americans were Protestant, and free-exercise rights abounded for most of them. Although Protestantism was dominant, free-exercise rights gradually were extended to Catholics, Jews, and others. Of course, in principle such groups could not constitutionally be denied free-exercise rights—yet they faced varying degrees of discrimination that in time gave way to acceptance of the pluralist reality of American religious life. Plenty of constitutional argument and political conflict occurred along the way.

Today, Americans generally enjoy a high degree of religious freedom encompassing many religious persuasions, groups, and practices, especially compared with other countries (see Box 12.1). This contemporary freedom does not deny the history of conflict that paved the road to free exercise, nor does it deny that some groups still struggle for their free exercise rights in the United States. There always will be religious groups that push against the margins of American political culture and its written and unwritten rules about the limits of acceptable religious practices. Even some of the largest and oldest religious traditions in the United States occasionally find themselves in conflict with those rules.

In attempting to interpret the Free Exercise Clause of the Constitution, the Supreme Court has distinguished between religious beliefs themselves and actions taken as a result of those beliefs. Beliefs are absolutely protected, but religiously motivated action, such as drug use as part of a religious ceremony, may be restricted when the Court decides it contravenes established law. That said, the Supreme Court has avoided addressing religious freedom under some circumstances; indeed, until the 1940s, federal courts often ducked religious issues altogether. For example, courts have been loath to adjudicate arguments among members of disbanded religious groups because getting involved in

BOX 12.1 RELIGIOUS FREEDOM IN CROSS-NATIONAL PERSPECTIVE

Article 18 of the United Nations Universal Declaration of Human Rights recognizes the "right to freedom of thought, conscience, and religion," and a series of global surveys by the Pew Research Center suggests that a majority of people around the world support the right to practice religion freely. What's more, most governments have included some provisions for religious freedom in their national constitutions. Nevertheless, most people worldwide live in countries that place high governmental restrictions on religious practice. Many people affiliated with minority religions also face widespread social hostility toward their faith from their fellow citizens. For example, this problem has grown dramatically in Europe over the past decade as migrants from war-torn parts of Asia and Africa have arrived there in search of a better life. An interesting twist is that countries with strict governmental restrictions on religion can have relatively low levels of social hostility toward religion (e.g., China), while other countries have greater social hostility than governmental restrictions (e.g., South Africa).

The United States tends to have low to moderate levels of both governmental restrictions and social hostility compared with other countries, but the news is less heartening when considering trends within the United States over time: Incidents of state limits on religious practice and social intolerance for religious nonconformity have been inching upward.

Sources: www.un.org; www.pewglobal.org; Katayoun Kishi, Pew Research Center, "Global Restrictions on Religion Rise Modestly in 2015, Reversing Downward Trend," 2017, http://assets.pewresearch.org/wp-content/uploads/sites/11/2017/04/24102207/Pew-Research-Center-Religious-Restrictions-2017-FULL-REPORT.pdf.

these often-bitter fights might mean improperly interfering with a religion and thus deterring free exercise. This standard remains today. Courts allow religious groups to resolve their own disputes, under their own rules, as much as possible. This is especially so when the basic doctrines of a religion itself are at issue (see Box 12.2).[4] If the courts generally have avoided becoming involved in arguments within religious organizations, they have also steered away from attempting to settle disagreements about what constitutes a religion. Judges realize that this matter is treacherous ground, but their policy of avoidance has, in fact, proven to be supportive of free exercise. After all, if the definition of religion were left to the government rather than to believers themselves, free exercise could quickly be threatened.

BOX 12.2 A PROPERTY DISPUTE
AT GEORGE WASHINGTON'S CHURCH

While courts generally avoid settling theological disputes, they often are drawn into conflicts over how to divide property and other tangible assets when congregations split or break away from a denomination. The Episcopal Church has experienced several such conflicts in recent years, as congregations have struggled mightily over various theological disagreements. We see a prominent illustration of this trend in the agonizing legal battles over Truro Church and Falls Church, both properties in Virginia with deep roots in colonial America (and famous members such as George Washington and George Mason). The conflict was triggered when a sizable majority of both congregations' members left the Episcopal denomination in 2006 out of concerns that leaders had become too liberal on homosexuality and a host of other social and theological matters. When the breakaway groups claimed a right to physical church property, the denomination resisted by filing a lawsuit to prevent the split, ultimately winning their argument before the Virginia Supreme Court in 2010.

Source: Michelle Boorstein, "Virginia High Court Rules Against Anglican Breakaway Churches," *Washington Post*, June 11, 2010.

It is not easy to resolve disputes involving what counts as religion, but the courts' standard policy has been to avoid deciding whether the claims of a given religion are true. For example, in *United States* v. *Ballard* (1944), the Supreme Court was asked to decide whether two people who were using the US Mail to solicit funds for the "I AM" spiritual movement were guilty of mail fraud. The parties to the case were the widow and son of the movement's founder, Guy Ballard, who said he was a divine messenger who could communicate with Jesus Christ. In its ruling overturning the Ballards' conviction, the Court stated: "Men may believe what they cannot prove. Religious experiences which are as real as life to some may be incomprehensible to others. . . . If one could be sent to jail because a jury in a hostile environment found his or her religious teachings false, little indeed would be left of religious freedom."[5] Even so, the Supreme Court has not been wholly successful in staying out of the business of defining religion, especially when fundamental roles of government are at stake. Consider the government's policies on taxation. In *Hernandez* v. *Commissioner* (1989), which involved the Church of Scientology, the Supreme Court ruled that fees for specific services (such as training in Scientology) could not be counted as nontaxable gifts. Critics of the Court's decision in this case complained that it implied Scientology was not a serious religion, thereby setting a dangerous precedent. If Scientology is not a religion, then what are the parameters of the religious and the secular—and who sets them?[6] The *Hernandez* case points to the continuing controversy over what exactly constitutes a religion—and what services an organized religion may provide. The nonprofit activities of organized religions are free from taxation, a policy that has long been in place. But just what is a "religion," and what is a "nonprofit activity"? The traditional approach has been that minimizing government interference in such matters maximizes religious freedom, but it also leaves room for abuse.

Some controversial religious practices make headlines. Often, the courts have decided cases in ways that affirm religious freedom. One example has to do with the issue of clergy malpractice. Clergy often provide advice to members of their congregations, but what happens if that advice is potentially harmful? The courts' usual response has been to avoid addressing such an issue when it arises.[7] Another thorny matter concerns the level of confidentiality clergy should be allowed to maintain. This is especially difficult when clergy learn, through pastoral counseling, that someone has committed a serious crime such as child abuse or murder. State policies differ, but the current trend is toward requiring clergy to report violations of the law when they learn of them. Some clergy argue that this requirement represents an erosion of their clergy–penitent privilege. Information gleaned through the seal of private confession in Roman Catholicism, however, remains sacrosanct. The confidentiality of pastoral counseling is far more controversial, all the more so in the wake of revelations of sexual abuse of minors by some Catholic priests.

Another sensitive question is the extent to which personal risk-taking should be allowed within a religious community. The issues almost always arise out of health risks incurred because of religious practices. Examples include Jehovah's Witnesses' refusal to accept blood transfusions, Christian Scientists' belief in faith healing (and their consequent rejection of modern medicine), the practice of serpent handling in a handful of Pentecostal churches, and rare instances of the practice of female genital mutilation in a few Muslim communities. Such issues may be approached from many directions—and, of course, it matters whether faith-based groups are honest with their members about possible consequences of any risky behaviors they might practice or encourage. The limits of religious freedom become especially important when the lives and fundamental health of children are at stake.[8] Disputes also swirl around the question of whether there should be limits to some religious groups' perpetual search for converts. Almost all religions assert that they seek only followers who knowingly choose their faith, so they renounce the use of fraud or manipulation to trick people into embracing their faith. But what constitutes a trick or a fraud? For many atheists, to use the extreme example, every religion is in the business of fraud. How much can government regulate what it—or society—determines to be fraudulent behavior without infringing on free exercise?

A classic exception to allowing free exercise was the Supreme Court's decision to allow a congressional ban on the Mormon practice of polygamy in *Reynolds v. United States* (1879). This decision came down long ago, however, and starting in the early twentieth century, the Court developed a broader free exercise perspective. In *Cantwell v. Connecticut* (1940), for example, the Supreme Court affirmed a generous range of free-exercise rights by invoking both religion clauses and other parts of the First Amendment to strike down local ordinances that interfered with Jehovah's Witnesses' desire to distribute literature to and request contributions from the general public. The Court's decision in *Cantwell* to allow religious groups the right to proselytize pursuant to their freedom of religion has been repeatedly reaffirmed, subject to restrictions on the setting.[9] Likewise, state attempts to penalize fund-raising by unpopular religious groups have been rejected.[10] The Court has also ruled that the state may not prevent clergy or religious organizations from becoming involved in politics.[11] Similarly, the Court has granted some religious freedom in federal institutions (most controversially, in prisons), but only so long as religious practices do not disrupt standard operating procedures.[12] In public schools, the courts have created a rather narrow zone of free exercise. Still, in *Pierce v. Society of Sisters* (1928), the Supreme Court affirmed the right of Roman Catholic schools (and thus other private schools) to exist alongside public ones. In *West Virginia State Board of Education v. Barnette* (1944), the Court held that Jehovah's Witnesses have the right to refuse to say the Pledge of Allegiance in school, as their religion forbids commitment to any nation-state. And in *Wisconsin v. Yoder* (1972), the Court upheld the refusal of Amish people to allow their teenagers to attend high school, accepting Amish religious doctrine that does not require or respect such schooling. All these decisions, especially taken together, demonstrate that public education must remain aware that it operates in an environment of modest protected religious free exercise (see Box 12.3).

THE LIMITS OF FREE EXERCISE

In principle, however, there is no debate about the government's, and the Constitution's, ultimate authority, including its power to restrict the free exercise of religion. While the First Amendment is written in absolutist language—"Congress shall make no law . . ."—it is not an absolute guarantee of religious practice anytime, anywhere, and in any manner. Even rights granted in the Constitution and the Bill of Rights must be balanced against other competing rights or when government has an important goal that clashes with religion. It is not self-evident from the Constitution how that balance ought to be struck, so judges must rely on their own judgment and the interpretations of the Supreme Court and other courts over the years.

This judicial balancing act raises an immediate question: Do court rulings that uphold competing rights claims or common-good legislation serve to

> ## BOX 12.3 SHOULD TEACHERS AT RELIGIOUS SCHOOLS BE TREATED AS CLERGY?
>
> Since the 1970s, the federal courts have maintained that the First Amendment allows houses of worship to hire and fire their own clergy without limitation by antidiscrimination laws. After all, it would be unreasonable to expect, say, a Jewish synagogue to open a clergy position to a Christian or Muslim. Does the same kind of "ministerial exception" to employment law apply to teachers in faith-based schools? In *Hosanna-Tabor Evangelical Lutheran Church and School* v. *Equal Employment Opportunity Commission* (2012), the US Supreme Court affirmed that it does. The Equal Employment Opportunity Commission (EEOC), an enforcement agency of the federal government, sued on behalf of a woman who was fired from a Lutheran school in Redmond, Michigan, after a lengthy sick leave. The agency argued that the termination violated the Americans with Disabilities Act, and that the school was not exempt from the lawsuit just because the teacher was not a minister. Writing for the majority of the Court, Chief Justice John Roberts rejected the EEOC's position that the exemption applies only to employees who perform "exclusively religious functions." It is enough, Roberts said, that a denomination has declared a position "ministerial" and that employees in that position perform some important religious function. Because the fired teacher fit that loose description of "minister," the school was exempted from the law.

promote particular moral positions at the expense of pure religious free exercise? This is precisely the concern voiced recently by many religious commentators who fear that governments at all levels slowly have been eroding religious freedom. They point to examples including the Obama administration's mandate that employers must fund contraception in their health-insurance plans, local and state governments revoking licenses of Christian foster-care agencies that refuse to place children in households with same-sex partners, and new state and federal restrictions on religious practices in public universities and the military, among other threats. These critics hope the Trump administration will alleviate some of these concerns, though early reviews are mixed.[13] In each instance, choices about morality and pluralism are at issue. The question becomes one of where religious free exercise ought to rank in comparison with other values. In the American legal system, free exercise is not always at the top of the list.

Many of the Supreme Court's most controversial free-exercise decisions in recent decades have addressed disputes in which the state's authority and need for security are at stake. In *Goldman* v. *Weinberger* (1986), the Court decided to uphold military regulations about appropriate dress, which forbade a Jewish person from wearing a yarmulke (skullcap) while on duty. At issue was not the wisdom of the regulation but whether the Court should defer to military rules and the reasons behind them, namely the military's need to maintain order and regularity. The Court concluded that it should defer to the military. Congress later passed a law allowing Jews to wear yarmulkes in the military, but in doing so it affirmed the authority of the federal government to decide such matters rather than leaving them to the individual believer. A similar issue arose in a New Jersey case, *O'Lone* v. *Estate of Shabazz* (1987), in which Muslims in state prisons claimed prison work rules interfered with their practice of Islam. The Court held that deference to prison rules and the administrators who make them (that is, the government) must take precedence over free exercise.

Other cases have considered challenges to public health regulations or other matters that touch on community values or the common good. For some time, the courts have endorsed the view that government provisions designed to protect the general welfare have priority over the First Amendment's guarantee of religious free exercise. A long series of cases has held that things such as requiring vaccinations to protect public health or legally forbidding child labor supersede free-exercise rights, even though some groups' religious freedoms might be violated. For example, in *Braunfeld* v. *Brown* (1981), the Court ruled against a group of Orthodox Jews who felt that their ability to earn a living was being compromised by Pennsylvania's Sunday closing laws. Their religion forbade them from working on Saturday, and the state forbade them from working on Sunday. The Court recognized that the Pennsylvania law made Orthodox Judaism "more expensive" than Christianity, but because the law did not prevent anyone from the actual practice of religion—"the Sunday law simply regulates a secular activity"—it did not violate the free-exercise clause.[14]

In complex legal areas such as these, the crucial question ultimately centers on where to draw the line between pursuit of government goals and protecting religious free exercise. The fact is that the US Supreme Court has never sent a clear message about where that line ought to be drawn. It usually has appeared to be more concerned with upholding government policy than with protecting some small, dissenting religious group. But no obvious or consistent pattern has emerged. From the late 1930s until the 1960s, however, it was a safe bet that most free-exercise appeals would meet with defeat in court. The Supreme Court usually sided with the federal and state governments and their laws in such conflicts. After the 1960s, however, the pendulum began to swing toward the expansion of free-exercise rights.

In the landmark free-exercise case of *Sherbert* v. *Verner* (1963), the Court decided that the standard of "strict scrutiny" (the most stringent level of judicial review) must apply to any law that conflicts with the free exercise of religion. By imposing this standard, the justices meant to underline the importance of free exercise, though they did not mean that any laws clashing with free exercise automatically would fail the strict scrutiny test. In *Sherbert*, a Seventh-Day Adventist won her claim against South Carolina for denying her unemployment benefits after she was fired from her job for refusing to work on Saturday (the Adventist Sabbath). The Court stated clearly that "the burden on the free exercise of appellant's religion must be justified by a compelling state interest."[15] Thus, the *Sherbert* case set a high standard for the government that the Court continued to use for many years in deciding a wide range of free-exercise disputes.

However, in the much-discussed 1990 case of *Employment Division* v. *Smith*, the Court specifically reversed the strict scrutiny doctrine that it had set forth in *Sherbert*. No longer would states be forced to demonstrate a compelling interest if their laws had the unintended effect of restricting free-exercise rights. Although the picture is complicated and the results mixed, the Court increasingly has been willing to uphold "common good" laws in the face of protests by religious groups and individuals contending that such laws infringe upon their religious freedom.

In the *Smith* case, the Supreme Court affirmed Oregon's drug policy. In that state, two Native American drug counselors had been fired for violating terms of their employment and were thus prevented from collecting unemployment compensation. The infraction was their use of peyote, an illegal hallucinogenic drug that plays a significant spiritual role in their religion as members of the Native American Church.[16] The Court essentially held that laws that do not target religion directly, such as Oregon's drug laws, are constitutionally valid even if they incidentally restrict religious practice. The Court's new direction in legal doctrine caused a real uproar. The Court had declared that it was no longer committed to automatic "strict scrutiny" of state laws that have the effect of restricting free exercise of religion, thereby undoing the decades-old *Sherbert* precedent. In *Sherbert*, of course, the Court had not said that laws restricting free exercise were inherently unconstitutional, but it did suggest they would face an uphill battle. The reversal of the *Sherbert* precedent seemed to conclude an era in which the Court provided an especially protected role for religious exercise in the United States.

Thus, the Supreme Court's 1993 decision in *Church of the Lukumi Babalu Aye* v. *City of Hialeah* came as some relief to critics of its *Smith* ruling. In this case, the Court struck down an ordinance passed by the city of Hialeah, Florida, prohibiting the ritual sacrifice of animals.[17] The justices ruled unanimously that this ordinance had been designed specifically to forbid animal-killing rituals which are practiced as part of Santeria, an Afro-Caribbean religion. The Court agreed with the Santerian Church of the Lukumi that the ordinance in question was extremely selective because it did not forbid other forms of animal killing, such as hunting or Jewish ritual preparation of kosher food. It was aimed instead at one group alone: practitioners of Santeria. What distinguishes the *Smith* case from the *Lukumi* case is that laws narrowly interfering with the free exercise of specific faiths may be ruled unconstitutional when they do not further a major state policy initiative designed for the common good. Laws pursuant to the common good that are not intended to oppress a specific religious group, however, are likely to be upheld under the *Smith* precedent.

In response to the Court's decision in *Smith*, religious groups united to push the Religious Freedom Restoration Act (RFRA) through Congress. This law, which President Bill Clinton signed in 1994, required the federal courts to return to the doctrine of strict scrutiny when reviewing any law that abridges religious free-exercise rights. But the Supreme Court declared the RFRA unconstitutional in *City of Boerne* v. *Flores* (1997). A Catholic parish in Boerne, Texas, wished to expand the size of its church sanctuary but had been denied a building permit. The city's policies about the protection of the historic district in which the church was located prevented any further development. Buoyed by the RFRA, the parish argued that the city did not have a compelling interest in preventing it from expanding. The Court supported the city's counterargument, simultaneously striking down the provision of the RFRA that called for the existence of a compelling state interest for state and local laws to restrict free-exercise rights.

Despite the *Boerne* decision, the legacy of the RFRA lives on. Congress passed scaled-back legislation in 2000 that applied only in certain land-use and prisoner-rights disputes.[18] And it is important to remember that the Supreme Court's decision in *Boerne* rejected only Congress's attempt to impose, via the Court's decisions, the old *Sherbert* standard on the actions of state and local governments. Those governments, however, could place restrictions on themselves—and many did in the wake of *Boerne*, passing their own state-level versions of the RFRA requiring that their own actions burdening religion have a compelling state interest.

By the same token, Congress could also impose the *Sherbert* standard on itself. In fact, the Supreme Court, in a case that must have provided the justices a sense of sweet irony, did apply the RFRA against Congress in a dispute over the importation of hoasca, a hallucinogen banned under federal drug law, which was used by a Christian spiritist movement in the Southwest.[19] The Court held that Congress and the executive branch had not shown a compelling reason under the RFRA for refusing to grant a faith-based exemption for the importation and use of the drug.

Pressure on the Supreme Court to strengthen free exercise, perhaps through a return to its pre-*Smith* standard, has changed, but not waned, over time. That pressure likely will intensify in coming years, as prominent religious groups face their own challenges regarding religious freedom. Some religious universities, for example, come out of traditions that reject same-sex marriage, which has created genuine moral conflict when those institutions attempt to comply with federal and state regulations that forbid hiring discrimination based on sexual orientation. Or consider that as part of the implementation of the Patient Protection and Affordable Care Act (popularly known as "Obamacare"), the US

Department of Health and Human Services announced a mandate in January 2012 that nearly all health-insurance plans pay for contraception. Enter the Catholic Church, which officially opposes the use of artificial contraception. Although the mandate exempts houses of worship, it would extend to the Catholic Church's vast network of hospitals, universities, and social-service agencies. US bishops reacted to this policy with vehement assertions that the mandate abridges these organizations' free exercise of the Catholic faith. Many other religious groups, as well as religiously observant owners of Hobby Lobby and other businesses, have followed the bishops' lead on the issue and protested the mandate. The Obama administration responded with some slight changes to the regulation, but that did not placate opponents enough to drop dozens of lawsuits or to cease intense congressional lobbying. These disputes over hiring discrimination and contraception access are harbingers of future battles between government and religious groups about the appropriate legal boundaries around reproduction, family life, and marriage (see Box 12.4).

BOX 12.4 SAME-SEX MARRIAGE AND RELIGIOUS CONSCIENCE

In *Obergefell* v. *Hodges* (2015), the US Supreme Court struck down bans on same-sex marriage in more than a dozen states. While the Court's decision was intensely controversial, it also reflected public opinion over the past decade, which has shifted dramatically in favor of legalizing same-sex marriage. Nevertheless, the landmark case raised a host of concerns for traditional religious believers. As Chief Justice John Roberts noted in his dissenting opinion: "Hard questions arise when people of faith exercise religion in ways that may be seen to conflict with the new right to same-sex marriage—when, for example, a religious college provides married student housing only to opposite-sex married couples, or a religious adoption agency declines to place children with same-sex married couples." It did not take long for the Supreme Court to be confronted with one of those questions. In 2017, the Court agreed to consider whether the constitutional protections of religious liberty and free speech extend to a baker who claimed his religious conscience would not allow him to provide a cake for a same-sex wedding celebration. This case is the first skirmish in what will likely be a new area of conflict about how far the religion clauses protect practices that are rapidly falling out of step with public opinion.

Sources: *Obergefell* v. *Hodges*, 576 US ___ (2015); Adam Liptak, "Justices to Hear Case on Religious Objections to Same-Sex Marriage," *New York Times*, June 26, 2017; *Masterpiece Cakeshop* v. *Colorado Civil Rights Commission*.

THE POLITICS OF RELIGIOUS ESTABLISHMENT

Separationist and anti-religion lobbies have had mixed success in attempting to dismantle subtler forms of establishment. For example, atheist leader Madalyn Murray O'Hair failed in her 1979 attempt to persuade the United States Court of Appeals (Fifth Circuit) to banish "In God We Trust" from the currency (*O'Hair* v. *Blumenthal*). Efforts to get the Supreme Court to eliminate prayer at the beginning of legislative sessions also have a long and unsuccessful history, with challenges at both the state (*Marsh* v. *Chambers*, 1983) and local (*Town of Greece* v. *Galloway*, 2014) levels. The weight of the traditional establishment of what may be called religion in general has been substantial throughout American history. Nonetheless, pressure against the symbolic establishment of Christianity has gathered steam over the years. The coalition against official endorsements of Christianity is often broad and includes some of the main players in the separationist coalition discussed in Chapter 11, such as the American Civil Liberties Union, Americans United for Separation of Church and State, the Secular Coalition for America, the Freedom from Religion Foundation, and the legal arms of prominent Jewish groups.

On the other hand, the technique most often used by those who wish to defend symbolic establishment has been to repackage establishment and present it as something that is not religious at all. In instances when these efforts succeed, courts appear to wink and move on, as has been evident in arguments over public crèches. In both *Lynch* v. *Donnelly* (1984) and *Allegheny County* v. *Greater Pittsburgh ACLU* (1989), the Supreme Court allowed crèches to stand on public land or alongside public buildings—but only if they are merely one element of what the Court has described as a "winter display." When crèches stand alone, however, as was the case in a Pittsburgh courthouse in *Allegheny County* v. *Greater Pittsburgh ACLU*, the Court has deemed them unconstitutional. In *Van Orden* v. *Perry* (2006), a similar line of reasoning led the Court to accept the display of the Ten Commandments at the Texas State Capitol. A plurality of justices argued the display had a historical significance that was not merely religious.[20]

The courts have also allowed the local, state, and federal levels of government to funnel tremendous amounts of financial aid to various religions. These practices, of course, certainly do not affirm the strict principle of separation of church and state. Government aid to nonprofit organizations (including religious groups) is vast. Examples of this practice, affirmed by the courts since 1899 in *Bradfield* v. *Roberts*, include assistance to religious hospitals and clinics, orphanages, halfway houses, retirement homes, refugee resettlement projects, and other social-service endeavors and programs. The exact amounts of aid and the specific rules governing its use vary from federal to state governments, from state to state, and from one policy area to another, but the general practice is widespread.

As we noted in Chapter 11, one of the Court's efforts to fashion a governing principle for establishment cases is the so-called Lemon test. Formulated in *Lemon* v. *Kurtzman* (1971), the Lemon test holds that laws are constitutional when they serve a secular legislative purpose, have a primary effect that neither advances nor inhibits religion, and do not foster an "excessive entanglement" between government and religion.[21] The Lemon test has been used in a variety of ways in establishment cases, and its implementation has been a controversial undertaking even within the Supreme Court. The late Justice Antonin Scalia, for example, bemoaned "the strange Establishment Clause geometry of crooked lines and wavering shapes [the Lemon test's] intermittent use has produced."[22] The Lemon test allows the constitutional provision of substantial government aid to religious organizations of all sorts. Thus, if governments decide that aid to nonprofit hospitals is in the public interest, then it is constitutional because the legislation from which the hospitals would benefit may be said to have a secular purpose, neither advance nor inhibit religion, and fail to foster any excessive entanglements between church and state.

It is nevertheless true that in such a situation government undeniably is aiding religious groups and thereby promoting some form of religious establishment. Granted, this sort of implicit establishment is by no means the same as the official establishments of the colonial era. During that era, government support was enjoyed exclusively by one church. Instead, the modern arrangement normally takes the form of "multiple establishment." Government provides aid in a specific policy area to all qualified applicants. For example, both secular and religious hospitals may receive government funds.

Contemporary establishment also arises in the common practice of exempting all nonprofit groups (again, including religious institutions) from paying property taxes. Because churches, synagogues, and mosques often occupy extensive and highly valuable properties, this arrangement is a tremendous financial boon for them. This policy has been defended not as a grant to religious groups per se but rather as a neutral law with the secular purpose of helping nonprofit (and only nonprofit) groups that benefit society. Although some separationists have argued strenuously against this arrangement as a flagrant form of establishment, they have not succeeded in the courts.

Education policy is another arena in which many conflicts have emerged around religious establishment. The battle over religion in schools has been waged throughout American history and continues unabated today. Sometimes the disputes deal with the place of religion in public education; in other instances, the issue is state support for private religious education. Regardless of the issue, American culture's faith in schooling ensures that struggles over education policy will continue because Americans believe a great deal is at stake.

All sorts of religious practices in schools, some of which have reflected the beliefs of one religious group or another, have been common throughout the history of American public education. Public prayers and Bible reading in class have been the most widespread of these practices. However, such policies began to face serious criticism in the mid-twentieth century when religious "release-time" education became a widespread fashion. Such programs allowed religious teachers to come into public schools during regular hours and teach religious lessons to students who had the permission of a parent or guardian. In the late 1940s and early 1950s, the Supreme Court was indecisive about the constitutionality of this practice. In *McCollum* v. *Board of Education* (1948), release-time classes held on school grounds were ruled unconstitutional. In 1952, the Court seemed to reverse itself in *Zorach* v. *Clauson*, but the release-time classes at stake in that case took place off school property.

Even though release-time programs are no longer popular in most places, the disputes surrounding them were an early sign of the courts' willingness to tackle establishment issues that relate to public education. Since the 1960s, courts steadily have brought about a sweeping disestablishment of religion in public schools. Separationist and antireligious groups that argue religion has no place in the classroom have seen this development as a great victory, but many other groups disagree strongly.

The Supreme Court's first step was to remove state-sponsored prayer from the schools in the monumental 1962 case of *Engel* v. *Vitale*.[23] One year later, the Court also put a stop to state-required Bible reading in public schools in *Abington School District* v. *Schempp* (1963). In 1980, they ruled the posting of the Ten Commandments in classrooms unconstitutional (*Stone* v. *Graham*). For some critics, the last straw came in *Wallace* v. *Jaffree* (1985), in which the Court struck down an Alabama law requiring public-school teachers to open each day with a moment of silence. The Court interpreted the law as Alabama's "effort to return voluntary prayer to our public schools" and did not accept the state's argument that the moment of silence served the secular purpose of encouraging good student behavior.[24] The latest issue of this nature to come before the Court is the constitutionality of prayer at public-school graduation ceremonies and other public events. The Supreme Court rejected clergy-led graduation prayers in *Lee* v. *Weisman* (1992) and student-led prayers at high-school sporting events in *Santa Fe Independent School District* v. *Doe* (2000).

Critics often argue that the exit of religion(s) from public schools has meant its replacement by a "religion" of secularism or secular humanism, a kind of anti-religion that celebrates humans or nature and implicitly or explicitly ridicules traditional religion(s). But in the 1987 case of Smith v. Board of Commissioners, the US Court of Appeals (Eleventh Circuit) disagreed, and that is where the matter rests in the courts at this point.

Some religious groups have welcomed judicial efforts to remove religion from public schools. They believe religion belongs at home and in church; they often have no use for vague nondenominational religion in the first place. Other observers, however, are uneasy about whether public schools should go to great lengths to avoid the presentation or teaching of anything traditionally religious.

Despite a long history of religious establishment in American public schools, the teaching of overtly religious lessons has now ceased in most school districts. This fact is reflected in the failure of efforts by conservative Protestants to force school districts in several southern states to provide instruction in creationism or intelligent design (the idea that some higher intelligence guides evolution). Courts invariably have deemed such efforts a manifest establishment of religion. On the other hand, the Supreme Court has protected the teaching of evolution. In 1968, in *Epperson* v. *Arkansas*, the Court struck down an Arkansas law forbidding the teaching of evolutionary theory. It is also unconstitutional for a state to require the teaching of both creationism and Darwinism, according to the Court's ruling in *Edwards* v. *Aguillard* (1987). In both instances, the Court ruled that the states in question were specifically attempting to establish Christianity.

Disputes over the judiciary's view of establishment also have raged in the context of financial aid to religious schools. Historically, this controversy was about aid to Roman Catholic schools, which was denied on establishment grounds because to give such aid would be to establish a branch of Christianity (Catholicism). Because public schools once were permeated by practices such as group readings from the Protestant King James Bible, skeptics have suggested that the real problem was not with establishment per se, it was rather a question of which Christian tradition would be given preference in most public schools. In recent decades, courts have removed much of the old Protestant establishment from public schools, but the record is complicated regarding financial aid to religious schools. Aid for teacher salaries, which is by far the greatest portion of school budgets, repeatedly has failed on establishment grounds, as was the case in *Lemon* v. *Kurtzman* (1971).

At the same time, the Supreme Court has upheld state laws allowing several significant forms of assistance to religious schools. According to the Court's 1947 decision in *Everson* v. *Board of Education*, public-school buses may be used to transport children to and from religious schools. The Court argued that this form of aid primarily benefited children, not schools, so transportation to religious schools did not violate the establishment clause. A similar logic drove the Court's 1968 decision in *Board of Education* v. *Allen*, in which it upheld New York's policy of allowing religious schools to borrow secular textbooks from public-school districts. In *Meek* v. *Pittenger* (1975), however, the Court ruled that neither state-paid staff nor instructional materials other than books could be loaned to religious schools. In *Wolman* v. *Walter* (1977), the Court affirmed *Meek* and further rejected state aid by declaring that public-school buses could not be used to transport children from religious schools on field trips. Finally, in *Aguilar* v. *Felton* (1985), the Court struck down a New York law providing state-financed remedial courses and guidance services in religious schools. But just over a decade later, the Court overturned *Aguilar* in *Agostini* v. *Felton* (1997), holding that public schoolteachers may provide state-mandated special services in religious schools. And following *Agostini* came the Court's decision in *Mitchell* v. *Helms* (2000), in which the Court upheld state aid to parochial schools in the form of computers and other instructional materials and equipment. The logic of the *Mitchell* case effectively overturned the Court's decisions in *Meek*.

In other cases, the Court has ruled that government funds may be used to pay an interpreter to accompany a deaf student attending a religious school, as it did in *Zobrest* v. *Catalina Foothills School District* (1993). Proponents could see no problem with this practice because insignificant establishment, at most, could result. Opponents, however, said that providing the interpreter was a serious breach of the no-establishment principle because taxpayers would be financing translation by the interpreter of sectarian events, such as Mass in the school. In *Kiryas Joel Village School District* v. *Grumet* (1994), however, the Court ruled that a special school district for disabled children in an Orthodox Jewish suburb of New York City was unconstitutional. Whereas only one student was being assisted in *Zobrest*, the Court saw the creation of an entire school district as another matter altogether.

What should we make of this bewildering array of cases? Can we point to a principle or even a pattern that unifies them? Answering yes to that question is a tall order. For many observers, twentieth-century establishment-clause jurisprudence amounted to nothing more than a confusing mess—and, thus far, the Roberts Court has added little clarity. As one commentator remarks:

> Bus trips from home to religious schools are constitutional, but bus trips from religious schools to local museums are unconstitutional. ... Standardized tests are o.k., but teacher-prepared tests are not. Government can provide parochial schools with books but not maps, provoking [the late] Senator Daniel Moynihan's quip: "What about atlases?" The Court has invoked Lemon to strike down a nativity scene surrounded by poinsettias and to uphold a nativity scene surrounded by elephants, teddy bears, Santa's workshop, and a talking wishing well.[25]

The Court's logic has been based on its attempt to balance two goals: ensuring no establishment and benefiting children. On the one hand, the Court's reasoning has been that establishment is especially dangerous in the schools because children are much more vulnerable to inculcation than are adults; on the other hand, that very vulnerability has led the Court to avoid disadvantaging children in any fundamental way if they happen to attend religious schools. Thus, the Court has been understanding if states decide that all children need textbooks and transportation to school. State-paid religious school teachers, however, would move too far toward establishment.

Obviously, there is room for argument on every point. Some contend that if religious schools may receive only a certain amount of aid for specific government services, then families of religious school students ought also to receive some compensation for the costs they incur in sending their children to these schools. Families that send children to religious schools commonly complain that they are forced to pay twice to educate their children—once through taxes to support public schools they do not use and again in tuition to the religious school. Opponents reply that no one is forced to send their children to a religious school and that public schools enhance the common good. They question why taxpayers should have to pay for the choices of one small portion of the population, especially when those choices may involve an establishment of religion.

However, some Catholics, evangelical Protestants, Muslims, and Orthodox Jews believe today that they must send their children to religious schools if they are to practice their religion freely—especially considering what they perceive to be growing secularism in public schools. For them, state support for religious schools, if it is made available to all, does not involve much establishment. Nor, they insist, does it hinder free exercise. Critics reply that such support does constitute unacceptable religious establishment because it makes all citizens contribute to the education of children in religious schools. Such critics sometimes find allies among supporters of religious schools who fear that the heavy hand of government regulation might accompany financial aid.

In the past, the courts have sided with citizens who oppose any form of financial relief for families sending children to private schools. State tuition grants, for example, have been held unconstitutional. The governing rule today, however, is not quite the same. In 1983, the Supreme Court decided in *Mueller* v. *Allen* that Minnesota's policy of allowing tax deductions for tuition, textbooks, and transportation to private schools—including religious ones— was permissible. The Court cast aside charges of establishment because Minnesota made such expenses deductible only if they were provided to all state-approved private schools. Minnesota has now expanded its program to allow tax deductions for any expense (within prescribed financial limits) for private education and has introduced a $1,000 tax credit for lower-income citizens who incur expenses other than tuition costs in sending their children to private schools.

The courts have addressed the efforts of many states and localities to adopt "school choice" plans, which permit families and students to choose between public and private schools at state expense—and have been receiving renewed attention with Betsy DeVos, a school-choice advocate, as Donald Trump's first secretary of education. Still, it is not obvious what the Supreme Court's reaction would be if school-choice plans were to become widespread.

In 2002, the Court upheld Cleveland's school-choice program in *Zelman* v. *Simmons-Harris*. Although nearly all students participating in the program used their grants to attend religious schools, the Court decided that the program was designed to enable a purely private choice. Parents, not government, choose to send their children to religious schools under the program, so there was no unconstitutional government support for religion. The decision clearly was a victory for school-choice advocates, including those who desire greater governmental accommodation of religion in public life. But the Zelman decision is unlikely to be the last word on broader-based voucher programs, which have been proposed with great controversy in places including Washington, DC, Florida, Louisiana, Colorado, Michigan, and others.

The courts consistently have ruled that aid directed to religious colleges and universities raises considerably less concern about establishment. The assumption here is that college students, as adults, are a good deal less vulnerable to religious propaganda than are children and youth in K-12 schools. Thus, aid may be provided to religious colleges for buildings as long as they are not used for worship or sectarian education, according to the Court's decisions in *Tilton* v. *Richardson* (1971) and *Roemer* v. *Board of Public Works* (1976).

EQUAL ACCESS: A HYBRID APPROACH TO CHURCH AND STATE

As we have noted, many legal observers have become frustrated by the Supreme Court's sometimes unpredictable approach to church–state relations, while many religious observers see the Court as a threat to religious freedom. Some evangelical legal strategists in the early 1980s shifted away from sole reliance on the First Amendment's religion clauses as the means of defending religious freedom and focused instead on the constitutional protection of speech and expression. By interpreting religious practices as a form of free expression, they put a well-developed and relatively predictable body of case law to work on their behalf. The basic free-speech principle is that government cannot limit expression—including religious expression—merely because it dislikes or fears the content of what is expressed.[26]

Some of the earliest efforts along these lines dealt with student-led religious groups in public schools. In *Widmar* v. *Vincent*—a case argued by the Christian Legal Society—the Supreme Court upheld such a policy for college campuses in 1981 by declaring that if a university offers the use of facilities to one extracurricular group, it must do so for all. In 1984, Congress passed the Equal Access Act, which applied the same principle to public high schools. This law provided that high schools had to allow student-led religious groups to meet after school if other extracurricular clubs were permitted to do so. Though many schools resisted, the Supreme Court affirmed the law in *Board of Education* v. *Mergens* (1990) by ruling that granting space to an after-school Bible club did not amount to an unconstitutional establishment of religion, provided a teacher (as a government employee) did not lead club meetings. To disallow such meetings would mean the state was unreasonably discriminating against a specific form of expression—in this case, religious expression—and therefore violating the bedrock principles of free speech.

The impact of the Court's decision to allow high-school Bible clubs to meet after school hours already has been felt, as an increasing number of schools have developed such clubs. High-school ministries, such as Young Life, the Fellowship of Christian Athletes, Youth for Christ, First Priority, and Student Venture (the high-school ministry of Campus Crusade for Christ) have been active on campuses across the country, in some cases for many decades.[27] Battles over such clubs and organizations continue, however. In 1993, the Court ruled that if a school district allows other community groups to use its buildings when classes are not in session, then religious groups must also be offered the same privilege (*Lamb's Chapel* v. *Center Moriches Union Free School District*). The Court also held in *Rosenberger* v. *Rector* (1995) that because the University of Virginia provides support to a wide variety of student publications, it must as a matter of equal access do the same for a campus Christian publication. The university at first had not assisted the Christian publication for fear of violating the establishment clause, but ultimately it was compelled to do so partly as the result of violating the free-speech clause.

It is important to note, however, that the principle of "neutrality" at the heart of equal access can cut both ways. Recently, schools including Vanderbilt University and the University of California have adopted policies requiring student groups to allow "all comers"—that is, any interested person—to join and even lead an organization. That presents obvious difficulties for religious groups that want to maintain their identity through control of their membership. But these university policies ostensibly are neutral because they apply the same way to all campus groups, religious or otherwise. In *Christian Legal Society* v. *Martinez* (2010), the Supreme Court, in its first significant religion-related case after John Roberts took over as chief justice, upheld the constitutionality of an all-comers policy at the University of California's Hastings College of Law. The Christian Legal Society, which required members to affirm a "Statement of Beliefs" to be considered for leadership positions, ironically lost its challenge partly because of a principle it had helped to pioneer in the *Widmar* case.

CONCLUSION

One of the most interesting questions in contemporary church–state politics is the relationship between free exercise and establishment. The framers of the Constitution took for granted that, by definition, establishment of religion meant restriction of free-exercise rights. And they were correct in instances when establishment means state sponsorship of a single religion. At least for practitioners of minority religions, free exercise was bound to be burdened (at best) in the face of a single established religion. At worst, minority religions would face drastic curtailment of their free exercise rights.

Much current church–state jurisprudence proceeds under the same assumption, namely that no official establishment can possibly enhance the free exercise of religion. But this assumption is not always true; sometimes, in fact, establishment may bolster free-exercise rights. The classic illustration is provided by the benefits that flow from state aid to religious schools. If state aid is given to all religious schools, religious free exercise may expand for families that desire a religious education for their children but cannot afford it. Some critics point out that implicit in this view is the idea that somehow government has an obligation to promote the free exercise of religion, an assumption at which they insist the First Amendment does not even hint. Instead, they read the First Amendment to mean that government should not interfere with religious free exercise, which is much different to providing active support for religion.

Such an interpretation of the First Amendment is just one possible understanding of how it might protect free-exercise rights. But even if one concludes that the First Amendment requires government to promote free exercise, it does not follow that it should also offer state aid to religious schools. The point is that it is not always obvious that an increase in establishment (of all religions) leads necessarily to a curtailment of free-exercise rights. In some instances, the opposite may be true. Some argue that sweeping formulas therefore should be replaced by case-by-case analysis and discussion. The courts have argued for decades that some forms of religious expression in public schools constitute unacceptable establishment. To say the least, these decisions have offended critics who contend that the resulting absence of religious expression in public schools amounts to an establishment of secularism.

It is also crucial to ask whether political conflicts should be fought out in the courts in the first place. And the issue is not only one of how elitist or democratic the courts may be, though that is certainly a subject that deserves reflection. Nor is the question as straightforward as deciding whether controversial religio-political issues should be removed from the public arena. The fact is that the legal remedy, given its focus on adversarial conflict, often exacerbates tensions and thus frequently fails to encourage the compromise essential in the increasingly multicultural and religiously pluralistic character of American society.

DISCUSSION QUESTIONS

1 What are some of the state interests or goals that the Supreme Court is most likely to uphold against free-exercise claims? Is it possible to categorize these interests along certain dimensions (e.g., perceived threats to state authority, challenges to community values or public welfare, etc.)?

2　What is the belief–action distinction, especially as laid out in the *Reynolds* case (i.e. the Mormon polygamy case)?

3　How does *Smith* change the way in which the Court scrutinizes free-exercise claims? How was its argument in *Smith* applied in the Santeria case? What did the US Congress do in the RFRA to respond to the *Smith* case, and how did the Court react to RFRA?

4　What is the Court's basic reasoning when deciding school prayer cases (see, e.g., *Engel* v. *Vitale, Lee* v. *Weisman, Santa Fe Independent School District* v. *Doe*)? Do the Court's decisions regarding the teaching of creation and/or evolution in schools follow a similar reasoning (*Epperson, Edwards*)?

5　What are the prongs of the Lemon test? Do you think it treats religion "neutrally"?

6　What is "equal access"? How has equal access law broadened over time, both through Court rulings (e.g., *Widmar* and *Rosenberger*) and congressional legislation (e.g., Equal Access Act of 1984)?

FURTHER READING

Brady, Kathleen A., *The Distinctiveness of Religion in American Law: Rethinking Religion Clause Jurisprudence* (Cambridge: Cambridge University Press, 2015). A carefully researched argument that religion should retain a special constitutional status rooted in the value of equality.

Drakeman, Donald L., *Church, State, and Original Intent* (Cambridge: Cambridge University Press, 2009). A strong critique of the Supreme Court's understanding of constitutional history.

Green, Steven K., *The Bible, the School, and the Constitution: The Clash that Shaped Modern Church-State Doctrine* (Oxford: Oxford University Press, 2012). A sweeping historical analysis of how eighteenth- and nineteenth-century concerns about schoolchildren led to modern views of church and state.

Greenawalt, Kent, *Religion and the Constitution: Free Exercise and Fairness* (Princeton, NJ: Princeton University Press, 2006). A nuanced and closely reasoned perspective in favor of strong religious-liberty protections.

Hertzke, Allen D. (ed.), *The Future of Religious Freedom: Global Challenges* (Oxford: Oxford University Press, 2013). A forward-looking compendium that provides a cross-national perspective on religious freedom in the United States today.

Meyerson, Michael I., *Endowed by Our Creator: The Birth of Religious Freedom in America* (New Haven, CT: Yale University Press, 2012). A careful historical treatment of the Constitution's framers' views of church and state.

Nussbaum, Martha, *Liberty of Conscience: In Defense of America's Tradition of Religious Equality* (New York, NY: Basic Books, 2008). A probing historical and legal analysis of the American tradition of religious freedom with an emphasis on the value of equality.

Witte, John and Joel A. Nichols, *Religion and the American Constitutional Experiment: Essential Rights and Liberties*, 4th edn (Oxford: Oxford University Press, 2016). A valuable introduction to the context for religious liberty in America.

NOTES

1. *Burwell* v. *Hobby Lobby Stores*, 573 US _____ (2014); *Trinity Lutheran Church of Columbia, Inc.* v. *Comer*; *Hosanna-Tabor Evangelical Lutheran Church and School* v. *EEOC*, 565 US (slip opinion) (2012); *Gonzales* v. *O Centro Espirita Beneficente Uniao do Vegetal*, 546 US 418 (2006); and *Christian Legal Society* v. *Martinez*, 561 US (slip opinion) (2010).

2. See, for example, Gregg L. Frazer, *The Religious Beliefs of America's Founders* (Lawrence, KS: University Press of Kansas, 2012); Michael I. Meyerson, *Endowed by Our Creator: The Birth of Religious Freedom in America* (New Haven, CT: Yale University Press, 2012); William L. Miller, *The First Liberty and the American Republic* (New York, NY: Knopf, 1986); and Steven Waldman, *Founding Faith: Providence, Politics, and the Birth of Religious Freedom in America* (New York, NY: Random House, 2008); William L. Miller, *The First Liberty and the American Republic* (New York, NY: Knopf, 1986); and Vincent Phillip Muñoz, *God and the Founders: Madison, Washington, and Jefferson* (Cambridge: Cambridge University Press, 2009).

3. Some scholars take a more pessimistic view. See David Sehat, *The Myth of American Religious Freedom* (Oxford: Oxford University Press, 2011).

4. See, for example, *Watson* v. *Jones*, 80 US 679 (1871); and *Jones* v. *Wolf*, 443 US 595 (1979).

5. *United States* v. *Ballard*, 322 US 78 (1944).

6. The IRS recognized the Church of Scientology as a charitable and religious organization in 1993, paving the way to tax-exempt status.

7. We draw much of the following discussion on clergy malpractice from Margaret P. Battin, *Ethics in the Sanctuary: Examining the Practices of Organized Religion* (New Haven, CT: Yale University Press, 1990); and Mark Weitz, *Clergy Malpractice in America: Nally v. Grace Community Church of the Valley* (Lawrence, KS: University Press of Kansas, 2001).

8. A particularly strong voice on these matters is constitutional lawyer Marci Hamilton. See Marci Hamilton, *God vs. The Gavel: The Perils of Extreme Religious Liberty* (Cambridge: Cambridge University Press, 2014).

9. See *Airport Commissioners* v. *Jews for Jesus*, 482 US 569 (1987).

10. See *Larsen* v. *Valente*, 456 US 228 (1982).

11. See *McDaniel* v. *Paty*, 435 US 618 (1978); *Catholic Conference* v. *Abortion Rights Mobilization*, 487 US 72 (1988).

12. See *Cruz* v. *Beto*, 405 US 319 (1972); *O'Lone* v. *Estate of Shabazz*, 482 US 342 (1987); *Cutter* v. *Wilkinson*, 544 US 709 (2005); and *Holt* v. *Hobbs*, 574 US ___ (2015). On the general question of the legal issues surrounding religious practice in prison, see Winnifred Fallers Sullivan, *Prison Religion: Faith-Based Reform and the Constitution* (Princeton, NJ: Princeton University Press, 2009).

13. See Emma Green, "Why Trump's Executive Order on Religious Liberty Left Many Conservatives Dissatisfied," *The Atlantic*, May 4, 2017.

14. *Braunfeld* v. *Brown*, 366 US 599 (1961). See also *Jacobson* v. *Massachusetts*, 197 US 11 (1905); *Prince* v. *Massachusetts*, 321 US 158 (1944).

15. *Sherbert* v. *Verner*, 374 US 398 (1963).

16. The legal status of these practices raise broader questions about the often painful relationship of the state to Native Americans. See Carolyn N. Long, *Religious Freedom and Indian Rights: The Case of* Oregon Division *v.* Smith (Lawrence, KS: University Press of Kansas, 2000).

17. The fascinating background to this case is described in David M. O'Brien, *Animal Sacrifice and Religious Freedom:* Church of Lukumi Babalu Aye *v.* City of Hialeah (Lawrence, KS: University Press of Kansas, 2004).

18. Religious Land Use and Institutionalized Persons Act (2000).

19. *Gonzales* v. *O Centro Espirita Beneficiente Uniao Do Vegetal*, 546 US 418 (2006).

20. *Van Orden* was decided at the same time as *McCreary County* v. *ACLU of Kentucky*, 545 US 844 (2006), which held that the context surrounding Ten Commandments displays in some county courthouses suggested that counties had no secular purpose and therefore violated the establishment clause.

21. On the matter of excessive entanglement, also see *Walz* v. *Tax Commission*, 397 US 664 (1970).

22. Justice Scalia made this comment in his opinion in *Lamb's Chapel* v. *Center Moriches Union Free School District*, 508 US 385 (1993).

23. Bruce J. Dierenfield discusses the effects of *Engel* on American culture in his *The Battle over School Prayer: How* Engel *v.* Vitale *Changed America* (Lawrence, KS: University Press of Kansas, 2007).

24. *Wallace* v. *Jaffree*, 105 S. Ct. 2479 (1985). Stephen D. Solomon, *Ellery's Protest: How One Young Man Defied Tradition and Sparked the Battle over School Prayer* (Ann Arbor, MI: University of Michigan Press, 2009).

25. Jeffrey Rosen, "Lemon Law," *New Republic*, 208 (March 29, 1993), p. 17.

26. Steven P. Brown, *Trumping Religion: The New Christian Right, the Free Speech Clause, and the Courts* (Tuscaloosa, AL: University of Alabama Press, 2002).

27. On Young Life, see www.younglife.org; on Fellowship of Christian Athletes, see www.fca.org; on Youth for Christ, see www.yfc.net; on Student Venture, see www.student venture.com.

13

BIG THEMES AND
NORMATIVE CONCERNS IN
RELIGION AND POLITICS

We have endeavored in this book to provide a wide and balanced treatment of the diverse relationships between religion, culture, politics, and government in the United States. Our focus has been on the empirical realm of documented facts, data, case studies, and historical accounts that illustrate the real-world impact of religion on American political outcomes. This kind of empirical rendering is precisely what political scientists strive to produce. On the other hand, as scholars and citizens we are not unaware of the many moral and normative concerns raised about whether, or under what conditions, religion's influence on American politics is a positive or negative force. In this brief chapter, we review some of the normative arguments raised in this book about whether and how religion ought to engage in public affairs. While we do not take any positions in these debates, we offer this account so readers can appreciate the diverse points of view and reach their own conclusions or moral judgments.

Before turning to this normative analysis, it is helpful to step back for a moment and look at the big themes that have emerged in this book. We see three such themes about the role of religion in American politics: it is powerful, it is pluralistic, and it is dynamic.

First, religion plays a variety of crucial roles in the politics and government of the United States. One cannot understand American culture and politics without comprehending the influence of American religion in all its complexity and diversity. Of course, one must not overstate religion's political role as there also are many other powerful groups and forces that influence politics and government in the United States. Indeed, sometimes what looks like the effect of religion is actually the result of a different set of factors such as race or gender. But, as we have shown, religious activism and values tend to find their political voice—whether in the voting booth, the halls of Congress, the Oval Office, or the chambers of the Supreme Court. Sometimes their influence is indirect, as when religious principles and cultural practices shape political attitudes or civic behavior. Other times, the influence is the direct result of active lobbying or social movement mobilization. Religious influence also waxes and wanes with the times and in changing contexts, but it is never entirely absent from the political arena.

To the extent that religion in the United States is politically powerful, it also is more pluralistic than ever. Religious pluralism has always played a significant role in shaping the nation's history, but today we see an increasingly diverse landscape of religious traditions—and, thus, religiously motivated political witnesses. Not only are there a multitude of Christian traditions, denominations, congregations, and other groups that engage in public life, but we also see growing communities of Christian immigrants, exiles, and refugees, all of whom bring their own distinctive concerns to the public square. Equally important, non-Christian constituencies have grown in number and diversity, with robust Jewish groups now joined by various (and sometimes competing) Muslim groups as well as Buddhists, Hindus, Sikhs, Baha'is, and others. Perhaps most importantly of all, the religiously unaffiliated sector of the US population (the "nones") is growing and becoming more politically cohesive and assertive against religious influences. One result of this pluralism is that no one group, constituency, or alliance can dominate political outcomes. In fact, different religious groups often check each other, just as James Madison predicted in "Federalist 10."

The third broad theme that emerges in this book is the dynamism of religion in American politics. While certain patterns of voting behavior or political affiliations do endure over time, specific religious groups gain and lose influence relative to one another. New national challenges emerge, priorities change on the political agenda, party coalitions fracture, judicial doctrines change, and global events ramify in powerful ways that affect religious communities. We have been especially struck by the dynamic changes that have transformed the religious landscape since the last edition of this book was written just five years ago: The Supreme Court nationalized same-sex marriage; the transgender movement burst onto the scene; healthcare policy became an arena of increasing contestation over the meaning of religious liberty; the surprising election of Donald Trump fractured old partisan alignments; and, on the international stage, the rise of ISIS and the Syrian civil war sparked various religious debates and brought new refugees to American shores. While this dynamism makes our task (and yours) more challenging, it also means that the general subject of religion's intersection with US politics will remain even more exciting and fascinating for future investigation.

Since religious engagement will remain a potent factor in our public life, it is valuable to reflect on the deeper moral and normative meaning of it all.

SECULAR VERSUS RELIGIOUS DEBATES

Because religion uniquely draws upon deeply held and often conflicting moral convictions, it is natural that a variety of normative concerns arise about whether, or under what conditions, religious engagement in politics is healthy, problematic, or even dangerous. Indeed, we see enduring and intense debates regarding these matters—debates that have also engaged some of the most influential political thinkers of the past and present. The most important thing to keep in mind is that the debates are not solely between religious activists and secular opponents but that they range across religious communities, often dividing specific religious traditions or denominations. Consider, for example, the cleavages that have emerged within mainline Protestant denominations over the ordination of LGBT clergy.

Nonetheless, one of the most salient lines of current debate does pit self-consciously secular groups and intellectuals against religious activists. Often debates between these two sectors of American society become hopelessly entangled in ideological clashes, as when conservative religionists challenge the liberal consensus on abortion, marriage, and sexuality. Sometimes the secular-religious cleavage manifests itself in differing constitutional interpretations, with groups like Americans United for the Separation of Church and State and the Secular Coalition for America seeking to check what they see as special legal privileges for religion. Religious actors and their defenders push back, saying they have every right to protect their autonomy and to participate politically in the same ways other citizens do.

This secular-religious debate reveals a timeless tension between individual liberty and the autonomy of religious communities. Legal scholar Leslie Griffin, for example, contends that when courts protect the autonomy of religious institutions such as Catholic schools or adoption agencies, those "patriarchal" institutions can discriminate against (or oppress) women and LGBT people.[1] Religious defenders respond that anyone is free to join or exit religious institutions, which are voluntary by nature and constitute a vital sector of a pluralistic civil society.

The debates between secular and religious groups rest on even deeper philosophical differences worthy of serious reflection. The most influential argument from the secular side was advanced by John Rawls, the famous Harvard political philosopher. Rawls was a liberal who argued that religious-based justifications should be kept out of public discourse. Because theological arguments for or against public policies are not comprehensible to all citizens, he argued, religious people should restrict themselves to making secular arguments when they enter the public square. Otherwise, their influence will unreasonably limit what he viewed as legitimate discourse in a liberal polity.[2] Others have followed in Rawls' footsteps, contending that it is illiberal or even dangerous for religious groups to influence political outcomes because by doing so they would impose their theological values on others. Why, critics ask, should we afford religion a privileged place, either legally or politically, when it represents a major force of resistance against a more tolerant, egalitarian, and progressive society?[3]

Religious thinkers have responded vigorously to this line of criticism, arguing that it is, in fact, illiberal to deny any group of citizens the right to draw upon their deepest values in asserting claims about which public policies are just or wise.[4] Some add the argument that while religious believers should be free to draw guidance and inspiration from their theological convictions, savvy religious activists know that to be effective they must employ publicly accessible arguments. The very nature of a pluralistic society also ensures that religious voices cannot dominate the discourse.

An especially influential response to Rawls was framed by the prominent intellectual Fr. Richard John Neuhaus, who feared that expelling religion would create a "naked public square" bereft of the deepest wellsprings of reflection on justice, the good society, and liberty.[5] Neuhaus and others also point out that neither liberals nor secularists are always consistent. If one lauds Martin Luther King or Jesse Jackson, both ministers who employed powerful biblical language and theological justifications to champion civil rights and social justice, one cannot also claim that religious traditionalists are wrong to bring their values into the public square.

Moreover, if only secular justifications are sanctioned in public discourse, or if religious devotion is viewed as merely a private concern, then the state will, in fact, be privileging secular voices and arguments over religious ones. As Yale Law Professor Stephen Carter argued, law and politics should not trivialize or marginalize religious devotion.[6] We often hear similar concerns expressed about the "secular environment" in public schools and the message that might convey to devout students: that their faith must not be important.

A final point is that secularization does not necessarily produce a more tolerant society. Peter Beinart, a liberal analyst writing in *The Atlantic*, recently contended that the toxic politics of the alt-right and white supremacists has been fueled in fact by the erosion of faith commitments, not because of them.[7] The perspectives that fill the societal void left by religion might not improve on any of religion's shortcomings.

While not all secular theorists share Rawls' categorical prohibition against bringing religious justifications to bear in national political discourse, they do express concern about how dominant religious groups in some local communities sometimes can monopolize public space and rhetoric, thus creating an oppressive environment for people who are religiously different. We should, they argue, not privilege some religious voices over others.

DEBATES BETWEEN RELIGIONISTS

Although "secular versus religion" disputes receive lots of attention, in some respects the more interesting normative debates have been among religionists themselves, or among intellectuals who are sympathetic to a vibrant religious culture. For example, some faith leaders worry about the corrupting influence of politics on their congregations and thus seek to keep a distance from entanglement in government. This concern recalls a famous argument made by Alexis de Tocqueville: that political activism by clergy or churches could undermine their vital role in cultivating mores of healthy family and community life. As a keen observer of early American society and politics, Tocqueville argued that religion was enormously influential in the civic life in the United States, but in a paradoxical way. Churches were "the first of the American political institutions," but not because they engaged in direct political advocacy. On the contrary, by avoiding most political entanglements, American clergy could exercise even greater influence by shaping the very habits of political culture in the young democracy. As a contrast, Tocqueville saw how the Catholic Church in France lost its legitimacy and influence because of its alignment with the old regime of monarchs and nobles, which was swept away by the French Revolution. The broader lesson to Tocqueville and his heirs is that religion will share in the "vicissitudes" of politics if it aligns itself too closely to any specific party or regime.[8]

Some commentators today echo Tocqueville's caution that religious institutions might be sacrificing their key cultural role due to their increasingly partisan activism. Thus, not only is political engagement potentially divisive, but it also takes time and energy that might be better spent elsewhere. For example, sociologist James Davison Hunter suggests that because politics is *downstream* from culture, political advocacy by churches diverts focus from more lasting initiatives of culture formation.[9]

Notwithstanding the peril of being coopted by the blandishments of political elites or the allure of power, advocates for a publicly engaged faith nonetheless point to the valuable perspectives religious actors bring to politics and the pivotal roles religious networks and convictions have played in the great social-justice movements throughout American history. Where would the United States be without the passion and networks of churches in the movements to end slavery, grant women's suffrage, and extend civil rights to African Americans? The independence of houses of worship—and the moral authority they wield—enables their leaders to offer a prophetic challenge to the state and to counteract the dominance of self-interest and money in politics. Religious advocates inject moral concerns into public deliberations that would otherwise be absent. At their best, religious advocates represent the needs of vulnerable people, including refugees and the impoverished at home and abroad. This capacity to broaden representation is especially evident in the way international faith-based humanitarian organizations raise awareness about the problems of famine, disease, persecution, and exploitation in the power centers of the United States, the global superpower. Who else would lobby as effectively as religious groups can on behalf of refugees in Central Africa or trafficked children in Southeast Asia?[10]

Finally, religious advocates argue that religious communities and institutions provide a necessary check on the intrusive power of the state. Hence, healthy civil society must maintain its independence from the state, and in the United States some of the most effective defenders of civil society are political advocates for religious communities. Their role is not surprising: after all, they represent the largest and perhaps most robust expression of civil society. If Jews, Sikhs, Muslims, or Catholics do not represent their rights of conscience or protect their institutions, who will? Indeed, religious litigants and activists have been at the forefront of the push for an expansive understanding of First Amendment liberties, which has made America a haven for exiles from abroad—including for those who have been religiously persecuted.

The themes of these debates have been with us for a long time, in part because the issues are timeless. But a relatively new dimension has emerged that produces an immediate sense of urgency and poignancy in the evaluation of religious politics in the United States. The question is: How will religious political engagement fare amidst political polarization?

RELIGIOUS ENGAGEMENT IN AN AGE OF POLARIZATION

The most significant development in American politics in the past quarter century has been the deepening of partisan polarization. The divided state of politics in the United States today often presents a grim picture of endless ideological combat and inevitable impasse, with deep-seated party rivalries that result far more often in disunity than in compromise for the common good. Political elites—elected officials, high-level bureaucrats, even judges—have resorted themselves into two durable partisan camps. In Congress, for example, Democrats and Republicans are farther apart ideologically than ever in recent memory. Scholars find few moderating voices among elites in the two major parties today; unlike three decades ago, it is rare to encounter liberals among Republicans or conservatives among Democrats. Centrists in both parties have almost vanished. As congressional members are pulled to the ideological extremes, often because they are elected in strongly partisan districts or states, bipartisan cooperation is rare.[11]

While most citizens are less polarized than their leaders, there is ample evidence of increasingly deep divides also emerging among average Americans in their perspectives on political authority and the importance of religion and morality in public life.[12] Fueled by regional and neighborhood sorting, new technologies, and partisan forms of media, many people live within ideological echo chambers where they are unlikely to encounter opposite points of view.[13] These physical and virtual divisions have produced an alarming level of antipathy between party identifiers.[14]

Partisanship consequently has been transformed from a mere brand loyalty to include aspects of social identity.[15] Like other markers of social identity such as gender, race, and religion, partisanship reinforces implicit assumptions about the groups we belong to and those we do not, assumptions that we rarely articulate and might not even realize we have. These assumptions can carry a lot of emotional and intellectual weight: Recent studies reveal that the most ardent partisans see their opponents as not merely wrong about policies or candidates for office but as untrustworthy, morally suspect, even an existential threat to the body politic.[16] Such partisans even say they would be upset if their children married outside of the partisan fold.[17]

This highly polarized political environment presents new challenges for religious engagement—sparking debates to be sure, but also, more importantly, spurring a profound normative questioning and reflection.

One concern is that religious political activism itself has helped drive this new polarization. As we saw especially in Chapters 8–12, leaders with a religious message, ranging from the conservative Christian right to the predominantly secular left, frequently have entered this partisan fray as party activists and even elected officials. They shape party platforms, provide a public stage to candidates, organize around specific issues and policies, weigh in on judicial decisions, and attempt to shape opinion on social media and elsewhere. To use political scientist Geoffrey Layman's terms, religious activists have helped define the "great divide" between the parties.[18]

While religious commitments can shape partisanship, another concern is that the influence can go the other way. If partisanship is becoming a form of social identity that affects personal choices beyond conventional politics, from housing to media consumption to life-mates, perhaps it is also subtly affecting religious commitments. The concern is that partisan identity may be shaping the lived experience of faith, including where and with whom we worship. Americans are in fact more likely to affiliate with houses of worship where members share assumptions about political ideas and personalities.[19] To some religious thinkers, this development seems like making an idol of politics or political identity.

Polarization raises a host of concerns for civil society in the United States. We described civil society in Chapter 10 as a set of voluntary associations and organizations that mediate between individuals and the state and provide a seedbed for good citizenship. The work of building thick civic dispositions in the United States—the necessary "social capital" of democratic citizenship—has often fallen to houses of worship, along with sports leagues, fraternal organizations, schools, and other networks that exist outside the state and market. But polarization can be anathema to a healthy civil society. Clustering people into silos with likeminded others arrests development of the civic skills and dispositions that foster decision-making across lines of difference.[20]

Moreover, the role of partisan identity in generating polarization not only erodes the quality of religion's role in civil society; it also threatens the extent of religion's reach. Social scientists have found that the rising level of partisanship within religious groups is pushing people away from religious affiliation, which of course simply intensifies partisan identity among those who remain.[21] If those patterns of disaffiliation continue, a key question is one of what might emerge in the cultural void religion could leave behind. Some commentators have answered this question by making rather disturbing predictions.[22]

Tocqueville noted that religion in early nineteenth-century America often provided a language and social norms that tempered democratic conflict and rhetorical vitriol against political opponents. But when religion declines, or when it becomes associated with one partisan identity by pledging loyalty to one ideological camp, it sacrifices its broad power to diminish political excesses. That was indeed one of Tocqueville's great concerns about the future of democracy in America.

RESPONDING TO POLARIZATION

This challenging era of polarization has sparked a variety of normative responses. One response is a withering critique of the ways in which religious actors have been "seduced" by party politics. Contemporary critics of both the "religious right" and the "religious left" have charged that religious advocates sometimes seem more driven by political ideology than faith, and that they too often baptize liberal or conservative positions with unreflective religious justifications.[23] As we noted in Chapter 9, the Trump presidency has provoked heated debates among conservative religionists about whether supporting him means compromising fundamental religious principles. We also hear charges that religious progressives often seem more committed to their political ideology than to their faith. A more general concern is that religious advocates sometimes move too slickly from voicing broad moral concerns to lobbying for specific, and contested, policy remedies.

If one response is to criticize religious actors for allowing themselves to be drawn into partisan camps, another proposal is for organized religion to retreat entirely from political engagement and work instead on creating cohesive faith communities. Only by renewing a religious culture of flourishing family and community life, the argument goes, can religionists regain a moral platform from which to engage political issues. Such a project, however, might take generations. Perhaps only after such a long term effort might religious voices be able to recover their prophetic independence and impact.[24]

For those who continue to believe that religious actors can make positive contributions to our polity—those who are not ready to retreat into modern-day cloisters—another response is to engage in politics with eyes wide open. The advice here is to be aware of the pitfalls and snares of political engagement: be humble and self-critical; resist the temptation to let political elites set the agenda; work in a bipartisan fashion; build bridges between people; and perhaps focus at the local level, where common ground most readily may be found. As teachers, we have noticed that many of our students, from the full range of religious backgrounds (or sometimes none at all), recoil from vitriolic partisan discourse. Still hoping to make a positive difference in the world, millennials seem drawn to issues around which common ground can be forged. However differently individual millennials might vote in elections, they do not wish to be defined by membership in any partisan team that demonizes its opponents. Instead, they seem to yearn to live in a more civil society.

We take heart in such aspirations, which give us hope for the future of our country. And on that positive note, we close.

DISCUSSION QUESTIONS

1 How do religious pluralism and dynamism shape the influence of religion in American politics?
2 Fundamental clashes have emerged over whether law should treat religion as a public good or as a potential harm. Where do you come down on that question? Or does it depend on circumstances?
3 Is declining religious affiliation a good or bad thing (or both) for American public life?
4 Tocqueville envisioned religion as most influential when it stood apart from politics. Why did he take that position? Is the United States at risk of losing influence because religion has become too wedded to politics?
5 Is religion partially responsible for polarization? Is it a potential solution to it? Why or why not?
6 Under what conditions should religious groups participate in, or retreat from, political engagement?

FURTHER READING

Carter, Stephen, *The Culture of Disbelief: How American Law and Politics Trivialize Religious Devotion* (New York, NY: Anchor Books, 1993). Too often, Carter argues, law and policy belittle the gravity of devout religious commitments.

Corvino, John, Ryan Anderson, and Sherif Girgis, *Debating Religious Liberty and Discrimination* (Oxford: Oxford University Press, 2017). Authors on opposing sides of same-sex marriage provide a model of how to conduct a civil conversation over the clashing values of religious conscience rights and non-discrimination on the basis of sexual orientation.

De Tocqueville, Alexis, *Democracy in America*, trans. Harvey Mansfield and Deborah Winthrop (Chicago, IL: University of Chicago Press, 2002), especially vol. I, part 2, chapter 9. Develops the famous argument that churches should avoid entanglement in partisan politics to ensure their cultural role in shaping the healthy mores of a democratic culture.

Dreher, Rod, *The Benedict Option: A Strategy for Christians in a Post-Christian Nation* (New York, NY: Sentinel, 2017). Argues for a conscious retreat from political engagement into radical Christian communities that, over time, can renew a fallen culture the same way early Benedictines did after the fall of Rome.

Griffin, Leslie, "Smith and Women's Equality," *Cardozo Law Review*, 32 (5) (2011): 1831–1855. Griffin argues against granting special legal protections for religious institutions that, in her view, represent barriers to women's equality.

Hunter, James Davison, *To Change the World: The Irony, Tragedy, and Possibility of Christianity in the Late Modern World* (Oxford: Oxford University Press, 2010). Argues that common strategies by Christians to shape political outcomes in America are ineffectual because Christianity has lost the cultural heights. Similar diagnosis to Dreher's but with somewhat different recommendations.

Leiter, Brian, *Why Tolerate Religion?* (Princeton, NJ: Princeton University Press, 2013). By arguing against special treatment of religion or religious freedom, Leiter exemplifies a new form of assertive secularism in American political thought.

Neuhaus, Richard John, *The Naked Public Square: Religion and Democracy in America* (Grand Rapids, MI: Eerdmans, 1988). In arguing against banishing religious values from public discourse, Neuhaus coined the celebrated phrase "the naked public square" to describe civic life shorn of fundamental moral convictions.

Rawls, John, *Political Liberalism* (New York, NY: Columbia University Press, 1993). One of the most influential of the secular critics of public religion, Rawls argues against religion-based justifications in public debate.

Wolterstorff, Nicholas, and Robert Audi, *Religion in the Public Square* (Lanham, MD: Rowman & Littlefield, 1997). The authors of this book take opposing sides in a civil debate over the proper role of religion in public life and politics. Nicely frames the contours of the debate.

NOTES

1. Leslie C. Griffin, "Smith and Women's Equality," *Cardozo Law Review*, 32 (5) (2011): 1831–1855.

2. John Rawls, *Political Liberalism* (New York, NY: Columbia University Press, 1993).

3. Brian Leiter, *Why Tolerate Religion?* (Princeton, NJ: Princeton University Press, 2013).

4. Nicholas Wolterstorff and Robert Audi, *Religion in the Public Square* (Lanham, MD: Rowman & Littlefield, 1997).

5. Richard John Neuhaus, *The Naked Public Square: Religion and Democracy in America*, 2nd edn (Grand Rapids, MI: Eerdmans, 1988).

6. Stephen Carter, *The Culture of Disbelief: How American Law and Politics Trivialize Religious Devotion* (New York, NY: Anchor Books, 1993).

7. Peter Beinart, "Breaking Faith," *The Atlantic*, April 2017.

8. Alexis de Tocqueville, *Democracy in America*, trans. Harvey Mansfield and Deborah Winthrop (Chicago, IL: University of Chicago Press, 2002).

9. James Davison Hunter, *To Change the World: The Irony, Tragedy, and Possibility of Christianity in the Late Modern World* (Oxford: Oxford University Press, 2010).

10. This theme of the pivotal role of transnational religious groups is made by Allen D. Hertzke, "The Globalization of Advocacy," in Andrew Dawson (ed.), *The Politics and Practice of Religious Diversity* (London and New York: Routledge, 2016), pp. 158–177.

11. Among other excellent sources, see Nolan McCarty, Keith T. Poole, and Howard Rosenthal, *Polarized America: The Dance of Ideology and Unequal Riches* (Cambridge, MA: MIT Press, 2016).

12. See, for example, Marc J. Hetherington and Jonathan D. Weiler, *Authoritarianism and Polarization in American Politics* (Cambridge: Cambridge University Press, 2009); and Jonathan Haidt, *The Righteous Mind: Why Good People Are Divided by Politics and Religion* (New York, NY: Pantheon, 2012).

13. Bill Bishop, *The Big Sort: Why the Clustering of Like-Minded America is Tearing Us Apart* (Boston, MA: Mariner Books, 2009); McCarty et al., *Polarized America*.

14. Pew Research Center, "Political Polarization in the American Public: How Increasing Ideological Uniformity and Partisan Antipathy Affect Politics, Compromise and Everyday Life," June 12, 2014, www.people-press.org/2014/06/12/political-polarization-in-the-american-public/.

15. Donald Green, Bradley Palmquist, and Eric Schickler, *Partisan Hearts and Minds: Political Parties and the Social Identities of Voters* (New Haven, CT: Yale University Press, 2002).

16. Shanto Iyengar and Sean J. Westwood, "Fear and Loathing across Party Lines: New Evidence on Group Polarization," *American Journal of Political Science*, 59 (2015): 690–707.

17. Pew Research Center, "Political Polarization in the American Public."

18. Geoffrey Layman, *The Great Divide: Religion and Cultural Conflict in American Party Politics* (New York, NY: Columbia University Press, 2001).

19. Bill Bishop, *The Big Sort*.

20. For a discussion of the role of cross-cutting networks in developing democratic citizenship, see Diana Mutz, *Hearing the Other Side: Deliberative versus Participatory Democracy* (Cambridge: Cambridge University Press, 2006).

21. Michael Hout and Claude S. Fischer, "Explaining Why More Americans Have No Religious Preference: Political Backlash and Generational Succession, 1987–2012," *Sociological Science*, 1 (2014): 423–447; Robert D. Putnam and David E. Campbell, *American Grace: How Religion Divides and Unites Us* (New York, NY: Simon & Schuster, 2010).

22. Peter Beinart, "Breaking Faith," *The Atlantic*, April 2017, www.theatlantic.com/magazine/archive/2017/04/breaking-faith/517785/.

23. This criticism is a staple of books against the Christian right but is also a common theme of critics (such as the Institute on Religion and Democracy) of the "left-wing" witness of mainline Protestant lobbies.

24. Rod Dreher, *The Benedict Option: A Strategy for Christians in a Post-Christian Nation* (New York, NY: Sentinel, 2017).

INDEX